Management of the Interconnected World

Alessandro D'Atri · Marco De Marco ·
Alessio Maria Braccini · Francesca Cabiddu
Editors

Management of the Interconnected World

ItAIS: The Italian Association for Information Systems

Physica-Verlag

Editors
Prof. Alessandro D'Atri
Centro di Ricerca sui
Sistemi Informativi (CeRSI)
Via G. Alberoni 7
00198 Roma
Italy
datri@luiss.it

Prof. Marco De Marco
Università Cattolica del Sacro Cuore
Facoltà di Economia
Dipto. Scienze dell'Economia e della
Gestione Aziendale
Via Necchi 7
20123 Milano Milano
Italy
marco.demarco@unicatt.it

Dr. Alessio Maria Braccini
Centro di Ricerca sui
Sistemi Informativi (CeRSI)
Via G. Alberoni 7
00198 Roma
Italy
abraccini@luiss.it

Francesca Cabiddu
Università di Cagliari
Dipto. Economia
Viale S. Ignazio 74
09123 Cagliari
Italy
fcabiddu@unica.it

ISBN 978-3-7908-2403-2 e-ISBN 978-3-7908-2404-9
DOI 10.1007/978-3-7908-2404-9
Springer Heidelberg Dordrecht London New York

Library of Congress Control Number: 2010927077

Cover design: WMXDesign GmbH, Heidelberg

Printed on acid-free paper

Physica-Verlag is a brand of Springer-Verlag Berlin Heidelberg
Springer-Verlag is part of Springer Science+Business Media (www.springer.com)

Foreword

Joey F. George*

I was honored to be asked to open the VI Conference of the Italian Chapter of the Association for Information Systems (ItAIS), held in Olbia, on the Costa Smeralda of Sardinia, Italy, in October 2009. Over 90 research papers were presented over two days, and over 120 people attended the conference. Each day, five parallel sessions featured papers on diverse information systems topics. Session themes included Information and Knowledge Management; Organizational Change and Impact of ICT; IS Quality, Metrics and Impact; E-Justice and Ethics of Information Systems; Information Systems Development and Design Methodologies; E-Services in Public and Private Sectors; Innovation Transfer of IT Research Projects; the Strategic Role of Information Systems; Accounting Management and Information Systems; Human Computer Interaction; and Emerging Issues in a Globalized and Interconnected World. The majority of attendees were from Italy, which would be expected for a meeting of the Italian Chapter of AIS. However, as much as 30% of participants came from elsewhere, from other parts of Europe to be sure, but also from as far away as Nigeria, Mexico and Australia. That the conference was so decidedly international provides support for the 2009 conference theme, "Achieving Fusion in the Interconnected World." Amid lively discussion and intellectual exchanges, professional networks were extended well beyond the Costa Smeralda and new connections and friendships were made.

The Italian Chapter of AIS has set standards to be emulated by the many other chapters and special interest groups in AIS. They have set the bar high. They have a healthy and growing membership, and yet they remain a tight-knit community. The annual ItAIS conference continues to prosper and to attract papers based on high quality research, from both inside and outside Italy. The list of session themes above attests to the breadth of research topics being pursued in the Italian IS community. While much of the work reported on at the conference contributes to scholarly IS research, much of it also contributes to practice. The papers presented at the conference also reflected a diversity of research methods and philosophies. The best of the conference's papers, which capture this mix of methods, and with the focus on both research and practice, have been collected in this volume.

Successful conferences result from the dedication and hard work of many individuals. Much of the credit for the success of the VI Conference of the Italian Chapter of AIS goes to the conference chairs, Gabriele Piccoli, Richard T. Watson, and Alessandro D'Atri. The rest of the credit goes to the organizing

---

* President Elect of the AIS 2009–2010, Florida State University, Tallahassee, FL, USA, jgeorge@cob.fsu.edu

committee, chaired by Francesca Cabiddu, and to the presenters and other attendees. It was a pleasure to attend the conference and to interact with my Italian (and non-Italian) colleagues. There is much this conference, and the papers presented there, can teach us. I urge other chapters of AIS to follow the example of the Italian Chapter in establishing a viable organization and a lively, stimulating IS conference.

Table of Contents

Part II: Organizational Change and Impact of IT

Part III: Information and Knowledge Management

Part VIII: Human Computer Interaction

Part IX: Emerging Issues in a Globalized and Interconnected World

Part X: IS Theory and Research Methodologies

Part XI: Accounting Management and Information Systems

Part XII: Innovation Transfer of IT Research Projects

Introduction

The decision to publish 63 selected papers from the 2009 sixth Conference of the Italian Chapter of AIS shows the willingness to discuss the issues raised by the work of the contributors on a larger scale than that of a conference. In fact the general theme addressed ('Achieving fusion in the interconnected world: exploring the connection between organizations and technology') drew the attention of researchers on the interplay of 'organizations' and 'technology' within a possible and workable set of planetary connections. Even though the questions at stake have been present for quite a while in the literature, the debate is far from being concluded. The search for frameworks capable of exploring the interconnections that link, for example, e-services providers to different groups (e.g.: customers for e-commerce, users for a wide variety of Internet services, citizens for e-government) is necessary to develop more effective utilizations. Such a search, however, is becoming more and more complex because Castells' *Internet Galaxy* has grown further and at an ever increasing pace since 2001. Thus the number of variables to be considered keeps expanding and there is no single set of assumptions, concepts, values, and practices able to view a reality that escapes framing because of its evolution. In fact, depending on the spreading in the production and uses of ICT-IS, the number of the relevant actors multiplies and a mass of organizations (different per size, industry, market, competences, function, entrepreneurial history, character, societal environment and so on) have become active and interacting on the rich turf of information exchange. Furthermore, different perspectives must be adopted when considering the 'individual' (be that a person or an organization) approaches to information technology versus the 'group' level ones or when examining the constraints that 'back offices applications' exert on the amount and kind of value that the institutions and enterprises would like to ensure through their 'front office application mediated' work. The dichotomies and facets developing in short periods of time make the results of IS research certainly incremental but denoted by a pro tempore slant in their validity and relevance. Moreover, the increasing amplitude of the field of inquiry reveals its heterogeneity, thus stressing the need for drawing on several contributing disciplines and highlighting the 'situated' character of investigations in a world that is experiencing the fiercest economic crisis since the years 30 of the past century.

The authors (from 15 countries, besides Italy, and mainly from Spain, Switzerland, Germany, Australia, and the United States) who have contributed to this collective work are well aware of the above mentioned challenges and have catalyzed their efforts around 12 themes which constitute the sections of this book. The research areas include 'macro' questions and 'organization specific' issues bridging theoretical aspects with the description of exemplary cases. Thus, for example, ethical implications of ICT, which remain in many respects controversial, have been studied in connection with the possibility of increasing the transparency and efficiency of courts by evaluating the results of change induced by the adoption of extensive IS (Part IV). The theoretical implications stemming from the encounter of human practices with tools and learning aims have been explored by examining a case of post graduate education (Part X).

A number of researcher looked into the opportunities that are coming to the foreground when considering the interplay of globalization and connectedness. In this respect there are companies that manage to combine in-house innovation with externally acquired technologies in order to enhance new businesses (the so-called 'open innovation' and 'lead users innovation' is examined in Part IX addressed to emerging issues). Also the question of transferring innovation of IT research projects (Part XII) relates to the possibility of cooperation among private and public partners by investigating models capable of harnessing different competences and knowledge. Since such choices of engaging in partnerships involve the overall objectives pursued by organizations (together with the ways they choose to pursue them), the strategic role of information systems is growing. Thus eight writings have explored some of the manners in which IS and the Internet can contribute to acquire and to sustain a competitive advantage (Part V). Within the strategic discourse related to the governance of an organization, accounting information systems have an important role to play both in operations and reporting (Part XI). The ways through which value is created and governed is particularly critical in exploring the ways through which e-services can be designed and delivered. Emerging services and novel models have been examined in nine essays addressing both the private and public sectors (Part I). The question concerning the overall equilibrium of an organization when new 'tools' are adopted (for example, to secure a new e-service) is crucial because such 'equilibrium' has a dynamic character. It requires people to undertake change in their behaviors and the context of processes and regulations to open up to innovation. Thus, 10 papers have studied the interplay of ICT impacts and organizational change (Part II). The impacts of ICT (considered specifically as a human-computer interaction) have been studied for a long time. In this book specific attention has been paid to the involvement of the user base of business interactive systems in the issues related to HCI (Part VIII) so that a better accessibility is achieved. The problem of 'access' is certainly crucial in the information society, as the European Union policies show, so that appropriate research in the ways in which new technologies (e.g.: service oriented architectures, tools for data and service integration) facilitate networked collaboration and knowledge exchanges are of high interest: nine papers concern this subject in Part III.

Of course, all the above mentioned efforts performed by private and public bodies have to be supported by appropriate IS development and design methodologies (Part VII) so that a proper balance can be achieved between business requirements and solution development. Such balance is certainly rooted in the availability of reliable criteria and metrics in the evaluation of IS, of their impacts and costs (Part VI).

Part I
E-Services in Public and Private Sector

Marco De Marco*

The rapid development of the Internet since the 1990s has spawned an increasingly variegated virtual landscape, in terms of both the services provided via the electronic networks – such as information, interaction, and transaction – and the user mix – firms, institutions, and individuals. The all-encompassing nature of the Internet, which is used by businesses but also society as a whole, means that the study of e-services cannot but straddle several disciplines. Thus, computer science and engineering investigate the development and provision of the e-services; economics and organization science deal with service quality and value research; and sociology examines emerging issues, such as the "digital divide" and "e-inclusion". These converging (or diverging) elements are key factors when it comes to analyzing, for ex-ample, the pros and cons of applying a private-sector perspective to the study of public-sector e-services. Defining integrated frameworks for the study of e-services in both the public and the private sectors underscores the need to shape new business models and increase the value of e-services integration by enhancing the collaboration between e-service providers and users (customers, citizens, peers). Technical advances in infrastructure integration, service-oriented architectures, and Enterprise Application Integration (EAI) overlap new revenue-generating models, in addition to expanding the scope for service improvement and building better customer/citizen relationships.

These issues are the focus of the contributions profiled below. The studies use different perspectives and research domains and draw on a broad research background: theoretical issues and empirical evidence developed in specific service areas (e.g. healthcare and government); processes (e.g. participation and innovation); and public or private environments. Thus, one study has used surveys to highlight the newspaper industry's evolution towards an emerging "media-as-a-service" approach, based on the adoption of extensively interactive features and user-generated content via social networks or aggregation sites. Another study employs the design of a causal loop diagram and a stock-and-flow simulation model to show the interaction of citizens with the public administration, emphasizing the significance of social and psychological factors in change management. The proliferation of social players has led one of the contributions to propose adopting an institutional perspective to leverage the growing number of intermediary actors in the implementation of the multichannel strategies deployed to enhance eGovernment plans. A further paper makes its research focus the literature on the emerging – and complex – issue of ageing and the possible role of IS-ICT.

* Università Cattolica del Sacro Cuore, Milano, Italy, marco.demarco@unicatt.it

Yet another paper explores the problem of participation (eDemocracy) and ICT (specifically open-source software). Complexity is the background of an essay on the properties of networks of collaborations, aimed at devising measures of structure and complexity to improve service system design. All these papers deal indirectly with the question of "innovation". Three articles deal explicitly with the fostering and management of innovative practices: one on the role of patent management systems, another on the adoption of "open innovation" processes by research libraries, and a third on the possibility of using typing behavior biometrics as an authentication method (thus exploring the relationship between technology and trust).

Open Innovation in Research Libraries-Myth or Reality?

Ada Scupola*[*] and Hanne W. Nicolajsen[†]

Abstract In this article we investigate open innovation in a non commercial setting: research libraries. The research questions are: Do academic libraries engage in open innovation processes? If so, what are the most important actors in e-services innovation and development and what is their role? By drawing on earlier research on open innovation, new product development and new service development, a case study at Roskilde University Library is conducted. We found that research libraries are indeed engaging in open innovation, especially they are involving competitors, government agencies and users. In particular collaboration with other Danish research libraries and governmental agencies are important in setting the visions and strategies for e-services innovations; users have a more limited role.

Introduction

Innovation has been and still is important to the survival of companies [1]. However while in the past companies were developing their innovation competences mainly internally, nowadays firms are more and more developing their innovation competences on the base of open innovation. That is companies do not only rely on their own capabilities to develop innovation, but they also co-operate with suppliers, customers, consultants and sometimes even with competitors [2]. Most literature on open innovation focuses on manufacturing firms, especially high tech (e.g. [3–5]), commercial service firms such as financial services (e.g. [6, 7]) or open source software as a model of open innovation. In previous research not much attention has been given to open innovation in non commercial service organizations such as research libraries. This lack of research has motivated our study, focusing on how library employees explore open innovation in developing e-services. Another study by Morrison et al. [8] investigated open innovation in academic libraries, but their focus was on lead users and on OLC library systems. Here we focus on all potential actors that might be involved in open innovations and on innovations related to library e-services. The basic research questions are: Do academic libraries engage in open innovation processes? If so, what are the most important actors in e-services innovation and development and what is their role? The results of this study are beneficial to both academics as well as practi-

* Roskilde University, Roskilde, Denmark, ada@ruc.dk
[†] Aalborg University, Aalborg, Denmark, westh@cmi.aau.dk

A. D'Atri et al. (eds.), *Management of the Interconnected World*,
DOI 10.1007/978-3-7908-2404-9_1, © Springer-Verlag Berlin Heidelberg 2010

tioners. Academics from different fields including MIS, innovation, policy and information science may benefit by better understanding open innovation processes in non commercial settings such as libraries. Libraries, other non-commercial industries and policy makers may benefit from the examples on success and failure to learn how to better exploit the potentials involving different actors in innovation.

We define open innovation as an innovation where suppliers, competitors, users and other actors have contributed to the problem solving process leading to a solution. E-services are defined as services whose production, consumption and/or provision takes place through the intermediation of an ICT-network such as Internet-based systems or mobile solutions [9]. We take the library perspective as only people employed in the library have been interviewed in this first phase of the project (see limitations).

The paper is structured as follows. The introduction presents the background and research question. The second session presents the theoretical background of the paper. The following session introduces the research method and the case library. The last two sessions present the analysis and results as well as discussion and conclusions.

Theoretical Background

The importance of involving customers, suppliers and even competitors in innovation has been the subject of innovation theory over the last decade or so (e.g. [3, 10, 11, 6, 12]. Recently, Chesbrough [3] has argued that the process of innovation has shifted from one of closed systems, internal to the firm, to a new mode of open systems involving a range of players distributed up and down the supply chain. The role of customers and suppliers is changing from a pure consumer/supplier of products or services to partners in a process of adding value [2, 3, 13]. Intentionally or not, most consumer goods have some solution space open to consumers or suppliers [14] making it meaningful to draw on them. The economic return of involving customers, suppliers and other actors has manifested through the creation of more superior and differentiated services [12], through shorter testing times and less market failures [13] and through user education and improved and long lasting relationships [12]. It is Chesbrough [2, 3]'s emphasis on the new knowledge-based economy that informs the concept "open innovation". Collaboration between suppliers, customers and users can lead to a mutual understanding of the users' needs and wishes, as well as an understanding of the technological opportunities [15–17]. For example, Bitner et al. [18] recommend close involvement of customers in the design process of technology-based services. Von Hippel has showed how lead users have invented the majority of products in certain industries and has given numerous examples of user driven innovations leading to product and service innovations (e.g. [19, 20]). However, a number of studies show an opposing view regarding the benefits of involving users or other actors in product or service development arguing that such input is of limited value and could even be damaging [13]. Innovation studies also point to the important role that top management and employees might have in the innovation process (e.g. [1]) like the importance of the organization and their employees to play an active role for motivating external actors' involvement and converting their input to usable innovations [5, 21, 22]. Kristensson et al. [23] and Matthing et al. [22] found that users are generating more original and valuable ideas in mobile service innovation than professionals. They also found that these ideas need to be thoroughly re-worked by professionals taking for example the technical constraints into consideration in order to become commercialized. Even though previous studies mainly focus on the commercial sector and therefore these theories might have a commercial bias, we use them to guide our study due to the challenges that libraries are facing and the proactive actions they have to take, to "know your users and keep close to them, integrate marketing in the library organization and in the way libraries approach strategy and service development, invest more in innovation and digital activities" [24].

Research Method

A case study [25] was conducted to explore the research questions of this study. As Rogers [1, p. 390] states: "data about the innovation process are obtained by synthesizing the recallable perceptions of key actors in the innovation process, written records of the organization adopting, and other data sources". The case under consideration is a research library located in Denmark, Roskilde University Library (RUB). The data mainly consists of primary data collected through qualitative explorative and semi-structured interviews, one workshop and several meetings with the library personnel. Secondary data such as reports and other material on e-services development provided by the library personnel and other material retrieved on the web were also used. Seven face-to-face qualitative interviews were conducted. The interviews lasted circa 2 h, were tape recorded and fully transcribed. The sampling was purposeful [26]. The respondents had to be involved in the e-services development process at top management level, managerial level or had to be librarians involved in using the e-services. Although the number of interviews is relatively small, the key role that the respondents had in the planning and development of e-services, gives higher level of reliability and validity to the research findings similarly to Ozdemir et al. [7]. By relying on Yin [25], the data were analyzed by following the "general strategy of relying on theoretical orientation" of the case study. Following Miles and Huberman [27, p. 58], a provisional "start list" of codes was created prior to the field work to guide the analysis. The coding was manual [25, 27]. To increase internal validity the article and partial reports of the study were presented and discussed with two of the library's top managers.

Roskilde University Library (RUB)

Roskilde University Library (RUB) is a research library serving the students and staff at Roskilde University. Roskilde University is a smaller university located in Roskilde, a city about 35 km. from Copenhagen, the capital City of Denmark. The university counts circa 10,000 students. The library counts approximately 46 employees. It holds a number of paper books, paper journals, the entire spectrum of media as for example videos, and circa 18,000 e-journals. RUB has developed a number of e-services including access to electronic journals and electronic books and chat with a librarian. According to Roskilde University Statute [28], Roskilde University Library has the following purposes:

(1) To give teachers and students at Roskilde University access to information and materials containing information that are necessary for research and teaching, as well as to ensure information on and access to the university's teachers and students' research;
(2) As a public research library to make available its collection to external users, among which are regional research and teaching institutions, business and citizens;
(3) To participate in the national and international library collaboration;
(4) To conduct research and development within the library subjects and functions, but also the surrounding community and businesses as well as anybody who would like to use the library being this a public library.

Analysis and Results

RUB does not have yet a formal, explicitly defined innovation strategy, but according to a top manager "is working systematically with 3-year plans including so called development plans which may be regarded as an innovation strategy". RUB engages in open innovation in e-services development. In the e-service innovation process we found that the most important actors involved were competitors, governmental agencies and library users. Library management and employees had an important role in understanding users' wishes and collaborating and negotiating goals and objectives with competitors and government agencies. We also found that competitors and government agencies had an important role in the initiation and implementation phases of the innovation process as defined by Rogers [1] or strategic planning and idea generation phases as defined by Alam and Perry [6]. Users play a more active role in the implementation stage [1] or the service testing and pilot run phases [6] which comply with two of the user roles defined by Nambisan [13]: customer as a resource and customer as a user. We found very little evidence of customer as co-creator (e.g. [13]).

RUB has both formal and informal processes to collect ideas and suggestions generated by the users [1]. On a formal level, RUB has established a "coordination committee" which is in charge of making several types of decisions including innovation related decisions. Everybody in the library can send an idea for approval, and often such ideas are based on user inputs collected by librarians or other personnel in direct contact with the users. RUB also has a formal online complaint box and systematically screen the users' e-mails for innovative ideas or suggestions, which are then reported to the "coordination committee". On an informal level, new ideas and suggestions get collected by all library employees and discussed in informal meetings such as e.g. lunch breaks. If the suggested changes are not so big, they get implemented by the employees themselves without approval from the coordination committee.

Competitors and Governmental Agencies

The most important source of inspiration and vision for e-service innovation for RUB is the participation in the national initiative called Denmark's Electronic Research Library (DEFF). This is an organisational and technological partnership between research libraries co-financed by the Ministry of Science, Technology and Innovation, the Ministry of Culture and the Ministry of Education. It is based at The Danish National Library Authority. Its purpose is to advance the development of a network of electronic research libraries that make their electronic and other information resources available in a coherent and simple way. This is obtained partly through government funding and partly by joint purchase of licenses [29]. The cooperation includes joint development when cooperation will result in a greater advantage than the sum of local initiatives, including a better and total utilization of the libraries' resources; further development of the joint network of information resources and collective dissemination of the research libraries' information resources to the public [29].

This collaboration with governmental authorities and competitor libraries has been very crucial for setting the vision and strategic goals for e-services innovation at RUB. DEFF is also an important source of innovation regarding the technological aspect of e-services implementation. Through DEFF, RUB can get ideas from and share experiences with other libraries. For example each library might be in charge of testing an IT solution, then they share experiences and finally they decide to choose and adopt a common system. DEFF is also important in financing new ideas or innovation projects, as RUB lack the financial resources to start all the projects they believe are worth pursuing. So in this case, competitors are really acting as co-creators of e-services innovations.

In a more indirect way, ideas may also come from other industries. For example one of the newer ideas of the management group is to develop a new e-service to allow customers to make reviews of books, articles, etc. This idea is inspired by the use of user forums in other industries such as the travel industry where customers rate hotels to inform other travelers. Or Amazon who allows users to rate books and provides information on similar readings. The library is currently facing two big barriers in implementing such a solution: how to get a technological feasible solution and how to motivate the users to write these reviews. Finally an important source of innovation comes from top management and library employees' participation to international meetings and conferences, where they get inspiration and ideas about what is going on at an international level [1].

Users in E-service Innovation

Overall we found that RUB involves users in e-services innovations, even though in a limited way. A systematic approach to user involvement is lacking. Users are mostly involved in the implementation stage of new e-services, thus contributing mainly to incremental changes [1] with small suggestions or improvements. User innovation is seen as a minor supplementary means to support the innovation process and not as a substitute for internal practices. At present the customers thus play a smaller role in the initiation phase [1] or the idea generation phase [6] but a bigger role in the implementation stage especially in e-service testing and pilot run [6, 13]. Finally, RUB does not employ any of the well known methods for user involvement such as lead users, user toolkits or idea competitions, which suggest an unexplored potential. RUB is relying on well known techniques such as survey questionnaires, observations and online mail boxes to understand the user needs and wants [12]. These methods primarily address what is and not what could be. At RUB users are mainly involved as a user and to a lesser extent as a resource [13]. The role of the customer as co-creator is at an infant stage, mainly due to the problem of involving the customer. This again points to areas where the involvement of users could be intensified, for example, as a resource or as co-creator exploiting the creative potential and the insights that customer possesses [21– 23].

Discussion, Conclusions and Limitations

This paper has presented the preliminary results of a case study about open innovation at a research library. To summarize we found that our research library does engage into open innovation. The most important actors are competitors, government agencies and to a limited extent library users. Competitors take on the role of co-creators and co-innovators. Especially the relationship and collaboration with competitors and governmental agencies is very important for e-services innovation at RUB. This collaboration is formalized through a partnership called DEFF [29]. This partnership contributes to co-financing and risk sharing of e-services innovation among the different co-creators of the e-services innovations. This partnership also serves as a basis for knowledge sharing and learning among the different participating libraries. Collaboration with competitor libraries is important both in the initiation stage as well as implementation stage [1]. This collaboration has been the result of a government plan of "IT for all" that the Danish government had made in the 1990s. This policy plan included the digitalization of the libraries to provide all the citizens with access to electronic resources.

Users are mainly involved as a user and to a very limited extent as a resource. Recently customers are fulfilling the role of co-creators [13]. A more systematic approach to user involvement is lacking. Users are involved by mainly responding to surveys, by using e-services, by expressing their dissatisfaction or irritation, by requesting information (e.g. [12, 13]). The more intensive role of users in the implementation than the initiation phase can be explained by library e-services being fairly new [18] or by the way customers are approached by the library. However we found that library management is aware of and would like to get hold of some of the few users (lead users) that might be able to provide valuable insights for innovation.

Finally, this study is not free of limitations. We only conducted in depth interviews in one research library; however we will argue that our findings regarding the innovation supported by the DEFF project cover the library e-services landscape in Denmark. Our findings regarding the involvement of users as well as other internal processes regarding innovation may be different across research libraries and thus call for further investigation. This limits the generalizations of the results to an international context and to some degree to the Danish national context. Also it is interesting to investigate the customers' and competitors' perspective. We plan to do so in a second phase of the study. Nevertheless the study provides interesting insights about open innovation in e-services at a research library, thus contributing to the debate on open innovation. This is done by providing examples on how innovation may be supported across competitors by launching a national initiative uniting competitive forces as well as discussing the potentials for involving users in service innovation by leaving a traditional view of customers as less interested and knowledgeable to a more inclusive approach.

References

1. Rogers EM (1995) *The diffusion of innovations*, 4th edn. Free Press, New York
2. Chesbrough (2006) *Open business model: How to thrive in the new innovation landscape*. Harvard Business School Press, Boston
3. Chesbrough HW (2003) *Open innovation: the new imperative for creating and profiting from technology*. Harvard Business School Press, Boston
4. Chesbrough H, Crowther AK (2006) Beyond high tech: early adopters of open innovation in other industries. *R&D Manage* 36(3):223–366
5. Jeppesen LB, Molin M (2003) Consumers as co-developers: learning and innovation outside the firm. *Technol Anal Strateg Manage* 15(3):363–383

6. Alam I, Perry C (2002) A customer-oriented new service development process. *J Serv Mark* 16(6):515–534
7. Ozdemir S, Trott P, & Hoecht A (2007) New service development: insights from an explorative study into the Turkish retail banking sector. *Innov Manage Policy Pract* 9(3/4):276–289
8. Morrison PM, Roberts JH, von Hippel E (2000) Determinants of user innovation and innovation sharing in a local market. *Manage Sci* 46(12):1513–1527
9. Hoffman KD (2003) Marketing+MIS=E-Service. *Commun ACM* 46(6):53–55
10. Christensen CM (1997) *The innovator's dilemma: when new technologies cause great firms to fail*. HBS Press, Cambridge
11. Griffin A (1997) PDMA research on new product development practices: updating trends and benchmarking best practices. *J Product Innov Manage* 14:429–458
12. Alam I (2002) An exploratory investigation of user involvement in new service development. *J Acad Mark Sci* 30(3):250–261
13. Nambisan (2002) Designing virtual customer environments for new product development: toward a theory. *Acad Manage Rev* 27(33):392–413
14. von Hippel E (2001) User toolkits for innovation. J Product Innov Manage 18(4):247–257
15. Anderson WL, Crocca WT (1993) Engineering practice and co development of prototypes. *Commun ACM* 36(6):49–56
16. Veryzer R (2003) Marketing and the development of innovative products. In Shavinina L (ed) *International handbook on innovation*. Pergamon Press, Canada, pp 43–54
17. Hennestad BW (1999) Infusing the organization with customer knowledge. *Scand J Manage* 15(1):17–41
18. Bitner MJ, Brown SW, Meuter ML (2000) Technology infusion in service encounter. J *Acad Mark Sci*, 28(1):138–149
19. von Hippel E (1988) *Sources of innovation*. Oxford University Press, New York
20. von Hippel E (1989) New product ideas from 'lead users'. *Res Technol Manage* 32(3):24–27
21. Magnusson P (2003) Benefits of involving users in service. *Eur J Innov Manage* 6(4): 228–238
22. Matthing J, Sandén B, Edvardsson B (2004) New service development: learning from and with customers. *Int J Serv Ind Manage* 15(5):479–498
23. Kristensson P, Gustafsson A, Archer T (2003) Harnessing the creative potential among users. *Prod Innov Manage* 21(1):4–14
24. Brindley L (2006) *Re-defining the library*. Libr HiTech 24(4):484
25. Yin RK (1994) *Case study research design and methods*, 2nd edn, vol. 5. Sage Publications, Newbury Park
26. Patton MQ (1990) *Qualitative evaluation and research methods*, 2nd edn. Sage Publications, Newbury Park
27. Miles MB, Huberman AM (1994) *Qualitative data analysis*. Sage Publications, Newbury Park
28. www.ruc.dk/library
29. www.deff.dk

News as a Service: Adoption of Web 2.0 by Online Newspapers

Soley Rasmussen*

Abstract This paper presents a study of the adoption of Web 2.0 by Danish online newspapers and discusses the future of the newspaper in the light of contemporary shifts from mass media and printed products to social media and web services. First the context of the study is presented. Then a methodology for collecting and analyzing data on Web 2.0 adoption is suggested. Data from two surveys carried out with an interval of 14 months (2008/2009) is discussed. These data reveal that most online newspapers have adopted blogs and commenting and many have adopted other interactive features such as voting and sharing of user-generated content, e.g. photos and video. The most significant development in the period between the two observation sets is a rapid diffusion of article tools for bookmarking and sharing of content via social networks or aggregation sites. The main conclusions are that the news industry will have to embrace the emerging "media-as-a-service" paradigm and that the future challenge for web services will be to leverage informational and social connectivity.

Context of the Study

Global providers of content and services have entered the media market, disrupting established value chains and business models of national, regional and local media companies. Google, Facebook, Flickr, YouTube etc. have long surpassed most national websites in terms of unique users and Google is currently outperforming many a national advertising channel. Printed newspapers (Western) are bleeding billions of dollars as consumers and advertisers are replacing print with web. Newspaper have been replaced by search engines and paid traffic and other traditional advertising channels are becoming obsolete, as more and more companies conduct business activities in the virtual space interacting directly with customers. Moreover, media content providers are not only challenged by the so-called "new media" companies, but by a new mode of producing and disseminat-

* Copenhagen Business School, Center for Applied ICT, Copenhagen, Denmark, sr.caict@cbs.dk

A. D'Atri et al. (eds.), *Management of the Interconnected World*,
DOI 10.1007/978-3-7908-2404-9_2,

ing informational and cultural goods, the non-market or commons-based production that is often associated with a new generation of web technologies, often referred to as Web 2.0.

For national, regional and local newspapers the virtualized and globalized media landscape seems to offer more threats than opportunities and the current financial crises seem merely to amplify the media revolution set in motion by ubiquitously available cheap processors and broadband. A recent study from Annenberg School of Communication [1] show that about 20% of American internet users stop buying printed newspapers, as they can get the same product online. The conclusion from Annenberg is clear:

> We're clearly now seeing a path to the end of the printed daily newspapers - a trend that is escalating much faster than we had anticipated. (…) Their cushion is gone, and only those papers that can move decisively to the Web will survive.

The first survey of the adoption of Web 2.0 by Danish newspapers was conducted as part of a Nordic research and innovation project, eMedia, funded by the Nordic Innovation Center [2]. This project was carried out from 2006 to 2008 and included five Nordic research institutions and seven Nordic media and/or e-business companies. The main aim of the project was to create new innovative products and service forms for e-business companies by utilizing existing media channels and to identify new business models in the broader area between media and e-business.

Recognizing that existing value chains and media channels might not exist in a few years time, we set out to explore the new paradigm that had become so popular in the blogosphere, the Web 2.0. The first survey of the adoption of Web 2.0 by traditional Danish newspaper was conducted to establish a better understanding of the impact of Web 2.0 on the media sector [3]. The second survey to be presented was carried out in April/May 2009 in order to consolidate and/or expand/dismantle the first survey.

The Survey Methodology

Web 2.0 is an umbrella concept that embraces technologies, applications and services, and a philosophy or a vision of the Web [4–9]. In the absence of common definitions, the process of finding a useful comprehensive framework for collecting data on adoption of Web 2.0 has to be iterative. While some features are widely accepted as Web 2.0 (e.g. RSS, blogs, tagging, multimedia sharing), others are less obvious. However, as Web 2.0 is considered the "second generation" of the Web a starting point is to look for features that distinguish a site from "Web 1.0". In this case it means that the feature must add something that distinguishes the site from an electronic version of the printed newspaper; an information silo. While the printed paper is a product, Web 2.0 is about platforms and services [4]. The registered features are not "back-end technologies", but those Web 2.0 features that can be registered by surfing on the site, i.e. those Web 2.0 features that the user will meet when visiting the site.

Thus, by starting with one of the online newspapers and registering which elements could be considered Web 2.0 a number of features were discovered. When looking for these features on the next online newspaper new features were found, and the first website had to be reviewed again and so on, until all the websites were examined and all potential Web 2.0 features registered. Categories were developed during the process of the survey. If a new feature was discovered that did not fit into the previous categories, the categories were changed or an additional was added. The result is categories that frame different aspects of the Web 2.0 umbrella (Fig. 1).

Web 2.0 Feature (examples)	Category	Web 2.0 Characteristics
RSS Newsletters	New forms of delivery	Scalability/Granular products Personalization
Blogs Bookmarking	Participation and sharing	Web as a "platform" Emergent outcome Interaction with content Involvement in content generation
Tickets Reader's webshop	Shopping	Immediate capitalization on traffic
Web search Cultural events	Search	Relevant content easily found Hyperlinking
Web TV	Hybrid media	Multimedia Rich User Experience
Google Ads	New advertising channels	Data as the "Intel Inside"

Fig. 1. Examples of Web 2.0 features and categories and their Web 2.0 characteristics

The two surveys covers the thirteen largest Danish newspapers with national distribution for print, excluding two niche papers for specific sectors (agriculture and engineering). It includes the websites of five traditional morning newspapers (Jyllands-Posten (JP), Politiken, Berlingske, Information, Kristeligt Dagblad), one business morning paper (Borsen), one weekly paper (Weekendavisen), two tabloids (B.T., Ekstra Bladet), four free daily papers (24timer, Urban, metroXpress, Nyhedsavisen (Avisen)). The free papers only publish in print during weekdays and are primarily distributed in larger cities. During the 14 months between the two observation sets one of the free papers, Nyhedsavisen, have closed down print activities and the international free paper MetroXpress have bought 24timer, formerly owned by JP/Politikens Hus. The four free papers do, however, still have online editions, and are still in the top 200 of Danish websites and as all but one of the online newspapers studied also the free papers' websites are clearly growing. Figure 2 is a count of unique visitors of the thirteen websites in the study (Official statistics March 2009, Association of Danish Interactive Media, fdim.dk).

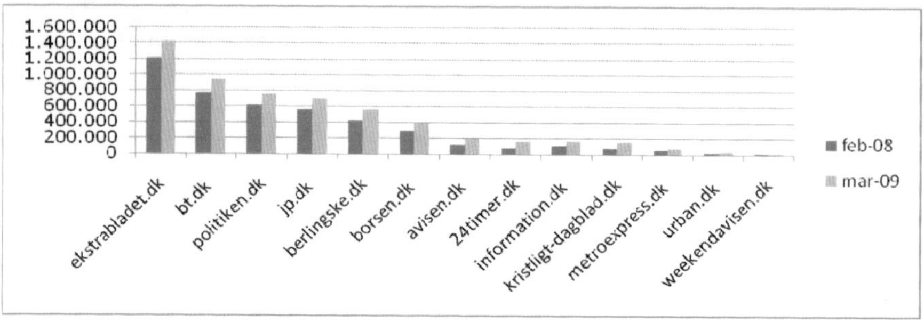

Fig. 2. Growth in unique visitors Feb. 08–Mar. 09 (Source: fdim.dk)

Survey Data

The aggregate results of the two surveys are shown in Fig. 3, where the distribution of the 20 features identified in 2008 are compared to the 2009 distribution.

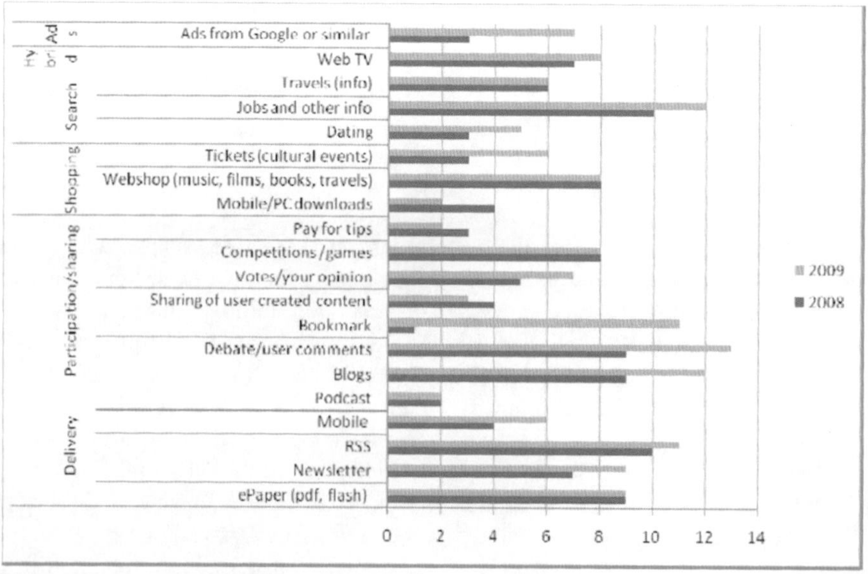

Fig. 3. Web 2.0 features of Danish online newspapers Feb. 2008/Apr. 2009

In February 2008 all except one of the sites (Weekendavisen) had adopted Web 2.0 features. Most sites had adopted new forms of delivery, interactive features, such as blogs and commenting, and different kinds of search options.

By 2009 all sites have adopted Web 2.0 features and the overall adoption has increased. The most significant development in the period between the two observation sets is a rapid diffusion of article tools for bookmarking and sharing of content via social networks or aggregation sites. By April 2009 all sites but one have an "Add This"-button – a web application that enable one click sharing to social networks, aggregation sites etc. Another remarkable development is the growth in the number of sites that display ads from Google or similar.

Just one of the little adopted features have spread in the period as two more sites have adopted Open Source (Berlingske.dk and B.T.), but new features have been adopted. By April 2009 five sites have a "Connect to Facebook" button and two sites a "Follow us on Twitter" button. In February 2008 just one site had "Add This" and none connected to Facebook/Twitter.

Without going into the details of the surveys, some conclusions from the comparison can be drawn. The main conclusions from the 2008 survey were that (1) the websites of the traditional newspapers seem to be far from reaching their potential for Web 2.0 adoption, (2) Changes are driven by the "new media companies"; traditional media adopts and promotes these changes, but are not drivers themselves, (3) the current adoption seems random and driven more by fashion and fascination than strategic implementation of business models [3]. This picture seems not to have changed. The rapid adoption of bookmarking tools is closely linked to the vast increase in the number of users of social networks. In the period between the two surveys Facebook has been booming in Denmark (see Fig. 4) and even if Twitter still has few Danish users, Twitter global growth rates in the period were about 1,400% [10].

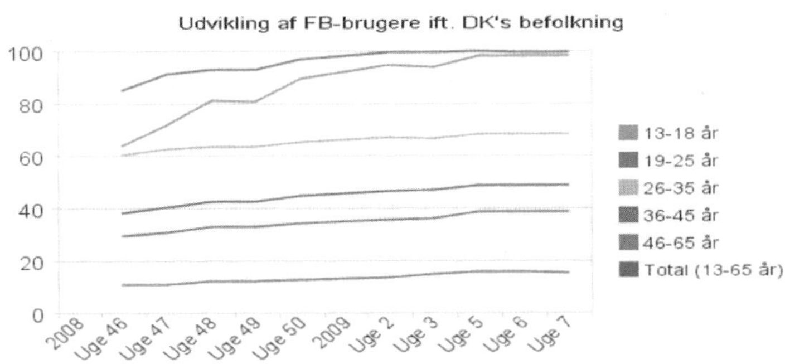

Fig. 4. Percentage of the Danish population using Facebook distributed on age groups (Period: Week 46, 2008 – Week 7, 2009. The average is about 45% in Feb. 2009 (Source: WeMind.dk)

Discussion and Outlook

Web 2.0 is an excellent example of one of the main characteristics of our time: That the cultural digitalization process moves faster than our ability to analyze it [11–13]. While traditional media companies and academia struggle to adapt to the 2.0 phenomenon, the electronic grapevine twitter about Web 3.0 or Web n.0.

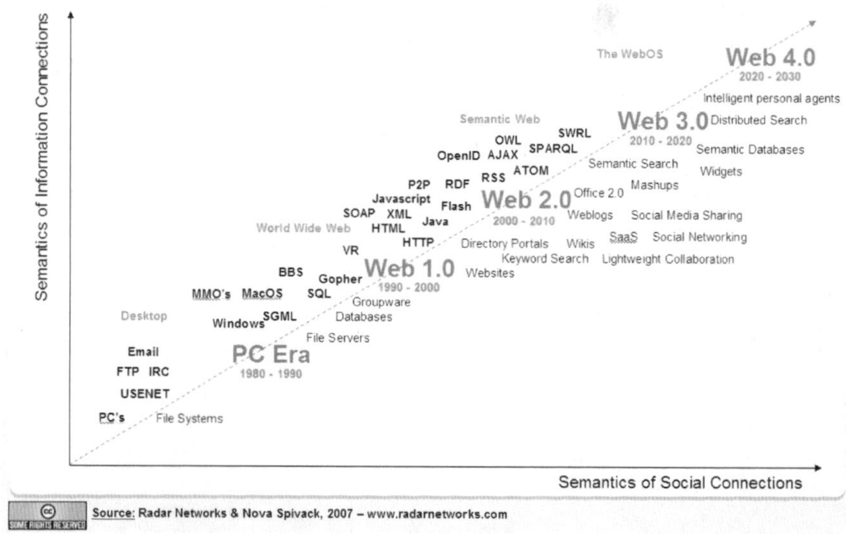

Fig. 5. Web evolution overview (Source: N. Spivack [14])

The development in the adoption of Web 2.0 by Danish Newspaper may be explained by looking at Spivack's model of Web-evolution (Fig. 5). Put somewhat simply Web evolution may be taken to develop in waves – an evolutionary shift between back-end and front-end innovations. New back-end or infrastructure technologies enable new front-end or user-technologies – and vice versa. According to Spivack [15, 16] and Davis [17] Web 2.0 is a front-end revolution that has created an explosion of content and social connectivity. The enormous amount of information created on this user friendly Web has necessitated a new Web infrastructure, the Web 3.0, a new back-end revolution that will enhance machine-machine and human-machine interaction. The evolutionary approach implies a Web of potential infinite informational and social connectivity, a Web n.0.

Applying these ideas to the two surveys indicate that even if the features adopted by the online newspapers have Web 2.0 characteristics (see Fig. 1) there is a great focus on informational connectivity. The services offered are not enhancing social connectivity, except perhaps for blogs and commenting in the category "participation and sharing". Adding bookmarking tools may increase traffic and informational connectivity, but it does not necessarily enhance social connectivity. This points to need for analyzing the phenomenon of social connectivity from the perspective of the user. This may have been understood better by the new media than by traditional media.

The question is whether newspapers – print or online – will survive the era of the service-oriented social Web. The adoption of new forms of delivery indicates that the core offer of traditional newspapers – the news – is shifting from being a product to becoming a service [18, 19]. Thereby the media companies may be undergoing "a paradigmatic shift as they are moving from the logic of exchange of 'goods,' which usually are manufactured output, to one in which service provision rather than goods is fundamental to economic exchange. The key assets in the context of the emerging paradigm of business are e-services like interactivity, connectivity, uncovering customer needs and providing customized offerings" [20].

Tapscott and Williams [21] argue that the border between producers and consumers is blurring, and emphasize that the power self-organizing *prosumer* communities are gaining leads to especially strong tensions in the media sector. Traditional producers and copyright owners will have to adapt to conditions under which open networks, open licenses, copying, remixing and even hacking are the rules of the game. This is a world where content is not merely user-*centered*, but created, managed and controlled by users. Similar conclusions can be found in Rheingold [22], Lessing [23], Anderson [24], Turow and Tsui [25]. Benkler [12] argue that a new mode of production is emerging: *Non-market-* or *commons-based peer production*. Throughout the industrial period the physical and financial costs of fixing information and cultural expressions in a transmission medium were high and increasing. The means of mass communication (the mechanical print press, photo-, film-, radio and television equipment etc.) were reserved companies (or states) that had the necessary capital. Today cheap processors have replaced the mass media technologies of the industrial society and this great reduction of cost has enabled a radical restructuring of our informational and cultural production system; a shift away from heavy reliance on commercial, concentrated business models and towards greater confidence in business strategies not based on intellectual property rights. In this system the access to existing information is almost cost free. As the costs of information management and communication also decrease the "human factor" becomes the only "scarce resource". As in the pre-industrial period, Benkler argue, the production of information and cultural goods no longer takes place on the market.

Thus, user-generated content and social networking are only the tip of the iceberg. The main outlook is that the media industry will have to embrace the emerging "media-as-a-service" paradigm and that the future challenge for web services will be to leverage informational and social connectivity.

References

1. Lindqvist U et al (2008) *New business forms in e-business and media "e-Media"*. Final report of the NICe Project 06212. VTT, Finland
2. CDF (2009) Annual internet survey 2009 – Highlights. Center for the Digital Future: Annenberg School of Communication. http://www.digitalcenter.org/pdf/ 2009_Digital_Future_Project_Release_Highlights.pdf. Accessed 10 Nov. 2009
3. Rasmussen S et al (2008) *Web 2.0 adoption by Danish news papers – urgent need for new business models?* Proceedings of international conference on new media technology, 2008. Graz, 185–193
4. O'Reilly T (2005) O'Reilly network: what is Web 2.0. http://www.oreillynet.com/pub/a/oreilly/tim/news/2005/09/30/what-is-Web-20.html. Accessed 10 Nov. 2009
5. O'Reilly T (2006a) O'Reilly radar > Web 2.0 compact definition: trying again. http://radar.oreilly.com/2006/12/web-20-compact-definition-tryi.html. Accessed 10 Nov. 2009
6. O'Reilly T (2006b) Web 2.0 Meme Map. http://www.oreillynet.com/oreilly/tim/news/2005/09/30/graphics/figure1.jpg. Accessed 10 Nov. 2009
7. Anderson P (2007) *What is Web 2.0? Ideas, technologies and implications for education. JISC Technology and Standards Watch*. JISC, Bristol, Feb. 2007
8. Vickery G, Wunsch-Vincent S (2007) *Participatory web and user-created content*. OECD, Brussels
9. IAB (2009) Social media Ad metrics definitions. Interactive advertising bureau. http://www.iab.net/media/file/Social-Media-Metrics-Definitions-0509.pdf. Accessed 10 Nov. 2009
10. Nielsen (2009) Nielsen NetView, 2/09, http://blog.nielsen.com/nielsenwire/online_mobile/twitters-tweet-smell-of-success/. Accessed 10 Nov. 2009
11. Castells M (2001) *The internet galaxy*. Oxford University Press, Oxford
12. Benkler Y (2006) *The wealth of networks*. Yale University Press, New Haven
13. Beer D, Burrows R (2007) Sociology and, of and in Web 2.0: some initial considerations. *Sociol Res Online* 12(5)
14. Spivack N (2007) http://novaspivack.typepad.com/nova_spivacks_weblog/2007/02/steps_towards_a.html. Accessed 10 November 2009
15. Spivack N (2006) The third-generation web is coming. http://www.kurzweilai.net/meme/frame.html?main=/articles/art0689.html. Accessed 10 Nov. 2009
16. Spivack N (2008) The semantic web. Video: bonnier GRID 2008 conference, Stockholm. http://link.brightcove.com/services/player/bcpid1803302824?bclid=1811464336&bctid=1812111640. Accessed 10 Nov. 2009
17. Davis M (2008) *Semantic wave 2008 report (executive summary)*. Project10X (www.project10x.com), Washington
18. PEJ (2008) The state of the news media 2008. Project for excellence in journalism. http://www.stateofthemedia.org/2008/. Accessed 10 Nov. 2009
19. Lenatti C (2009) How can publishers join the social networking conversation? Futur Newspapers, The Seybold Report, 9(5)

20. Sheth JN, Sharma A (2007) E-services – a framework for growth. In: Evanschitzky H, Iyer GR (eds) *E-services – opportunities and threats.* (pp. 8-12). New York: Springer
21. Tapscott D, Williams AD (2006) *Wikinomics.* Portfolio, New York
22. Rheingold H (2001) *Smart mobs: the next social revolution.* Basic Books, Cambridge
23. Lessing L (2004) *Free culture.* The Penguin Press, New York
24. Anderson C (2008) *Long tail, the revised and updated edition: why the future of business is selling less of more.* Hyperion, New York
25. Turow J, Tsui L (ed) (2006–2008) *The hyperlinked society: questioning connections in the digital age.* University of Michigan Press, University of Michigan Library, Ann Arbor

Citizens Participation in Public Decisions: The Open Source Role

Lucia Scudu*

Abstract This article explores the emerging challenges and opportunities of Open Source Software used in Public Sector as an instrument and method to ensure and to encourage citizen participation in public decisions in e-Democracy projects. The main aim is to verify the presence of these projects and to check if they're realized using Open Source Software and what are the reasons which support this choice. The Open Source can be considered also as an operating model which is used to the development of the software itself. This operating model is based on the democratic principle of sharing information and results, of transparency and participation among community members, in order to achieve common goals. For these characteristics it can be successful used in other fields. The paper will verify, through a research regarding the Italian Regional Administrations how the OSS can be considered a useful operating model that allows to include citizen in public decisions as well as a software.

Introduction

In recent years Information and Communication Technology (ICT) has reached a very high level of development, improving work and communication between people and public/private organizations. The strong development of Internet has contributed to reduce the distances between citizens and Public Administration. E-Democracy (electronic Democracy), in fact, has captured the attention of those Public Administrations interested in communication with citizens. The main goal is to realize a citizen-oriented administration, through actions and projects that can satisfy specific citizens needs. Among the different technologies currently available, the Open Source Software (OSS) seems to be the most suitable solution to achieve this important target. OSS is not just a software, it is a successful operating mode, based on democratic principles. Usually the OSS use in Public Sector is supported only by technical or economic advantages, but the democratic values should be considered too.

---

* University of Cagliari, Cagliari, Italy, lucia_scudu@hotmail.it

A. D'Atri et al. (eds.), *Management of the Interconnected World*,
DOI 10.1007/978-3-7908-2404-9_3,

The purpose of this paper is to verify the presence of e-Democracy project made by OSS, and in particular to check if in this choice there is certain awareness about the characteristics and potentiality of this software, used for citizen participation in public decisions. Then, considering Open Source as an operating model, the paper will check if there are some positive effects for citizen participation in the e-Democracy projects found.

The research method used to test these objectives is the analysis of some case studies, using data collected from multiple sources.

The paper is organized as follow. The next paragraph introduces a review of prior literature, then there is the description of the research methodology; the following paragraph describes data collected and the results of the analysis, the last section concludes the paper.

Background and Literature Review

Open Source refers to software programs that are distributed with their source code; in fact "Open Source" term[1] refers to the availability of source code. OSS involves a variety of fields, and in every sector are considered different aspects [1]. OSS is analysed not only by informatics science, but also from economics, psychology and sociology. Sometimes researchers refer to OSS as well a solution for many problems, for example, the reduction of the digital-divide, the decrease of costs for ICT in Public Sector, and to solve the problems connected with security of e-voting software .

Furthermore, Open Source can be seen in a largest view, not just as a software, but also as an operating model characterized by a community of participants who share information, knowledge and results to achieve common goals, waiving the rights to the critical knowledge component of the innovation, programming code or chemical formula [2]. The OSS operating model has been found also in others fields [2], in which working in a sharing community is an important element for reaching goals. Researchers consider also if the implications of its use for others virtual communities and work groups can be positive [3]. Here, for example, are considered the benefits that should arrive in Public Sector if decisions are taken jointly by a community made up by citizens, experts and administrators with the support of the ICT and the possibility that the OS operating model can offer to users. Creating on-line communities, using this operating model is possible to cover the space-temporary difficulties connected with the use of traditional inclusive model of decisions, outside a local contest.

Literature has investigated OSS use in Public Administration, too. Usually its use is justified by technical/economic reasons, but democratic values should be considered too. In the public choice of software only the firsts aspects are gener-

[1] The term was introduced by the Open Source Initiative founded by Raymond .

ally considered, while the democratic values are neglected [4]. On the contrary, in this choice, these elements should be considered, through combining technical/economic and democratic reasons, especially if the instrument is introduced to promote transparency in government processes, citizen participation, awareness and citizen control in public action, that is democracy itself. Moreover, if Public Sector considers the new possibility of communication offered by the ICT just as a technological evolution, it cannot exploit its real potentiality in this sense [5]. OSS and its characteristics are also analysed as an instrument to realize e-Democracy project [4–10], which can be defined as the use of the ICT to support citizen participation in public decisions [11]. Furthermore, it can be seen as an operating model that can be used for e-Democracy project [5]. This is possible for its characteristics, as described above, which also are the features that an inclusive process of public decision should be have (co-operation, participation, transparency). From this standpoint, a parallelism between Open Source operative model and citizen participation to public decisions can take place. In addition to the operating model, also the technical characteristics that allow a real participation and interaction among users have been considered. The users, in fact, can upload, review and modify document, and this is possible for administrators, experts and citizens too. In this way the data and every useful information to make a conscious choice can be analyzed from every stakeholder, and make public participation more constructive. The use of these instruments is proposed to encourage the dialogue in the urban planning processes in particular [12], and in every process in which the different stakeholder's inclusion in decisions is necessary to create shared solutions. In addition it has been analysed a system which support co-operation, spatial planning and decision making by an integrated concept of shared virtual workspace, Internet mapping and discussion forum and allow public participation in the processes. This way of working also makes urban planning more efficient, less time-consuming and less expensive [13].

Another factor that deserves attention here, is transparency. Using OSS, as described, citizens are able both to get useful information about the problem they are interested in, and to control and verify the correctness of software working at the same time. This is possible only if citizens have informatics skills, and if Public Sector's really aim is to involve them. Moreover, this availability is seen as an openness sign of Public Administration, while the use of proprietary software, without the code, is seen as a synonymous of closure of government processes itself [4].

The OSS use in Public Administration is also analyzed for its security. This is an important feature that public software should have, especially in e-Democracy and e-voting projects [9, 10]. The use of proprietary software, in fact, sometimes has failed, as Diebold case shows [4]; this is a proprietary software used for United State municipality elections, in which code appears in the Internet with some information about the voters.

Obviously, OSS is only an instrument that can support democratic processes, but its use needs some important preconditions. First of all, political legitimacy, awareness about the importance of jointly choice to realize shared actions. Finally, it is necessary to overcome the problem connected with the digital divide.

Research Method

The research method used to test these objectives is the analysis of some case studies. This method is used to analyse and understand the dynamic of considered situation, it can be used to describe, to build and also to test theories, as this paper tries to do. The research is organized as follow:

- definition of a questionnaire to be submitted to Regional Governments for the collection of data;
- selection of cases coherent with the testing goals;
- collection of data from multiple sources (web, questionnaire, forum, interview) to have the possibility of triangulation. and to analyse the argument going from general to particular;
- drawing the final report to compare the theories with empirical results.

The research, which has been developed in 2 months (April/May 2009), is divided into 3 phases. First of all, it has been considered some conferences about e-Democracy and OSS use. In this way it can be considered the guidelines, and in which direction Public Sector is going. Then it has been considered the web site of Regional Administration, to find a "place" dedicated to public discussion, or what else e-Democracy project. Finally, it has been sent a questionnaire to the managers of these projects to understand if the literature reflections are considered in planning e-Democracy project. Analysing these multiple data it can be seen the direction which is taken by Public Administration, what is the situation in practice and how these aspects are considered by the managers of the e-Democracy projects realized by the administrations interviewed.

Data Collect

The Conferences

As told, the first step takes into account the conferences. By analysing these data, it emerges that Public Administration is experiencing a period of great change to became more efficient, without money and time wasting. It is true for technological changes too, in fact the ICT can bee successful used to promote and motivate citizen participation in public choices. This is a core element to grow citizen trust in Public Administration, and to realize public actions that can really satisfy their needs. The central element of the conferences analysed, is the growth of Internet's use, and the increase of social network use. This consideration permits to say that Internet is a very important instrument for information and communication and this fact starts to be considered by Public Sector too, especially for the ones which want to increase citizen engagement in public choice with e-Democracy project. The conferences consider also some case studies in which successful experiments of e-Democracy realized with Open Source Software are described [14, 15].

The Web Site Analysis

The second step of the research is characterised by the individuation of Public Administration consistent with the proposition to test. The choice has regarded Regional Administration, first because it is a territorial entity, in which important decisions are taken for citizens who live in, and because it is out of a local contest, in which traditional inclusive model of decisions can be used. So their web sites have been monitored to find out the presence of e-Democracy projects. In this phase it is emerged that in Italy 16 Regions out 20 have carried out this kind of project, but sometimes it hasn't been easy to individuate.

The Questionnaire

The third step of this research consisted in a questionnaire to submit to the project's managers. The questionnaire is made up by 9 open questions, this structure has been chosen in order not to influence the answers with closed questions. The issues proposed considered all the element of the Open Source both as a software and as an operating model. So the 16 regions have been contacted to ask the availability to participate on this research. Only 12 of them answered positively, but just 10 of them resubmitted the questionnaire completed.

By using open questions is more difficult to summarise the results, but they can be represented using Tables 1 and 2; the follow regards the use of OSS, the reasons that have driven the choice, results and difficulties of the projects considered:

Table 1. Summary of results for e-democracy projects and open source use

	Use of OS	Reasons	Participation	Results	Difficulties
E. Romagna	YES	Ec, Tech, De	YES	Sustainability of the project	Political legitimacy, participation

Friuli V.G.	n.a	n.a	n.a	Suggestion to bills	n.a.
Liguria	NO	–	–	–	–
Marche	YES	Ec, De	YES	Young to policy	Lack of trust
Piemonte	YES	Tech	YES	Document access	Participation
Puglia	YES	Ec, Tech, De	YES	7.5 ml pg read	Lack of trust
Toscana	YES	Ec, Tech, De	YES	Results to Council	Participation
Trentino	YES	Ec, Tech, De	Independent to the instrument	Started various Experiment	Political, procedurals, organizational
Umbria	YES	Ec	YES	Participation's path	Participation
Veneto	YES	Ec	n.a.	n.a.	n.a

Ec: economic, De: democratic, Tech: technological.

To start the questionnaire it has been asked if the project is activated using an Open Source technology, and the reasons for this choice. So, it is possible to know if democratic values of this software are considered in practice. The majority of the interviewed has indicated technical and economic element, but someone has considered also these aspects. In one case emerged that OSS has been chosen for the coherence of its movement and the project principles (activation and participation). Continuing in the analysis of the answers, it emerged that, tendentially, OSS can help citizen participation in public decision, but a first difficult emerges; this is participation itself, because sometimes it is hard to involve citizens. Then it should be considered the importance of political legitimacy and the lack of trust in politics by citizen. Then the questionnaire analyses the community. This element refers to the Open Source operating model, as previous defined. These questions have the aim to verify if this operating model is used in e-Democracy project, and if its use can origin positive implication for participation in public decisions. Then, it has been verified what kind of community developed, and what kind of topic they discuss. The results can be summarize in the following Table 2:

Table 2. Summary of the results for the online community use

	Tipology	Theme discussed	Positive influence in participation
E. Romagna	Software development	Town planning	NO [1]
Marche	Discussion group	Needs, politics	YES
Puglia	Community of practices, of interests, of learning	Access support, comparison	YES
Toscana	Debate's community	Climatic change renewable energies	YES

[1] This question is been certainly misunderstood, the answer in fact refer to community of software, not citizen participants in public life. But looking at the web site is possible to individuate a reference to the community as here considered.

Analysing these questions emerges that only 4 Regions have found the community element in their project. But in one of these 4 cases, it is a software's community rather than a citizen's one interested in their own problems or opportunities. So, in this case, it is obvious that its presence can't have some positive influence for participation. In the other 3 cases the community presence has a positive impact, and in 2 of these 3 cases, the community isn't a spontaneous element, but a factor contemplated by the project itself. This is a very important element, because it permit to underline the value of a collective dimension of participation, typical of OSS, and because only in this way it is possible to attract the interest of discouraged citizen in public life. Moreover it has been claimed that "before promoting the access to decision, it is necessary to promote participation to social, civil, political and cultural life. On-line's community can be the new strategic instrument to give back "participation sense", in particular to younger citizen". Analysing the theme discuss by these community, it emerges that the citizens discuss subjects like policy, needs, trust and sometimes themes like climatic changes and renewable energies.

Conclusion

Open Source is taking an increasing relevance in academic research, and also in researches connected with Public Administration. In particular this software can be used with the aim to reduce ICT costs, but not just for this reason. OSS is analysed for its democratic values of participation and transparency, so it should be used in Public Administration which wants to open itself to citizens. In this paper Open Source is considered also as an operating model, referring to the method used by the developers of the software, who work together sharing information, results and objectives. These are the typical features of inclusive decision making processes too. The aim of this paper is to verify if literature's concept are considered in practice. Here have been analysed some conferences about these themes, then the web site of Regional Administration and final it has been proposed a questionnaire to e-Democracy project's managers in order to see what they really think about it. Considering all data collected, it emerges that the literature reflection are slowly starting to capture the interest of Public Sector, in fact the central guidelines are going toward this direction. Analysing the web site, it appears clear that a space to citizen's communication with administration is present in 16/20 regions, so interaction among citizens, administrators and experts is becoming a very important ingredient to obtain shared programs and actions. By analysing questionnaire answers it can be noting an emerging awareness about the literature considerations described above, because, for example, OSS has been chosen not only for its economic or technical elements, but also for its democratic values, which are viewed as a synonymous of the opening of the Public Sector to citizens. As regard to the operating model, it is emerging its positive impact in involving citizens in public decision, although it is in a starting phase, and this is caused by the lack of the necessaries precondition mentioned above, particularly the political legitimacy. Although the cases in which this operating model is emerged are just 3, the results, as presented, seem to demonstrate an operating model that can be successful used to increase citizens involvement and participation in public life, also making easy the communication between them and the public administrators.

References

1. von Krogh G, Spaeth S (2007) The open source software phenomenon: characteristics that promote research. *J Strateg Inf Syst* 16(3):236–253
2. Ulhoi JP (2004) Open source development: a hybrid in innovation and management theory. *Manage Decis* 42(9):1095. ABI/INFORM Global
3. Feller J, Fitzgerald B (2000) *A framework analysis of the open source development paradigm.* University College Cork, Ireland
4. Berry DM, Moss G (2006) Free and open source software: opening and democratising e-government's black box. *Inf Polity* 11(1):21–34
5. Rushkoff D (2003) *Open source democracy how online communication is changing offline politics.* DEMOS, London
6. Jayasena GN, Karunaratna DD (2007) Towards an enabling framework for eDemocracy through the integration of citizen participation along the spatial dimension using free and open source technologies. *Spec Issue Int J Comput Internet Manage* 15(SP4)
7. Kavanagh E (2006) Citizen auditors-web-enabled, open-source government. *Public Manager* 35(1):20–25
8. Brito J (2008) Improving government transparency online. *Public Manager* 37(1): 22–26
9. Moynihan DP (2004) Building secure elections: e-voting, security, and systems theory. *Public Adm Rev* 64(5):515–528
10. Rios Insua D, Kersten GE, Rios GC (2008) Towards decision support for participatory democracy, *Information Systems and E-Business Management,* 6(2):161–191
11. Formez (2004) Linee guida per la promozione della cittadinanza digitale: e-democracy. Supema srl
12. Gordon TF, Richter G (2002) Discourse support systems for deliberative democracy. Lecture Notes in Computer Science, 2456:325–334
13. Schmidt-Belz B, Gordon TF, Voss H (1998) Urban planning with GeoMed first user experiences. In Proceedings of the 6th ACM International Symposium on Advances in Geo-praphic Information Systems, (pp.82–87), New York: ACM
14. Marzano F, Pubblica Amministrazione 2.0? http://www.tosslab.it/documentazione even-ti/edemocracy-marzano, Accessed April 2010
15. Manzari V, Il contributo delle nuove tecnologie al processo di e-Demoracy. http://iniziative.forumpa.it/files/documents/file/portal/websemantico_29ottobre/eDemocracy _Mi lano_ottobre2008_a_101.pdf, Accessed April 2010

A System Dynamics Model to Identify and Measure the Paper Digitization Advantages in Public Administration

Nunzio Casalino*, **Stefano Armenia**† and **Mauro Draoli**‡

Abstract This study provides a System Dynamics model built to identify the benefits arising from the process of digitization in the Italian Public Administration. The paper describes the process in terms of the causal relationships between systemic variables that define the underlying structure of the problem. The analysis focuses on the interaction between the "outer world" of the citizens and the "inner world" of the Italian Administrations, by designing a causal loop diagram and a stock and flow simulation model. The systemic approach allows considering many crucial aspects for the digitization problem and provides a rich analysis that shows how those obstacles brought forward by social and psychological factors may become a great obstacle to organizational change.

Introduction

The process of managing digital documents is recognized as faster, safer and cheaper than the paper one. Granting fast process and reducing costs both for the public and for the private sectors, it can be used as a high leverage tool in order to gain a higher efficiency rate [1, 2]. The e-government is a broad process of innovation in public administration with particular reference to the internal administrative process and to the relations with the outside world. There is a positive correlation between the gradual diffusion of technology within the Public Administration and increasing socio-economic well-being [3]. Paper dematerialization is an issue that has affected mostly the existing rules making a radical transformation, still in place, of the activities of public and private institutions. In particular, the collection of norms known as "Codice dell'Amministrazione Digitale" is on a real overhaul that transforms the existing digitization in a strong requirement for the institutions, introducing at the same time, in relation to the documentation to be submitted to the administration, new guaranteed rights to citizens and companies [4, 5]. The following government plan, known as "Piano E-gov 2012" is another key initiative for the future of the Italian country. In a context of economic crisis this Plan, in line

* Dipartimento di Scienze Economiche ed Aziendali, Università degli Studi "Guglielmo Marconi", Roma, Italy, n.casalino@unimarconi.it

† CATTID, Università degli Studi di Roma "La Sapienza", Roma, Italy, armenia@cattid.uniroma1.it

‡ DigitPA, National Centre for Informatics in PA, Roma, Italy, draoli@digitpa.gov.it

A. D'Atri et al. (eds.), *Management of the Interconnected World*,
DOI 10.1007/978-3-7908-2404-9_4,

with the Lisbon strategy, deals the problem of competition distance between Italy and more advanced Countries, aiming to renew the institutions and to improve the efficiency of Public Administration. Among the main objectives of the new E-gov Plan, there is one relating to paper digitization whose goal is to reduce, within 2012, the conventional paper flows and to increase totally digital documents.

A Perspective on Document Digitization

While seeking streamlined processes and better customer satisfaction, many Italian Public Administrations are also looking at the document workflow management aspect as a potential solution to gain in efficiency while maintaining a high customer satisfaction. However, the simplification process of administrative activity goes back to the early 90s when the public institutions was concerned by rules involved to improve the quality of services for the citizens. In this context, the process of paper digitization is an example of "change" in the Italian Public Administration, both in technical and organizational/managerial aspects, led by the ICT development and especially for their diffusion and adoption. The declared purpose is the progressive reduction of the number of paper administrative documents handled by the administrations, while managing a proportional and gradual increase of the digital document management combined with the replacement of traditional hard copies.

The introduction of specific technologies such as digitization, the certified mail, digital signatures, the electronic ID and the card of national service, was part of change inside the PA Italian. The digital document is the "computer representation of actions, facts or data legally relevant" (art. 1, lett. P, CAD), which is valid for the purposes of the law and may meet the same requirements of the paper document. Digital documents offer significant benefits for the Public Administration. It will allow faster drawing up and transmission, can be multimedia; presents ease of management and storing. The digitization of the document is essential for the Public Administration change because it is from and in it that diverge and converge the different administrative activities; the introduction of on-line documents are different options for computer-based processes (such as payments on-line) and the digitization allows a paper to become computer-based. The certified e-mail and digital signature represent additional tools to overcome the "weakness" of their predecessors, introducing the concept of legal validity of the information thus exchanged. Legislation on digitization field has led to define the concept of data-management protocol such as the widespread adoption of document management system and electronic administrative processes, with protocol information. Indeed, there are more opportunities to search, greater availability of information, greater security and faster time of transmission. All of these instruments represent the most important means of radical administrative transformation that digitization entails because permit, in addition to a substantial change in the way of working inside the Public Administrations, significant advantages in terms of cost, time and human resources management.

A Dynamic Analysis of the Digitization Process

Our study has focused mainly on the analysis, by means of the system dynamics approach, of how the document digitization process in the Italian public administration may contribute to the vision of the so called "digital administration" which, according to this vision, ought to produce great benefits for the citizens and for the same public administration.

Our starting point was the identification of the two main interacting "worlds", the "inner" world (or PA world) and the "outer" one (or citizens world), which in turn has allowed us to first study the specific dynamics of these two sub-models and then the dynamics due to the interaction between them. On the Administration side, we studied the whole document management process, pointing out how the introduction of new IT technologies (like the Certified Mail and Digital Signature services) may influence the volume of internal digital documents, thus saving both on average document production and archiving costs. On the citizens' side, we analyzed how IT alphabetization and being used to interact online with PA-offered services by means of the new technologies constitute important variables which are able to reduce the Italian Digital Divide with respect to the European average. However, some obstacles still exist which prevent a full and satisfying interaction experience between administrations and citizens, and these are mainly due to cultural issues and attitude towards change. In fact, the digitization process implies a deep change in many domains inside the PA, both on a technological perspective and from the tools needed to accomplish all the activities, up to the eventual redefinition of the whole document management system.

Methodological Approach

The main hypotheses that we assumed while conceptualizing our model concern the resources which are available for the PA to be spent on the marketing and promotion of the new online services, thus ultimately stimulating the citizens to use them. The final objective of our policy analysis will be to show to what extent the digitization process may lead to sensible advantages for the PA, also trying to analyze how such a process may get spread out in the actual context. It was however necessary to recur to some "simplified" modeling or functions for some of the systems variables; such hypotheses have been validated by domain experts as totally realistic [1, 4, 5]. Our analysis also includes a few elements usually not considered in "classic" digitization literature, like the word of mouth effect, whose impacts on the technical digitization process are hard to forecast without a systemic analysis; according to our approach [6], those variables are instead crucial if we want to understand how eventually the system is able to succeed in its mission.

The Causal Relationships Diagrams

According to the System Dynamics approach, the model has been designed starting from a qualitative analysis carried out by causal mapping, which describes the main relations and interconnections between various parts of the system. This map is represented by an oriented di-graph G(V,E), where the vertex set V represents the variables, while the edges set E represents effects (positive or negative) that a particular variable causes on the next linked one. Each causal link is described by an algebraic sign that shows either the direct (positive) or inverse (negative) proportionality between each couple of elements. The cycles appearing in the graph are called causal feedback loops, and they may be Reinforcing Feedback Loops (those having an even number of "minus" signs) and Balancing Feedback Loops (those having an odd number of minus signs). The relations among the reported systemic variables have been validated both by CNIPA experts and by previous studies [1].

The first reinforcing feedback (R1) loop shows that if online interaction between PA and citizens increases, then IT alphabetization grows and consequently Internet usage, and this will increase the number of accesses to the PA websites. In this way the online service usage will grow, together with actual users of these services. This growth is followed by an increased introduction of digital documents and a consequently increased quantity of digital documents inside the PA and of documents registered, decreasing the documents average unit cost of production; thus, the advantage perceived from PA grows, and so the latter increase its computerization (Fig. 1).

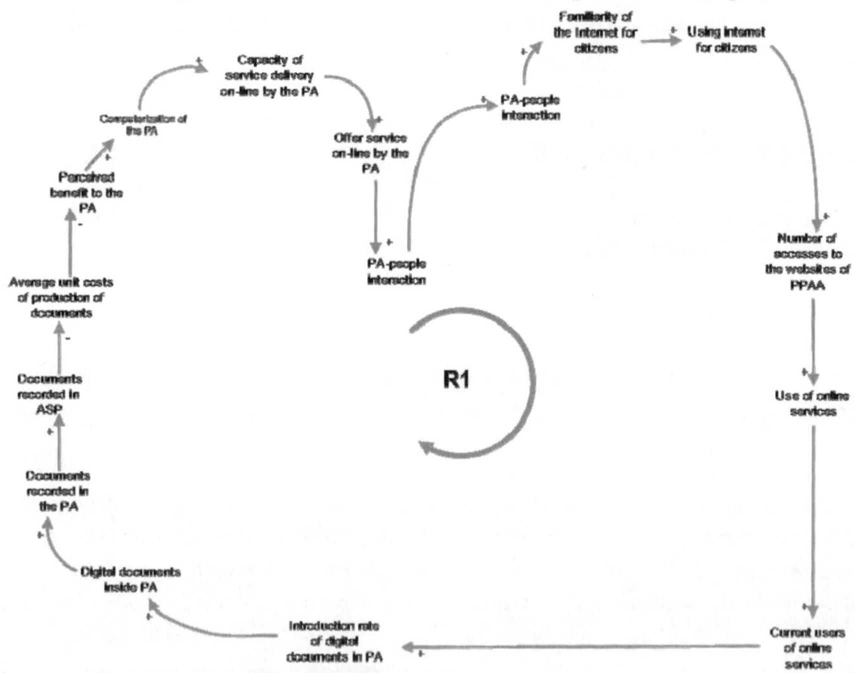

Fig. 1. R1: Loop describing the impact due to on-line services utilization by the citizens on public administrations cost savings from protocol procedures

The self-balancing feedback (B1) puts in evidence how online interaction between PA and citizenship causes, through Internet use and number of accesses to PA websites, to increase the online services usage with a consequent growth of the digital documents introduction and so of documents that can be filed. In this way digital archives dimension will increase together with their operative costs, which are in inverse proportion with PA obtainable advantage from digital documents storage versus paper documents storage. Public Administration, perceiving an advantage, will continue to computerize its processes (Fig. 2).

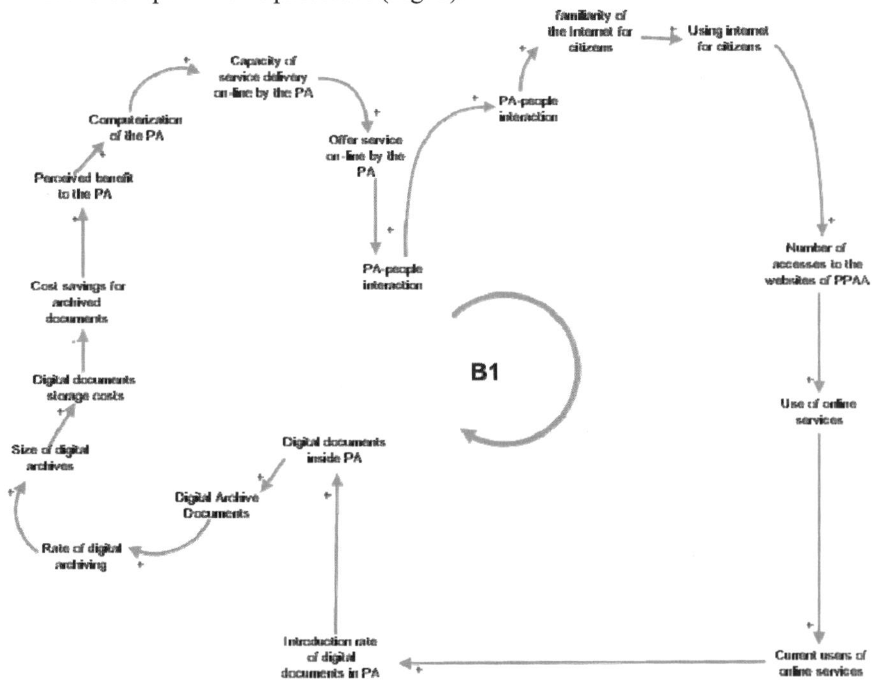

Fig. 2. B1: Use cycle of online services by citizens' savings on storage costs for the administration

A System Dynamic Based Digitization Process Model

The causal maps are just the starting point for creating a *stock and flow* model, which can then be simulated to study the system if a policy reach its goal or not. In general, the Stocks (or Levels) are accumulators that shows the state of the system, and works as memory of the system; their values aren't instantaneously calculated, creating an implicit delay effect on the system. Every stock has variations due to Flows, that can increase (Inflows) or decrease (Outflows) the stock level. This representation works well to analyze the feedback loops aforementioned, that are the depiction of the context surrounding the document management procedures. Implemented model describes five main processes: the document flow in PA, the model of the adoption of PEC and FD in Public Administration, the model of the quality of offered services, the model of interaction between PA and citizens, the model of the adoption of online services by citizens. At the end of the simulation (which will be detailed later in this work), it will be clear which leverages and governance policies ought to be implemented in order to make the digitization technology successful, and which advantages may be obtained through its use [7–10].

The main variables to describe the documents flow into the PA are the archive dimensions and the total of paper documents, digital documents, documents archived in both ways that, granting the reduction of the average unit cost of production, can allow to quantify savings for PA against the only paper documents usage.

Notably, from this model it can be seen how the paper digitization brings to interesting cost savings for the Public Administration.

In the model of the adoption of Certified mail (PEC) and Digital Signature (FD) in Public Administration it was used the Bass Model, conveniently modified for this case, in which the adoption rate is given by the interaction probability among users that were already using the technology and the ones that, potentially, could use it.

The adoption model of the offered services quality wants to represent how the citizens satisfaction increase with the quality supplied by the PA employed.

The model of PA and citizenship interaction represents the union between this two worlds. In fact, it has been seen how this interaction is influenced by both services offered by the PA and services demanded by citizens to the PA itself.

The most significant change concerns the adoption rate that empty the potential users stock to fill up the actual online services users level. This rate is influenced by word of mouth adoptions, through the contact between actual users and potential users and by marketing effect adoptions, influenced themselves by the percentage of ICT expenses in marketing, that makes aware potential users of these services.

Analysis of Simulation Results

As a first step, we put the systemic variables under the so called condition of "simulation stress", to provide realistic and acceptable values for them. The time line considered for our simulation scenario is 5 years. After a few warm-up simulation runs, based on the elaboration of some historical data [2, 11], the values which were identified for the following listed input variables were:

- paper document archiving cost: €18.00;
- digital document archiving cost: €9.00;
- average unit costs of production of paper documents: €1.8;
- average unit costs of production of digital documents: €0.9;
- percentage of marketing expenditure: 3–5%;
- percentage of employees trained on ICT: 50–70%.

Output variables subject to examination are actual and potential users number, the word of mouth adoption and the marketing effect adoption, average unit costs of production and storage saving, service quality and citizens satisfaction and actual and potential PA that uses PEC and FD. In the following we report the results related to storage costs saving given by the digital to paper document substitution and the average unit costs of production of digital documents saving thanks to the ASP mode registration (Table 1).

Table 1. Savings in the cost of storage and in average unit costs of production of documents

Time	Cost of storage (€)	Time	Average unit costs of production (€)
2009/01/01	0	2009/01/01	0
2010/01/01	1,054,012.97	2010/01/01	398,510.43
2011/01/01	7,337,007.72	2011/01/01	2,216,152.69
2012/01/01	20,418,682.75	2012/01/01	5,005,948.37
2013/01/01	40,667,728.24	2013/01/01	8,288,606.73
2014/01/01	68,913,115.89	2014/01/01	12,035,753.75

With the digital documents usage, costs saving for Public Administration will increase from year to year.

Table 2. Trends for savings in the cost of storage and in average unit costs of production of documents

Time	Cost of storage (€)	Time	Average unit costs of production (€)
2009/01/01	0	2009/01/01	4
2010/01/01	1,054,339.68	2010/01/01	398,641.08
2011/01/01	7,344,947.14	2011/01/01	2,218,902.18
2012/01/01	20,471,374.75	2012/01/01	5,022,167.28
2013/01/01	40,882,112.64	2013/01/01	8,348,202.47
2014/01/01	69,539,831.75	2014/01/01	12,192,170.10

The results shown in Table 2 were obtained through the use of two managerial levers: percentage of expenses in marketing and percentage of employed that follows ICT courses. These variables were varied respectively from 5 to 7% and from 50 to 70%. The simulation shows how, after the actuation of both the cited policies, there is a considerable growth of PA costs saving, with a +1.30% average unit costs of production saving and +0.90% of storage costs saving.

Conclusions

The study carried out how paper digitization constitutes a big challenge for the Public Administration to reach many benefits. Paper digitization is the set of activities to solve the typical problems of the paper such as the access and transmission difficulties, high costs of handling, search, storing, space, costs and timing. The introduction of a fully computer-based document management within Public

Administrations and companies, although it represents only a small improvement can be applied in the reengineering of administrative processes, it is a goal that could take place quickly. The document management system, however, gives the possibility of several improvements within the administrations. With the digitalization of administrative processes, it is possible to obtain very large savings in time and in economic terms. The study shows that there are at least two variables on which the government should "leverage" to optimize [11] its internal structure and, consequently, derive all possible advantages [12]. First, we have seen as raising awareness of citizens plays a key role for the system. Second, another major challenge to introduce innovation in Public Administration concerns the improvement of ICT and organizational skills through proper training and recruitment. It should be emphasized that the benefits arising from the process of paper digitization within the administrations are obtained mainly on a large scale basis [13]. It is needed, in essence, to overcome the breakeven point to cover investments and, consequently, derive its benefits.

References

1. Armenia S, Canini D, Casalino N (2008) A system dynamics approach to the paper dematerialization process in the Italian public administration. In *D'Atri et al. (Eds.), Interdisciplinary Aspects of Information Systems Studies*. Springer, Heidelberg, Germany
2. CNIPA (2006) La dematerializzazione della documentazione amministrativa. Quaderno 24, Rome
3. CNIPA (2006) La dematerializzazione della documentazione amministrativa – Libro bianco del Gruppo di lavoro interministeriale per la dematerializzazione della documentazione tramite supporto digitale, Rome
4. Senge P (1992) *The fifth discipline*. Bantam Doubleday Dell Publishing Group, New York
5. Sterman JD (2000) *Business dynamics – system thinking and modeling for a complex world*. Irwin McGraw Hill, Boston
6. Ridolfi P (2007) Dematerializzazione e semplificazione dei procedimenti: l'Innovazione possibile. In Dal protocollo alla conservazione sostitutiva: la gestione efficace di contenuti e processi, Torino
7. Radzicki MJ (2007) *Foundation of system dynamics modeling*. Office of Policy and International Affairs
8. Casalino N (2008) *Gestione del cambiamento e produttività nelle aziende pubbliche. Metodi e strumenti innovativi*, Cacucci Editore, Bari
9. Piano E-gov (2012) Ministero per la pubblica amministrazione e l'innovazione
10. Morecroft JDW, Sterman J (2000) *Modeling for learning organization*. Productivity Press, Oregon
11. Bass F (1969) A new product growth model for consumer durables. *Manage Sci* 15(5):215–227
12. Burns JR (2002) A matrix architecture for development of system dynamic models. In *Proceedings of the 20th International Conference System Dynamics Society*, Palermo, Italy
13. Burns JR (2002) A component strategy for the formulation of system dynamics model. In *Proceedings of the 20th International Conference System Dynamics Society*, Palermo, Italy

ICTs in an Ageing Society: An Overview of Emerging Research Streams

Francesca Ricciardi *

Abstract Because of the paramount demographic changes involving the western world, the so-called "Information Society" is going to be also an "Ageing Society". Severe problems are emerging, involving for example the pension system, the healthcare system, or the labor market. Of course, ICTs and IS are called to action in this scenario. How are the researchers addressing the issue of the technological needs in an ageing world? To answer this question, a systematic Literature Survey was conducted, during which 419 papers and books were identified and analyzed in their disciplinary approaches and main outcomes. What came out is that whilst the issue of the technological needs of our ageing society is quite thoroughly investigated from other disciplinary fields, such as Medicine or Engineering or Human–Computer Interaction studies, it is quite overlooked by Organizational Studies. A new brief Research Agenda, identifying some possible new Research Questions about this topic for Information Systems/Organizational Studies researchers, is the outcome of this work.

Demographic Change, New Needs

Population ageing, resulting from low birth rates and increasing longevity, is now well established in the western world. Moreover, because of other important social changes (e.g. growth of female work), traditional solutions for elderly assistance are fading: a large and growing part of elderly population does not live with their family, and can't count (or can count only partially) on the traditional assistance of their loved ones. The Information Society, in other words, is going to be also an Ageing Society. These changes are severely challenging the existing healthcare, pension, labor market systems.

New needs are emerging:

- *On the part of elderly people:* tools and systems that provide information, advice, advocacy, warnings, facilities, supports, prosthesis, as for: security; safety; mobility; health; personal care; shopping; household administration;

* Catholic University, Milan, Italy, francesca.ricciardi@unicatt.it

A. D'Atri et al. (eds.), *Management of the Interconnected World*,
DOI 10.1007/978-3-7908-2404-9_5, © Springer-Verlag Berlin Heidelberg 2010

housework; work environment and work conditions (for older workers); sport, fun, social and cultural activities; asserting one's rights as a citizen and as a consumer, etc.

- *On the part of caregivers*: (both for family and professional caregivers) tools and systems that can make care-giving easier and more effective; tools and systems that let caregivers concentrate on the most important, i.e. human and social aspects of care-giving, alleviating the other tasks; (for family caregivers only) tools and systems that make care-giving less time- and money- consuming.
- *On the part of the Public Administration*: enhancing prevention of accidents and diseases amongst elderly population; keeping the percentages of hospitalizations and use of public retirement homes under control; identifying saving strategies to compensate for increasing assistance/healthcare/pension expenses due to ageing population; enhancing the efficiency of services offered to elderly people.
- *On the part of the society as a whole*: keeping social costs of ageing population under control; having more healthy, active, informed old members; having younger people (especially the women) available for the labor market and for other activities, even when they have old parents and /or grandparents to care for.

Research Question

The situation, of course, dramatically calls the ICTs to action. The possibilities offered by the new technologies in order to meet the needs of an ageing society had already been taken into consideration in "before-the-web" years [1]; today, with the world-wide spread of net services, the field of studies is potentially even more vast and rich.

The Research Questions, then, are the following:

How are the researchers addressing the issue of the information society in an ageing world? What writings are being published on the international scene about this subject? With what focuses, what disciplinary approaches, what outcomes? Are there any streams of studies which result overlooked, and which on the contrary would deserve more thorough attention?

To answer to the Research Questions, a survey of the available literature in the field of ageing – AAL has been conducted.

Literature Search Method

The methodological reference model for the Literature Search that will be presented below is the work of Vom Brocke et al. [2], according to which «the process of searching the literature must be comprehensibly described. Only then can readers assess the exhaustiveness of the review and other scholars in the field can more confidently (re)use the results in their own research». Vom Brocke et al. propose a five phases circular framework for the literature search process.

In a first phase, the *literature review scope* must be clearly defined. In this case, the literature search *focus* will span all the types of writings, from theoretical to application-centred ones, given that the main goal of this study is understanding the whole range of different approaches existing to the topic of ICTs in an ageing society. The literature search *goal* consists in identifying the central issues (both those which are already thoroughly studied, and those which are quite neglected at the moment) of the topic. The literature search, consequently, will be *organized* by identifying a limited number of core issues/disciplinary approaches and by classifying the identified writings on the basis of such a framework. The literature search *perspective* is essentially neutral: there is no interest here to promote one or another position or policy about the issue. The *audience* of the search is made up of specialized scholars; the *coverage* of the literature search is not meant to be exhaustive, but reasonably representative of the main groups of writings available in this field.

The second phase consists in *identifying the key concepts* of the topic. In this search, the key concepts identified were the emerging needs of the ageing society; they have been synthesized in the first paragraph, entitled "Demographic Change, New Needs".

The third phase is the literature search itself. During literature search, the researcher must choose the databases to explore; then, the most convenient keywords and search criteria must be selected; finally, the processes of backward search and forward search must be addressed. «Whereas the process of backward search [...] refers to reviewing older literature cited in the articles yielded from the keyword search [...], forward search [...] means both reviewing additional sources that have cited the article and reviewing the authors' following publications» [2]. Evaluation of writings, aimed to restrict the review only to literature relevant to the topic, may be conducted essentially on titles and abstracts. Database search, keyword search, backward search and forward search choices of this study will be described in the following paragraph entitled "Literature Search".

During the fourth phase, the identified *literature must be analyzed and synthesized.* In this case, a simple concept matrix has been studied, to give a systematic order to the search outcomes and to facilitate the process of answering the Research Questions. The concept matrix will be presented in the paragraph entitled "Literature Search outcomes".

The literature search process never comes to a definitive end. A good literature review is expected to result in a new *research agenda* that usually is more insightful than the research question posed in the first place. This may easily call for further, more specific literature search, in a circular process, which may involve other scholars. The research agenda resulting from the literature search hereby presented will be described in the last paragraph.

Literature Search

The on-line databases selected for this literature search are the following: Springer Publishing (books); Springer (books); Business Source Premier; Econlit; E-journals; Health Technology Assessment.

Springer Publishing was selected because of its strong focus on gerontology, health care and social work. The Springer Publishing website provides a search interface. Two different searches were conducted (in April, 2009): in the first search, the system was requested to search the word "technology" in the title and/or description of the book. The system found 80 books. In the second search, the system was requested to search the words "aging", "web" and "internet" in the title and/or description of the book (no Boolean choice was possible: the system apparently used the Boolean operator OR automatically). The system found 120 books. Among the 80+120 identified books, 23 were considered relevant for this search.

Springer was selected because of its strong tradition in the fields of technology and social sciences. The Springer website provides a navigation tool that lets the user see what is published in the different disciplinary fields covered by the publishing house. The search was conducted in this way (April–May, 2009): first, the discipline "social sciences" and the sub-discipline "aging" was investigated. The system found 113 books, 18 of which were judged relevant for this work. Then the discipline Informatics was explored, and particularly the sub-disciplines User Interfaces, HCI and Ergonomics: 85 books were found, of which 1 was considered relevant. In the Sub-discipline Information Systems, 184 books were found, of which 1 was considered relevant. Finally, the Discipline Economics was examined, and particularly the sub-discipline Economy of Populations: 26 books were found, of which 1 was judged relevant.

The on-line databases *Business Source Premier, Econlit, E-journals, Health Technology Assessment* were chosen because they span a vast field of publications (papers and journal articles above all), which may focus on the issue of interest. They were investigated through the EBSCO on-line system. In this case, the search was conducted in the months of February and March 2009. The query asked the system to search in the Abstracts the following words: "(aging OR ageing OR elderly) AND (e-services OR web OR internet OR divide OR information technology OR information systems)". The system found 820 writings, among which 197 were considered relevant for this work.

Considering that 23 + 18 + 1 + 1 + 1 + 197 = 241 writings had been already identified, it was decided to dramatically restrict Backward Search. Among the 241 writings, one book was chosen, which demonstrated particularly focused on the issue at hand, and particularly rich in reference lists [3]. Moreover, this book is quite recent (2003) and it is edited by scholars with a long experience and several publications in the field. These reasons were considered sufficient to start concentrating on this book for backward search. Backward search conducted on this sole book yielded as many as 776 writings, among which 178 were considered relevant for this search (the remaining were mostly medical writings, strongly focused on specific medical problems such as osteoarthritis or dementia).

At that point, the search had yielded 241 + 178 = 419 writings, most of which quite recent (published after 1995). This amount of writings was considered a sufficient pool to identify the main issues on which scholars are focusing in these years, and then to answer the Research Questions. Consequently, it was decided not to perform any Forward Search in this case, nor any further Backward Search, postponing them until further, more specific Research Questions will make a more restricted search process possible.

Literature Search Outcomes

The 419 identified writings were organized into a concept matrix (Table 1) to assess the different research streams that researchers are developing in these years about the issue of ICTs in an ageing world.

Table 1. Concept matrix designed to organize the search outcomes into a references database

Cod.	Reference	Abstract	Source	Full text	Backward Search	Disciplinary standpoint(s)
(1)	(2)	(3)	(4)	(5)	(6)	(7)
…	…	…	….	…	…	…
…	…	…	…	…	…	…

The matrix includes a progressive code (1, on the table) that unambiguously identifies each writing; the complete reference in standard format (2, on the matrix); the abstract (3); the source (4) that made the identification of the writing possible (Springer Publishing website; Springer website; EBSCO databases; Backward Search); the URL of the full text, when available on the Internet (5); weather or not a backward search was carried out starting from the writing (6). The analysis of the identified literature confirmed that the issue "how could new technologies enhance successful ageing?" is a typically *interdisciplinary* one, which can be seen from many standpoints. Seven main disciplinary standpoints were identified, and each writing was given a minimum of 1, maximum of 3 disciplinary standpoint(s) code (see column 7 of the Concept matrix of Table 1). The outcomes were the following:

1. *Physiology and Pathology of Ageing* disciplinary standpoint. It mainly focuses on assessing elderly people cognitive, perceptive, mobility and psychological problems/abilities, providing clues about what their main (technological) needs could be. Eighteen Percent of the 419 identified writings have been classified as addressing the issue from this standpoint; see [4] in the Reference List as an example of one of the most relevant publications within this group.
2. *Social Sciences* disciplinary standpoint. It mainly focuses on elderly people and on caregivers as new, important subjects of the "Information Society". Thirty Four Percent of the 419 identified writings have been classified as addressing the issue from this standpoint; see [5] in the Reference List as an example of one of the most relevant publications within this group.
3. *Engineering/architecture/design Sciences* disciplinary standpoint. It mainly focuses on artifacts (tools, devices, hardware+software systems, prosthesis, etc.) that may support independent living, and on the so-called "gerontechnology". Sixteen Percent of the 419 identified writings have been classified as addressing the issue from this standpoint; see [6] in the Reference List as an example of one of the most relevant publications within this group.
4. *Human Factors – Human Computer Interaction* disciplinary standpoint. It mainly focuses on Task Analysis, Performance analysis, Interfaces design, Training design, considering the elderly as users of systems; in this field, a growing amount of studies is focusing on *web acceptance and web usability* on the part of old people. One could say that the Human Factors disciplinary standpoint is part of the more general discipline of Design, and then should be included in previous Point 3; nevertheless, the paramount percentage of identified studies and the important peculiar characteristics of this approach led to the creation of a specific Disciplinary Standpoint. As many as 46% of the 419 identified writings have been classified as addressing the issue from this standpoint; see [7] in the Reference List as an example of one of the most relevant publications within this group.

5. *Organizational Studies* disciplinary standpoint. It mainly focuses on how the organizations (both of private and public sector) dealing with elderly customers/users/citizens (and their caregivers) should organize their processes and manage their knowledge base. Five Percent of the 419 identified writings have been classified as addressing the issue from this standpoint; see [8] in the Reference List as an example of one of the most relevant publications within this group.
6. *Healthcare* disciplinary standpoint. It mainly focuses on the specific topic of how to provide (public) healthcare to the growing number of elderly people, and on how to keep the related costs under control. Again, one could consider the Healthcare disciplinary standpoint as a particular case (dedicated to the healthcare industry) of the Organizational Studies disciplinary standpoint of previous Point 5; nevertheless, the creation of a specific Disciplinary Standpoint was deemed appropriate because of the astonishing amount of studies dedicated to the healthcare industry, in comparison to all the other industries having the elderly as customers/users, and also because of the approach of these studies, often starting from a medical, more than organizational, background. Twenty-seven Percent of the 419 identified writings have been classified as addressing the issue from this standpoint; see [9] in the Reference List as an example of one of the most relevant publications within this group.
7. *Policies and Strategies* disciplinary standpoint. It mainly focuses on general strategic challenges of public and private organizations facing the issue of ageing population. Five Percent of the 419 identified writings have been classified as addressing the issue from this standpoint; see [10] in the Reference List as an example of one of the most relevant publications within this group.

(Please note that the sum of all the percentages is above 100%, because each writing could be given up to 3 disciplinary codes).

Conclusions and New Research Agenda

The literature survey conducted in this study reveals that there are disciplinary areas already showing a strong interest in the emerging issue of the ageing society and its (technological) needs. Scholars with a background in Social Sciences, Medicine, Psychology, Engineering, Web design, Human–Computer Interaction and Human Factors are focusing on the ageing society issue, and are producing a considerable amount of literature about what the role of ICTs in this field could be. On the other hand, scholars with a background in Organizational Studies and Information Systems seem to substantially overlook this topic. The percentage of writings addressing the issue from this standpoint is very low (5%); moreover, among this 5%, most writings are not specifically focused on the elderly, but on more general categories, such as disadvantages persons needing social services; and several of these writings are not recent, dating back to the before-the-web era. In other words, ICT (web) based solutions for enhancing independent living of the elderly are being taken into consideration essentially in their technological dimension (how do they work? What can they do?) and as for their interface performances (Are they easy to use for the elderly?). On the contrary, questions such as "how should *the process* of providing (ICT based) solutions for elderly customers/users/workforce *be managed* (by the private or the public sector)?" appear quite overlooked by the 419 writings identified in the literature survey, with the sole, but important exception of those focused on the healthcare industry. A new research agenda may, then, be drawn: a specific, in-depth literature search is needed, focused on the organizational issues of the information *and* ageing society.

In conclusion, the outcome of this paper is a strong encouragement to identify and investigate the most fertile and promising research streams of this (still) almost uncultivated topic.

References

1. Pollack GR (1982) Information system design and implementation: strategies for success. *J Appl Gerontol* 1(1):104–114
2. Vom Brocke J, Simons A, Niehaves B, Riemer K, Plattfaut R, Cleven A (2009) Reconstructing the giant: on the importance of rigour in documenting the literature search process. Paper presented at the 17th European Conference on Information Systems (ECIS 2009), Verona, Italia. Accepted for publication.
3. Charness N, Schaie W, (eds) (2003) *Impact of technology on successful aging*. Springer Publishing, New York
4. Capezuti E, siegler EL, Mezey M (eds) (2007) *The encyclopedia of elder care*. Springer Publishing, New York
5. Mollenkopf H, Walker A (eds) (2007) *Quality of life in old age. International and multi-disciplinary perspectives*. Springer, Dordrecht
6. Beula Devamalar PM, Thulasi Bai V, Srivatsa SK (2009) Design and architecture of real-time web-centric tele-health diabetes diagnosis expert system. *Int J Med Eng Inform* 1(3):307–317
7. Morrell RW, Dailey SR, Feldman C, Mayhorn CB, Echt KV (2001) *Older adults and information technology: a compendium of scientific research and web site accessibility guidelines*. National Institute of Aging, Washington
8. Christianson J, Applebaum R, Carcagno G, Phillips B (1988) Organizing and delivering case management services. *Home Health Care Serv Q* 9(1):7–27
9. Bath PA (2008) Health informatics: current issues and challenges. *J Inf Sci* 34(4):501–518
10. Siebert H (ed) (2002) *Economic policy for aging societies*. Springer, Berlin

Analyzing the Structure and Complexity of a Service Provision Network: Potential Applications to Network Assessment

Miguel Ángel Sicilia Urban* **and Manuel Jesús Prieto Martín**†

Abstract Measuring service structure is a requirement to advance our scientific understanding of service provision. This paper describes a method to analyze some aspects of service complexity from the viewpoint of the number of collaborating elements and their relations. All these relationships determine to some extent the complexity of the service production and indirectly, its final quality and the possible incidents during service provision. The properties of these networks of collaborations are candidates to devise measures of structure and complexity that are meaningful for system design. The approach to measuring complexity in this paper provides an analytical framework for the assessment of the design of the service, focusing on critical structural points.

Introduction

Services represent the front stage of business [1]. Customers perceive the service as a whole, but many service provision systems nowadays are actually made of a chain of combined services provided by the same or different partners. It can be hypothesized that the complexity of that chain determines to some extent the efficacy and success of the final provision of service to end users. Some studies [2] have defined this interdependency as a shift in focus, going away from the way the organization allocates and structures its own activities from the consideration of resources of the other parties constituting its context.

---

* Departamento de Ciencias de la Computación, Universidad de Alcalá de Henares, Madrid, Spain, msicilia@uah.es

† Departamento de Ciencias de la Computación, Universidad de Alcalá de Henares, Madrid, Spain, vitike@gmail.com

A. D'Atri et al. (eds.), *Management of the Interconnected World*,
DOI 10.1007/978-3-7908-2404-9_6, © Springer-Verlag Berlin Heidelberg 2010

The analysis of the network of interrelated elements that supports a service can be used as a point of departure to assess and to improve the service as a whole. The study of these networks is also the subject of increasing attention in the management and marketing literature, and the structure of the networks influences in the complexity of the services [3]. For years, the most popular vision of the companies is a linear one (with collaborators considered but not explicitly modeled), based in theories as the value chain [4] but the increasing complexity of services requires also more sophisticated models. Nowadays, collaborations between companies are represented as networks, with internal and external nodes, and this representation is more flexible to account for the complexity inherent to the arrangement of services in the real world. The value creation in these networks is based in a strong relationship between parts [5].

The study of this network of collaborators gives the possibility of analyzing the best options to deploy the elements required to provide the service. Doing this in an early stage of the service configuration will produce a better final service, with higher quality and with less incidents [6]. Complexity based in the structure of interactions is a formal tool and indicator that can be used for that assessment. This paper explores structural measures that are considered useful to evaluate service providing networks. The measures proposed are intended as a point of departure for further studies on metrics relating service outcomes with the structure of interactions in the service system.

The scope of this study and analysis of the complexity of the configuration of the network that supports the service, not the service itself. It's clear that there are closely related and the first has a very important influence in the second, but they are different things. Another important point is that not all the complexity is bad. Sometimes, the complexity is needed to achieve a better service or to provide a service according to the law [7].

The rest of this paper is structured as follows. The second section provides a model and formal notation for service networks, with interaction points at the nodes. Then, Section "Measuring Service Network Complexity" describes a basic measurement framework. A practical example is provided in Section "A Practical Example". Finally, conclusions and outlook are provided in Section "Conclusions and Outlook".

Modeling Services as Networks

A service can be defined and structured like a network of elements that collaborate in its production. A conceptual model that represents this vision of the services will permit a better understanding of the services and how each agent contributes with partial value to the global final value [3]. One key point of this is that even when the internal structure is a network, the final evaluation is done by the consumer [6] that perceives the service just as an integrated whole. All the internal parts, agents and relationships usually are transparent to this final customer.

All the elements in the network should theoretically add some value to the service. We can study how each participant collaborates by adding value to the system. It should be noted that collaboration might be related to tasks that are not directly involved in the service provision itself. For example, checking regulatory compliance and quality control tasks are not part of the flow of activities of the interaction with the customer, but they clearly add some value to the service system. The network can be formalized as a graph $G=(V,E)$ with a set of value-providing interaction points $V=(V_1,...,V_n)$ and a set of edges $E=(E_{11},..,E_{ij})$ where E_{ij} represents the adjacent connection between the nodes *i* and *j*.

Measuring Service Network Complexity

The representation and analysis of services as networks of elements that collaborate in order to generate a global value, opens new opportunities to research how services works and how it can be improved or optimized [3, 8].

The complexity of a service network depends of several factors including the following: the number of actors and the probability that these actors are involved in delivering the services; the integration of the elements with the main (director) element; the relationships in the network, that determine its structure, and how the actors connections are done. Then consideration of the links between nodes or actors in the network as one of the complexity factors has two components:

The existence of the link – When two elements in the network must collaborate to exchange information, documents, knowledge or other resources, a link must be created.

- The communications or uses of the link – The link is created just one time, but can be used in several ways and for different things.

- With these premises, a first approach to conceptualize the complexity of a service network could be:

$$c=\sum_{i=1}^{N} cn_i+\sum_{j=1}^{L} cl_j+\sum_{k=1}^{U} cu_k$$

Where *N* is the number of the nodes in the network; cn_i is the complexity of each node; *L* is the number of links in the network; cl_j is the complexity of each link, just for its existence; *U* is the number of uses of the links; cu_k is the complexity added to the global measure (*C*) for each way of use of the links. The complexity of the network will show the probability of incidents.

The integration of the elements emphasizes the level of collaboration between the actors. The complexity is based in several types of parameter, some requiring subjective assessment, and others measurable from structural parameters. For example, when two nodes of the network are from the same company, they can be considered to share vision, culture, procedures and technology, and it can be hypothesized that this reduces the complexity and makes the relationships easier.

The complexity of a network has been studied from several viewpoints, but in our case, we focus on the business view as a network of companies, departments and entities that collaborate in the construction of a service. So, the complexity inherent to each node or actor is not relevant for the analysis, as that complexity will exists in any case, so we just measure how the complexity changes when the structure of the network is changed. Taking the structure as the actors, the links and how these links are used to provide the service. Some measures can be derived from network structure, for example, measures the prominence of a node based on its position [9] but also the influence of the node in information or activity passed to other nodes. Considering a graph, the betweenness for vertex u is:

$$C_B(u) = \frac{\sum_{s \neq u \neq t \in V} \sigma_{st}(u)}{(n-1)(n-2)}$$

Where $C_B(u) = 1$ if and only if the shortest path from s to t passes through v and 0 otherwise. Betweenness can be the basis to interpret roles such as the "gatekeeper" or the "broker" which are studies extensively in communication networks.

Each different way of use of this links adds complexity in the system. For example, once an electronic communication based in standards is considered for the complexity measure, each different way of use of this communication adds its own complexity. If the connection is used to send just one file from node *A* to node *B*, the final complexity of the service will be less than if the connections is used to send a file from node *A* to node *B* and to send back another file with the first file process result. It is important to note that we are measuring the complexity of the service as a network, based on the complexity added for each component. The objective is compare between different configurations of the network, changing the links, the actors or the uses of the connections. But all the processes, tasks and other elements that the nodes provide to the service must stay unaltered. With this condition we can see what structure for the network is better.

A Practical Example

In this example, we will calculate the complexity level of a network that provides a finance service. This case is taken from a real experience and the information has two main sources: the users and people involved in the service provision and the consultancy workgroup that has analyzed the service network. A short explanation of the process done to provide the service is:

- Somebody (the customer) buys something in a retailer, for example a car, and decides to finance it, responding to the offering of the salesman.
- A finance staff at the retailer makes a request to the finance partner company via Web or phone call (through a call center which is an independent service), providing all the necessary data.

- The financer studies the request using automatic tools and with a group of analyst that decides if the request is accepted or not. This decision is communicated to the retailer via web and via email.
- If the request is accepted, the retailer must print a contract from the web application that the buyer must sign, take some documents copies from the buyer and send all this to the finance company. These physical documents must arrive to the financer to continue the process.
- When the financer gets all the documentation, makes some checks to verify that all the data provided by the vendor is correct. In this task, some external companies (A and B) collaborate.
- If everything is correct, the operation is paid to the vendor, and the finance is granted to the buyer.
- Finally, all the documentation is archived.

The network with all the actors and intermediate service points that collaborate in the provision of this overall service is shown in the Fig. 1, with the direction of the arcs representing the actor initiating the interaction. All the actors are totally independent except for numbers from 6 to 10 and the commercial representative (#3).

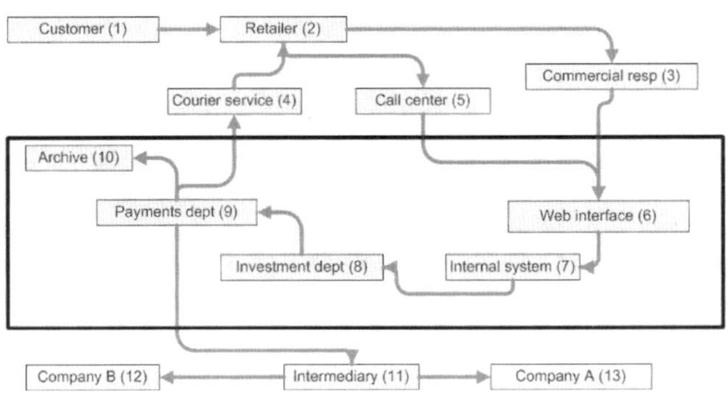

Fig. 1. Network agents and links for the example

The parameters defined to apply in the measure to each type of element in the network are: nodes, links and uses. These parameters are relevant for this example and they will be different in the evaluation of each network and service. In this concrete case, the parameters are and their values are provided by the service provider and obtained from interviews with the people implicated in the service and from analytical data of years of service provision (Table 1).

Table 1. Parameters for nodes (pn), links(pl) and uses (pu)

Parameter	Name	Description
pn_1	Company	If the node is part of the main company of the service or not
pn_2	Location	The distance between where the service is provided and the node may add complexity
pn_3	Experience	The knowhow of the node in this type of services or even in this service specifically
pn_4	Service network knowledge	The global vision of the network usually improves the quality of the work of each partner. With a better knowledge, the capability to take decision of each node will be improved
pn_5	Rel. sevice/core business	In the service is part of the core business of a node the complexity will be lower and its contribution will be better
pn_6	Responsibility	If the responsibility in the service and its provision is formalized via a contract, a QA control or via legal documents, the network will be more robust
pl_1	Physical or electronic	The physical connection between nodes usually adds more complexity to the network than an electronic one
pl_2	Security needed	If the link must be secure, and depending of the level of security wanted, the complexity will be higher or lower
pl_3	Broker	If the node is a broker in the network and it integrates several sources (other nodes), this key node will add complexity
pl_4	M2M or personal relations.	If the link is between machines, without human interaction, complexity will be lower than when a human is in charge
pl_5	Changes in the nodes	If the extremes of the link change with some periodicity, the complexity will be higher
pl_6	Technology	If a concrete technology is involved in the link, the know of this, its habitual use, its quality and other parameters will influence the complexity of the network
pu_1	Standards	If the use of the link is based on standards, the network will be more robust and flexible
pu_2	Quality assuracen taks	Better if the use has QA tasks in order to check its function
pu_3	Sync needed	Need of sync between the nodes will up the complexity
pu_4	Known parts	If the elements of the node that uses the link to make the use are known each other, the complexity will be lower
Pu_5	Feedback or acknowledge	If after the use of the link there is some feedback or even and acknowledge, the service will generate less problems
Pu_6	Same language	This is applicable for human interactions and for computers too. In this last case is clear that different languages or protocols will make the use of the link harder. In the case of interaction between humans, the perfect knowledge of a common language will help in any communication

The complexity estimation can be used by assessing potential values for each parameter in a tabular form, with the nodes, links and uses in the rows, and parameters at the columns. The weaknesses in our network will show a higher value and the weak nodes, links or uses, are the elements where the probability of incident is higher.

For example, to detect the weak nodes in the network configuration described according to the parameters defined previously we have the next Table 2 (complexity range for values, from 1, min, to 5, max).

Table 2. Complexity matrix for nodes

	Node	Pn1	Pn2	Pn3	Pn4	Pn5	Pn6	
Final client	1	5	2	5	5	3	2	22
Retailer	2	3	2	3	3	3	2	16
Commercial	3	1	3	1	1	1	1	8
Courier	4	4	2	1	3	1	3	14
Call center	5	2	1	2	2	2	2	11
Web	6	1	1	1	1	1	1	6
Systems	7	1	1	1	1	1	1	6
Investment	8	1	1	1	1	1	1	6
Payments	9	1	1	1	1	1	1	6
Archive	10	2	1	2	2	2	1	10
Data Controller	11	2	2	1	2	1	2	10
Company A	12	5	2	4	3	4	4	22
Company B	13	5	2	4	3	4	4	22
								159

This network, with the valuation parameters defined, has a weak point in the final client and in the relationships with companies A and B. This is logical because this three elements appears once in a operation and they don't know the process and they learn what must to do just before do it. Besides, their vision of the network is totally partial.

Another key point to control in order to minimize the incidents is the retailer, who knows the service, plays an important role in the process but it's no its core business, even being the interface with the weakness element, the final client.

In this concrete case, based on real experience, the online search in public databases of some information as part of the tasks done by the core nodes (investment and payments), has removed from the network the interaction with one of the companies (nodes 12 and 13) and has simplified the tasks of the retailer, another weak poing. This task is now done as a new use within and existing link and node, so the matrix of complexity for the nodes has decreased its global value from 159 to 137, which means a 14% improvement. This analytical information is supported for the result of the changes done in the network in the same direction. The final process is better and so the service.

Social network analysis is useful in the example above to assess pl_3, which can be measured as node betweenness. In the example above, node 9 is the main broker in the service, followed by node 2, identifying the more critical actors.

Conclusions and Outlook

Complexity in service networks is a multi-dimensional concept that includes aspects related to the actors that interact in the network, but also other aspects related to the ties between the actors and their usage. Graph models can be used to assess the complexity of the network, indentifying points with some influence.

Future work will further refine and develop the set of complexity aspects initially proposed, and evaluate how they can be assessed and aggregated resulting in significant measures of complexity. Also, the notion of complexity itself needs further conceptual inquiry, eventually resulting in a breakdown of the concept into several aspects that depart from the notion of complexity as the quantification of the amount of relations and relation kinds between parts.

References

1. Teboul J (2006) *Service is front stage: positioning services for value advantage*. Insead Business Press. Palgrave Macmillan
2. Hakansson H, Snehota I (2006) No business is an island: the network concept of business strategy. *Scand J Manage* 22(3):256–270
3. Basole RC, Rouse WB (2008) Complexity of service value networks: conceptualization and empirical investigation. *IBM Syst J* 47(1):53–70
4. Porter M (1985) *Competitive advantage: creating and sustaining superior performance*. Simon & Schuster, New York
5. Kothandaraman P, Wilson D (2001) The future of the competition. Value creating networks. *Industrial Mark Manage* 30:379–389
6. Bradley L, Stewart K (2003) The diffusion of online banking. *J Mark Manage* 19(9/10):1087–1109
7. Mitleton-Kelly E (2002) *Measuring complex systems*. Seminar notes from London School of Economics, London
8. Allee V (2002) *A value network approach for modelling and measuring intangibles. Conference on the transparent enterprise*. The value of intangibles, Madrid
9. Freeman LC (1979) Centrality in social networks: conceptual clarification. *Soc Networks* 1(3):215–239

Biometric Authentication and Authorization Infrastructures in Trusted Intra-Organizational Relationships

Matthias Olden[*]**, and Stefano Za**[†]

Abstract Today, the lives of both people and organizations are strongly focused on the creation, development and maintenance of relationships. These are influenced by several factors, amongst which trust plays an important role. Same as in traditional relationships, trust is considered crucial in their digital equivalent; here we can speak of the concept of trust in technology. An example for trust in technology is given by biometric authentication and authorization infrastructures. A possible approach is the use of typing behavior biometrics as authentication method. This provides a higher security, considering several biometric specific problems like replay attacks or template aging. The intra-organizational environment allows an interesting solution to these problems, namely the synchronization of biometric data within a federation of applications running in the same company. This paper presents the influence of the proposed authentication model on trust by means of the technical-formal-informal model inside an organization.

Introduction

Relationships among individuals or organizations have always been playing a relevant role in their private, social or business lives. This role has become fundamental, as people and organizations are often centered on creating, developing and maintaining relationships. Usually, there are several components that can influence relationships, the most important being the trust level among the parties. According to Chiles and McMackin [1], trust is a key factor for relational exchange.

In literature, there are several studies that give a definition of trust or make a review in order to find a common definition among several contexts; i.e. sociologi-

---

[*] Institute for Epidemiology and Preventive Medicine, University of Regensburg, Regensburg, Germany, matthias.olden@klinik.uni-regensburg.de

[†] CeRSI – Centro di Ricerca sui Sistemi Informativi, LUISS Guido Carli University, Roma, Italy, sza@luiss.it

A. D'Atri et al. (eds.), *Management of the Interconnected World*,
DOI 10.1007/978-3-7908-2404-9_7, © Springer-Verlag Berlin Heidelberg 2010

cal, psychological, organizational and computer science [2–5]. Levi [6] writes: "Trust is not one thing and it does not have one source; it has a variety of forms and causes". Also, some authors consider trust as a result of a combination of beliefs, attitude, intention and behavior [7], while others see trust only as a risk liability [4].

From the organizational point of view, trust is strongly linked with opportunistic behavior [1]. If there is a high perception of trust, the parties can adopt less elaborate safeguard rules. The opposite is also valid. If we consider the transaction cost theory [8] and the agency theory [9], transaction costs and agency costs are meant to protect against and to control the potential opportunistic behavior of the other party involved. Due to the continuous expansion of IT technologies and the enormous diffusion of internet, we distinguish between two kinds of relationships:

- Traditional relationships: they take place in ordinary life where information technology plays a marginal role. In this case, we can speak only of two concepts of trust: institutional [10] and social (often defined as customer trust [11]).
- Digital (or online) relationships: these focus strictly on IT. In this context (E-business/E-service/E-commerce), IT influences the institutional and social trust concept. Digital relationships are strongly associated with technological trust (trust in technology) [12–14].

Important attention is given to digital relationships inside an organization. For this, it is important to understand the role of IT and how this role can increase the trust perception or the opportunistic behavior control.

For this, we must consider relationships inside an organization through the TFI (technical-formal-informal) model. The trust concepts, especially the technological trust, are directly influenced by the security level provided by IT systems.

We consider an IT system where access is granted based on a standard user name/password routine; its security level is accordingly low.

The security of this system can be increased by Authentication and Authorization Infrastructures (AAIs) [15]. These are standardized methods to authenticate users and to grant them access to distributed web contents of several web providers.

At the moment, the combination AAI with password authentication does not present enough security, as it replaces the individual passwords from all applications with one "master" password used to access the federation. Additional security is given by enhanced authentication methods like biometrics, the only mechanism that can provide a bond between a user name and a real person. The gain of security must be considered upon solving several biometric specific problems, which will be presented in this paper.

Theoretical Framework

An information system is composed of technical, formal and informal (TFI) parts in a state of continuous interaction [16].

The informal ways of managing information in organizations are critical and cannot always be replaced by rules or embedded in technical systems. The informal elements (i.e. perception of risks, awareness) which are very context related drive the design and the selection of formal (i.e. policies, business processes) and technical solutions (i.e. software and hardware platforms, network infrastructures). For information systems, the relationship between these three levels is complex and therefore requires consideration of issues such as trust and privacy by means of new technical, formal and informal mechanisms. In order to understand the influence of IT systems on technological, institutional and social trust in intra-organizational relationships, critical issues identified in information systems literature can be summarized as follows [17, 18]: the perception of security embedded in the technical system (Informal level); the presence of formal mechanisms which regulate the interactions (Formal level); the reliability of IT systems, assured by the agreement on technical and procedural standards (Technical level).

By means of a biometric AAI with an enhanced security mechanism, the technological trust will have a positive influence over the institutional and social trust and will help to control the opportunistic behavior (i.e. this system does not allow users with different privileges to exchange credentials among each other).

Research Design: Trust Definitions and Trust Conceptual Model

Same as in traditional relationships, trust is crucial in the digital world [19]. As internet is an insecure environment [20], IT influences trust [12]:

- social trust, strongly linked to the risk perception in exchanging information with other parties [21];
- organizational trust, concerning the relationships between customers and organizations supported by information technology [22, 10, 23–25];
- technological trust, which reflects above all the relation with IT used as support for information exchange [14].

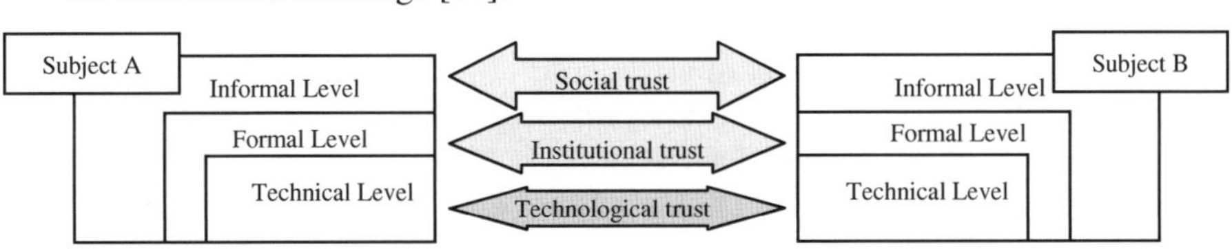

Fig. 1. The relationships between the three trust concepts and the TFI levels

Viewing the electronic relationships through the TFI model, the relations appear split in three levels, as shown in Fig. 1.

This work concentrates upon mechanisms acting on the technological trust level, disconsidering the other IT mechanisms that improve the institutional or social trust level (i.e. feedback mechanisms that aim to improve the subject reputation). Starting from the seven IT mechanisms table defined by Ratnasingam [20], we consider only two of them: authentication and access control within a biometric AAI.

Biometric AAIs Within an Organization

A biometric AAI with more identity providers (IdPs) is subject to several biometric specific problems, such as replay attacks, template aging or low recognition quality due to the use of multiple sensors. As the configuration proposed involves different IdPs belonging to the same company, it is possible to synchronize biometric data between the different user accounts.

Following situations can lead to biometric problems:

- the user possesses several accounts (user names) in the federation;
- the user has more biometric profiles (under the same user name), for example in the case of multiple sensors. These profiles are also stored at different IdPs.
- some of the profiles are not actualized and therefore outdated.

These problems can be solved by a stricter user management policy in which either the data is stored with a single IdP in the federation or the biometric data is located at different IdPs that synchronize it between themselves.

As the different IdPs are part of the same organization (and therefore share the same user database), it is possible to make a synchronization of the biometric data amongst IdPs. This process can be made either at database level or at the circle-of-trust level. By synchronization, the biometric data will be actualized between all IdPs.

The synchronization of biometric data directly on the database level is very efficient as it is uncoupled from the overlying AAI that remains responsible of authentication and authorization, Single Sign On and exchange of remaining attributes. An advantage is a better performance and a lower implementation effort as there are various software solutions for database mirroring [26]. On the other hand, most of these solutions presume a master-slave relationship between the database servers, which is not the case in a federated environment.

Basically, there are two possible scenarios for database synchronization: a first variant assumes that biometric data is managed via a central repository. An alternative is a decentralized configuration; however, no replication mechanism allows a completely decentralized synchronization of multiple servers.

This solution also implies considerable restrictions, as it assumes a close trust relationship between the participating partners, where all IdPs must grant each other access to their user databases. A further requirement for the synchronization on database level is that user data has to be identical at all IdPs, meaning identical user names on all servers in the circle of trust. This makes it impossible for the user to assume different user names, e.g. for privacy protection. It also automatically creates user accounts at all IdPs, although the user may use only some of them.

Due to these restrictions, biometric data must be treated in the same way as other user attributes and therefore synchronized on the AAI level. Nevertheless, this raises the problem of different user names assignment (it must be possible for a user to have different user names stored at different IdPs). For this, a mapping table must be created, where different user names from different IdPs are joined together. This process can be very difficult to complete and maintain manually and it is subject to errors.

A different approach is to forego mapping tables and to identify the same user on different servers by means of biometrics. If the user registers via biometrics at one IdP from the federation, the biometric samples will be sent to the other providers that will match them against all profiles stored locally. If the achieved match score is higher than a certain threshold, the other IdPs assume that the current sample belongs to one of their registered users. The user can now log in to all other IdP and the biometric sample will be correctly added to the identified profile for synchronization purposes.

This solution saves disk space and increases availability as it requires no update of a mapping table and no contact to dedicated servers. Nowhere does it become apparent under which user name a user is registered at other IdPs, which insures user privacy. A disadvantage is the fact that this variant requires a high computational effort. In the worst case, all profiles on the server have to be matched against one biometric sample. This worst case is not improbable; it occurs always when a user does not have an account on a server and therefore no matching profile can be found. Another problem occurs when the achieved match score is too small to ensure a clear biometric identification. In this case, the synchronization can not be executed automatically, but only by means of manual mapping by the administrator or even by the user himself.

The optimal solution is a combination between biometric identification and mapping tables. For this, when the user registers to an application within the circle of trust, the identification process is started at every other IdP. As the user provides more samples for the registration (biometric enrolment), the identification process can find the proper correspondent user account stored at every IdP. For privacy reasons, the IdP that submits the enrolment samples can choose to anonymize them by means of a random user id, which will be marked in its mapping table. As soon as the user is identified on all IdPs, the mapping tables are automatically completed and no further biometric identification is necessary, thus reducing the computational effort.

Another problem of biometric data synchronization occurs when the transfer of a typing sample or a whole profile fails, for example if an IdP is offline. To avoid this case, the IdP that received the latest typing sample and started the synchronization process must remember with which other IdP the synchronization failed and retry at a later date. Another solution is that the server which was not accessible inquires whether new typing samples were delivered at the other participants during the time when it was offline. As additional information, the IdP can send the date of the latest sample from its database (it is assumed that the providers have also synchronized times).

By means of synchronization, biometric data is kept up to date, thus ensuring that all samples can be checked for replay attacks, that the biometric template did not age on any server and that conflicts caused by the lack of profiles for different sensors are avoided.

Conclusions and Future Work

Starting from the relationship between IT and trust in inter-organizational relationships, we constructed a technical solution for an AAI system based on enhanced authentication technologies. This system allows a better access protection to restricted information and prevents credential exchange among users.

In the TFI model, a biometric AAI allowing both authentication and identification results in a better respect of bureaucracy roles (e.g. each person must use only his/her own credentials to access, create or manipulate a subset of information). It also has a positive influence on the trust in technology inside the organization.

This work can be the basis for future research of the organizational and technological aspects of this topic.

From an organizational point of view, user's perception of trust in a biometric AAI must be evaluated. This can be made by submitting a survey to several users inside an organization and understanding the references to the different types of trust.

From a technological point of view, the process of synchronizing biometric data must take into consideration other facts like data redundancy, the quantity of data that has to be transferred and the fact that some AAI protocols may not support real time synchronization upon login. For the case of typing behavior biometrics, the mechanisms of recognizing replay attacks or determining the template aging must be researched. Another interesting use case is the situation when the biometric template is not centrally stored at one or more IdP, but kept entirely in possession of the user.

References

1. Chiles TH, McMackin J (1996) Integrating variable risk preferences, trust, and transaction cost economics. *Acad Manage Rev* 21(1):73–99
2. Rousseau MT, Stikin SB, Burt SB, Carmerer C (1998) Not so different after all: across-discipline view of trust. *Acad Manage Rev* 23(3): 393–404
3. Kramer RM (1999) Trust and distrust in organizations: emerging perspectives, enduring questions. *Ann Rev Psychol* 50(1):569–598
4. Mayer RC, Davis JH, Schoorman FD (1995) An integrative model of organizational trust. *Acad Manage Rev* 20(3):709–734
5. McKnight DH, Chervany NL (2001) Trust and distrust definitions: one bite at a time. In: Falcone R, Singh MP, Tan Y (eds) In *Proceedings of the workshop on deception, fraud, and trust in agent societies held during the autonomous agents conference: trust in cyber-societies, integrating the human and artificial perspectives lecture notes in computer science*, vol. 2246. Springer, London, pp 27–54
6. Levi M (1996) Social and unsocial capital: a review essay of Robert Putnam's "making democracy work". *Polit Soc* 24(1):45–55
7. Bhattacherjee A (2002) Individual trust in online firms: scale development and initial test. *J Manage Inf Syst* 19(1):211–242
8. Williamson OE (1985) *The economic institutions of capitalism*. Free Press, New York
9. Eisenhardt K (1985) *Control: organizational and economic approaches*. Manage Sci 31(2):134–149
10. McKnight DH, Cummings LL, Chervany NL (1998) *Initial trust formation in new organizational relationships*. Acad Manage Rev 23(3): 473–491
11. Granovetter M (1985) *Economic action and social structure: the problem of embeddedness*. Am J Sociol 91(November): 481–510
12. Misiolek NI, Zakaria N, Zhang P, (2002) *Trust in organizational acceptance of information technology: a conceptual model and preliminary evidence*. In Proceedings of the decision sciences institute 33rd annual meeting 2002, San Diego
13. Ratnasingam P, Pavlou P (2002) *Technology trust: the next value creator in B2B electronic commerce*. International resources management association conference, Washington, Seattle
14. Reeves B, Nass C (1996) *The media equation. How people treat computers, television, and new media like real people and places*. Cambridge University Press, New York
15. Schläger C, Sojer M, Muschall B, Pernul G (2006) *Attribute-Based authentication and au-thorisation infrastructures for e-commerce providers*. Springer, Krakow, pp 132–141
16. Liebenau J, Backhouse J (1990) *Understanding information: an introduction*. Macmillan, London
17. Gambetta D (1988) *Trust: making and breaking cooperative relations*. Basil Blackwell, Oxford
18. Kumar K, Becerra-Fernandez I (2007) *Interaction technology: speech act based information technology support for building collaborative relationships and trust*. Decis Support Syst 43(2):584–606. DOI= http://dx.doi.org/10.1016/j.dss.2005.05.017
19. Ba S, Whinston AB, Zhang H (1999) *Building trust in the electronic market through an economic incentive mechanism*. In: Proceedings of the 20th international conference on information systems (Charlotte, North Carolina, United States, December 12–15, 1999). International conference on information systems. Association for Information Systems. Atlanta, GA, pp 208–213
20. Ratnasingam P (2002) *The importance of technology trust in web services security*. Inf Manage Comput Secur 10(5):255–260
21. Koller M (1988) *Risk as a determinant of trust*. Basic Appl Soc Psychol 9(4):265–276

22. Lewicki RJ, Bunker BB (1996) *Developing and maintaining trust in work relationships*. In: Kramer RM, Tyler TR (eds) Trust in organizations: frontiers of theory and research. Sage Publications, Thousand Oaks, pp 114–139
23. Pavlou P, Tan YH, Gefen D (2003) *Institutional trust and familiarity in online interorganizational relationship*. In Proceedings of the 11th European conference on information systems, Naples, Italy, June 19–21, 2003
24. Spagnoletti P, Za S, D'Atri A (2007) *Institutional Trust and security, new boundaries for virtual enterprises*. In Proceedings of 2nd international workshop on interoperability solutions to trust, security, policies and QoS for enhanced enterprise systems, IS-TSPQ2007, Funchal, Portugal
25. Tyler TR, Degoey P (1996) *Trust in organizational authorities. The influence of motive attributions on willingness to accept decisions*. In Kramer RM, Tyler TR (eds) Trust in organizations: frontiers of theory and research. Sage Publications, Thousand Oaks, pp 331–350
26. Qarchive (2008) *Database synchronization*, database-synchonization.qarchive.org. Retrieved 1 Oct 2008

Reshaping eGovernment Through Institutional Agents

Maddalena Sorrentino* **and Luca Solari**†

Abstract The eGovernment stage is being populated by a cast of intermediary actors from both the private and the not-for-profit sectors, as a result of the multichannel strategies with which many countries are seeking to give new impulse to their eGovernment plans. This paper claims that a fuller understanding of these players' role is crucial in developing socially-aware eGovernment policies and suggests the usefulness of adopting an institutional perspective to place the intermediaries in an adequate frame of reference. In particular, it suggests that it might be fruitful to slot the intermediaries into the "institutional agent" category. Some implications ensuing from this study are proposed and discussed.

Introduction

Future eGovernment will be increasingly built on public-private partnerships and on the deployment of new intermediaries in the public service delivery chain and democratic processes [1]. Some countries already have adopted multichannel (blended) management strategies to give fresh momentum to their overall eGovernment plans. The UK has coined the phrase "electronic mixed economy" to describe the delivery of public services through private or not-for-profit intermediaries [2]:184, as launched by the British government in 2003. Similarly, the Italian government introduced the Reti Amiche (Friendly Networks) project at end-2008, coupling the State with pharmacies, lottery retailers, post offices, and professional associations to bring some e-services – booking/payment of healthcare tickets; delivery of medical reports; passport applications, renewals, and visas; payment of

* Dipartimento di Scienze economiche, aziendali e statistiche, Università degli studi di Milano, Milano, Italy, maddalena.sorrentino@unimi.it

† Dipartimento di Studi del lavoro e del welfare, Università degli studi di Milano, Milano, Italy, luca.solari@unimi.it

A. D'Atri et al. (eds.), *Management of the Interconnected World*,
DOI 10.1007/978-3-7908-2404-9_8, © Springer-Verlag Berlin Heidelberg 2010

contributions for home helpers/carers; issue of resident permits – within reach of the citizens.

The eGovernment stage is thus becoming populated by a variegated cast of intermediary actors whose role is to serve businesses and households. Generally, the business (especially SME) users of the public e-services turn mainly to professional structures/actors, while the private individuals (at least in the economically developed countries) have access to both informal and formal channels: family or friends, libraries, public internet access points, and community telecenters.

In this paper we argue that a fuller understanding of the potential role of these players is crucial to the development of socially-aware eGovernment policies. Above all, we refer to the problem of e-inclusion, meant both as a lack of inclusive ICT – i.e. an information society in which the technology itself creates barriers – and the failure to harness ICT to advance economic and social inclusion in general [3]:8. This study recognizes that e-inclusion – as a multidimensional phenomenon – should be understood as a political and social rather than a primarily technical or development issue. For the purpose of this study eGovernment "is the use of information and communication technologies, and particularly the Internet, as a tool to achieve better government" ([4]:11). The complexity of our chosen theme has prompted us to adopt a perspective [5] that sees the organizations as open systems – strongly influenced by their environments – but where rational or efficiency-based forces are not the only drivers at work. "Socially constructed belief systems and normative rules exercise enormous control over organizations – both how they are structured and how they carry out their work" (ibidem:117). Public institutions in particular "are highly differentiated, multifaceted, often loosely coupled congeries of organizations" (ibidem:207).

The purpose of this study is to examine two questions:

1. *To what extent has the scientific debate adequately reflected on eGovernment intermediation?*
2. *In what way do formal and informal intermediaries help to solve the inclusion challenge?*

The paper is designed to first offer a review of the relevant literature and then comment on it. The third section explores the usefulness of adopting the institutional perspective as an alternative approach to placing the intermediaries in the social inclusion frame of reference. Finally, we discuss the main implications and limitations of the study.

Related Literature

Intermediaries, eGovernment, and inclusion present a number of overlaps and interconnections, both conceptual and practical. Precisely the need to explore these interconnections spurred us to embark on the study illustrated in this paper. In covering the many issues related to the intermediary theme, the authors trawled the publications contained in the ISI Web of Knowledge database, inserting the following terms (used in two or more combinations) as research keys: intermed*, eGovernment, inclusion, public sector. We then manually eliminated those contributions deemed irrelevant or not significant. To ensure coverage of not only the theoretical but also the practical aspects, we added reports from government sources to our sample basket of publications (38 papers).

Importantly, we found that there is no agreed definition of the term "intermediary" or a generally accepted classification proposal. The many labels proposed in the studies obviously point to a fragmented framework and reflect the different assumptions made by the various authors. We identified two main categories of intermediaries: *virtual* and *physical*, in which spheres the authors adopt different tags. Following are some definitions of "physical intermediary" (or equivalent terms) used in the studies examined; the underscored terms are used by the authors to sum up the role attributed to the intermediaries:

> [intermediaries] act as <u>facilitators</u> and bridges to help citizens interact with eGovernment or eHealth applications [6]:34;
> a new <u>interface</u> (…) between the citizens/business and public sector [7]:88;
> (…) the intermediary is acting as an <u>agent</u> of the end-customer [8]:18.
> (…) social <u>moderators</u> of internet adoption, access and use [9]:244.

While there are diverse ways of understanding the intermediaries' influence on the citizen-PA relationship these are often incomparable. The debate is dominated by two viewpoints. The *organization-centric* view, in which the intermediaries (especially the virtual type) are considered part of a delivery strategy guided by rational arguments, such as the cost-efficiency of the channels:

> [intermediaries] reduce the intervention of government in micro operational issues [10]:84.
> (…) intermediaries (…) increase eGovernment service take-up [11]:5.

On the other hand, the *citizen-centric* view perceives the intermediaries as, above all, a way to help specific groups of citizens access the information/resources they need through more tailored services. In that sense, the intermediaries have the potential to bridge inequalities, especially in terms of the adoption, access and use of the ICT resources:

> Intelligent intermediaries add human skills and knowledge … [are] critical for projects that want to reach disadvantaged groups in society [12]:19.
> [partnering with intermediaries] provides a more appropriate route for delivering improved customer service and value for money [13]:381.

Midway between the organization-centric and citizen-centric views are the studies (e.g. [14, 15]) that recognize a gap between how governments want their citizens to use channels and the citizens' actual preferences.

However, the articles do not always enable the reader to deduce the theoretical framework of reference. There is a vast amount of empirical research on the implications of ICT in general. To date, an instrumental perspective, in terms of economic value, has prevailed in the research on intermediaries, whereby these are understood as one of the possible delivery channels in the scope of a blended strategy, or even a way to ensure a capillary access (and relatively inexpensive for the PA) to the public services, using existing ICT infrastructures or networks. Recurrent themes are: intermediation vs. disintermediation; and the intertwining relationship between offline and online channels.

In short, while there is a substantial body of knowledge on the subject of eGovernment implementation, adoption and diffusion, other streams of research rarely undertake an in-depth discussion of intermediary issues.

Commentary

The brief review just carried out, which is far from exhaustive, shows how the intermediary theme has yet to be consolidated. Below, we summarize the main shortcomings of the literature in the belief that identifying the "critical knowledge gaps" will help to stimulate the debate on intermediary-related issues.

Most of the studies analyze the intermediaries in relation to the channel diversification strategies, only in rare cases do these highlight the fact that the internal structure of the intermediaries and their role can evolve in time, as it did in the case of the US public libraries, which have started to become "one-stop shops" [16]. The key focus is on the more visible aspects (e.g. the user interface or service accessibility), neglecting equally important aspects like improving service quality.

The organizational dimension appears underdeveloped. Most studies keep ICT change separate from the public administrations (PA): "e-government is only loosely coupled to organizational action" [17]:88. That separation delimits the extent of the problems and therefore seems to simplify the analysis. However, in reality, that delimitation reduces the organizational scientific community's perception of the relevance and interest in eGovernment-related issues.

That the multichannel strategies create inclusion seems obvious, giving the citizens the opportunity to "switch and make choices between technology, human and other channels suited to preference, location, service and task" [18]:1. Generally, like in other policy areas, the outcome (positive) of these strategies is almost a given, while the pernicious effects – which can actually heighten those inequalities they were expected to remove – are overlooked. Often the digital exclusion cited in many studies has no "special or political meaning" ([19]:268). If that widespread perspective were to prevail also in the future, we risk falling into the technological determinism that characterized the first round of eGovernment studies.

In brief, the intermediaries are primarily associated with the first types of goal identified as "pillars" in the IPTS report [20], i.e. the cost-effectiveness and efficiency pillar and the creation of public value pillar. The report underscores that these two pillars should not be treated as independent and equal goals, but as "means" and "ends" with the interrelationship that this implies. Further, and still more important, is the fact that public value is recognized as a greater burden ("public value is the superior ends of the operational means", ibidem:17). The ultimate purpose of ICT in supporting government and governance thus becomes not public sector modernization itself, but the modernization that *maximizes* public value.

Intermediaries as Institutional Agents

Institutional theory is a theoretical approach able to encompass all three points of the Intermediaries-eGovernment-Inclusion triangle. In particular, we claim it might be fruitful to slot the intermediaries into the "institutional agent" category (a concept worked on by Scott [21, 22]). The capacity of this framework to incorporate all three core elements facilitates the research that explores how eGovernment-related reforms affect social capital.

Our theoretical choice is also motivated by the fact that the institutional perspective is coherent with the concept of organization adopted in the paper (see Introduction). Assuming that the interaction between the service takers and the service providers, mediated by the intermediaries, creates norms and organizational frameworks, this, in turn, affects the behavior of the different actors and, therefore, of society as a whole. Our proposal – which we illustrate solely in exemplary form due to space limitations – enables us to shed light on some aspects that have been little investigated up to now, including: the public value of the intermediaries. Specifically, institutional agents: (i) are "definers, interpreters, and appliers of institutional elements", [21]:223, i.e. "regulatory, normative or cultural elements, or various combinations of them" [22]:882; (ii) have an "impact on social behavior" [21]:222; (iii) are never neutral conveyers, but must adapt and translate their messages to fit specific recipients and varying local circumstances. They are "crafters of institutions" [21]:223.

Adopting Scott's perspective is beneficial because it enables us to place the diverse categories of eGovernment intermediaries into one sole conceptual framework, in turn underpinned by a solid theoretical paradigm (by which we mean institutional theory) well known to the scholars. That setting has both a descriptive and a prescriptive value for eGovernment-related issues. In *descriptive* terms, the intermediaries can be regarded as relational agents (i.e. "systems made up of connections between actors, both individual and collective" [22]:886) and symbolic agents (i.e. "systems that can be used to convey information about rules (…), values and norms (…), or mental schema or models" (ibidem, 882)). In the first role, the intermediaries (such as one-stop shops and professional associations) reshape the organizational boundaries (since the information, resources and knowledge flows transcend the formal borders between different organizations) and "stimulate managers to reconsider who and what are inside vs. outside" (ibidem:887). The second role played by the intermediaries, especially those who interact directly with individuals, appears to be particularly crucial in carrying tacit knowledge, i.e. uncodified knowledge embedded in the skills and routines of performers. For instance, the user sees the pharmacist as a kind of access point to an abstract system, i.e. the national health service. Nevertheless, codified knowledge can be also embedded in ICT artifacts (as in the case of the virtual intermediaries). In turn, the artifacts, like other agents, can be viewed as associated with, and affected by, regulatory, normative or cultural elements.

In *prescriptive* terms, Scott's proposal enables us to say that, as institutional agents, the intermediaries are a key reference point for the policymakers, the public managers, and the researchers, who should learn to recognize and value them. Disclosing the institutional values of the intermediaries means, on the one side, recognizing the multitude of interests mobilized in the eGovernment programs and, on the other, that the diverse stakeholder groups have a different weighting in the distribution of the public resources and the right to access these.

We still need to consider the usefulness of Scott's proposal in terms of public value, an aspect less developed in the studies examined. Given that public value is a slippery and articulated concept [20]:17, in this paper we merely outline a general hypothesis (yet to be fully verified) on social inclusion.

The previous pages have underscored the unrealistic scenario in which public services are delivered mainly through electronic means. Equally, the implementation of a multichannel strategy can be a source of concern for those who view such redundancy as potentially expensive and inefficient [23]. The answer to that trade-off can be sought by acknowledging that the PA is charged with managing a broader set of objectives than private firms. Like the private firms, the public sector is interested in efficiency, but is also expected to provide services that ensure equity and accountability. Inclusion is a priority value (an "end" [20]) that must anyway be pursued and managed (with or without ICT support), even at the cost of demoting the efficiency goals. The goal of inclusion presumes a high tolerance of what, at first sight, might be labeled as complexity and redundancy.

How do the intermediaries fit into the processes that generate social value? The intermediaries perform informational and transactional services on behalf of the citizens, building value by institutionalizing new practices and personalizing the offerings. A prominent role (in terms of social value) played by these actors is to reproduce and strengthen trust in institutions and public authorities [24]. A number of research (e.g. [25, 26]) show how the trust between the people and the intermediary organizations is positively associated with the use and take-up of the public services. The "production and propagation of trust is a *sine qua non* in respect of public value" [27]:138.

Implications and Conclusions

This exploratory study aims to close a gap in the literature by providing a first and partial overview of eGovernment intermediaries, thus spurring the accumulation of knowledge on this theme. The goal of the paper is twofold: to understand to what extent the scientific debate has adequately reflected on eGovernment intermediation; and to discover how formal and informal intermediaries help solve the inclusion challenge.

In answer to the first question, our research revealed that while many studies have approached the intermediary theme, the authors have never attempted to interpret the intermediaries at the conceptual level. That means we face a relatively unexplored field requiring an investigative effort by, above all, the eGovernment academic community.

As to the second, the response is potentially favorable, leading us to suggest using the institutional concept to approach and develop the topic of eGovernment intermediaries-inclusion. eGovernment intermediaries are "institutional agents". Public value is the bridge-concept that connects Intermediaries, eGovernment and Inclusion.

Our work reveals that the research agenda can be enriched by a number of interesting possibilities; we especially highlight:

- the possible contribution of the intermediaries to the (re)construction of relations of trust between government and citizens;
- the opportunity to analyze how the integration of old and new channels reflects on the network governance systems;
- the search for the most appropriate ways of combining diverse types of intermediaries to ensure the maximum return in terms of social value.

These issues need to be addressed adequately by the scholars, also from diverse disciplinary spheres. Investing in empirical research is a key step in helping to empower the existing theories on intermediaries. Longitudinal studies could help to highlight not only the positive implications, but also the negative and/or unexpected consequences of the diffusion of eGovernment intermediaries. For instance, a growing reliance on these "go-betweens" also carries the risk of widening (instead of narrowing) the PA-citizen gap. To assess such a hypothesis, research could investigate the conditions in which the presence of intermediaries activates or neutralizes these "perverse mechanisms".

Accreting our knowledge could help the public managers to cast light (from a bottom-up perspective) on the "street level bureaucracy", i.e. all those processes and practices that underpin the chain of command but that are nonetheless decisive because in direct contact with the "real" recipients of the public policies.

Based on the above, we can say that the Intermediaries-eGovernment-Inclusion challenge is hard to approach from the "top-down planning" perspective, as if we are dealing with a problem that needs to be solved once and for all. Conversely, it is far more reasonable to adopt a bottom-up approach of discovery and experimentation, of learning by doing.

Like all studies (especially those of the exploratory type), our reflections also present limitations. First, the review conducted is far from exhaustive and, therefore, future studies on the eGovernment intermediaries theme will need to be based on the analysis of a higher number of scientific sources. Second, the use of the institutional perspective does not rule out the possibility of other frameworks finding application in the study of eGovernment intermediaries.

References

1. Frissen V, Millard J, Huijboom N (2007) *The future of eGovernment*, Seville
2. Burt B, Taylor J (2003) Constructing new ways of living together: government relationships with the voluntary sector in the information polity. *Inf Polity* 8:181–192
3. European i2010 initiative (2007) *To be part of the information society*, Brussels
4. OECD (2004) *The e-Government imperative*. OECD, Paris
5. Scott WR (1998) *Organizations. Rational, natural and open systems*. Prentice-Hall, Upper Saddle River
6. Zinnbauer D (2007) *What can social capital and ICT do for inclusion*. European Commission Joint Research Centre, Seville
7. Pasic A, Sassen AM, Garcia A (2004) e-Government Intermediation. *Lecture Notes in Computer Science,* 3183: 88-92
8. e-Envoy (2003) *Policy framework for a mixed economy in the supply of e-Government services. Implementation Guidelines* 1 London
9. Hill R, Beynon-Davies P, Williams MD (2008) Older people and internet engagement. *Inf Technol People* 21(3):244–266
10. Liou KT:(2008) E-Government development and China's administrative reform. *Int J Public Adm* 31(1):76–95
11. Lowe C (2003) Ten steps to massive take-up of eGovernment in Europe. *Int J Commun Law Policy* 8:1–9
12. Rajalekshmi K (2007) E-Governance services through telecenters: the role of human intermediary and issues of trust. *Inf Technol Int Dev* 4(1):19–35
13. De', R (2006) E-Government systems in developing countries: issues and concerns. *IIMB Manage Rev* 18(4):277–288
14. Millard J (2006) User attitudes to e-government citizen services in Europe. *Int J Electronic Gov Res* 2(2):49–58
15. Ebbers WE, Pieterson WJ, Noordman HN (2008) Electronic government: rethinking channel management strategies. *Gov Inf Q* 25(2):181–201
16. Gibson A, Bertot JC, McLure C (2009) Emerging role of public librarians as e-Government providers. In: *HICSS-42 Hawaii international conference on systems science*, Hawaii
17. Akesson M, Skalén P, Edvardsson B (2008) E-Government and service orientation: gaps between theory and practice. *Int J Public Sector Manage* 21(1):74–92
18. Millard J (2006) eGovernance and eParticipation: lessons from Europe in promoting inclusion and empowerment, Citeseer
19. Klecun E (2008) Bringing lost sheep into the fold: questioning the discourse of the digital divide. *Inf Technol People* 21(3):267–282
20. IPTS (2006) Towards the eGovernment Vision for the EU in 2010: research policy challenges. European Commission Directorate General
21. Scott WR (2008) Lords of the dance: professionals as institutional agents. *Organ Stud* 29(2):219–238
22. Scott WR (2003) Institutional carriers: reviewing modes of transporting ideas over time and space and considering their consequences. *Ind Corp Change* 12(4):879–894
23. Warner ME, Hefetz A (2008) Managing markets for public service: the role of mixed public-private delivery of city services. *Public Adm Rev* 68(1):155–166
24. Avgerou C, Ciborra C, Cordella A, Kallinikos J (2006) e-Government and trust in the state: lessons from electronic tax systems in Chile and Brazil, LSE, pp 1–38
25. Carter L, Weerakkody V (2008) E-government adoption: a cultural comparison. *Inf Syst Front* 10(4):473–482
26. Bekkers V (2007) The governance of back-office integration. *Public Manage Rev* 9(3):388–400
27. Grimsley M, Meehan A (2007) e-Government information systems: evaluation-led design for public value and client trust. *Eur J Inf Syst* 16(2):134–148

Patent Information System in R&D Strategies: Tasks, Techniques and On-line Search Tools

Daniela Baglieri* **and Fabrizio Cesaroni†**

Abstract Conventional patent analysis has commonly focused on factual information, while less scholarly attention has been devoted to the strategic role of Patent Information System in supporting decision-making in R&D investment. This paper attempts to fill this gap and proposes an integrated conceptual framework which lies upon a process view of R&D strategy formulation, which is split into four stages. For each stage, PIS task and nature of information are highlighted. Moreover, some public and private on-line research tools are analyzed to compare services and support.

The Emergence of a Pro-patent Era: Implications for Information Systems

Over the last decades, an intensification of firms' patent activity has been observed in several countries and technological fields. During the 1980s and the 1990s, the number of US patent applications has grown from a range of 40–80,000 in the 1980s to at least 120,000 patents in 1995 [1]. This discontinuous growth has also been examined by Hall [2], who has shown a structural break in the time series of the growth of the number of patents in the mid-1980s. Despite this patent explosion, some scholars have found that patents are not the most effective means to protect inventions, except to chemical and pharmaceutical industries [3, 4]. Mansfield et al. [5] found that 60% of patented inventions were imitated successfully in less than 4 years. Badaracco [6, p.37] noted that in the electronics industry it sometimes takes only a few weeks after a new American-made product is introduced in the United States for it to be copied, manufactured and shipped to the United States from an Asian country. Against these criticisms to patents (and the patent system) as an effective appropriability mechanism, there is no doubt that the emergence of a pro-patent era has brought to the attention of managers both

* Dipartimento di Studi e Ricerche Economico-Aziendali ed Ambientali, Università di Messina, Messina, Italy, Daniela.Baglieri@unime.it

† Departamento de Economía de la Empresa, Madrid, Spain, Universidad Carlos III de Madrid, fabrizio.cesaroni@uc3m.es

A. D'Atri et al. (eds.), *Management of the Interconnected World*,
DOI 10.1007/978-3-7908-2404-9_9,

the need of an adequate patent management system, and the possibility to exploit available patent information for strategic purposes. Following Rivette and Kline [7], patents can be used in the processes of product diversification or of development of new product lines, in order to define which technologies the company needs to develop or acquire. Also, in the case of merger decisions, patents can be used to assess potential targets' technological profiles. Furthermore, in the case of businesses whose growth rate is slowing down, profits are falling, and products have become commodities, patents can be used to identify potential targets for a patent licensing program aimed at generating new revenues. In this situation, which is similar to the classical "Cash Cow" area of a BCG matrix, the most effective strategy is to boost incremental revenues. Finally, in the case in which a business is no more profitable and has to be abandoned, patents can be useful as well. The point here is to find a company that would find one's patents of value. Patent statistics, and patent search methodologies can be helpful in this case.

We build on Rivette and Kline's study [7] and state that Patent Information System (PIS) can help firms along four main dimensions:

1. In product development and R&D management in general, to define the most appropriate, less risky technology trajectory;
2. In the processes of mergers and acquisitions, to identify potential targets whose technological profiles respond to the firm's needs;
3. In the competitive arena, to monitor main competitors' technological competences and their evolution over time;
4. For external stakeholders, to control the firm's technological activity.

While the importance of patent analysis in strategic planning has therefore become increasingly evident [8], conventional patent analysis has commonly focused on factual information. Less scholarly attention has been devoted to the efforts to integrate a range of patent information supporting decision-making in R&D activities. In this paper, we propose an integrated conceptual framework to understand which tasks, technicalities and on-line search tools are more helpful to enhance the supporting role of PIS to R&D strategy formulation.

Patent Analysis for R&D Strategies: A Process View

Strategies in planning, acquiring and utilizing technological assets have become an important element in deciding how best to use limited resources and to achieve a competitive advantage. According to Chesbrough [9], technological innovation is not only developed *in-house*, but external sources (i.e. universities, PROs, other high-tech firms) may supply valuable scientific and technological knowledge through selling and licensing patent rights. As a consequence, high-tech firms have to make more efforts to link technologies and markets in order to profit from innovation [10, 11]. In this direction, patent analysis shows several benefits in terms of supporting strategic decision-making. Since several emerging technological trajectories are *general purpose*–see, for example, nanotechnologies, biotechnology, ICT – their applications may be deployed in a wide range of markets. Therefore, understanding which market fits better in terms of economic and societal benefits is not irrelevant. We believe that PIS may be valuable in identifying promising new business opportunities, if firms integrate technological information with market issues. In so doing, we suggest to adopt a *process view* in order to better understand linkages and relations among patent information in the following stages: (i) R&D planning; (ii) Technology planning; (iii) Product planning; and (iv) Market planning (Fig. 1).

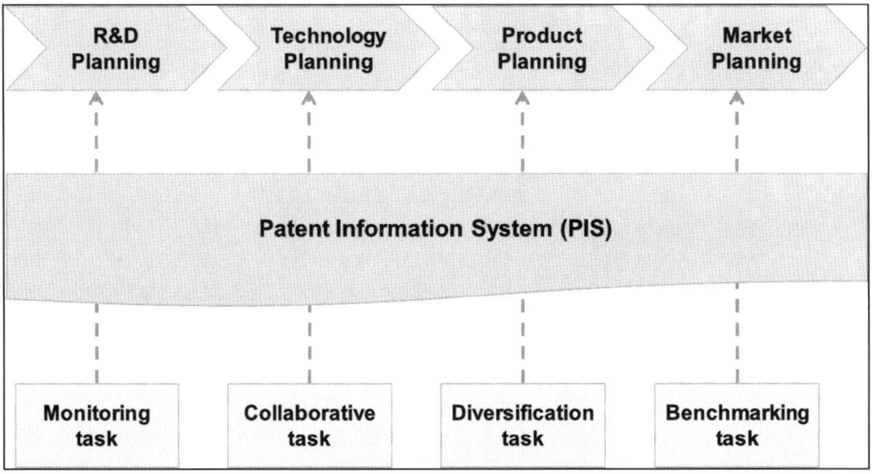

Fig. 1. Patent information system: a process view

R&D Planning

Initially, firms need to identify those leading technologies they choose to invest in, and which technology source to exploit – either an internal source, *via* in-house R&D investment, or an external source, *via* R&D collaborative agreements. Patents can be a source of valuable technological information which may be visualized through patent maps. Patents may also highlight various elements of knowledge about competitive positions [12, 13], infringement risks [14], etc. In other words, if carefully analyzed, patents can show technological details and relationships among firms that have been doing similar research and which are leading the industry. At this stage, patent analysis can provide useful information about competitors, and therefore PIS plays a *monitoring task.*

Technology Planning

Once R&D planning is completed, firms have to consider their chance of technology realization by collaborating with others, according to the open-innovation model. Patent analysis can help a firm make strategic decisions for collaborative R&D, and therefore PIS plays a *collaborative task.*

Product Planning

The next step is "product planning", and it is devoted to find new business opportunities based on technologies that will become available. Since a general purpose technology – though developed for a specific context – may turn out to be applicable in various industries with a minimum modification, the most important task at this stage is to discover such industries. Patents may offer a picture of technology applications in different industries using patent citation analysis. In this way, firms may assume that industries with more technological flows may offer greater possibilities for technology applications. Accordingly, at this stage, patent analysis can help a firm to identify promising business areas where existing or to-be-developed technological assets might be exploited. In turn, PIS plays a *diversification task.*

Market Planning

Technological aspects of possible product development avenues, got from the previous stage, need to be integrated with market conditions and trends. Hence, "market planning" seeks to identify markets where other firms with similar technological assets are competing in order to understand the potential linkages between products and markets. In other words, if two firms have similar combinations of patents, it is likely that their technological assets may be similar and their affinity value becomes high. Among competitors, those with high affinity values are identified, and their business areas are analyzed for benchmarking. It is worth noting that an industry where many firms with similar sets of patents are already doing business offers good possibilities of further technology applications, but may be an arena of strong competition. As a result, patent analysis can offer valuable information for future product and market planning, and PIS plays a *benchmarking task.*

To wrap up, patent analyses are meaningful in themselves, but they can be more powerful when used together, according to the suggested process view.

Getting Patent Information: On-line Patent Search Tools

Starting from the mid-1990s, firms have become more sensitive on how to obtain patent information. Several patent offices have made available patent information through on-line (Internet-based) search tools free of charge. This has been the case not only of Trilateral Patent Offices (that is, the European Patent Office, United States Patent & Trademarks Office, and Japanese Patent Office), but also of smaller patent offices from China, Korea, Australia and New Zealand, and other international organizations concerned with patent protection (such as the World Intellectual Property Organization – WIPO). Thus, even before the advent of the information technology revolution, patent information was readily available to people [15].

Simple on-line search tools (such as those integrated into patent offices' web sites) let users to search patent documents and to retrieve basic information out of them, but hardly can be used to perform more complex analyses. To support R&D strategy formulation a careful analysis of technological information in patent documents is needed, which allows highlighting various elements of knowledge about technologies, firms' competitive positions, intellectual property rights' infringement risks, and so forth [14]. Such possibilities depend on the application of methodologies and computational solutions that are not offered by freely available patent search engines. More sophisticated software applications have been developed in this respect.

Among these, a first category of solutions consists of more user-friendly search engines, such as Delphion and MicroPantent (both owned and operated by Thomson Reuters), and QPAT (produced and owned by Questel-Orbit).[1] Apart from slight differences among the three systems [16, 17], all of them represent an improvement with respect to basic patent search engines, mainly because they permit a quicker and easier patent information collection, because they facilitate the organization of search outcomes, and because they overcome some limits that are implicit in on-line free services (such as the impossibility to link all patents assigned to different firms belonging to the same industrial group, or the difficulty to convert patent technology classes into commercial classes of practical use).

Even so, such software applications do not perform analyses that help describe complex technological fields and trajectories, such as the bio-chemical industry, the pharmaceuticals industry, and the software industry. To this purpose, a patent map is often needed. A patent map can be simply defined as "a collection of patent statistics that include but are not limited to, patent count analysis, country analysis, competitor analysis, inventor analysis, citation analysis, and classification analysis, resulting in a number of statistical indicators that capture different aspects of patenting activities" [18, p. 508]. By revealing the underlying implicit rela-

[1] For further information, refer to: http://www.delphion.com, http://www.micropatent.com, http://www.qpat.com. Last assessed: June 30th, 2009.

tionships among patents, patent owners and patent inventors, patent maps do represent a powerful yet difficult analytical tool which better supports technology managers in R&D decision making. More specifically, taking into account the four stages previously analyzed, technology managers may apply an "actor-similarity map" in the first stage (R&D Planning) to understand relationships between the main actors in a specific business area based on their technological similarity. Unstructured textual information may be handled through text-mining (TM), and then through social network analysis. To elaborate a technology planning, it is more worthwhile to analyze knowledge flows among firms through their patents. Consequently, an "actor-relation map", based upon citation analysis, is needed. As mentioned before, after the technological assessment, firms need to analyze business and market opportunities. To do this, they may exploit a "technological-industry map" which helps identify other industries where the technologies to be developed (or which already exist) might be applied. In the end, a "technology-affinity map" of technologies can be developed based on an affinity index. This map helps analyze knowledge flows among firms.

Due the breadth of patent map techniques, providers of similar services have constantly grown over time. Table 1 illustrates a summary of these techniques.

Table 1. Patent maps techniques

Stage	PIS task	Method	Patent map	On-line services
R&D planning	Monitoring	Text mining	Actor-similarity map	Thomson reuters' "Aureka" (http://thomsonreuters.com) NeoPatents (http://www.neopatents.com) Metrix group (http://www.metricsgroup.com) Dolcera (http://www.dolcera.com/website_prod/services/ip-patent-analytics-services) Invengine (http://www.invengine.net/) M-Cam (http://www.m-cam.com/)
Technology planning	Collaboration	Citation analysis	Actor-relation map	
Business planning	Diversification	Citation analysis	Technology-industry map	
Market planning	Benchmarking	Index analysis	Technology-affinity map	

Finally, an emerging (and still not completely developed) type of software applications builds on the previous category and tries to forecast technological areas that have not been fully exploited but whose expected application potential is very high (or, at least, increasing). In turn, these software systems may support managers in making decisions concerning technology roadmapping processes [19, 20], with an especial emphasis on the connections between product and technology planning. The key advantage of using such applications is that of making the roadmapping exercise more quantitative. Indeed, traditional technology road maps tend to overstate the qualitative and expert-dependent knowledge rather than incorporating quantitative and objective information. In contrast, the new approach makes use of available patent data in order to discover undeveloped technological fields, thus making the result of the analysis more reliable.

Concluding Remarks

Performing effective patent analysis is an endeavour firms must take on. Traditionally, PIS are perceived in terms of information extraction and visualization, with no emphasis to their supporting role of strategic decision-making in R&D setting. We focus on this issue and propose to adopt a process view to analyze the multiple tasks of PIS in R&D strategy formulation.

In particular, we analyze the monitoring, collaborative, diversification, and benchmarking tasks, highlighting the proper analytical techniques (such as text-mining, network analysis, citation analysis and index analysis), patent maps and relative on-line services. This approach leads us to recognize several streams in PIS research, such as: *patent intelligence,* aimed at analyzing the use of patent information to develop corporate strategy; *patent mapping*, which uses published patent data to create a graphical or physical representation of the relevant art pertaining to a particular subject area or novel invention; *analysis methods,* which refer to the study of patent citations for determining a patent's potential value or, perhaps more reliably, the identification of potential licensing partners based on the citation of an organization's patents by another company in the same or a completely different market space.

By its nature, this study is an exploratory one and needs more elaboration in terms of methodology and application. We strongly believe that it will promote further research in PIS and deepen understanding on the managerial side.

References

1. Kortum S, Lerner J (1999) What is behind the recent surge in patenting. *Res Policy* 28(1):1–22
2. Hall BH (2004) Exploring the patent explosion. National bureau of economic research (NBER) Working Paper, #10605, Cambridge
3. Levin RC, Klevorick AK, Nelson RR, Winter SG (1984) Survey research on R&D appropriability and technological opportunity: part 1. Yale University Working Paper, New Haven, July 1984
4. Levin RC (1986) A new look at the patent system. *Am Econ Rev* 76(2):199–202
5. Mansfield E (1981) Composition of R&D expenditures: relationship to size of firm, concentration, and innovative output. *Rev Econ Stat* 63(4):610–615
6. Badaracco JL (1991) *The knowledge link.* Harvard Business School Press, Boston
7. Rivette KG, Kline D (1999) *Rembrandts in the attic: unlocking the hidden value of patents.* Harvard Business School Press, Boston

8. Ernst H (2003) Patent information for strategic technology management. *World Patent Inf* 25(3):233–242
9. Chesbrough H (2003) *Open innovation: the new imperative for creating and profiting from technology*. Harvard Business School Press, Boston
10. Teece DJ (1986) *Profiting from technological innovation*. Res Policy 15(6):285–305
11. Grindley PC, Teece DJ (1997) Managing intellectual capital: licensing and cross-licensing in semiconductors and electronics. *Calif Manage Rev* 39(2):8–41
12. Abraham B, Morita S (2001) *Innovation assessment through patent analysis*. Technovation 21(4):245–252
13. Liu S, Shyu J (1997) Strategic planning for technology development with patent analysis. *Int J Technol Manage* 13:661–680
14. Daim T, Rueda G, Martin H, Gerdsri P (2006) *Forecasting emerging technologies: use of bibliometrics and patent analysis*. Technol Forecast Social Change 73(8):981–1012
15. Siddiquee Q, Bhattacharya P (2003) Online patent searching techniques: an overview. *DESIDOC Bull Inf Technol* 23(4):3–17
16. Lambert N (2004) Internet patent information in the 21st century: a comparison of Delphion, Micropatent, and Qpat. In *Proceedings of 2004 international chemical information conference & exhibition*, Annecy (France), 17–20 October 2004
17. Stock M, Stock WG (2006) Intellectual property information: a comparative analysis of main information providers. *J Am Soc Inf Sci Technol* 57(13):1794–1803
18. Wu YJ (2006) Assessment of technological innovations in patenting for 3rd party logistics providers. *J Enterp Inf Manage* 19(5):504–524
19. Lee S, Lee S, Seol H, Park Y (2008) Using patent information for designing new product and technology: keyword based technology roadmapping. *R&D Manage* 38(2):169–188
20. Lee S, Yoon B, Park Y (2009) *An approach to discovering new technology opportunities: keyword-based patent map approach*. Technovation 29(6-7):481–497

Part II
Organizational Change and Impact of IT

Ferdinando Pennarola[*] and Maddalena Sorrentino[†]

In the modern corporate world, Information and Communication Technologies (ICT) absorb a dominant share of a firm's total capital investments. Organizations expect to use the new ICT to run new processes, innovate products and services, gain higher responsiveness, and implement new corporate environments aimed at transforming their internal structures into better achieving organizations.

To date, practice and literature have both widely shown that one of the most challenging tasks faced by managers is the effective implementation of new ICT, since it requires people to understand, absorb, and adapt to new requirements. It is often said that people love progress but hate change. Therefore, the ultimate impact of ICT is mediated by a number of factors, many of which require an in-depth understanding of the organizational context and human behavior.

Despite the many change strategies and tactics applied so far and the fact that many research findings have associated successful tactics with organizational contexts, it is proving difficult to develop a comprehensive theory of change management and change implementation. Empirical investigation must be conducted hand-in-hand with theory building if we want to better interpret today's corporate environments.

The nine papers accepted by this Track discuss a broad spectrum of organizational and technical aspects and provide perspectives from different organizational settings. The reader will find an overview of these contributions below.

The article by Rocco Agrifoglio and Concetta Metallo: "ERP Acceptance: The Role of Affective Commitment" investigates the process of acceptance and use of Enterprise Resource Planning (ERP) systems by users, with the aim of understanding the reasons that drive their behavior. The authors use the Technology Acceptance Model to illustrate the case of an Italian public transport firm. The paper's findings underscore the importance of affective commitment in determining user acceptance and use behavior.

Leonardo Caporarello and Assia Viachka in their article titled "Individual readiness for change in the context of Enterprise Resource Planning System" take a fairly innovative approach to investigating the organizational implications of Enterprise Resource Planning (ERP) systems implementation in several companies, adopting diverse interpretive keys, i.e. people integration, process integration and information integration. The authors discover the ERP-specific sources of resistance that could negatively affect the deployment of the software in organizations.

[*] Bocconi University, Milan, Italy, ferdinando.pennarola@unibocconi.it

[†] University of Milano, Milan, Italy, maddalena.sorrentino@unimi.it

In their article “Changing Spaces for Social Learning in the Implementation Biography of an ERP System: A Longitudinal Case Study” Gian Marco Campagnolo and Samantha Ducati focus on four different periods of implementation choices in the history of an Italian public organization as ERP software support shifts from an in-house to a market-based supply. The case illustrates a deeply contextual reflexivity between the various compositions of supply and use space, and the social learning that provides the technical knowledge shaping members representations of the technical feature of the ERP system that drives implementation choices.

Pierluigi Rippa, Guido Capaldo, Nancy Jones and Gail Corbitt are the authors of the article “A Planning-Oriented Approach for ERP Implementation in SMEs”, in which they highlight a set of organizational and technical capabilities that influence successful ERP projects. The model prepared in this study shows how an SME’s various enterprise capabilities can influence the implementation process. The authors draw on this model and a case study to reveal how SMEs can select better strategic and change management activities.

Small and medium-sized tourism companies is the theme of Carla Wilkin’s paper “Motivators and Inhibitors to IT Infusion in Tourism SMEs”. In the busy operational environments of small and medium enterprises (SMEs), the challenge for owners is to achieve a balance between “working in the business” and “working on the business”. The study reports on the IT experiences of 158 Australian firms and suggests the need to understand mediating factors like organizational context, the role of key personnel, and human attitudes and behaviors in relation to successful IT infusion (i.e. the use of technology to its fullest potential).

In their paper “Information Systems Security in Small and Medium Sized Enterprises in the South East of Ireland”, Amanda Freeman and Liam Doyle seek to close a gap in the literature on information protection in SMEs. The purpose of the research was to gain an understanding of the growing role of information system security in SMEs in South East Ireland. The study reports on the security technologies implemented and examines the related issues.

The paper by Matthias Kießling, Mauricio Marrone and Lutz Kolbe on the “Influence of IT Service Management on Innovation Management: First Insights from Exploratory Studies” delves into the relation between innovations and standards in companies that have implemented an IT Service Management framework. The research shows that most of the companies that have adopted an IT Service Management framework first implemented the framework and then the Innovation Management process. This has enabled them to reap benefits such as faster adoption of the innovations and an enhanced ability to recognize improvement potential.

Tommaso Federici and Alessio Maria Braccini in their paper “Technological and Organizational Structures: A Case of Adaptation in the Archaeological Sector” explore an underdeveloped theme in the academic literature, i.e. the implementation of Information Systems (IS) in an application field where intensive ICT use has made few inroads to date. The authors highlight the difficulties and the challenges that accompany computerization projects in the archeological sector and propose an interpretive approach that harnesses the assumptions of structution theory.

In her paper "Organizational Readiness and Success of the EHR-S Adoption" Valentina Albano illustrates the hurdles encountered in the adoption of Health Information Systems, particularly Electronic Health Record Systems (EHR-S). The author suggests that the risk of failure in these types of projects can be mitigated by identifying some of the organizational and cultural factors that prepare the internal environment for the innovation. The article describes the preliminary steps of a study that aims to define a framework to support the analysis and diagnosis of the "organizational readiness" to EHR-S adoption.

ERP Acceptance: The Role of Affective Commitment

Rocco Agrifoglio* **and Concetta Metallo**†

Abstract This study investigates the process of acceptance and use of ERP system by its users. The TAM is used as a starting point for this work. We assume that affective commitment directly also affects both the behavioral intention to ERP system use and it moderates the relationships between perceived usefulness, perceived ease of use, and behavioral intention. A survey methodology was used to gather data from an Italian public transport firm. Findings show the importance of affective commitment in determining acceptance and use behavior by users.

ERP Acceptance and Affective Commitment

Enterprise Resource Planning (ERP) systems are comprehensive packaged software solutions that support all business processes and integrate the various functional areas [1]. Despite the advantages associated with ERP systems, their adoption is often problematic [2]. Some firms consider the adoption of ERP systems to be an instrument for promoting and realizing organizational and managerial changes. ERP implementation is often associated with mechanisms of rejection by potential users, such as a sense of confusion and inability to achieve their innovation potential. User acceptance was found to be one of the main factors contributing to ERP implementation success [2]. Therefore, understanding the conditions that lead users to adopt a new technology represents a high-priority research issue.

The process of user's technology acceptance and use has been investigated by many researchers [3–5]. Davis' (1986) Technology Acceptance Model (TAM) is one of most widely used models to explain users' behavioral intention to use a technological innovation. According to Davis [3, 4], the intention to use an information system (BI) is determined by two beliefs: perceived usefulness (PU) and perceived ease of use (PEOU). PU is defined as "the degree to which a person believes that using a particular system would enhance his or her job performance" [4]:320. PEOU refers to "the degree to which a person believes that using a particular system would be free of effort" [4:320]. Moreover, PEOU is also related to

* Management Department, Parthenope University, Naples, Italy, agrifoglio@uniparthenope.it
† Management Department, Parthenope University, Naples, Italy, metallo@uniparthenope.it

A. D'Atri et al. (eds.), *Management of the Interconnected World*,
DOI 10.1007/978-3-7908-2404-9_10,

PU. The TAM has served as a basis for numerous studies of technology acceptance and usage behavior, and it has been widely tested in different situations [see 6 for review].

Some research [7–11] has highlighted the key role of commitment in determinmining PU, PEOU, and, in turn, the BI to use an information system. Particularly, Malhotra and Galletta [7, 8] have developed the new construct of user commitment, users' psychological attachment to system use (drawn from O'Reilly and Chatman's [12] affective commitment), and they assumed that it affects the volitional acceptance and usage of the system and, therefore, the following aspects: PU, PEOU, and BI. Some authors [11] have investigated the links between Allen and Meyer's [13] organizational commitment (affective, continuance, and normative) and organizational change. On this, IT adoption and use should be conceptualized as a form of organizational change. In particular, Kwahk and Lee [11] assumed that organizational commitment affects users' attitudes toward change that, in turn, affect the TAM's constructs (PEOU, PU, and BI). Other authors [14, 10], instead, have argued that affective commitment may be positively related to user beliefs. Results of Magni and Pennarola's [10] study showed that AC is positively related to PU, but it is not positively related to PEOU. On the contrary, results of Thatcher and his colleagues' [14] study showed that AC positively affects PU and PEOU. Finally, Li and colleagues [9] argued that an individual's decision to continue to use a Web site may be influenced by two dimensions of organizational commitment: affective commitment, and calculative commitment (CC). Results highlighted that AC and CC are positively related to a person's intention to continue to use a Web site.

However, these studies don't show a direct relationship between AC, as "an affective or emotional attachment to the organization such that the strongly committed individual identifies with, is involved in, and enjoys membership in, the organization" [13:2–3], and user's BI to use a new technology and, particularly, an ERP system that is characterized by high complexity and very high failure rates.

Research Model and Hypotheses

According to the TAM [3], the BI to use a technology is determined by two constructs: PU and PEOU; moreover, PEOU also affects PU.

We assume that the behavioral intention to use derives from the ease of use and usefulness that users perceive around the new system: the more users consider it easy and useful the more they will be willing to use it. Moreover, if the system is easy to use, users perceive greater usefulness. Consequently, our hypotheses are:

H1: PU is positively associated with BI.
H2: PEOU is positively associated with BI.
H3: PEOU is positively associated with PU.

Moreover, we believe that AC plays a key role in determining user technology acceptance and use. Some previous research has highlighted the role of AC on IT adoption. In particular, these studies have shown that AC affects BI to use the IS mainly through the two basic TAM constructs: PU and PEOU. Affectively committed users believe that the implementation of new technology could represent an important change within the organization, improving individual and organizational performance, and, therefore, they are more likely to understand the perceived usefulness and perceived ease of use. Moreover, users that express positive beliefs about new technology may demonstrate their identification with, and involvement to organizational goals and values. Consequently, our hypotheses are:

H4: AC is positively associated with PU.
H5: AC is positively associated with PEOU.

However, AC should also directly affects BI. Prior research has highlighted that commitment may affects work attitudes and individuals' behavior. Users believe that the implementation of a new system promotes individual and organizational performance, perceiving the necessity for and importance of the system. Moreover, affective committed users may use the new system with affection, happiness, and pleasure because they know that the IT use encouraging the implementation success and ability to achieve innovation potential. Therefore, we assume that high degrees of user's AC to the goals and values of the organization increases their BI. Consequently, our hypothesis is:

H6: AC is positively associated with BI.

Finally, AC should also moderates the relationships between PU, PEOU, and BI. Users who perceive the new system's usefulness and easy, and with a high level of AC, will be characterized by a higher level of BI to use a new information system. In fact, beyond the user's PU and PEOU, a high degrees of AC to the goals and values of the organization increases their BI to use IT and intensify the positive effect of PU and PEOU on BI. Consequently, our hypotheses are:

H7: AC moderates the relationship between PU and BI, such that the positive effects of PU become stronger as the AC increases.
H8: AC moderates the relationship between PEOU and BI, such that the positive effects of PEOU become stronger as the AC increases.

Research Methodology

Sample and Procedure

A survey methodology was used to gather data. The survey data was collected a public transport firm that was implementing a SAP R/3. The firm has 2,500 employees, of which 250 ERP users. The firm was using several modules of the SAP software: FI, CO, MM, PM, and PS. The Go-Live phase started on 01/01/2008.

Of the 250 users surveyed, 172 returned questionnaires (response rate 68.8%). 86.8% of the respondents are men and the average age is about 50 years while the level of education was classified into the following levels: 68.5% of the respondents have a high school diploma, 14.8% have a bachelor's degree and 3.7% have a master's degree. As for their ICT experience, it varies from a minimum of 4 months, to a maximum of 31 years, with an average of approximately 12 years.

Measurements

BI, PU, and PEOU were measured using respectively two, four, and four items of Venkatesh and Davis' [15] scale, adapted from Davis [4] and Davis and colleagues [16].

AC was measured using Allen and Meyer's [13] eight-item scale.

Finally, we identified the following control variables: age, gender, educational level, and ICT experience.

Results

The structural equation modeling technique of Partial Least Squares (PLS) has been used to analyze the data. PLS is a structural equation modeling technique particularly useful to predict a set of dependent variables from a large set of independent variables [17]. This technique has been must used in IS research and, particularly, IT acceptance (e.g. [5, 10]).

The process of data analysis consists of two phases. In the first phase we established the psychometric validity of the scales used. The correlations among the variables are represented in Table 1.

Table 1. Mean, standard deviation, composite reliability, AVE, and correlations

	Mean	SD	Reliability	AVE	1	2	3	4	5	6	7	8
1. Age	50.30	7.75	–	–	–							
2. Gender	0.13	0.34	–	–	−0.35	–						
3. Educational level	13.31	2.87	–	–	−0.33	0.22	–					
4. ICT experience	12.21	8.30	–	–	0.13	−0.02	0.35	–				
5. AC	3.82	1.48	0.76	0.76	0.16	−0.27	−0.08	−0.12	–			
6. PEOU	4.01	1.59	0.91	0.77	−0.16	0.05	0.13	−0.06	0.38	–		
7. PU	4.50	1.04	0.94	0.84	0.03	−0.04	−0.13	−0.16	0.38	0.61	–	
8. BI	5.37	1.32	0.79	0.83	−0.19	0.11	0.09	−0.14	0.36	0.45	0.60	–

Table 1 also shows the mean, the standard deviation, the Cronbach's coefficients for the variables (composite reliability), and the Average Variance Extracted (AVE) as well as the correlations between constructs. The Cronbach Alphas (0.91 PEOU, 0.94 PU, 0.76 AC, 0.79 BI) for the items within each construct are sufficiently high. Moreover, the results do not show high levels of correlation between the independent variables. These results show a high degree of internal coherence with the scales used and, therefore, the measures testing the model shown a good psychometric properties.

In the second phase we tested our hypotheses. The results of Partial Least Squares are shown in Fig. 1.

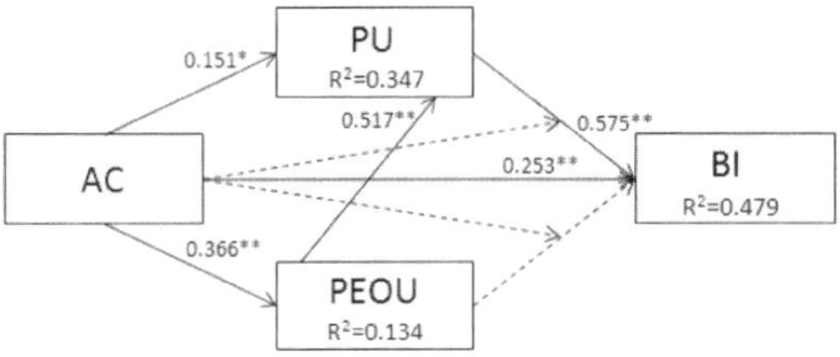

** $p \leq 0.001$; * $p \leq 0.05$;

— The relationship is significant; -- The relationship is not significant.

Fig. 1. Results of partial least squares

Figure 1 shows PLS results on dependent variable BI. The control variables used are age, gender, educational level, and ICT experience. Results show that the control variables are not related with BI. Therefore, in the final model the control variables are not displayed.

Figure 1 highlight that PU is positively related to BI (β=0.575; $p \leq 0.001$), thus supporting H1. Moreover, PLS results show that PEOU is positively related to PU (β=0.517; $p \leq 0.001$), thus supporting H3, while it has not a significant influences on BI (β=−0.035; $p \geq 0.05$), thus H2 is not supported.

Providing support for hypotheses 4 and 5, AC is positively associated with PU (β=0.151; $p \leq 0.05$) and PEOU (β=0.366; $p \leq 0.001$). Moreover, results show that AC is positively associated with BI (β=0.253; $p \leq 0.001$), thus supporting H6.

Finally, we tested the moderator hypotheses H7 and H8. Results show that AC does not moderate the relationship between PU and BI ($\beta=-0.029$; $p\geq0.05$) and between PEOU and BI ($\beta=0.098$; $p\geq0.05$). Thus, H7 and H8 are not supported.

PLS results show a good explanation of users' behavioral intention to use variance (BI R2=0.479). Moreover, the contribution of independent variables on BI has been tested through path analysis. Path analysis results are shown in Table 2.

Table 2. Path analysis

	PU	PEOU	AC
Correlation coefficient	0.612	0.435	0.349
Pathway	0.575	–0.035	0.253
Correlation coefficient*Pathway	0.352	–0.015	0.088

Table 2 highlights the explanatory role of PU (0.575), PEOU (–0.035), and AC (0.253) on BI. Particularly, path analysis results show that AC is more explanatory than PEOU.

Discussion

The aim of this study was to analyze the process of acceptance and use of technology by users. Using the TAM, we analyzed the relationships between PEOU, PU, and BI. We highlight the role of AC as a key variable in determining the process of acceptance and use of new technology such as ERP system.

Our results show that PEOU positively affects PU, and that PU, in turn, positively affects BI. In particular, PU represents a mediator variable between PEOU and BI. These results are consistent with a lot of research investigating technology adoption based on Davis' TAM [6]. In fact, many researchers had shown that PU affects IT adoption, but others had mostly failed to do so regarding PEOU [18]. Users believe that IT use will increase their job performance and, therefore, they will be more willing to use it [4, 16]. Davis [4] already failed to find a direct linkage between PEOU and users' BI, and he argued that "ease of use operates through usefulness" [4]:332. For this reason, some authors [see 18 for a review] have investigated the importance of PEOU in IT adoption. In particular, Ma and Liu [19] conducted a meta-analysis based on 26 selected empirical studies on the TAM's constructs. Results have suggested a strong relationship between PU and acceptance, and between PEOU and PU. The authors have concluded "that the relationship between ease of use and acceptance is weak, and its significance does not pass the fail-safe test" [19:59].

Moreover, our results show that AC positively affects user's beliefs such as PU and PEOU. In particular, Kwahk and Lee [11] demonstrated that affective commitment indirectly affects PU and PEOU; it operates through attitude to organizational change. Moreover, other authors [14, 10] assumed that AC is directly related to

PU and PEOU. However, results of Magni and Pennarola's [10] study had shown that AC is positively related with PU, but the relationship between PEOU and AC is not significant. In agreement whit previous study, we argue that affectively committed users perceive the ERP system as a tool to improve the individual and organizational performance, developing their awareness about the processes of organizational change and supporting organizational goals and values. In this way, users with high level of AC may be more willing to expend time and effort learning to use new systems and, consequently, they PEOU and PU more [14].

Compared with these studies, our results highlight the role of AC in determining the BI to use ERP system. Particularly, AC is directly and positively associated with user's BI. However, results show that the effect of PU and PEOU on BI is not moderated by AC. Employees may perceive the implementation of a new information system as either a threat or an opportunity. IT implementation is often associated with mechanisms of rejection by potential users, and a sense of confusion and inability to achieve their innovation potential. On the other hand, workers may perceive the adoption of new IT, and in particular an ERP system, as an instrument to promote and realize organizational and managerial changes. In this case, highly affective committed employees have a greater emotional attachment to, identification with, and involvement in the organization than non-committed colleagues, perceiving the implementation of a new information system as beneficial for individual and organizational performance. Affective committed users believe that implementing an ERP system could represent the best way for the organization to achieve success and, for this reason, they put up less resistance to change and facilitate the implementation processes. Therefore, users with goals and values congruent to organization feel and believe that the use of a new IS is the "right thing" to do [11], increasing their intention to adopt and use it.

Conclusions

In summary, our findings show the key role of affective commitment in determining the process of acceptance and use of ERP system. Compared with previous research, our results highlight that AC affects BI trough user's beliefs such as PU and PEOU, but, above all, it affects BI directly and positively. Therefore, organizations may adopt human resource management practices favouring AC in order to improve their behavioral intention to adopt the ERP system.

We believe that this study has several limitations. The first limitation comes from having tested our hypothesis within a single firm. Moreover, we have not conducted a longitudinal study, thus, we cannot compare results over time.

Despite these limitations, we believe that this study contributes further to explain user behavior regarding new technology acceptance. Future research can extend our study to other firms and sectors using longitudinal data collected in order to compare results. In particular, additional research could also make a comparative analysis between voluntary and mandatory use of technology verifying the role of affective commitment in these different contexts. On the other hand, longitudinal study could explain how affective commitment influences the process of adoption and use of new technology over time.

References

1. Davenport TH, Stoddard DB (1994) Reengineering: business change of mythic proportions?. *MIS Quarterly*, 18(2):121–127.
2. Markus ML, Axline S, Petrie D, Tanis SC (2000) Learning from adopters' experiences with ERP: problems encountered and success achieved. *Journal of Information Technology*, 15(4):245–265.
3. Davis FD (1986) *Technology acceptance model for empirically testing new end-user information systems: theory and results*. MIT: Doctoral dissertation. Cambridge
4. Davis FD (1989) Perceived usefulness, perceived ease of use, and user acceptance of information technology. *MIS Quarterly*, 13(3):319–340.
5. Venkatesh V, Morris MG, Davis GB, Davis FD (2003) User acceptance of information technology: toward a unified view. *MIS Quarterly*, 27(3):425–478
6. King WR, He J (2006) A meta-analysis of the technology acceptance model. *Information & Management*, 43(6) :740–755.
7. Malhotra Y, Galletta DF (1999) Extending the technology acceptance model to account for social influence: theoretical bases and empirical validation. In: *Proceedings of the Hawaii international conference on system sciences*. IEEE Computer Society Press, Los Alamitos
8. Malhotra Y, Galletta DF (2005) A multidimensional commitment model of volitional systems adoption and usage behavior. *Journal of Management Information Systems*, 22(1):117–152.
9. Li D, Browne GJ, Chau PYK (2006) An empirical investigation of web site use using a commitment-based model. *Decision Sciences*, 37(3) :427–444.
10. Magni M, Pennarola F (2008) Intra-organizational relationships and technology acceptance. *International Journal of Information Management*, 28(6) :517–523.
11. Kwahk KY, Lee JN (2008) The role of readiness for change in ERP implementation: theoretical bases and empirical validation. *Information & Management*, 45(7) :474–481.
12. O'Reilly C, Chatman J (1986) Organizational commitment and psychological attachment: the effects of compliance, identification and internalisation on prosocial behaviour. *Journal of Applied Psychology*, 71(3):492–499
13. Allen NJ, Meyer JP (1990) The measurement and antecedents of affective, continuance and normative commitment to the organization. *Journal of Occupational Psychology*, 63(1):1–18
14. Thatcher JB, McKnight DH, Ahuja MK (2002) The work environment and technology acceptance: the influence of affective commitment, autonomy and trust. *Information systems technical reports and working papers*.Kellyschool of Business, Indiana University, Bloomington, IN.
15. Venkatesh V, Davis FD (2000) A theoretical extension of the technology acceptance model: four longitudinal field studies. *Management Science*, 46(2):186–205
16. Davis FD, Bagozzi RP, Warshaw PR (1989) User acceptance of computer technology: a comparison of two theoretical models. *Management Sciences*, 35(8):982–1003
17. Abdi H (2003) Partial least squares (PLS) regression. In: M Lewis-Beck M, A Bryman A, T Futing T (eds.), *Encyclopedia of social sciences research methods*. Thousand Oaks: Sage, Thousand Oaks.
18. Gefen D, Straub T (2000) The relative importance of perceived ease-of-use in IS adoption: a study of e-commerce adoption. *Journal of the Association for Information Systems*, 1(8):1–30.
19. Ma Q, Liu L (2004) The technology acceptance model: a meta-analysis of empirical findings. *Journal of Organ and End User Computing*, 16(1):59–72.

Individual Readiness for Change in the Context of Enterprise Resource Planning System Implementation

Leonardo Caporarello* **and Assia Viachka**†

Abstract The present study takes a rather innovative approach and investigates the organizational implications of the implementation of Enterprise Resource Planning (ERP) systems in companies from people integration, process integration and information integration perspectives. In this manner we discover the ERP-specific sources of resistance that could affect negatively the deployment of the software in an organization. Then, we argue that a general set of beliefs shapes employees readiness to change to IT use and provides the foundation for resistance or for adoptive behavior. We define the concept of readiness for change in the context of ERP implementation and introduce a readiness for change assessment approach. Then, we test empirically the study hypotheses upon which the research model was build. The results obtained offer insights into factors that can improve the effectiveness of ERP implementation strategies.

Introduction

This research explores mainly two streams of literature. Firstly, the literature related to Enterprise Resource Planning (ERP) system software, and secondly the organizational change literature. Based on that research we develop a model that is designed to assess the impact of several variables on employees' readiness for change in the context of ERP implementation. The motivation to undertake such research was based on the aspiration to contribute to the development of ERP literature by finding proves for the importance of change management for the successful implementation of the software. Our goal is to demonstrate that the functional logic of ERP software leads to a wide organizational transformation that can be very disruptive for companies and could encounter employees' resistance to change. In fact, some researchers believe that a lot of ERP projects fail because

* Institute of Organization and Information Systems, Bocconi University, 20136 Milano, Italy
† CEMS Candidate, Master of International Management, Bocconi University, Milan, Italy

A. D'Atri et al. (eds.), *Management of the Interconnected World*,
DOI 10.1007/978-3-7908-2404-9_11,

companies underestimate the efforts involved in managing the implied organizational transformation (e.g. [1]). We argue that there is a need to develop change management tools and strategies that acknowledge the specifics of an ERP environment. For this purpose, we first analyze the organizational consequences that could result from the deployment of ERP, in order to discover what forces could cause organizational resistance to integrated system environment.

Given that in literature creating readiness for change (RFC) has been proposed as a major prescription for reducing resistance [2], we propose a research model build upon several variables that are expected to influence employees' readiness to adopt ERP technology. A statistically significant relationship between the proposed variables and RFC would indicate that employees' reaction to ERP could be managed and would bring tangible evidence for the importance of change management for the success of ERP projects. The argument goes that if managers correctly assess how employees feel about the proposed factors and outline actions to reduce negative perceptions, then organizations will be more successful in implementing ERP.

Theoretical Framework

In this study RFC is seen not as a general perception, but as the attitude and the intention of employees towards the implementation of an ERP system in their concrete organization. Specifically, RFC refers to the predisposition of individuals to adopt supportive (readiness) rather then rejective (resistance) behavior with respect to ERP. In that sense, we define RFC as a continuum with readiness on one hand and resistance on the other. Without underestimating the wide implications of ERP for organizations that could generate various individual reasons to go against such projects, the paper argues that there are some conditions that could create general willingness to support the related changes. The question is: are interventions to enhance RFC possible in the context of ERP? To answer this question we first need to study the organizational consequences of ERP deployment. This would allow us to discover factors that could influence RFC in a positive way.

Factors Influencing RFC in the ERP Context

The first step in constructing the present research has been the analysis of the specifics of ERP software, in order to discover the variables that influence the readiness of employees to work in an ERP environment. ERP Systems are software platforms that help companies integrate all the operational information across functions, departments and locations [3, 4]. In order to achieve the desired level of integration, companies need to rethink and integrate all their business processes making them compatible with the ERP logic which very often implies a shift from functional to process-based operational logic [5]. In that sense we can argue that ERP creates an integrated structure that involves a whole new perspective on business and deeply affects the way people in organizations interact [6]. Mismanaging this transition could indeed lead to a failure of the implementation project as it could encounter organizational resistance to change [1].

Following this logic, we have proposed to analyze the ERP integration process from processes, information and people perspectives, in order to discover in what way ERP affects organizations. We base this analysis not only on a wide literature review, but also on different case studies and company examples. Here below, the paper summarizes briefly the findings of this analysis, making reference to several of the reviewed papers, and then considers a likely point of view of employees in looking for potential sources of change resistance. Next, we put forward organizational variables which capture factors that are expected to reduce resistance and, consequently, to create RFC. In that manner we discover the factors that build up our research model and formulate the research hypothesis that are presented at the end of this section.

Information integration means sharing data in a standardized way allowing for real-time access to all business and information transactions, operating and financial data. Supervisors have the possibility to monitor the performance at any point in time. This increases transparency but could create vertical tension as it tolerates surveillance. Furthermore, information integration leads to the introduction of new tools that require extensive training on all levels in the organization. More importantly, it requires a passage from a skill-based logic, on which functional division of work is based, to a customer-oriented logic, on which ERP process division of work is based. In fact, Martin and Huq [1] claim that employees' understanding of ERP is the most common obstacle to implementation. Moreover, if employees do not understand the benefits of adopting ERP as a business strategy, it is probable that they resist the implementation or try to avoid using the system to the extent possible, causing information loss and lower ERP benefits [7]. For these reasons, we have chosen to study the relationship between RFC and the following variables. First of all, we argue that Perceived usefulness, or the belief that using a particular system would enhance job performance [8], increases users' motivation to adopt ERP. We base this argument also on Amoako-Gyampah [7] empirical proves that managerial efforts aimed at increasing users' perception of the personal relevance of technology, contribute to implementation success and on Holt et al. [9] who suggest that RFC is influenced by the belief that the change is beneficial to organizational members. Furthermore, we study whether Holt et al. [9] positive relationship between Change efficacy, or the degree to which organizational members feel confident they will be able to implement the change and to perform well after the transformation, and RFC holds also in the ERP context. Additionally, based on Miller et al. [10] who proved the positive link between RFC and employees' relationship with their managers, the paper investigates whether Faith in the good intentions of management, or the perception of employees that management is trustworthy and cares about them, can cause employees to be more positive towards the possibility of increased level of control implied by the new system.

Process integration implies wide structural changes in organizations: some positions are eliminated; new ones appear; some tasks are reduced; others are amplified. This makes ERP implementation an important organizational event as it affects to a great extent the way people work and can render previous knowledge obsolete. Weeks et al. [11] have discovered that people are reluctant to cooperate when they are not sure of how the proposed change will affect their current relationships at work, their status, their future. Moreover, when processes change, people have to be able to adapt to the new settings, recognize the differences and make the necessary adjustments [12]. Managers are the primary change agents that have to guide people through this transformation. Reicher et al. [13] argue that change efforts are likely to fail if employees lose faith in senior management as change agents. We argue that a company might expect resistance to ERP in case employees feel that there is not enough organizational support and commitment in order for the proposed changes to be implemented. Two variables reflect these considerations. First, based on Weeks et al. [11] who have discovered a significant negative relationship between readiness for change and Individual fear of change, we argue that people can resist ERP if they perceive the changes as personally not beneficial and disruptive for their current work relations or status. A further concept that we develop concerns Change Leadership, or the perceptions of employees on whether the efforts of management to guide them through the change process are sufficient and adequate. We have based this argument on the research of different authors such as Parr et al. [14] who point out the importance of leaders for the ERP implementation success.

People integration is an inevitable result of process integration. The more processes are integrated, the more operations are conducted in a cross-functional way and the higher is the need of interactions and cooperation across the value chain [6]. ERP creates interdependencies between the various organizational units and leads to a higher degree of people integration through the organization. However, change towards cross-functional integration can be seen as very disruptive and can result in conflicts. This study argues that the lack of Cooperative working environment (where personal contribution is recognized and employees work in teams and trust each other) might result in employees' resistance to work in a situation where job performance depends on cross-functional collaboration.

Formally:

H1 Perceived usefulness is positively related to RFC

H2 Change efficacy is positively related to RFC

H3 Faith in the good intentions of management is positively related to RFC

H4 Individual fear of change is negatively related to RFC

H5 Change leadership is positively related to RFC

H6 Cooperative working environment is positively related to RFC

Method

Research Design and Measurements

In this study we used an individual-level survey to empirically assess the proposed research model.[1] The survey consisted in 53 questions in the form of self-administered questionnaire and it was distributed to companies in several countries. The target companies were in the process of implementing an ERP system or were expanding their software platforms in a "second wave" logic. Finally, a total of 23 companies participated to the research. The total amount of retained responses for the data analysis was 107.

All the constructs in the study were taken from measures that have already been validated by prior research. Minimum adjustments to the questions have been made, in order to relate them to the ERP context. All variables were measured on Likert scales ranging from "strongly disagree" to "strongly agree".

Two control variables were included in the study. Nationality was included because previous findings indicated that national culture can influence ERP implementation [15]. Gender was included based on the argument that there are differences between men and women when it comes to adopting new technologies [16].

Data Analysis

The first step of the data analysis focused on ensuring that the research instruments were valid and reliable. Briefly, we controlled for convergent validity through inter-item correlations among measures of the same construct. All items that had item-to-total correlations of less than 0.5 were dropped. Moreover, only items with factor components above 0.7 (the correlation of the items with the unique factor that best explains the variance of the respective construct) were retained in the analysis.

Furthermore, all variables scored higher than the suggested theoretical 0.7 threshold for Cronbach's Alpha coefficient [17], showing good reliability of the constructs. Moreover, we controlled for discriminant validity of the constructs by confirming that the squared root of the average variance extracted (AVE) of each construct (the diagonal line of the correlation matrix in Table 1) was higher than

---

[1] Tables with more detailed information about the study variables, the demographics of the research and the results of the factor analysis are available upon request from the corresponding author.

the inter-construct correlations. Additionally, the structure of the model was assessed through a confirmatory factor analysis (PCA extraction method and Varimax rotation). In saving factor scores we applied Kaiser's criterion of eingenvalue >1. All items loaded respectively on their corresponding factor, reconfirming the discriminant validity of the constructs. Based on all these considerations, we concluded that the measures used to test the proposed model had adequate psychometric properties.

Table 1. Descriptive statistics, reliability of constructs, correlations and AVE

Construct	Mean	SD	Cronbach's Alpha	Items	Items Retained	CWE	IFC	CL	FIM	PU	CE	RFC
CWE	2.48	0.86	0.86	5	4	***0.78***						
IFC	0.53	0.65	0.89	3	3	–0.16	***0.90***					
CL	4.74	1.70	0.92	11	8	0.38	–0.43	***0.78***				
FIM	1.68	0.73	0.80	3	3	0.45	–0.18	0.63	***0.85***			
PU	4.31	1.33	0.95	6	6	0.23	–0.18	0.38	0.36	***0.89***		
CE	3.22	1.13	0.89	6	5	0.24	–0.35	0.48	0.29	0.34	***0.78***	
RFC	4.50	1.54	0.92	14	7	0.28	–0.43	0.44	0.15	0.39	0.55	***0.83***

Second, we tested the direction and the statistical significance of the proposed relationships through a Regression analysis (Fig. 1). Factor scores were used to conduct the analysis. Four of the research hypotheses were statistically confirmed, these are (H1) perceived usefulness (t = 2.532), (H2) change efficacy (t = 4.062), (H4) individual fear of change (t = 2.467), (H5) change leadership (t = 2.376). The positive relationship between cooperative working environment and RFC (H6) was confirmed but was not statistically significant. (t = 1.829). Our third hypothesis was also not confirmed due to the fact that in the analysis faith in the good intentions of management and RFC had a negative relationship. Finally, the control variables did not show any significant influence. Overall, the model seemed to have relatively good fit to the data ($R^2 = 0.46$, p • 0.001, adjusted $R^2 = 0.43$).

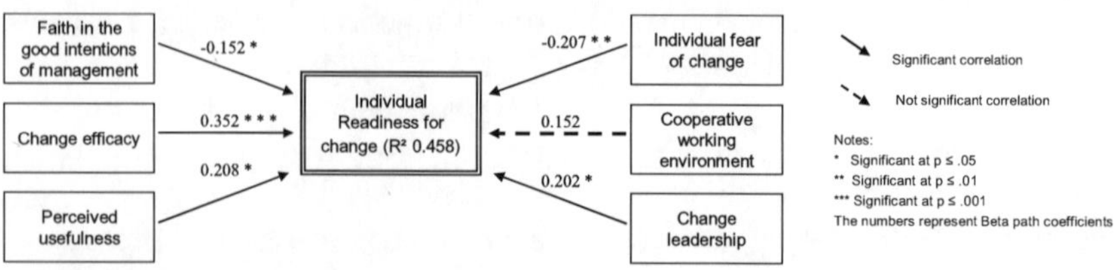

Fig. 1. Model and regression results

Discussion and Implications

Our study aimed at contributing to the construction of an ERP-specific change management tool that would allow managers to assess RFC to ERP at individual level in their organizations. However, the study had an exploratory nature and did not aim at providing a complete definition of RFC, but rather to set the basis for future research of the concept. First of all, our results suggest that the belief that the proposed technology could increase job performance, and that one has the necessary capabilities to confront the changes involved, is positively related to his/her willingness to support the project.

However, if employees perceive the change as personally not beneficial, there is a possibility of change resistance. Furthermore, the analysis supported our initial hypothesis that the perception of employees on the capabilities of managers to lead the change in an adequate manner could result in a higher degree of organizational support for the project. Moreover, even though from significance point of view we cannot confirm this hypothesis, the presence of cooperative working environment was found to have a positive relationship with RFC. Finally, faith in the good intentions of management produced negative regression score which leads us to reject our third hypothesis.

These results show that managerial efforts in guiding the change initiative could impact positively the adoption of supportive behavior towards ERP and, consequently, could increase the probability of project success.

All these considerations lead to the conclusion that change management should be an essential element of ERP implementation strategies. Consequently, several managerial implications can be deducted from the present study. Managers need to: (1) communicate clearly the benefits of the system implementation and "promote" the change within the organization by emphasizing the benefits of the software in terms of individual performance gains; (2) acknowledge that employees might have a different perspective on whether leaders' efforts in managing the change are sufficient; (3) mitigate the individual fears of organizational actors concerning the changes that will take place by meeting employees' doubts in an open dialogue; (4) assess whether the training initiatives are perceived as efficient and whether employees feel that they have the necessary capabilities to work with ERP systems.

References

1. Martin TN, Huq Z (2007) Realigning top management's strategic change actions for ERP implementation: how specializing on just cultural and environmental contextual factors could improve success. *J Change Manage* 7(2):121–142
2. Kwahk K-Y, Lee JN (2008) The role of readiness for change in ERP implementation: theoretical bases and empirical validation. *Inf Manage* 45(7):474–481

3. Davenport TH (1998) Putting the enterprise into the enterprise system. *Harv Bus Rev* 76(4):121–131
4. De Marco M (2000) *I sistemi informative aziendali: temi di attualità*. Franco Angeli, Milano
5. Caporarello L, Basaglia S (2008) *Sistemi ERP: un'innovazione tecnologica ed organizzativa*. Egea, Milano
6. Amrani EI, Frantz R, Geffroy-Maronnat B (2006) The effects of enterprise resource planning implementation strategy on cross-functionality. *Inf Syst J* 16:79–104
7. Amoako-Gyampah K (2007) Perceived usefulness, user involvement and behavioural intention: an empirical study of ERP implementation. *Comput Human Behav* 23(3):1232–1248
8. Davis FD (1989) Perceived usefulness, perceived ease of use, and user acceptance of information technology. *MIS Q* 13(3):319–340
9. Holt DT, Armenakis A, Hubert A, Field S, Harris SG (2007) Readiness for organizational change. The systematic development of a scale. *J Appl Behav Sci* 43(2):232–255
10. Miller D, Madsen SR, John CR (2006) Readiness for change: implications on employees' relationship with management, job knowledge and skills, and job demands. *J Appl Manage Entrepreneurship* 11(1):3–16
11. Weeks WA, Roberts J, Chonko LB, Jones E (2004) Organizational readiness for change, individual fear of change, and sales manager performance: an empirical investigation. *J Pers Selling Sales Manag* 24(1):7–17
12. Leban B, Klein A, Stone R (2006) *Managing organizational change*. Wiley, New York
13. Reicher A, Wanous J, Austin J (1997) Understanding and managing cynicism about organizational change. *Acad Manage Exec* 11(1):48–59
14. Parr AN, Shanks G (2000) A taxonomy of ERP implementation approaches. *In Proceedings of the 33rd Hawaii international conference on system sciences*, Maui, USA
15. Sawah S, Abd El Fattah T, Hassan Rasmy M (2008) A quantitative model to predict the Egyptian ERP implementation success index. *Business Process Manage J* 14(3):288–306
16. Venkatesh V, Morris MG (2000) Why don't men ever stop to ask for directions: gender, social influence and their role in technology acceptance and usage behaviour. *MIS Q* 24(1):115–139
17. Oppenheim AN (1992) *Questionnaire design, interviewing and attitude measurement*. Continuum, London/New York

Changing Spaces for Social Learning in ERP Implementation: A Situational Analysis

Gian Marco Campagnolo* **and Samantha Ducati†**

Abstract The research presented in this paper focuses on two different periods of implementation choices in the history of an Italian public sector organization as ERP software support shifts from being provided in-house to a market-based supply. The case illustrates a deeply contextual reflexivity between the various compositions of supply and use space and the social learning that shapes organizational members' representations of ERP system implementation choices. Data on distinctive situational maps of organizational resources concerning implementation choices and post-implementation enhancements of the system were gathered through biographic interviews and observations of the system in use. Two different situational maps of IT related expertise were identified across different time periods: the "Steering Committee" period (1998–2001) and the "Key Users" period (2002–2005). We explore the role played across time by the reconfiguration of actors and their interactions along the ERP system support chain in patterning the way project participants make sense of notions like "customization" or "standardization".

Research Approach

This paper presents an analysis of how the notions of standardization and customization changed according to the varied distribution of responsibilities for realization of the software in Dante Province from one time period to the next. This is organized as one "organizational move" representing a major change in the supply/use space. The empirical data are used to illustrate how different strategies of knowledge mobilization enacted different learning spaces and how representations of implementation choices emerging from each historical period were interlinked. We want to show how the varied composition of the supply and use space at different times was enlisted in knowledge formation. Our analysis highlights the distributed [1] and abductive [2] nature of technical knowledge formation in ERP implementation and post-implementation at Dante Province. The analytical tools adopted to interpret time periods are situational maps [3] including (i) the map of the supply/use space; (ii) the implementation trajectory of the ERP system from supply to use; (iii) the moving locus of implementation choices and (iv) the mean-

* Università di Trento, Trento, Italy, gianmarco.campagnolo@soc.unitn.it
† Univeristà di Trento, Trento, Italy, samantha.ducati@studenti.unitn.it

A. D'Atri et al. (eds.), *Management of the Interconnected World*,
DOI 10.1007/978-3-7908-2404-9_12,

ing of standardization versus customization emerging from each time period constituency. The following section analyzes the move from the period when the Steering Committee was in place to manage a cross-organizational project to the time when the adoption of SAP – the ERP system selected by Dante Province – was managed by the appointment of key users representing each organizational unit involved. We organize the narrative around the "move" from one time period to another in order to highlight how changes in the meanings given to notions like "customization" or "standardization" were due to changes in actors' roles and implementation management devices coupled with the varying size of the supply/use space from one period to the next, and how implementation choices in each historical period were interlinked with each other as resources for sense making.

From the "Steering Committee" (1998–2002) to the "Key Users" (2002–2005) Time Period

In the supply/use space enacted during the "Steering Committee" time period, implementation actors worked within a "hum" of "continuous reporting among participants" [4]. Communication from the use side to the supply side was ensured by the Committee, on which Dante Province's organizational Department and the implementation support providers were all represented. The supply space consisted of a limited number of intermediaries, the most important of which was the in-house IT company. The use space comprised representatives of Dante Province's Departments of Organization, Planning and Accounting. More global communication about SAP implementation issues was limited by various factors. Despite the technology provider's efforts to disseminate SAP implementation experiences across user organizations, SAP had been translated into Italian only in 1997. A verticalization for the public sector was not yet available. The only public administrations implementing SAP at that time were in foreign countries–Austria and Spain. And they have different accounting practices from Italy's:

> they have an Anglo-Saxon accounting model. We have a Latin model. In the Anglo-Saxon model controls are all final. Ours are estimates (Project Manager).

Another example of the limited access to specialist knowledge about SAP at that time is the fact that the local university consultants were described by the project manager as possessing information about the implications of customization which they had gathered from newspapers.

Communication among members of the implementation project's "hum" took place within this limited learning space on implementation choices. However, the presence of the General Director of the in-house IT company and of a number of Dante Province heads of department ensured the fundamental management commitment to the project [5] and empowered cross-sectorial project management functions. The goal was also limited: namely to implement the Financial module (FM/FI), together with the module hosting the deliberations of the political apparatus (DDP) (Fig. 1).

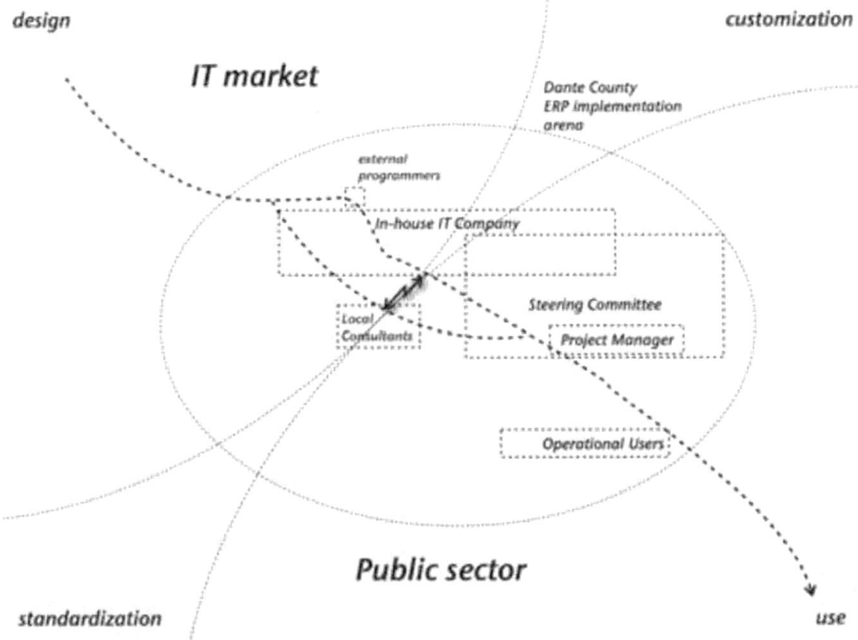

Fig. 1. Supply/use space adapted from [6]: the "Technological experiment". Broken lines represent the ERP implementation trajectory. Zigzag lines denote key tensions between actors.

According to the Social Learning in Technological Innovation (SLTI) framework, this is the typical supply/use space configuration of a technological experiment, where users, developers and suppliers [7, 8] often deliberately construct a constituency of certain key players to provide a framework of ideas and resources to shape innovation [9]. The idea emerging from this constituency was that SAP should be implemented to meet the year 2000 milestone for system roll-out, without too many customizations concerning reporting-controlling-monitoring functions.

According to the aim of administrative decentralization, the implementation of the SAP financial module would distribute accounting functions from the Staff Structures directly to all 14 Operational Services. The system at that time "intended to serve the Operational Services users" was a system "in which each single user, each single unit, was responsible for the data input and for the controls". "Information that does not have an added value for all", that is, the control requirements performed by each single Staff Service for its own monitoring purposes, "should not be included". The Dante Province ERP implementation project manager said about her role at that time:

> I have always promoted the Operational Services' point of view... I played the role of the Operational Services (Project Manager).

This view was shared by the majority of the members of the Steering Committee, whose role was to maintain control over the amount of customizations requested by the key users of each Department involved. Customizations were considered to impact heavily on future module implementations and migrations to further versions of the system. The amount of work days devoted to customizations, however, even under the very tight control of the Steering Committee, was much higher than expected: an estimate of 1,300 work days rose to a final 3,000.

In 2002, having achieved the goal of rolling out the FM and the DDG modules, the Steering Committee dissolved and the Project Manager was moved from the IT Department to the Accounting Department. At that time, together with some additional applications in the accounting area ("Borrowing Transactions" and "Electronic Payment"), also implemented was the PS "Project System". The PS module's implementation involved Dante Province personnel that did not belong to the Accounting Department. Rather, the PS key user was selected from among members of the Planning Department. With reference to the literature on SAP as an accounting application [10, 11], PS represented the case of a SAP implementation that extended beyond accounting logics and involved key users that did not belong to the Accounting Department. In this context, moving the project coordinator from the IT Division to the Accounting Division, considered by the management as the most important requirement provider for the implementation of SAP, was perceived by the other Service's key users as a loss of impartiality and trust–especially at a time when the SAP project was no longer limited to accounting functions but spread across the entire organization. The project manager perceived that the logic had changed between the Steering Committee period and the 2002–2005 period:

> We wanted to see SAP from the point of view of the project or of the plan, not from the accounting point of view [...]. But the logic had been changed (Project Manager).

Seven key users were appointed at that time for as many business processes. The logic of appointing most key users from the same organizational Unit (the central Accounting Department) contributed to changing the logic by customizing the system in such a way that more and more sector-specific reporting functions were required in the form of system customizations. According to the key users' logic, the on-line controls and the reports did not constitute information that was without "an added value for all". Indeed, and contrary to what the Steering Committee had supported in the former period, the key users maintained that controls and reports "are mainly made for the operational structures. With the controls, the Operational Services are confident that they cannot make mistakes. And reports allow them to have all information, like willingness to invest" (Key User Planning Service).

The ERP project manager had neither the position nor the necessary management devices to control the increasing amount of customization. At that time, owing to the increasing amount of customization, an agreement had been signed between the in-house IT company and Dante Province to pay for the work hours for customization a fixed price. While generating a saving, the introduction of that practice reduced the ERP project manager's control over the exact amount of customizations with an impact on future versions of the system. Another practice that did not contribute to empowering the project manager's control over the key users was that each customization requiring fewer than 10 work days was not submitted to the project manager. The only way for the PM to control key users' decisions was via a ex-post indirect check that took place every 2 months and was reported yearly by the tutors to her as the project coordinator.

As a result of these dynamics of distrust between key users and shallow empowerment of the project manager role, she concluded that: “We have only an interface, not a real integration. We have to make an effort to reduce customization every time we have to migrate to the next version to allow integration”.

Another factor creating a supply/use space where the locus of implementation choices moved towards the “customizing the system” corner was the dissatisfaction of key users with consultants procured by the in-house IT Company. Owing to the absence of a Steering Committee and to the shallow position of the Project Manager, the key users occupied a role of prime responsibility. They were often direct intermediaries with external technology providers: the in-house IT company and the external consultants it procured to support the different system development phases. Key users reacted to their role as Dante Province intermediaries for implementation choices in a situation of consultants with experience only in the private sector by advancing many “demands for policy” [12]. Thus, they stated, in order to be fully compliant with the regulation, the overall customized version of the system had to include all possible exceptions from each of the 14 different Operational Services’ long-term budget plans management particularities (Fig. 2).

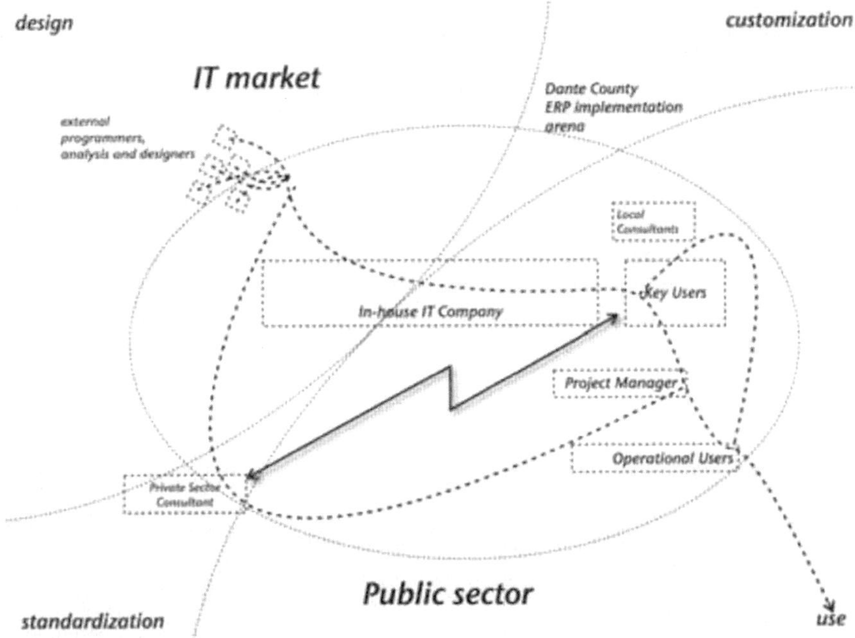

Fig. 2. Suppy-use space adapted from [6]: “intermediary and proxy user centered design”. Broken lines represent the ERP implementation trajectory. Zigzag lines denote key tensions between actors.

According to the specific service they provided, some Operational Services had specific management requirements not shared by other Operational Services:

> There are some plans that can directly commit budget. They do not have to book funding. They are the highway administration, the local autonomies and the disaster management services. Then plans working with this particular typology have to be foreseen for control of budget commitment availability. Then, in the registry information of the plan, a function has been added to specify: ‘Does this plan require the booking of funding?’ since

> the system has to identify what kind of control to apply. Then there are some plans that are divided into sections. The aggregated vision of the sections at the level of the plan has been added as a further function to the module. (Key User Planning Service).

The configuration of the interactional space between design and use was not a temporary ad-hoc configuration like that of the "technological experiment"that we found from 1998 to 2002. It was more like an institutionalized functional division of labour. According to our framework, this time period supply/use space was one of "proxy and intermediary user centered design" [6]. Key users were kinds of "proxy users", and "intermediary users" as well. Key users were "proxy users" in that, while working closely with the in-house IT developers, they had to represent both their requirements as a Staff Unit and the Operational Services requirements. But key users were also "intermediary users" in that, since the developers were not members of the same organization (they were part of an in-house company), they often acted as an interface between the entire Dante Province organization and external IT suppliers. The notions of what the "standard" and "customized" versions of the system were, and what the purposes of "standardization" and "customization" were, changed over time. While in the former period, implementing a SAP module standard version meant "giving responsibility to the Operational services", in the latter period "standard" meant a system "coming from the private sector". By contrast, whilst in the former period a "customized" system carrying too many control requirements as "information that [does] not have an added value for all" was considered to be unfortunate, in the latter period "customizations" were important for Operational Services users to be "confident that they cannot make mistakes" since all possible controls and blocking messages were "coherent with regulatory provisions". The changes in the meaning given to notions like "customization" or "standardization" were due to changes in actors roles and in implementation management devices coupled with the varying size of the supply/use space. Whilst in the 1998–2002 period the Steering Committee was a "hum" of "continuous reporting among participants" where the distance between supply and use was covered by a few intermediary actors, the Steering Committee being the central locus of implementation choices, in the 2002–2005 period, owing to the absence of the Steering Committee and the ERP Project Manager's transfer from the IT Department, key users acquired a central position in defining implementation choices.

Conclusions

We have explored how Dante Province's ERP implementation choices evolved across the extended range of historical times and locales of the emerging market of software service supply in the public sector. We have addressed the way in which the changing spaces for social learning affected actors' sense-making concerning notions such as "standardization" and "customization". While in the 1998–2002 period at Dante Province, implementing a standard version meant "giving responsibility to Operational Service users" and customization concerned "information that does not have an added value for all", in the 2002–2005 period, because of changing conditions in the supply/use space, these notions changed radically. The standard system became the symbol of a system "coming from the private sector" and the customized one was "coherent with regulatory provisions". We have shown the deeply contextual reflexivity between the varied compositions of supply and use space and the social learning leading to implementation choices in each time period. Our situational analysis has illustrated the configurational nature of ERP technology consumption in organizations as a formative space that involves an extended network of practice that traverses occupational, task and even organizational boundaries to include the broader dynamics of the supply/use space.

Our analysis is an illustration of how the representation of a system's technical features changed over time according to the relative positions of intermediary actors and their goals in a constantly changing and growing supply/use space. In direct contrast to other analyses, which regard ERP adaptations as given and argue about their various forms [13–16], our findings illustrate the relational and historically situated meanings of these notions. Each representation and the space in which it resides does not merely react to the local network of actors interests.

In our narration, implementation options have emerged as organizational moves [1] to distribute responsibilities for the realization of software [12] across an extended network of practice [17]. In many circumstances, our story illustrates that these "moves" do not reveal available technological choices and analyze the forces determining which designs are eventually adopted in terms of "conflicts" (see e.g. [18]). We have found evidence that the situation is often characterized by an apparent absence of choice as a "blame-shifting" type of organizational move found in the academic literature as "deferral of decisions" [12]. For example, it was due to the absence of a Steering Committee and the shallow position of the project manager that key users in the 2002–2005 period started to perform the role of direct intermediaries with the IT providers increasing the amount of sector-specific customizations.

References

1. Pentland B (1992) Organizing moves in software support hot lines. *Adm Sci Q* 37(4): 527–548
2. Almkov PG, (2008) Standardized data and singular situations. *Soc Stud Sci* 38(6):873–897
3. Clarke A (2005) *Situational analysis: grounded theory after the postmodern turn*. Sage, Thousand Oaks
4. Knorr-Cetina K (1999) *Epistemic cultures: how sciences make knowledge*. Harvard University Press, Cambridge
5. Ciborra C (2000) *From control to drift: the dynamics of corporate information infrastructures*. Oxford University Press, Oxford
6. Williams R, Slack R, Stewart J (2005) *Social learning in technological innovation—experimenting with information and communication technologies*. Edgar Elgar Publishing, Cheltenham
7. Jaeger B, Slack R, Williams R (2000) Europe experiments with multimedia: an overview of social experiments and trials. *Inf Soc* 16(4):277–302
8. Brown HS, Vergragt P, Green K, Berchicci L (2003) Learning for sustainability transition through bounded socio-technical experiments in personal mobility. *Technol Anal Strateg Manage* 15(3):291–315
9. Molina A (1995) Sociotechnical constituencies as processes of alignment: the rise of a large-scale European information technology initiative. *Technol Soc* 17(4):385–412
10. Hislop D (2002) The client role in consultancy relations during the appropriation of technological innovations. *Res Policy* 31(5):657–671

11. Newman M, Westrup C (2005) Making ERPs work: accountants and the introduction of ERP systems. *Eur J Inf Syst* 14(3):258–272
12. Pollock N, Cornford J (2004) ERP systems and the university as an 'unique' organization. *Inf Technol People* 17(1):31–52
13. Richmond WB, Nelson P, Misra S (2006) An empirical analysis of software life spans to determine the planning horizon for new software. *Inf Technol Manage* 7(2):131–149
14. Liang H, Xue Y, Boulton W, Byrd T (2004) Why Western vendors don't dominate China's ERP market: examining cases of failed ERP system implementation in China and explaining the unique circumstances. *Commun ACM* 47(7):69–72
15. Kumar K, Maheshwari U, Kumar U (2003) An investigation of critical management issues in ERP implementation: empirical evidence from canadian organizations. *Technovation* 23(10):793–807
16. Light B, Holland C, Wills K (2001) ERP and best of breed: a comparative analysis. *Bus Process Manage J* 7(3):216–224
17. Brown JS, Duguid P (2001) Knowledge and organization: a social-practice perspective. *Org Sci* 12(2):198–213
18. Wagner E, Newell S (2004) Best for whom: the tension between 'best practice' ERP packages and diverse epistemic cultures in a university context. *J Strateg Inf Syst* 13(4):305–328

A Planning-Oriented Approach for ERP Implementation in SMEs

Capaldo Guido[*], Corbitt Gail[†], Jones Nancy[‡] and Rippa Pierluigi[π]

Abstract Despite the many advantages of Enterprise Resources Planning (ERP) or integrated systems, the research is inconclusive when it comes to the adoption of ERP in small and medium sized enterprises (SMEs). At the very least a comprehensive ERP system is not easily implemented by SMEs. This paper seeks to explore the following question: what can be done to enhance the chance of success of the ERP implementation process in SMEs? The paper shares some insight into research aimed at identifying the technical and organizational requirements of SMEs in the implementation of an ERP. It highlights a set of organizational and technical capabilities which influence implementation project success. In addition, the results of a case study are discussed that test the methodological approach. This model expounds on how the various enterprise capabilities in an SME can influence the implementation process. By drawing upon this model and case study, we can show how SMEs can select better implementation strategic and change management activities.

[*] Business and Managerial Engineering Department, University Federico II, Naples, Italy, guido.capaldo@unina.it

[†] SAP AG, Director–United States University Alliances Program, Global Communications, Chico, CA, USA, g.corbitt@sap-com

[‡] Accounting and Management of Information Systems Department, California State University, Chico, CA, USA, njones@csuchico.edu

[π] Business and Managerial Engineering Department, University Federico II, Naples, Italy, pierluigi.rippa@unina.it

A. D'Atri et al. (eds.), *Management of the Interconnected World*,
DOI 10.1007/978-3-7908-2404-9_13, © Springer-Verlag Berlin Heidelberg 2010

Introduction

The ever growing number of successful ERPs in large, mid and small businesses likely indicates that ERPs share utility and perceived value for businesses of all sizes, although this topic warrants additional research. Whether the business is a small or mid-market organization of limited scope or a large, multinational organization, the business complexities, implementation challenges, and resulting lessons learned are essentially the same [1]. However, the ERP vendors have an advantage when it comes to working with larger customers. Big companies realize the seriousness of ERP projects, not only because of the money invested, but also in the context of the restructuring and redefining core business functions. This awareness is often absent in SMEs who may not assign the same importance to business process reengineering. Change management may look absurd to the smaller companies or not even be considered important to the implementation processes. SMEs may also be more focused on limitations of time, funding, and expertise within their organization and may thereby seek to approach implementation differently than a larger organization [2].

It is well know, that the adoption of an ERP can be disruptive in an organization. In addition, while change management is a normal part of a large organizational implementation, the management of change is sometimes incompatible with SMEs' characteristics. Generally, SMEs who may be immature in terms of IT sophistication lack many technical and managerial skills and competences. Thus, information systems in SMEs don't play a crucial role in the strategic activities [3]. The system may be essentially managed by a single employee with his own experience, following informal rules, with tacit objectives. Sometimes, the adoption of an information system like an ERP is assigned to a specific firm's unit or, in many cases, is outsourced to a consulting firm. More than 50% of SMEs turn to consulting firms for ERP implementation and management, primarily for the following reasons (www.erpwire.com): SMEs don't consider ERP management as a strategic activity, thus they find it better to outsource such services; technical skills are not acquirable within the firm, and; due to the scarce financial and human resource, SMEs need to implement the system as fast as possible.

The unit or consulting firm engaged in the management of the system is mainly focused on the operational management of the architectural technology infrastructure. Consequently the advantages achievable by an efficient management of the information supporting the business strategy are unknown or underestimated. The system represents simply an operative support to the core business processes. The absence, within the SME, of specific informatics skills is the main reason for the SME's dependence on the consulting firm engaged to manage the ERP and provide those skills.

This paper proposes a methodological approach to help SMEs and their consultants choose the most appropriate ERP implementation strategy for the firm. In addition, the model is prescriptive in terms of business process reengineering and change management interventions needed on the basis of the firm's predisposition of its organizational and technical context. Within this model, the proposed strategy is selected on the basis of organizational and technical configuration of the firm, realized through the analysis of appropriate indicators which measure the capabilities of the firm within given areas considered critical success factors for implementation of ERPs.

The Methodological Approach

The methodological approach seeks to develop a tool that can help firms identify the most appropriate implementation strategy for their ERP system derived from an assessment of the firm prior to ERP implementation. Change management strategies are identified on the basis of the result of the assessment, and are aimed at driving the firm to a successful implementation.

The assessment is based on the analysis of the organizational capabilities of the firms [4]. Such capabilities are the results of previous research conducted by the authors. Organizational capabilities are divided in two main categories: business process reengineering capability and change management capability. The firm is evaluated before the implementation starts on the basis of its capabilities to deal with organizational issues determined by an ERP implementation process and on the basis of the results of this assessment. The more appropriate implementation strategy (and the related change management interventions) is then suggested. This study examines two predominant implementation strategies, the "Big Bang" approach, which assumes the reengineering of all the processes, the closure of all the old legacy systems, the training of all the employees, the re-definition of roles and responsibilities, and the acceptance of the new routines by the employees at a predefined cut-off date; and the incremental approach, which infers a more measured, methodical implementation of the new system over an extended time period. The incremental approach carries less of a risk to the organization in this case. Using fuzzy logic principles and argumentation theory, a model was developed to assess the capabilities of the organization, allowing it to address the associated risks of implementation using one of these two strategies or a combination thereof.

The model was developed to assess the firm's business process re-engineering capabilities and its change management capabilities and suggest appropriate implementation strategy as follows. First of all, because the assessment of "capabilities" requires verbal judgment, we decided to use the dual truth model [5], where it provides a framework for a more comprehensive use of the results of the assessment model (Table 1).

Table 1. Organizational capabilities

Scale capabilities	1	2	3	4	5	6	7	8	9
1. Orientation of the organization toward processes	Functional structure						Process, interdepartmental communications and collaboration		
2. Level of organizational flexibility	Process never change in the last few years, lack of experience in CM						Positive business processes change in the last few years		
3. Cross functionality of the individual and performance systems	Objective and performance systems based on a division						Adequate systems to evaluate the cross-functional performance, coordination among functional units		
4. Capability to monitor the quality of the processes	No use of any quality system approach						Certified quality system, adequate quality monitoring system		
5. Cross-functional project team	Sporadic cross-functional meetings to manage projects						Cross-functional coordination, existence of steering committee, appropriate use of PM schedule		
6. Availability of potential project manager	Few project management skills and competences in the firm						Many PM skills and competences in the firm, adequate PM resources, full time team-member availability		
7. Capability to deal with resistance to change	No use of systems to analyze and evaluate the organizational climate						Organizational climate evaluation system raised periodically		
8. Capability to deal with skill development and job conversion activities	No specific capability						Development and conversion plan are periodically made		
9. End users background	Few employees with a undergraduate-graduate title, high age average (~50)						Mainly graduate-undergraduate employees, mostly young people (~30)		
10. Experience in the use of IS/IT	Expertise in IS customization and program language						Few skills on IS parameterization and customization		
11. Frequency of job rotation	Sporadic job conversion activities raised in the last years						Vertical and horizontal job conversion plan periodically raised		
12. Human capital	No planning in the evaluation of HR development, lower use of competences' monitoring systems						HR development activities and evaluation are raised periodically, competences' monitoring system		
13. Commitment of top management	Top management is not involved in innovation/implementation project						Executive participation in change project, good understanding of IT capabilities and limitations,		
14. Incentives towards innovative attitude	Incentives based only on employees' results						Adoption of new reward system, employees empowerment		

The dual truth model enables us to formulate an assessment scale whereby the assessor can choose the most suitable degree of precision for expressing his or her judgment. We start with the truth couple which measures an assessment of precision, ambivalence and ambiguity in verbal judgment. For each capability, the two antonyms, as well as representing the two opposite poles of an assessment, also represent bipolar meaning. If we combine the scale model and the dual truth model we can measure the ambiguity inherent in the assessment, or give it a numerical value. The bar has been divided into nine boxes, and a fuzzy triangular function can be associated with the judgment expressed in any one box. In the next table, the organizational capabilities are represented with all the couples of antonyms. In order to make it more precise, the middle values have been identified along with the scale limits. The dual truth model represents and combines in quantitative ways the verbal judgment, while at the same time preserving vagueness, ambivalence and ambiguity of verbal sentences. The fuzzy algorithm deduces the final score on the basis of the contributor's judgment. The final score is a synthesis of both categories of capabilities of organizational issues. Thus, the model provides a numeric value for both the business process reengineering propensity and change management propensity of the firm.

Table 2. Implementation methodology matrix

BPR Propensity	High	HR Development	Big Bang
	Low	Reorganization	BPR Intervention
		Low	High
		End Users Propensity	

The results are then represented in a matrix in which the propensity of the firm to business process reengineering (BPR) and the propensity of end users to change management is compared. This in turn, identifies the implementation strategy that best fits with the characteristics documented. In the next figure, the matrix shows that for the higher values in all the capabilities, the firm has a higher chance to successfully implement an ERP using a "Big Bang" strategy. In all other situations, an incremental strategy would be better. Change management activities to enable the success of the implementation are also suggested for each different position in the matrix (Table 2).

Case Study and Results

The model has been tested in the course of a retrospective field study within a small/medium enterprise. The firm operates in the manufacturing and import of building products. The number of employees is more or less 120, and it is located on the west coast of the United States. The firm implemented an ERP system because of the additional functionality promised by the new system and because of the poor performance of the old legacy system.

We interviewed managers from the firm to test the model. The implementation occurred all at once, as in the "Big Bang" implementation strategy, but no formal assessment was done prior to the implementation process. The company hired a consulting firm to implement the system. The company Controller was resistant to the system change. In this case, the results of the implementation project were actually good, but the company took a couple of years after the go-live to realize the full benefits. The main perceived critical issues encountered in the course of the implementation process were lack of understanding of system capability, lack of experience in IS implementation processes, lack of understanding of best practice in the industry, and the lack of IT personnel (Table 3).

Table 3. Results of initial interview for test case

Indicators	1	2	3	4	5	6	7	8	9
Orientation of the organization toward processes				X	X				
Level of organizational flexibility				X	X	X			
Cross functionality of the individual and performance systems			X	X					
Capability to monitor the quality of the processes			X						
Cross functional project team				X					
Availability of potential project manager		X	X						
Capability to deal with resistance to change	X	X							
Capability to deal with skill development and job conversion activities			X	X					
End Users background					X				
Human capital				X					
Commitment of top management				X	X				
Incentives towards innovative attitude		X	X						

After these descriptions, we asked participants to try to use the methodology thinking about the firm's situation before the implementation process. Based on the perception of the managers, results of the methodology showed a position of the firm in the middle level of End User Propensity, a middle-low position in the BPR propensity scale. Those results are shown below.

The output of the case study survey created a matrix surprising close to the participants' original perception of the organization's capabilities. The exhibit of the output matrix follows.

Based on these results, an incremental implementation strategy would have guaranteed better and faster results for this organization. For example, a process reengineering and full involvement of the employees in the project plan, or the acquisition of information skills would have lead to a better implementation.

Table 4. Results of "fuzzy" elaboration of data for test case

BPR Propensity	High	HR Development	Big Bang
	Low	Re-organization	BPR Intervention
		Low	High
		End Users Propensity	

However, the real value of the case study is that it is at least one case that validated the model. Obviously, more cases of this type are needed. In addition, the model needs to be used in the field with companies implementing ERP systems and then comparing the predictive values with the actual outcomes. Ideally, enlargement of the data set would strengthen the hypothesis of the predictive value of the model, perhaps providing SMEs with a tool to facilitate their ERP implementation projects.

Discussion and Conclusion

The proposed methodological approach is based on the dual truth model using an uncertainty scale and fuzzy indicators and relating those data to the ERP implementation methodology most likely to incur success for an SME. The approach was tested using a case study and interviews of involved personnel. Based on the results of the case study, the model demonstrated positive results in the way the model more accurately assessed behavior in terms of attitude towards uncertainty; it enables us to limit the problem of diminished comprehension inherent whenever we formalize knowledge; and the model may allow consultants and others to validate implementation methodology most appropriate for SME's under their advisement.

Feedback from the case study participants was positive regarding the survey and use of the fuzzy scale factors. In addition, the graphical representation of the survey input was seen as a strong i

ncentive for project managers at the SME to adopt the recommended implementation model rather than overriding recommendations, a likely occurrence without the graphical output.

Certainly, additional field surveys are needed to further validate the model. Field validation studies are currently planned, with surveys to be conducted with SME's within the United States and parts of Europe. We hope to show that having a tool such as our planning model can help SMEs in the implementation process of ERPs, thereby reducing the rate of failure of such implementations worldwide. In fact, the capabilities may go beyond the critical factors. Critical success factors, in fact, are not the same across countries, but the capabilities of the firm to implement an ERP are always the same because of the intrinsic rigid characteristics of an ERP.

References

1. Esteves J, Bohorquez V (2007) An updated ERP systems annotated bibliography: 2001–2005. *Commun Assoc Inf Syst* 19(18):386–446
2. Snider B, de Silveira GJC, Balakrishnan J (2009) ERP implementation at SMEs: analysis of five Canadian cases. *Int J Operations Prod Manage* 29(1):4–29
3. Holland C, Light B (2001) A stage maturity model for enterprise resource planning systems use. *Database Adv Inf Syst* 32(2):34–45
4. Capaldo G, Rippa P, (2008) A methodological proposal to assess the feasibility of ERP systems implementation strategies. *Proceedings of the 41st Hawaii international conference on systems science*, Waikoloa, 7–10 January 2008
5. Iandoli L, Zollo G (2008) *Organizational cognition and learning: building systems for the learning organization*. IGI Global, New York

Motivators and Inhibitors to IT Infusion in Tourism SMEs

Carla L. Wilkin*

Abstract In the busy operational environment of Small-to-Medium enterprises (SMEs), the challenge for owners is to achieve a balance between "working in the business" and "working on the business". Often SME's invest in Information Technology (IT) to achieve operational efficiencies and facilitate development of new business initiatives without really planning for the required new structures and processes. This paper reports on the IT experiences of 158 firms in one tourism sector in one Australian state. Results suggest a need to understand mediating factors like organizational context, the role of key personnel, and human attitudes and behaviours as they relate to successful IT infusion.

Introduction

Much has been written about the role of Information Technology (IT) in large firms as it becomes ubiquitous in business processes. Here the principal focus has been on adoption and acceptance of IT. One area that has received little attention is the final stage of implementation called IT infusion [4, 16], where IT is increasingly embedded across a firm's business processes and used to its fullest potential by satisfied users [4, 10] resulting in increased business performance. Like their larger business counterparts, the benefits afforded to Small-to-Medium Enterprises (SMEs) by cheaper and better IT and off-the-shelf software necessitate new structures and processes. However, the ability to procure such software without specialist advice, together with the interactive working relationships in SMEs, means it is often put to different use. This can impact the benefits that are acquired and moreover create challenges for change management.

Whilst the definition of SMEs varies between countries, they are commonly defined by: number of employees, annual sales and fixed assets. In Australia the Bureau of Statistics defines an SME based on the number of employees with small enterprises employing less than 20 people and medium, 21–200. Regarding importance to the national economy, there's an estimated 130,000 SMEs in Australia. Annual turnover is $2–250 million; they pay around 15% of total tax collected; contribute a further 12% of total tax through amounts they withhold in payments

* Department of Accounting and Finance, Monash University, Victoria, Australia, carla.wilkin@buseco.monash.edu.au

A. D'Atri et al. (eds.), *Management of the Interconnected World*,
DOI 10.1007/978-3-7908-2404-9_14, © Springer-Verlag Berlin Heidelberg 2010

to employees; and employ more than 26% of the Australian workforce [3]. Worldwide SMEs are important: in Canada they provide 64% of private sector employment [15]; in the European Union, firms with 250 or less employees provide 67% of jobs outside the financial industry [11]. This makes SMEs a valuable research environment.

Given SMEs significantly differ from large firms [14], yet the business benefits afforded by implementing IT are equally significant, exploration of the motivators and inhibitors that affect IT infusion in SMEs provides insight into how to manage the change process. This study aims to address this by looking at the experiences of SMEs in one tourism sector. The paper begins with a literature review of SMEs' use of IT and factors that impact IT infusion. The research method and context is then presented. After reporting on survey findings, motivators and inhibitors to successful IT infusion are discussed and then conclusions are presented.

SME Use of Technology and IT Infusion

As with larger firms, IT offers SMEs efficient means to manage business processes, facilitate customer relationships, maintain financial records and monitor staff and business performance. Yet SMEs are different. In SMEs the role of users is more interactive, with owner/managers more likely to use IT at operational as well as reporting/strategic levels. This enhances flexibility, enables quicker responses to issues and facilitates closer work-place interactions [18].

In SMEs all end-users make a significant contribution to the success of the firm and any change it may pursue, making it a rich environment in which to explore factors related to realising IT benefits. Herein success in organizational change is related to: SMEs' knowledge and involvement [7]; building on internal rather than external IT expertise; end-user level of computer literacy [19]; and managerial enthusiasm [5]. In understanding IT infusion past research has explored implementation by breaking it down into six stages [29] (see Table 1).

Table 1. Six stages of IT implementation

Stage	Meaning
Initiation	Analysis of business processes and IT solutions
Adoption	Sorting organizational mechanisms for implementation
Adaptation	Development, installation and maintenance of the IT
Acceptance	Fostering commitment to IT usage
Routinization	Encouragement of IT usage as routine process
Infusion	Use of IT is integrated and comprehensive for organizational gains

As shown, IT Infusion refers to the stage in which IT is used to its fullest potential [29]. In a sense it captures organizational implementation success [16]. When exploring this most infusion studies have investigated enablers of IT implementation. For example, Winston and Dologite [29] reviewed 54 articles on IT implementation in small businesses and identified four sets of factors that contribute to successful efforts to implement IT, namely:

- *Organizational:* structural attributes and experience in the organization with IT. Despite literature that empirically demonstrates a relationship between organizational structure and IT infusion, it is seen as "earliness of adoption", and measured by the years of organizational experience with IT [9, 30].
- *End-user*: refers to the characteristics of individuals who contribute to IT success. These include experience, training, involvement and incentives to use the technology. This factor may also affect future use of technology.
- *Owner*: In SMEs owners typically work full-time in the business with a dominant role in business decisions. Consequently their personal abilities and motivations impact the firm [21, 28]. Other aspects include owner characteristics [23], owner attitudes and IT-gatekeeper assumptions [6, 29]. Where the owner is off-site, management support and involvement play a role.
- *Extra-organizational situation*: factors or situations that affect an organization's innovation process, including strategic alliances, social networks, IT consultants and changes in the environment. Business partners and regulators can also apply pressure [22].

In addition, innovation and diffusion also enable IT infusion. Here innovation compatibility (the degree to which innovation is seen as consistent with the existing values), past experiences and needs of potential adopters [24], were found to be related to organizational strategy, and in turn to IT infusion behaviors [16]. Other characteristics of innovation (relative advantage, complexity and compatibility with tasks) were found to relate to IT diffusion not IT infusion [4].

Research Method and Context

Given its exploratory nature, this research sought to investigate the problem in a common business sector, across a range of firm sizes. Commonality of sector gave consensus regarding the purpose and use of IT, but variation in firm size gave scope to appreciate differences. The author's background led to a focus on one tourism sector in one Australian state. In exploring this understanding survey research was used. The method enabled a current view of practice [13] across a range of firms to be acquired and link this to information about respondent's attitudes, opinions and behaviors [20]. It also facilitated the discovery of common relationships across a population [26, 12]. The anonymous survey was mailed to participants with reply-paid envelopes to enhance response rates.

With respect to survey items, aspects of standard instruments were used as much as possible. For example, questions probing participants to evaluate their firm's performance in applying IT to support business strategy relative to other firms were drawn from Armstrong and Sambamurthy [2]; attitude toward change from Larsen [17]; understanding on system restrictiveness from Silver [25] and DeSantics and Poole [8]; and computer playfulness from Agarwal and Prasad [1].

Contextually this study investigated SME tourist accommodation firms that are individually owned and operated. In 2006/2007 tourism contributed $9.9 billion

(3.7% of Australian Gross Domestic Product); employed 482,800 people (4.7% of total employed); and was responsible for $85 billion in consumption [27]. Technology used in the surveyed firms is summarized in Table 2 below.

Table 2. Technology used in the surveyed firms

Technology	% Uptake	Technology	% Uptake
EFTPOS	91.8	Online reservations	53.8
Computerised reservation management system (CRMS)[a]	69.6	Online reservations with payment gateway	33.5
Own website	82.3	Computerised accounting	77.2
Email	97.5	Wireless hot spot	41.8
Fax	99.4	Internet café	24.7

[a] A transaction processing system that manages bookings, financial records etc. in a structured and routine manner.

Findings

Data was gathered from a sample of 158 adult respondents representing a 39.3% response rate (i.e. 158 from 402). Drawn from one Australian state, respondents were relatively evenly divided between male (45%) and female (55%) with 79.7% being over 41 years of age. They included front-office staff (operational users), but the majority (88%) were middle management or owner/operators. 68.4% of firms employed between 2 and 4 staff, with most staff using the technology. 78.5% of respondents had 6+ years experience with computers (66.5% had 10+ years). Actual experience with the firm's systems was less (37.4% had 6+ years).

Training is an important mechanism for improving IT knowledge and uptake. Respondents had high levels (high/very high) of self taught training (73.4%). 48.1% had received high levels of training when working in this or another firm, 22.8% high levels of vendor training and 19% high levels of training provided by schools/TAFE/tertiary institutions. This suggests that much IT knowledge was acquired on site through experimentation. 84.2% of respondents indicated practical experience with their firms' systems, 68.4% indicated some breadth of knowledge with different systems and 59.5% enjoyed playing with software.

Regarding technology used, need was judged by asking respondents to consider the frequency of need for given technologies (frequently, hourly, daily, through to not at all) and then considering separately how regularly they used it (same scale). Table 3 considers daily or higher use. In every case perceived need was higher than actual use. Interestingly need and actual use of a Computerised Reservation Management System (CRMS) was lower than expected.

Table 3. Perceived need vs. actual use of the technology

Technology	Perceived need (% of respondents)	Actual use (% of respondents)
CRMS	75.3	67.7
Online reservation system	68.4	60.1
Online reservation system with payment gateway	55.1	44.9
Email	97.5	94.3
Computerised accounting package	89.2	81.0
Ability to update content on the firm's website	80.4	72.8

Investigation of attitude and behaviour towards change and technology (see Table 4) identified (as reflected in agree/strongly agree answers) that most considered themselves to be innovative (70.2%) and enjoyed problem solving (74%). Telling was that 29.8% avoided risk, suggesting the majority were reasonably flexible and accepting of change.

Table 4. Attitude and behaviour towards technology

Attitude towards change	% Respondents agreeing	Extent of flexibility regarding use of IT	% Respondents agreeing
Innovative behaviour	70.2	Tailorability seen in CRMS	49.3
Enjoys problem solving	74.0	Willing to be playful with CRMS	57.0
Models originality	63.3	Views CRMS as constraining	35.5
Inventiveness with existing practices	60.8	Manages CRMS inflexibly	27.2
Avoids risk	29.8	Sees CRMS as restrictive	42.4

When attitude and action are compared (left vs. right side of Table 4), respondents seemed less responsive. 29.1% did not answer these questions. Of those who did, 49.3% agreed (agree/strongly agree) that the firm's CRMS could be tailored and 57% were willing to be playful with it. Given only 35.5% saw the system as constraining, education/training could be inhibiting IT infusion here.

In Table 5, customer service has been understood as efficient service whilst the customer is present, not the more sophisticated customer relationship management. 13.2% of respondents failed to compare IT in their firms with industry best practice and 5.85% failed to evaluate their firms' performance regarding operations, marketing, sales and customer service. The lower ratings of IT performance in marketing and sales compared to operations and customer service suggest that IT infusion has yet to substantially move beyond daily practice. Support for this can be found in respondents' evaluation (mid/most successful) of their firms' performance compared to industry best practice with respect to less tangible activities (Column 1 of Table 5). Similar, but slightly higher patterns were found in respondents' comparison of performance in applying IT to business strategy with industry best practice. Here customer service was rated highest (mid/most successful) with a rating of 69.1%, closely followed by operations.

Table 5. Firm use and strategy for IT vs. industry best practice

Evaluation of IT use in own firm vs. industry best practice	Extent of correlation	Evaluation of IT business strategy in own firm vs. industry best practice	Extent of correlation
Being a low-cost provider	52.5%	Operations	68.3%
Having operations flexibility	61.4%	Marketing	56.4%
Enhancing customer linkages	48.8%	Sales	58.3%
Providing value-added service	48.2%	Customer service	69.1%

Discussion

Data analysis suggests that within the surveyed tourism SMEs, technology is being used at reasonable levels in various forms particularly in normal practices like operations and customer service. Use is less evident in more sophisticated processes like sales, marketing, customer relationship management or creating new markets and services. Whilst what has been achieved should/will enhance business performance, there is scope to use it more fully.

Although Stages 1–5 of IT implementation (see Table 1) have been handled reasonably confidently, IT infusion (Stage 6) is less evident. By comparing Winston and Dologite's [29] factors affecting IT infusion with results from this survey, the following motivational and inhibiting responses (see Table 6) were identified. This suggests the lack of IT infusion relates to a lack of appreciation of what can be achieved with IT rather than an unwillingness to achieve it. Lack of sophisticated education and training seem to be the cause, which has impacted change.

Table 6. Motivational and inhibiting responses to IT infusion

Winston & Dologite (1999) Category	Factors	Findings from this study on IT infusion in tourism SMEs: Motivational Responses	Inhibiting Responses
Organizational	Structure Centralization Formalization	Interactive style fosters free flow of ideas	No internal IT specialist means that IT is seen as an add-on
	IT experience	General IT experience high	Experience with firm systems was low
End-user	Experience	General IT experience high	Experience with firm systems was low and preference was to avoid risk
	Training		Mostly self-taught so options seen as too hard, overlooked, or not significant
	Involvement	Owner interacts with end-users so exchange of awareness about needs	Owner interactions with end-users encourage a focus on immediate needs (operational and service)
	Incentives		System use is mandatory
Owner	Knowledge	Presence of motivating qualities like playfulness	Avoidance of risks hinders willingness to experiment with IT to draw out strategies like direct marketing and to fully implement online bookings
	Strategy		Lack of technical knowledge and disparity between attitude and action affect decisions re IT selection and purchase

	Involvement		Involved in implementation but not fully aware of opportunities
Extra-organizational situation	Strategic Alliance	No data available	
	IT Consultants		Not utilized which may be inhibiting knowledge and opportunities

Conclusions and Future Research

This study investigated IT infusion in operationally busy SME tourist accommodation firms in one Australian state. Here IT investment related to operational efficiencies and development of new business initiatives without really planning for the required new structures and processes. Results suggest that:

- the interactive nature of the work environment means there's a focus on short term needs (operations and sales) rather than strategies to grow the business through IT infusion (marketing and sales);
- purchasing off-the-shelf software reduces the role of IT consultants to that of tailoring and supporting individual products. This reduces owner's capacity to access knowledge about wider IT alternatives and how to implement them;
- the centrality of owners to both IT purchases and IT functions reduces their capacity to see the broader picture;
- the dependence of the business on the IT function, when linked to self-training, risk aversion and lack of regular contact with IT specialists, may discourage extended IT use (infusion); and
- knowledge about options is present, but education is lacking e.g., resources needed (inhibiting), returns (motivational) and operationalization (inhibiting).

The contribution being made here to knowledge about IT infusion in tourism SMEs is that the owner is central to the process, but that his/her lack of education about the potential of IT is a key inhibitor. This is different from knowledge, for there is evidence that owners know what IT initiatives are available. Future research may investigate the lack of focus by owner/managers beyond operational issues and ways to help individuals to take the next step. It may also explore other factors that can moderate the effect of IT infusion.

References

1. Agarwal R, Prasad J (1998) A conceptual and operational definition of personal innovativeness in the domain of information technology. *Inf Syst Res* 9(2):204–215
2. Armstrong CP, Sambamurthy V (1999) Information technology assimilation in firms: the influence of senior leadership and IT infrastructures. *Inf Syst Res* 10(4):304–327
3. Australian Taxation Office (2008) *Compliance program 2008–2009*, http://www.ato.gov.au/corporate/content.asp?doc=/content/00155156.htm&page=38&H38&mnu=42758&mfp=001. Accessed 25 April 2009
4. Cooper RB, Zmud RW (1990) Information technology implementation research: a technology diffusion approach. *Manage Sci* 36(2):123–139
5. Cragg PB, King M (1993) Small-firm computing: motivators and inhibitors. *MIS Q* 17(1):47–60, March

6. Davidson RA, Hart SD (1995) Managing the adoption of new technologies: does personality affect the acceptance of new audit technologies?, *Revue Canadienne des Sciences de l'Aministration* 12(4):268
7. DeLone WH (1988) Determinants of success for computer usage in small business. *MIS Q* 12(1):51–61, March
8. DeSanctis G, Poole MS (1994) Capturing the complexity in advanced technology use: adaptive structuration theory, *Org Sci* 5(2):121–147
9. Eder LB, Igbaria M (2001) Determinants of intranet diffusion and infusion. *Omega* 29(3):233
10. El Sawy O (1985) Implementation of cultural infusion: an approach for managing the introduction of information technologies. *MIS Q* 9(2):131–140 June
11. Eurostat (2007) *European Business – 2006 Edition* – Chapter 1: Business Economy Overview, available at: http://epp.eurostat.ec.europa.eu/cache/… Accessed 25 April 2009
12. Gable GG (1994) Integrating case study and survey research methods: an example in information systems. *Eur J Inf Syst* 3(2):112–126
13. Galliers RD (1992) Choosing information systems research approaches. In Galliers RD (ed) *Information systems research: issues, methods, and practical guidelines*. Blackwell Scientific Publications, Oxford, pp 144–162
14. Ghobadian A, Gallear DN (1996) Total quality management in SMEs. *Omega* 24(1):83–106
15. Industry Canada (2006) *Key small business statistics* – July 2006. Available at: http://strategis.ic.gc.ca/epic/site/sbrp-rppe.nsf/en/rd02030e.html. Accessed 25 April 2009
16. Kishore A, McLean ER (2007) Reconceptualizing innovation capability as organizational alignment in secondary IT adoption contexts: an investigation of software reuse infusion. *IEEE Trans Eng Manage* 54(4):756
17. Larsen TJ (1993) Middle managers' contribution to implemented information technology innovation. *J Manage Inf Syst* 10(2):155–176
18. Malone SC (1985) Computerizing small business information systems. *J Small Bus Manage* 23(2):10–16, April
19. Montazemi AR (1988) Factors affecting information satisfaction in the context of the small business environment. *MIS Q* 12(2):239–256, June
20. Neuman WL (2003) *Social research methods: qualitative and quantitative approaches*. Allyn and Bacon, Massachusetts
21. Palvia PC, Palvia SC (1999) An examination of the IT satisfaction of small-business users. *Inf Manage* 35:127–137
22. Premkumar, G (2003) A meta-analysis of research on information technology implementation in small business. *J Organ Comput Electron Commer* 13(2):91–121
23. Quaddus M, Hofmeyer G (2007) An investigation into the factors influencing the adoption of B2B trading exchanges in small businesses. *Eur J Inf Syst* 16:202–216
24. Rogers EM (2003) *Diffusion of innovations*, 5th edn. Free Press, New York
25. Silver MS (1988) User perceptions of decision support system restrictiveness: an experiment. *J Manage Inf Syst* 5(1):51–65
26. Sonquist JA, Dunkelberg WC (1977) *Survey and opinion research: procedures for processing and analysis*. Prentice-Hall, Englewood Cliffs, London
27. Tourism Australia (2007) *Market insights tourism facts 2007*, Retrieved 11 January 2009, from http://www.tourism.australia.com/content/Research/Factsheets/Key_Tourism_Facts_07.pdf
28. Walker B, Brown A (2004) What success factors are important for small business owners? *Int Small Bus J* 22(6):577–594
29. Winston ER, Dologite DG (1999) Achieving IT infusion: a conceptual model for small businesses. *Inf Res Manage J* 12(1):26–38
30. Zmud RW, Apple LE (1992) Measuring technology incorporation/infusion. *J Product Innov Manage* 9(2):148

The Utilization of Information Systems Security in SMEs in the South East of Ireland

Amanda Freeman* **and Liam Doyle†**

Abstract The protection of information has always been a challenge. There is a lack of academic research regarding the protection of information in small to medium sized enterprises (SMEs). The purpose of this research study was to gain an under-standing of the role of information systems security in SMEs in the South East of Ireland. This paper outlines the importance of SMEs in Ireland and examines the implementation of information systems security in those organisations. The study reports on the security technologies that are implemented and examines issues re-garding the implementation of those technologies. This study employed a quanti-tative approach to gather empirical data.

Introduction

There is no globally accepted definition for what constitutes an SME. Definitions vary from country to country. In general, SMEs are classified by number of employees, turnover, and balance sheet total [1]. The European Commission [2] have adopted a definition of SMEs. Medium sized enterprises are defined as enterprises with less that 250 employees, annual turnover of less than 50 million and a balance sheet total of less that 43 million. Small enterprises are defined as enterprises with less than 50 employees, a turnover less than 10 million and a balance sheet total less than 10 million. Micro enterprises are defined as enterprises with less than 10 employees, an annual turnover less than 2 million and a balance sheet total less than 2 million. SMEs represent 99% of all enterprises in the European Union and provide more than 65 million jobs. Micro enterprises represent 93% of all European enterprises [2]. In Ireland, SMEs account for 99.55% of enterprises and are responsible for 68.44% of employment [3]. SMEs are a key driver of economic growth as they stimulate competition, innovation and productivity throughout the economy as a whole [4, 5].

---

* Waterford Institute of Technology, Waterford, Ireland, afreeman@wit.ie

† Waterford Institute of Technology, Waterford, Ireland, ldoyle@wit.ie

A. D'Atri et al. (eds.), *Management of the Interconnected World*,
DOI 10.1007/978-3-7908-2404-9_15,

SMEs have become increasingly reliant on information technology (IT) to conduct business globally, improve their competitive strategy and speed up business processes [6–8]. Consequently there is an increasing importance on security and control procedures to ensure that information embedded within organisational information systems retain its integrity, confidentially and availability [9, 10]. Growing dependence on IT has led to increased risks which can be mitigated through the use of information systems security (ISS) measures. Organisations should adopt a mix of physical, technical and operational security controls that are appropriate to their needs [11].

In recent years companies have made large investments in security technologies in order to prevent unauthorised access to networks and the causing of serious financial damage [12, 13]. Security breaches cause continuing problems for companies conducting business on-line. In addition to direct financial loss companies risk damage to their corporate reputation if they do not adequately secure their customer data [14]. Companies face pressures for cost containment and to respond to their competitors. These pressures lead companies to adopt IT, often without careful planning or adequate attention to security concerns [15, 16]. An IT disruption can impede a company's ability to create products, deliver services and connect with trading partners. Despite this, many companies have not adequately identified or tempered their vulnerabilities [17, 18].

Awareness of security in SMEs is generally low and many SMEs struggle to find the appropriate combination of technologies to protect their business [19]. In Ireland SMEs find it difficult to recruit staff with appropriate security expertise [20]. Due to resource constraints many SMEs do not have dedicated in-house staff to support their IT. As a result IT security is not always given the prominence it deserves and IT security expenditure may be regarded as an overhead rather that as an investment [21]. An understanding of the technical aspects of IT security attention must be matched by attention to the business aspects such as the role of security procedures [22, 23]. A common failing among SMEs is their lack of formal IT security policies [24]. The development of a formal policy is a signal that management are committed to IT security, communicates an expectation that staff are expected to follow that policy [25] and is a major tool for information systems security management [26, 27]. The implementation and success of information systems security is dependent on the role played by both management and staff [15, 28]. If information system security is regarded as a purely technical concern there may be a resulting lack of attention at senior management and board level. As senior management are ultimately responsible for information systems security, and are also ultimately legally responsible for data protection, it is important that they play a leading role in information systems security management [29, 15, 9, 30, 11, 31].

Research Motivations and Objectives

Most studies of information systems security are commercially oriented and also tend to focus on large organisations. There is a dearth of academic research on the topic of IS security in SMEs. In order to address this gap this empirical study examined the role of IS security in SMEs in the South East of Ireland. This paper reports on the IS security problems faced, the types of security technologies being used, and socio-technical issues associated with IS security.

The main objective of this paper are to:

- Investigate what is the perception among Irish SMEs of information systems security
- Examine what is happening to Irish SMEs in terms of security attacks and breaches
- Investigate how Irish SMEs address information systems security issues.

Methodology

This study used a quantitative approach. A postal questionnaire was chosen as the data collection mechanism. This allowed for wide coverage while overcoming the costs associated with personal interview questionnaires and telephone questionnaires. It also helps overcome interviewer bias. Also, it was felt that, given the sensitive nature of the topic, respondents may be reluctant to provide information over the phone.

A draft questionnaire was developed based upon a review of the current literature. As there are few published academic papers explicitly addressing the use of information systems security in SMEs, the literature was used to generate ideas and insights into the issues of importance, rather than as a source of specific questions. A sample of 100 companies was selected at random from a commercial database listing SMEs within Ireland. Each company was contacted by phone in order to identify the person responsible for information systems security and in order to explain the nature of the study. This step was considered important given the nature of the study and in order to overcome reluctance to provide information which might be considered sensitive. The questionnaire was issued to the 100 companies and a response rate of 57% was achieved. The questionnaire was organised into six sections examining Organisational Environment, Computer Security Environment, Computer Security Threats and Technologies, Staff and Training, Policies and Procedures, and Further Information.

The draft questionnaire was initially validated through a series of pre-tests, firstly with an expert statistician and then by four experienced IS researchers. The pre-testers were asked to critically appraise the questionnaire, focusing primarily on issues of instrument content, clarity, question wording and validity, before providing detailed feedback, via an evaluation form. The pre-tests resulted in a number of enhancements being made to the structure of the survey and the wording of specific questions. A pilot study was also undertaken with five SMEs of varying sizes, which provided valuable insights into the likely response rate and analytical implications for the full survey.

Sample Characteristics

The sample can be characterised in terms of both the size of the responding organisations and the sectors in which they are primarily operating. Of the valid respondents, 24.6% were employed in micro-sized organizations having fewer than 10 employees, 40.4% were based in small organisations with between 10 and 49 employees and the remaining 35.1% in medium-sized organisations with between 50 and 250 employees. The responses came from a number of sectors as follows: Agriculture, Forestry & Fishing (7.0%), Other Production Industries (19.3%), Construction (15.8%), Wholesale & Retail Trade (8.8%), Hotels & Restaurants (10.5%), Transport, Storage & Communication (7.0%), Financial & Other Business Services (5.3%) and Other Services (26.3%).

Research Findings

The companies rated their dependence on computer systems on a scale of 1–5. The average response was 4.61 indicating a high level of perceived dependence. Dependence was consistently high among micro, small and medium categories. It was apparent from the data analysis that all the SMEs surveyed are using some form of security protection within their organisations. While the findings show that awareness of security is on the increase within SMEs (71.9%) senior management do not seem to have much involvement in the security process as 57.1% receive ad-hoc reports on security issues. Also, while over 75% of respondents reported a high dependence on their IT systems a high percentage of them said that they did not feel that their company was prepared for a security attack (74.5%). The SMEs that completely outsource their security (10%) are most confident with their level of security protection, however, the most popular types of security systems being used are systems that are being controlled internally (40%) by the companies or a mixture of outsourced and internally managed solutions (45.6%). Notably, the remaining respondents do not know how security in managed in their companies.

The most commonly reported types of security breaches faced by Irish SMEs are viruses (52.63%), spyware (52.63%) and insider abuse of Internet access

(24.56%). None of the companies surveyed reported abuse of wireless networks and only small companies have suffered from mobile or laptop theft (5.3%). The most popular security technologies used by SMEs are anti-virus software (96.5%), firewalls (80.7%) and reusable passwords (68.4%). The literature shows that in America and England companies are suffering from as many insider attacks as they are external attacks [31, 32]. However in this research, external attacks are still the most prevalent with a very low percentage of SMEs reporting insider attacks (9.1%). For those companies that outsource their security none of them reported suffering from an insider attack.

According to Stitch [19] effective security is not just about having the right technology; it is also about having the right staff that are appropriately trained. Most respondents reported that they did not find it hard to find staff with the appropriate security expertise (90.8%). However, this research shows that over 70% of the people responsible for security within these organisations do not have a formal IT qualification. Overall, 61.4% of companies reported that security training was important or very important. Less than half of micro companies (42.9%) and over a quarter of small (31.8%) and medium (25%) companies say that security training is not important within their organisation and quite a few companies provide no training at all (31.2%) as illustrated in Fig. 1. Of those that do provide training the most common methods used are internal company trainers (32.1%) and consultants (25%).

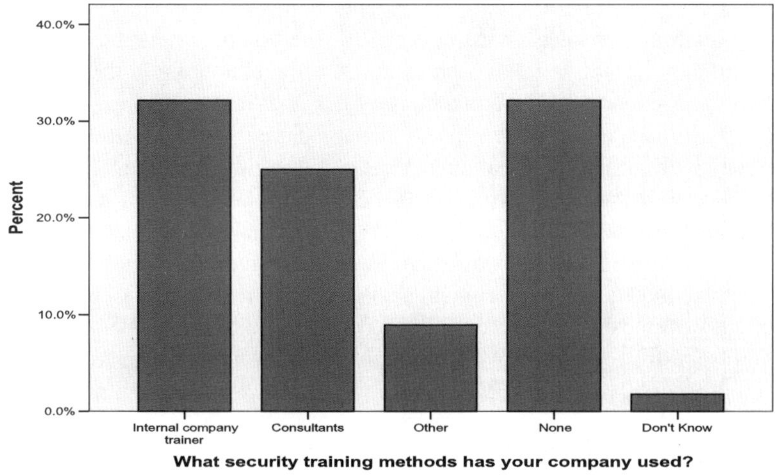

Fig. 1. Training methods used

The literature states the one of the most common problems with SMEs in terms of security is their failure to set out policies [24]. In terms of this research only 15 companies (27.31%) reported having a formal comprehensive security policy; however, the vast majority of companies do have individual policies. The most common policies used are password (52.14%), Internet usage (56.14%) and email policies (40.3%). Very few of the companies surveyed actually have a data protection policy (15.79%) despite their legal obligation to protect staff and consumer information. The most popular method for disseminating the polices are through providing staff with a copy of the policies upon induction (40.35%) and issuing them a copy with their contract of employment (33.3%), which according to the literature are the best methods to use.

Budget constraints (28.1%), technical challenges/complexity of products (22.8%) and lack of end user awareness (15.8%) were identified as the three main obstacles that the SMEs felt they faced in terms of securing their organisation. Other obstacles mentioned were lack of internal security policies (8.8%), lack of managerial support (7.0%) and unclear responsibilities (7.0%). It is clear that non-technical issues play a large role in information systems security within Irish SMEs.

Conclusion

The results of this paper show that although information systems security awareness is on the increase within SMEs in the South East of Ireland many SMEs are still not confident that they are prepared for a security attack. The hands-on approach seems to be popular with respondents as 40% of respondents control their security internally. However the companies who outsource their security are the most confident in their level of protection. A paradox appears in these findings in terms of staff expertise. Respondents said that they did not find it a problem to find staff with the appropriate security expertise, yet, just over a quarter of them have staff with an IT qualification. What is interesting about this finding is that over a quarter of the respondents say that their company does not provide any security training to their staff which indicates the person responsible for security in a lot of these organizations has no formal training in security. This further explains why the respondents named technical challenges and complexity of products as on the biggest obstacles that they faced in terms of information systems security. It appears from this research that although awareness of information systems security is on the increase in these SMEs many of the companies are still not implementing it to its full potential.

While this research presents many important new insights into the use of information systems security within SMEs it raises many issues that need to be further studied. The sample size was limited due to the time and cost constraints of contacting each company by phone. A further, larger scale quantitative study would provide more generalisable results. In addition, a qualitative approach could be used to investigate a number of cases selected by company size and/or industry sector, in order to provide a more in-depth understanding of the issues.

References

1. Curran J, Blackburn R (2001) *Researching the small business*. Sage Publications, London
2. European Commission (2003) Commission adopts a new definition of micro, small and medium sized enterprises in Europe [Online]. Available from http://www.eurexcel.org/sme_definition.pdf, Accessed 16th May 2006
3. OECD (2002) *OECD small and medium enterprise outlook*. OECD Publications, Paris
4. Levy M, Powell P (1997) SME flexibility and the role of information systems. *Small Bus Econ* 11(2):183–196
5. Forfas (1998) *Annual competitiveness report 1998 – SME Performance*, Dublin
6. Golden W, Griffin M (1998) *A survey of internet commerce in small and medium sized enterprises*. National University of Ireland, Galway
7. Ballantine J, Levy M, Powell P (1998) Evaluating information systems in small and medium-sized enterprises: issues and evidence. *Eur J Inf Syst* 7(4):241–251
8. Levy M, Powell P, Yetton P (2002) The dynamics of SME information systems. *Small Bus Econ* 19(4):341–354
9. Whitman M, Mattord H (2002) *Principles of information security*. Course technology, 1st edn. Thomson/Course Technology, Boston, 16 December 2002
10. Dhillon G (2006) *Principles of information systems security*. Wiley, New Jersey
11. Posthumus S, Von-Solms R (2004) A framework for the governance of information security. *Comput Secur* 23(8):638–646
12. Saltzman S (2004) *Fraudulent bugs*. Irish Comput 28(5):18
13. Williams N (2004) *Security – stop outside getting in*. Irish Comput 28(5):36–38
14. Bednarz A (2004) *Crime and punishment*. Network World 21(37):49
15. Dhillon G, Backhouse J (2000) Information system security management in the new millennium. *Communications ACM* 43(7):125–128
16. Garg A, Curtis J, Halper H (2003) Quantifying the financial impact of IT security breaches. *Inf Manage Comput Secur* 11(2):74–83
17. Carr N (2003) IT doesn't matter. *Harv Bus Rev* 81(5):41–49
18. Austin R, Darby C (2003) The myth of secure computing. *Harv Bus Rev* 81(6):120–126
19. Stich P (2005) IT security: the human factor. *ISSA J*:27–29, February 2005
20. CCI (2005) *SME e-business survey 2005*, Chambers of Commerce of Ireland. Dublin
21. Collins J (2005) *Staying within the law*, Sunday business post, October, 1–35
22. Winkler I (2003). Zen and the art of cyber security. In *Proceedings of the IDC security conference*. Croke Park, Dublin
23. Leach J (2003) Improving user security behaviour. *Comput Secur* 22(8):685–692
24. Robinson F (2001) High-end IT security: no longer a distant pipe dream for SMEs. *Comput Fraud Secur* (9):12–14
25. Weil S (2003) Creating high-quality security policies. *Inf Syst Secur Assoc J*:10–14, May 2003
26. Higgins HN (1999) Corporate system security: towards an integrated management approach. *Inf Manage Comput Secur* 7(5):217–222
27. Karyda M, Kiountouzis E, Kokolakis S (2004) Information systems security policies: a contextual perspective. *Comput Secur* 24(3):1–7

28. Dhillon G (2001) Violations of safeguards by trusted personnel and understanding related information security concerns. *Comput Secur* 20(2):165–172
29. Dinnie G (1999) The second annual global information security survey. *Inf Manage Comput Secur* 7(3):112–120
30. Ernst and Young (2004) *Global information security survey 2004*, Ernst and Young
31. Schneier B (2004) Customers, passwords, and web sites. *Computer* 37(4):88
32. CSI/FBI (2005) *Computer crime and security survey 2005*, Computer Security Institute

Influence of IT Service Management on Innovation Management: First Insights from Exploratory Studies

M. Kießling[*], M. Marrone[†] and L. M. Kolbe[‡]

Abstract The paper explores the relation between innovations and standards in companies that have implemented an IT Service Management framework. Six German companies were asked which process was implemented first: the framework or the Innovation Management process. In addition, the companies were queried on the impact of IT Service Management frameworks on innovation. The resultant research shows that a great majority of companies that adopted an IT Service Management framework first and later implemented the Innovation Management process. Benefits observed include a faster adoption of innovations and an enhanced ability to recognize potential for improvement.

Introduction

The adoption of IT Service Management (ITSM) frameworks is on the rise. It is estimated that 90% of US companies are considering or currently using an ITSM framework [1]. One of the goals of ITSM is to attain a particular level of standardization of operational processes in the Information Technology (IT) department. Innovation, moreover, is a process requiring creativity. Hence a specific degree of freedom is needed for the development of new ideas. The processes – innovation and standardization – are seen as either mutually exclusive [2]: 6 or complementary, as in the study by Allen and Sriram [3]: 180, in which they found that standardization spurred innovation in 50% of the cases.

Relevant to this research is the impact of a standard per se on innovation in IT departments. IT is one of the most frequently changing departments. As stated by

[*]Faculty of Economic Sciences, Chair of Information Management, University of Göttingen, Göttingen, Germany, mkiessl@uni-goettingen.de

[†]Faculty of Economic Sciences, Chair of Information Management, University of Göttingen, Göttingen, Germany, mmarron@uni-goettingen.de

[‡]Faculty of Economic Sciences, Chair of Information Management, University of Göttingen, Göttingen, Germany, lkolbe@uni-goettingen.de

A. D'Atri et al. (eds.), *Management of the Interconnected World*,
DOI 10.1007/978-3-7908-2404-9_16,

Nolan [4]: 399, by adopting the stage theory as a foundation, methods for managing the department must evolve over time if the management of IT in the long term is to be successful. Further, Mohr [5]: 112 suggests that an organization may be more likely to produce innovative ideas when its environment is rapidly changing. Consequently we focus in this paper on companies that have implemented the ITSM standard, and we explore below their different views on managing innovation.

In this context, the following three research questions are addressed:
(1) Which process – ITSM or Innovation Management – is implemented first in the majority of cases?
(2) Are ITSM and Innovation Management independent processes?
(3) What is the impact of ITSM on Innovation Management?

Theoretical Foundation

Management of Innovations

Rogers [6]: 5 defines innovation as "the application of new ideas to the products, processes or any other aspect of a firm's activities." Furthermore, innovations can be understood as improvement, and when implemented in the market, they expand the competitiveness of the innovator for at least a limited amount of time [7]: 43. Organizational innovation can be defined as "the adoption of an idea or behaviour that is new to the organization adopting it" [8]: 197. Ven et al. [9]: 592 describe an innovation as an idea that is new to the people involved, even though it may appear to others as an imitation.

To stay competitive and to promote innovation, companies cannot rely on chance alone. It is crucial to manage the innovation process systematically, providing both structure and goals [10]: 43. This necessity is based on limited financial, material and human resources [11]: 47.

In general, "Innovation Management is about learning to find the most appropriate solution to the problem of consistently managing this process" [12]: 762. It can also be defined as planning, organizing, executing and controlling all activities related to the development and implementation of innovations [13]: 57. Moreover, Drejer et al. [14]: 5 describe Innovation Management as consisting of five activities: technological integration, the process of innovation, strategic technology planning, organizational change and business development.

Fundamentals of ITSM

The ITSM framework can be defined as "a set of processes that co-operate to ensure the quality of live IT services, according to the levels of service agreed to by the customer" [15]. It can also be seen as a philosophy for orientation toward market, service, life-cycle and process in general [16]: 13. The main focus of the framework is not the development of IT applications, but rather the management of services. The most frequently adopted ITSM resource is the IT Infrastructure Library (ITIL), the de facto standard for IT Service [17]. Other ITSM frameworks include HP ITSM, CobiT and ISO 20000.

Methodology

To examine objectives and experiences reflecting the impact of ITSM on Innovation Management, partially structured expert interviews were conducted. Chief Information Officers (CIOs) of eight IT Service Providers were approached, of whom six agreed and were interviewed between November, 2008, and January, 2009. Interviewees came from different fields and levels of responsibility. The interviews averaged 20 min and were primarily held by telephone. Some were conducted by e-mail, with the potential for further questioning to supplement incomplete information.

Based on the theoretical foundations, interview topics were outlined and grouped into four sections: (1) personal information on the interviewees' background and responsibilities; (2) reasons for ITSM adoption; (3) the conducting of Innovation Management; and (4) possible links between ITSM and Innovation Management. In order to encourage interviewees to express their opinions, many questions were open-ended. The order and direction of topics varied, as openness and flexibility allowed new points to be raised. Each interview was recorded in order to permit information to be extracted and compared in a systematic and objective fashion.

The limiting of our sample to companies in Germany allows for greater comparability as well as a simplification of the data collection. One criterion is the use of ITSM within the company. In Table 1, the interviewed companies are introduced, along with a description of their respective IT services.

Table 1. Interviewees' sample demographics

Case	Company size	Company description
A	Large	Internal IT service provider
B	Mid-size	IT consultant
C	Mid-size	External IT service provider
D	Small	Software management and software distribution
E	Small	External IT service provider
F	Large	Internal IT service provider

Results

The following section presents

(1) the results, considering separately ITSM adoption and Innovation Management implementation; and

(2) the interviewees' perception of the impact of ITSM on their Innovation Management.

Results are later summarized in Table 2.

ITSM Adoption

The length of time that ITSM has been in place in the various companies differs. Cases A, B and C have implemented ITSM over a period of 7–10 years; cases D and F for 5 years; and case E for 3 years.

Since different perceptions of maturity levels exist, it is important to know what is meant by "maturity" in the various cases. Five out of six respondents employ the Capability Maturity Model Integration (CMMI), or models based on CMMI, such as the CobiT maturity levels, as their basic definition.

Following the CMMI model, cases A, D and E show a "defined process" maturity level, in which the processes have been standardized and documented. Cases B and F reflect a "managed and measured" maturity level, where procedures are monitored by the management.

Case F is alone in reporting difficulties in specifying a maturity level. They have installed Key Performance Indicators (KPIs) for the assessment of central processes, but not for all processes.

Case C has an "optimized" maturity level, in which processes have been polished to a level of good practice. Areas of improvement targeted were customer satisfaction, internal processes, standardization of processes, service quality, efficiency, and return on investment.

Innovation Management Implementation

In case A, Innovation Management is conducted on an interdepartmental basis. The various ideas for improvement of products and services are collected as part of the Innovation Management process, after which they undergo review and are considered for implementation.

Case B focuses not only on internal processes but also on innovation geared at customers. A special team is solely responsible for research and innovation. Suggested innovations are evaluated by a standardized process.

Innovation Management in case C is essential to their business strategy, to improve the effectiveness and efficiency of their products, services, processes and structures.

Case D implemented Innovation Management and holds yearly reviews of their internal processes in order to assess efficiency and effectiveness. They expressed that a more systematic Innovation Management will be implemented in the future, once a higher maturity level of their Service Management and other processes has been reached.

Due to their size, case E does not yet see Innovation Management as an independent process within their company. Finally, in case F the main focus of Innovation Management is on collaboration with customers to identify improvements in products and services.

Link Between ITSM and Innovation Management

On the question of the noted effect or impact of ITSM on Innovation Management, companies submitted different feedback.

In case A, no direct impact of ITSM on Innovation Management is noted, thus the two need to be considered as separate processes. As a first step, ITSM needs to be aligned with customers' needs and interests. Only when all ITSM processes have been installed properly and reached a certain maturity level can Innovation Management follow as a next step, to optimize and develop processes.

Case B describes ITSM and Innovation Management as "natural enemies," for they represent contrary goals. According to their perception, that is, the adoption of an innovative process distracts from the main objective of ITSM frameworks, which is to have clearly defined standard processes. Innovation Management has to be seen as a separate process in which innovations are identified, developed and implemented; and the implementations of these innovations need to proceed under controlled circumstances in order to be able to evaluate the results in a standard fashion.

In contrast, case C claims that they could identify impact of ITSM on Innovation Management. Using a "Plan-Do-Check-Act" cycle to recognize potential for improvement, they believe that Innovation Management within their ITSM framework shows three basic types of impact: (1) significant increase of customer satisfaction; (2) image improvement; and (3) product and service quality improvement.

Case D definitely noticed the effect of ITSM on their Innovation Management; for them it is not a question of whether there is an impact, but rather how great this impact is. Specifically, they have noticed that, due to the faster adoption of innovations via the ITSM, customers' needs can be handled more efficiently. In this the company differentiates itself from its competitors

In assessing the impact of ITSM on Innovation Management, case F sees ITSM as the superior model. After first implementing ITSM, they later introduced Innovation Management into the framework as an independent process. This opportunity to employ Innovation Management as a new strategic process was possible since case F's ITSM consists of not only operational processes (e.g. Incident Management) but also strategic processes (e.g. IT Strategy, IT Business Assessment).

Table 2. Interview results

Case	Years of adoption	Maturity level	First implementation	Independent processes
A	10	Defined	ITSM	No
B	8–10	Managed	Innovation Mgt.	Yes
C	7	Optimized	ITSM	No
D	5	Defined	ITSM	No
E	3	Defined	ITSM	No
F	5	Managed	ITSM	No

Discussion

When companies were asked which process was implemented first – the ITSM framework or Innovation Management – interviewees more frequently responded that ITSM frameworks preceded implementation of Innovation Management. One possible reason for this could be the inherent capacity of the ITSM framework for continuous improvement of extant services. This process – Continual Service Improvement (CSI) – is "responsible for managing improvements to ITSM Processes and IT Services" [18]. Rather than considering Innovation Management as a separate entity, ITSM includes innovation in its very structure.

Additional insight was gleaned when the companies were asked if in fact they had implemented an Innovation Management process, and if so, where it was introduced. This revealed case B as the only company to have implemented Innovation Management independently of the ITSM framework. This was done to give enough space for innovations to evolve without obligation to integrate them within current business operations. It thus eliminates the risk of affecting business processes already defined in line with ITSM. By separating the two, they reduce the risk of compromising the quality of either process.

On the contrary, cases A, C and F have fully integrated Innovation Management into their ITSM. This can lead to an Innovation Management that is more directly related to business operations as well as to customers, incorporating improvements through the CSI process. It can however be suggested that this process yields if not favours incremental rather than radical innovations.

One particularly interesting aspect of the interviews merits further examination. For the two small companies, who have not yet implemented systematic Innovation Management, nonetheless reveal that innovations are developed more quickly than in the cases of the larger companies. This appears to contradict researchers' conclusions that there is a positive association between organizational size and innovation [19]: 395. Furthermore, these two small companies explain that they not only incorporate their customers' innovative requirements, but also emulate innovations observed in suppliers and competitors. Ven [9] confirms these ideas, but also points out that an innovation can also be an imitation. We observe, then, that this behaviour again favours incremental rather than radical innovations.

Finally, when the companies were queried on the impact of Innovation Management on ITSM, five out of six described a modification in both speed and quantity of innovations, as well as an improved ability to recognize potential for improvement.

Conclusion

Three principal observations from the study show that (1) in its yield of incremental improvements, Innovation Management as a subset of the ITSM frameworks is able to contribute to standardization efforts; (2) companies develop an Innovation Management process due to adoption of an ITSM, employing the concurrent Continual Service Improvement built into the ITSM; and (3) companies recognize that one impact of ITSM on Innovation Management is an increased ability to adopt innovations and to identify areas for potential improvement.

As limitations to this study, we identify: (1) the lack of understanding of the different types of Innovation Management in the companies (systematic, non-systematic or prescribed from ITSM specifications); and (2) the focus on companies in Germany alone. Thus the paper and the conducted expert interviews are merely explorative in nature. Further research should include a larger-scale survey employing the same factors to understand adoption of Innovation Management inside and outside of ITSM. Moreover, the perception of maturity level of the ITSM should be explored as it relates to the adoption of Innovation Management.

References

1. Galup SD, Dattero R, Quan JJ, Conger S (2009) An overview of IT service management. *Commun ACM* 52(5):124–127
2. Kondo Y (2000) Innovation versus standardization. *TQM Mag* 12(1):6–10
3. Allen RH, Sriram RD (2000) The role of standards in innovation. *Technol Forecast Soc Change* 64(2):171–181
4. Nolan RL (1973) Managing the computer resource: a stage hypothesis. *Commun ACM* 16(7):399–405
5. Mohr LB (1969) Determinants of innovation in organizations. *Am Polit Sci Rev* 63(1):111–126
6. Rogers M (1998) *The definition and measurement of innovation. Melbourne Institute of Applied Economic and Social Research*, Melbourne
7. Jetter M, Satzger G, Neus A (2009) Technologische innovation und die Auswirkung auf Geschäftsmodell, Organisation und Unternehmenskultur – Die Transformation der IBM zum global integrierten, dienstleistungsorientierten Unternehmen. *Wirtschaftsinformatik* 2009(1):43–52
8. Daft RL (1978) A dual-core model of organizational innovation. *Acad Manage J* 21(2):193–210
9. van de Ven AH (1986) Central problems in the management of innovation. *Manage Sci* 32(5):590–607
10. Pleschak F, Sabisch H (1996) *Innovationsmanagement.* UTB, Stuttgart
11. Burmester R, Vahs D (2005) *Innovationsmanagement.* Schäffer-Poeschel, Stuttgart
12. Bessant J (2003) Challenges in innovation management. In: Shavinina LV (ed) *International handbook on innovation* (pp. 761–774) Elsevier Science, Boston
13. Gerpott TJ (2005) *Strategisches technologie- und innovationsmanagement.* Schäffer-Poeschel, Stuttgart
14. Drejer A, Christensen KS, Ulhoi JP (2004) Understanding intrapreneurship by means of state-of-the-art knowledge management and organizational learning theory. *Int J Manage Enterp Dev* 1(2):102–119
15. Young CM (2004) *An introduction to IT service management.* Gartner Research
16. Zarnekow R, Hochstein A, Brenner W (2005) *Service-orientiertes IT-management: ITIL-best-practices und Fallstudien.* Springer, Berlin
17. IT Governance Institute (2008) IT governance global status report – 2008. Resource document. ISACA, http://www.itgi.org/AMTemplate.cfm?Section=ITGI_Research_Publications&Template=/ContentManagement/ContentDisplay.cfm&ContentID=39735. Accessed 13 October 2009
18. Great Britain Office of Government Commerce (2007) Continual service improvement. The Stationery Office, London
19. Damanpour F (1992) Organizational size and innovation. *Org Stud* 13(3):75–402

Technological and Organizational Structures: A Case of Adaptation in the Archaeological Sector

Alessio Maria Braccini* **and Tommaso Federici**†

Abstract In the archaeological sector, information about finds and related documents is highly relevant, but no information system (IS) is available to manage it. Professionals working in the field are often not used to managing information by means of technology and, moreover, work practices are not standardized. The introduction of a new IS to track events and record information in such an environment is therefore a big challenge. An adaptation between technology and organization is then to be expected, in order to find an appropriate form of integration. By adopting a structuration theory perspective, this work analyses the case of a project in which an IS to manage finds was designed, experimented with, discussed, and then developed.

Introduction

Once discovered, an archaeological find (like a jug, a statue, a fragment, or even a site) starts a sort of new "life cycle", throughout which it will cross several, even repeated, events (among them storage, cleaning, restoration, study, exhibition, grouping, or consolidation with other finds …).

Sometimes such actions change the nature of the find (e.g. after a consolidation of fragments found at different moments) and its interpretation (e.g. after a study that details its origin or dating), generating a lot of new information. The traceability of all the events in the life cycle of an archaeological find is fundamental to deepening the scientific contribution received by it, to making the best decision about its management every time, and, in the end, to making sense of its discovery and overall of its expensive conservation.

Despite the relevance of information in the archaeological sector, even to warrant the security and safeguarding of the finds, the retrieval and collection of data related to them does not follow standardized procedures, and neither are they managed through computer-based information systems. The operational procedures are

* University LUISS Guido Carli, Rome, Italy, abraccini@luiss.it

† University of Tuscia, Viterbo, Italy, tfederici@unitus.it

A. D'Atri et al. (eds.), *Management of the Interconnected World*,
DOI 10.1007/978-3-7908-2404-9_17, © Springer-Verlag Berlin Heidelberg 2010

highly diversified, and are specific to each agency, organization, or even individual that works on finds. Very often operations follow individual practice or context pressure (like in case of an urgent excavation during works on a railway).

The issue of recording, retrieving, and sharing all the information on an archaeological find and its related documents and photos is further complicated by the presence throughout the life cycle of several professionals (archaeologists, restorers, storekeepers, archivists, photographers ...), who usually work separately, even when their activities intersect. Moreover, these professionals often have low levels of IT literacy.

The introduction of a new computer-based IS in order to track events, by recording all the possible information, is then a big challenge. On the one hand, such a system has to be designed in detail to reach its aims; on the other hand, organizational structures are neither fit (diverse, not standardized procedures) nor ready (novelty of IT use in operations) to adopt it profitably. An adaptation between technology and organization is then to be expected, to overcome these difficulties.

This work analyses from a structuration theory perspective the case of the project named "giSAD – Recouvrement du Potentiel Informatif des Sites Archéologiques Démontés" ("Potential Information Retrieval of Archaeological Mobile Sites"), during which an operational IS was designed, discussed, and finally developed. After the description of the theoretical framework, and of the research methodology, this paper will analyse the project context and history. A discussion on the findings and some conclusions will follow.

Theoretical Framework

The theoretical perspective adopted in this paper is based on Anthony Giddens's Structuration Theory (ST) [1], which describes the relationship between individuals and society [2]. Rejecting the two alternative hypotheses of social structures and human agents' radicalism, Giddens claims that they both draw on each other [1]. ST does not directly address technology. As reported by Jones and Karsten [2] and Poole and DeSanctis [3], the technology artifact is neglected by Giddens. Nevertheless, ST is credited to be a great influence on IS research [2–4]. Therefore, due to the relevance of IT in organizations' everyday life, some seminal works have attempted to include the IT concept more explicitly [4].

Among all the seminal works that extend and adapt ST, DeSanctis and Poole propose Adaptive Structuration Theory (AST) [5]. AST extends ST by introducing concepts that have found broad acceptance in the IS community [6]: "structural features" ("specific types of rules and resources, or capabilities offered by the system" [5:126]), "spirit" ("the general intent with regard to values and goals underlying a given set of structural features" [5:126]), and "appropriation". Citing Dennis and Wixom [7] and Rao and Jarvenpaa [8], Niederman et al. affirm that AST "has been used extensively as a framework for investigating and consolidating findings regarding Group Support Systems for more than a decade" [9]. Since AST adds constructs to study relationships among groups and technology, it appears to be a suitable extension of ST for the present empirical case.

According to AST, not only do social structures shape human agency (and vice versa) but technology itself is a source of structures, as it possesses features that can shape the way human agents manipulate information (what Giddens calls "signification" [5]:126). Structures provided by technology can also be described by the spirit, that is, the "official line which the technology presents to people regarding how to act when using the system, how to interpret its features, and how to fill in gaps in procedure which are not explicitly specified" [5]:126 (what Giddens calls "legitimation" [5]:126).

When information technology is implemented, complex patterns of behaviours that lead to users' appropriation can be observed. Foreseeing appropriation processes is difficult, as the introduction of a new technology might lead to unexpected outcomes, due to the interplay among social structures, structural features, and human agency. The intended uses of IT may be distorted by users, who appropriate IT for purposes different from those initially intended [10]. Even if the present case deals with a development process (and not with a post-implementation analysis), AST has been adopted because the project also involved software experimentation by the users.

Research Methodology

The unit of analysis this paper focuses on is formed by multiple groups of actors (professionals working in the archaeological field) across the different organizations (the different archaeological departments) involved in the project as partners.

Data for the analysis have been collected by means of direct observation and analysis of documents. One of the two authors of this paper was able to attend all the project meetings and has had, as a result, direct access to primary sources of data. Moreover, minutes of meetings and copies of relevant project documents were available to both authors for investigation.

Due to the lack of specific guidance on the application of ST [3], the case is analysed using the key concepts of social structures (ST), structural features (AST), spirit (AST), and appropriation (AST). The entire operational method of AST proposed by DeSanctis and Poole [5]:131–141 is not adopted, because it appears too restrictive and, furthermore, it seems not to have been literally adopted in other works. The methodology rather relies on the sequence of events and the three groups of actors (promoters and leaders, technology experts, and final users) used by Boudreau and Robey [11] to analyse the implementation process of a technology. Such events include: the "inertia" (that Boudreau and Robey [11] assimilate to the kind of technology use described by Orlikowski [12]: users try not to modify their existing way of doing things), the "reinvention" (users develop new practices in order to accomplish their work using the system, despite the problems and limitations of the technology), and the "improvised learning" (the transition process in between, through which users acquire knowledge of the system in a way that is neither planned nor anticipated).

Case Description

The case analysis begins with a description of the institutional context of the project, together with its aims and characteristics. As already stated, by following the approach of Boudreau and Robey [11], the project history is then reported in three steps: initial inertia, improvised learning, and reinvention of the IS.

Project Context and Characteristics
In 2001, the Italian autonomous Region Valle d'Aosta, by means of its Co-financed Projects and Research Direction under the Monuments Department, promoted a project named giSAD, co-financed by the European Union. A partnership was established with other six regional Monuments Departments, both Italian and European (from France, Portugal, and Spain). Even though each partner's context was different (in terms of laws, practices, resources, size of the territory, number of finds), they operated in the same field (archaeological heritage management), in a scenario similar to the one described at the beginning of this paper.

Summarizing, in the finds management, the organizational structures (like procedures, workflows, and hierarchies) were both not strict and not incontrovertible, whereas the technological ones did not substantially exist (information about a find or an event was collected only in some cases and on paper registers).

The project [13] had the aim of designing and developing an operational IS addressing multiple objectives, common to all the partners: the exploitation of the huge amount of finds not studied, the availability of much more information based on more trustworthy data, an improvement in resources' usage, the achievement of a higher finds protection, and a reduction in management costs. In the background, the initiative promoters also had more general intents (the "spirit" as in DeSanctis and Poole [5]), which can be classified in three dimensions (see Table 1).

Table 1. Dimensions of the intents characterizing the "spirit" of the initiative

Dimension	Description
Integration	Promoting continuous co-operation among the diverse professionals, through the use of the same platform
Knowledge management	Fostering the creation of knowledge through the availability and sharing of much more information
Ease of adoption	Minimizing the initial impact on users' daily practices and the changes in organizational structures (roles, rules …)

In order to point out the human agency in the emergence of structures, the persons intervening in the project can be classified in three groups (see Table 2). In this context, the role of each individual appears hugely relevant, because of the multiplicity of involved disciplines and the high level of everyone's specialization.

Table 2. Groups of actors involved in the project

Group	Description
Project promoters and leaders (PL)	Director and project local leader of the seven departments; global project leaders
Technology experts (TE)	Persons in charge of the drawing of technical aspects of the system
Final users (FU)	Different professionals of the seven departments

Taking into account the innovation brought into the environment by the project, giSAD was planned involving several phases and stages for presentation and discussion with the users of the outputs produced so far (see Table 3). Also for this reason the project took a long time, ending with the final IS development in 2007.

Table 3. Phases of the project with outputs and actors involved (summarized)

Phases	Outputs	Who
1. Analysis of practices and needs	Set of information needed (on the characteristics of finds, depots, archives, events ...); thesauri for each piece of information; map of the events to be managed	PL, FU
2. Preliminary design of the system (performed only on the basis of documents)	Documents including technical solutions (database model, structure of the software, hardware ...) and new workflow model	TE
3. Trial of pilot software (pre-existing)	Acceptance and hints by the users about this software (limited to some functions in respect of the target one)	FU
4. Discussion on the preliminary design and trial results	List of comments, suggestions and criticism by the users, both on pilot experience and new software design	PL, TE, FU
5. Revised software design	Detailed project to proceed as the system development	TE, FU
6. Development	Final software to be implemented	PL, TE

Initial Inertia

When the project started, almost all the users were very curious about the possibility of innovating in their work ("it's time to have more modern and efficient tools to improve our work"). At the same time, they were not at all used to resorting to managerial software (keying in each datum, retrieving information) and to co-operating with other professionals (both from the same and different fields) in their tasks.

The users then began the planned trial of pilot software with great interest and some difficulties, as with any like innovation. Such software had been developed some years before by the cited Direction of the Region Valle d'Aosta with similar aims, but a less broad perimeter than that to be realized by the giSAD project.

The technical experts were introduced to the project only at the end of the analysis phase, without any previous contact with the final users. They then produced the preliminary design of the system only on the basis of the available documents. Both for this reason, and for their cultural bias, they stressed the security and efficiency objectives by pursuing total process certainty, data completeness, and trustworthiness. Moreover, they paid much attention to the issue of distributing the same software to several partners in partially different situations. Therefore, they proposed a rational design, where technical structures (structural features [5], like data model, workflow model, architecture of the system, mandatory data) featured strongly, then involving a correspondent organizational structuration (in terms of procedures, flow of events, task content, and so on).

Improvised Learning

The central phase of the project was devoted to the presentation and discussion with the users of the preliminary study elaborated by the technical experts, and to the examination of the reactions of the same users after the pilot trial.

Regarding the former, the final users generally noticed that it tended to force them too much in many relevant aspects: a restrictive data model ("I could guess that an internal automatic code can help *you* to univocally identify a find, but *I* need a mnemonic code created *by myself*"); standardized forms, unsuitable for anyone in particular ("you put that data in this form, I don't know to be used by whom, but I don't need them and they generate confusion to me"); a set of mandatory data ("we cannot key up that data at all times at this stage of the process, even if it would be both correct and useful"); and overall workflow rigidity ("yes, we agree, yours would be an ideal flow, but we can very hardly follow it. Let's think on an open excavation: we must bring away all the finds in a while, no matter about the complete registration of their data"). Structural features of the technology were then rejected by the users.

Similar comments came out during the evaluation of the pilot trial. Even though this prototype was developed to collect a lot of information on a find, useful for many users, it was designed to support the restoration activity. For this reason, its concept and forms were especially conceived to meet the restorers' needs. Furthermore, this software presented some enforcements, such as for the workflow model and the introduction of the finds' parcel concept, unusual for most users.

The trial of the pilot was then abandoned by many users before the forecasted term. At the same time, however, having experienced the use of computerized systems to record data, some users started to create individual shadow systems, by using a spreadsheet or a database on their own PCs. As could be expected, every single data collection was different in structure, codification, and completeness.

Reinvention

The technical experts learnt many lessons during the several meetings with the users, mainly the specificity of the archaeological sector in terms of the organization and variety of the cultures. At the same time, the relevance of the issues proposed by the users gave new strength to the dimension "Ease of adoption" of the original spirit, mitigating the weight of some other objectives for the technical experts, and also for the promoters and leaders. All these factors led to a new, less prescriptive, concept for the system, which was designed together with the users, involving many changes in the technical structures:

- an extensible "core" data model, including information common to all the partners, was designed: any user has the chance to obtain new fields in some cases (i.e. for finds' codes), which will automatically appear in the specified form;
- the set of mandatory data in each situation was reduced to the minimum (e.g. a find can be registered initially in the system without the specification of its material or discovery location);
- forms and navigation tools were differentiated on the basis of each professional habit, leaving at the same time the option to add data or change their position;
- the workflow model was deconstructed, becoming a collection of single events: users can insert data on a new find starting from the event considered more appropriate in that case, and then proceed with any other event (or stop there).

As regards this last point, having lost the track-recording feature implicit in any workflow while still being the traceability of a find fundamental, a new function to rebuild each find history ex post was conceived. It retrieves and reports on a timeline all the data about treatments, movements, and other activities related to a find.

Discussion on the Findings

The giSAD project is a valuable example to shed light on the interplay of human actors and technology across the three phases described by Boudreau and Robey [11]. The project history shows the phase of technology radicalism, producing a system whose structural features were not aligned to social structures, finally leading to signs of rejection. From this perspective, the actors in the giSAD project show behaviours compatible with the constructs and outcomes of ST and AST.

Nevertheless, the human actors (especially the end-users) in the giSAD project have also shown another aspect. During the improvised learning phase, the users started to show patterns of unfaithful appropriation [5], but instead of using the system in a different manner from the planned or intended one [10], they decided to reject the artifact completely. However, as they supported the spirit of the giSAD project [5], they appropriated the main concept of the system, creating their own shadow systems.

Then, the improvised learning phase outcomes helped the technological partners and users to converge to a less restrictive [5] reinvention [11] of technology. The new structural features [5], described in the previous paragraph, played a major role in this phase and increased their chance of fitting the social structures.

Conclusions and Limitations

This paper analyses the interplay of technology and organization in the giSAD project, through the study of the process of designing, evaluating, and fixing up of an IS addressed to the management of archaeological finds.

The first element of novelty of this paper lies exactly in the IS analysed, which has been the first, and so far the only, system devoted to archaeological finds management. The second novel element is the adoption of the ST and AST perspective to analyse the whole development process of an IS, instead of the usual post-implementation study.

The adopted theoretical perspective also seems to be suitable in such a case, since its constructs fit the reality of the empirical case and contribute interesting insights on the action of the actors involved in the giSAD project. Due to the relevance and novelty of the case, further research will be addressed to deepening the findings, and to grasping the whole scientific contribution of this project.

References

1. Giddens A (1984) *The constitution of society*. University of California Press, Berkeley
2. Jones MR, Karsten H (2008) Gidden's structuration theory and information systems research. *MIS Q* 32(1):127–157
3. Poole MS, DeSanctis G (2004) Structuration theory in information systems research: methods and controversies. In: Whitman ME, Woszczynski AB (eds) *The handbook for information systems research* (pp.206–249). Idea Group Inc., Hershey
4. Pozzenbon M, Pinsonneault A (2005) Challenges in conducting empirical work using structuration theory: learning from IT research. *Org Stud* 26(9):1353–1376
5. DeSanctis G, Poole MS (1994) Capturing the complexity in advanced technology use: adaptive structuration theory. *Org Sci* 5(2):121–147
6. Markus ML, Silver MS (2008) A foundation for the study of IT effects: a new look at desanctis and poole's concepts of structural features and spirit. *JAIS* 9(10–11):609–632
7. Dennis AR, Wixom BH (2002) Investigating the moderators of the group support systems use with meta-analysis. *J Manage Inf Syst* 18(3):235–257
8. Rao VS, Jarvenpaa SL (1991) Computer support of groups: theory-based models for GDSS research. *Manage Sci* 37(19):1347–1362
9. Niederman F, Briggs R, de Vreede GJ, Kolfschoten GL (2008) Extending the contextual and organizational elements of adaptive structuration theory in GSS research. *JAIS* 9(10–11):633–652
10 Schultze U, Orlikowski WJ (2004). A practice perspective on technology-mediated network relations: the use of internet-based self-serve technologies. Inf Syst Res 15:87–106
11.Boudreau MC, Robey D (2005) Enacting integrated information technology: a human agency perspective. *Org Sci* 16(1):3–18
12.Orlikowski WJ (2000) Using technology and constituting structures: a practice lens for studying technology in organizations. *Org Sci* 11(4):404–428
13. Braccini AM, Federici T (2008) Knowledge sharing in a cultural heritage context: an exploratory study. In: *Proceedings of the Mediterranean conference on information systems*, MCIS 2008, Hammamet, Tunisia, 24–26 October 2008

Organizational Readiness and Success of the EHR-S Adoption

Valentina Albano*

Abstract Despite institutional programs and enthusiastic declarations of eHealth potential, the adoption of Health Information Systems, and Electronic Health Record Systems (EHR-S) in particular, has progressed very slowly. Thus, the expected benefits have not fully surfaced. This can be partly ascribed to the lack of attention to organizational and individual variables influencing the success of the EHR-S adoption, in practice as well as in literature. A possible strategy to reduce the risk of failure is to identify some organizational and cultural factors that get the internal environment "ready" for the innovation. This makes it able to manage the change process needed to effectively enact the EHR-S potential and to assure the satisfaction of all stakeholders involved. Using this hypothesis, in this contribution, the preliminary steps of a study aiming to define a framework supporting the analysis and diagnosis of the "organizational readiness" to the EHR-S adoption will be presented. More in detail, the critical dimensions of organizational readiness and the relationship between this construct, project outcomes and the success of EHR-S adoption will be discussed.

Introduction

The systematic adoption of Health Information Systems, and especially of Electronic Health Record Systems (hereby EHR-S), is broadly considered as a promising strategy to improve the economic sustainability and quality of the healthcare service provision.

Several definitions of EHR-S were provided over time. For the purpose of this work, EHR-S is defined as system managing digitally stored healthcare information, collected during the patient's lifetime [1] by a diverse range of professionals in any care delivery setting. EHR-S is widely considered as a key element of the "integrated care" paradigm [2] and the patient-centered approach. This increases communication and interoperability in a highly heterogeneous network of healthcare professionals, home care workers and patients across institutional, organizational and professional boundaries, fostering shared decision-making, team work, open access and a greater outcome responsibility.

---

*Research Center on Information Systems (LUISS-CeRSI), LUISS Guido Carli University, Rome, Italy, valbano@luiss.it

A. D'Atri et al. (eds.), *Management of the Interconnected World*,
DOI 10.1007/978-3-7908-2404-9_18,

These beliefs have convinced several countries worldwide to develop national roadmaps fostering and managing eHealth programs and projects. Nevertheless, despite institutional programs and enthusiastic declarations of eHealth potential, EHR-S adoption has progressed very slowly: in 2006 only 28% of U.S. physicians had embraced a fully functional EHR-S as a routine part of practice, while just 23% in Canada [3]. Moreover, in the cases of adoption, clinical data effectively exchanged across providers often remains low [3] and physicians refuse to use the system [4].

These failures could be partially ascribed to the lack of attention to organizational and individual variables influencing EHR-S adoption, in practice as well as in literature [5]. Many contributions, recognizing shared information across organizational and professional boundaries as the main critical aspect of the "integrated care", seem to suggest a direct causal connection linking the introduction of the ICT to a self-sustaining change of organizations towards this new organizational paradigm. Nevertheless, difficulties arising from the EHR-S projects demonstrated that the expected benefits are only "potential" or "permissive" [6] and transforming these into concrete advantages strictly requires adequate and coherent organizational decisions.

An interesting approach, recently embraced by healthcare practitioners and change experts [7], focuses on the evaluation of organizational readiness as a critical precursor to successful change implementation. Readiness assessment could provide organizations with a solid plan to integrate the new technology and might contribute to establishing appropriate expectations.

Using this hypothesis, this contribution will presents the first steps to the realization of a conceptual framework aiming to support the analysis and diagnosis of the "organizational readiness" to adopt the EHR-S. More in detail, the critical dimensions of organizational readiness and the relationship between this construct, project outcomes and success of EHR-S adoption – here expressed in terms of stakeholders satisfaction to the innovation – will be discussed.

The reminder of this paper is organized as follows: the next Section introduces the concept of organizational readiness, and reviews main readiness frameworks, while the third Section presents the conceptual framework. Further remarks and some proposals on future works are provided in the last Section.

The "Organizational Readiness": A Literature Review

The concept of "organizational readiness" is widely considered as a critical precursor to the successful adoption of any organizational change [8, 9] and of an IT-based change in particular [10, 11]. Two concepts of "organizational readiness" arise from the literature [7].

A first approach emphasizes the psychological state of organizational members in respect to a specific organizational change. In fact, "readiness" has been defined as the extent to which individuals are prepared to participate in organizational development activities. Furthermore, it is manifested in organizational members' beliefs, attitudes, and intentions regarding the extent to which changes were needed, and the organization's capacity to make those changes [8]. Following this approach, Campbell et al. [12] introduced six dimensions of eHealth readiness related to the professional willingness to change (turf, efficacy, practice context, apprehension, time to learn and ownership).

The focus limited to the professional' viewpoint also characterizes the framework proposed by Demiris et al. [13] which, however, adopts the second concept of organizational readiness.

In fact, according to the second approach, "readiness" is described in structural terms, focusing on the availability of resources and capabilities to perform the change. Resources, capabilities and indicators vary greatly depending on the type of organizational change analyzed. For instance, focusing on IT-based change, organizational readiness has been considered as one of the main factors influencing the adoption of inter-organizational systems (with perceived benefits of IT and external pressures) [10, 11]. It is characterized by two dimensions: the first one concerns the level of financial resources supporting installation, implementation, enhancement and on-going expenses. The second one refers to the level of IT sophistication within the organization, expressed in terms of technological expertise, and the level of management understanding of, and support for, IT to achieve organizational objectives.

In several studies on eHealth adoption, financial capabilities, and IT sophistication in particular, are considered as the main dimensions of organizational readiness [14–16]. Nevertheless, this approach does not allow a full understanding of the organizational readiness. IT Sophistication is only one of the many cultural and structural factors involved in the process of adoption of an EHR-S [17]. It actually represents a disruptive change in the healthcare workplace and culture, introducing new objectives, rules, work processes, and the importance of knowledge-sharing among professionals; i.e., a new different vision of care management for which healthcare organizations must be ready.

Organizational Readiness' and Success of EHR-S Adoption: The Proposed Framework

As highlighted in the previous paragraph, existing readiness frameworks suffer from an inconsistent coverage of the evaluation components as well as from a narrow definition of the construct. In fact, organizational readiness should be considered as a two-dimensional construct that refers to both organizational members' motivation and organization capability to implement intentional change [7]. Therefore, the concept adopted should include both psychological and behavioural implications. Consequently, a new organizational readiness assessment framework has been developed.

The Organizational Readiness Dimensions

Three components have been recognized as relevant in the assessment of the overall organizational readiness for the adoption of EHR: the *innovation-oriented climate*, the *information maturity* and the *cooperation maturity*.

Innovation-oriented climate. The innovation oriented climate refers to the presence of a climate where new ideas are welcomed and accepted and where management and professionals feel motivated to engage in improvement activities. This dimension is particularly challenging in the healthcare domain where a rule-based culture exists, seeking compliance rather than entrepreneurship, innovation and improvement. More specifically, there are three areas that seem particularly important:

- *Performance orientation*: a climate of openness and willingness to face the realities of service performance level;
- *Openness to change*: management and professionals' interest and effort in keeping up with change and general resilience to use new and changing technologies or new procedures;
- *Professional commitment*: capability to involve healthcare professionals in major hospital initiatives. It might be expressed by a previous collaborative effort between management and professional staff to improve care quality and reduce practice variation.

Information maturity. Considering the nature of the change introduced by EHR-S adoption, we can suppose that readiness is also influenced by the capability to treat information in a consistent and conscious way. These are generally influenced by the characteristics of the "information ecology" of the organization, including the existing system practices, terminology, knowledge, behaviours and values related to the use of information, as well as technologies in use.

From this perspective, *IT sophistication* – concerning the existing ICT infrastructure, the style of IT manager, and IT skills, knowledge and attitudes – represents only one of the critical areas of the information maturity. In fact, it is also necessary to evaluate:

- *Information culture*: the role attributed to the information by professional and managers (performance evaluation, communication, continuity of care) in order to verify its compliance with the information objectives of EHR-S.
- *Information structure*: the level of care standardization (care pathways) and the capability to reduce practice variation in a paper-based process in

order to be supported by the system. It also refers to the strategies adopted by physicians to collect and retrieve information.

Cooperation maturity. As far as EHR-S adoption requires coordination between at least two organizations, the capability to develop and manage inter-organizational relationships becomes a critical factor to assure an effective use of the system. Traditionally, in healthcare systems there are particularly strong obstacles to inter-organizational coordination due to the increasing specialization required to ensure high quality of work. Therefore, functional boundaries are reinforced by professional identities, status differentials, specialized knowledge and specific interpretations on patients needs and roles in the healthcare process. All these factors undermine relationships and make the enactment of workflow and knowledge-sharing particularly complex. From this viewpoint, three areas are crucial for the evaluation of cooperation maturity:

- *Collaboration climate*: the sense of professional autonomy, collaboration and trust between professionals. Technological and semantic interoperability can only be effectively enacted if professionals have already accepted the reduction of their professional independence and the cultural barriers to cooperation have been overcome. Indeed, the sense of autonomy is particularly strong – especially among physicians in small practice settings – and EHR-S is generally viewed as a potential threat to professional autonomy.
- *Coordination mechanisms*: the presence of a pre-existing multidisciplinary approach to problem solving that includes medical staff, nursing and pharmacy (e.g. team working, case management).
- *Communication maturity*: the nature and the frequency of communication among healthcare providers; between them and their management, as well as among institutions. This also refers to the tools adopted to communicate.

The Relationship Between Organizational Readiness and Project Outcomes

For the most part, theories and research carried out on organizational readiness start from an interpretation of the organizational change as the result of a deliberate effort initiated by the management. From this perspective, organizational issues become critical only when strategies aiming at reducing the "resistances" and assuring a "perfect adaptation" of the organization to the selected innovation have to be defined. In fact, focusing on the two general stages of the adoption process of innovation (the *initiation stage* and the *implementation stage*) [18], readiness assessment precedes the implementation process, in order to support the definition of the right policies of change management. However, it comes after the initiation stage, when the decision to adopt the change has already occurred.

The main limitation of this approach is that it does not take into account the different time needed to implement a change in the organizational structure or culture (e.g. the construction of trust and willingness to cooperate) with reference to the duration of an IT adoption project. The development of organizational resources/capabilities results from the history of a specific reality and depends on the organizational choices made over time; therefore, they can only partially evolve during the different phases of the IT project. Consequently, as previously suggested by [19], pre-conditions able to make the healthcare organizational context prepared to succeed in the change should already be assessed in the initiation stage of the innovation adoption process. Thus, according to the "level" of readiness detected, the management could evaluate the opportunity to reconsider the project, eventually postpone it and define specific actions targeted to improve the level of readiness during the implementation stage.

Subsequently, organizational readiness influences *project outcomes* both directly, improving the quality of the decisions of adoption, and indirectly, orienting change management policies, the *quality of the implementation process*. Obviously, *technological quality*, expressed in terms of technological choices performed (e.g. architecture, IT development methodology selected, etc.), is the other key factor influencing the project outcome.

The Definition of "Success" in EHR-S Adoption

EHR-S adoption is successful when expected benefits – improved clinical outcomes or patient satisfaction – have been achieved. Nevertheless, due to the complexity of the system and of the environment where benefits are identified, EHR-S evaluation becomes really challenging. The main problem concerns the definition of measurable parameters reflecting targeted benefits, due to the difficulties related to the identification of meaningful, measurable outcomes directly affected by EHR-S. In order to overcome this challenge, many authors have adopted surrogate or proxy measures focusing on the work process, such as improved quality metrics (e.g. increased provider adherence to guidelines for cancer screening), more optimal laboratory test ordered or reduction of medical errors [20]. Other areas of measuring are clinical productivity (e.g. working time optimization and healthcare costs [21]).

Nevertheless, the adoption of proxy measures also encounters the limits of the performance analysis based on quantitative parameters. This is due to the impossibility to isolate the ICT impact from the influence of other variables. A different approach widely adopted in the IS literature focuses on the selection of a qualitative parameter such as stakeholders satisfaction (e.g. patient perceived quality or professional satisfaction [22]). This perspective suggests that success can be assessed measuring the satisfaction of the main class of stakeholders directly impacted by the EHR-S: healthcare professionals and managers. Actually, even though many works focus on patients, EHR-S does not directly have an impact on them but through the clinician users.

The proposal to borrow the concept of customer satisfaction from the Marketing domain in order to assess IT adoption is particularly interesting. Customer satisfaction is measured using the gap between customers' expectation of performance and their perceived experience of performance [23]. According to this definition, success is influenced not only by the experiences of usage but also by the stakeholders expectations generated by information and promises provided by producers (or by "innovators", when the "product" is a change to be implemented) and other users, personal attitudes and past experiences. This perspective highlights that readiness assessment, providing an insight on personal attitudes in respect to the use of the system and on past experiences, gains an important role also for the establishment of appropriate expectations (Fig. 1).

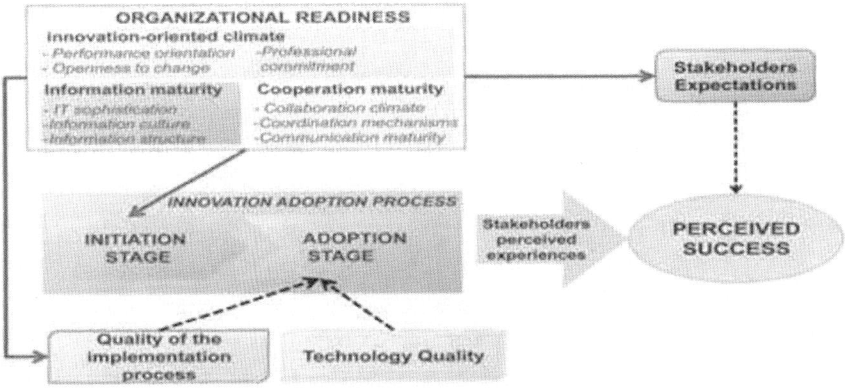

Fig. 1. Relationship between organizational readiness, project outcomes and success of EHR-S adoption

Conclusions and Future Works

The preliminary steps of a study aiming at defining a framework supporting the analysis and diagnosis of the "organizational readiness" to the EHR-S adoption have been presented. Furthermore, the following aspects were discussed: the critical dimensions of organizational readiness and the relationship between this construct, project outcomes and success of EHR-S adoption – here expressed in terms of stakeholders satisfaction to the innovation.

The framework proposed could become particularly relevant for healthcare organizations, progressively forced to deal with an institutional request of change. More specifically, it could support healthcare managers to recognize the critical factors that should be carefully considered during the planning phase of the EHR-S adoption project. This is necessary to verify the adequacy of the innovative process, to assure the satisfaction of all stakeholders involved, and to identify past or present actions of the adoption project, increasing the success of the initiative.

The next steps will be an in-depth observation of a set of projects fostered by a selection of Local Health Organizations in order to validate the main assumptions of the study. Organizational readiness will be studied within different healthcare organizations involved in the same program of EHR-S adoption in order to try to reduce the influences of other variables (such as technology quality) on the project outcomes.

References

1. Jakovidis I (1998) Towards personal health record:current situation, obstacles and trends in implementation of EHR in Europe. *Int J Med Inform* 52(1–3):105–115
2. Ovretveit J (1998) *Integrated care: models and issues*. Health Rev–Online
3. Jhaa AK et al (2008) The use of health information technology in seven nations. *Int J Med Inform* 77(12):848–854
4. Ash JS, Bates DW (2005) Factors and forces affecting EHR-S system adoption: report of a 2004 ACMI Discussion. *JAMIA* 12(1):8–12
5. Amatayakul M (2008) EHRs are not IT projects. *HFMA* 62(11):128–130
6. Barras R (1986) Towards a theory of innovation in services. *Res Policy* 15(4):161–173
7. Weiner BJ, et al (2008) Conceptualization and measurement of organizational readiness for change. *Med Care Res Rev* 65(4):379–436
8. Armenakis A et al (1993) Creating readiness for organizational change. *Hum Rel* 46(6):681–703
9. Kotter JP (1996) *Leading change*. Harvard Business Press, Boston
10. Iacovou CL et al (1995) Electronic data interchange and small organizations: adoption and impact of technology. *MIS Q* 19(4):465–485
11. Chau PY, Hui KL(2001) Determinants of small business EDI adoption: an empirical investigation. *J Org Comput Elect Commer* 11(4):229–252
12. Campbell JD et al (2001) Introducing telemedicine technology to rural physicians and setting. *J Family Pract* 50(5):419–424
13. Demiris G et al (2004) Home telehealth: the Missouri telehospice project. Background and next steps. *Home Health Care Technol Rep* 1:55–57
14. Amatayakul M (2005) EHR? Assess readiness first. *HFMA* 59(5):112–113
15. McGowan et al (2008) Formative evaluation: a critical component in EHR implementation. *JAMIA* 15(3):297–302
16. Wickramasinghe NS, Fadlalla AMA, Geisier E, Schaffer JL (2005) A framework for assessing eHealth preparedness. *IJEH* 1(3):316–334
17. Stablein D et al (2003) Understanding hospital readiness for computerized physician order entry. *J Qual Saf* 29(7):336–341
18. Zaltman G et al (1973) *Innovations and organizations*. Wiley, New York
19. Caruso A, Marchiori M (2003) The adoption of information systems in SMEs: organizational issues and success factors. In *Proceeding of ECIS 2003*, Naples, Italy
20. Bates DW et al (2001) Reducing the frequency of errors in medicine using information technology. *JAMIA* 8(4):299–308
21. Hillestad R et al (2005) Can electronic medical record systems transform health care? Potential health benefits, savings, and costs. *Health Aff* 24(5):1103–1117
22. Sittig DF et al (1999) Evaluating physician satisfaction regarding user interactions with an electronic medical record system. In Proceedings of AMIA Symposium (pp. 400-404), vol. 1999
23. Parasuraman A et al (1994) Reassessment of expectations as a comparison standard in measuring service quality: implications for further research. *J Mark* 58(1):111–124

Part III
Information and Knowledge Management

Valeria De Antonellis[*] and Katia Passerini[†]

Modern organizations, in the era of internet and web-based scenarios, have started to experience networked collaboration by information and knowledge sharing in order to improve business process, to extend business knowledge and to collaborate with all potential partners, to share and access the huge number of available resources over the network. New requirements for Information and Knowledge Management Systems must be considered in such distributed collaboration scenario. Specifically, advanced methods and tools for semantic interoperability, integration support and dynamic collaboration are strongly required.

The track Information and Knowledge Management aims at presenting the latest research on information and knowledge management and collaboration in modern organizations. The track serves as a forum for researchers, practitioners, and users to exchange new ideas and experiences on the ways new technologies (e.g., semantic web, semantic web services, service oriented architectures, P2P networks, OLAP systems, tools for data and service integration, information wrapping and extraction, data mining, process mining) may contribute to extract, represent and organize knowledge as well as to provide effective support for collaboration, communication and sharing of information and knowledge.

Main topics of the track include:

- Advanced requirements of integrated Information and KM Systems;
- Distributed collaboration in networked enterprises;
- Integration and discovery of information sources and services;
- Knowledge sharing in distributed and virtual organisations;
- Designing systems and solutions to support knowledge work;
- Workflow, process modelling and web services in networked enterprises;
- From DBMS to OLAP;
- Data mining;
- Emerging areas of research for Information and KM.

Sixteen contributions were originally submitted to the track, ten were selected for publication in this book. They look into Information and Knowledge Management from different perspectives, and along different dimensions in various domains of discourse.

[*] Università di Brescia, Brescia, Italy, deantone@ing.unibs.it

[†] New Jersey Institute of Technology, Newark, NJ, USA, pkatia@njit.edu

Four papers look into techniques and tools for effective knowledge and information management, querying and searching.

Razia Haider, Federica Mandreoli, Riccardo Martoglia, Simona Sassatelli and Paolo Tiberio in "Toward a Flexible Data Management Middleware for Wireless Sensor Networks" propose innovative solutions for the flexible querying of distributed data collected by heterogeneous devices.

In the paper by Davide Martinenghi and Riccardo Torlone, "A Logical Approach to Context-Aware Databases" a logical model and an abstract query language are presented as a foundation for context-aware database management systems.

Devis Bianchini, Valeria De Antonellis and Michele Melchiori in "Semantic Search of Distributed Information and Knowledge" define a computer aided methodology for service-based semantic search of resources in P2P networks, based on the efficient retrieval and the effective suggestion of suitable services.

Silvana Castano, Alfio Ferrara and Stefano Montanelli in "The iCoord Knowledge Model for P2P Semantic Coordination" present iKM, a three-layer peer knowledge model developed in the framework of the iCoord system for P2P semantic coordination.

Four papers address relevant issues in the area of information and knowledge integration, sharing, discovery and transfer.

Sonia Bergamaschi, Laura Po, Serena Sorrentino and Alberto Corni in "Uncertainty in Data Integration Systems: Automatic Generation of Probabilistic Relationships" propose a method for the automatic discovery of probabilistic terminological relationships in the environment of data integration systems.

Alessia Barbagallo, Antonio De Nicola and Michele Missikoff in "Social Validation in the Ontology Evolution Process" focus on the ontology definition and evolution process and on the correct assignment of the roles played by the members of a community of interest (COI).

In "Automatic Definition of KDD Prototype Processes by Composition", Claudia Diamantini, Domenico Potena and Emanuele Storti discuss one of the most interesting challenges in Knowledge Discovery in Databases (KDD), that is, how to support users in the composition of tools in order to form a valid and useful KDD process.

Chris Rivinus, Peter Baloh and Kevin C Desouza in "Improving Data Visualization for High-Density Information Transfer in Social Network Analysis Tools" suggest three areas in which SNA software designers should focus efforts to evolve more effective tools for organizational and IS design: realism, detail and changes over time.

Finally, two papers discuss methods and tools for intensional knowledge extraction and datawarehouse semantic annotation.

Devis Bianchini, Paolo Garza and Elisa Quintarelli in "Semantic-Enriched Data Mining Techniques for Intensional Service Representation" propose the application of data mining algorithms to service repositories, to properly extract useful information about services.

Claudia Diamantini and Domenico Potena in "Exploring Strategic Indexes by Semantic OLAP Operators" discuss a novel set of OLAP operators resulting from a previously defined model for the semantic annotation of a Data Warehouse (DW) schema.

Toward a Flexible Data Management Middleware for Wireless Sensor Networks

Razia Haider[*], **Federica Mandreoli**[†,‡], **Riccardo Martoglia**[π], **Simona Sassatelli**[§] **and Paolo Tiberio**[#]

Abstract In this paper we present the research activity we are carrying out in the "Mobile Semantic Self-Organizing Wireless Sensor Networks" Project at the Department of Information Engineering of the University of Modena and Reggio Emilia. In this context, the main aim of our research is to study solutions for the flexible querying of distributed data collected by heterogeneous devices providing measurement readings. To this end, we propose a middleware for wireless sensor networks which is able to autonomously configure the communication and the operations required to each device in order to reduce energy and temporal costs.

Introduction

In recent years, the advances made in the miniaturization, processing, storage and communication technologies have allowed the creation of new families of small and cheap devices capable of wireless communication and significant computation. Thanks to their peculiarities, these devices may be distributed in large quantities in the environment in order to perform data collection, goods movement control or, broadly speaking, to implement new and advanced forms of interaction with the world around them. Sample fields of application include domotics, logistics, biomedicine, remote control systems, distributed sensing of environmental phenomena and more general applications of measurement, detection and monitor-

---

This work is partially supported by the "Mobile Semantic Self-Organizing Wireless Sensor Networks" Project.

[*] University of Modena and Reggio Emilia, DII, Modena, Italy, razia.haider@unimore.it

[†] University of Modena and Reggio Emilia, DII, Modena, Italy, federica.mandreoli@unimore.it

[‡] BO/CNR, IEIIT, Bologna, Italy

[π] University of Modena and Reggio Emilia, DII, Modena, Italy, riccardo.martoglia@unimore.it

[§] University of Modena and Reggio Emilia, DII, Modena, Italy, simona.sassatelli@unimore.it

[#] University of Modena and Reggio Emilia, DII, Modena, Italy, paolo.tiberio@unimore.it

A. D'Atri et al. (eds.), *Management of the Interconnected World*,
DOI 10.1007/978-3-7908-2404-9_19, © Springer-Verlag Berlin Heidelberg 2010

ing in "ambient intelligence" scenarios. Wireless Sensor Networks (WSN) represent one of the best known and widespread technologies of this kind.

This is the stimulating scenario of the "Mobile Semantic Self-Organizing Wireless Sensor Networks" 3-years project at the Department of Information Engineering (DII) of the University of Modena and Reggio Emilia. This research activity adopts an interdisciplinary approach by integrating aspects in the areas of computer science, electronics and telecommunications such as design of microelectronic systems, ad-hoc radio communications, digital information management, applied electromagnetism and electronic measures. The high profile scientific and technological challenge is to deploy a mobile network of intelligent radio sensors, requiring enormous inputs from all the traditional disciplines of ICT.

In this context, our research activity is focused on data management and, in particular, on studying solutions for the flexible querying of distributed data collected by heterogeneous devices providing measurement readings. In order to allow a flexible querying of sensor data, in this paper we present a specifically devised Data Management Middleware which is able to autonomously configure the communication and the operations required to each device in order to satisfy the temporal, energetic and accuracy requirements of the specific usage scenario. Users can express their informative needs by composing queries in declarative form, such as "Return the maximum value of the refrigerator temperature each hour for a day, with an accuracy of 0.1%". The middleware receives the queries from user devices, abstracting from all technical issues related to the communication with the specific sensors and devices in use. Then, it produces execution plans maximizing power consumption and temporal efficiency w.r.t. the desired measure accuracy, and finally executes the query, gathering its results and presenting them to the users. Further, the middleware may enact network topology reconfiguration and selectively reprogram some of the nodes capabilities, in order to better distribute communication and computation load.

This paper is organized as follows: we first analyze the state of the art on sensor data management, focusing on query processing issues arising in our project; then, we present our data management middleware for wireless sensor networks, describing the different functionalities and how the modules interact in order to provide them; finally, we conclude by introducing possible application scenarios.

Related Work

Wireless sensor networks have been a very active area of research in latest years (see [1] for a survey) and this trend has led the database community to begin a number of research activities focusing on the different aspects of managing sensor data [2–13].

Some recent works [2, 3] have proposed the powerful vision of a sensor network as a distributed database which is programmed and queried by means of a declarative language. The vision of declarative querying is attractive since it allows programmers to "task" an entire network of sensors nodes, rather than requiring them to worry about programming individual nodes. As an example, the Cougar Project [2] treats the entire sensor network as a single streaming database where data collection is performed using declarative queries, allowing the user to focus on the data itself, rather than on the collection operation. Another notable example of such kind of systems is the TinyDB Project [3]. It uses an acquisitional query processing approach which requests data to sensors on the basis of the current query corpus. The adopted SQL-style language allows both data collection and aggregation. Also the work in [4] proposes a deductive framework where an even more expressive language for programming high-level applications is used. None of these projects, however, copes with issues related to the heterogeneity of the specific sensors and devices in use.

One of the most important constraints when dealing with a network of sensors is power consumption. Indeed, because communication is orders of magnitude more expensive than local computations, several research groups have focused on optimized in-network query processing (that is, the pushing of operations into the network) as a means of reducing energy consumption.

As an example, in the Cougar Project, given a user query, a central query optimizer generates an efficient query plan aiming at minimizing resources usage within the network by means of in-network processing performed at specialized sensor nodes, called *leaders*, which are statically chosen when sensors are deployed [2]. A more dynamic roles differentiation and network topology adaptation has instead never been studied.

Also the Acquisitional Query Processor (ACQP) of TinyDB adopts energy-efficient techniques which minimize resource usage by tuning frequency and timing of data sampling [5]. The sensor network project at USC/ISI Group has then proposed Direct Diffusion [6], an energy-efficient data dissemination paradigm which is data-centric and offers reinforcement-based adaptation and in-network data aggregation and caching. There has been some work on operator placement [7] too, but a number of challenges still remain.

Particularly interesting are issues concerning heterogeneity [8], which involve, for example, the choice of where to place operators given that the nodes in the network may have different processing power or battery life and may be experiencing different computational or communication loads. Dealing with dynamic heterogeneity, such as variations in load or energy charge, suggests some form of adaptive query optimization which has not been investigated till now. Further, the possibility to selectively send some specific execution code to few properly chosen sensors during network operation has not yet been explored.

Another key issue concerning sensor data is that they usually contain incomplete and noisy measurements of environmental phenomena, such as temperature and light, which are continuous in both time and space. This problem is coupled with different sources of noises induced by the transmission process. Then, statistical analysis and probabilistic modeling are perhaps the most suitable solutions for appropriately managing such kind of uncertain data.

Regarding modeling, the work in [9, 10] presents the BBQ system which improves TinyDB by building statistical data models which capture correlations among attributes and attribute value changes; the aim is to enable reduced sensing rates while meeting a query-specified confidence. Ken [11] equally deals with the issue of reducing power consumption, this time by using replicated dynamic probabilistic models to minimize communications in the sensor network. A framework for representing uncertainty of sensor data is presented in [12] which also proposes techniques for qualitatively and quantitatively representing answers imprecision. The work in [13] goes further and quantifies uncertainty of query results as noisy data pass through various processing stages. In these approaches, the data uncertainty is due to the sampling process [9, 10], to the low communication rate among sensors [11], or to the outdated data used for answering queries [12]. Nevertheless, none of them seems to model accuracy by exploiting information on the sensors current status and on the inherent uncertainty due to the physical measurement process.

A Flexible Data Management Middleware

Querying distributed data related to measurement readings collected by sensor devices is currently not a simple operation for users. Even for very simple informative needs, such as "The mean temperature of room A over the last hour", to formulate and execute the appropriate query can be a very difficult task. Indeed, sensor devices only react to low level commands and can not understand and process declarative queries. Thus, in order to query sensor data, users would be required to know how data is acquired, what sensors are available, what is their power status and what are the specific protocols, languages and communication modes each of the sensors supports; this would clearly be unfeasible. As a further complication, we should note that heterogeneity strongly comes into play not only from sensors but also from the devices requesting the information, which could be computers, PDAs, mobile phones, and so on.

In order to allow a flexible querying of sensor data, we envision a specifically devised Data Management Middleware (Fig. 1a) which is interposed between user devices (application layer) and sensors (data source layer) and is able to autonomously configure the communication and the operations required to each device in order to satisfy the user needs, while always reducing energy and temporal costs. In particular, the middleware should:

- communicate with user devices, providing a simple unified interface to compose declarative queries while abstracting from all technical issues related to the specific sensors and devices in use;

- parse the query and find the best (i.e. temporally and energetically efficient) execution plan, possibly rewriting the query for a balanced distributed execution;
- configure the network nodes and topology w.r.t. the specific computation and communication needs (*auto-adaptivity*);
- execute the query on the network and present the final results to the user.

Since the middleware has to support different user needs, our design provides different query types: *instant queries* (involving specific measures to be acquired at the time the query is executed, and possible calculations to perform on them, such as "return the current average noise level in the factory premises"), *event-based queries* (involving specific trigger events, such as "return the temperature of all the rooms when one of the temperatures exceeds 40C") or *lifetime-based queries* (involving lifetime clauses, such as "return the light level of the office each minute for 1 day"). Further, in all situations, the user should be able to specify the level of measure *accuracy* which is most suited to the application requirements. The middleware will thus produce a plan that best satisfies all user needs: for instance, the execution of a lifetime query should primarily focus on optimizing power consumption w.r.t. the given accuracy goal, while an instant query should also achieve a satisfying temporal efficiency.

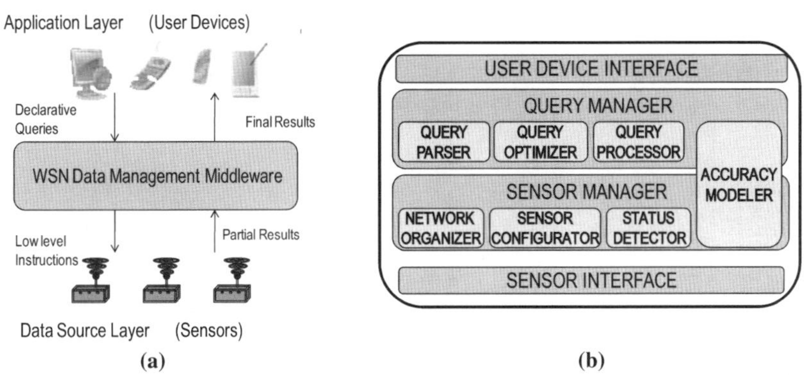

Fig. 1. WSN data management middleware overview (**a**) and inner organization detail (**b**)

In order to achieve such a vision, our middleware has been designed in a modular way. Let us analyze the composing modules, depicted in Fig. 1b, and their specific functionalities:

User device interface. It exploits a web and application server which user devices connect to. In this way, just by using a simple browser, users can easily express their requirements and compose their query with an easy to use interface; finally, the module outputs the query in declarative language form.

Query manager. This module offers all the functionalities required for understanding the query (*query parser*), producing execution plans maximizing power consumption and temporal efficiency w.r.t. the given accuracy goal (*query optimizer*), and finally executing the query and gathering its results (*query processor*). The *accuracy modeler*, whose services are shared with the sensor manager module, contributes with the probabilistic modeling of the measurement accuracy, which includes the inherent uncertainty due to the physical measurement process and the communication noise. It thus helps the query optimizer to understand the current sensors' capabilities and the query processor to answer queries based on accuracy figures associated to the data.
Sensor manager. It is in charge of managing the sensor network and configure it for specific requirements. In particular, the *network organizer* module takes care of the network topology: it interacts with the query optimizer to automatically derive the best topology for executing a query. If a network reconfiguration is advisable, the *sensor configurator* is able to enact it. Further, it can re-configure each of the sensors' communication modes (for instance streaming or on-demand mode) and even send them specific software allowing them to make ad-hoc computations, thus maximizing the exploitation of the limited capabilities of each device. Finally, the *status detector* monitors the status of the different sensors, desumes their availability, i.e. power level, signal strength, etc., and makes the query optimizer aware of it.
Sensor interface. This module takes care of handling all the actual low-level communications with the sensors, managing and understanding all the relevant protocols in use (e.g. ZigBee, Bluetooth, etc.)

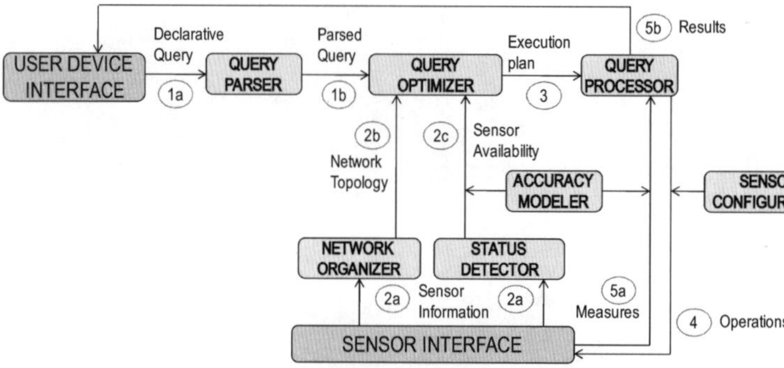

Fig. 2. How the middleware modules handle a query

Let us conclude our analysis by following in detail the interactions and the steps performed by the different middleware modules after a query is issued (Fig. 2):
Step 1: The query is issued through the user device interface and is sent to the query parser (1a), which then sends it in parsed form to the query optimizer (1b);
Step 2: The query optimizer gathers all the information needed for its computations. First, it analyzes the query and identifies the requirements, such as the kinds

of computations and functions employed and the desired accuracy level. Then, it analyzes the current status of the sensor network: this includes the network topology (2b) and the availability of each sensor (2c) (i.e. power level, signal stregth and an estimate of measure accuracy), which are derived from the sensor information acquired at the sensor interface (2a);

Step 3: The query optimizer analyzes the gathered information and produces different execution plans, evaluating which sensors to involve, what kinds of communication modes to employ, and, for complex queries, how to re-organize network topology and distribute the required computations among the available devices. This could also involve the reformulation of the query following algebraic properties (for instance, a mean could be split into sum and cardinality operations) and reprogramming the software of specific sensors. The execution plans are then sorted according to temporal and/or energetic efficiency, and the best one is sent to the query processor;

Step 4: The query processor enacts the selected execution plan, by communicating with the sensor configurator and sensor interface to configure the network and execute the query;

Step 5: The measurements and partial results are then sent back to the query processor together with their accuracy Fig. (1a); then, the query processor performs possible final computations and sends the results to the user device interface Fig. (1b).

Application Scenarios and Concluding Remarks

In this paper, we presented the results of the study we conducted in the "Mobile Semantic Self-Organizing Wireless Sensor Networks" Project which includes the preliminary proposal of a flexible data management middleware we are currently working on. Thanks to a variety of upcoming collaborations and supported by the newly established Wireless Sensor-Network Laboratory (WiSe-NetLab) of our Department and its recently ad-hoc engineered Alpha Node sensor, in the near future we plan to thoroughly test our sensor network middleware in a wide range of application scenarios. Among the planned applications, our proposed data management middleware could be used for medical care purposes with some specific hardware equipment devised for medical care. In hospitals, patients could have attached wearable wireless sensors to their bodies that would allow the doctors and nurses to continuously monitor their status. In a disaster scenario or an emergency, this technology would enable medics to more effectively care for large numbers of patients.

The proposed system can also be employed in the military field, where the same technology would allow the captain to know about his soldiers' conditions. The soldiers would have attached specific wireless sensors to their bodies, helmets and weapons, monitoring their body temperature and body position (e.g. standing, laying down, etc.).

Further possible applications of the proposed system could be in industrial working environments. In manufacturing, wireless sensors could be attached to specific points of processing pipelines in order to constantly measure the temperature, pressure etc. during the manufacturing process. Depending on the speed of the production line, very high frequency data rates should be monitored in real time and, from the performed analysis, possibly critical situations could be identified or even predicted as soon as possible. Finally, sensors could also enhance the security of the workers in dangerous environments, such as construction sites, for instance by constantly monitoring if they are wearing all their protecting gear, such as belts or helmets.

All these application scenarios will benefit from the flexibility and optimization capabilities of our middleware, each one primarily focusing on specific requirements, such as, high measurement accuracy for medical care or fast response time for military.

References

1. Akyildiz IF, Su W, Sankarasubramaniam Y, Cayirci E (2002) Wireless sensor networks: a survey. *Comput Netw* 38(4):393–422
2. Yao Y, Gehrke J (2002) The cougar approach to in-network query processing in sensor networks. *SIGMOD Record* 31(3):9–18
3. Madden S, Franklin MJ, Hellerstein JM, Hong W (2005) TinyDB: an acquisitional query processing system for sensor networks. *ACM Trans Database Syst (ACM TODS)* 30(1):122–173
4. Gupta H, Zhu X, Xu X (2009) Deductive framework for programming sensor networks. In *Proceedings of the 25th international conference on data engineering* (ICDE), Shanghai, pp 281–292
5. Madden S, Franklin MJ, Hellerstein JM, Hong W (2003) The design of an acquisitional query processor for sensor networks. In *Proceedings of the SIGMOD conference*, ACM Press, New York, pp 491–502
6. Intanagonwiwat C, Govindan R, Estrin D, Heidemann JS, Silva F (2003) Directed diffusion for wireless sensor networking. *IEEE/ACM Trans Network* 11(1):2–16
7. Bonfils, BJ, Bonnet P (2004) Adaptive and decentralized operator placement for in-network query processing. *Telecommun Syst* 26(2–4):389–409
8. Hellerstein JM, Hong W, Madden S (2003) The sensor spectrum: technology, trends, and requirements. *SIGMOD Record* 32(4):22–27
9. Deshpande A, Guestrin C, Madden S, Hellerstein JM, Hong W (2004) Model-driven data acquisition in sensor networks. In *Proceedings of the 30th International Conference on Very Large Data Bases (VLDB)*, Toronto, pp 588–599
10. Deshpande A, Guestrin C, Madden S (2005) Using probabilistic models for data management in acquisitional environments. In *Proceedings of the 2nd Biennial Conference on Innovative Data Systems Research (CIDR)*, Asilomar, pp 317–328
11. Chu D, Deshpande A, Hellerstein JM, Hong W (2006) Approximate data collection in sensor networks using probabilistic models. In *Proceedings of the 22nd international conference on data engineering (ICDE)*, Atlanta, pp 48–59
12. Cheng R, Prabhakar S (2003) Managing uncertainty in sensor database. *SIGMOD Record* 32(4):41–46

13. Diao Y, Li B, Liu A, Peng L, Sutton C, Tran T, Zink M (2009) Capturing data uncertainty in high-volume stream processing. In *Proceedings of the 4th biennial conference on innovative data systems research (CIDR)*, Asilomar

Semantic-Enriched Data Mining Techniques for Intensional Service Representation

Devis Bianchini[*], **Paolo Garza**[†], **and Elisa Quintarelli**[‡]

Abstract The adoption of Web service technologies to enable collaboration in distributed environments has been made possible by the availability of huge amount of service repositories, that, if not properly controlled, leads to information overload rather than facilitating collaboration. Data mining provides well known exploratory techniques to extract relevant and frequent information from data repositories. This paper presents a preliminary effort to apply data mining algorithms to service repositories, to properly extract useful information about services. Our purpose is two-fold: (i) we study a proper Web service representation extracted from available Web service standards, to enable the application of data mining techniques; (ii) we propose the application of data mining algorithms to infer patterns representing summarized and integrated representation of service functionalities. These patterns can be used to facilitate the formulation of service requests on the underlying repositories. Semantic heterogeneities will be also addressed, in order to improve the recall of data mining results.

Introduction

Collaboration in distributed environments is often enabled through the sharing of data and services. Data and service discovery becomes a crucial aspect to be considered for information and knowledge management systems. However, the availability of huge amount of data and service repositories, if not properly controlled, leads to information overload that may cause confusion rather than facilitating collaboration. Moreover, shared information is often described using different vocabularies, thus rising semantic heterogeneity issues. Starting from these considerations, effective techniques to extract relevant information from data and service repositories are required [4].

---

[*] Dipartimento Di Elettronica per l'Automazione, Università di Brescia, Brescia, Italy, bianchin@ing.unibs.it

[†] Dipartimento Di Automatica e Informatica, Politecnico di Torino, Torino, Italy, paolo.garza@polito.it

[‡] Dipartimento Di Elettronica e Informatica, Politecnico di Milano, Milano, Italy, quintare@elet.polimi.it

A. D'Atri et al. (eds.), *Management of the Interconnected World*,
DOI 10.1007/978-3-7908-2404-9_20,

Data mining provides well known exploratory techniques (e.g., clustering, association rules) to discover frequent properties holding in huge repositories. The application of data mining techniques to Web Service technology is relatively new (see [11] for an overview), spanning over a lot of applications, such as classification [11], clustering [10], association and sequential pattern discovery [3, 8] and deviation analysis. Classification and clustering approaches are usually applied on execution logs in order to figure out Web Service properties. In [3] authors introduce the notion of executable sequence of Web Service operations and propose an efficient mining algorithm for sequential patterns discovery. In [8] Web Service usage patterns and pattern discovery are treated through mining techniques at three different levels: user request, template and instance level.

Our contribution. In this paper we present a preliminary effort to apply data mining algorithms to identify recurrent patterns in the representation of service functionalities. In particular, data mining techniques are used to enable intensional, although approximate, representation of services. Such representation of functional service interfaces, in terms of performed operations and inputs/outputs parameters, provides decision support for the user that is looking for suitable services in huge repositories, where browsing is based on available (in general, fixed) categorization schemes, that only reflect the category in which the Web Service is classified. However, it is sometimes difficult to identify the categories that best describe a given set of services, either manually or automatically [7]. With respect to existing approaches, we do not rely only on service execution logs, but we extract a summarized representation of service repository contents to facilitate browsing. Moreover, given the inner semantic heterogeneity of the considered environment, semantic-enriched service descriptions are also adopted to improve the results of data mining application. Descriptive approaches based on faceted classification have been proposed for indexing Web Services into repositories. Web Services are classified according to a set of keywords extracted from WSDL documents and grouped into one or more (possibly orthogonal) facets, thus enabling a multi-dimensional space, where each facet corresponds to a dimension [6, 12]. However, these efforts do not consider semantic-enriched service descriptions and use classification and indexing techniques to speed up the production of extensional search answers, that are not always feasible to provide decision support when dealing with huge repositories. We try to overcome these limitations with the intensional representation of available services.

A motivating example. To show the practical impact of our proposal, an eligible application scenario is the one of an international exhibition, where a huge amount of data and services are available, including information on how to visit the exhibition and services for booking hotels or events. Let us imagine a casual user accessing for the first time the exhibition Web application in order to discover information about accommodation in the neighborhood of the exhibition. His/her intention is to book the flight directly from the Web application. Rather than retrieving a flat list of available search results, the user could be interested in quickly obtaining a first summarized intensional description such as "the 98% of flight booking services do not admit flexible departure and arrival dates". This kind of answer, although approximate, could be useful to better focus the future service requests submitted by the user; indeed, the user has to plan in advance the exact period of her staying in the city where the exhibition is located.

In the following we propose the Web Service representation to apply data mining algorithms, we show the kind of patterns we are able to extract and we present some preliminary evaluations.

Web Service Representation

Among data mining techniques, association rules are often applied to detect the co-occurrence of data items in a large amount of collected data [1]. Rules are usually represented as implications in the form $X \Rightarrow Y$, where X and Y are two arbitrary sets of data items, such that $X \cap Y = \emptyset$. The quality of an association rule is usually measured by means of *support* and *confidence*. Support corresponds to the frequency of $X \cup Y$ in the dataset, while confidence corresponds to the conditional probability of finding Y, having found X and is given by $\frac{\sup(X \cup Y)}{\sup(Y)}$.

The goal of the preliminary experiments described in this paper is to apply data mining techniques to a poorly organized dataset of services and verify which kind of association rules can be mined. Coarse-grained organization of services makes browsing more difficult. The mined rules will be exploited to support the user in browsing the dataset and finding the most suitable services. Since data mining techniques work at the syntactical level, a pre-processing phase in which service descriptions are semantically enriched through ontologies should improve the set of identified association rules.

The first step consists in extracting a proper Web Service representation from existing standards. According to the service-oriented architecture, services are described through their WSDL (Web Service Description Language) document [5]. The WSDL standard distinguishes between the service abstract interface, that describes a service through the service operations and inputs/outputs parameters, and the message formats and data types for service invocation (*service bindings*). To make the service available to consumers, service providers register them in a Universal Description, Discovery and Integration (UDDI[1]) registry. In the UDDI, services are associated with their corresponding WSDL document and are classified according to pre-defined, coarse-grained categorization schemes (e.g., UNSPSC, NAiCS). However, WSDL and UDDI only provide keyword-based matching to

[1] `http://uddi.org/pubs/lru_UDDI_Tech-nical_paper.pdf`

identify suitable services [13]. Well-known efforts have been introduced to add semantics to Web service descriptions, such as OWL-S [9], where operation and I/O parameter names are annotated with ontological concepts. OWL-S models a service through three elements: (i) a *service profile*, that describes what the service does, that is, its functional interface through the service name, service inputs/outputs, pre-conditions (that must be satisfied before service execution) and post-conditions (that are satisfied after service execution); (ii) a *process model*, that describes how the service operates in terms of its internal workflow; (iii) a *service grounding*, that defines the formats and data types for service invocation. The service profile contains relevant information for service discovery. The process model is used for service composition. Service grounding is used to relate the OWL-S representation to the corresponding WSDL document.

We apply data mining techniques to service representation extracted from WSDL and OWL-S specifications. Each service is represented as a set of data items, that must be considered together and collectively constitute what we call a *service itemset*. Each data item is a pair in the form `(service-element,value)`, e.g., `(serviceOperation,bookHotel)` or `(serviceInput, paymentMethod)`. For each service, we extract the following items:

- a data item `(serviceCategory,value)`, representing the category associated to the service, extracted from the UDDI registry;
- a data item `(serviceName,value)`, extracted from the WSDL/OWL-S document associated with the service;
- one or more data items `(serviceOperation,value)`, representing service operations, extracted from the OWL-S process model;
- one or more data items `(serviceInput,value)`, representing service inputs, extracted from the OWL-S service profile;
- one or more data items `(serviceOutput,value)`, representing service outputs, extracted from the OWL-S service profile.

For what concerns operation and I/O parameter names, ontological concepts associated to them are considered. Semantic annotation unifies element names, thus enabling better results after the application of pattern discovery techniques. Starting from the representation of service items, co-occurrences of data items are identified, as explained in the next section.

Data Mining Application to Web Service Representation

The extracted rules are frequent combinations of the data items in the service dataset. To perform our experiments, we have used a public available dataset[2] with services belonging to seven general categories, namely communication, economy, education, food, medical, travel, weapon. We identified two main classes of rules.

Class 1 – Rules describing the correlation of the outputs and the inputs of services. In this first class, we mine rules of the form:

$\{(serviceOutput_i, value_i)\} \rightarrow \{(serviceInput_j, value_j)\}$ (support, confidence)

This class of rules can be used whenever we desire to gain knowledge about the (frequent) inputs required for services, when the desired outputs are known. Examples of Class 1 rules are:

{(serviceOutput,Hotel)} => {(serviceInput,Country)} (1.09, 47.82%)
{(serviceOutput,Hotel)} => {(serviceInput,City)} (1.28, 56.52%)

describing the fact that, when searching for services providing information about hotels, the user has to specify the information about the desired location. In particular, with a confidence 47.82% the location is identified by the country, whereas with a confidence 56.52% by the city. The sum of the confidence values of the two rules is strictly greater than 100% because some services require to specify both the country and the city of the hotel to search. These rules help the user to select the right service by knowing in advance which kind of information must be frequently provided as input to obtain the desired outputs.

Class 2 – Rules describing the correlation between a service category and the output (or input) offered by services in that category. Such rules are of the form:

(ServiceCategory, name) $\rightarrow \{(serviceOutput_i, value_i)\}$ (support, confidence)
(ServiceCategory, name) $\rightarrow \{(serviceInput_i, value_i)\}$ (support, confidence)

This second class can be used to improve the knowledge about services offered by a very general category, in terms of their inputs and/or outputs. Examples of Class 2 rules regarding services in the "education" category are the following:

[2] http://projects.semwebcentral.org/projects/owls-tc/

(serviceCategory,education) => {(serviceOutput,Funding)} (1.00, 3.52%)
(serviceCategory,education) => {(serviceOutput,SkilledOccupation)} (3.75, 13.38%)
(serviceCategory,education) => {(serviceOutput,company)} (1.00, 3.52%)
(serviceCategory,education) => {(serviceOutput,Scholarship)} (2.17, 7.75%)
(serviceCategory,education) => {(serviceOutput,Publication)} (1.09, 3.87%)
(serviceCategory,education) => {(serviceOutput,Profession)} (2.76, 9.86%)
(serviceCategory,education) => {(serviceOutput,Book)} (1.38, 4.93%)

These rules can help the user for discovering the services offered in the education class and their frequencies; e.g., he can find services about books, scholarships, etc. In fact, the user usually does not know in advance which are the categories that contain the right services; this is particularly true for coarse-grained classifications. Class 2 rules guide the user towards the best categories given the desired service outputs.

We imagine an advanced search engine acting upon the service repository that is able to provide such kind of summarized information. By clicking on the provided results, the corresponding services can be displayed. The user can select the subset of services of interest by considering the available information.

Preliminary Experimental Results

We performed a set of preliminary experiments to analyze the applicability of the proposed approach on a real repository; we have considered the number and the kind of mined rules and the execution time. The experiments have been performed on a public available repository composed of 1,013 services, associated with their OWL-S descriptions. OWL-S service descriptions have been parsed by means of an ad-hoc XQuery script, while a publicly available version of Apriori[3] tool has been used to mine the frequent association rules. All the experiments have been performed on a 3.2 GHz Pentium IV system with 2 GB RAM, running Kubuntu 6.10.

The association rule mining algorithm has been applied by setting the minimum support threshold to 0.5%. The total execution time of the mining process is 10.2 s and the total number of mined rules is 17,084. We analyzed in details the Class 1 rules (90 results) and Class 2 ones (91 results) that have been identified. Some of the extracted rules are those already reported in the previous section. We focus here on the following example:

---

[3] `http://www.adrem.ua.ac.be/~goethals/software/`

Class 1
{(serviceOutput,Book)} => {(serviceInput,Title)} (0.59, 25.00%) {(serviceOutput,Book)} => {(serviceInput,Author)} (0.49, 20.83%) {(serviceOutput,Book)} => {(serviceInput,Publication-Number)} (0.49, 20.83%)

Class 2
(serviceCategory,economy) => {(serviceOutput,Book)} (1.00, 2.79%) (serviceCategory,education) => {(serviceOutput,Book)} (1.38, 4.93%)

The extracted rules highlight some (previously unknown) interesting characteristics of the analyzed repository. The set of rules allows the end user to obtain new knowledge that can be profitably exploited to perform more easily service search.

The rules reported in this section can be exploited, for example, to search for services concerning books. Let suppose a user is interested in buying a new book. In order to find a new book she needs first to find the most appropriate book service for her purpose. Service categorizations not always reflect what the user has in mind while searching for something and category browsing for large dataset is often time-consuming. The user can exploit the Class 2 rules to focus her research exclusively on the service categories providing book services. This information allows her to find more quickly the service of her interest.

Moreover, the user has usually not a priori knowledge about which inputs are required by the available book selection services. Since the user probably knows only partial information about the book she is searching (e.g., the name of the author, but not the book title), she may need to learn which inputs are required by the available services. By exploiting the Class 1 rules, she can acquire the needed information. Three different service types are available: the first one requires as input the book title, the second one the author name and the last one the publication number.

Conclusion and Future Work

In this paper we proposed the application of data mining techniques to service repositories to properly extract useful information about services. Data mining algorithms have been applied to infer patterns representing summarized and integrated representation of service functionalities. These patterns provide succinct (intensional) knowledge on available services to facilitate the formulation of service requests on the underlying repositories. Semantic service descriptions have been adopted to solve semantic heterogeneities and to increase the recall of data mining results. A preliminary evaluation on available datasets has also been presented, showing the effectiveness of the proposed techniques although the coarse-grained organization of services in the available datasets. Future efforts will be devoted to the extension of traditional service repositories (e.g., UDDI) with the summarized representation of registry contents, in order to provide novel query languages for service retrieval. Evaluation of the proposed approach will be performed on wider collections of services, expressed through other languages for semantic service description (e.g., WSDL-S [2]). A more in depth integration of semantic Web tools in data mining algorithms will be also studied.

References

1. Agrawal R, Srikant R (1994) Fast algorithms for mining association rules in large databases. In: *Proceedings of the 20th international conference on very large data bases* (pp. 487–499), Morgan Kaufmann Publishers Inc
2. Akkiraju R, Farrell J, Miller J, Nagarajan M, Schmidt M, Sheth A, Verma K (2005) Web service semantics – WSDL-S. A joint UGA-IBM technical note, v1.0, `http://lsdis.cs.uga.edu/Projects/METEOR-S/WSDL-S`
3. Asbagh M, Abolhassani H (2007) Web service usage mining: mining for executable sequence. In *Proceedings of the 7th WSEAS international conference on applied computer science* (pp. 266–271), Venice, Italy
4. Baralis E, Garza P, Quintarelli E, Tanca L (2004) Answering queries on XML data by means of associations rules. In *Current trends in database technology*, vol 3268. Springer, Heidelberg
5. Christensen E, Curbera F, Meredith G, Weerawarana S (2001) Web service description language (WSDL). World wide web consortium (W3C), `http://www.w3.org/TR/2001/NOTE-wsdl-20010315`
6. Fluit C, Sabou M, van Harmelen F (2005) *Ontology-based information visualization: towards semantic web applications. Visualizing the semantic web*, 2nd edn. Springer, New York
7. Globe C, Wroe C, Sabou M, Mishne G (2005) Learning domain ontologies for web service descriptions: an experiment in bioinformatics. In *Proceedings of the 14th international world wide web conference (WWW'05)* (pp. 190–198), ACM Press, Chiba
8. Liang QA, Chung JY, Miller S, Ouyang Y (2006) Service pattern discovery of web service mining in web service registry-repository. In *Proceedings of the IEEE international conference on e-business engineering* (pp. 286–293), Shanghai
9. Martin D, Burstein M, Hobbs J, Lassila O, McDermott D, McIlraith S, Narayanan S, Paolucci M, Parsia B, Payne T, Sirin E, Srinivasan N, Sycara K (2004) *OWL-S: semantic markup for web services*, v1.1
10. Nayak R, Lee B (2007) Web service discovery with additional semantics and clustering. In: *Proceedings of IEEE/WIC/ACM international conference on web intelligence* (pp. 555–558), Silicon Valley, USA
11. Nayak R (2008) Data mining in web services discovery and monitoring. *Int J Web Serv Res* 5(1):63–81
12. Rouached M, Gaaloul W, van der Aalst WMP, Bhiri S, Godart C (2006) Web service mining and verification of properties: an approach based on event calculus. In *Proceedings of Cooperative Information Systems conference (CoopIS'06)* (pp. 408–425), Monterrey, Mexico
13. Sabou M, Pan J (2007) Towards improving web service repositories through semantic web techniques. Journal of Web Semantics, 5(2):142–150

Semantic Search of Distributed Information and Knowledge

Devis Bianchini[*], **Valeria De Antonellis**[†], **and Michele Melchiori**[‡]

Abstract Services are more and more provided for semantic search of different types of information and knowledge (resources) from multiple heterogeneous sources, by gaining platform independence and transparent access. The growth of service provisioning and the advent of advanced service registries have led to the design of sophisticated techniques and tools to retrieve services apt to access required resources. This paper describes a computer aided methodology SELF-SERVICE based on formal service specifications, scoring mechanism and thresholds, to support – in a user-transparent and cost effective way – semantic search on multiple heterogeneous sources in P2P environments.

Introduction

Services are more and more provided for semantic search of different types of information and knowledge (resources) from multiple heterogeneous sources, by providing platform independence and transparent access. Each Web service is described by means of its functional interface, where we distinguish among inputs and outputs. Inputs correspond to data to be provided by the user to access the sources, while outputs represent search results, provided through the execution of the service. The growth of service provisioning and the advent of advanced service registries have led to the design of sophisticated techniques and tools to retrieve usable services. When semantic search is performed in open environments, such as P2P networks, characteristic aspects to be considered are the high dynamicity, the absence of a common resource conceptualization and the presence of different service registries, which are autonomous and heterogeneous. This paper

[*] Dipartimento Di Elettronica per l'Automazione, Università degli Studi di Brescia, 25123 Brescia, Italy, bianchin@ing.unibs.it

[†] Dipartimento Di Elettronica per l'Automazione, Università degli Studi di Brescia, 25123 Brescia, Italy, deantone@ing.unibs.it

[‡] Dipartimento Di Elettronica per l'Automazione, Università degli Studi di Brescia, 25123 Brescia, Italy, melchior@ing.unibs.it

A. D'Atri et al. (eds.), *Management of the Interconnected World*,
DOI 10.1007/978-3-7908-2404-9_21, © Springer-Verlag Berlin Heidelberg 2010

describes SELF-SERVICE, a computer aided methodology for semantic search of digital resources in P2P networks, based on the efficient retrieval and the effective suggestion of suitable services. SELF-SERVICE relies on a formal specification for services registered across a Distributed Service Registry (DSR) in a P2P environment, and exploits service semantic descriptions to retrieve and suggest services apt to satisfy user semantic searches.

The proposed methodology consists of four phases: (i) semantic description of services in the DSR; (ii) definition of semantic links between similar services published on different registries; (iii) dynamic evolution of the DSR and change assimilation; (iv) semantic search interactive specification, by supporting user in "self-service" selection of ranked suitable services from the DSR. The SELF-SERVICE approach, based on formal service specifications, scoring mechanism and thresholds, can support – in a user-transparent and cost effective way – semantic search on multiple heterogeneous sources in P2P environments. The methodology is strongly based on semantic description formalisms and semantic matching criteria and techniques that have been previously developed for service discovery [1, 2] and that are summarized in this paper. The aim of this paper is to present a general methodological framework for semantic search and, in particular, we introduce the novel user SELF-SERVICE selection approach for semantic search interactive specification.

The paper is organized as follows: firstly the reference scenario is introduced; then the SELF-SERVICE methodological phases are illustrated in detail; a brief discussion of existing approaches in literature is given; finally, some conclusive considerations are given.

Reference Scenario

As a reference example, consider the classical case of a traveler who wants to organize a week holiday in one of the European cities and is searching for a low-cost flight. First, she looks for available low-cost flights and, on the basis of the collected offers, decides which city to visit. Secondly, she has to find a cheap accommodation for the final destination of the journey. To support answering this kind of requests, the SELF-SERVICE approach helps the traveler to discover suitable services, to find availability and prices of flights and hotel booking facilities and display retrieved services ordered by relevance. The traveler, uses the DSR to submit its request. In particular, the considered user search, in our approach, can be supported in two ways: (i) given a request for low-cost-flight booking services submitted on a peer registry, say Rx, not only local services of Rx can be suggested, but also services, with similar interfaces, registered on different registries; (ii) once the user selects a service for low-cost-flight booking, say Sx, the system is able to suggest possible related services (accepting as INPUT what is OUTPUT of Sx), as for example hotel booking services. In SELF-SERVICE, the first kind of search is supported by establishing semantic links between similar services (functional similarity links). The second functionality is supported by establishing semantic links between services that can be coupled for composition (coupling similarity links).

The SELF-SERVICE Methodology

Phases of the methodology are shown in Fig. 1 and described in the following sections.

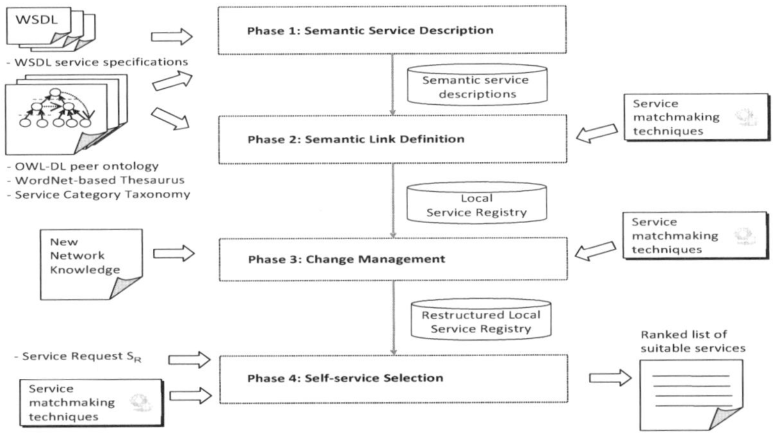

Fig. 1. Phases of the SELF-SERVICE methodology

Semantic Service Description

Starting from the WSDL specifications of services (that represent functional service interfaces), this phase produces semantic-enriched service descriptions. The inputs required for this methodological are the following ones.

WSDL service specifications. To keep backward compatibility with existing service description technologies, the representation of functional interface of services is based on the WSDL specification. According to this specification, the service functional interface is identified by a set of input and output parameters. Services are advertised in the UDDI registry of the peer.

OWL-DL peer ontology. WSDL specification provides service functional descriptions from a syntactic viewpoint, but to automate service discovery semantic ambiguities must be solved. To this purpose, each peer has a domain ontology, formally expressed in OWL-DL. Service I/O parameters are associated to concepts defined in the peer ontology.

Service category taxonomy. According to the UDDI standard, published services are categorized through service categories, extracted from available standard taxonomies (e.g., UNSPSC, NAiCS).

The outputs produced by the first methodological phase are semantic descriptions of service functional interfaces.

Semantic service descriptions. Semantic descriptions are obtained by semantically annotating the service I/O parameters described in the WSDL-S documents with suitable concepts of the peer ontology.

Semantic Links Definition

Given the semantic service descriptions in each local registry (*peer local knowledge*), the aim of the second phase is to establish semantic links towards similar services registered on other peers of the P2P network (*peer network knowledge*). This phase accepts as inputs the semantic service descriptions produced in the previous phase, the OWL-DL peer ontology and the Service Category Taxonomy. Moreover, this phase requires the following additional inputs.

WordNet-based Thesaurus. Since we do not constrain registries in the DSR to adopt a common shared conceptualization, different peer ontologies can be used. To bridge the gap between slightly different terminologies, peer ontologies are extended with a Thesaurus [1] of terms related by terminological relationships to the names of ontological concepts. The Thesaurus is built from the WordNet lexical system.

Service matchmaking techniques. These techniques are used to compare semantic service descriptions and have been detailed in [1]. They are based on the OWL-DL peer ontology, the Service Category Taxonomy and the Thesaurus and combine deductive-based and similarity-based service matchmaking models. The aim is to provide matching information that *qualify* the kind of match (total or partial) and *quantify* the degree of similarity between similar services. Matchmaking techniques are applied to establish semantic links between similar services and obtain the peer network knowledge.

Peer network knowledge. Two kinds of semantic links between a local service S1 and a remote one S2 can be established:

- *functional similarity links*, denoted with S1≈S2, to relate similar semantic service descriptions, that is, services with similar functionalities;
- *coupling similarity links*, denoted with S1→S2, to assert that outputs of S1 are semantically related to the inputs of S2; S1 and S2 are defined as *coupled* if they do not match but they can be taken into account as suitable for composition.

Each peer maintains an OWL-DL representation of the network knowledge. Local and network knowledge constitute a semantic overlay built and maintained over the underlying logical P2P network. In Fig. 2, the overall structure of the Distributed Service Registry is shown: in the logical overlay, peer registries are connected through the P2P network and in the semantic overlay, semantic service descriptions and semantic links are established.

In the next sections, we explain how semantic links are maintained and exploited within the DSR.

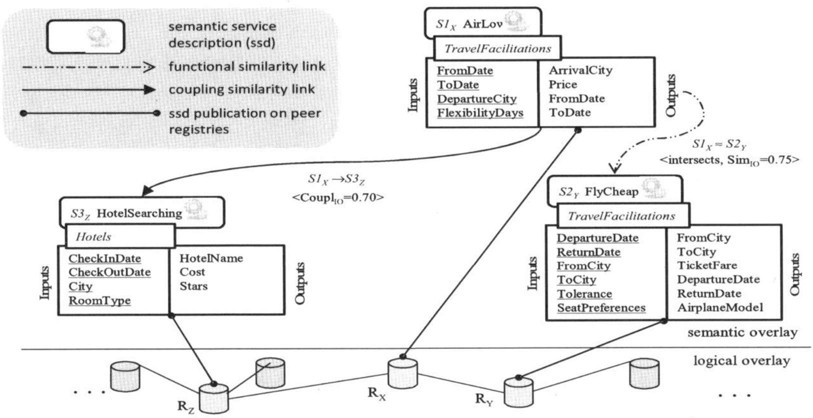

Fig. 2. Distributed service registry

Change Management

The purpose of this phase is to keep updated the network knowledge of a registry in the DSR with respect to dynamic changes occurring in the network of peer registries. Different situations are possible: (i) new peer registries are detected at the logical level; (ii) new services are published on known registries.

The collection of knowledge about new available services on the network is triggered by:

- periodical sending of *probe requests* to registries connected on the network;
- discovery at logical level of new available registries on the network.

This phase is therefore responsible of detecting the availability of new services on other registries and to update consequently the network knowledge assimilating the discovered changes. A probe request is sent for each locally available service and contains the semantic description of the service. When a peer Ry receives the probe request, matchmaking techniques are applied to the request and each semantic service description on Ry. For each similar or coupled service, a reply is sent back to the registry from which the request came. Semantic links are established for each received reply and involved registries become *semantic neighbors*. Semantic links towards a peer registry are removed if a given number of service requests sent to it are not answered.

SELF-SERVICE Selection

This phase is devoted to semantic search interactive specification, by supporting user in "self-service" selection of ranked suitable services from the DSR. Semantic links are here exploited. The SELF-SERVICE selection of suitable services is further organized in five steps, as shown in Fig. 3 and described in the following.

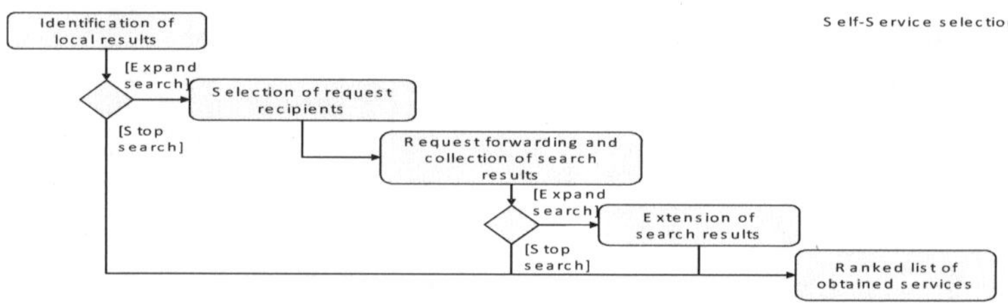

Fig. 3. Steps of the SELF-SERVICE selection phase

(A) *Identification of local results.* In the first step, the search request S_R submitted to a registry Rx is matched against the local semantic service descriptions of Rx and a list $MS(S_R)$ of matching service descriptions is obtained. If local results are not completely satisfying (i.e., partial match), S_R can be forwarded to the other nodes of the DSR to extend the list of matching services (first *expand search* branch).

(B) *Selection of request recipients.* The request S_R can be forwarded to the other nodes of the DSR to extend the list of matching services. To prune the set of registries to be investigated, thus avoiding time-consuming distributed service search, peers *semantic neighbors* of Rx that are related to services $Sx \in MS(S_R)$ through functional similarity links (of Rx) are selected as request recipients according to the forwarding policies on the basis of the matching information labeling the semantic links. According to a minimal forwarding policy, search over the network stops when matching services which fully satisfy the request have been found. Exhaustive policies can be applied following the same rules, but the search does not stop when matching services that fully satisfy the request are found: the request S_R is forwarded to semantic neighbors to find other services that could present, for example, better non functional features. In [2] a detailed presentation of different forwarding rules based on functional similarity semantic links is provided.

(C) *Request forwarding and collection of search results.* Once the candidate semantic neighbors have been selected, the search request S_R is forwarded towards them in order to obtain required search results on the DSR. Each semantic neighbor receiving the request checks for locally available matching services: if matches have been found, the semantic neighbor replies to the registry Rx, from which the request started and it repeats the forwarding procedure based on its semantic neighbors. Search results are collected and ranked according to their similarity value with the request S_R.

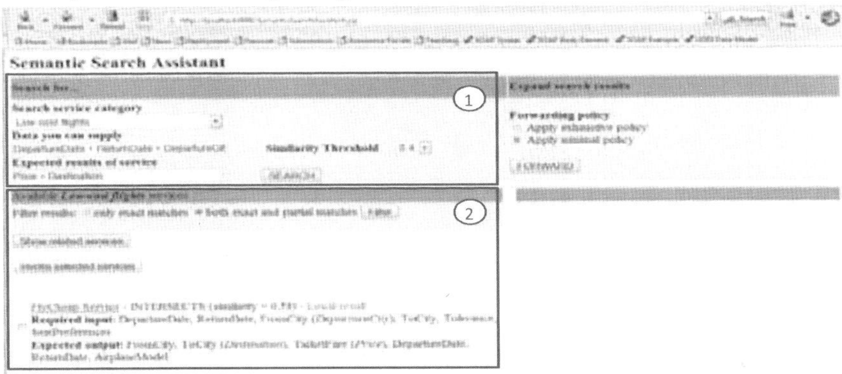

Fig. 4. Semantic search assistant web interface: (1) submission of request; (2) identification of local results

(D) *Extension of search results.* When the user selects one of the search results, coupling similarity links can be exploited to propose additional results regarding those services that can offer additional functionalities with respect to the user request (second *expand search* branch in Fig. 3). As an example, if the flight booking `AirLow` service (Fig. 2) is selected, the system exploits the coupling semantic link `AirLow`→`HotelSearching` to propose the coupled `HotelSearching` service to the user as a complementary service with respect to `AirLow`.

To automate this phase, a Semantic Search Assistant (SSA) has been defined, with a user-oriented interface (Fig. 4). The use of semantic links ensures scalable system performances by guiding in the selection of suitable registries in the DSR for service request propagation.

Related Work

Various approaches for service discovery in distributed environments have been proposed in literature. Some of these architectures require a centralized structure as in METEOR-S [3] and ad-UDDI [4]. With respect to these approaches, SELF-SERVICE does not require a centralized organization for service classification, for adding or removing peers, or for managing neighboring relationships among peers. In this way, it avoids system bottleneck and presence of a single point of failure. An approach for service discovery based on a two layers semantic overlay over peers network is proposed in [5], where offered services are semantically described according to peer local ontologies. Peers offering services in the same domain are clustered to form SemSets. In each SemSet, a coordinator peer is elected. Coordinators of semantically related SemSets (e.g., Rental and Transport) are associated through semantic relationships that are exploited for inter-SemSet query routing. With respect to SELF-SERVICE [5], relies on SemSet coordinators for service discovery and adopts a coarse-grained routing, that is, among SemSets. Our approach gives a contribution to scalable service discovery in P2P network without assuming the presence of centralized structures/coordinators nor a priory agreement on shared conceptualization among peers.

Conclusions

In this paper we proposed SELF-SERVICE, a computer aided methodology for semantic search of resources in P2P networks, based on the efficient retrieval and the effective suggestion of suitable services. SELF-SERVICE relies on a formal specification of services registered across a Distributed Service Registry (DSR). Some modules automating single functionalities of the methodology have been developed: the service matchmaker, to automate matchmaking functionalities that support the most methodology phases; the evolution manager, to update network knowledge at the semantic layer of the DSR; the semantic search assistant that supports the self-service selection with part of the interface shown in Fig. 4. These modules must be integrated to properly support the whole methodology. Experimentations on some DSR building blocks have been presented in [2] and [3]. The methodology will be validated on real case scenarios.

Acknowledgments This work has been partially supported by the TEKNE FIRB Project (http://www.tekne-project.it/), funded by the Italian Ministry of Education, University and Research.

References

1. Bianchini D, De Antonellis V, Melchiori M (2008) Flexible semantic-based service matchmaking and discovery. *World Wide Web J* 11(2):227–251
2. Bianchini D, De Antonellis V, Melchiori M, Denise Salvi (2008) A semantic overlay for service discovery across web information systems. In *Proceedings of 9th international conference on web information systems engineering (WISE'08)*. Auckland, New Zealand, pp 292–306
3. Verma K, Sivashanmugam K, Sheth A, Patil A, Oundhakar S, Miller J (2005) METEOR-S WSDI: a scalable infrastructure of registries for semantic publication and discovery of web services. *J Inf Technol Manage Special Issue on Universal Global Integration* 6(1):17–39

4. Du Z, Huai J, Liu Y (2005) Ad-UDDI: An active and distributed service registry. In *Proceedings of 6th international workshop on technologies for e-services (TES'05)*. Trondheim, Norway, pp 58–71
5. Sapkota B, Nazir S, Vitvar T, Toma I, Vasiliu L, Hauswirth M (2007) Semantic overlay for scalable service discovery. In *International conference on collaborative computing: networking, applications and worksharing (CollaborateCom 2007)*, Orlando, pp 387–391

Exploring Strategic Indexes by Semantic OLAP Operators

Claudia Diamantini* **and Domenico Potena†**

Abstract At strategic and decision levels of information systems, information models are defined by a set of high-level measurable performance indexes, calculated by composition of more basic pieces of information, and aggregated along a number of different dimensions. Although the multidimensional model is able to effectively capture the aggregative characteristics of strategic information, it fails to represent its compound nature. Hence, index semantics is not completely specified and OLAP operators allow only to analyze indexes through the different aggregation dimensions. In this paper we discuss a novel set of OLAP operators resulting from a previously defined model for the semantic annotation of a Data Warehouse (DW) schema. These operators perform the analogous of drill down operators on index components instead of dimensions, both at intensional and extensional level. This means that both the definition of an index in terms of components and compositions operators and the actual values of the components can be hierarchically explored on-line, giving final users better ways to understand the meaning of the complex information encoded in a DW, its correctness, and more powerful tools to analyze it. A prototype implementing the proposal is presented.

Introduction

Anybody who has been present at a budget discussion in a firm, or has watched a political debate about government results, has experienced at least once a dispute on "numbers". Not rarely, the dispute depends on different definitions of measures used for the evaluation of results. To give an example, somebody states that the amount of investment in higher education in Italy is too low (far below EU average), while others state it is too high. Digging into this apparent contradiction, one discovers that both evaluate the amount of investment as the *ratio* between the

* Dipartimento di Ingegneria Informatica, Gestionale e dell'Automazione, Università Politecnica delle Marche, Ancona, Italy, diamantini@diiga.univpm.it
† Dipartimento di Ingegneria Informatica, Gestionale e dell'Automazione, Università Politecnica delle Marche, Ancona, Italy, potena@diiga.univpm.it

A. D'Atri et al. (eds.), *Management of the Interconnected World*,
DOI 10.1007/978-3-7908-2404-9_22,

total expenditure and the student population, but whereas the former considers as student population those officially enrolled in a course, the latter wants to *subtract* from this population those who are not actually attending a course. Without dwelling on which is the right measure, this example wants to enlighten the fact that, when dealing with complex measurable performance indexes, the definition of the categories or concepts involved in is a tricky issue, and it cannot leave out of consideration their compound nature, that is the fact that they are calculated from others more basic categories.

Traditionally, the multidimensional data model is adopted to represent performance indexes and to enable flexible analysis by means of OLAP operators. The multidimensional model captures the aggregative nature of performance indexes, defining datacubes as multi-level, multidimensional database with aggregate data at multiple granularities [1]. It does not take the compound nature of indexes into consideration. As a consequence, OLAP operators allow only to analyze indexes through the different aggregation dimensions.

In this paper we discuss a novel set of OLAP operators enabled by a model of semantic enrichment of Data Warehouse (DW) schema previously introduced by the authors [2]. These operators perform the analogue of drill down/roll-up OLAP operators, but they act on index *components*, instead of dimensions, both at intensional and extensional level. This means that both the definition of an index in terms of components and composition operators and the actual values of the components can be hierarchically explored on-line, giving final users better ways to understand the meaning of the complex information encoded in a DW, its correctness, and more powerful tools to analyze it.

The need for a semantic enrichment of DW is recently recognized in the literature as a means to fill the gap between the technical and managerial views of indexes. Results from traditional semantic web research have been applied to DW to represent hierarchical relations among datacubes for data-information integration [3], to support datacube design [4, 5] or ETL process design [6] and to improve OLAP functionalities [7, 1]. Our work extends previous researches since semantic enrichment by means of traditional ontologies is extended with the use of a mathematical ontology supporting the definition of the actual index calculus. This allows us to take all advantages deriving from the classical definition of index semantics to support integration and design activities, plus others deriving from the knowledge of "operational" relations among concepts. In practice, indexes are no more viewed as atomic elements of which we can know the meaning in logical terms; rather they appear as structured concepts, having mathematical relations with other concepts. Among the advantage of this approach, the ability to explore indexes in more flexible and deeper ways by the OLAP operators described in this paper, and also the capability to enhance integration techniques by mathematical formulas manipulation.

In the next Section we give a general overview of the proposed architecture and the semantic annotation model. In subsequently Section, details on the semantic OLAP operators are given.

System Overview

This Section is devoted to give an overview of our approach, discussing the DW annotation model and the main modules of the system devoted to the management of annotations and implementation of semantic OLAP operators (see Fig. 1).

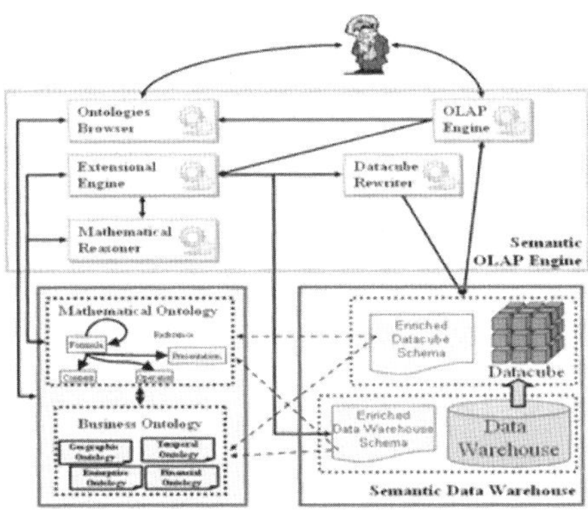

Fig. 1. The system architecture

In the Figure, we can distinguish three main elements: the *ontologies*, the *Semantic Data Warehouse* (SDW), and the *Semantic OLAP Engine* (SOE).

The SDW is formed, as usual, by a Data Warehouse and its datacubes. Measures, levels and dimensions of both datacubes and DW schemata are semantically annotated by means of references to ontological concepts describing the meaning of elements in the domain. In particular we refer to two classes of ontologies: *Business Ontology* and *Mathematical Ontology (MathOnto)*. The former contains concepts of the application domain, while the latter describes mathematical formulas by which the SDW elements are computed. The division of concepts and formulas is needed because domain ontologies, typically expressed in description logics (DLs), are not able to semantically describe a mathematical formula, with its operators and operands. Note that, in order to describe the application domain several ontologies have been considered, to represent the different kinds of information (temporal, geographic, financial and economical, enterprise-related) that typically appear in DWs. We will give more details on the annotation model in the following subsection. Here we like to note that, although information contained in datacubes is strictly related to information in the DW, semantic annotation is realized for datacubes and DW schemata separately. The use of two different mappings is needed because (1) a datacube is a view of the whole DW, so only some elements of the DW are contained in the datacube schema; (2) viceversa, a datacube schema could be formed by measures of the DW as well as new indexes defined as combination of measures of the DW, but actually not belonging to its schema. Note also that, although for sake of simplicity Fig. 1 shows only one datacube, the annotation model and the proposed system are able to work with any number of datacubes defined over the DW.

The SOE is devoted to provide analysis functionalities by means of both classical and semantic OLAP operators. In particular, the *OLAP Engine* module interprets the semantically enriched schema of a datacube, allowing users to perform semantics-based navigations, in the form of *extensional index drill-down/roll-up*. To this end, the OLAP Engine exploits the *Ontology Browser* to query ontologies and extract concepts, properties and relations. This is mainly devoted to obtain intensional definitions of dimensions and measure. The *Extensional Engine* and *Mathematical Reasoner* are devoted to implement reasoning capabilities on the structure of an element, mainly measures, and hierarchically extract from datacubes and DW the values of measure sub-components. Finally, the *Datacube Rewriter* is devoted to rebuild a datacube structure for visualization. We will come back to the description of both semantic OLAP operators and modules introduced for their execution in the third section.

The Semantic Annotation Model

The model we present in this work for the semantic annotation of a Data Warehouse, extends the model we proposed in [2] for the annotation of a datacube. The main idea is that the semantics of a multidimensional schema is made explicit by linking each schema element (i.e. dimensions and measures) to both a concept in the Business Ontology, and a *Formula* (i.e. an instance of the MathOnto). Since Business Ontology is typically represented in DLs, we assume it is written in OWL standard, while we define a new XML-based language for the MathOnto, whose formulas cannot be represented in DLs. Figure 2 gives an example of such a language for the measure *Return on Investment (ROI)*.

A formula is described by the name, its presentation and the formal description of its operators and operands. The *formula presentation* describes how the formula should be visualized, and it is based on the presentation part of the MathML standard [8]. In the example, the ROI presentation is not reported due to lack of space, but it would be rendered as: $ROI = ROS \cdot \frac{net\_income}{total\_costs}$. The *formal description* of operators and operands is divided in three parts: (a) content, (b) operators definition and (c) references. The content exploits the content part of the MathML standard to express the scope of operators. The formal operators definition is given by exploiting the OpenMath ontology [9]. Finally, references are used to give the formal definition of operands. This is in turn given by the two attributes *BO* and *MO* that link to an element of the Business and of the Mathematical Ontology respectively. For example, the operand named *total_costs* is associated to the concept *PR_totalcost* in the Financial Ontology and to the formula *total_costs* in the MathOnto. Hence, each operand is described both by referring to a concept that helps to understand its meaning (e.g. *total_costs* is a cost, which is a property of a project, ...), and recursively by a link to another formula that explains how the operand is computed (e.g. *total_costs* is linked to its formula, that has a name, a presentation, and so on). In this way a *tree* of formulas is built. Finally, the formula itself can be contextualized in the domain by referring to a concept of the Business Ontology by exploiting the *BO* attribute. For lack of space we do not further detail the annotation model, but refer interested reader to [2], where some examples are also available.

```
<formula>
  <name BO="financialOntology.owl#PR ROI">ROI</name>
  <semantics>
    <annotation-xml encoding="MathML-Presentation">
    ...
    </annotation-xml>
    <annotation-xml encoding="MathML-Content">
            <apply>
                <eq/>
                    <ci> ROI </ci>
                    <apply>
                        <times/>
                            <ci> ROS </ci>
                            <apply>
                                <divide/>
                                    <ci> net income </ci>
                                    <ci> total costs </ci>
                            </apply>
                    </apply>
            </apply>
    </annotation-xml>
    <annotation-xml encoding="OpenMath">
            <OMA xmlns="http://www.openmath.org/OpenMath">
                <OMS cd="arith1" name="times"/>
                <OMS cd="arith1" name="divide"/>
                <OMS cd="relation1" name="eq"/>
    </annotation-xml>
  </semantics>
  <reference>
    <obj BO="financialOntology.owl#PR ROS" MO="ReturnOnSales" name="ROS">
    <obj BO="financialOntology.owl#sales" MO="net income" name="net income">
    <obj BO="financialOntology.owl#PR total cost" MO="total costs" name="total costs">
  </reference>
</formula>
```

Fig. 2. The formula of ROI in the mathematical ontology

Since each schema element in the datacube and the DW is linked to concepts in the two ontologies, the overall system turns out to be easily *navigable*: starting from any datacube index we can move through its formula, and recursively through formulas defining its operands, down to retrieve the measures into the DW that have been exploited to derive the datacube index. This is the mechanism at the basis of the intensional and extensional index drill-down/roll-up.

Semantic OLAP Operators

Exploiting the proposed semantic annotation model, we are able to define new functionalities supporting the user: from semantic OLAP operators to mechanisms for building on-line datacubes. In particular, we introduced two novel OLAP operators:

intensional and *extensional index drill-down/roll-up*. The former, provides functionalities for browsing the ontological descriptions of an index, allowing the manager to better understand the meaning the index assumes in the business domain, how the index is computed (i.e. its formula), the relationships between the index and its components (i.e. other indexes in the formula), and so forth.

On the other hand, the extensional operator, as classical OLAP drill-down/roll-up, transforms the schema of the datacube by allowing to expand/collapse the information in it; but whereas classical OLAP operators change the datacube dimensions (or their levels), the extensional index drill-down/roll-up adds/drops measures, which are the operands of the formula used to derive the index.

In order to validate our proposal, we have developed a prototype of system presented in this work[1]. In such prototype, the datacube management is based on Mondrian [10], an open-source project for the development of an OLAP server; whereas we chose MySQL as RDBMS for managing the DW. Since in Mondrian the schema of a datacube is built by means of a XML-based description language, we simply extend this language for semantically annotating a datacube schema, by means of tags referring to concepts of both the ontologies. As already stated, the DW schema is enriched by another XML-based mapping document. As concerns the SOE, Mondrian is exploited to perform the classical OLAP navigations, like slice and dice, pivot, drill-down, roll-up and drill-through; whereas others modules have been developed for implementing the semantics-based operators. In both cases we exploit JPivot [11] for building the GUI, by which the user may perform OLAP operations and view the results by means of both tables and charts.

As an illustrative example hereafter we refer to a DW storing the annual budgets of Italian medium enterprises, where measures in the DW are only the 155 elements of an Italian balance sheet, e.g. net incomes, mortgages, taxes, employee costs and so on. Furthermore, we consider a datacube having the average ROI of these enterprises as measure, which is not into the DW; whereas dimensions are years and geographical places. The ROI index is computed as described in Fig. 2.

When an analysis starts, the *OLAP Engine* reads and interprets the schema of the datacube to analyse; then for each annotated measure, it shows two new buttons (the two arrows in Fig. 3(a, b), close to measures) enabling intensional and extensional index drill-down/roll-up operators.

If an intensional index drill-down/roll-up is requested, the *Ontologies Browser* module queries the ontologies on the basis of *MO* and *BO* tags of the datacube and reports to the user the domain meaning of the index, the underlying formula, its components and operators. Furthermore, SPARQL queries are exploited to extract from the Business Ontology useful properties of the index, like aliases, class hierarchy, and so forth. The output of this OLAP operation is shown in Fig. 3(c). Note that this is a starting point for browsing the ontologies. As a matter of fact, by interacting with the Ontologies Browser, the analyst may recursively retrieve the meaning of any components of the index under analysis.

---

[1] The prototype is available at http://backus.diiga.univpm.it:8080/semDW

As concerns the execution of the extensional operator, the *Extensional Engine*, the *Mathematical Reasoner* and the *Datacube Rewriter* are been developed.

		Measures
year	place	ROI
+All	-All	7,67%
	-Marche	7,62%
	+Ancona	7,17%
	+Ascoli_Piceno	7,39%
	+Macerata	9,13%
	+Pesaro-Urbino	7,39%
	+Puglia	6,34%
	+Umbria	9,98%

(a)

		Measures			
year	place	ROI	ROS	net_income	total_costs
+All	-All	7,67%	4,28%	142.656.624,96	144.776.118,73
	-Marche	7,62%	4,17%	139.429.156,14	141.972.997,74
	+Ancona	7,17%	,91%	79.591.877,43	79.508.847,66
	+Ascoli_Piceno	7,39%	6,58%	16.095.296,93	18.120.349,01
	+Macerata	9,13%	7,36%	18.946.629,79	18.089.201,78
	+Pesaro-Urbino	7,39%	6,53%	24.795.351,99	26.254.599,28
	+Puglia	6,34%	9,77%	21.645,43	34.464,8
	+Umbria	9,98%	7,76%	66.942,93	51.137,62

(b)

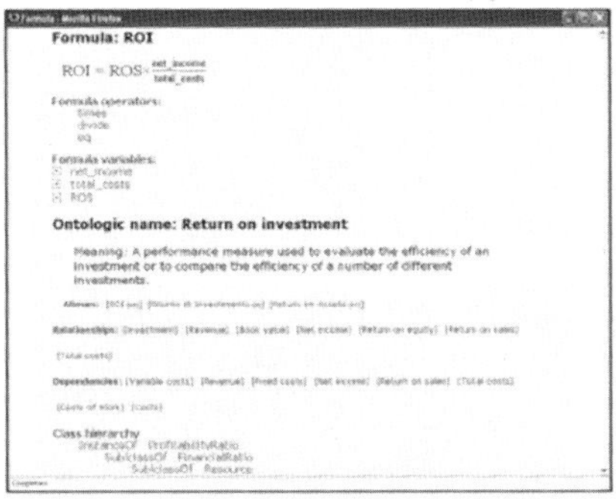

(c)

Fig. 3. (**a**) The GUI of the prototype, (**b**) the output of the extensional drill-down of the ROI index, (**c**) the output of the intensional drill-down/roll-up of the ROI index

As first step, the Extensional Engine searches in the MathOnto for the formula, which the index refers; then from the formula the *references* to its components are extracted (see Fig. 2). Starting from the *MO* of each component the module recursively visits the formulas tree of the MathOnto, searching for nodes that can be matched with measures of the DW schema. A match exists if a DW measure and the node refer to the same ontological concept. At the same time, the Mathematical Reasoner is activated for deriving a new formula allowing to compute the ROI components on the basis of the found DW measures. To this end, such a module exploits the information of the MathML-Content part of formulas, substituting recursively each operand *ci* with the related formula, that is the one referred through the attribute *MO* of the tag *reference*. In our case, this procedure provides a new formula for the calculus of total_costs on the basis of 74 different measures of the DW, which is obtained after several recursions.

The joint use of the Extensional Engine and the Mathematical Reasoner provides all information we need for drill-down the datacube index: the way to compute the values of its operands. The remaining activity is entrusted to the Datacube Rewriter, which adds these new measures to the datacube schema. This mainly means to transform formulas in SQL queries, and to insert them according to the Mondrian description language. The new datacube is now ready for other analysis. The output of the extensional index drill-down is shown in Fig. 3(b), where we can see that other extensional drill-down operation are enabled, but for net_income which is a leaf of the formulas tree. Note also that, the extensional button of ROI changes form, pointing out that an extensional roll-up is now enabled. This last operator is simply performed by removing from the datacube schema the components of the chosen index.

Conclusion

This paper focus on a semantic model for the annotation of Data Warehouses, which allows to describe besides the domain meaning of DW elements also the way they are computed. From such a model new support functionalities can be derived. In particular, her we present novel semantics-based OLAP operators and show the implementation of a prototype. The model contains all information needed to allow a manger to build datacubes on-line. At present, we are developing a module performing such functionality.

Furthermore, we are working on the enrichment of the Mathematical Reasoner, allowing more reasoning capabilities, like for instance to derive new formulas, to solve equations systems, and so forth.

References

1. Lakshmanan LVS, Pei J, Zhao Y (2003) Efficacious data cube exploration by semantic summarization and compression. In *Proceedings of the 29th international conference on very large data bases* (pp. 1125–1128), Berlin
2. Diamantini C, Potena D (2008) Semantic enrichment of strategic datacubes. In *Proceedings of the 11th ACM international workshop on data warehousing and OLAP*, Napa Valley, pp 81–88
3. Huang S-M, Chou T-H, Seng J-L (2007) Data warehouse enhancement: a semantic cube model approach. *Inf Sci* 177(11):2238–2254
4. Xie GT, Yang Y, Liu S, Qiu Z, Pan Y, Zhou X (2007) EIAW: towards a business-friendly data warehouse using semantic web technologies. In *Proceedings of the 6th international semantic web conference* (pp. 857–870), Busan
5. Niinimäki M, Niemi T, Toivonen S, Nummenmaa J (2007) Ontologies with semantic web/grid in data integration for OLAP. *Int J Semant Web Inf Syst* 3(4):25–49
6. Skoutas D, Simitsis A (2006) *Designing ETL processes using semantic web technologies*. In Proceedings of the 9th ACM international workshop on data warehousing and OLAP (pp. 67–74), New Orleans
7. Priebe T, Pernul G (2003) *Ontology-based integration of OLAP and information retrieval*. In Proceedings of DEXA workshops (pp. 610–614), Prague
8. W3C Math Working Group. Mathematical markup language (MathML) Version 2.0, 2nd edn. http://www.w3.org/Math/. Accessed 18 Sept 2009
9. OpenMath Society. The OpenMath Standard Ver. 2.0. http://www.openmath.org/. Accessed 18 Sept 2009
10. Pentaho Analysis Services: Mondrian Project site. http://mondrian.pentaho.org/. Accessed 18 Sept 2009
11. JPivot Project site. http://jpivot.sourceforge.net/. Accessed 18 Sept 2009

Automatic Definition of KDD Prototype Processes by Composition

Claudia Diamantini[*], Domenico Potena[†] and Emanuele Storti[‡]

Abstract The design of a Knowledge Discovery in Databases (KDD) experiment implies the combined use of several data manipulation tools that are suited for the discovery problem at hand. This implies that users should possess a considerable amount of knowledge and expertise about functionalities and properties of all KDD algorithms implemented in available tools, for choosing the right tools and their proper composition. In order to support users in these demanding activities, we introduce a goal-driven procedure to automatically discover candidate prototype processes by composition of basic algorithms. The core of this procedure is the algorithm matching, which is based on the exploitation of an ontology formalizing the domain of KDD algorithms. The present work focuses on the definition and evaluation of algorithm matching criteria.

Introduction

Knowledge Discovery in Databases (KDD) is aimed to extract from a given database useful, valid, unknown and potentially useful knowledge. To achieve such a goal, a KDD process, involving different tools of various nature and interacting with human experts, has to be designed and executed. Since each tool has its own characteristics, performances, and is suitable for a specific task, users should have technical skills and a strong expertise in order to choose, to set-up, to compose and to execute tools. Such a situation sketches process design as a highly complex activity, which is hard to manage by both domain managers, with limited knowledge of KDD tools, and KDD experts, which typically master only few techniques.

[*] Dipartimento di Ingegneria Informatica, Gestionale e dell'Automazione, Università Politecnica delle Marche, Ancona, Italy, diamantini@diiga.univpm.it

[†] Dipartimento di Ingegneria Informatica, Gestionale e dell'Automazione, Università Politecnica delle Marche, Ancona, Italy, potena@diiga.univpm.it

[‡] Dipartimento di Ingegneria Informatica, Gestionale e dell'Automazione, Università Politecnica delle Marche, Ancona, Italy, storti@diiga.univpm.it

A. D'Atri et al. (eds.), *Management of the Interconnected World*,
DOI 10.1007/978-3-7908-2404-9_23,

For these reasons, one of the most interesting challenges in KDD field involves the possibility to give support to any kind of users in both tool discovery and process composition. Such two activities are closely related because composition requires to discover suitable tools, which are then linked together in order to build valid and useful knowledge discovery processes. We adopt an automatic top-down process composition strategy: at first we define a process, at a conceptual level, as composition of algorithms; then this process is instantiated by appropriately substituting each algorithm with one of the tools implementing it. We would like to point out that the proposed strategy allows us to produce prototype KDD processes, which are general and reusable; moreover, generated processes can be themselves considered as useful, valid and unknown knowledge. The design of a process can be ultimately reduced to the sub-problem of algorithm matching, which is a basic step for automatically composing processes. The present work focuses on defining and evaluating algorithm matching criteria.

Given two algorithms, matching is based on the comparison between the output of the first and the input of the second, in order to determine if they can be executed in sequence, i.e. if their interfaces are compatible. In order to guide the matching we described algorithms, their properties and interfaces in KDDONTO, a formal domain ontology [1]. In such a way, it is possible to perform reasoning on the ontology for deducing not explicit and hidden relations among algorithms. In particular, by using semantic relations it is possible not only to find suitable algorithms on the basis of an exact match between input and output, but also to define approximate matches. These matches are based on subsumption relations and, unlike many previous works, also parthood relations among a compound data structure and its subcomponents. A score can be assigned to each kind of match according to a semantic distance function. In such a way, the generated processes are ranked and users can choose the most suitable with respect to their requests.

In the rest of this paper we first present KDDONTO, and then we introduce algorithm matching criteria, which are used as basic step for the process composition procedure. Successively, we discuss relevant related works.

KDD Ontology

KDDONTO is an ontology describing the domain of KDD algorithms, conceived for supporting the discovery of KDD algorithms and their composition.

In order to build KDDONTO, we used a formal approach based on a goal-oriented step-wise strategy, where quality requirements and formal criteria are taken into account, with the aim to make meaning explicit and not ambiguous [2].

The key class is `Algorithm`, because it is the basic component of each process. Other top-level classes, from which any other is defined, are the following:

- Method: technique used by algorithms to extract knowledge from input data;
- Phase: a phase of a KDD process;
- Task: the goal at which aims who executes a KDD process;
- Data: models (a set of constructs and rules for representing knowledge), datasets (a set of data in a proper format) and parameters (any information required in input or produced in output by an algorithm);
- DataFeature: specific preconditions/postconditions that an input (or output) must have in order to be used by a method or an algorithm. Such conditions concern format (normalized dataset), type (numeric or literal values), or quality (missing values, balanced dataset) properties of an input/output datum;
- PerformanceIndex and PerformanceClass: an index and a class of values about the way an algorithm works;

Then, subclasses are defined by means of existential restrictions on main classes, which can be considered as fundamental bricks for building the ontology. Many relations are defined among classes, but for lack of space we introduce only the most relevant for the purposes of this work:

- has_input/has_output, n-ary relations with domain Algorithm, Method or Task and co-domain Data. For each I/O data, optional relations has_condition and is_parameter are defined. The former specifies a pre/postcondition on the input/output at hand. The latter is a Boolean property allowing us to distinguish between an input on which the algorithm works, and an input which is used for tuning the functionalities of the algorithm (i.e. a parameter). For instance, an MLP requests among others as input the dataset and as parameter the number of training epochs: the algorithm elaborates upon the dataset until the chosen number of epochs is reached. As regards precondition, a value expressing the *precondition strength* may be provided: a value equal to 1 corresponds to a mandatory precondition, whereas lower values to relaxable ones. The property in_contrast is used for representing two contradictory conditions, e.g. the condition NUMERIC is in contrast with the condition LITERAL, because a datum cannot be numeric and literal at the same time;
- uses links an instance of Algorithm to one ore more implemented instances of Method, whereas specifies_task assigns an instance of Method to related instances of Task;
- in_module/out_module allow to connect an instance of Algorithm to others, which can be executed respectively before or after it. These relations provide suggestions about process composition, representing in an explicit fashion KDD experts' experience about process building;
- part_of (and its inverse has_part), between a compound datum and an its component (Data instances). Many different meanings of parthood relation have been studied by works in mereology theory. According to the terminology firstly introduced in [3], in this work we refer to a *component/integral* part-of, i.e. a configuration of parts within a whole. Hence, such a transitive relation allows describing a model in terms of the subcomponents it is made of and is useful for identifying algorithms working on similar models, which are models having common substructures, as discussed in next section.

At present, KDDONTO is represented in OWL-DL, and an implementation is available at http://boole.diiga.univpm.it/kddontology.owl. For further details about KDDONTO classes and relations, we refer the interested reader to [2].

Algorithm Matching

For the purposes of this work, we define a KDD process as a workflow of algorithms that allows achieving the goal requested by the user. The basic issue in composition is to define the *algorithm matching*, that is to specify under which conditions two or more algorithms can be executed in sequence. Each algorithm takes data with certain features in input, performs some operations and returns data in output, which are then used as input for the next algorithm in the process. Therefore, two algorithms can be matched if the output of the first is *compatible* with the input of the second. An *exact match* between a set of algorithms $\{A_1,\ldots,A_n\}$ and an algorithm B is defined as:

$$\mathbf{match}_E(\{A_1,\ldots,A_n\},B) \leftrightarrow \forall in_B^i(is\_parameter(in_B^i) \vee \exists A_k \exists out_{A_k}^j : out_{A_k}^j \equiv_o in_B^i \wedge valid(out_{A_k}^j, in_B^i))$$

where in_B^i is the ith input of the algorithm B, out_{Ak}^j is the jth output of A_k. The symbol $\equiv_o$ represents the conceptual equivalence and is defined as follows: let a and b be two data, $a \equiv_o b$ if $C_a \subseteq C_b$ i.e. a and b refer to the same concept[1] or C_a is a subconcept of C_b. The predicate *valid(out,in)* is satisfied if none of the postconditions of *out* are `in_contrast` with any of the *in* preconditions.

By exploiting properties of algorithms, described in the previous section, it is possible to define a match based not only on exact criteria, but also on similarity among data. We can define a match among algorithms even if their interfaces are not perfectly equivalent: the relaxation of constraints results in a wider set of possible matches. Hence, an *approximate match* between a set of algorithms $\{A_1,\ldots,A_n\}$ and an algorithm B is defined as:

$$\mathbf{match}_A(\{A_1,\ldots,A_n\},B) \leftrightarrow \forall in_B^i(is\_parameter(in_B^i) \vee \exists A_k \exists out_{A_k}^j : similar(out_{A_k}^j, in_B^i) \wedge valid(out_{A_k}^j, in_B^i))$$

where the similarity predicate *similar*(*x*,*y*) is satisfied if $a \equiv_o b$, or a and b are similar concepts, i.e. if there is a path in the ontology graph that links them together. An approximate match is useful not only when an exact match cannot be performed, but also for extracting unknown and non-trivial processes.

[1] Hereafter we use "class" and "concept" as synonyms.

The similarity between concepts can be evaluated on the basis of various ontological relations. Previous works about matching (see the next Section) commonly take into account only relations at *hierarchic* level: a specific datum is similar to its superclass, e.g. a Labeled Vector Quantization model (LVQ) is similar to a more general classification model.

However, generalization/specialization is not enough for exploiting complex data structures which are common in Data Mining field; for such a reason we consider similarity also at a *structural* level: a compound datum can be made of simpler data, according to part_of/has_part relationships. To give a practical example, a LVQ has_part a VQ model and a Labeling function (L). As shown in Fig. 1, if an algorithm requires VQ model in input, LVQ model can be provided in place of it because the latter contains all the needed information.

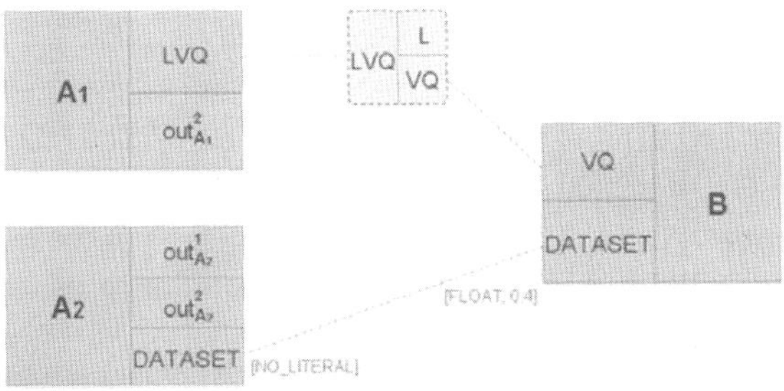

Fig. 1. An approximate match: *VQ* is part of *LVQ* and DATASET $\equiv_o$ DATASET. A precondition on the input DATASET exists and its value is FLOAT that is a specialization of NO_LITERAL, which in turn is the value of the postcondition, with strength 0.4, of the output DATASET

In order to evaluate degrees of approximation, it is useful to assign a numeric weight to each match such that the higher is the weight, the less accurate is the match. Given two similar data, a *path* is the shortest sequence of is-a or part_of edges that are needed to link them in the ontological graph. We define *ontological distance* between two data the summation of the weighted edges in the path: $D_o(out_A, in_B) = \sum_{i=1}^{|path|} \delta_i$, where δ_i is the weight of the ith edge in the path, and its value depends on the relation type, such that $\delta_{spec(ialization)} \leq \delta_{part(hood)} \leq \delta_{gen(eralization)}$. Unlike many previous works (e.g. [4, 5]), we weight differently a generalization and a specialization; such asymmetry is due to the different amount of information carried by the two relations. For instance, since LVQ is a specialization of a CLASSIFICATION_MODEL, LVQ contains all the information of the superclass and can be easily used when a CLASSIFICATION_MODEL is required, but the vice-versa does not occur. For such a reason, $\delta_{spec} \leq \delta_{gen}$ and, since we use subsumption relation in exact match, δ_{spec} is weighted 0.

The part-of relation could be considered as a kind of specialization and weighted in the same manner, e.g. a LVQ could be also viewed as a specialization of a VQ, because a LVQ adds features to a VQ. However this approach, besides to be incorrect from a conceptual point of view, is also wrong from a pragmatic perspective. As a matter of fact, part-of intrinsically requires an additional manipulation (that implies an additional cost) in order to extract the needed subcomponents from the compound datum; in the example, this means to separate the VQ model from its Labeling function (the dotted square in Fig. 1).

Finally, given two algorithms A and B, we define *cost* of their match: $C_m(A,B) = \frac{\alpha\gamma}{n_B}\sum_{i=1}^{n_B} \beta D_o^i$, where n_B is the number of input of the algorithm B, whereas α, β and γ coefficients are introduced for taking into account other weighting factors, as follows:

α – *use of link modules*: given two algorithms linked through the `in_module` and `out_module` properties, C_m is decreased because these relations state that a specific connection among them was proved to be effective;

β – *precondition relaxation*: in algorithm matching, postconditions of the first algorithm must not be in contrast with preconditions of the second one, as regards the same data. Preconditions on some data can be relaxed if they have a `condition_strenght` value lower than 1. Relaxing preconditions increases terms in the C_m summation, because in such cases algorithm execution may lead to lower quality outcomes;

γ – *performance evaluation*: algorithm performances can affect C_m, e.g. the higher the complexity, the higher the cost.

Based on algorithm matching, we define a goal-driven procedure for composing KDD processes. Our approach is aimed at the generation of an ordered list of all valid prototype processes satisfying the user requests; this allows the user to choose among processes with different characteristics and to experiment more than a single solution. In each phase of the procedure, a reasoner is exploited to make inference on the ontology for searching matchable algorithms. The proposed process composition procedure is formed of the following phases:

- *dataset and goal definition*. The user provides characteristics of the dataset to mine (i.e. instances of `DataFeature` class) and specifies the goal to achieve (i.e. instance of the `Task` class);
- *process building*. Process building is an iterative phase, which starts from the given task and goes backwards adding one or more algorithms to a process. Firstly, through the `specifies_task` and `uses` relations, all instances of the `Algorithm` class performing the given task are extracted. From these starting algorithms, prototype processes are generated by means of the algorithm matchmaking criteria defined in the previous section. This backwards procedure goes on until the first algorithm of each process is compatible with the given dataset;

- *process ranking*. Generated processes are ranked on the basis of the *process cost*, i.e. the summation of all the matching costs C_m in the process.

Due to page limitations, we refer the interested reader to [1] for further details about the composition procedure.

Related Works

In last years researchers in Data Mining and KDD fields have shown growing interest in techniques for supporting the design of knowledge discovery processes.

Some earlier researches were proposed for supporting process composition, but no automatic procedure is defined for most of them, and only recent works have dealt with this issue [6, 7]. In detail, in [6] authors define a simple ontology of KDD algorithms, that is exploited for designing a KDD process facing with cost-sensitive classification problems. A forward composition, from dataset characteristics towards the goal, is achieved through a systematic enumeration of valid processes, which are ranked on the basis on accuracy achieved on the processed dataset, and on process speed. Reference [7] introduces a KDD ontology representing concrete implementations of algorithms and any piece of knowledge involved in a KDD process (dataset and model), that is exploited for guiding a forward state-space search planning algorithm in the design of a KDD workflow. Such ontology describes algorithms in very few classes and a poor set of relationships, resulting in a flat knowledge base. Both in [6, 7], ontologies are not rich enough to be extensively used both for deducing hidden relations among algorithms and for supporting approximate matches. Our approach, moreover, is aimed to achieve a higher level of generality, by producing abstract and reusable prototype processes.

Outside KDD and Data Mining, some related works can be also found within Web Service Composition field. Very few proposals deal with only exact match, while most of them (e.g. [4, 8–11]) consider also the subsumption relation for matching services.

To the best of our knowledge the only previous approach considering also parthood in matching is [5], which describes a procedure for Web Service discovery using semantic matchmaking. To this end, authors exploit relations of the lexical ontology Wordnet, including the meronymy relation, i.e. part-of.

As concerns the functions used to assign a score to a match, some of the above-cited works weight in the same way generalization/specialization relations [4, 5]. On the contrary, like [8, 9, 11], we assign them different weights as previously explained in previous Section. Furthermore, like [4, 5, 8] we define a numeric value for the matching cost instead of a discrete score as in [10, 11]: this allows us to define an overall cost for a process with more accuracy.

Conclusion

The main contribution of this work is to introduce criteria for matching KDD algorithms, which are used as basic brick for the automatic composition of KDD prototype processes. These matching criteria are based on KDDONTO, a domain ontology formalizing knowledge about algorithms and their interfaces.

In particular, we exploit KDDONTO for defining approximate matches, which are based on the subsumption and parthood relations. In the proposed approach we weight each match on the basis of the ontological path linking algorithms, the kind of ontological relations in the path and other elements which affect the quality of the match, namely preconditions, linkable modules and performance indexes.

As future extensions, in order to provide an effective ranking of the generated processes, we are evaluating specific values for weighing both matches and processes. Furthermore, we are working on techniques for translating a KDD prototype process into an executable process of tools.

References

1. Diamantini C, Potena D, Storti E (2009) Ontology-driven KDD process composition. In Proceedings of the 8th international symposium on intelligent data analysis, *LNCS*, 5772, Lyon, France, pp 285–296
2. Diamantini C, Potena D, Storti E (2009) KDDONTO: an ontology for discovery and composition of kdd algorithms. In: *Proceedings of the ECML/PKDD workshop on third generation data mining: towards service-oriented knowledge discovery*, Bled, Slovenia, pp 13–24
3. Winston ME, Chaffin R, Herrmann D (1987) A taxonomy of part-whole relations. *Cogn Sci* 11(4):417–444
4. Akkiraju R, Srivastava B, Ivan A, Goodwin R, Syeda-Mahmood T (2006) SEMAPLAN: combining planning with semantic matching to achieve web service composition. In *Proceedings of the IEEE international conference on web services*, Chicago, IL, USA, pp 37–44
5. Bianchini D, De Antonellis V, Melchiori M (2008) Flexible semantic-based service matchmaking and discovery. *World Wide Web* 11(2):227–251
6. Bernstein A, Provost F, Hill S (2005) Towards intelligent assistance for a data mining process: an ontology based approach for cost-sensitive classification. *IEEE Trans Knowl Data Eng* 17(4):503–518
7. Žáková, M, Křemen P, Železný F, Lavrač N (2008) Using ontological reasoning and planning for data mining workflow composition. In *Proceedings of the ECML/PKDD workshop on third generation data mining: towards service-oriented knowledge discovery*, Antwerp, Belgium, pp 35–41
8. Arpinar IB, Aleman-Meza B, Zhang R, Maduko A (2004) Ontology-driven Web services composition platform. In *Proceedings of IEEE international conference on e-Commerce technology*, San Diego, CA, USA, pp 146–152
9. Fuji K, Suda T (2004) Dynamic service composition using semantic information. In *Proceedings of 2nd international conference on service oriented computing*, New York, NY, USA, pp 39–48
10. Lemmens R, Arenas H (2004) Semantic matchmaking in geo service chains: reasoning with a location ontology. In *Proceedings of international workshop on database and expert systems applications*, Zaragoza, Spain, pp 797–802
11. Ni Q (2005) Service composition in ontology enabled service oriented architecture for pervasive computing. In *Proceedings of workshop on ubiquitous computing and e-Research*, Edinburgh, UK

Social Validation in the Ontology Evolution Process

Alessia Barbagallo[*], **Antonio De Nicola**[†], **and Michele Missikoff**[‡]

Abstract Ontology building is a social process requiring, as a first step, the collaborative work of a group of people to create a shared understanding of a specific domain of interest. This process typically involves an heterogeneous group of people: from ontology engineers to domain experts, to end users. A crucial aspect of ontology building is to reach consensus among all the involved actors. For this reason, it is important that every step of the process is clearly defined and the roles played by the members of a community of interest (COI) are precisely assigned. In this paper we present the guidelines for social validation in the ontology evolution process. In particular, we describe the process and we identify the milestones where the COI is asked to reach a consensus. Then, we present the different roles to be played in the COI, the procedures to reach consensus and the result of a first experimentation in the domain of semantic technologies.

Introduction

An ontology is a formal specification of a shared conceptualization [1, 2]. Ontology engineering is an emerging discipline studying the process of building ontologies. Besides technical aspects, ontology engineering needs to take into account social aspects to ensure that the built ontologies are accepted and, consequently, adopted by ontology users. According to [3], by adopting a *collaborative approach* to ontology building, an ontology is developed as a joint effort reflecting experiences and viewpoints of persons who cooperate and interact with each other. To this end, it is necessary to create a community of interest (COI), that should reach a consensus on the ontology scope and purpose (why the ontology is built [4]), on ontological commitments (agreement on the content) [5], and, finally, on concepts and relationships that represent the actual ontology content.

[*] TXT e-solution, Milan, Italy, alessia.barbagallo@txtgroup.com
[†] IASI – CNR, Rome, Italy, denicola@iasi.cnr.it
[‡] IASI – CNR, Rome, Italy, missikoff@iasi.cnr.it

A. D'Atri et al. (eds.), *Management of the Interconnected World*,
DOI 10.1007/978-3-7908-2404-9_24, © Springer-Verlag Berlin Heidelberg 2010

In this paper we present the guidelines for social validation in the ontology evolution process. Here we assume that one (or more) ontology already exists and the goal is its evolution. Therefore, we describe a process aimed at extending existing shared ontologies by using knowledge coming from documents related to an application domain and, more generally, domain resources. The process, described in the following, is partly automated and partly manual. The main focus of this paper is on manual aspects requiring the COI to take decisions. In particular, we have identified the procedures to reach consensus on decisions on ontological modelling, involved actors, and produced artifacts.

The rest of the paper is organized as follows. In the next section, we present related works. In the third section, we describe the ontology evolution process and we identify the milestones where the COI is asked to reach a consensus. Then, we present the different aspects of the consensus process: the community of interest, how to reach consensus, and a first experimentation in evolving an ontology in the semantic technologies domain. Finally, in the last section, we present conclusions and future work.

Related Works

The collaborative approach for ontology building was firstly proposed by [3]. The authors propose to structure collaborative consensus processes using an approach based on the Delphi method, i.e. a formal technique for collecting and integrating the views of multiple persons about some topic. The idea is that an initial ontology is critiqued and iteratively revised by participants until they collectively agree on an ontology. With respect to this approach, we focus on extending an existing ontology rather than revising an existing one.

Reference [6] presents a framework to support ontology evolution in collaborative environments. One of the major contributions of the paper is the classification of scenarios for collaborative ontology evolution and the discussion of the related benefits and weaknesses. In particular, they present: synchronous and asynchronous ontology construction; continuous and periodic archiving of ontology; ontology building with and without a designated curator to resolve conflicts; monitored (i.e., recording the changes) and non-monitored editing of ontology.

Finally, other important contributions on consensus building techniques applied to ontology engineering are presented by [7, 8].

With respect to [6–8], in the next sections, we present the complete ontology evolution process and we provide a detailed description of the collaborative processes (i.e., selection, voting, and debating) and when they are needed (i.e., milestones).

The Ontology Evolution Process

The *ontology evolution process* here presented is derived from the UPON methodology [4, 9]. It is, currently, applied in the COIN IP [10]. UPON is a methodology for ontology building from scratch, developed along the line of the Unified Process [11], a widespread and accepted method in the software engineering community. A characterizing feature of the UPON methodology is its incremental nature, reflected by the outcomes produced in the different phases of the process. First the relevant terms in the domain are identified and gathered in a *lexicon*; then the latter is progressively enriched with definitions, yielding a *glossary*; adding to it the specialisation relationships allows a *taxonomy* to be produced, until further enrichments and a final formalization produces the sought *domain ontology*.

The proposed ontology evolution process (Fig. 1) is structured in phases, according to the UPON methodology. The key idea is to start from the documents of the enterprise and to analyse them to see if the reality they reflect has changed, and therefore, the ontology needs to change accordingly. Starting from an existing ontology, we extract the terminological part, i.e., *O-Lexicon*. Then, new relevant terms in the domain are automatically extracted, by analysing the Enterprise Corpus of documents, and gathered in a lexicon, i.e., *E-Lexicon*. The terms belonging to the *E-Lexicon*, and not belonging to the *O-Lexicon* represent the potential candidate concepts, to be considered for the ontology update. However, it is not sufficient to perform a set difference, the list must be socially validated by the community of reference, under the supervision of the COI (milestone 1), and gathered in the new lexicon: *N-Lexicon*. The latter is progressively enriched with definitions extracted from existing resources (e.g., Wordnet), yielding a glossary, i.e., *E-Glossary*. Then the COI validates the glossary entries (i.e., the pairs "term-definition"). The validation consists of analysing the glossary entries of the E-Glossary, in order to choose the most suitable definition from the list and to find synonyms within the E-Glossary and with respect to the terms of the initial ontology, i.e., *O-Glossary*. The result of this step is gathered in the *N-Glossary* (milestone 2). Another important step is the categorization of every *glossary entry* by associating a *kind* to it (Object, Process, Actor, according to the OPAL framework [12]). The kind is assigned by the COI with a consensus building process (milestone 3). Starting from the newly acquired concepts definitions, an advanced NLP technique allows us to identify hypernyms and other related concepts, producing a set of micro-taxonomies: *Eμ-Taxonomies*. An *Eμ-Taxonomy* is a specialization hierarchy between two concepts. Then, the *Eμ-Taxonomies* are merged with the initial taxonomy (i.e., *O-Taxonomy*) producing the *N-Taxonomy* by means of a social consensus process (milestone 4). Finally, the ontology is enriched with other relationships (e.g., partOf) by the COI (milestone 5).

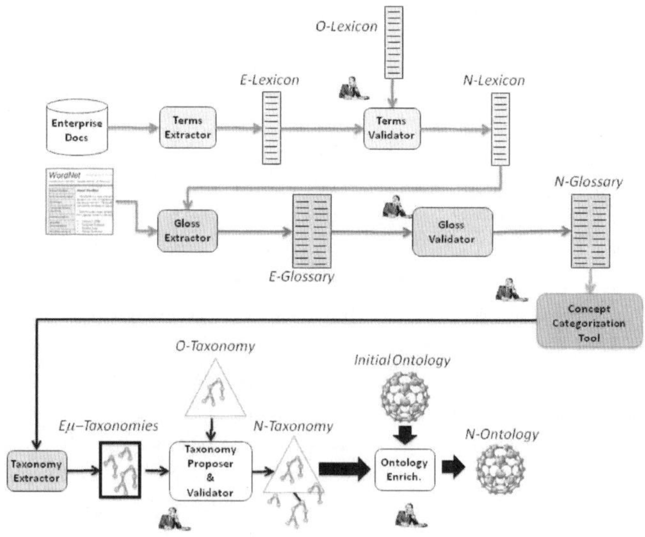

Fig. 1. Overview of the ontology evolution process

The Consensus Process

The process starts with the specification of an issue requiring a decision. Then a group of people, starting from diverging positions, collaborates to make the best possible decision. Concerns are raised and resolved, sometimes one by one, until all voices are heard. Since, after a while, the proposal is no longer the property of the presenter, a solution can be created more cooperatively. A consensus process, based on cooperative dynamic interactions, is more a social process than a technical activity. Social decision making techniques are used to support and smooth this process.

The Community of Interest

The community of interest is composed by knowledge engineers, ontology users, and ontology stakeholders. Knowledge engineers are classified as ontology engineers (OE), domain experts (DE), and application experts (AE). OE are supposed to have skills in technical issues (e.g., conceptual modelling, OWL), whereas DEs and AEs are experts, respectively, of the domain of interest and of the particular application addressed. Ontology users are the group of people who will operationally interact with ontology-based applications. Ontology stakeholders are people who are interested in the successful achievement of the ontology building project.

The above mentioned actors, belonging to the COI, play different roles in the collaborative work. For the ontology evolution process we identified two roles: *ontology owner* and *ontology participant*. The *ontology owner* is the responsible of the overall quality of the ontology content. He facilitates the consensus processes, by pushing the harmonization of different points of view. Finally, he takes care of the discussion content, periodically summarizes different positions emerging in the debate, identifies the points that can be considered fixed (not to be further discussed), and concludes discussion. The *ontology participant* takes part to consensus activities, like voting and debating.

How to Reach Consensus

There is a vast literature on the social decision making. Here we adopted a simple approach, based on free debate and a final democratic determination.

We identified three different activities aimed at reaching consensus in the ontology evolution process: *debating*, *voting*, and *selection*.

Debating. Debating is the process allowing to discuss, share ideas and converge on agreed decisions. To structure this process, we applied a modified version of the speech act theory (SAT) [13]. A speech act is a sentence that an actor utters when interacting with other actors, with a defined intent. Speech act theory mainly concerns sentences that are related to the acts like: proposing, supporting, rejecting, informing, requesting and so on. To properly convey the speech act to the hearer, one possible solution should be to "tag" the conversation of the speaker, with a label that can help the hearer to identify what the speaker wants to achieve by his speaking. From the classification of the speech act kinds, we have identified several relevant types to be used in the consensus process. These kinds are: *proposal*, *support*, *concern*, *rebuttal*, *pros*, *cons*, *counterproposal*, *comment*, *revision*, *withdrawal*, *request for information/clarification*, and *mediation*. By using SAT kinds in an explicit form, the communication among people is typically highly-structured and less fuzzy. For example, when someone asks a question, he/she usually expects either an answer or a request for clarification. After a request, a typical response is to fulfill the request or to explain a reason for declining it. We experimented that, in a consensus process, a correct communication structure based on SAT significantly supports the achievement of a consensual outcome.

Voting. Votes are expressed using an ordinal Likert's-like scale [14], widely used to measure attitudes, opinions and preferences. The format of a typical five-level Likert's item is: *strongly disagree*, *disagree*, *neutral*, *agree* and *strongly agree*. These levels are anchored with consecutive integers from 0 to 4. The adopted Likert's item is constituted by a set of levels, with specific format features, related to the topic to be decided.

The responses are combined by adding or averaging the anchored integers in order to produce an overall score.

Selection. Selection is the process of expressing a preference, selecting one among different elements of a list (e.g., terms, definitions of terms).

Case Study: The Evolution of an Ontology on Semantic Technologies

The procedures for social validation were applied in the context of the evolution of an ontology on semantic technologies. The COI was composed of 8 members: 2 ontology users, 1 ontology stakeholder, 2 application experts, 2 domain experts, and 1 ontology engineer. We started from a corpus of approximately 150 documents and, by using an automatic tool, the ***E-Lexicon*** of 1,073 terms was extracted. Then, after the social validation process, we obtained the ***N-Lexicon*** of 178 terms (5 terms extracted were already included in the ***O-Lexicon***). The number of valid definitions in the ***N-Glossary*** was 93. Since the overall number of glossary extractions was 178, the 47.7% of definitions had to be established directly through debating. The number of the terms having at least one synonym is 4 (e.g., *ontological issue* and *ontological problem*) while the 3.3% of pairs <*term,definition*> required debating for the category's selection. After the categorization of the concepts, we obtained 20 concepts associated to the kind actor, 49 to kind process, and 109 to kind object. Finally, the COI designed the taxonomy and the final ontology.

In the following, we briefly introduce some clues obtained in the experimentation in the domain of semantic technologies, achieved mainly to test the illustrated process: from the documents to the *N-Lexicon,* to the *ontology*. Tables 1 and 2 present an excerpt respectively from the *N-Lexicon* and from the *N-Glossary*. Table 3 shows some OPAL concepts. Finally, Figs. 2 and 3 illustrate an excerpt respectively of the *N-Taxonomy* and of the final *ontology* in UML notation.

Conclusions

In this paper we presented a methodology for social validation in the ontology evolution process. We tested it in the evolution of an ontology on semantic technologies to demonstrate the viability of our methodology. The introduction of our procedures for consensus building in the ontology evolution process makes the process itself more structured, less error prone, less time consuming and ensures that the ontology will be broadly useful to the community. As future works, the ontology evolution process will be further automated to allow a larger scale applicability.

Table 1. Excerpt of the N-lexicon on semantic technologies

Annotation tool, domain ontology, ontology-based reconciliation, ontology building, ontology engineering, ontology management system, reasoning system, reconciliation rule, and reconciliation suite

Table 2. Excerpt of the N-glossary on semantic technologies

Term	Definition
Annotation tool	A tool that facilitates annotation
Domain ontology	A domain ontology is an ontology tied to a specific domain
Ontology-based reconciliation	A semantics-based reconciliation mechanism, which requires the existence of a reference ontology for building reconciliation rules
Ontology building	Collaborative process of ontology construction for knowledge worker support
Ontology engineering	Ontology engineering is a subfield of knowledge engineering concerning methods and methodologies for building ontologies
Ontology management system	A software system that facilitates the creation and maintenance and use of ontologies
Reasoning system	A reasoning system is a piece of software able to infer logical consequences from a set of asserted facts or axioms contained in a logic theory formalized in a logic language. Intuitively a reasoning system aims at making explicit the knowledge implicitly represented in a logic theory
Reconciliation rule	A rule for enacting the mediation between two counterparts
Reconciliation suite	A set of software tools for enabling the mediation of hindering aspects between two counterparts (e.g. documents, processes)

Table 3. OPAL concepts concerning semantic technologies

Annotation tool [Actor_Kind], Domain ontology [Object_Kind], ontology-based reconciliation [Process_Kind], ontology building [Process_Kind], ontology engineering [Process_Kind], ontology management system [Actor_Kind], reasoning system [Actor_Kind], reconciliation rule [Object_Kind], reconciliation suite [Actor_Kind]

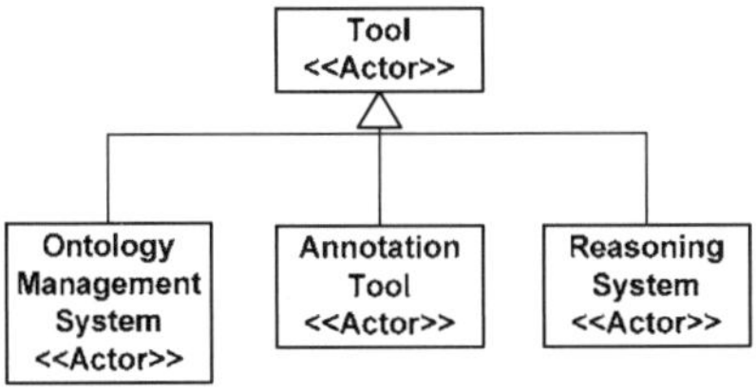

Fig. 2. Excerpt of the N-taxonomy on semantic technologies

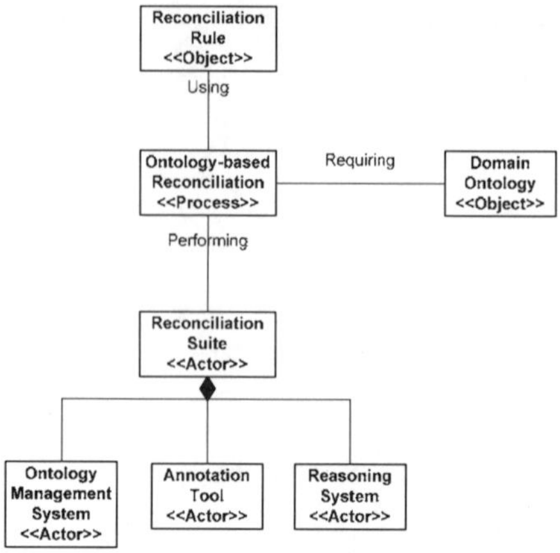

Fig. 3. Excerpt of the ontology on semantic technologies

Acknowledgments This work is partially supported by the COIN IP, 7th European Union Framework Programme.

References

1. Gruber TR (1993) A translation approach to portable ontology specification. *Knowl. Acquis* 5:199–220
2. Borst WN (1997) *Construction of engineering ontologies for knowledge sharing and reuse*. University of Twente, Enschede, The Netherlands
3. Holsapple CW, Joshi KD (2002) A collaborative approach to ontology design. *Commun ACM* 45(2):42–47
4. De Nicola A, Navigli R, Missikoff M (2009) A software engineering approach to ontology building. *Inf Syst* 34 (2):258–275
5. Guarino N, Carrara M, Giaretta P (1994) Formalizing ontological commitments. In *Proceedings of AAAI 94*, vol. 1, pp 560–567, Seattle, WA, USA
6. Noy FN, Chugh A, Liu W, Musen MA (2006) A framework for ontology evolution in collaborative environments. The semantic web – ISWC 2006, *LNCS* 4273, pp 544–558, Athens, GA, USA
7. Tempich C, Simperl E, Luczak M, Studer R, Pinto HS (2007) Argumentation-based ontology engineering. *IEEE Intell Syst* 22(6):52–59
8. Karapiperis S, Apostolou D (2006) Consensus building in collaborative ontology engineering processes. *J Universal Knowl Manage* 1(3):199–216
9. Velardi P, Cucchiarelli A, Petit M. (2007) A taxonomy learning method and its application to characterize a scientific web community. *IEEE transactions on knowledge and data engineering,* 19(2):180–191
10. COIN (2007). *Enterprise Collaboration & Interoperability*. VII European Framework Integrated Project. http://www.coin-ip.eu/, Accessed on September 2009
11. Jacobson I, Booch G, Rumbaugh J (1999) *The unified software development process*. Addison-Wesley, Reading

12. D'Antonio F, Missikoff M, Taglino F (2007) Formalizing the OPAL eBusiness ontology design patterns with OWL. In: *Proceedings of the 3rd international conference on interoperability for enterprise applications and software*, I-ESA, Funchal, Portugal
13. Searle J (1969) *Speech acts*. Cambridge University Press, Cambridge, ISBN 0-521-09626-X
14. Likert R (1932) A technique for the measurement of attitudes. *Arch Psychol* 140:1–55

A Logical Approach to Context-Aware Databases

Davide Martinenghi* **and Riccardo Torlone†**

Abstract Context awareness is an enabling technology of ubiquitous computing aimed at utilizing the location, the time, and other properties that characterize the context of use to select the information that is most appropriate to final users. Although it is widely considered a fundamental ability of modern applications, current database technology does not provide any support to context awareness yet. In this paper, we propose a logical model and an abstract query language as a foundation for context-aware database management systems. The model is a natural extension of the relational model in which contexts are first class citizens and can be described at different levels of granularity. This guarantees a smooth implementation of the approach with current database technology. The query language is a conservative extension of relational algebra where special operators allow the specification of queries over contexts.

Introduction

Nowadays, context awareness is widely recognized to be a fundamental means to guide users through the wealth of information available in digital form [8]. Basically, a context aware application provides some ability to filter, adapt, and personalize the accessible content according to a set of features characterizing the user context. These features may include the location, time, device as well as any available aspect that allows the identification of the most appropriate information for the final user.

In spite of this fact, the support of current database technology to context awareness is very limited. The only examples are some ad-hoc functionality provided by specialized systems, such as temporal and spatial DBMS, that explicitly take into account some specific contextual property. Conversely, we believe that context-aware applications can benefit greatly from applying the relational database technology enhanced with a comprehensive support for the management of context. In particular, it will become possible to formulate as queries much more sophisticated search requests, such as those required by geographic and location-based applications [7]. In the light of these

* Politecnico di Milano, Milan, Italy, martinen@elet.polimi.it

† Università Roma Tre, Rome, Italy, torlone@dia.uniroma3.it

A. D'Atri et al. (eds.), *Management of the Interconnected World*,
DOI 10.1007/978-3-7908-2404-9_25, © Springer-Verlag Berlin Heidelberg 2010

considerations, we propose in this paper a logical data model and an abstract query language for context-aware databases with the goal of providing a solid foundation to the problem of adding context awareness to database systems. The data model is a natural extension of the relational model in which contexts are first class citizens: this guarantees a smooth implementation of the approach with current database technology. As it happens in practice, contexts can be expressed at different levels of detail: this is made possible by a partial order relationship defined over contexts both at the schema and at the instance level. Basically, a context c associated with a relational tuple t specifies that t is valid in c and in any other context c' that includes c according to the partial order defined on contexts: it follows that t can be selected in a query that refers to c'.

The query language we propose, called Contextual Relational Algebra (CRA), is a conservative extension of relational algebra that allows the specification of queries over contexts. CRA allows a simple, natural embedding of contexts into ordinary queries through some special operators for contexts that extend the capabilities of standard projection, selection and join operators. These operators make it possible to formulate complex context-aware queries, such as those required by location-based search (find an opera concert in or close to Rome next summer), multifaceted product search (find a cheap blu-ray player with an adequate user rating), social search (find the objects that the friends of Jane like), and device adaptation (resize the picture to fit my screen).

The rest of the paper is organized as follows. In the next section we present our context model. CRA, the query language for this model, is illustrated in the section on querying contextual data. In the section that follows we compare our approach with related works and finally, in the last section, we draw some conclusions.

A Data Model with Contexts

In this section, we present an extension of the relational model in which contexts are first class citizens. We assume the reader is familiar with partial orders [3] and lattices [2], which are basic ingredients of our model.

We represent a context by means of a set of dimensions, each of which represents an autonomous aspect that should influence the delivery of data, such as the time and the location in which the source is accessed, the access device and the network used. Each dimension is described by means of a set of levels representing the dimension at different degrees of granularity. For instance, the time dimension can be organized in levels like day, week, month and year.

Definition 1 *A (contextual) dimension* d *is composed of:*

- *a finite set* $L = \{l_1, \ldots, l_k\}$ *of levels, each of which is associated with a set of values called the members of the level and denoted by* $M(l)$*;*
- *a partial order* $\leq_L$ *on* L *having a bottom element, denoted by* $\perp_L$*, and a top*

element, denoted by $\top_L$*, such that:*

- $M(\bot_L)$ *contains a set of ground members whereas all the other levels contain members that represent groups of ground members;*
- $M(\top_L)$ *contains only a special member* $m_\top$ *that represents all the ground members;*

- *a family* CM *of containment mappings* $cmap_{l_1}^{l_2}: M(l_1) \to M(l_2)$ *for each pair of levels* $l_1 \leq_L l_2$ *satisfying the following consistency conditions:*
  - *for each* $l \in L$*, the function* $cmap_l^l$ *is the identity on the members of* l*;*
  - *for each pair of levels* l_1 *and* l_2 *such that* $l_1 \leq_L l \leq_L l_2$ *and* $l_1 \leq_L l' \leq_L l_2$ *for some* $l \neq l'$*, we have:* $cmap_l^{l_2}(cmap_{l_1}^l(m)) = cmap_{l'}^{l_2}(cmap_{l_1}^{l'}(m))$ *for each member* m *of* l_1*.*

Example 1 The contextual dimension time has a bottom level whose (ground) members are timestamps and a top level whose only member, anytime, represents all possible timestamps. Other levels can be day, week, month, quarter, season and year, where $\mathrm{day} \leq_L \mathrm{month} \leq_L \mathrm{quarter} \leq_L \mathrm{year}$ and $\mathrm{day} \leq_L \mathrm{season}$. A possible member of the Day level is 23/10/2009, which is mapped by the containment mappings to the member 10/2009 of the level month and to the member Summer of the level season.

Note that the poset $(\mathrm{L}, \leq_\mathrm{L})$ is a lattice and therefore every pair of levels l_1 and l_2 in L has both a glb and a lub. Actually, a partial order $\leq_\mathrm{M}$ can also be defined on the members M of a dimension D: it is induced by the containment mappings as follows.

Definition 2 *Let D be a dimension and* m_1 *and* m_2 *be members of levels* l_1 *and* l_2 *of D, respectively. We have that* $m_1 \leq_M m_2$ *if: (i)* $l_1 \leq_L l_2$ *and (ii)* $cmap_{l_1}^{l_2}(m_1) = m_2$*.*

Example 2 Consider the dimension of Example 1. Given the members $\mathrm{m}_1 = 29/06/2009$ and $\mathrm{m}_2 = 23/08/2009$ of the level day, $\mathrm{m}_3 = 06/2009$ and $\mathrm{m}_4 = 08/2009$ of the level month, $\mathrm{m}_5 = 2\mathrm{Q}2009$ and $\mathrm{m}_6 = 3\mathrm{Q}2009$ of the level quarter, $\mathrm{m}_7 = 2009$ of the level year, and $\mathrm{m}_8 = \mathrm{Summer}$ of the level season, we have: $\mathrm{m}_1 \leq_\mathrm{M} \mathrm{m}_3 \leq_\mathrm{M} \mathrm{m}_5 \leq_\mathrm{M} \mathrm{m}_7$, $\mathrm{m}_2 \leq_\mathrm{M} \mathrm{m}_4 \leq_\mathrm{M} \mathrm{m}_6 \leq_\mathrm{M} \mathrm{m}_7$, and $\mathrm{m}_1 \leq_\mathrm{M} \mathrm{m}_8$ and $\mathrm{m}_2 \leq_\mathrm{M} \mathrm{m}_8$.

Example 2 shows an interesting property: differently from the poset on the dimension levels, the poset on the members of a dimension is not a lattice in general. Consider for instance the members m_1 and m_2 of this example: they have no lower bounds, since their intersection is empty (more precisely, the intersection of the ground members that they represent is empty), and have two incomparable minimal upper bounds: 2009 at the year level and Summer at the season level. Indeed, it is possible to show that the poset $(\mathrm{M}, \leq_\mathrm{M})$ can be converted into a lattice by adding to M all the elements of the powerset of the ground members (including the empty set, which would become the bottom level). This however would imply an explosion of the number of members and an unnatural representation of a contextual dimension. We are ready to introduce our notion of context.

Definition 3 *Let D be a set of contextual dimensions. We denote by* $C = (A_1: l_1, \ldots, A_k: l_k)$ *a context schema where each* A_i *is a distinct attribute name and each* l_i *is a level of some dimension in D. A context* c *over* C *is a function that maps each attribute* A_i *to a member of* l_i.

Given a context c over a schema C and an attribute A_i occurring in C on level l_i, we will denote by $c[A_i: l_i]$ the member of level l_i associated with c on A_i. Also, for a subset C' of C, we will denote by $c[C']$ the restriction of c to C'. Moreover, for the sake of simplicity, often in the following we will not make any distinction between the name of an attribute of a context and the name of the corresponding level when no ambiguities can arise.

Example 3 A context schema over the dimensions time, location and weather conditions can be the following: (Time: day, Location: city, Weather: brief). A possible context over this schema is: c = (12/05/2009; Rome; Sunny). Then we have: c[Location: city] = Rome. A partial order relation on both context schemas and contexts can be also defined in a natural way.

Definition 4 *Let* C_1 *and* C_2 *be context schemas over* D_1 *and* D_2 *respectively. We have that* $C_1 \leq_C C_2$ *if: (i)* $D_2 \subseteq D_1$, *and (ii) for each* $A_i: l_i \in C_2$ *there is an element* $A_i: l_j \in C_1$ *such that* $l_j \leq_L l_i$.

Definition 5 *Let* c_1 *and* c_2 *be contexts over* C_1 *and* C_2 *respectively. We have that* $c_1 \leq_c c_2$ *if: (i)* $C_1 \leq_C C_2$, *and (ii) for each* $A_i: l_i \in C_2$ *there is an element* $A_i: l_j \in C_1$ *such that* $c_1[A_i: l_j] \leq_M c_2[A_i: l_i]$.

Note that, in these definitions, we assume that levels of the same dimension occur in different contexts with the same attribute name: this strongly simplifies the notation that follows without loss of expressibility. Basically, it suffices to use as attribute name the role played by the dimension in the application domain.

Example 4 Let us consider the context c_1 = (10/05/2009; 12/05/2009; Rome; Sunny) over the context schema C_1 = (StartTime: day; EndTime: day; Location: city; Weather: brief); the context c_2 = (11/08/2009; Rimini) over C_2 = (StartTime: day; Location: city); the context c_3 = (2Q2009; Lazio) over C_3 = (StartTime: quarter; Location: region); and finally the context c_4 = (Summer; Italy) over C_4 = (StartTime: season; Location: country). Then, it is easy to see that: (i) $C_1 \leq_C C_2 \leq_C C_3$, and $C_2 \leq_C C_4$, and (ii) $c_1 \leq_c c_3$ and $c_2 \leq_c c_4$.

Note that the same considerations done for the poset on dimension levels also apply for the poset on context schemata: the poset $(C, \leq_C)$ is a lattice, where C is the set of all possible context schemas over a set of dimensions D. Conversely, the poset on contexts is not a lattice in general since, it is easy to show that, given two contexts, they can have more than one minimal upper bound (but necessarily at least one) as well as more than one maximal lower bound (possibly none).

As usual, we denote by $X = (A_1\colon V_1, \ldots, A_k\colon V_k)$ a relation schema, where each A_i is a distinct attribute and each V_i is a set of values called the domain of A_i. A tuple t over a relation schema X is a function that associates with each A_i occurring in X a value from V_i. A relation r over a relation schema X is a finite set of tuples over X. A contextualized relation, or simply a c-relation, is a database relation whose tuples include contexts. Basically, a context c associated with a tuple t means that t represents a valid piece of information in c.

Definition 6 *Let D be a set of contextual dimensions. We denote by $R(X^s \parallel X^c)$ a c-relation schema, where R is the name of the schema, X^s is a relation schema and X^c is a context schema. A c-relation over $R(X^s \parallel X^c)$ is a set of tuples $t = (s \parallel c)$ where s is a tuple over X^s and c is a context over X^c. The members of X^c are called contextual attributes.*

We recall that, for the sake of simplicity, we will often make no distinction between the name of a contextual attribute and the corresponding level.

Example 5 We now give some examples of c-relations that will be used for query answering purposes in the next section. A c-relation over the schema $R_1(\text{Opera: string, Director: string} \parallel \text{Time: day, Location: theater})$ is:

$r_1 =$

Opera	Director	Time:day	Location:theater	
La Traviata	Abbado	11/05/2009	La Scala	$t_{1,1}$
La Bohème	Chailly	24/04/2008	Opéra	$t_{1,2}$
Turandot	Maazel	24/07/2009	Arena	$t_{1,3}$
Rigoletto	Muti	24/04/2008	La Scala	$t_{1,4}$

A c-relation over $R_2(\text{Price: real} \parallel \text{Location: theater, Time: quarter})$ is:

$r_2 =$

Price	Location:theater	Time:quarter	
150	La Scala	1Q 2009	$t_{2,1}$

The following c-relation is over $R_3(\text{Company: string} \parallel \text{Location: airport})$.

$r_3 =$

Company	Location:airport	
Alitalia	Villafranca	$t_{3,1}$
Air France	Roissy	$t_{3,2}$

Finally, a c-relation over $R_4(\text{Discount: percentage} \parallel \text{Time: month})$ is:

$r_4 =$

Discount	Time:month	
10%	03/2009	$t_{4,1}$
20%	06/2009	$t_{4,2}$

Note that a tabular representation has been chosen here for a c-relation but other solutions are possible. For instance, we could represent the non-contextual part of the tuples in an array in which the context provides the coordinates. The following is a representation of r_1.

	La Scala	Opéra	Arena
11/05/2009	La Traviata, Abbado	-	-
24/04/2008	Rigoletto, Muti	La Bohème, Chailly	-
24/07/2009	-	-	Turandot, Maazel

As shown in the previous example, our model is a logical model that can therefore be implemented in several ways.

Querying Contextual Data

In this section we present CRA (Contextual Relational Algebra) an extension of the relational algebra over c-relations. This language provides insights on the way in which contextual data can be manipulated and, for its procedural nature, can be profitably used to specify query optimization. The goal is provide a solid foundation to querying over contexts. Similarly to what happens with the standard relational algebra, the operators of CRA are closed, that is, they apply to c-relations and produce a c-relation as result. In this way, the various operators can be composed to form the *c-expressions* of the language. CRA is a conservative extension of basic relational algebra (RA) and so it includes its standard operators: selection (σ), projection (π), and natural join ($\bowtie$).

Definition 7 [Upward extension] Let r be a c-relation over $R(X^s \parallel X^c)$, A be a contextual attribute in X^c defined over a level l, and l′ be a level such that $l \leq_c l'$. The upward extension of r on l′, denoted by $\hat{\varepsilon}_{A:l}^{A:l'}(r)$, is the c-relation over $R'(X^s \parallel X^c \cup \{A:l'\})$ defined as follows:

$$\hat{\varepsilon}_{A:l}^{A:l'}(r) = \{(s \parallel c) \mid \exists(\bar{s} \parallel \bar{c}) \in r : s = \bar{s}, c[X^c] = \bar{c}, c[A:l'] = cmap_l^{l'}(\bar{c}[A:l])\}$$

Definition 8 [Downward extension] Let r be a c-relation over $R(X \parallel X)$, A be a contextual attribute in X^c defined over a level l, and l′ be a level such that $l \leq_c l'$. The downward extension of r on l′, denoted by $\check{\varepsilon}_{A:l}^{A:l'}(r)$, is the c-relation over $R'(X^s \parallel X^c \cup \{A:l'\})$ defined as follows:

$$\check{\varepsilon}_{A:l}^{A:l'}(r) = \{(s \parallel c) \mid \exists(\bar{s} \parallel \bar{c}) \in r : s = \bar{s}, c[X^c] = \bar{c}, c[A:l] = cmap_{l'}^{l}(\bar{c}[A:l])\}$$

For simplicity, in the following we will often simply write $\hat{\varepsilon}_l^{l'}$ or $\check{\varepsilon}_l^{l'}$, when there is no ambiguity on the attribute name associated with the corresponding levels.

Example 6 Consider the c-relations r_1 and r_2 from Example 3. The result of $\hat{\varepsilon}_{Theater}^{City}(r_1)$ is the following c-relation.

r_5 =

Opera	Director	Time:day	Location:theater	Location:city	
La Traviata	Abbado	11/05/2009	La Scala	Milan	$t_{5,1}$
La Bohème	Chailly	24/04/2008	Opéra	Paris	$t_{5,2}$
Turandot	Maazel	24/07/2009	Arena	Verona	$t_{5,3}$
Rigoletto	Muti	24/04/2008	La Scala	Milan	$t_{5,4}$

The result of $\check{\varepsilon}_{Month}^{Quarter}(r_2)$ is the following c-relation.

$r_6 =$

Price	Location:theater	Time:quarter	Time:month	
150	La Scala	1Q 2009	01/2009	$t_{6,1}$
150	La Scala	1Q 2009	02/2009	$t_{6,2}$
150	La Scala	1Q 2009	03/2009	$t_{6,3}$

The main rationale behind the introduction of the upward extension is the need to relax a query with respect the level of detail of the queried information. For example, one might want to find events taking place in a given country, even though the events might be stored with a finer granularity (e.g., city). Similarly, the downward extension allows the relaxation of the answer with respect to the level of detail of the query. For instance, a query about products available in a given day may return the products available in that day's month. Both kinds of extensions meet needs that arise naturally in several application domains.

CRA also include some variants of the standard selection and join obtained by combining them with the upward and downward extension. We refrain from introducing formally these operators due to space constraints and just describe them by means of an example.

Example 7 Consider again the c-relations r_1 and r_2 from Example 5. In CRA the selection comes in two forms upward ($\hat{\sigma}$) and downward ($\breve{\sigma}$). Their behavior is shown in following examples: $\hat{\sigma}_{City=Milan}(r_1) = \{t_{1,1}, t_{1,4}\}$ and $\breve{\sigma}_{Day=13/03/2009}(r_2) = \{t_{2,1}\}$. The CRA join has also the upward ($\hat{\bowtie}$) and the downward ($\breve{\bowtie}$) forms. The result of $r_1 \hat{\bowtie}_{City} r_3$ is the following c-relation:

$r_7 =$

Opera	Director	Company	Time:day	Location:theater	Location:airport	
La Bohème	Chailly	Air France	24/04/2008	Opéra	Roissy	$t_{7,1}$
Turandot	Maazel	Alitalia	24/07/2009	Arena	Villafranca	$t_{7,2}$

Consider now the c-relations r_2 and r_4 from Example 2.3. The result of $r_2 \breve{\bowtie}_{Theater,Day} r_4$ is the following c-relation:

$r_8 =$

Price	Discount	Location:theater	Time:quarter	Time:month	
150	10%	La Scala	1Q 2009	03/2009	$t_{8,1}$

Related Work

Context awareness has been studied in very diverse application domains including, among others, interface adaptation, information retrieval, service discovery, and artificial intelligence (see [1] for a survey on context-aware systems). In this paper, we have focused on the problem of selecting the most appropriate data according to a context of reference and in particular on context-aware query answering [5]. Actually, several context data models have been proposed and a comprehensive survey of the most interesting data-oriented approaches has been presented in [4]. We have not considered the rich features provided by these models but rather we have concentrated on the basic ingredients that need to be added to the relational model with the aim of adding context-aware capabilities to current database technology. In this respect, the most relevant characteristic is the ability of the model to represent contexts at different levels of detail [4]. The model we have proposed is indeed a variation of a multidimensional model, which provides this ability for data warehousing applications [6]. Recently, some proposals of multidimensional context models similar to our approach have been presented [9, 10], but, unlike ours, they cannot be considered strict extensions of the relational model. A multidimensional data model for dealing with contexts has also been proposed in [12, 13], but the goal of the authors is rather different and focuses on contextual preferences, a problem that we have not addressed in this paper.

To our knowledge, CRA is the first proposal of a query language for context-aware relational databases that extends the classical relational algebra. The algebra presented in [9] is in fact rather informal and does not interact with standard operators. A query language with a similar objective has been proposed in a different framework [11].

Conclusion

In this paper, we have presented a logical model and an algebraic language as a foundation for querying context-aware databases. In order to facilitate the implementation of the approach with current technology, they rely on a natural extension of the relational model. The hierarchical organization of contexts allows the specification of queries that refer to contexts at different levels of details, possibly different from those associated with data.

References

1. Baldauf M, Dustdar S, Rosenberg F (2007) A survey on context-aware systems. Int J Ad Hoc Ubiquitous Comput 2(4):263–277
2. Birkhoff G (1967) Lattice theory. Colloquium publications, vol XXV, 3rd edn. American Mathematical Society, Providence
3. Birkhoff G, MacLane S (1999) Algebra, 3rd edn. AMS Chelsea Publishing, Providence
4. Bolchini C, Curino C, Quintarelli E, Schreiber FA, Tanca L (2007) A data-oriented survey of context models. SIGMOD Rec 36(4):19–26
5. Bolchini C, Curino C, Orsi G, Quintarelli E, Rossato R, Schreiber FA, Tanca L (2009) And what can context do for data? *Communications of the ACM*, 52(11):136–140
6. Cabibbo L, Torlone R (1998) A logical approach to multidimensional databases. In: *Proceedings of the 6th international conference on EDBT*, Springer, Berlin/Heidelberg, pp 183–197
7. Chen Y, Suel T, Markowetz A (2006) Efficient query processing in geographic web search engines. In: *Proceedings of the SIGMOD*, ACM New York, NY, USA, pp 277–288
8. Coutaz J, Crowley JL, Dobso S, Garlan D (2009) Context is key. Commun ACM 48(3):49–53
9. Roussos Y, Stavrakas Y, Pavlaki V (2005) Towards a context-aware relational model. In: *Workshop on context representation and reasoning*, Informal proceedings
10. Stavrakas Y, Gergatsoulis M (2002) Multidimensional semistructured data: representing context-dependent information on the web. In: *Proceedings of the CAiSE*, Springer, Berlin/Heidelberg, pp 183–199

11. Stavrakas Y, Pristouris K, Efandis A, Sellis TK (2004) Implementing a query language for context-dependent semistructured data. In: *Proceedings of the ADBIS*, Springer, Berlin/Heidelberg, pp 173–188
12. Stefanidis K, Pitoura E, Vassiliadis P (2006) Modeling and storing context-aware preferences. In: *Proceedings of ADBIS*, Springer, Berlin/Heidelberg, pp 124–140
13. Stefanidis K, Pitoura E, Vassiliadis P (2007) Adding context to preferences. In: *Proceedings of the ICDE*, IEEE, Los Alamitos, CA (USA) pp 846–855

Uncertainty in Data Integration Systems: Automatic Generation of Probabilistic Relationships

Sonia Bergamaschi[*], **Laura Po**[†], **Serena Sorrentino**[‡], **and Alberto Corni**[π]

Abstract This paper proposes a method for the automatic discovery of probabilistic relationships in the environment of data integration systems. Dynamic data integration systems extend the architecture of current data integration systems by modeling uncertainty at their core. Our method is based on probabilistic word sense disambiguation (PWSD), which allows to automatically lexically annotate (i.e. to perform annotation w.r.t. a thesaurus/lexical resource) the schemata of a given set of data sources to be integrated. From the annotated schemata and the relathionships defined in the thesaurus, we derived the probabilistic lexical relationships among schema elements. Lexical relationships are collected in the Probabilistic Common Thesaurus (PCT), as well as structural relationships.

Introduction

Traditional data integration systems are systems interconnecting a limited number of resources, which are relatively stable in time and which have been typically built with sophisticated designs that have taken several time. On the other hand, data applications broaden more and more and ask for flexibility and handling of uncertainty. Applications like Google Base or involving a large number of sources as in the deep web or tool dealing with biological data [1], require that the semantic mappings between the mediated schema and the data sources, may be approximate as they need to be automatically extracted.

[*] Information Engineering Department, University of Modena and Reggio Emilia, Modena, Italy, sonia.bergamaschi@unimore.it

[†] Information Engineering Department, University of Modena and Reggio Emilia, Modena, Italy, laura.po@unimore.it

[‡] Information Engineering Department, University of Modena and Reggio Emilia, Modena, Italy, serena.sorrentino@unimore.it

[π] Information Engineering Department, University of Modena and Reggio Emilia, Modena, Italy, alberto.corni@unimore.it

A. D'Atri et al. (eds.), *Management of the Interconnected World*,
DOI 10.1007/978-3-7908-2404-9_26, © Springer-Verlag Berlin Heidelberg 2010

Using a probabilistic view, our approach allows to insert potential matches and to assign a probability value to them. This significantly reduces the cost of schema integration by allowing it to be fully automated and thus scalable to a large number of data sources [2].

Starting from our previous works on automatic discovery of semantic mappings in the environment of the MOMIS data integration system [3], we propose a method for the automatic discovery of probabilistic relationships in the context of new dynamic data integration system, i.e. systems where semantic mappings among schemata of different sources have to be discovered on the fly without or with a minimal human intervention.

The PWSD method, introduced in this paper, will automatically annotate the labels of sources schemata and associate to each annotation a probability value. The probabilistic annotations generated by PWSD are used to derive probabilistic lexical relationships between local sources. PWSD has been implemented in the ALA (Automatic Lexical Annotator) tool [4] that is integrated in the MOMIS system. However, PWSD but can be easily generalized to other data integration systems. Moreover, our method can be used by ontology merging and data integration system, adopting OWL as conceptual language[1].

Probabilistic Automatic Annotation in a Data Integration System

The data integration methodology proposed by MOMIS in previous articles [3] has been modified to cope with the treatment of uncertainty. Instead of building a global schema, we focus on the automatic generation of probabilistic relationships. The process is organized in three steps which are described in the following.

(1) Source schema extraction
Specialized software (wrappers) logically convert the format of the source schemata into the internal object language ODL_I^3.

(2) Lexical knowledge extraction
The extraction of lexical knowledge from data source is performed by ALA. ALA allows the user to choose a set of WSD algorithms and a way to combine their outputs. ALA supports a sequential (or pipe) combination and a parallel combination of the outputs. The parallel combination is based on PWSD.

During the annotation process, ALA interacts with the lexical resource WordNet extended with WND (WordNet Domains[2]) and the WNEditor [5]. ALA supplies a set of probabilistic annotations of the source terms. From these annotations

[1] The MOMIS system uses ODL_I^3 as an internal language, but supports the translation of OWL/ODL_I^3 and ODL_I^3 /OWL schemata

[2] http://wndomains.fbk.eu/

ALA calculates the probabilistic lexical relationships among source schema elements.

Definition 2.1-*(Probabilistic Annotation). Let T be a schema and t be a label of an element e ∈ T. We define St = {t#1; :::; t#n} as the set of all meanings for t w.r.t. a lexical resource. The probabilistic annotation of the term t is the triple <T; t; At>, where At = {a1; :::; ak} is the set of annotations associated to t. In particular, ai is defined as the couple (t#i; P(t#i)), where t#i ∈ St is a meaning for the term t, and P(t#i) is the probability value assigned.*

Definition 2.2-*(Ordinary Annotation). An ordinary annotation for t is a probabilistic annotation where there is only an annotation associated to t (||At|| =1) and the probability value assigned is equal to "1".*

(3) Probabilistic Common Thesaurus generation
The PCT is a set of ODL_I^3 relationships describing inter- and intra-schema knowledge among the source schemata. ODL_I^3 relationships can be structural or lexicon derived, and ordinary or probabilistic.

Definition 2.3-*(Structural ODL_I^3 relationship).The structural ODL_I^3 relationships are:*

- *SYN_{EXT} (t1 is equivalent to t2 iff extension(t1) = extension(t2));*
- *BT_{EXT} (t1 subsumes t2 iff extension(t2) $\subseteq$ extension(t1));*

Definition 2.4-*(Lexical ODL_I^3 relationship).The lexical ODL_I^3 relationships are defined on the basis of thesaurus relationships:*

- *SYN: (Synonym-of),defined between two terms that are synonymous;*
- *BT: (Broader Term),defined between two terms where an hypernym relationship holds between their meanings (the opposite of BT is NT, Narrower Term);*
- *RT: (Related Term) defined between two terms when a holonym or meronym relationships holds between their meanings.*

Structural relationships are automatically extracted by the MOMIS wrapper and ODB-Tools [6]. Lexical relationships are automatically extracted on the basis of the probabilistic annotations obtained.

Definition 2.5-*(Probabilistic ODL_I^3 relationship). A probabilistic ODL_I^3 relationship is a pair (Rel ODL_I^3; P(Rel ODL_I^3)), where Rel ODL_I^3 is a ODL_I^3 relationship and P(Rel ODL_I^3) is a probability value, in the interval [0, 1].*

Definition 2.6-*(Ordinary ODL_I^3 relationship). An ordinary ODL_I^3 relationship is a probabilistic ODL_I^3 relationship with probability value equal to "1".*

Lexical ODL_I^3 relationships can be both probabilistic and ordinary; structural ODL_I^3 relationships are only ordinary. In addition to these relationships, other ordinary ODL_I^3 relationships can be supplied directly by the designer, interacting with the MOMIS Ontology Builder. MOMIS exploits description logic techniques

[6] to infer new relationships by applying subsumption computation to "virtual schemata" obtained by interpreting BT and NT as subclass relationships and RT as domain attributes.

PWSD

PWSD is based on a probabilistic combination of different WSD algorithms. In our previous works [7, 8], we have developed and tested on a real data scenario different types of WSD algorithms. These algorithms constitute an evolution of the ones proposed in the area of Natural Language Processing to disambiguate text, because they have been adapted to the case of structured and semi-structured data sources. At present, we have developed five algorithms[3]: Structural Disambiguation, WordNet Domain Disambiguation, WordNet first sense, Gloss similarity, Iterative gloss similarity. All this algorithms need to be configured about their reliability, although each algorithm has a default reliability based on its precision evaluated on a benchmark.

Example 1 As a case in point, let us consider the term "name". In WordNet we found six different meanings for "name" (*name#1*, *name#2*, .., *name#6*). Suppose we have to combine three algorithms that give different outputs: WSD1 that chooses a set of meanings formed by *name#1*, *name#2*, WSD2 that provides *name#1* as the correct meaning and WSD3 that does not give any result. What we want to obtain is a rate of confidence to be assigned to each possible meaning of the term "name".

Uncertainty in Disambiguation – The Use of the Dempster-Shafer Theory

The set of WSD algorithms defines a type of evidence that can be consistent or arbitrary. These types of evidence cannot be handled by the traditional probability theory without resorting to further assumptions. That is why we decided to support the use of the Dempster-Shafer theory [9, 10]. This theory allows us to model ignorance through lack of knowledge.

The theory deals with the so-called *frame of discernment*, the set of base elements θ in which we are interested (in our case, θ is the set of all possible meanings for the term under consideration), and its power set 2^{θ}, which is the set of all subsets of the interesting elements (in our case, all the possible subsets of the possible meanings). The basic of the measure of uncertainty is a *probability mass*

[3] More details available http://www.dbgroup.unimo.it/publication/d2_1.pdf

function m(·). The mass function is defined for every element A of 2^{θ}, it assigns zero mass to empty set and a value in the range [0, 1] to each A of 2^{θ}. The total mass distributed being 1 so that:

$$\sum_{A \subseteq 2^{\theta}} m(A) = 1 \tag{1}$$

We can apportion the probability mass exactly as we wish, ignoring assignment to those levels of detail that we know nothing about. In our case, we derive the mass functions from the output and the precision of each WSD algorithm. To combine several algorithms we use the *Dempster's rule of combination* [9, 10]:

$$m(a) = K \sum_{\cap A_i = a} \prod_{i=1}^{n} m_i(A_i) \tag{2}$$

$$K = \sum_{\cap A_i = \varnothing} \prod_{i=1}^{n} m_i(A_i) \tag{3}$$

where n is the number of algorithms that supplied a disambiguation output for the term under analysis.

In the end, to obtain the probability assigned to each meaning we split the belief mass function concerning a set of meanings.

$$P(a_i) = \sum_{a_i \in A} \frac{m(A)}{\|A\|} \tag{4}$$

where a_i is a meaning and A are all the sets of meanings that contain a_i.

Let us see the application of PWSD to the element "name" in Example 1. In order to combine different outputs, PWSD does not consider the algorithms that do not supply any annotations for the term. In the example, PWSD will be executed only on the outputs of WSD1 and WSD2. Each algorithm has a reliability value and an ignorance value, (the complementary value of the reliability), i.e. the mass function assigned to the entire set of possible meanings. Let us suppose that WSD1 has a reliability of 70% and WSD2 a reliability of 50%.

The application of the Dempster's rule of combination is shown in Fig. 1. As WSD1 supplies a set composed of two meanings, the probability will be assigned to this set.

mass function	WSD1	WSD2	Dempster-Shafer combination
m{name#1}		0,5	0,5
m{name#1,name#2}	0,7		0,35
m{name#1,name#2, ... name#6}= m{ignorance}	0,3	0,5	0,15

probability function	PWSD
P{name#1}	0,67
P{name#2}	0,17
P{ignorance}	0,15

Fig. 1. Application of the Dempster-Shafer theory on the WSD algorithms output and generation of the probabilistic annotations

The results obtained after the application of the Dempster's rule of combination show the probability assigned to different sets of meanings. In order to compute lexical relationships, we have to bring back to the case of probabilities assigned to individual meanings. As shown in Fig. 1 on the right, the probability assigned to the set of meanings *{name#1,name#2}* is splitted in probabilities assigned to *name#1* and *name#2*.

From Annotation to Probabilistic Relationship Discovering

MOMIS derives lexical ODL_I^3 relationships between local sources terms from the semantic relationships defined in WordNet between meanings, by using the following WordNet constructors:

- *synonymy* (similar relation) corresponds to a SYN ODL_I^3 relationship;
- *hyponymy* (sub-name relation) corresponds to an NT ODL_I^3 relationship;
- *hypernymy* (super-name relation) corresponds to a BT ODL_I^3 relationship;
- *holonymy* (whole-name relation) corresponds to an RT ODL_I^3 relationship;
- *meronymy* (part-name relation) corresponds to an RT ODL_I^3 relationship.
- *correlation* (two terms that share the same hypernym) corresponds to a RT ODL_I^3 relationship.

The application of PWSD associates a set of probabilistic meanings to a term in a source. So, a term *t* is described by a meaning *t#i* with a certain probability. When we assign the meaning *t#i* to the term *t*, *t* will inherit the same lexical relationships that occur for the synset *t#i* within the WordNet relationships network.

We restrict to the sub-network of relationships that branch off from *t#i*, in the context of analysis of the sources to be integrated. From the sub-net of lexical relationships between meanings we derive lexical ODL_I^3 relationships among schemata terms. Thanks to the formula of the *join probability*, the probability value associated with an ODL_I^3 relationship holding among *t#i* and *s#j* is defined as:

$$P(\text{REL}_{\text{ODL}_{\text{I}^3}}(t_i, s_j)) = P(t_i) \times P(s_j) \quad (5)$$

Evaluation: Experimental Result

We experimented PWSD over real data sources, for sake of simplicity, we considered only three data sources, but the process is scalable and applicable to a large set of data sources. We used three ontologies from the benchmark 2008 of the OAEI project[4] to run the automatic annotation.

Table 1. PWSD compared with other WSD methods

	Accuracy (%)	Error (%)	Precision (%)	Recall (%)	Fmeasure (%)
CWSD	0.78	0.22	0.66	0.55	0.60
PWSD	0.75	0.25	0.56	0.76	0.65
PWSD with threshold=0.2	0.84	0.16	0.80	0.70	0.75
WordNet first sense heuristic	0.83	0.17	0.81	0.53	0.64

The golden standard for the benchmark is the annotation selected by an expert. The expert may select more than one meaning for each term and the evaluation is done on each possible selected meaning. We calculate statistics of accuracy, error, precision, recall and F-measure. All these measures are express as percentage, with 100% being the best score, except of error measure where 0% is the best.

We compared the results of PWSD with our previous combined algorithm, CWSD [8], and with the WordNet first sense heuristic (this heuristic is often used as baseline for WSD systems and often outperforms many of these systems which take surrounding context into account [11]).

As Table 1 shows, precision and recall of PWSD do not increase with respect to CWSD (a method that combines only 2 WSD algorithms), this is due to a high number of annotations performed by PWSD with a very low probability value. Filtering the PWSD annotation output refines the annotation results. The threshold chosen was quite low (the average probability value of PWSD was 0.34), this allowed to filter out only the annotations that were not supported by a lot of WSD algorithms (the annotations that can introduce noise) without decreasing the recall.

[4] http://oaei.ontologymatching.org/2008/

Conclusions and Future Work

We presented a method for the automatic discovery of probabilistic relationships in the environment of data integration systems. We proposed PWSD, a probabilistic method to automatically annotate the terms of source schemata w.r.t a lexical resource. PWSD associates a probability value to each annotation that is determined combining the results of many WSD algorithms through the application of the Dempster-Shafer theory. The PWSD has been implemented in ALA tool and integrated in the MOMIS system; the annotations are used in MOMIS to derive probabilistic lexical relationships between among sources.

We noticed that, to improve the relationships discovery of this process, it is crucial that the probabilistic annotations are as much accurate and robust as possible. Future work will be devoted to improve the annotation process inserting techniques able to deal with acronyms and abbreviations [12].

Acknowledgments The work reported in this paper has been funded by the MUR FIRB Network Peer for Business project (http://www.dbgroup.unimo.it/nep4b) and by the IST FP6 STREP project 2006 STASIS (http://www.dbgroup.unimo.it/stasis).

Reference

1. Louie B, Detwiler L, Dalvi NN, Shaker R, Tarczy-Hornoch P, Suciu D (2007) *Incorporating uncertainty metrics into a general-purpose data integration system, SSDBM*, 19. IEEE Computer Society, Los Alamitos, California
2. Dalvi NN, Suciu D (2007) *Management of probabilistic data: foundations and challenges, PODS.* ACM Press, New York, pp 1–12
3. Beneventano D, Bergamaschi S, Guerra F, Vincini M (2003) Synthesizing an integrated ontology. *IEEE Int Comput* 7(5):42–51
4. Bergamaschi S, Po L, Sorrentino S, Corni A (2009) Dealing with uncertainty in lexical annotation. ER 2009. *J Theor Appl Inform* 16(2):93–96
5. Benassi R, Bergamaschi S, Fergnani A, Miselli D (2004) *Extending a lexicon ontology for intelligent information integration.* ECAI. IOS Press, Amsterdam, pp 278–282
6. Beneventano D, Bergamaschi S, Sartori C (2003) Description logics for semantic query optimization in object-oriented database systems. *ACM Trans Database Syst* 28:1–50
7. Bergamaschi S, Bouquet P, Giacomuzzi D, Guerra F, Po L, Vincini M (2007) An incremental method for the lexical annotation of domain ontologies. *Int J Semantic Web Inf Syst* 3(3):57–80
8. Bergamaschi S, Po L, Sorrentino S (2007) Automatic annotation in data integration systems. OTM Workshops (1). *LNCS Springer* 4805:27–28
9. Parsons S, Hunter A (1998) A review of uncertainty handling formalisms, applications of uncertainty formalisms. *LNCS Springer* 1455:8–37
10. Shafer G (1976) A mathematical theory of evidence. Princeton University Press, Princeton
11. McCarthy D, Carroll J (2003) Disambiguating nouns, verbs, and adjectives using automatically acquired selectional preferences. *Comput Linguist* 29(4):639–654
12. Sorrentino S, Bergamaschi S, Gawinecki M, Po L (2009) Schema normalization for improving schema matching. In: Laender AHF et al (eds) ER 2009. *LNCS* 5829:280–293

The iCoord Knowledge Model for P2P Semantic Coordination

Silvana Castano[*], **Alfio Ferrara**[†], **and Stefano Montanelli**[‡]

Abstract In this paper, we present iKM, the three-layer peer knowledge model developed in the framework of the iCoord system for P2P semantic coordination. iKM grounds on the notion of *knowledge chunk* embedding the information about concepts to be shared/exchanged across peers for coordination. The main functionalities of iCoord for exploiting an iKM knowledge repository, namely *knowledge browsing* and *data search*, will be also presented.

Introducion

In a modern vision, P2P systems are seen as effective collaboration platforms where knowledge and data belonging to a possibly large set of peers have to be managed in an efficient way as collective knowledge. In this context, social relationships among individuals and similarity relations among ontology concepts belonging to different peers are the basis to construct an integrated knowledge sharing system capable of handling different layers of knowledge in a coordinated way [1]. The problem is not only to detect those peers that are relevant for a certain query, but also to establish appropriate relationships for acquiring data of interest from selected sources. As a result, the problem shifts from a mere discovery issue to a more comprehensive semantic coordination need. In P2P environments, semantic coordination can be defined as the capability to discover and maintain content mappings between pairs of independent peers in a "harmonized" way [2, 3]. This kind of mappings can be exploited for lightweight integration purposes with the goal of establishing a network of P2P semantic relations [4]. In this context, we have developed iCoord, a framework for P2P semantic coordination whose general overview and architecture have been presented in [5].

In this paper, we present the knowledge model of iCoord, called iKM, which allows a peer to organize knowledge in a three-layer repository. With respect to previous

[*] Università degli Studi di Milano – DICo, Milano, Italy, castano@dico.unimi.it

[†] Università degli Studi di Milano – DICo, Milano, Italy, ferrara@dico.unimi.it

[‡] Università degli Studi di Milano – DICo, Milano, Italy, montanelli@dico.unimi.it

A. D'Atri et al. (eds.), *Management of the Interconnected World*,
DOI 10.1007/978-3-7908-2404-9_27, © Springer-Verlag Berlin Heidelberg 2010

work, this paper focuses on the notion of knowledge chunk, an innovative feature of iKM employed to effectively and efficiently represent peer concept knowledge during the semantic coordination tasks of iCoord. With respect to the existing solution in the field, iCoord enables a peer to support P2P semantic integration on a single concept of interest, thus allowing to build a unified peer-view of the matching knowledge harvested from the network about the target concept specifically considered.

P2P Semantic Coordination with iCoord

P2P semantic coordination in iCoord is realized by a three-layer architecture on top of a set of independent peers, without prior reciprocal knowledge and without predefined relationships (see Fig. 1).

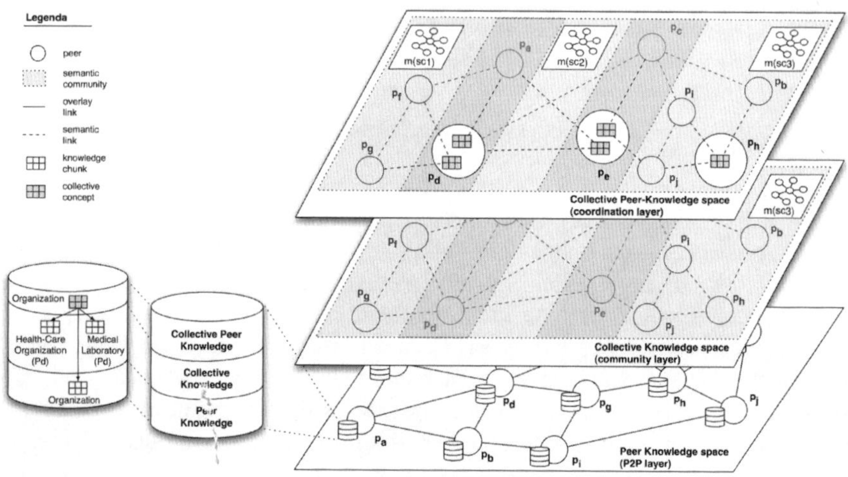

Fig. 1. Architecture of the iCoord system and of the iKM repository

At the bottom, peers are inserted in a basic P2P layer, called *Peer Knowledge space*, responsible of maintaining the peer connectivity by means of a shuffling-based mechanism based on overlay links. The basic idea of shuffling is to maintain connectivity by keeping each node connected to a small set of other nodes that are continuously varying through random exchange of neighboring nodes [6].

In the P2P layer, each peer is considered as a single agent having view only of its personal knowledge, namely the peer ontology, describing its own contents/resources. By joining semantic communities of interest, a peer is inserted in a community layer, called *Collective Knowledge space*. This space is organized in a set of semantic communities which are autonomously emerging from the P2P layer by handshaking those nodes that have similar contents and spontaneously agree on a proposed topic of interest expressed through an ontology-based manifesto[1]. Within the Collective Knowledge space, peers are interconnected by semantic links, denoting the existence of semantic relations between concepts of their respective peer ontologies. Semantic links are progressively discovered and established through harvesting techniques. Goal of harvesting is to enable a peer *P* interested in a concept *c'* to discover and to acquire knowledge chunks semantically matching the concept *c'* from the peer ontologies of other nodes.

On top of the community layer, a coordination layer, called *Collective Peer-Knowledge space*, is defined. In this layer, the harvested knowledge chunks and the semantic links are used to move from a network of peers to a network of *collective concepts*. A collective concept *cc'* is a reference view of the peer *P* about a concept *c'* derived from a coordinated representation of the matching knowledge chunks collected during harvesting, using semantic links to keep track of the source peers from which the chunks have been acquired.

The iKM Knowledge Model

The iKM knowledge model is based on the notion of knowledge chunk to give explicit formalization to the basic unit of knowledge relevant for P2P semantic coordination.

Knowledge chunk. Given an ontology *O*, let *NC* be the set of concept names in the signature of *O*, *NR* the set of relation names in *O*, *D* the set of datatypes in *O*, and *NP* the set of peer identifiers of the considered P2P network. A knowledge chunk *kc* is a structured representation of an ontology concept $c \in O$ in terms of its constituent axioms, both explicitly and implicitly defined. To this end, *kc* is defined as a set of axioms $kc = <a_1(kc), a_2(kc), \ldots, a_n(kc)>$ constituting the specification of the corresponding ontology concept *c*. An axiom $a_i(kc)$ with $i \in [1,n]$ has the form $a_i(kc) = <n(kc), r(a_i), v(a_i), p(kc)>$ where:

- $n(kc) \in NC$ is the name of the knowledge chunk *kc*, which coincides with the name of *c*.
- $r(a_i) \in R$ is a semantic relation contained in the specification of *c*, with $R = NR \cup \{equivalentClass, subClassOf\}$.
- $v(a_i) \in V$ is the value of the corresponding relation $r(a_i)$, with $V = NC \cup D$.
- $p(kc) \in NP$ is the provenance of *kc*, namely the identifier of the peer from which the knowledge chunk originates (e.g., the peer MAC address).

An iCoord peer *P* organizes its knowledge repository according to iKM by distinguishing a *peer knowledge layer*, a *collective knowledge layer*, and a *collective peer knowledge layer*, respectively (see Fig. 1).

[1] Details about handshake of P2P semantic communities are provided in [7].

- *Peer knowledge layer*. It stores the personal knowledge of *P* in the form of a peer ontology *PO*(*P*) and a set of local knowledge chunks *KC*(*P*).
- *Collective knowledge layer*. It stores the knowledge retrieved by *P* from communities in the form of a set of harvested knowledge chunks.
- *Collective peer knowledge layer*. It stores the collective concepts of *P* in the form of a set of collective knowledge chunks built on the basis of the harvested knowledge chunks.

The knowledge repository of an iCoord peer is implemented as a relational database according to the ER schema shown in Fig. 2.

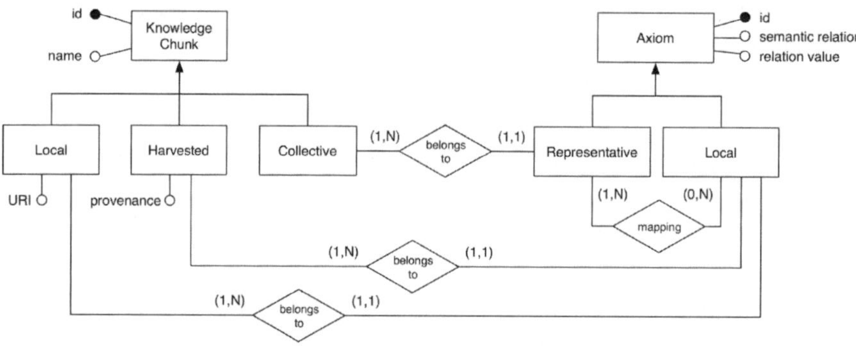

Fig. 2. ER schema of the iCoord knowledge repository

In the following, we describe the construction of the specific repository layers together with examples in the health-care domain.

The Peer Knowledge Layer

This layer stores the peer ontology *PO*(*P*), a Semantic-Web compatible description (i.e., RDF(S), OWL) of the peer contents/resources that are made available for sharing. For each ontology concept $c \in PO(P)$, a corresponding knowledge chunk $kc \in KC(P)$ is created. Standard techniques for DL reasoning are employed to classify *PO*(*P*) and to determine the set $S_c \cup E_c$ which represents the complete set of super and equivalent concepts of the considered concept $c \in PO(P)$. For example, considering OWL-DL ontologies, for each concept $c' \in S_c \cup E_c$, the following extraction rules are used to automatically create the knowledge chunk related to *c*:

1. If *c'* is an OWL property restriction, we add to *kc* the axiom $a(kc) = <n(c), r(c'), f(c'), p>$, where *n*(*c*) denotes the name of the original OWL concept *c*, *r*(*c'*) denotes the name of the OWL property involved in the property restriction *c'*, *f*(*c'*) denotes the property filler of *c'*, and *p* is the identifier of the peer *P*.

2. If $c' \in NC$ is a concept name in the signature of *PO*(*P*), we add to *kc* the axiom $a(kc) = <n(c), r, c', p>$, where *n*(*c*) denotes the name of the original OWL concept *c*, *r* is subClassOf if *c'* is a super concept of *c* or *r* is equivalentClass if *c'* is equivalent to the concept *c*, and *p* is the identifier of the peer *P*.

Example 1. We consider a peer P_d and the OWL-DL specification of the concepts Health-Care_Organization and Medical_Laboratory belonging to the peer ontology $PO(P_d)$ as follows:

Health-Care_Org. ⊆ ∃employs.Professional_Group

Health-Care_Org. ⊆ ∃mission.Health-Care

Medical_Lab. ⊆ Health-Care_Org.

Medical_Lab. ⊆ ∃produces.Test_Result

Through standard DL-reasoning techniques, we calculate the set S(Health-Care_Organization) = {owl:Thing, ∃employs.Professional_Group, ∃mission.Health-Care} which represents the complete set of super concepts of Health-Care_Organization. Each element in this set produces an axiom a_i of the knowledge chunk Health-Care_Organization as follows:

a_1(Health-Care_Org.) = < Health-Care_Org., rdf:subClassOf, owl:Thing, peer P_d >

a_2(Health-Care_Org.) = < Health-Care_Org., employs, Professional_Group, peer P_d >

a_3(Health-Care_Org.) = < Health-Care_Org., mission, Health-Care, peer P_d >

Similarly, for the concept Medical_Laboratory, the axioms of the knowledge chunk Medical_Laboratory are defined as follows:

a_4(Medical_Lab.) = < Medical_Lab., employs, Professional_Group, peer P_d >

a_5(Medical_Lab.) = < Medical_Lab., rdf:subClassOf, Health-Care_Org., peer P_d >

a_6(Medical_Lab.) = < Medical_Lab., produces, Test_Result, peer P_d >

a_7(Medical_Lab.) = < Medical_Lab., mission, Health-Care, peer P_d >

The Collective Knowledge Layer

This layer stores the harvested knowledge chunks that a peer *P* collects from other nodes with respect to a certain concept of interest by exploiting the communities to which *P* participates. For knowledge harvesting, a requesting peer *P* formulates a probe query *pq* containing an ontological specification of a target concept of interest expressed in the form of a knowledge chunk. This probe query *pq* is submitted to the network by choosing as recipients those communities whose members are most likely capable of providing knowledge chunks matching the target. A routing-by-community mechanism based on shuffling is defined to this end, and the query *pq* is sent to the peer members of the selected recipient communities for processing [7].

Receiving *pq*, a peer *P'* compares the incoming probe query against its peer ontology by invoking a semantic matchmaker to identify possible semantic affinities.

In iCoord, the HMatch 2.0 ontology matching engine is exploited, which performs matching at the level of knowledge chunks and calculates a value of semantic affinity *SA*(*pq*, *kc*) for each knowledge chunk $kc \in CK(P')$ [8]. A (possibly empty) list of matching knowledge chunks (i.e., concepts semantically related to the target query *pq*) is produced by HMatch 2.0 and it is returned to *P* as answer to *pq*.

The peer *P* stores the answers to the query *pq* in the collective knowledge layer as harvested knowledge chunks. Furthermore, the provenance *p*(*kc*) contains the identifier of the peer from which *kc* has been harvested. We observe that also local knowledge chunks in the peer knowledge layer can be relevant for the query *pq*. If it is the case, matching knowledge chunks of *KC*(*P*) are also stored in the collective knowledge layer as harvested knowledge chunks, coming from *P* itself.

The collective knowledge layer requires to be periodically updated with the purpose of refreshing the harvested knowledge chunks due to creation of new communities and/or to membership updates of existing ones. Periodic knowledge harvesting on the probe query *pq* is executed by the peer *P* to this end.

Example 2. The peer P_a is interested in harvesting knowledge about health-care institutions. A probe query pq_1 = {<Organization, has_goal, Health-Care, peer P_a>} is then formulated and submitted to the semantic communities sc_1 and sc_2 related to health-care organizations and hospitals, respectively. The peer P_d, member of both sc_1 and sc_2, receives pq_1 and it invokes HMatch 2.0 obtaining back Health-Care_Organization and Medical_Laboratory as matching knowledge chunks.

At the same time, the probe query pq_1 is locally processed by the requesting peer P_a itself, and the local knowledge chunk Organization is also stored by P_a as an harvested knowledge chunk in its collective knowledge layer.

a_8(Organization) = < Organization, rdf:subClassOf, owl:Thing, peer P_a >
a_9(Organization) = < Organization, involve, Professional_Society, peer P_a >
a_{10}(Organization) = < Organization, function, owl:Thing, peer P_a >
a_{11}(Organization) = < Organization, member, Person, peer P_a >

The Collective Peer Knowledge Layer

This layer stores the collective concepts of a peer *P* in the form of collective knowledge chunks, representing a unified view of the underlying harvested knowledge chunks about a certain concept of interest. Compared with knowledge chunks, a distinguishing feature of collective knowledge chunks is that (i) they are built considering a set of harvested knowledge chunks, and (ii) the provenance is expressed in terms of a set of axiom mappings expressing the correspondences with the axioms of the harvested knowledge chunks from which the collective concept has been derived.

The definition of a collective concept is articulated in two main phases, namely the *classification of knowledge chunks*, and the *construction of collective knowledge*.

The classification phase has the goal of clustering those axioms of the harvested knowledge chunks that denote the same or similar element using the HMatch 2.0 ontology matching engine. A hierarchical and agglomerative clustering algorithm is used to group together axioms according to their semantic affinity value produced by HMatch 2.0. The construction phase has the goal of creating a set of collective knowledge chunks out of the clusters previously computed, by defining a representative axiom for each cluster of matching axioms. A detailed procedure of collective concept construction is described in [7].

Example 3. Considering the peer P_a and the harvested knowledge chunks with the associated axioms $a_1,\ldots, a_{11}$ (see examples above), an example of the collective concept Organization is provided in Table 1.

Table 1. Example of the collective concept organization

Represent. axiom ID	Collective concept name	Semantic relation	Relation value	Axiom mapping
u_1	Organization	rdf:subClassOf	owl:Thing	$<a_1, a_5, a_8>$
u_2	Organization	Involve	Professional_Society	$<a_2, a_4, a_9>$
u_3	Organization	Function	owl:Thing	$<a_3, a_7, a_{10}>$
u_4	Organization	Member	Person	$<a_{11}>$

Usage of an iKM Knowledge Repository

Two main functionalities are available for exploiting the three-layer knowledge stored in an iKM repository, namely *knowledge browsing* and *data search.*

Knowledge browsing. This functionality enables a peer to explore both its personal knowledge (peer knowledge layer) and the harvested knowledge chunks collected from communities (collective knowledge layer). Through knowledge browsing, a peer can visualize the list of knowledge chunks and associated axioms related to a certain concept of interest by invoking the following command:

RETRIEVE {*peer|collective*} [<*concept name*>]

The {*peer|collective*} clause specifies the name of the repository layer to be considered in the query, while the [<*concept name*>] clause allows to specify the name of the concept requested for visualization. The *RETRIEVE* command is processed by invoking HMatch 2.0 and by matching the requested <*concept name*> against the knowledge chunks stored in the specified repository layer (i.e., peer/collective). A list of matching knowledge chunks is returned as a result.

Data search. This functionality enables a peer to query the network for searching data/resources of interest by exploiting the collective concepts stored in the repository. The idea is that a single query, called *collective query*, is posed on the collective concepts of a peer and it is automatically rewritten in a set of *peer queries* to be sent to a number of related peers spread across the network. To specify a collective query, the following command is defined:

SEARCH [<*collective concept name*>]
WHERE [<*condition*>]

The [<*collective concept name*>] clause specifies the name of the collective concept to be queried, while the [<*condition*>] clause specifies the constraints that need to be satisfied for including the associated data in the result. The *SEARCH* command is rewritten in a set of corresponding peer queries according to the mapping set of the specified <*collective concept name*>. These peer queries are sent to the appropriate nodes (by exploiting the provenance of the involved axioms) for processing and data acquisition. Examples of data search according to the iKM knowledge model are provided in [7].

Concluding Remarks

In this paper, we presented the iKM knowledge model for P2P semantic coordination in iCoord (http://islab.dico.unimi.it/icoord/). The development of the iCoord knowledge repository according to the iKM model has been completed. Currently, we are working on the development of the iCoord query engine where both knowledge browsing and data search functionalities will be implemented. Evaluation and experimental tests are planned to assess the effectiveness of iKM on real scenarios of P2P knowledge coordination.

References

1. Jung JJ, Euzenat J (2007) Towards semantic social networks. In *Proceedings of the 4th European semantic web conference (ESWC 2007)* Innsbruck, Austria
2. Bouquet P, Serafini L, Zanobini S (2004) Peer-to-peer semantic coordination. *J Web Semant* 2(1):81–97
3. Sabou M, D'Aquin M, Motta E (2008) Exploring the semantic web as background knowledge for ontology matching. *J Data Semant* XI:156–190
4. Calvanese D, De Giacomo G, Lenzerini M, Rosati R (2004) Logical foundations of peer-to-peer data integration. In *Proceedings of the 23rd PODS*, Paris, France
5. Castano S, Ferrara A, Montanelli S (2008) A reference architecture for semantic knowledge coordination. In *Proceedings of the 5th itAIS Conference*, Paris, France
6. Voulgaris S et al (2005) CYCLON: inexpensive membership management for unstructured P2P overlays. *J Netw Syst Manage* 13(2):197–217
7. Castano S et al (2009) *P2P semantic coordination for collective knowledge organization*. (Tech. Report) Università degli Studi di Milano. Submitted for publication
8. Castano S, Ferrara A, Montanelli S (2006) Matching ontologies in open networked systems: techniques and applications. *J Data Semant (JoDS)* V:25–63

Part IV
e-Justice

Francesco Contini*

In the last 15 years, the development of ICT has been one of the main and most complex challenges faced by European justice systems. Together with other pressures for change such as new public management, and most recently the serious budget constraints of the public sector, ICT has been one of the prominent drives of innovation. In this framework, policy makers used technological innovation and e-justice to pursue many different goals: efficiency and cost reduction, but also transparency, accountability and access to justice.

Applications developed in the last 15 years cover almost all the activities performed within judicial systems. On one side they have been used for the automation of administrative tasks (case tracking, case management systems, and more broadly office automation). On the other, ICT has been designed to support judges' operations offering an easier access to legal information, supporting decision making or other tasks performed by judges.

In all these areas, many judiciaries around the world have developed applications that are well integrated in the functioning of courts and judicial agencies. More recently, many judiciaries took seriously the challenge of e-justice to improve the access to dispute resolution and to increase the efficiency and effectiveness of the systems [1]. Indeed, justice systems can be described as networks of independent organizations (courts, law firms, police, prosecutors, prisons department etc.) exchanging data and document following pre-established formal procedures. Just apparently easy, the challenge of translating such exchange of information from paper to electronic media has been very problematic for practitioners in many EU countries.

First of all, e-justice does not deal just with the automation of paper based tool and procedures. It entails the development of an information infrastructure shared by the members of the network [2]. It requires the creation of new working practices and new "technological artifacts" with well established legal value, such as electronic summons, digital signatures, and on-line payment orders just to mention few of them [3]. Such developments require several changes in the normative framework regulating the functioning of judicial agencies and judicial procedures, such as the rules governing the correct identification of the persons entitled to access (and protect) data and documents. Even more complex is the question of authenticity, integrity, non repudiation of the documents exchanged electronically. The solutions found in the different countries to these techno-juridical knots,

---

* Istituto di Ricerca sui Sistemi Giudiziari, Consiglio Nazionale delle Ricerche (IRSIG-CNR), Bologna, Italy, francesco.contini@irsig.cnr.it

going from strong authentication based on PKI (Italy) to ultra-simplified systems based on "regular" e-mail (Finland), have strong consequences on the features of information infrastructure supporting the exchange, and on the development rate of the systems [4]. These innovations require an extensive organizational adoption of highly standardized procedures and technologies that may conflict with specific working practices adopted locally or by individual judges. In several cases, judges perceive these constraints as threats to their judicial independence and resist to their full adoption.

In addition, from a governance point of view, the development of e-justice requires the involvement of lawyers, bar associations, and other judicial agencies. Therefore, in comparison to other technological innovations successfully exploited in judicial system, the development of e-justice entails the management of several complex institutional and organizational issues, and the mediations between multiple contradictory interests. Therefore, the deployment of e-justice has to face a very high level of complexity and build systems interoperable not only at the technological level, but also from organizational, institutional and legal perspectives. It represents therefore a major challenge. More than a digitalization of the services provided by courts, it is an institutional reconfiguration of judicial proceedings and of the network of the different judicial agencies [5].

Given such complexities and the resources spent – especially in Italy – for technological and organizational developments the evaluation of the results achieved with e-justice and ICT in courts is a key issue. Lepore, Agrifoglio and Metallo, with their paper "Measuring Performance of Italian Courts: The Role of IS Success" move from the assumption that the outcomes of ICT must be strictly related with the broader outcomes of courts systems. Following the approach of the balanced score cards, the evaluation model developed in the paper relates indicators used to assess courts performances such as Courtools and indicators used to measure IS success inspired by the DeLone and McLean approach. The model proposed has now to be empirically tested in one or more courts, to verify its effectiveness.

References

1. Fabri M (2001) State of the art, critical issues and trends of ICT in European judicial systems. In Fabri M, Contini F (eds) *Justice and technology in Europe. How ICT is changing the judicial business*. Kluwer Law International, The Hague
2. Hanseth O, Lundberg N (2001) Designing work oriented infrastructures. *Comput Support Coop Work* 10:347–372
3. Contini F, Cordella A (2007) Information system and information infrastructure deployment: the challenge of the Italian e-justice approach. *Electron J e-Gov* 5(1):43–52

4. Fabri M (2009) E-justice in Finland and Italy: enabling versus constraining models. In Contini F, Lanzara GF (eds) *ICT and innovation in the public sector. European studies in the making of e-government*. Palgrave, Trowbridge
5. Lanzara GF (2009) Building digital institutions: ICT and the rise of assemblages in government. In Contini F, Lanzara GF (eds) *ICT and innovation in the public sector. European studies in the making of e-government*. Palgrave, Trowbridge

Measuring the Performance of Italian Courts: The Role of IS Success

Luigi Lepore[*], Rocco Agrifoglio[†] and Concetta Metallo[‡]

Abstract The aim of this research was to develop a decision support tool to measure the performance of Italian courts. This tool consists of five perspectives for measuring court performance, four of which are based on BSC perspectives, and one on the IS success perspective. We believe that this decision support tool could respond to the needs of court managers and presiding judges to improve the effectiveness and efficiency of dispute resolution, and overall court performance.

Introduction

Over the last 20 years the Italian Judicial System (JS) has been facing a dramatic crisis of performance. The JS plays an important role in socio-economic progress in every country. Like other public services, efficient and effective judicial services (e.g., dispute resolution) may be a critical factor in creating development opportunities for businesses, credit availability, and in attracting financial resources from other countries [1].

Italy has been one of the Countries in Europe that has spent the most on ICT and IS implementation to improve the efficiency and effectiveness of its JS [2]. The Italian legislator, through considerable investment in ICT, is trying to develop an "e-government approach" to the judicial sector (e-justice), that will adopt mechanisms of accountability and respect the principle of independence, satisfying the needs of the stakeholders [3]. The expected result is that e-justice will allow full on-line transaction between courts, lawyers, and the other actors within the JS. Many European countries have adopted e-justice solutions. Despite Italy being been one of the biggest spenders in this field [2], to date the results achieved have been very few. In fact, the Italian Court System is still characterized by bad performance, such as the unacceptable length of its proceedings, a very large amount of pending civil and penal proceedings and a significant amount of money invested [3].

---

[*] Management Department, Parthenope University, Naples, Italy, lepore@uniparthenope.it
[†] Management Department, Parthenope University, Naples, Italy, agrifoglio@uniparthenope.it
[‡] Management Department, Parthenope University, Naples, Italy, metallo@uniparthenope.it

A. D'Atri et al. (eds.), *Management of the Interconnected World*,
DOI 10.1007/978-3-7908-2404-9_28,

In this context, a Performance Measurement System (PMS) able to evaluate the performance, and particularly, the IS success contribution to improving the efficiency and effectiveness of the Court System can obviously be of value. In fact, "performance measurement is crucial to a court's ability to provide high quality yet cost-effective and efficient services to its customers. Court managers and presiding Judges increasingly embrace the idea of systematically integrating performance measurement into the daily operations of the courts" [4]:1.

The aim of this research is to develop a decision support tool to evaluate the Italian courts' performance based on the (Balanced Scorecard) BSC framework. Concerning this, we believe that the performance should also include an IS perspective and we therefore add another dimension to the BSC framework: IS success. Thus, the decision support tool developed for measuring performance consists of five perspectives, four of which are traditional BSC perspectives (financial, customer, internal operating, innovation, and learning), and one is related to IS success.

PMS in Non-profit Organizations

Several PMS have been developed to evaluate the business performance of both profit and nonprofit oriented organizations such as: Balanced Scorecard [5, 6]; Integrated Performance Measurement System [7]; Intangible Asset Monitor [8]; Piramide SMART [9]; Macro Process Model [10]; the Performance Prism [11]; Skandia Navigator [12]. These systems assume a very important role in organizations, supporting their strategic and operational decision making. Scholars and practitioners have used the BSC framework to investigate performance in nonprofit organization [13, 14] and, especially, in court [4].

The BSC is a management tool that provides a periodic assessment of how well the organization is progressing towards achieving its strategic goals. The model was created by Kaplan and Norton in the early 1990s and has grown in popularity ever since. BSC provides a concise view of the business performance through 4 perspectives: financial, customer, internal process, and innovation and learning. To each strategic objective of the organization are associated some measurements on the 4 perspectives of the Balanced Scorecard. Furthermore, this tool has been used to evaluate IT investments and IS performance in different kinds of organizations, both profit and non-profit oriented [15–18].

Courts are complex non-profit organizations that provide users with different types of services. According to Ostrom and colleagues [4]:9 their mission is to deliver justice, and for this purpose "the court will, in a fair, accessible, effective, and efficient manner, resolve disputes arising under the law and will interpret and apply the law consistently, impartially, and independently to protect guaranteed rights and liberties". Courts, therefore, pursue a plurality of goals through their services: ensuring legal certainty and effective legal protection of individuals, providing security and order.

In this context, the BSC is a useful instrument to measure how well a court is progressing toward achieving its strategic goals. It, in fact, identifies essential court activities, spells out their intended goals, and suggests indicators to measure the degree to which goals are achieved. The BSC framework, therefore, represents a leverage to assess the court's current performance and develop a workable strategy to achieve higher performance in the future. Indicators included in the 4 perspectives of the BSC give Judges and Court Managers information about a court's ability to be effective, satisfying its stakeholders (customer perspective), being efficient, saving money (financial perspective), timely in dispute resolution (internal operating perspective), and able to improve performance through processes of innovation and learning (innovation and learning perspective). As outlined above, we believe that adding a fifth dimension to the BSC is also possible to monitor the IS success contribution to improving the court's overall performance.

Information System Success

"IS success or effectiveness is critical to our understanding of the value and efficacy of IS management actions and IS investments" [19]:10. Many scholars recognize the need to evaluate IS success (or effectiveness) and a large number of systems success measures exist [20–22].

Bailey and Pearson [20] defined user satisfaction as the sum of an individual's reactions to a set of factors affecting IS success. They identified thirty-nine factors that influence IS user satisfaction and developed an instrument to measure them. Bailey and Pearson's instrument has been adopted in numerous research as a basis to measure IS satisfaction and success [e.g., 23–25].

DeLone and McLean [22] classified the dimensions of IS success into six categories: (1) system quality, the measurements of IS itself; (2) information quality, the measures of the IS output; (3) information use, recipient consumption of IS output; (4) user satisfaction, recipient response to the use of IS output; (5) individual impact, the effect of information on the behavior of the recipient; and (6) organizational impact, the effect of information on organizational performance. Particularly, system quality concerns the consistency of the user interface, the quality of documentation, and whether there are bugs in the system. Information quality concerns the relevance, timeliness and accuracy of information generated through the system. IS use concerns the use of the system by the user. User satisfaction, instead, is the sum of an individual's reactions to a set of factors affecting information system success [20]. Finally, individual and organizational impacts are the outcomes attributed to IS use [26] and user satisfaction [22].

DeLone and McLean's model is based on 3 levels: (a) technical, the accuracy and efficiency of the communication system that produces information; (b) semantic, the success of the information in conveying the intended meaning; (c) effectiveness, the effect of the information on the receiver. Therefore, the systems quality dimension measures technical success; information quality dimension measures semantic success; and effectiveness success is measured from several dimensions such as use, user satisfaction, individual and organizational impacts. Moreover, DeLone and McLean [22, 19] argued that this model is based on both process and causal considerations and, therefore, these dimensions of success are interrelated rather than independent. According to the authors, the aim of their model was to investigate a process understanding of IS and their impacts. Therefore, the process model analyzed 3 components: the creation, use, and consequences of system use. Really, they argued “each of these steps is a necessary, but not sufficient, condition for the resultant outcome(s)” [19]:16.

Seddon [26] proposed two dimensions for classifying IS effectiveness measures: type of system and stakeholder. Compared with DeLone and McLean’s Model, Seddon [26] argued that different IS success measurements are needed to assess not only the individual and organizational impact, but also the effectiveness of a system for different groups of stakeholders. Moreover, they substitute perceived usefulness for IS use because they believed that system use dimension represents a behavior, appropriate for inclusion in a process model, but not in a casual model. DeLone and McLean [22, 19], on the other hand, argued that system usage is an appropriate measure of success in most cases. In this way, Saariner [25] also highlighted that IS use represents a necessary condition for success.

Since 1992, DeLone and McLean’s IS success model has served as a basis for numerous successive studies and empirical investigations of IS success [e.g., 27, 28]. Other authors [15–18] have tried to evaluate IS success using the BSC model. Particularly, Wright and colleagues [17] argued that it could be reasonable to apply BSC also for the evaluation of software performance. In fact, in their BSC, software evaluation is included in the innovation and learning perspective. Rosemann and Wiese [18]: 774, however, used the BSC for the evaluation of IS tasks such as the process of implementation and operational use. As for the 4 dimensions of the BSC, they add a new project perspective, increasing the completeness and the quality of IS reports including measures such as processing time along the critical path or remaining time to the next milestone. Finally, Martinsons and colleagues [16] developed a BSC for IS. They used Kaplan and Norton’s BSC framework, adapting it to IT application projects and/or an IS department or functional area. Particularly, they suggested four perspectives to measure and evaluate IS: user orientation, business value, internal processes, and future readiness.

The Proposed Research Model

We have chosen the BSC to measure court performance because it, more than any other PMS, provides a range of information that goes beyond mere economic and financial performance. The BSC, in fact, makes extensive use of qualitative and non-financial indicators to demonstrate the overall ability of the organization to adequately satisfy the stakeholders. The BSC, thus, appears to be particularly suited to measuring the results in complex institutions such as courts, whose mission includes the achievement of several goals, not just financial ones.

Some authors [15, 18] have argued that although the innovation and learning dimension of BSC could also provide the measurement and evaluation of IS performance, in some cases it is not suitable for this purpose.

We believe that business performance should also include an IS perspective. Particularly, we assume that the profit and non-profit oriented organizations' business performance could be measured and evaluated using a decision support model based on both the classic four dimensions of the BSC and another that measures IS performance: IS success. Therefore, we developed a decision support tool that evaluates court performance based on different kinds of measures included in the following 5 perspectives: customer, internal operating, financial, innovation and learning (based on the BSC framework), and IS success. The indicators included in the customer, internal operating, and financial dimensions have been developed and validated using "CourTools" by the Institute for Court Management at the National Center for State Courts. This tool is a PMS used in the USA to evaluate first instance court performance. Based on the literature, we have selected and adopted other indicators. Figure 1 shows our decision support tool.

Fig. 1 Court performance measurement system (CPMS)

Customer Perspective	Internal Operating Perspective	Financial Perspective	Innovation and Learning Perspective	IS success Perspective
Access and fairness	Clearance rate	Cost per case	Number of professional Judges	System quality
	Case turnover ratio		Number of administrative staff	Information quality
	Disposition time		Number of IS end-users	Information use
			ICT hardware investment	User satisfaction
			ICT software investment	Individual impact
			CCAI	Organizational impact

The five dimensions comprising our decision support tool are the following:

(1) *Customer perspective*: the customer/user of a court is a person or an organization that receives the services provided by the court. The indicator that we use is "access and fairness". It is a measure of a court's accessibility and treatment of customers in terms of fairness, equality, and respect. Access and fairness will be measured using a 5 point scale developed by the National Center for State Courts;

(2) *Internal operating perspective*: the indicators used in this perspective measure the court's ability to be efficient, controlling its internal procedures and environments. The efficiency measurements used inform presiding judges and court administrators about how well resources are used to achieve intended goals. For this perspective we use the "clearance rate" indicator, which is the number of cases resolved as a percentage of the number of incoming cases. Another indicator is the "case turnover ratio" measured as the resolved cases/unresolved cases ratio. Finally, we use the "disposition time" calculated as the 365/case turnover ratio. These measurements are a fundamental management tool that evaluate the length of time it takes a court to process cases;

(3) *Financial perspective*: the indicator we use is a cost indicator such as "cost per case". It is a measurement of the average cost of processing a single case by case type (e.g., civil and/or penal cases). Cost per case will be measured using an indicator developed by the National Center for State Courts. This measurement aids managers in decision-making in order to improve efficiency and effectiveness of court;

(4) *Innovation and learning perspective*: in this dimension we include some indicators that measure the contribution of human resources, the information capital, and court culture to support innovation and learning. Particularly, for human resources, we use the following indicators: the number of administrative staff, the number of professional judges, and the number of IS end-users. Information capital, on the other hand, will be measured using the following indicators: ICT software and hardware investments. Finally, court culture will be measured using a specific scale [29], the Court Culture Assessment Instrument (CCAI), which has been adapted from the Organisational Culture Assessment Instrument (OCAI) scale [30]. The indicators used to measure human resources have been adapted from "CourTools" developed by the National Center for State Courts;

(5) *IS success perspective*: DeLone and McLean's model measures IS success classifying the dimensions of information system success into six categories: (1) system quality, (2) information quality, (3) information use, (4) user satisfaction, (5) individual impact, (6) organizational impact. DeLone and McLean [19] argued that "systems quality" measures technical success; "information quality" measures semantic success, while "use, user satisfaction, individual impacts and organizational impacts" measure effectiveness success. DeLone and McLean's model investigates IS performance by a process understanding of IS and their impacts. Therefore, their model represents a temporal and process model that analyses three components: the creation, use, and consequences of system use. IS success will be measured using Rai and colleagues' [28] scale.

Conclusion and Future Perspectives

The aim of this research has been to develop a decision support tool able to measure business performance in the Italian Court System. This tool is based on the BSC framework. It consists of 5 perspectives for measuring performance: financial, customer, internal process, innovation and learning, and IS success.

The IS plays an important role in the "modernizing" process of the JS. Through considerable investment in ICT, the Italian legislator is trying to develop an "e-government approach" to the judicial sector (e-justice), adopting mechanisms of accountability and respecting the principle of independence, satisfying the needs of the stakeholders [3]. Despite the large amount of money invested, however, very few results have been achieved after several years of effort.

This tool could be useful to support managers in decision-making in order to improve the allocation of resources and the achievement of intended goals. Moreover, our BSC could allow presiding Judges to reduce the length of dispute resolution and the backlog of cases, improving the quality of services provided to different groups of stakeholders. The information collected through this instrument, used at JS level, could also be useful for the legislator to understand whether the investments in ICT have produced the expected results.

In the future we will test our decision support tool in some Italian courts involved in the project named "Processo Civile Telematico" (PCT). This project, through widespread use of ICT in the courts' activities, aims to allow full on-line transaction between the ministry of justice, courts, lawyers, and other JS actors. In the Italian JS, the spread of ICT represents an important initiative in the modernization process that has been involving the Public Administration for the last decade. Particularly, we will use a quantitative method of data collection. We will administer a structured questionnaire to Court managers and IS end-users in order to test our decision support tool, measuring, and evaluating court performance.

References

1. Masciandaro D (ed) (2000) *La giustizia civile è efficiente? Primo rapporto sull'economia delle regole*. Laboratorio ABI-Bocconi. Bancaria Editrice, Roma
2. Fabri M (2001a) State of the art, critical issues and trends of ICT in European judicial system. In Fabri M, Contini F (eds) *Justice and technology in Europe: how ICT is changing judicial business*. Kluwer Law International, The Hague, The Netherlands
3. Contini F, Cordella A (2007) Information system and information infrastructure deployment: the challenge of the Italian e-justice approach. *Elect J e-Gov* 5(1):43–52
4. Ostrom B, Schauffler RY, Clarke TM, Ostrom C, Hanson R (2008) *A unifying framework for court performance measurement*. NCSC, Williamsburg
5. Kaplan RS, Norton DP (1992) The balanced scorecard: measures that drive performance. *Harv Bus Rev* 70(1):71–79
6. Kaplan RS, Norton DP (1996) *The balanced scorecard: translating strategy into action*. Harvard Business Scholl Press, Boston

7. Nanni AJ, Dixon JR, Vollmann TE (1992) Integrated performance measurement: management accounting to support the new manufacturing realities. *J Manage Account Res* 4(fall):1–19
8. Sveiby KE (1997) The intangible assets monitor. *J Hum Resour Cost Account* 2(1):73–97
9. Lynch R, Cross K (1991) *Measure up-yardsticks for continues improvement*. Blackwell, Oxford
10. Brown MG (1996) *Keeping score-using the right metrics for world class performance*. Quality Resources, New York
11. Neely A, Adams C (2001) *Perspectives on performance: the performance prism*. Cranfield School of Management, Cranfield
12. Edvinsson L, Malone MS (1997) *Intellectual capital: realizing your company's true value by finding its hidden brainpower*. Harper Collins, New York
13. Niven PR (2003) *Balanced Scorecard step by step for government and nonprofit agencies*. Wiley, Hoboken
14. Busco C, Riccaboni A, Saviotti A (2008) *Governance, strategia e misurazione delle performance. Le nuove frontiere della balanced scorecard*. Knowità, Arezzo
15. Martinsons MG (1992) *Strategic thinking about information management*. Keynote Address to the 11th annual conference of the international association of management consultants, Toronto
16. Martinsons M, Davison R, Tse D (1999) The balanced scorecard: a foundation for the strategic management of information systems. *Decis Support Syst* 25(1):71–88
17. Wright WF, Smith R, Jesser R, Stupeck M (1999) Information technology, process reengineering and performance measurement: a balanced scorecard analysis of compaq computer corporation. *Commun Assoc Inf Syst* 1(2):1–61
18. Rosemann M, Wiese J (1999) Measuring the performance of ERP software-a balanced scorecard approach. In *Proceedings of the 10th Australasian conference on information systems*, Hobart
19. DeLone WH, McLean ER (2003) The DeLone and McLean model of information systems success: a ten-year update. *J Manage Inf Syst* 19(4):9–30
20. Bailey JE, Pearson SW (1983) Development of a tool for measuring and analyzing computer user satisfaction. *Manage Sci* 29(5):530–545
21. Cheney PH, Mann RI, Amoroso DL (1986) Organizational factors affecting the success of end-user computing. *J Manage Inf Syst* 3(1):65–80
22. DeLone WH, McLean ER (1992) Information systems success: the quest for the dependent variable. *Inf Syst Res* 3(1):60–95
23. Ives B, Olson MH, Baroudi JJ (1983) The measurement of user information satisfaction. *Commun ACM* 26(10):785–793
24. Montazemi AR (1988) Factors affecting information satisfaction in the context of the small business environment. *MIS Q* 12(2):239–256
25. Saariner T (1996) An expanded instrument for evaluating information system success. *Inf Manage* 31(2):103–118
26. Seddon PB (1997) A respecification and extension of the DeLone and McLean model of IS success. *Inf Syst Res* 8(3):240–253
27. Goodhue DL, Thompson RL (1995) Task-technology fit and individual performance. *MIS Q* 19(2):213–233
28. Rai A, Lang SS, Welker RB (2002) Assessing the validity of IS success models: an empirical testand theoretical analysis. *Inf Syst Res* 13(1):50–96
29. Ostrom B, Ostrom Jr. C, Hanson R, Kleiman M (2007) *Trial courts as organizations*. Temple University Press, Philadelphia
30. Cameron KS, Quinn RE (2006) *Diagnosing and changing organizational culture*. Wiley, San Francisco

Part V
The Strategic Role of Information Systems

Gabriele Cioccarelli[*] and Ernestina Giudici[†]

This part of the book covers different issues related to the strategic role of Information Systems (IS), intended as the way in which IS can contribute to the creation and appropriation of value and the creation and sustainability of firm competitive advantage.

Recently the literature has begun to explore the role of capabilities and agility, and therefore the way in which competitive advantage is continuously developed and renewed through the development of IS dynamic capabilities and the capacity to streamline and quicken the reaction time to competitive changes. The emphasis is on the incorporation of IS into organizations' strategic thinking, strategy alignment, change management and innovation, knowledge management and organizational learning, as well as the exploration/exploitation of peculiar resources and competencies.

Seven papers have been selected to extend our current understanding on different aspects related to the strategic role of IS. Due to the wideness of this topic, the papers collected in this section face very different issues, as briefly reported below, to reflect the multiplicity of aspects and the complexity of the real world.

The paper of De Marco, Imperatori and Isari aims at giving a contribution to the current discussion around the interconnections between IS, Strategy and Organization researches. Based on a meta-analysis on a sample of 170 articles published in 2008 on leading AIS ranking journals, it addresses questions such as the most relevant topics and issues within the IS field of study, their linkages with Organization and Strategy issues and theoretical perspectives, and the research methods adopted.

The interconnections between IS, strategy and organization is faced also by the paper of Francesconi and Dossena. Their case study is focused on Web Reputation Management Systems, intended as strategic tools to protect and to manage – within the world of Web 2.0 – one of the most important firm resource, that is corporate reputation. Opportunities to exploit IT/IS to support decision making in this scenario and the need for specific capabilities are addressed in this work exploiting the experience of a young Italian consulting firm and its customer base of 35 firms.

The key role of Web is also dealt by Dessì, Floris and Melis, in terms of e-CRM development and the opportunities to generate knowledge on the gap between the "created value" and the "perceived value" within Web sites. This drives also towards the exploitation of learning chances that arise from wrong customer

---

[*] Faculty of Economics, University of Pavia, Pavia, Italy, gabriele.cioccarelli@unipv.it
[†] Faculty of Economics, University of Cagliari, Cagliari, Italy, giudici@unica.it

perceptions, as argued in their case study, to better support managerial decisions, CRM practices and the definitions of Web sites goals.

Marchi and Caserio also deal with the opportunity of knowledge generation, within decision-making processes. The authors propose what they call "Knowledge Generating Decision Support System" together with some applications in the specific field of "prediction and planning" and "variance analysis" to support their arguments.

Pinna, Carrus and Pettinao face firm performance and competitive advantage issues focusing on Supply Chain Management and its performances. Their work, based on a case study, suggests a more comprehensive framework to study the buyer-supplier relationships, in order to contribute to the research stream on logistics integration.

Virtual Reality and its organizational implications for business innovation in Small and Medium Enterprises start up is highlighted by Tampieri. The work is based on the case study of a simulated fashion enterprise established in Second Life (SL), one of the most diffused virtual worlds. Particular attention is made on the relations between real and virtual environments.

Finally, end-users capabilities and their consciousness on IS security issues are key issues in the paper of Cavallari. He starts from the consideration that information security policies and procedures can be often misinterpreted, misused, or not followed by end-users, thus undermining the organizational policies and practices related to strategic aims.

In conclusion, we acknowledge authors for their compelling works that challenge our thinking regarding taken-for-granted assumptions, models, and research practices related to a key topic, that is the strategic role of IS.

Information Systems Security and End-User Consciousness – A Strategic Matter

Maurizio Cavallari*

Abstract "Information security consciousness" (also cited in literature as awareness) is referred to the condition in which information systems users (end-users principally) in an organisation are well informed, prepared to – and committed – the security issues concerning the use of those systems. There is no doubt in doctrine that security of IS represents a central strategic matter. In adherence to Mathieson's thought about the use of Information Systems (IS) information security consciousness is, within that view, of fundamental importance. It is foreseen by a number of studies that a higher level of consciousness should significantly reduce "user related faults" and maximize the overall information system. Understanding of the context and of the original reasons of users-level errors, are crucial to achieve, at a strategic level, the above mentioned goals. The motivation of different organisational levels, e.g., to comply with information security policies and procedures is an activity that falls into the "content category". Technology Acceptance Model (TAM) of Davis and the Theory of Planned Behaviour of Ajzen are taken into account. Communication and moreover, the "persuasive communication" turned out to be one of the main key points. It is suggested that the persuasion strategy should start from communication of reasons and explanations, providing answers about rules and security procedures.

The Theoretical Framework

With respect to the types of security consciousness, this work focuses on the content part, which suggests the research for robust organisational theoretical foundations. Current approaches [1–3], are descriptive. Their partially unsatisfactory approach is also recognized by McLean [1], who states that the approaches commented do not ensure learning. As learning can be also descriptive it makes it an unacceptable objective for end-user security consciousness. On one hand it is true that learning and the other concepts and approaches are relevant in the case of end-user security consciousness, via education or training actions but, on the other hand, these approaches need a well established contextualisation as a starting point, in order to achieve relevancy. This level of descriptiveness is not considered an adequate objective for a security activity. Also with respect to the content part,

* Università Cattolica del Sacro Cuore, Milano, Italy, maurizio.cavallari@unicatt.it

A. D'Atri et al. (eds.), *Management of the Interconnected World*,
DOI 10.1007/978-3-7908-2404-9_29, © Springer-Verlag Berlin Heidelberg 2010

the crucial role of motivation (and behaviour) about end-users and security of Information Systems has been largely recognised [4–9], but, nonetheless, solely on an abstract level. Motivation is a matter, however, where an in depth view may be appropriate with respect to the efficaciousness of approaches which relies on it. In literature it is generally accepted that ability, motivation and working conditions greatly affects performance [10]. The mentioned factors interact naturally: the impact of motivation on performance depends on ability and viceversa (ibidem). Motivation is described as to be dynamic in nature (short term) in comparison with attitude which is more static and assimilated element (long term). Attitude regards mainly the quality of actions, while motivation correlates itself with activity levels. Some authors [11] states that there are two ways of inducing change in human beliefs: active participation and persuasive communication. A general review of these motivational and behavioural theories can be found in [1].

The Method

Conceptual analysis, as defined in the clear work of Jaervinen [12], is used as the main research method in this paper. Questions of how to be aware of "security consciousness" and how to increase the degree of consciousness to the management or within external entities go beyond the focus of this paper, which focuses on "human aspects" as thoroughly referenced on end-users at the strategic organisation level. The present work is organized within the following conceptual scheme. It is identified a behavioural scheme, which outlines selected motivation and behavioural theories that will be used to pursue the matter of the paper. Additional parts consider the response at the organizational level to security-consciousness activities. The currently available methods available in literature to increase user- consciousness are analyzed from the viewpoint of the identified theoretical scheme. The particular nature of consciousness, i.e. prescriptive, will be considered and commented, as well as a some approaches taking into account the prescriptive nature of consciousness are presented.

The Approach

Authors and studies had proven that performance depends greatly on ability – as considered the capability of workers to accomplish tasks, motivation – which finely adjust behaviour, and the working conditions [10]. The same authors demonstrate that the influence of motivation on performance depend on ability and viceversa. Motivation is known in literature as to be dynamic while attitude is defined as a static, stable factor. Attitude refers basically to the quality of actions, while motivation correlates itself with activity levels. Fishbein and Ajzen [11] identified two main ways to induce change in human beliefs (whether beliefs would lead towards motivation and attitude, is still unclear as a general scheme): active participation and persuasive communication. The Theory of Planned Behaviour [11], i.e. TPB, and TAM [13] had been observed to be valid [14] and should be, therefore, constantly taken into account within the present work. Many scholars, such as Mathieson [14], Adams et al. [15], had used and/or compared TAM and TPB. What makes the theory of intrinsic motivation more attractive for our purposes is that it seems to consider the role of motivation deeper than TPB.

Intention. An interesting analysis of motivational – behavioural theories is pursued in Locke [16] and it leads to the formulation of the theories of Fishbein and Ajzen [11] and Ajzen [17] which consider the "intention" as «the immediate determinant of the corresponding behaviour». Furthermore "intention" is divided into «attitude toward behaviour» and «subjective norm concerning behaviour». In subsequent developments of Ajzen's mentioned theory [17] we can find developments in terms of definition of planned behaviour, in which arises a new element. i.e. «Perceived behavioural control».

Attitude. On the other hand we find "attitude", defined as a threefold, consisting of: (a) confidence regarding the consequences of a specific behaviour, (b) subjective norm which refers to normative beliefs as an exogenous element, and (c) motivation to comply [11]. The effects in the field of security policies and procedures of normative beliefs may greatly increase due to an «organizational norm/culture» or role responsibility, including compliance to own mission or role. About attitude, the preset work is interested in users' concerns about the consequences of complying with the security norms. In facts, the satisfying of the "attitude" element shows that it is desirable to live up to security practices. In Ajzen's theory of planned behaviour there is a third element, the concept of "Control Beliefs and Perceived Facilitation" (also known as CBPF), which points to «people's perception of the ease or difficulty of performing the behaviour of interest» [17]. Looking at the Technology Acceptance Model (TAM) [13], systems use relies on behavioural "intention" of use, which implies also "attitude" towards use. This can be divided into the following elements of perception: "perceived usefulness", and "perceived ease of use". We can clearly see that the TAM and the TPB require both that must be desirable, in the perception of the users, the consequences of complying to security procedures. Ease of use is a rather common aspect, present into TPB's as "perceived behavioural control". As we can appreciate, TAM is close to TPB. It is interesting to point out how "perception" is, in this context, a most important subjective element to take into account, hence further investigation are foreseen towards what are the main influences about that highly subjective element, i.e. perception in general and moreover "perception of security" [18].

Intrinsic motivation. With regards to Deci's "intrinsic motivation" who had been extensively discussing the matter, [19, 20], it has to be noticed that the definition consists of «feeling to be free to make own choices concerning each individual's behaviour»; something very close to the concept of "self-determination". At the end, self-determination is shown to be the principal factor in deciding whether we are in presence of intrinsic or external motivation. Bear this in mind, and with respect to security policies, it seems that users are usually more externally motivated than intrinsically. An interesting question is whether internal aspirations, abilities and external forces (security policies in this case, along with normative beliefs in terms of TPB) reflect people's feeling of freedom. Certain studies show that active programmes and active participation could be useful in this respect. According to Deci [19], intrinsic motivation includes excitement and a feeling of being challenged. Other researchers also state that the feeling of being respected is also to be taken into account while designing training programmes. Organisational culture and working atmosphere, team spirit and more general view of life also have reflections on intrinsic motivation and on intention (subjective norms, motivation to comply, in terms of Ajzen's TPB). Wise organisational culture, good leadership and healthy working environment shows themselves to be surely important and necessary factors in achieving wide security consciousness throughout the organisation, as they affect the creation of intrinsic motivation and of intention and also have a definitive impact on perceived usefulness (also in terms of TAM). It has been proven that labour dissatisfaction can spring in unethical and immoral behaviour of employees and can give a way to a number of security threats [10].

Enhancing Consciousness

In order to comprehend, within the scope of this work, the response from people involved into organisational actions pointing to increased consciousness, it is important to outline the variety of non univocal type of responses of (any) human being to different stimuli [16]. According to some studies, there is a wide choice for the adoption of different steps in the direction of commitment [21, 22].

The mentioned study demonstrates that there are a multitude of levels of acceptance and commitment in every organisation (from very low to very high), and that all the different levels are always represented. Acceptance and commitment are here referred as the dynamic state of mind after the introduction of a consciousness activity. With respect to this studies, the various levels seem to a constant in the organisations. The success or otherwise of security consciousness activities depends greatly on the appropriateness of the action as addressed considering the level of acceptance in which is being implemented. Misunderstanding of the context in terms of the mentioned levels, might lead to failure of the action or even worst. "Positive" responses are, e.g., readjustment, co-operation, acceptance and assimilation, while "negative" responses are, as a example, hostility, even leading to stronger kinds of contrasting feelings. User acceptance and assimilation should be regarded as slow, long terms, goals. It has been argued, by Spruit et altrii [23], that algorithmic evaluation of human attitude may not be feasible and even appropriate as it is subject to major changes and greatly depends on the person [24]. So generalisation of such an element would not be included in the present work, although some general results of qualitative research in the field may give an option in trying to understand user behaviour.

Some authors suggest that campaigning could be an appropriate approach in order to disseminate security education [1]. From these studies we learn that it is included the so called "selling" the idea of information security to users through campaigns. Such a kind of action, i.e. campaigning, could in theory prove itself very useful in terms of stimulation and creation of motivation, hence pointing towards attitude about information systems security, as it helps to maintain high the relevance of security in the eyes of users. Those studies highlighted, however, that security campaigns may also provoke undesirable effects in terms of motivation and attitude, e.g. negative feelings, irritation, hate and various forms of resistance.

A wise utilisation of the mentioned method should be regarded to, and aimed at, carefully, controlled, and with support actions. An interesting method was proposed by Perry [2] and it is resembling campaigns. Its main idea is rendering information systems security an "in" topic, a fashion within an organization, we would call this method the "fashionable of security" (ibidem). Evidences suggest that campaigns and fashionable topics can be used alongside with consciousness programmes and that they may prove useful in providing incentives for end-users about the importance of security. Moreover, security consciousness involves education and training. Education should enhance users' insight and clarify the question about "why" (and this surely enhance motivation), while training should point towards skills and competence (i.e. the ability aspect of performance, in terms of TPB and perceived behavioural control, which should lead to make easy the compliance to security policies and procedures), and give an answer to the question "how". Since the reasons (the "why" part) of security policies are very important (probably the most), users cannot be motivated with statements like "just do it this way", or "this is the rule", or "the procedure says so", and so on. This seems to be a largely spread out approach, let's say, a "traditional approach".

On the other hand, and from the behavioural theories point of view, the simple announcement of security procedures, in the hope that they will be spontaneously implemented, is also clumsy and inappropriate. These traditional approaches do not have any support from motivational theories, either. Moreover if we regard to the theory of the Cognitive Moral Development (CMD) of Kohlberg [25], it is clear that the mentioned approaches are just not adequate. The CMD theory proves that, about moral matters, with rational people orders per se, i.e. "this is the rule", do not meet the expectations. The statement «the facts do not force us logically to make one moral judgement rather than another», has proven to be valid, in addition to moral norms, to other norms or "duties", such as the one implied in information systems security.

We can then also assume that the CMD can be adopted in our context. There is a definite normative nature of security, which ought to be understood.

The Prescriptive Nature of Security

Considering the intrinsic nature of information system security policies and procedures, which is authoritative and goal-oriented, there little doubt that the information security consciousness should be prescriptive.

Warman gives us a good statement when affirming that the real problem is that users very often acknowledge the rules and the procedures but avoid to apply them in practice [9]. To be aware of the procedures does not guarantee their correct implementation. This is a wider problem when considered in terms of standard and legal compliance throughout the whole organisation.

The kind of commitment related to the term "prescriptive" is bound to the situation in which people shows a form of interiorised motivation and within the role responsibility and, as an ideal situation, moral responsibility. Thus, to be effective the security actions must be regarded as moral and desirable. Norms and exogenous hints even if accepted in the short term tend to show, in a longer run, adverse and negative effects, like resistance and irritation (affecting labour effectiveness). It is very clear at this point of the work what security actions and enhanced security consciousness require more then just a set of policies and procedures to strictly adhere to. Justification and explanation of the reasons of security procedures turns out to be an important factor.

As an example the so called "social engineering" actions show a particular auto-immune effect: nobody likes to be manipulated, so once somebody has been the target of social engineering manipulation (or other forms of manipulation) it won't be an easy target any more [26]. This is a pretty explicit confirmation of intrinsic motivation power, cfr. Locke [16] and Bartol and Martin [10]. Motivation and attitudes change greatly if arguments and justifications are given in order to explain the reasons for security procedures.

Active participation and persuasion through communication should be the actions undertaken to a successful implementation of security processes which would eventually lead to an enhanced user consciousness. This kind of approach has proven itself within behavioural studies [11], even though not with particular reference to information systems.

Communication and Enhanced User Consciousness – The Strategic Issue

Communication turns out to be a strategic critical success factor while designing programmes to achieve enhanced end-user security consciousness. In the view "prescriptive consciousness" appears to be a rational objective with robust theoretical background. Strategic implementation of information security consciousness programmes requires a structural approach.

The present work started with a division of the literature about consciousness in general. The framework should be thought in a systematic way with the help of appropriate standards and complying to external rules (law and best practices). As far as end-user motivation and attitude of the security policies and procedures is the final goal, the content part of the security consciousness should also come under wise consideration.

Particular notice should be given to the presented difference between descriptive and prescriptive (factual-normative, respectively) and the understanding of the relevance of the prescriptive nature is crucial. It's a well-established opinion of the author that all effective organisational approaches related to, or affecting the behaviour of user should take into serious account the requirements of behavioural theories.

Communication and moreover, the "persuasive communication" is one of the main key points. The persuasion strategy should start from communication of reasons and explanations, providing answers about rules and security procedures.

The persuasive communication and actions should state clearly there is no bias between organisational levels and, moral and ethics motives should be communicated and internalised by end users. There is a limitations of this work, which rely on the research method used, e.g. conceptual analysis. Empirical studies are needed to consider the validity of the presented study.

References

1. McLean K (1992) Information security awareness – selling the cause. In *Proceedings of the IFIP TC11/Sec'92*, Singapore, 27–29 May
2. Perry WE (1985) *Management strategies for computer security*. Butterworth Publisher, Boston
3. Morwood G (1998) Business continuity: awareness and training programmes. *Inf Manage Comput Secur* 6(1):28–32
4. Parker DB (1998) *Fighting computer crime – a new framework for protecting information*. Wiley Computer Publishing, New York
5. Baskerville R (1989) Logical controls specification: an approach to information system security. In Klein H, Kumar K (eds) *Systems development for human progress*. North-Holland, Amsterdam
6. SSE-CMM (1998a) *The Model*, v2.0, http://www.sse-cmm.org
7. SSE-CMM (1998b) *The Appraisal Method*, v2.0. http://www.sse-cmm.org
8. Thomson ME, von Solms R (1998) Information security awareness: educating our users effectively. *Inf Manage Comput Secur* 6(4):21–39
9. Warman AR (1992) Organisational computer security policy: the reality, *Eur J Inf Syst* 1(5)
10. Bartol KM, Martin DC (1994) *Management*. McGraw-Hill, New York
11. Fishbein M, Ajzen I (1975) *Belief, attitude, intention and behaviour: an introduction to theory and research*. Addison-Wesley, Reading
12. Jaervinen P (1997) The new classification of research approaches. In: Zemanek H (ed) *The IFIP pink summary – 35 years of IFIP*. IFIP, Laxenburg
13. Davis F (1989) Perceived usefulness, perceived ease of use, and user acceptance of information technology. *MIS Q* 13(3):189–211
14. Mathieson K (1991) Predicting user intentions: comparing the technology acceptance model with the theory of planned behaviour. *Inf Syst Res* 3(2):173–191

15. Adams DA, Nelson RR, Todd PA (1992) Perceived usefulness, easy of use, and usage of information technology: a replication. *MIS Q* 16(2):227–247
16. Locke EA (1991) *The motivation sequence, the motivation hub, and the motivation core.* Organ Behav Hum Decis Process 50:288–299
17. Ajzen I (1991) The theory of planned behaviour. Organ Behav Hum Decis Process 50:179–211
18. Straub DW, Welke RJ (1998) Coping with systems risk: security planning models for management decision making. *MIS Q* 22(4):441–469
19. Deci EL (1975) *Intrinsic motivation.* Plenum Press, New York
20. Deci EL, Ryan RM (1985) *Intrinsic motivation and self-determination in human behaviour.* Plenum Press, New York
21. Conner DL, Patterson RW (1982) *Building commitment to organizational change*. Train Dev J 36(4):18–30
22. Taylor WA (1995) Senior executives and ISO 9000: attitudes, behaviours and commitment. *Int J Qual Reliab Manage* 22(4):40–57
23. Spruit MEM (1998) Competing against human failing. In *Proceedings of the 15th IFIP world computer congress.* The global information society on the way to the next millennium. Proceedings of the SEC '98, TC11, Vienna
24. Senge PM (1990) *The 5th discipline: the art and practice of the learning organization.* Doubleday Currency, New York
25. Kohlberg L (1981) *The philosophy of moral development: moral stages and the idea of justice*. Harper and Row, San Francisco
26. Ceraolo JP (1996) Penetration testing through social engineering. *Inf Syst Secur* 4(4):34–57

The Simulation by Second Life of SMEs Start Up: The Case of New Fashion Perspectives

Laura Tampieri*

Abstract The aim of the paper is to analyze and discuss the organizational implications of the Virtual Reality (VR) in Small and Medium Enterprises (SMEs) start up. To this purpose the case of the simulated enterprise in the fashion sector New Fashion Perspectives (NFP) will be examined, with its establishment from 2008 in Second Life (SL), one of the most diffused 3D world in last years. In particular the analysis wants to underline the impact of ICT implications on organizational processes and structures according to the networking approach based on the net of relationships that an organization can establish during its cycle of life and mainly in the start up phase.

The Use of Virtual Reality in Business Management

The increasing interest of the scientific community [1] on the strategic role of IT in business management, mainly in terms of impacts on technological competencies, capabilities and behaviors, has been extended to VR that recent studies [2] recognized as primary research field in business innovation.

As most of business transactions are carried out using Internet, the issues of managing these relationships among the VR actors within bounded resources and with the required level of trust, need to be analyzed, in connection also with the progresses made in this field [3].

The diffusion of Information Systems (IS) and VR applications as Metaverse, There, SL accelerated in many organizations the process of virtualization [4] in order to restructure and implement innovative solutions considering the organizational strategies of resources exploring and exploiting [5].

VR become a very diffused tool to establish electronic communities or virtual playgrounds in which people participate simultaneously in an interactive environment provided by computer technologies, according to an immersive perspective [6].

A controversial topic is linked to the researches on the symmetry and the relations between the real environment and the virtual one and, particularly, on the effective impact of the second on the first one. To this purpose a reconfigurable vir-

---

* Forlì Faculty of Economics, University of Bologna, Bologna, Italy, laura.tampieri@unibo.it

A. D'Atri et al. (eds.), *Management of the Interconnected World*,
DOI 10.1007/978-3-7908-2404-9_30,

tual platform for virtual testing based on real time data and communication between virtual environment and real one has been proposed [7].

A relevant question to be considered is the individuation of the adequate level and the modalities of competitiveness achieved by the entrepreneurial initiatives into the virtual world.

Many Studies, undertaken on this topic [8, 9], underlined the connections between IT and business management particularly if we consider the virtual world where the relationships with suppliers and customers are very relevant for the creation of a network that allows the enterprises to start up and to survive in the market.

These virtual relationships created in SL seem to be mostly weak owing to the rapidity and multiplicity of transactions among all the residents, especially in the start up phase. However these links are considered as the basis for the trade of virtual products/services that interfaces the real world by using virtual money convertible in the real one[1].

The analysis is focused on the enterprises start up that is a concept argued by many Authors [10, 11] that distinguished two organizational approaches: the clustering and the networking. They defined the clustering as a resource based process that stresses the relevance of financial assets and information in a stock taking perspective, quite far from the attitude of action management that characterizes the networking, highly involved in start up activities and in the survival struggle of new initiatives [12].

The networking is based on the continuous building and maintenance of the net that the enterprises have to manage with customers and suppliers on the basis of a clear and strong commitment [13]. In these terms the commitment, as the first order of work, represents the main impulse for the organizations in the process of relationships creation with customers and suppliers, that allows them to insert and survive in the market.

The research analyzes the networking approach as a very diffused organizational and managerial tool in SMEs [14, 15] on the basis of an internal and external perspective. The internal perspective considers the relationships created inside the organizations, while the external one refers to the links established among organizations of a common network and among different networks. In this way it is possible to set a more dynamic system's boundary.

In the virtual world the establishment of the commitment and of the practice of networking is still discussed considering that the virtualization process of structures, actually in a development phase for SMEs, involves the following entities of the framework: the real enterprise (A), the simulation as a reproduction of the real business by real agents (B) and virtual ones (C) and the 3D asset in Virtual World (D) (Fig. 1).

---

[1] The virtual trade in SL is based on the currency Linden™ dollar (L$). Residents can buy and sell L$ on the LindeX™, the official virtual currency exchange of SL. In 2008 more than USD $100 million worth of L$ were bought and sold on the LindeX. http://secondlife.com.

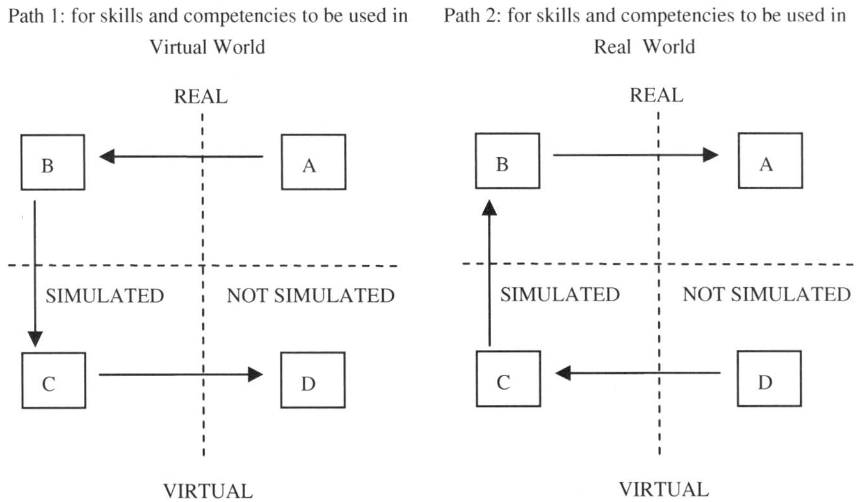

Fig. 1. The different paths from real to virtual and from virtual to real organization

This interrelation between the process and the structure determined two different paths in the start up approach. The first path specifies the start up of a real enterprise that, passing through the simulation models in real and virtual environment, creates a virtual platform to test innovative processes and products for real and virtual businesses. This platform produces itself a virtual organization to increase the business also in the virtual world, mainly for marketing and branding targets. The second path is linked to the start up as virtual organization used to improve managerial capabilities and skills for the establishing of a real enterprise operating in the real market.

According to the networking approach both these paths are based on the process of organizational links creation that assumes different characteristics in the real and virtual world. If we consider SL, the virtual contacts are linked to the rapidity and multiplicity of transactions among SL entrepreneurs, especially in their start up phase, making these relationships mainly weak and with a high renewal.

The Methodological Approach

The dynamic of virtual relationships in SMEs start up, according to the networking approach, is the main research topic that is discussed in the paper through the case analysis with the distinction of three entities involved in the start up and in the routine activities : (1) the real business, (2) the simulation unit and (3) its reproduction in VR.

The survey on the networking approach is carried out by analysing the organizational implications of the creation of a net of virtual contacts that SMEs addressed to establish mainly in the start up phase.

The research path can be summarized as follows: (1) The different profile of the networking level, that can be measured by the number and the persistence of contacts that an enterprise can create, is influenced by the change of organizational set ups. (2) The interrelations among real, simulated and virtual worlds can be connected to different expressions of the networking approach, particularly as it concerns its level and time. (3) The acceleration of the start up time for new entrepreneurial initiatives is made by simulation and VR.

The variables considered in a significant period of time refer to the number of contacts with visitors as the expression of the level of networking achieved by an enterprise. In other terms the networking, with the main aim of creating a net based on the relationships among the organizations, can be measured by the number of visitors considered as potential customers and suppliers.

Moreover the number of primitives, that are the basic elements used to create equipments in virtual space, are the main operative resources available for the virtual enterprises.

The Case of New Fashion Perspectives

The research, still in progress, considers the case of New Fashion Perspectives (NFP), the simulated micro enterprise of fashion sector established on October 2008 with the support of Perting[2], the first simulated unit certified by Europen Network and established in an Italian University (Bologna University- Forlì Faculty of Economics), that operates in the field of organizational and network consulting with the merchandising of ICT products.

NFP, that is the specular initiative of a micro enterprise operating in the real business of fashion, produces and sells clothes and accessories.

The simulation was realized in Forlì Laboratory managed by Bologna University-Faculty of Economics that begun to operate since 2001 with students, as participants, carrying out the organizational functions, assuming managerial responsibilities, roles and tasks, working in team, as happen in a real enterprise, under the mentoring of teachers and tutors, according to the learning by doing strategy [16].

[2] http://www.perting.altervista.org

In NFP land[3] the residents can easily access and use the equipments and operative tools as clipper, sewing machine and cutter to create clothes and fashion products and where it's possible to realize the trade, reproducing and simulating the activities of a real micro enterprise (Fig. 2).

Fig. 2. The NFP in SL

The infrastructural change of the NFP building moved from an experimental atelier-laboratory in 2008 with the main aim of testing fashion products attractiveness, to an atelier-pavilion on March 2009, with the structure of a store, for the production and trade of clothes and fashion accessories. In this pavilion posters and models of clothes are showed.

Considering the number of primitives as a parameter that influences the organizational settings, the survey shows an increasing trend from the initial laboratory to the store, passing from 76 to 104 used primitives (Fig. 3).

Initial Infrastructure from 14/10/08	**Renewed Infrastructure from 13/03/09**
Primitives materials: 76 - Sewing machine: 51 - Dummy: 7 - Raw materials: 8 - Computer and magazines: 4 - Poster:1 - Final products: 5	Primitives materials:9 - Sewing machine: 51 - Dummy: 7 - Raw materials: 8 - Computer and magazines: 4 - Poster:1 - Final products: 8 - 2 vendors with 2 models of clothes (2 primitives) - 3 vendors for 3 different models of clothes (3 primitives) - 4 promotional materials (4 primitives) - 1 bag (3 primitives)

Fig. 3. The primitives in the initial and renewed infrastructure (On 8th May 2009)

[3] http://slurl.com/secondlife/Kouhun/246/248/54

According to the first level of analysis about the impacts of VR on the implementation and the development of organizational set ups in SMEs, the virtual world is considered as the environment where the start up activities are addressed to build the strategic and operative conditions mainly toward the realization of links with customers and suppliers, according to the networking approach based on the creation of relationships with other virtual entities symmetrically connected with companies existing in the real world.

The analysis shows that with the change of NFP infrastructural setting the number of visitors increased especially in few days after the renewed form building (Fig. 4).

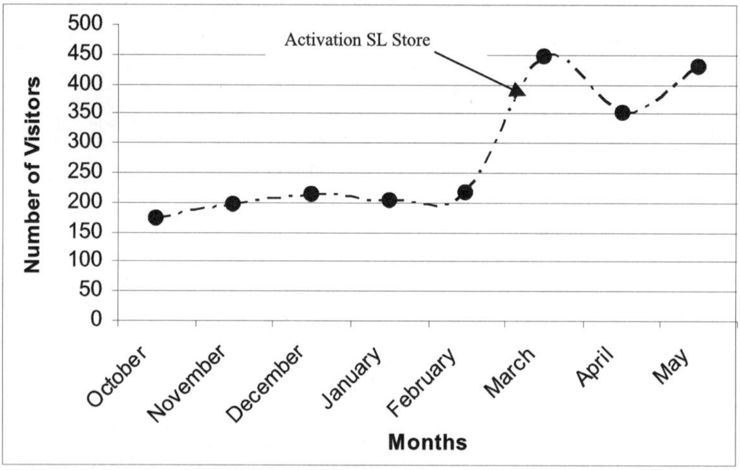

Fig. 4. The trend of the number of visitors October 2008 – May 2009

In this way we can state that the level of networking, expressed by the number of visitors interacting with NFP in the start up phase, is linked to the change of organizational set ups.

As it regards the second level of analysis, the interrelations among real, simulated and virtual worlds move on the basis of different orientations to networking approach. These orientations are confirmed by NFP behaviour that, from the start up of the virtual store in SL on March 2009 till the end of May[4], registered 10 sales (from a catalogue of 8 products) to 5 different customers[5]. In particular the different expressions of the networking approach in start up phase underlined the connections between the number of visitors and the sales of NFP in SL.

A different orientation of the networking can be referred to the behaviour of real enterprises that, especially in the start up phase, aims to realize strong commitments for stabilizing and fidelizing the customers.

[4] Up to 25th May 2009.

[5] Poka Rokocoko, Zanthian Loire, Alty Saphir, Ambre Jenkins, ChasityLace001 Baxton.

The third level of analysis regards the acceleration of the start up time of new entrepreneurial initiatives that is made by simulation and VR. The reduction of start up timing, as the main recent trend, moved from a dimension of years as forecasted by the regulations of enterprise incubator in the maximum period to be hosted in this artificial environment and crated to facilitate the start up of new enterprises[6] to a month as indicated by recent studies in the formal processes needed for the enterprises start up also with the support of municipal organisms[7]. In terms of weeks, the time of start up is linked to the decision making processes and the networking[8]. Especially in the virtual world the dynamism and the velocity to create relationships among organizations accelerated the process of start up passing from the unit of weeks to those of days. In this process the simulation models can facilitate the passage from real to virtual world and vice versa reducing the time of operative processes and improving technological and managerial skills.

Conclusions

The research underlined the perspective of the key role of IT in networking approach for achieving a competitive advantage in the dynamic market [17] and facing the challenges provided in knowledge management [18]. In this way the possibilities of using IS, especially with the main aim of integrating the different activity areas solving the structural and processual problems related to the coordination of business functions [19, 20] and in some cases for the outsourcing purposes [21], clearly emerged in last years. The networking activities are particularly relevant in SL where the transactions are carried out in a fast way and the interactions with suppliers and customers, personalized by Avatars, provide on time a feedback in order to establish a net of contacts. In comparison to the traditional techniques of simulation enterprise, in the examined case the use of virtual reality determined a relevant impulse to the development of contacts with customers and suppliers that are considered as the basis for the enterprise start up.

References

1. Turban E, McLean E, Wetherbe J, Bolloju N, Davison R (2002) *Information technology for management. Transforming business in the digital economy*, 3rd edn. Wiley, New York, pp 250–261
2. Lattemann C, Kupke S, Stieglitz S, Fetscherin M (2007) How to govern virtual corporations. *E-Bus Rev* VII:137–141

---

[6] See www.sviluppoitalia.it; www.ri.camcom.it

[7] For instance the public transport sector with the chart of services. See www.atr.fc.it

[8] "The time required for business start up (registration and licensing procedures) measures calendar days for a firm to obtain all necessary permits, and to notify and file with all requisite authorities, in order to legally operate a business". See www.worldbank.org

3. Li Y, Fu SS, Chung JY, Chao KM (2007) Emerging technologies for e-business engineering. *Inf Syst E-Bus Manage* 6(1):1–3
4. Overby E (2008) Process of virtualization theory and the impact of information technology. *Org Sci INFORMS* 19(2):277–291
5. Lazer D, Friedman A (2007) The network structure of exploration and exploitation. *Adm Sci Q* 52(4): 667–694
6. Suh KS, Lee YE (2005) The effects of virtual reality on consumer learning: an empirical investigation. *MIS Q* 29(4):673–697
7. Wu WY, Zhao Z (2005) Realization of reconfigurable virtual environments for virtual testing. *Int J Autom Comput* 2(1):25–36
8. Dittrich K, Duysters G (2007) Networking as a means to strategy change: the case of open innovation in mobile telephony. *J Product Innov Manage* 24(6):510–521
9. Barabasi AL (2004) Link. La nuova scienza delle reti. Einaudi, Torino, pp 211–230
10. Baker T, Nelson RE (2005) Creating something from nothing: resource construction through entrepreneurial bricolage. *Adm Sci Q* 50(3):329–366
11. Bianchi M (2005) Cluster analysis or NewBuc? Some lessons from projects of SME creation in transition countries. In: Bianchi M, Tampieri L (eds) *Life long learning and managerial development in transition countries* (pp. 11–18). Il Ponte Vecchio, Cesena
12. Tampieri L, Zaric S (2007) Improving intangible assets through project management in transition countries. In: Babic S, Cerovic B, Jaksic M, Prascevic A (eds) Challenges of globalization and transition. In *Proceeding of contemporary challenge of theory and practice in economics* (pp. 417–427), Faculty of Economics, University of Belgrade, Belgrade
13. Bruni A, Perrotta M (2007) Apprendimento inter-organizzativo e biotecnologie: dai network al networking. *Studi Organizzativi* 1:97–214
14. Tsai T, Zhou C, Cheng B (2007) Internal networking and organisational capability: towards a new perspective of the firm. *J Gen Manage* 33(2):25–40
15. Tappi D (2003) On the unit of analysis in the study of networks. In: Fornahl D, Brenner T (eds) *Cooperation, networks and institutions in regional innovation systems*. Edward Elgar, Cheltenham, pp 149–170
16. Gualdi D (2001) *L'impresa simulata*. Paravia Bruno Mondadori, Varese
17. Mason RB (2008) Management actions, attitudes to change and perceptions of the external environment. A complexity theory approach. *J Gen Manage* 34(1):37–53, Braybrooke Press, UK
18. Ratcheva V (2008) The knowledge advantage of virtual teams-processes supporting knowledge synergy. *J Gen Manage* 33(3):53–67, Braybrooke Press, UK
19. Carignani A (2005) *IT is…Il ruolo delle Tecnologie dell'Informazione nella teoria e pratica dei Sistemi Informativi*. FrancoAngeli, Milano
20. De Marco M (2004) *Le metodologie di sviluppo dei sistemi informativi*. FrancoAngeli, Milano
21. Virtuani R (2005) *L'organizzazione del processo di outsourcing nei sistemi informativi aziendali*. FrancoAngeli, Milano

Web Reputation Management Systems as Strategic Tools

Alberto Francesconi* **and Claudia Dossena**†‡

Abstract Accordingly to the Resource Based View, the online corporate reputation is seen as a resource for a sustainable competitive advantage. The Internet and "Web 2.0", in particular, have radically altered the dynamics of corporate reputation formation and management by creating newly accessible channels and ways of communication, shifting the balance of power of "voice". The result is that corporate reputation is increasingly defined not (only) by what companies do or say, but also by how stakeholders perceive and respond to their actions and words. Effective online corporate reputation management requires companies to develop new capabilities, also in terms of IT exploitation. Our work is focused on Web Reputation Management Systems, emerging software systems to monitor and to manage online corporate reputation. We aim at highlighting main criticisms, opportunities and managerial needs through the analysis of an explorative case study, based on the experience developed with 35 customers in the last 2 years by an Italian consulting firm. Finally, we provide some suggestions for future researches.

Introduction

Firms act to legitimate their business activities especially through external approval and consent [1–5]. As a consequence, a good corporate reputation (CR) provides a competitive advantage to the firm [6–8] thanks to a better stakeholders' perception compared with competitors [9].

Web technologies, user-generated contents and social networks diffusion, which characterize the "Web 2.0" [10], are catalyzing an increasing interest because of new opportunities and new challenges to be faced in the arena of online CR [11]. In a traditional way of thinking, firm's communications were largely controlled and regulated both when internally and externally addressed. Firms were used to assume that details about their internal workings were valuable or protectable keeping them secret. Nevertheless, Web 2.0 has inverted the "social physics" of information [12]. Now "You can't hide anything anymore", as argued

* Business Research Department, University of Pavia, Pavia, Italy, afrancesconi@eco.unipv.it

† Business Research Department, University of Pavia, Pavia, Italy, claudia.dossena@eco.unipv.it

‡ Though this work and its conclusions are jointly authored, Alberto Francesconi is author of the first two paragraphs, and Claudia Dossena of paragraph "method, case description and discussion".

A. D'Atri et al. (eds.), *Management of the Interconnected World*,
DOI 10.1007/978-3-7908-2404-9_31,

by Tapscott and Ticoll [13] in their book on corporate transparency. Web 2.0 represents a discontinuity point in the more traditional approaches. It is based on the idea that everybody can interact with each other, sometimes beyond any schemes or filters, within and outside the – even more weak – firm boundaries. Wiedmann and others [14] have observed, for instance, that many bloggers merge their personal opinions with business aspects, commenting decisions, anecdotes, incidents happened in the firms where they work. What are the consequences in terms of CR and which is the emerging role of IT in this scenario?

The aim of this exploratory study is to highlight main criticisms, opportunities and managerial needs and to provide some suggestions for future researches on online CR. At the same time we aim at emphasizing some opportunities for firms to exploit IT in this new scenario. Due to the relative novelty of this topic, both in theory and practice, we developed a case study based on the experience of a young Italian consulting firm[1] (founded in 2004) which offers both consultancy and a software system for "online reputation intelligence" and management.

Theoretical Framework

Fombrun and van Riel [15]:10 defined CR as *a collective representation of a firm's past actions and results that describes the firm's ability to deliver valued outcomes to multiple stakeholders. It gauges a firm's relative standing both internally with employees and externally with its stakeholders in both its competitive and institutional environment.* CR is considered one of the most important intangible resource [8, 16–19]. Previous research suggests a positive reputation can lead to a sustainable competitive advantage being a scarce, valuable, not perfectly imitable resource, not substitutable and not easily transferable [6–8, 20, 21]. Literature has focused on the role of traditional media – such as TV, radio, and newspapers – as means capable to reduce information asymmetries and to affect the *media reputation*, that is the whole evaluation of a firm widespread by media [21, 18]. Due to the peculiar characteristics of Web, *online (or Web) corporate reputation (WCR)* emphasizes a shift from a *push* approach to a *pull* approach in the creation and diffusion of information contents compared with traditional media. Web "spaces", such as blogs, forums, chat, wikis, social networks, etc., allow users to generate information contents directly and to share them easier than in the past. This also highlights the role of online communities as key information sources for *reputation intelligence* [19].

Though reputation is a resource cumulated in time, it is quite "fragile" and quickly damageable [22–24], sometimes by malicious information, thus making more important a fast detections of possible threats as well as proactive interventions. A common opinion, still to be fully demonstrated, argues that Web

[1] Called fictitiously "Alpha".

2.0 would make reputation more fragile and quickly damageable, due to the viral and space/time boundary spanning characteristics of Web 2.0. For example, in a recent experiment, Park and Lee [25] demonstrated that just one negative comment contributes to worsen CR within a forum online while the perception of a positive reputation is strictly proportional to the number of positive comments.

Since the early 1980s, considerable research attention has focused on the strategic role of IT, its potential for creating and sustaining competitive advantage, and the central role of barriers to erosion [26]. We propose the protection of a fragile resource such as reputation for firms as well as their capability and agility to streamline and quicken the reaction in the world of Web 2.0 is consistent with the strategic role of IT. Moreover, IT allow firms to exploit an increasing amount of not structured contents as sources, for example, for knowledge management, a more informed decision-making, and for innovation and marketing purposes [27–29]. Nevertheless, as confirmed in the case, a narrow focus on IT is misleading. IT capabilities and a better comprehension of threats and opportunities of Web 2.0 are central for a full exploitation of IT potential.

Our work is focused on particular software systems, we name *Web Reputation Management Systems* (WRMS), intended as sets of "tools" to support:

- the evaluation and management of a complex, dynamic and multidimensional resource such as WCR;
- the reduction of time between contents diffusion on the Web and decision-making, acting also as *early warning systems* [30, 31] for a proactive WCR management;
- the collection and synthesis of information contents, in particular low-structured, typical of Web 2.0, for business intelligence [32–35] and competitive intelligence [36] aims.

In particular, the WRMS internally developed by Alpha combines *semantic intelligence* technologies, a search engine, *web content mining*, *natural language processing* and *information retrieval* algorithms [37], with traditional databases. Strengths of Alpha's WRMS are the ability to self-learn, thanks to inductive analysis, and the possibility to exploit the whole web as well as precise domains to assess the WCR of a firm or its competitors.

Method, Case Description and Discussion

We analyzed the experience developed by Alpha in the last 2 years with 35 customer firms (Table 1). We collected data on WRMS through 4 semi-structured interviews with the service product manager, the managing director and an analyst. We analyzed the customer database to collect key information in terms of aims, needs, experience on WCR, competencies involved, and so on. Moreover, after a short training of about 1 h, we have tested the software to evaluate its main features.

Table 1. Alpha's customer firms

Size (recomm. 2003/361/EC)	Small: 2.8%	Medium: 5.8%	Big: 91.4%
Market	Regional: 0%	National: 14.3%	International: 85.7%
Product/service firms	Products: 42.9%	Services: 45.7%	Both: 11.4%
Web-based business?	Yes: 31.4%	No: 62.9%	Strongly related: 5.7%

Using qualitative and quantitative criteria (Table 2), and defining semantic categories and keywords, the system can analyze both large web portions and focused domains. We noticed that objective criteria are easily embedded and managed through software applications, thus exploiting full IT potentials for routine analysis and the synthesis of huge amount of data. On the contrary, subjective criteria, though fundamental, still limit a complete automation of WCR analysis and management, deeply related to user capabilities.

Table 2. Main objective and subjective criteria used by Alpha to weigh information contents

Subjective criteria	Objective criteria
Relevance assigned to the domain (URL) by the user (reliability /credibility/authoritativeness of the content source)	Content visibility on the Web (e.g. positioning in the Google serp)
Relevance assigned to the issue by the user	Date creation of the content
Content consistency/semantic correctness of the content	Page rank web page/home page
Reliability and credibility attributed to the author of content by the user	Number of contents
Terminology, language and communication style	Number of content views
	Number of comments (tot.)
	Number of related links (viral effect)

The system classifies the results by categories on the basis of different thematic areas, channels (i.e. blog, forum, news, etc.), positive and negative contents for WCR, associating coefficients and alarms related to critical levels. Therefore, an important characteristic is the possibility of collecting, filtering and classifying a huge amount of information contents, mainly not structured. But, most important, is the automatic production of semi-structured reports, whose widening level can be selected by users. In this way, the system can be adopted not only as a web content mining tool but also as a decision support system. Moreover, workflow features to support managerial interventions in critic situations and the production of related documentation are available. On the bases of a generic "intentionally rational" decision-making process, it is possible to distinguish between automatic and user/manual tasks (Table 3).

In the previous paragraph we argued that a narrow focus on IT is misleading, and IT capabilities as well as a better comprehension of "Web 2.0" are central. Though Alpha's WRMS application is available in Application Service Providing too, Alpha's customers preferred a full consultancy support so far. And this is not due to the characteristics of the software, which is quite simple to use as we verified during our test (Table 4).

Table 3. The support to management decision-making, automated and manual tasks

Decision-making phase	Software (primarily automated task)	User (primarily manual task)
Problem recognition (intelligence)	First level monitoring and categorization of the results on the basis of: criticality content (positive or negative); topic date; channel; URL; keyword Viral alert Anti phishing Second level monitoring of link/url particularly important Customized reporting (trend) Post processing Bookmarking Reporting sources of discussion (channels) more active	Checking results (contents) proposed by the system
Solution research (design)	–	Consultancy support
Evaluation and selection of alternatives (choice)	Advanced reporting Filters Alternative scenarios/economic evaluation (partially automated)	Consultancy support
Implementation of decision (implementation)	–	Consultancy support
Monitoring of results and adjustment of actions (control)	Detailed forms of interventions Daily monitoring and categorization of results In-depth monitoring of important link/url customized report (trends)	Regular check of results (contents)

Table 4. Corporate reputation dimensions and most important fields on web

RQ dimension	Trends/emerging challenges	Abs. freq.
Products and services	Focus on quality, functionality, innovativeness. For products, defects and pre/post-sales assistance are main topics	35
Emotional appeal	Strongly related to the brand, often in blogs and forums	29
Social responsibility	Main contents are related to environmental ethics	22
Vision and leadership	Rarely vision is a topic; on the contrary, leadership is important	18
Workplace environment	Emphasis on employees' opinions (both positive and negative)	11
Financial performance	Contents often confined to financial sites/specialized forums	3

Conclusions and Suggestions for Future Research

Alpha experience well represents the opportunities offered by IT to support the protection and management of such a fragile resource as CR, as well as the need for specific IT and managerial capabilities and an organizational culture oriented towards a proactive exploitation of Web 2.0. In our opinion, from the limitations of our study – first of all the role of content receivers which is underestimated in our collected data – some interesting suggestions for useful insights arise such as, for instance, the analysis, for reputational aims, on what is truly perceived from those who read/write data on the web. Moreover, we need a more precise definition of the WCR concept – and whether it is more fragile than traditional CR – to better define its drivers, its dimensions and antecedents as well as its measurement criteria. Therefore, we argue that some specific questions for further analysis on the role of IT/IS could be: What information are more suitable to give a measure of reputation on the web? Can WRMS be made more resistant to "content/information manipulation"? Which are the impacts of WRMS on business models and corporate performances? Which are the implications from an organizational point of view and for IS management and development?

Considering Alpha experience and the current evolution of semantic intelligence field, it is plausible that IT will increasingly affect both the level of automation in monitoring and management of WCR and the trade-off showed in Fig. 1. This could be useful to reduce the difficulty in translating the large amount of semi-structured web information and the risk of information over-load. And it could be also useful to support a better articulation and use of knowledge both within the process of WCR management and decision-making.

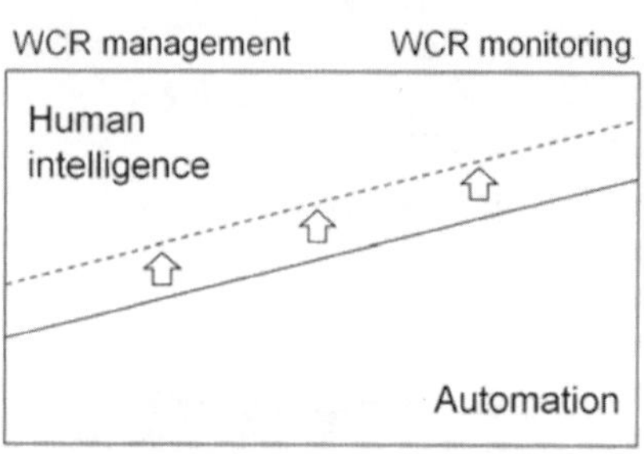

Fig. 1. Trade-off between human intelligence and routines associated with a software in the activities of WCR monitoring and management

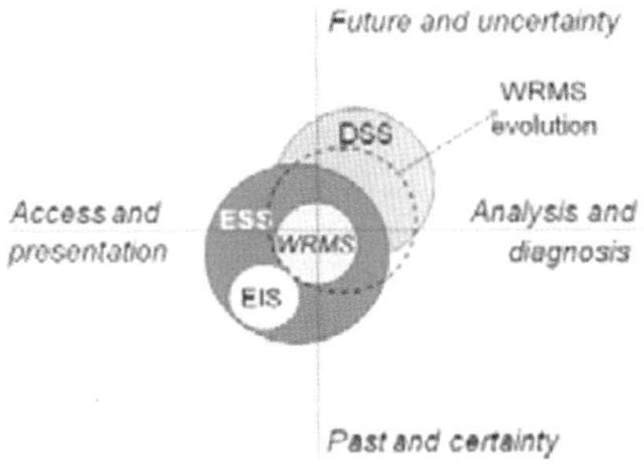

Fig. 2. WRMS and a possible evolution path (adapted from [38])

Based on the experience of Alpha in these years, we also suggest that WRMS will follow an evolutionary path as in Fig. 2, thus integrating with typical features of Decision Support System.

References

1. Coda V (1991) Comunicazione e immagine nella strategia d'impresa. Giappichelli, Torino
2. Donaldson T, Preston L (1995) The stakeholder theory of the corporation: concepts, evidence and implications. *Acad Manage Rev* 20(1):65–91
3. Vicari S (ed) (2001) Il management nell'era della connessione. Egea, Milano
4. Brammer S, Pavelin S (2004) Building a good reputation. *Eur Manage J* 22(6):704–713
5. Freeman RE, Rusconi G, Dorigatti M (eds) (2007) *La teoria degli stakeholder.* FrancoAngeli, Milano
6. Dierickx I, Cool K (1989) Asset stock accumulation and sustainability of competitive advantage. *Manage Sci* 35(12):1504–1511
7. Barney JB (1991) Firm resources and sustained competitive advantage. *J Manage* 17(12):99–120
8. Hall R (1992) The strategic analysis of intangible resources. *Strateg Manage J* 13(2):135–144
9. Fombrun CJ, Rindova V (1999) Constructing competitive advantage: the role of firm-constituent interactions. *Strat Manage J* 20:691–710
10. O'Reilly T (2004) The Web 2.0 conference at the hotel Nikko in San Francisco. http://www.web2summit.com/web2con/
11. Bunting M, Lipski R (2000) Drowned out? Rethinking corporate reputation management for the internet. *J Commun Manage* 5(2):170–178
12. Tapscott D, Williams A (2007) *Wikinomics: how mass collaboration changes everything.* Penguin Books, New York
13. Tapscott D, Ticoll D (2003) *The naked corporation. How the age of transparency will revolutionize business.* Free Press, New York
14. Wiedmann KP, Langner S, Hennig N (2007) *Collaborated marketing – towards a multidimensional model of motivation in open source oriented marketing projects.* Academy for global business advancement and the Asian academy of management joint conference, Penang, Malaysia (Conference proceedings)
15. Fombrun CJ, van Riel CBM (1997) The reputational landscape. *Corp Reput Rev* 1(1):5–13
16. Kay J (1993) *Foundations of corporate success.* Oxford University Press, Oxford

17. Whetten DA, Mackey A (2002) A social actor conception of organizational identity and its implications for the study of organizational reputation. *Bus Soc* 41(4):393–414
18. Fombrun CJ, van Riel CBM (2004) *Fame and fortune. How successful companies build winning reputations*. Prentice Hall, Upper Saddle River
19. Cullen J (2005) Corporate identity and reputation intelligence: emerging opportunities for information professionals. *Bus Inf Rev* 22(2):101–106
20. Teece DJ, Pisano G, Shuen A (1997) Dynamic capabilities and strategic management. *Strateg Manage J* 18(7):509–533
21. Deephouse DL (2000) Media reputation as a strategic resource: an integration of mass communication and resource-based theories. *J Manage* 26(6)1091–1112
22. Hall R (1993) A framework linking intangible resources and capabilities to sustainable competitive advantage. *Strateg Manage J* 14:607–618
23. Alsop RJ (2004) Corporate reputation – anything but superficial: the deep but fragile nature of corporate reputation. *J Bus Strategy* 25(6):21–29
24. Grant M (2005) *Contemporary strategic analysis*, 5th edn. Blackwell, Oxford
25. Park N, Lee KM (2007) Effects of online news forum on corporate reputation. *Public Relations Rev* 33(3):346–348
26. Piccoli G, Ives B (2005) It-dependent strategic initiatives and sustained competitive advantage: a review and synthesis of the literature. *MIS Q* 29(4):747–777
27. Prandelli E, Sawhney M (2000) Beyond customer knowledge management: customers as knowledge co-creators. In: *Malhotra Y (ed) Knowledge management and virtual organizations*. Idea Group Publishing, Hersey
28. Abrams C (2006a) Determine how Web 2.0 may affect your organization. Gartner Res. http://www.gartner.com/DisplayDocument?doc_cd=144276&ref=g_rss
29. Abrams C (2006b) Seven ways your organization can benefit from Web 2.0. Gartner Res. http://www.gartner.com/DisplayDocument?ref=g_blog&id=498328
30. Gilad B (2006) Early warning revisited. *Compet Intell Mag* 9(2):17
31. Comai A, Tena J (2007) Early warning systems for your competitive landscape. *Compet Intell Mag* 10(3):57–58
32. De Marco M, Salvo V, Lanzani W (eds) (1999) *Balanced scorecards: dalla teoria alla pratica*. FrancoAngeli, Milano
33. Rajola F (ed) (2000) *L'organizzazione dei sistemi di business intelligence nel settore finanziario*. FrancoAngeli, Milano
34. Pasini P (2004) *I sistemi informative direzionali*. Egea, Milano
35. Bracchi G, Motta G, Francalanci C (2005) *Sistemi informativi per l'impresa digitale*. McGraw-Hill, Milano
36. Fleisher CS (2003) Competitive intelligence education: competencies, sources and trends. *Inf Manage J* 38(2):56–62
37. Liu RL (2007) Dynamic category profiling for text filtering and classification. *Inf Process Manage* 43(1):154–168
38. Anderson G (1989) The ESS revolution: decision support software reaches the boardroom. *Ind Manage Data Syst* 7:4–5

IS, Organization and Strategy: Convergence or Divergence? A Meta-Analysis

Marco De Marco*, Barbara Imperatori†, and Daniela Isari‡

Abstract This paper aims to provide some evidences to contribute to the ongoing debate about IS discipline domain and its theoretical boundaries and backgrounds. In order to investigate the main issues and topics related with the IS discipline and the most recurrent relationships and ties among IS, Organization and Strategy we performed a meta-analysis based on the 170 papers published in 2008 in the six reference IS journals. Our findings point out the convergence towards some theoretical and research issues and moreover suggest the emerging of a new "two-ways" form of interaction that requires original directions for the future IS and management research.

Research Aim and Theoretical Background

The definition of IS field of study, its epistemological background and its relationship with other disciplines has been long debated in the literature [1–6].

Among other contributions, two influential opinions pointed out that IS discipline has today become a mature field and its relationship with other disciplines needs to be redefined. According to some authors [2], besides relying on other reference disciplines, IS can play a leading role in itself and fertilize other disciplines; other authors foster more interplay between the IS research and other fields like organization studies, encouraging hybrid research and theory development at the intersection of different disciplines [3].

The paper aims to give a contribution to the current discussion examining the interconnections between research on IS, Strategy and Organization fields of study. We focused on what has been published in the last year in the leading journals of the IS field in order to define the state-of-the-art of IS research relationships with other management disciplines (Organization and Strategy).

In the first part of the paper, we present the results of a meta-analysis based on the 170 papers published in 2008 in six reference IS journals; in the second part, based on our findings, we propose some considerations on IS discipline

* Department of Economics and Management Science, Catholic University of Milan, Milan, Italy, marco.demarco@unicatt.it

† Department of Economics and Management Science, Catholic University of Milan, Milan, Italy, barbara.imperatori@unicatt.it

‡ Department of Economics and Management Science, Catholic University of Milan, Milan, Italy, daniela.isari@unicatt.it

A. D'Atri et al. (eds.), *Management of the Interconnected World*,
DOI 10.1007/978-3-7908-2404-9_32, © Springer-Verlag Berlin Heidelberg 2010

and its convergence and/or divergence with other management disciplines for future research directions.

Intersection Between IS, Organization and Strategy: A Meta-Analysis

In the following paragraphs we illustrate first the research questions that guided our meta-analysis, secondly the research method and finally the main findings of the study.

Research Questions

As stated before, the aim of the meta-analysis is to analyze the most recent contributions appeared in 2008 on the leading journals in IS, which represent the reference journals for IS scholars at international level.

In order to present a synthesis and a critical analysis of the literature examined, the research is designed to addresses the following questions:

- Which are currently the most relevant topics and issues within the IS field of study?
- What are the most frequent cross issues and theoretical perspectives with organization and strategy disciplines?
- Which are the research methods adopted?

Research Method

The nature of our research goal led us to adopt a quantitative research strategy based on a meta-analysis. The sample includes all articles published in 2008 on the leading journals and reviews in AIS ranking. In particular, we took in consideration a basket of six journals selected by the AIS Senior Scholars Forum Subcommittee on Journals in 2006 and recommended as excellent reference journals for IS scholars. This basket of journals, which includes MISQ, ISR, JAIS, JMIS, EJIS and ISJ, can be accordingly considered representative of current trends in IS research.

We analyzed overall 170 papers, representing different research contexts, background and approaches, recognized by the Academic Community as rigorous and value adding contributions to the research field.

The issues of the six reference journals we analyzed are: MIS Quarterly (Vol. 32); Information Systems Research (Vol. 19); Journal of AIS (Vol. 9); Journal of MIS (Vol. 24); European Journal of Information Systems (Vol. 17) and Information Systems Journal (Vol. 18).

For each journal we considered all articles published in the volume (year 2008) and we analyzed the titles and abstracts provided by authors.

The papers have been codified according to a number of dimensions of analysis based on the research questions; paper contents have been codified in a data set for subsequent analysis.

The dimensions of analysis and the coding categories are the following:

- Research topics
  This dimension was codified according to the taxonomy proposed by Davis [4] and re-proposed by Baskerville and Myers [2] which we integrated – based on the evidence emerging from the papers analyzed – with a sixth category. These are the five plus one categories: IS management; IS development processes; IS development concepts; Representations in IS; Application systems; the sixth category we added is IS Discipline domain and research.

- Research issues
  Through a content analysis of the abstracts we identified the more specific research issues and topics within the papers, in order to codify the main trends within the discipline. The categories emerged through content analysis of titles and abstracts are: Knowledge management, Project management, Collaboration and virtual teams, IT and change, Electronic markets.

- Cross issues and theoretical perspectives with organization and strategy disciplines
  According to our research question, this dimension was coded into five categories in order to measure the relevance of the ties among IS, Organization and Strategy. Our classification is based on the three main areas of organization discipline, plus two other categories that were considered relevant for this work: Organization Theory (OT); Organizational Behaviour (OB); Human Resource Management (HR); Strategy (Str.); other (i.e. all contributes that have no relationships with the previous ones).

- Research methodology adopted
  This dimension was coded into six traditional categories including both quantitative and quantitative approaches: case studies and field projects, surveys, meta-analyses, theoretical papers, laboratory experiments and simulations, action research.

Results

The results are synthetically represented by frequency analysis in Figs. 1 and 2, which allow us to make some first considerations about the state-of-the-art of the most recent research in IS and its interconnection with organization and strategy disciplines.

Research Topics

Regarding the broad research topics, results are presented in Fig. 1. There is a prominence of studies connected to IS management and organization, followed by contributions related to IS discipline and research field. Contributions related to technical issues and application systems are less frequent.

Fig. 1. Meta-analysis results: research topics

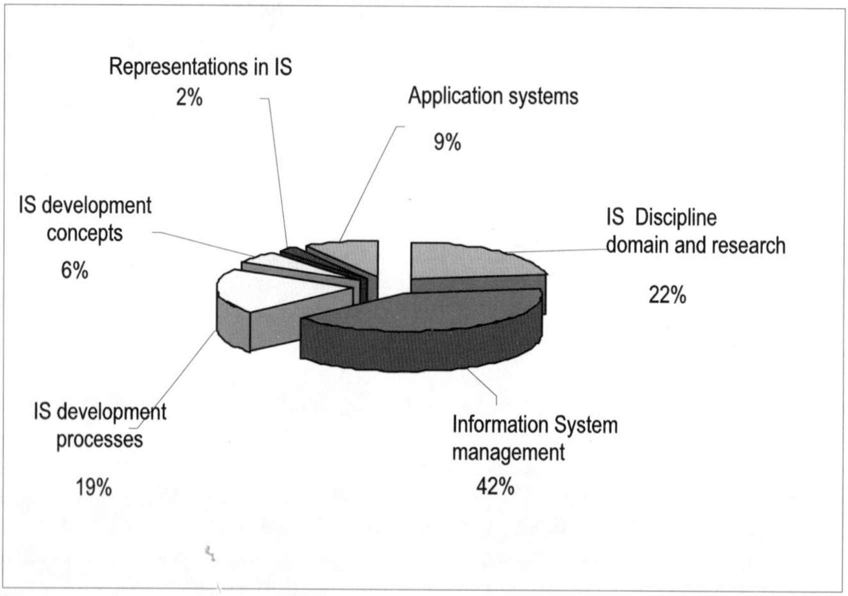

This strong presence of papers focused on IS discipline and research field testifies that a deep reflection within the discipline for the definition of its identity is still in course. The relevant presence of contributions on IS management issues shows that the link with Organization and Strategy disciplines is stronger and stronger in this field of studies.

Research Issues

Content analysis based on titles and abstracts allowed to identify some most frequent research issues, as follow: Electronic markets 13, 5%; Knowledge management 6%; Project management 5, 3%; Collaboration and virtual teams 5, 3%; IT and change 3%.

These results, though related to one single year and thus not representative of the dynamics in course, are pointing out two emergent phenomena within IS discipline. First, the development of new technology based industries and business models (i.e. electonic markets), and related research areas. Secondly, results confirm the interconnection with some main managerial topics (i.e. knowledge management and coordination processes).

Cross Issues and Theoretical Perspectives with Organization and Strategy Disciplines

As stated, we focused the content analysis on research cross issues specifically related to Organization and Strategy disciplines, in order to make some considerations on the interconnection between IS, Organization, and Strategy fields of study.

Figure 2 shows the width of ties and interconnections, within the papers examined, with the macro-areas of Organization discipline (Organization Theory, Organizational Behaviour, Human Resource management) and with Strategic issues. The table presents the absolute value numbers of papers dealing with issues which can be classified according to the taxonomy proposed.

Fig. 2. Meta analysis results: interconnections with organization and strategy

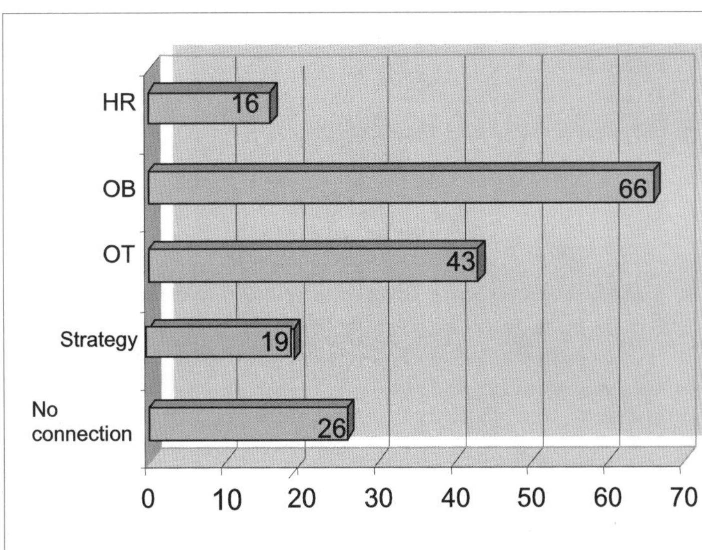

We recall that the overall sample includes 170 observations. The figure shows that only twenty-six out of 170 papers deal with issues which show no ties with Organization and Strategy area of studies. Nineteen papers deal with strategy

issues and up to one hundred and fifteen contributions are directly related to organizational issues, with a prominence of papers which deal with contents and theories from the field of Organizational Behaviour, followed by Organization Theory and design and finally by contributions dealing with Human Resource management issues.

To add more details, it is interesting to point out the main theories and conceptual frameworks recurring in these papers, because they are common within other disciplines, such as Organization theory, design and behaviour. When explicitly cited into the abstract, the most frequent theoretical backgrounds are the following: Motivation theories [7–9]; Decision making theory [10]; Stakeholder theory [11]; Social construction approaches [12]; Knowledge perspectives [13]; Transaction Cost Economics [14].

Research Methods

As far as methodology is concerned, results are presented in Fig. 3.

The variety of methodologies adopted suggests a plurality of epistemological approaches.

Fig. 3. Meta analysis results: research methodologies

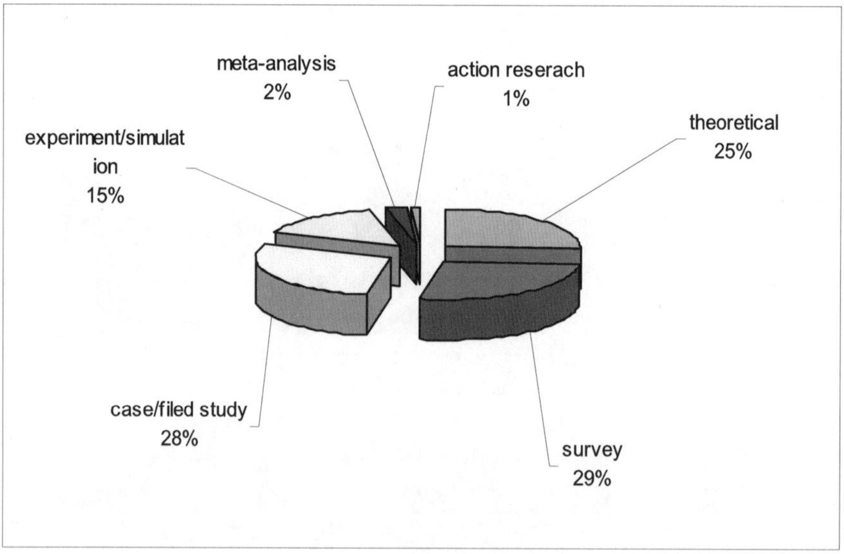

In particular, there is a prominence of empirical studies, compared to theoretical papers. Quantitative methods are prevailing, but, not surprisingly, qualitative methods are also significantly represented.

IS, Organization and Strategy: Two Way Ticket

It is not the aim of this paper to draw conclusions about the long and ongoing debate concerning the relationship among IS and other disciplines like Organization and Strategy; nevertheless our findings enable us to suggest some considerations to contribute to the present day discussion.

First of all, the results confirm the relevance of the debate on IS discipline domain that is still open, but that also points out the maturity of the discipline and its progressive consolidation.

Secondly, the presented findings show a consistent interconnection among the investigated disciplines, regarding research topics, issues, theoretical perspectives and methods.

Third, the interconnections analysed suggest an emerging "two-way nature" of the relationship, which does not mean a complete fusion, but mostly a new form of intersection. IS discipline has been building on Organisation and Strategy studies and theory, but, in its turn, IS discipline is, at present, contributing to the Organization and Strategy Theory building. New organizational forms, new business models, new innovation paths, new way of working, new information and decision practices are now enabled by ICT innovations and IS discipline development. This of course requires organizational and strategic approaches within the IS domain, but it also demands new theoretical approaches and research questions within Organization and Strategy domain.

Moreover, this emerging new form of intersection is consistent with relevant previous analysis and contributions [3, 2, 15] and confirms the relevance of an integrated socio-technical approach for the future "intersected research".

Limits and Future Research

The main limitation of this paper is about the research sample. The aim of the study is explorative, but the observation time is narrow (i.e. 1 year), and this could bias the analysis. For these reasons, to convalidate the proposed findings and moreover to define research trends and trajectories a longitudinal research is required.

Finally, the presented quantitative analysis has also to be integrated with a more qualitative approach to better understand the papers contents and to propose more articulated reflections and discipline suggestions.

References

1. Avison DA, Pries-Heje J (eds) (2005) *Research in information systems: a handbook for research students and their supervisors*. Elsevier Butterworth-Heinemann, Oxford
2. Baskerville RL, Myers MD (2002) Information systems as a reference discipline. *MIS Q* 26(1):1–14

3. Orlikowski WJ, Barley S (2001) Technology and institutions: what can research on information technology and research on organizations learn from each other? *MIS Q* 25(2):145–165
4. Davis G (2000) Information systems conceptual foundations: looking backward and forward. In: Baskerville R et al (eds) *Organizational and social perspectives on information technology*. Kluwer, Boston
5. Benbasat I, Weber R (1996) Research commentary: rethinking diversity in information systems research. *IS Res* 7(4):389–399
6. Galliers RD (1991) Choosing appropriate information systems research methods. In: Nissen H, Kelin HK, Hirschheim R (eds) *Information systems research: approaches and emergent traditions*. North Holland, Amsterdam
7. Maslow A (1954) *Motivation and personality*. Harper & Row, New York
8. Mc Clelland DA (1985) *Human motivation*. Scott, Foresman, Glenview
9. Locke EA (1968) Towards a theory of task motivation and incentives. *Org Behav Hum Perf* (3):152–189
10. Kahneman D, Tversky A (1979) Prospect theory: an analysis of decision under risk. *Econometrica* 47(2):263–229
11. Freeman RE (1984) *Strategic management: a stakeholder approach*. Pitman, Boston
12. Weick K (1979b) Cognitive processes in organizations. *Res Org Behav* 1:41–74
13. Nonaka I, Takeuchi H (1995) *The knowledge-creating company: how Japanese companies create the dynamics of innovation*. Oxford University Press, New York
14. Williamson O (1975) *Markets and hierarchies: analysis and antitrust implications*. Free Press, New York
15. Lee AS (2001) Editorial. *MIS Q* 25(1): iii–vii

The Strategic Role of Business Intelligence Systems: An Assessment Model

Cecilia Rossignoli[*], **Antonella Ferrari**[†], **Lapo Mola**[‡], **and Elisa Bertoni**[π]

Abstract This work includes an analysis of the most significant studies in the academic literature on the evaluation and measurement of Decision Support Systems and Business Intelligence Systems (BIS).

The evaluation model of BIS success proposed by Clark et al. has been studied in depth and a new model has been proposed.

The conclusions will describe the most meaningful factors that influence the new proposed evaluation model of BIS success. Particularly important are commitment to the system development and users' training, while technology does not seem to be one of most critical elements.

Introduction

This work belongs to the field of studies on the analysis and evaluation of intangible assets in using Information and Communication Technology (ICT).

The objective of this research is to give a useful contribution to the identification of the critical success factors in implementing a peculiar type of ICT, namely, a Business Intelligent System (BIS). An analysis of the most meaningful studies in the academic literature on the measurement and evaluation of BIS has been carried out. The model proposed by Clark et al. [1] has been deeply investigated.

The authors have chosen a multiple case study approach as research methodology, aware of the limits of this method. However the multiple interpretative case study can be considered an useful instruments for preliminary study as the one proposed in this paper.

The model considers five important factors of a BIS and their iterative behavior over time: the objectives of the system, its environment, its resources and its management, which influences over time the results. The research methodology

[*] University of Verona, Verona, Italy, cecilia.rossignoli@univr.it

[†] University of Verona, Verona, Italy, lapo.mola@univr.it

[‡] University of Verona, Verona, Italy, antonella.ferrari@univr.it

[π] University of Verona, Verona, Italy, elisa.bertoni@sdgconsulting.net

A. D'Atri et al. (eds.), *Management of the Interconnected World*,
DOI 10.1007/978-3-7908-2404-9_33,

adopted in this paper is a multiple case study. Following all the phases suggested by the literature, i.e., first selecting the cases, then defining the research protocol and finally collecting the data to reach the conclusions, a new model has been proposed to measure the success levels of BIS. The new model has been developed following two phases: in the first phase, the traditional model has been simplified, removing those variables that did not achieve substantial results during the empirical research. In the second phase, all the new variables emerged during the study have been included in the model. The conclusions describe the most significant factors. These seem to be commitment to the system development and users' training, while information technology does not appear to be the most important variable.

Business Intelligence Systems and Their Strategic Role

Business Intelligence Systems (BIS) are systems able to transform data in useful information and knowledge to support decision-making processes, in view of the objectives that enterprises must pursue in order for them to sustain their competitive advantage [2]. In the last 30 years, Decision Support Systems have been widely discussed by the Information System (IS) literature. These debates started with a category named DSS. Over the years, the academic literature has produced a common definition of the meaning of the systems belonging to this category. Today BIS are included in the DSS category: they allow easy access to data, information and knowledge able to satisfy the needs of individuals and groups. They support, moreover, the interaction among actors in their decision-making process [3–7]. BIS, as decision support systems, play a strategic role for the enterprises, where the concept of decision-making process is considered a critical success factor as it is by strategic management [8–10]. The theoretical approach of this study concerns the *Knowledge Based View*, according to which enterprises are a depot of capabilities and knowledge that organizations can transform in value to create competitive advantages [11, 12].

Clark's et al. Model

The work of Clark et al. [1] is significant because it identifies the right factors and actions that must be taken in order to reach a successful implementation of a BIS [4, 13]. His model thoroughly analyzes the main elements and the specific components of a BIS. To represent the elements that define the success of a BIS, the analyses are developed at an individual and organizational level. Fourteen critical success factors are identified that can be considered the starting hypotheses able to influence the success level of a BIS. For each of these 14 factors, the main concept is made explicit, together with the most important factors that influence in a positive or negative way the 14 factors. The specifications of these 14 hypotheses (from H.1 to H.14) are explained. The objective of the empirical research is to validate or not these hypotheses. When they are not validated, the new critical factors that emerge from the empirical study are indicated. Figure 1 shows in brief the 14 hypotheses. The arrows represent the connections and influences existing between the 14 hypotheses. The numbers 1, 2, 3, 4 in the figure indicate further interdependencies among the considered hypotheses.

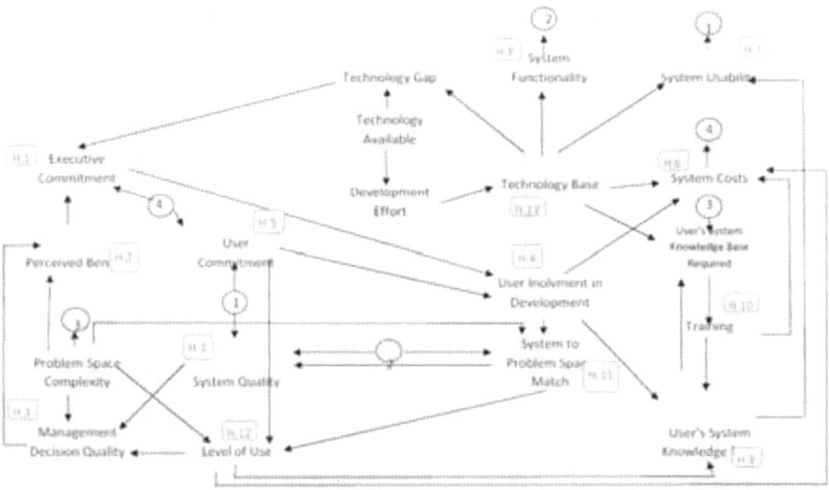

Fig. 1. The original model of Clark et al. [1]

H.1: ***Executive Commitment.*** This is influenced by two main variables: perception of obtainable benefits [14–16] and costs of the investment.

H.2: ***Perceived Benefits***. One of the most important benefits deriving from the use of a BIS is the improvement of the efficiency of DSS [17–20].

H.3: ***Management Decision Quality.*** Some factors that influence the quality of decisions are the level of use, the quality and complexity of the system, the approach of people to the system.

H.4: ***User Involvement in Development.*** The main interactions occur between users and analysts [21]. The involvement of the final user in the design of the system causes a high level of satisfaction and a positive perception of the usefulness of the system [22].

H.5: ***User Commitment in Development.***

H.6: ***Costs.*** These are costs of technology, human resources and training.

H.7: ***Usability.*** This is the quality of the interaction between user and DSS and depends on how easily users can interact (interface) with the system [23]. Other two factors influence the usability: the adopted technology and the users' knowledge of the system.

H.8: ***Functionality***. This includes the capacity to provide decision-makers with what is necessary throughout the various phases of the decision-making process [24, 25]. Moreover, it includes flexibility and infrastructure of the system, which must be able to easily support the possibility to rapidly modify some parts of the system to adapt it to the changes that are necessarily required by the complexity of the organizational context [26–29]. Finally, it includes the capacity to receive the changes without totally redesigning the architecture of the global model [30, 31].

H.9: ***User's MSS Knowledge Base***. This is considered the experience that the organizations gain and maintain as regards uses and activities of the system in a defined area [32]. The knowledge base is influenced by three main factors: level of use, user involvement in the development of the system and training.

H.10: ***MSS Training.***

H.11: ***MSS to Problem Space Match***. This is the meeting point between the system and the organizational context to be managed.

H.12: ***Level of MSS Use***. This is influenced by the accuracy and relevance of the output of the system and by the experience and knowledge of the decision-maker as regards the domain in which the system has to be applied.

H.13: ***MSS Base Structure***. Choosing the right instrument depends on the available market alternatives and on the capacity of the organization to receive and integrate the selected technological solution [33, 34].

H.14: ***MSS Quality***.

The Multiple Case Study

Following the definition of the hypothesis used by *Clark* et al. [1] to identify the success level of a BIS, the objective of this study was to test the model by means of an empirical research. The research methodology is the multiple case study [35–38]. Five enterprises were selected with a BIS experience of 3–5 years. Afterwards, to validate the results, the research has been extended to other 10 enterprises with a similar experience as regards the use of a BIS, in terms of quality and quantity data. The main sources used for this research were observations, informal talks and interviews based on a questionnaire. By means of a *cross-case analysis* [37] the case studies have been compared. Based on the results, Fig. 2 highlights the relationships that have not been validated (in red) while Fig. 3 shows the new relationships (in green). Moreover, the new relationships among variables are noted in small letters.

H.1: Executive Commitment. Partially validated hypothesis.
H.2: Perceived Benefits. Validated hypothesis.
H.3: Management Decision Quality. Validated hypothesis.
H.4: User Involvement in Development. Validated hypothesis.
H.5: User Commitment in Development. Partially validated hypothesis.
H.6: Costs. Partially validated hypothesis.

H.7: System Usability. Validated hypothesis.
H.8: System Functionality. Validated hypothesis.
H.9: Users' System Knowledge. Validated hypothesis.
H.10: Training. Partially validated hypothesis.
H.11: System to Problem Space Match. Partially validated hypothesis.
H.12: Level of Use. Partially validated hypothesis.
H.13: Technology Base. Validated hypothesis.
H.14: System Quality Validated hypothesis.

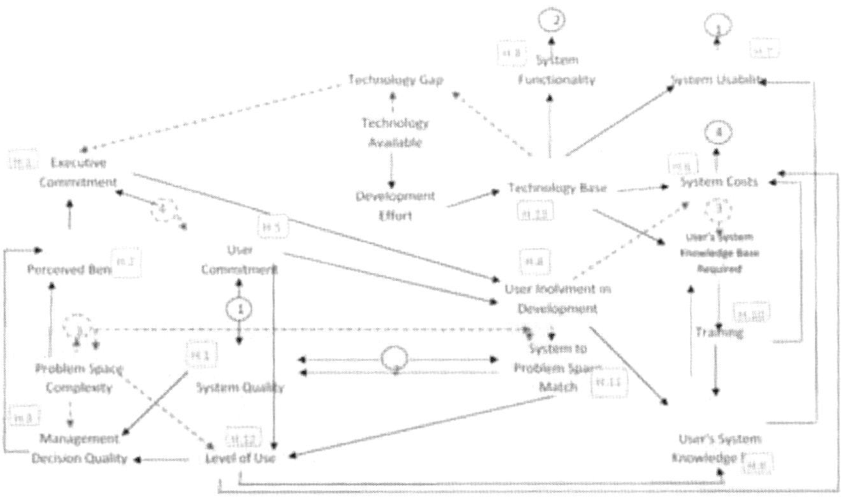

Fig. 2. The simplified model of Clark et al. [1]

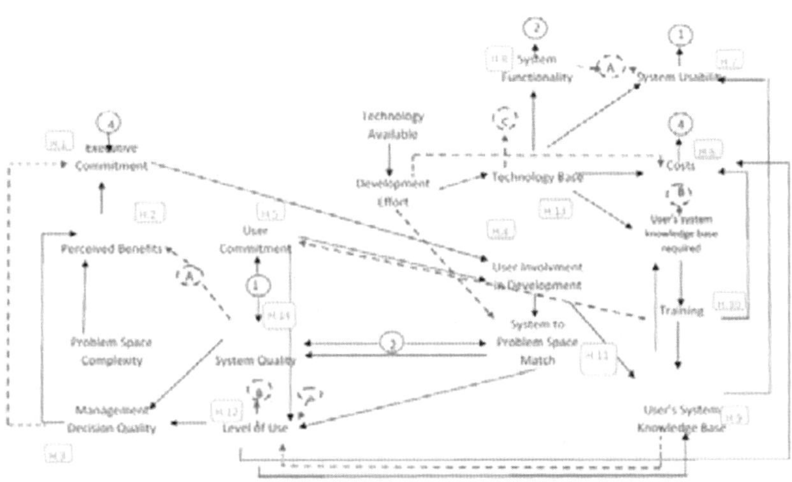

Fig. 3. The new proposed model

Conclusions, Limits and New Research Proposals

Based on the interviews and questionnaires, it has emerged that the current economic and organizational scenario has changed from the one outlined by Clark et al. [1]. Some variables considered essential in the past are now less important. From the cross-case analysis it can be inferred that the "complexity of the context and problems to be solved" is no longer considered so important (see H.3, 10, 11, 12). Also the "costs" are no longer considered particularly decisive elements. In some cases, in fact, the relationship has been denied (see H.5) and in other cases it has been considered less relevant than other factors.

Nowadays, other aspects are considered more important to evaluate the level of success of a BIS. Primary importance is given to the user and management commitment to BIS development and training of final users. The technology base does not constitute the most significant variable. The key element is the willingness of the people involved in the project to take special care of the system development. Oftentimes, training of end users is underestimated. On the contrary, investing in the training on the system allows users to exploit, in the best possible way, the capabilities of the implemented system. Moreover it enables the proposal and integration of new system developments. In a BIS process, a cyclic interaction between the two main actors, i.e., user developer and end user, is fundamental. They have different needs and competencies, and this is why they must cooperate in the system development to reach the best possible results. Finally, the authors are aware of the limits of the research method chosen. However the multiple interpretative case study can be considered, at this stage, an useful approach responding to the objectives of a preliminary study as the one proposed in this paper.

References

1. Clark DT, Jones MC, Armstrong CP (2007) The dynamic structure of management support system: theory development, research focus, and direction. *MIS Q* 31(3):579–615
2. Davenport TH, Prusak L (1998) *Working knowledge: how organization manage what they know*. Harward Business School Press, Boston
3. Alavi M, Leidner DE (2001) Review: knowledge management and knowledge management systems: conceptual foundations and research issues. *MIS Q* 25(1):107–136
4. Anderson-Lehman R, Watson HJ, Wixom BH, Hoffer JA (2004) Continental airlines flies high with real-time business intelligence. *MIS Q Exec* 3(4):163–176
5. Lee H, Choi B (2003) Knowledge management enablers, processes, and organizational performance: an integrative viewand empirical examination. *J Manage Inf Syst* 20(1):179–228
6. Rouibah K, Ould-ali S (2002) Puzzle: a concept and prototype for linking business intelligence to business strategy. *J Strateg Inf Syst* 11:133–152
7. Schultze U, Leidner DE (2002) Studying knowledge management in information systems research: discourses and theoretical assumptions. *MIS Q* 26(3):213–242

8. Chandler Jr AD (1962) *Strategy and structure: chapters in the history of the industrial enterprise*. MIT Press, Cambridge
9. Ansoff HI (1965) *Corporate strategy: an analytical approach to business policy for growth and expansion*. McGraw Hill, New York
10. Andrews KR (1971) *The concept of corporate strategy*. Dow-Jones Irwin, Homewood
11. Polany M (1966) *The tacit dimension*. P. Smith, Gloucester
12. Kogut B, Zander U (1992) Knowledge of the firm, combinative capabilities, and the replication of technology. *Org Sci* 4:383–397
13. Arnott D, Pervan G (2005) A critical analysis of decision support systems research. *J Inf Technol* 20(2):67–87
14. Belcher LW, Watson HJ (1993) Assessing the value of Conoco's EIS. *MIS Q* 9:239–253
15. Watson HJ (1999) Introduction to the organizational systems and technology track, hicss, *Thirty-second Annual Hawaii international conference on system sciences* (7): 7701
16. Watson HJ, Wixom BH, Hoffer JA, Anderson-Lehman R, Reynolds AM (2006) Real-time business intelligence: best practices at continental airlines. *Inf Syst Manage* 23(1):7–18
17. Dennis AR, Carte TA, Kelly GG (2003) Breaking the rules: success and failure in groupware-supported business process reengineering. *Decision Support Systems* 36(1):41–47
18. Van der Aalst WMP, Berens PJS (2001) Beyond workflow management: product-driven case handling. In Ellis C, Zigurs I (eds) *Proceedings of the international ACM SIGGROUP conference on supporting group work 2001*, Boulder, pp 42–51
19. Williams S, Williams N (2004) *Capturing ROI through business-centric BI development methods*. DM Review
20. Chen JQ, Lee SM (2003) An exploratory cognitive DSS for strategic decision making. *Decis Support Syst* 36(2):147–160
21. Keen PGW (1980b) Decision support systems: translating useful models into usable technologies. *Sloan Manage Rev* 21(3):33–44
22. Franz CR, Robey D (1986) Organizational context user involvent & the usefulness of information systems. *Decis Sci* 17(3):329–356
23. Housdeshel G, Watson HJ (1987) The management information and decision support (MIDS) System at Lockheed-Georgia. *MIS Q* 11(1):128–140
24. Kottermann J, Remus W (1989) A study of the relationship between decision model naturalness and performance. *MIS Q* 13(2):171–181
25. Gass SI (1983) Decision-aiding models: validation, assessment, and related issues for policy analysis. *Oper Res* 31(4):603–631
26. Simon HA, Newell A (1971) Human problem solving: the state of the theory in 1970. *Am Psychol* 26(2):145–159
27. Donovan JJ, Madnick SE (1976) Virtual machine advantages in security, integrity and decision support systems. *IBM Syst J* 15(3):270–278
28. Franz LS, Lee SM, Van Horn JC (1981) An adaptive decision support system for academic resource planning. *Decis Sci* 12(2):276–293
29. Gibson CF, Singer CJ, Schnidman AA, Davenport TH (1984) Strategies for making an information system fit your organization. *Manage Rev* 73:8–14
30. Kendall KE, Kendall JE (1984) Structured observation of the decision-making environment: a reliability and validity assessment. *Decis Sci* 15:107–118
31. Inmon B (2005) World-class business intelligence. *DM Review*, pp 60–61
32. Sprague Jr RH, Carlson ED (1982) *Building effective decision support systems*. Prentice-Hall, Englewood Cliffs
33. Hult GTM (2003) An integration of thoughts on knowledge management. *Decis Sci* 34(2):189–195

34. Malhotra A, Gosain S, El Sawy OA (2005) Absorptive capacity config.tions in supply chains: gearing for partner-enabled market knowledge creation. *MIS Q* 29(1):145–187
35. Zahra SA, George G (2002) Absorptive capacity: a review, reconceptualization, and extension. *Acad Manage Rev* 27(2):185–203
36. Yin R (1994) Case study research: design and methods, 2nd edn. Sage Publishing, Beverly Hills
37. Eisenhardt KM (1989)Building theories from case study research. *Acad Manage Rev* 14(4):532–550
38. Voss C, Tsikriktsis N, Frohlich M (2002) Case research in operations management. *Int J Oper Prod Manage* 22(2):195–219

Learning from a Wrong Consumer Perception: Bridging the Gap Between Created Value and Perceived Value

Cinzia Dessì[*], Michela Floris[†], and Giuseppe Melis[‡]

Abstract In the light of the development of E-CRM, the right customer perception of web site can improve management and customer relationships and better orients web site goals. This is true particularly in a specific market as well as the online tourism. The aim of this work is to underline how a wrong consumer perception may affect goals of a web site and consequently what management have to learn from this misunderstanding. The theoretical analysis is established on a tourism site web called Terremobili (Italy) through a learning approach that shows the misinterpretation between management and customer perception about the offer of this web site. Interviewing management and analyzing information, we demonstrated that the web site initially did not meet consumer needs and beliefs, and, moreover, its structure generated a wrong perception of consumer observation. The study offers useful details about which consequences firms may suffer because of a wrong customer perception of the web site generating opportunistic behaviors. Conclusion underlines the need of a perceptive concordance between management and customer perception as a way for the businesses to aim their goals.

Introduction

In the last decades the number of e-customers has been increased underlining that Internet and e-commerce provide an interesting possibility for firms in customer relationship management.

---

[*] Department of Business Economics, Technology and Environment, University of Cagliari, Italy, Cagliari, cdessi@unica.it

[†] Department of Business Economics, Technology and Environment, University of Cagliari, Italy, Cagliari, micfloris@unica.it

[‡] Department of Business Economics, Technology and Environment, University of Cagliari, Italy, Cagliari, gemelis@unica.it

A. D'Atri et al. (eds.), *Management of the Interconnected World*,
DOI 10.1007/978-3-7908-2404-9_34,

Customer Relationship Management (CRM) as a key competitive requires a deeper understanding of thoughts, opinions and beliefs of customer needs. Despite this significance the field of relationship research is still underdeveloped above all regarding perceptions aspects where studies are still little.

In fact, literature has been paid little attention on how management perceptions aspects can weight customer relationships development in order to verify if the existence of an erroneous perception may affect business outcomes and consequently competitive advantages. In this sense, managers need to verify if their mental construct of customer beliefs are confirmed by consumer's opinion such as a part of the key development of competitive advantage for firms.

In light of this, based on CRM and eCRM literature will analyse an opportunistic use of a tourism web site from costumer dues to a wrong perceptions between customers and management supply.

Literature Review

CRM and E-CRM

A knowledge management perspective of customer relationship management (CRM) argues that firms must invest in developing and acquiring the right awareness of customer preference. Through these efforts they can modify their behaviour in case of neglected construct. This is not always an automatic bent for managers customer oriented, probably because managers used to organise their customer interaction in centralized marketing functions to better accomplish service production for their customers.

In this way relationships with customers are relatively more emotional and behavioural, centred on such variables such as bonding, empathy, reciprocity and trust.

Although this aspect of CRM has not received wide spread support in the literature, its analysis serves to emphasize that a certain degree of right perception is needed to effectively manage customer relationships. After all, the emerging literature suggest that effective CRM demands that a firm be capable of gathering knowledge about its current and prospective customers and applying this knowledge to shape its subsequent interactions with them, for example changing its behaviour towards them.

The implication on filling this underdeveloped fields permits to better achieve a business customer orientation with the understanding of customer leanings and to increase and improve management tacit knowledge in relation to the customer.

While it observes that there has been an increase in the attention paid to CRM by practitioners and academics there is not a systematic attempts to develop a valid measure of it. It is no longer sufficient to advise practitioners and researchers that the key to business successful is through CRM without providing information on to what dimensions actually involve relationship. In this sense little research has focused on creating measurement scale and testing the CRM concepts empirically. CRM improves, on one hand, customer retention and loyalty and, on the other hand, increases customer profitability.

There are different ways to sustain the use of CRM's strategy inside a firm through the information technology. This peculiar aspect of CRM is commonly defined as Electronic Customer Relationship Management (e-CRM) and is one of the latest technique that firms use for developing their marketing proficiency. This found confirmation in what Purba [1] defines, or better e-CRM is "the application of e-technology – or Internet-based technology – to achieve CRM objectives."

This means that e-CRM finalizes and completes the CRM strategies used by firms for building stronger customer relationships through Internet.

Other authors more specifically define e-CRM as the use of databases, web use (e-mail website visits, newsgroups, chat groups, web casts and other) to accomplish CRM objectives [2, 3].

It is allegorical what Yaeckel et al. [4] suggest defining e-CRM as a marriage between CRM and electronic commerce (e-commerce) where the second one indicates doing business online [5]. In particular, e-commerce is strictly related to digital information required for understanding customer preferences and comprises e-CRM or web-based applications. It is in this aspect of e-commerce that e-CRM is applied. Through the online use of digital information customers become self-users and active players in the purchase and service process, felling their self more powerful in managing and controlling all procedures through the web. Furthermore, services in this way may become more convenient for customers improving their satisfaction and loyalty [6].

Purba makes clear that e-CRM can be considered superior to traditional CRM as well as managing relationships with customers through the easy use of Internet access.

All this underlines the importance for the firm that use web applications for customer retentions to know and understand deeply electronic customer relationship management. This requires firm's investments on a high-quality e-CRM.

Few studies analyzed the relation between e-CRM and customer satisfaction underlining that sometimes a huge amount of features in the web sites can be unimportant for customer. This can cause discomfiture for customers.

For this aspect Zeithaml and Bitner [7] underlined that it is very important to monitor over time the quality of customer retention especially through the web.

In this scenario firms need to better know customers' perceptions of value received, and satisfaction with services and the provider [8]. Customers in fact have different perception and for this reason it is important to know their perceptions as well as foundation for building effective relationship strategies for retaining customers.

Perception and Perceived Value

Calling into question the "perception" derive from the increasing competition that forces manager to create new and different offers from competitors. *Perception* is the process by which people select, organize and interpret their perspectives of the world [9]. This is important because people perceive reality in different ways and the final result is produced by a combination of various situational elements.

Scholars of marketing underline the importance that perception has in consumers behaviour comprehension in terms of the brand [10] and the logo while others have analyzed consumers perceived quality in services field [11] and through the use of gap analysis introducing important concepts as perceptional gaps and perception of gaps [12–15].

Also in the e-business world, perception acquires an increasing importance. This is due to the fact that to attract more visitors to shop on the internet, e-retailers have to deliver preferred value to their target customer. In this sense, firms have to learning to know customer perceived value, in order to create better responses to consumers' need.

Many scholars have underlined that value and perceived value are a multidimensional construct in which the variety of notions are all embedded [16] [17]. In this scenario, perceived value has been described as complex [18], dynamic [19], multifaced and subjective. This means that the concept of customer-perceived value is a complex theoretical and practical construct that touches upon a number of concepts as well as quality, satisfaction, loyalty, trust, etc.

In light of this, the knowledge of consumer perceived value have to become a key factor in building and sustaining competitive advantage. Managers not always have not the correct perception of consumer perceived value. In this case, the risk of misunderstanding consumer value and behaviour may emerge and can cause the need of a revision of the whole of the firm's offer. Especially in the online market, where the eye-to-eye contact is absent the misunderstanding events are numerous, but this may be the opportunity for the firm to learn from a wrong perception.

Method

Learning from a failure is not always easy or automatic. From a classical view few authors [20] define the common approach to learning while innovating when people change behavior after a failure. This behavior change is in accordance with Cyert and March [21] and March et al. [22] that underline the necessity to search alternatives when there is a failure. Also Prosbt [23] emphasize that learning from a failure means to innovate within the firm. In this work we used a learning approach from the analysis of a case [24] because: (a) the survey refers to a contemporary phenomenon based on real life contexts; (b) the boundaries between the phenomenon and its context are not clearly identifiable; (c) some resources demonstrate our assumptions. The case is an unusual instance of a online tourism in a specific sector (*unique case*) and represents a *critical case* that allows us to observe and analyze a phenomenon (management-customer relations) rarely studied in a scientific manner (*revelatory case*).

At the same time, this work offers a pilot survey as a prelude to subsequent studies and other investigations. Thus, it can function as the first step of a subsequent *multiple-case study.*

The case

We chose "Terremobili", a brand of the firm "GH Impresa turistica", that plays in the on-line tourism also through other brands as well as: *Ferias*, *Sailtosee*, *Orme nel parco* and *GHnet*. The brand was born in 2007 with the aim to run in the specific market segment of high quality hotels, in which *GH Impresa Turistica* didn't still work. This brand represents a particular combination of touristic activities, starting from the idea that the "holiday market" shouldn't be exported or implanted: it is founded upon a relationship between hosts and guests, rooted in a context of experiences that take place and assume meaning in each location. This brand operates in Dalmatia, Morocco, Sardinia, Sicily, Puglia, Basilicata, Campania and Calabria. Rich people, couples or large families are the customers of the brand *Terremobili*. These people are from 25 to 80 years old and they comes from Germany, United Kingdom, Ireland, Sweden, Norway, Denmark, Finland, Holland, Russia, Belgium, Luxembourg, Switzerland, Italy. The link among the brand and customers is managed throw a customized and not aggressive system of newsletter, based on a low frequency and with a targeted content. The Marketing Information System (MIS) of this brand is enforced when the potential client moves to be potential to become effective, through filling a questionnaire regarding: personal data, interests and value of the journey experience. The case is very interesting because the brand when was at its beginnings had changed by the management after short time.

Initially, the brand forecasted the opportunity for the customer to fill, through the web site, his journey obtaining a customized budget with details about services and costs.

The on line offer has divided into the following options: (1) "do all you": in this case, customers can create their personal journey alone; (2) "we and you": in this section – in addition with the first option – the customer was able to pay in three steps (look>book>pay) his holiday; (3) "we do all": the firm provide a closed tourist offer without the possibility for customer to change it.

Characteristic of these three options was a strong *transparency* of the brand's offer. This feature would be as a strength for the firm while it suddenly became a weakness. In fact, even if customer contacts were high they didn't be converted in contracts. The level of interest of the potential customer was really elevated but economic results were absolutely unsatisfactory.

What happened was a paradox: there was a tourist consultant able to process purpose so interesting and detailed for the customer that this leads the consumer to organize the journey independently, perhaps modifying just the hotels. Above all the way "do all you" doesn't require to close the entire on line process with the payment. While the customer had the possibility to print the whole offer proposed.

Since September 2008 management has done an analysis in depth through customer web contacts carried out also by phone. This had been done examining the closed web purposes, customer level satisfaction and sales proceeds obtained. Through this analysis management discovered that the potential client built its itinerary but after quantifying the amount of the journey he decided to find arrangements individually or he bought just a share of the web offer.

In fact, the transparency of supply wasn't converted into value for the firm. In this way, result for the firm has been to gather "mercenary" customers due by the over-transparency of the web procedure about the estimated costs and itinerary. On one hand, in fact, the customers had a positive perception of the firm supply but, on the other hand, consumers had a negative perception of the sacrifice (the price of the entire itinerary) they had to face. Consequently, in the month of April 2009, Terremobili modified its strategy changing the web structure and supply mechanism in the following two steps: (1) *Tour*: option that produces close blocks as well as the previously procedure "We do all"; (2) *Dimore*: option that propose for each territory a choice of selected hotels with excellent quality/price relation.

These two options allow for the potential customers the possibility to look/book/pay all in real time by the web site. This is strictly related with two aspects of this new web procedure: the first one is the reduction of the interaction among the firm and the client, and the second one is connected to the profitability for the firm. In fact, the profitability for the firm increases when the web purpose has been converted in the online purchase.

Conclusion

The main purpose of this study is to investigate the positive effects of wrong customer perception due to the gap existing between created value and perceived value. Results of the research provide us with some meaningful insights.

For academic, the paper offers a different approach in E-CRM and perception studies. Often the positive side of a negative event is not adequately considered. Instead, we argue that from an unfavorable situation, a systemic improvement can derive. Moreover, this study provides to enlarge the field of study on customer and management perception, analyzing the cases in which managers changes completely their way to propose their offer in order to better responding to consumer needs. In fact, the well noted importance of perception in management research is still emphasized thanks to the observation of our empirical case – Terremobili – in which managers have learn to the consumer misunderstanding. This highlights that website can be improved studying consumer perception about offer and the following behavior, in an optic of learning by doing.

In addition, results of the above mentioned observation suggested a change and improvement of the website structure, that now is more functional and interactive than in the past, when the immoderate transparency of information caused an incorrect consumer behavior (mercenary consumer).

Finally, Terremobili can suggest managers to pay attention on consumer perception. Generally, managers do not seek consumer feedback, and this means do not deeper understand consumer needs and image consumer behaviors. E-business, instead, claims a different behavior, based on perception analyzes, especially, in the observation of value perceived.

The paper has many limitations, but the main is the reference to only one firm, that does not allow the results generalization. To obviate this limitation, the sample analyzed will be enlarged in future researches, in order to better understand the way to create a bridge between what management image and what consumer really does.

References

1. Purba S (2001) *Architectures for e-business systems*, building foundations for tomorrow's success. CRC Press, Boca Raton
2. Chaffey D, Mayer R, Johnston K, Ellis-Chadwick F (2003) *Internet marketing, financial times*. Prentice Hall, Harlow
3. Bergeron PB (2004) *Essentials of CRM: a guide to customer relationship management*. Wiley, New York
4. Yaeckel B, Kania D, Allen C (2002) *One to one Web marketing, 2nd edn. Build a relationship marketing strategy one customer at a time*. Wiley Computer Publishing, Wiley, New York
5. Vacca J, Loshin P (2003) *Electronic commerce, 4th edn*. Charles River Media Inc. Hingham
6. Feinberg R, Kadam R (2002) E-CRM Web service attributes as determinants of customer satisfaction with retail Web sites. *Int J Serv Ind Manage* 13(5):432–451
7. Zeithaml AV, Binter JM (2002) *Services marketing, integrating customer focus across the firm, 2nd edn*. Irwin McGraw Hill publications, Boston
8. Weinstein A, Johnson WC (1999) *Designing and delivering superior customer value*. CRC press, Boca Raton
9. Solomon M (2007) *Consumer behaviour (Enhanced media edition)*. Financial Times Press, London
10. Gurviez P, Korkia M (2003) Test of a consumer-brand relationship model including trust and three consequences. In *Proceedings of the 30th international research seminar in marketing*, La Londe les Maures, Francia
11. Minjoon J, Zhilin Y, DaeSoo K (2004) Customers' perceptions of online retailing service quality and their satisfaction. *Int J Qual Reliab Manage* 21(8):817
12. Parasuraman A, Zeithaml VA, Berry LL (1988) SERVQUAL: a multiple-item scale for measuring consumer perceptions of service quality. *J Retail* 64(1):12–40
13. Dessì C, Floris M (2008) *Management and customer relations in small and medium-sized family businesses: the perceptive concordance index*. Academy of Management Annual Meeting, Anaheim
14. Cabras S, Dessì C, Floris M (2008) *Stressing management-customer relations in small/medium-sized family businesses. The importance of management perceptions*, paper presented at 4th EIASM workshop on family business management research, Napoli, 8–10 giugno
15. Cabras S, Dessì C, Floris M, (2009) When management and customer see eye to eye: the agreement factor and performance. *J Small Bus Enterp Dev* (forthcoming)

16. Mathwick C, Malhotra N, Rigdon E (2002) The effect of dynamic retail experiences on experiential perceptions of value: an internet and catalogue comparison. *J Retail* 78:51–60
17. Sweeney JC, Soutar GN (2001) Consumer perceived value. The development of a multiple item scale. *J Retail* 77:203–220
18. Lapierre J (2000) Customer perceived value in industrial contexts. *J Bus Ind Mark* 15(2/3):122–140
19. Parasuraman A, Grewal D (2000) The impact of technology on the quality-value-loyalty-chain: a research agenda. *J Acad Market Sci* 28:168–174
20. Van de Ven A, Polley D (1992) Learning while innovating. *Org Sci* 3(1):92–116
21. Cyert RM, March JG (1992) *A behavioral theory of the firm, 2nd edn*. Blackwell Publishing, Oxford
22. March JG, Sproull LS, Tamuz M (1991) Learning from samples of one or fewer. *Org Sci* 2:58–71
23. Probst G (2002) Putting knowledge to work: case writing as an organizational learning and knowledge management tool for the new economy. In Probst G, Davenport TH (eds) *Knowledge management case book*. Wiley, New York, pp 248–261
24. Yin RK (1994) *Case study research. Design and methods, 2nd edn*. Sage, Thousand Oaks

Supply Chain Coordination and IT: The Role of Third Party Logistics Providers

Roberta Pinna*, **Pier Paolo Carrus**†, **and Daniela Pettinao**‡

Abstract Logistics Service Providers have become important players in supply chain management as increasing numbers of firms are outsourcing their logistics activities. In a highly competitive context characterized by "time compression", IT alignment between supplier and logistics service provider has a direct positive impact on, strategic and operational performance. The success of logistics outsourcing relationship is entrenched in the third party's technological ability to improve the supply chain reactivity.

Introduction

The philosophy of supply chain management (SCM) is founded on collaboration among supply chain partners to achieve greater benefits [1, 2]. It consists of many organizations acting together, with each organization dependent on the performance of other organizations in the chain. Supply chain management (SCM) seeks to improve performance through elimination of waste and more efficient use of internal and external supplier capabilities and technology, creating a seamlessly coordinated supply chain and thus elevating interfirm competition to intersupply chain competition [3]. Indeed, SCM "extends the concept of partnerships into a multiform effort to manage the total flow of goods from suppliers to the ultimate customers" [4]. According to Mentzer et al., in this paper the supply chain is defined as a set of three or more entities (organizations or individuals) directly involved in the upstream and downstream flows of products, services, finances, and information from a source to a customer.

Logistics management is the part of SCM that plans, implements and controls the efficient, effective forward and reverse flow and storage of goods, services and related information between the point of origin and the point of consumption in order to meet customers' requirements. With the increasing globalization of markets, companies began to view logistics as more than simply a source of cost sav-

* Faculty of Economics, University of Cagliari, Cagliari, Italy, pinnar@unica.it
† Faculty of Economics, University of Cagliari, Cagliari, Italy, ppcarrus@unica.it
‡ Faculty of Economics, University of Cagliari, Cagliari, Italy, pettinao@unica.it

A. D'Atri et al. (eds.), *Management of the Interconnected World*,
DOI 10.1007/978-3-7908-2404-9_35, © Springer-Verlag Berlin Heidelberg 2010

ings and recognize it as a source of enhancing product or service offerings as part of the broader supply chain process to create competitive advantage [5, 6]. However, because logistics users often lack the competence to operate logistics activities internally, they tend to develop outsourcing with third-party logistics (3PL). By outsourcing logistics activities, firms can better focus on their core competencies, such as manufacturing and retailing, while allowing third-party specialists to take care of functions such as transportation, distribution, and warehousing to satisfy the ultimate needs of their customers. One distinguishing characteristic of contemporary logistics providers, by contrast, is a focus both on formal long term relationships between the service providers and their customers, and on mutually beneficial relationships. This study explores the connection between strategic buyer– 3PL relationships and logistics integration, along with the subsequent impact on a firm's agility performance.

Literature Review

Firm integration is a fundamental element of SCM and is accomplished through coordination of activities throughout the network of buyers and suppliers. Central to collaboration is the exchange of large amounts of information along the supply chain, including planning and operational data, real time information and communication. Optimization of information storage and use requires that the organization and storage of data throughout the supply chain be consistent so that all the data are accessible to multiple entities at different levels. The results are well coordinated movements of inventories, products that are delivered quickly and reliably when and where they are needed, high responsiveness to short lead times, the elimination of bullwhip effect, and improved firm performance [7]. As the practice of logistics outsourcing and SCM have become increasingly important as a source of competitive advantage, researchers have started to explore various research topics related to logistics outsourcing and the role of 3PLs in SCM [8–11]. In a highly competitive context, effective leadership of logistics service providers lies in their capacity to innovate in the area of information flows management [12]. Specifically, the type of IT used largely determines the nature and quality of interactions the company has with customers, suppliers, and trading partners. Numerous researchers have found that when buyers and logistics services providers communicate and share information they are more likely to improve the quality of their products or services; cycle time reduction; reduce the costs of protecting against opportunistic behaviour and improve cost savings through greater product design and operational efficiencies [13–17]. A high level of IT capability has been shown to provide a clear competitive advantage and can be a differentiating factor in terms of company performance [18, 19].

Methodology

To identify appropriate research methods for this research, we used a taxonomy of IS research methods proposed by Galliers [20]. In his proposal, the Author outlines the importance of the use of case studies as a research technique for the analysis of organisational aspects; techniques which may be identified as the most common method of qualitative research utilized in IT studies [21]. The research methodology selected for the achievement of the aforementioned objectives is, in any case, qualitative. In particular, it will be decided to employ the case study technique [22] adapted to develop the theory through the understanding of the phenomenon in its proper context. According to Yin [23], for this study we stet up a single case study. In order to this, multiple sources of information was utilized. The access to a multiplicity of information sources has favoured the principles of interaction and the triangulation of the sources [24]. Once the primary observations are developed these are further compounded which the interview material which seems to emerge from the analysis. These cross-comparisons have been useful for the final compilation of the proposed interpretative model and for the individuation of the future direction of this research [25].

Case Description: The Laziale-Interlaziale Logistic Group

The Laziale Distribuzione was born in 1978 in order to offer Italian companies modern shipments and logistic services. Over the years it succeded in consolidating its position in the market: by differentiating its offer; by expanding its field of action just to international markets; by investing in structures, training and IT infrastructures, becoming one of the most important logistics & distribution centres in Italy nowadays. The Logistic Group LD is composed of 6 companies: Laziale Distribuzione, Interlaziale, Laziale express, LOG.DI. srl, Logigraf s.r.l. and inLog. The Logistic Group LD has been celebrated as the most innovative logistic Italian business by Assologistica, Euromerci and SITL Italia. In the Italian market, the Logistic Group is between the first 100 enterprices of logistics services providers (Confetra 2005). In the 1997 the Laziale-Interlaziale Logistic Group have obtained the certification of own Quality System based on UNI EN ISO 9002:1994 rules. In the 2003, they have renewed the certification of Quality System in agreement to UNI EN ISO 9001:2000 (Vision 2000).This important result permit, to consolidate the business process of continuous improvement, guaranteeing a service level of the proven reliability and professionalism that it answers to the satisfaction of the Customers. At the present, the LD Group is starting a new project: creation of Santa Palomba's logistic polo, the first logistic polo in the middle-south Italy. In function about two factors, the number of sectors manage and the number of services supplies, the LD to take in the integrator logistic operators quadrant (Fig. 1).

Indeed, LD Group's works in different sectors[1], each one has got a specifics markets with rules and different tecnics. With reference to numbers and type of services suppliers, the LD Group offers different services[2] that can classify in two different principals classes: *distribution* and *logistics services*. The LD Group offers distribution services fit for needs, thanks to their widespread network that allows fast and customized deliveries. The LD Group Network is composed of 15 platforms located throughout Italy. These platforms distribute any kind of goods (raw materials, semi-finished products, and finished products) both an a national and an international scale, according to appointed times, thanks to selected carriers.

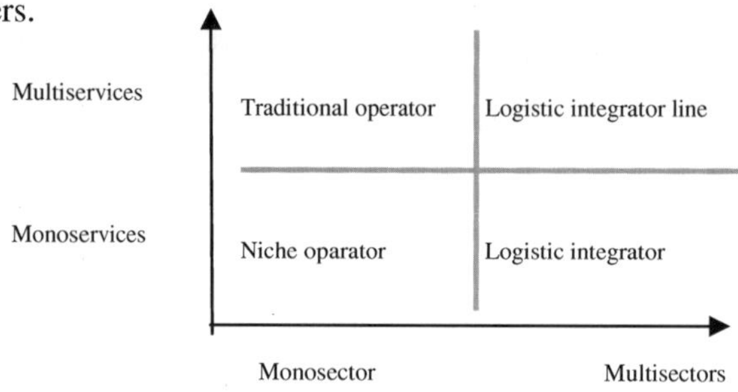

Fig. 1. Matrix positioning

Over the years, the LD Group has become skilled in logistics, creating purpose-built plants. Thanks to skilled technical and computer structures, in Italy the company is a competitive reality in terms of costs and services. The added value of logistic solutions derives from the concentration in a single production unit of all operational activities: from directly receiving the products to handling and distribution. This system architecture allows logistic costs to be reduced by about 25%, thereby determining huge savings in management costs. Thanks to skilled technical and computer structures the logistic services allowing the customers to: manage bigger volumes (getting thereby economies of scale); reduce handling of products; reduce internal management costs; improve performance efficiency; respect lead time; offer its own customers new services; greater flexibility; reducing communication errors. An important aspect of LD Group's strategic orientation is the philosophy of leveraging IT to create superior product and services and to build solutions to respond to customer and partner requirements. In other words, the provider customized its services to the buyer's needs, and the relevant services are provided in a consistent and reliable manner: *The LD culture leads us to listen and understand the reasons and needs of our beloved customers, discussing with them the diagnosis and the relative solution to adopt. A progressive engagement*

[1] Pharmaceutical, Promotional, Publishing, Automotive, I.T. Eletctronics and Telecommunications, Banking, Insurance, Fashion.
[2] Assembly and packaging, Development of distribution strategy/SYSTEM,EDI capability, Management of performance reports, Information management, Warehousing, Intermodal services, Export operations, licensing assistance, Import operations, Letter of credit review and compliance, Reverse logistics, Tracking & tracking operation, Customers services.

made of attention and empathy. What they get undoubtedly is an overwhelming satisfaction to be recognized as catalysts of process of amazing steps ahead towards the street of success. With IT the LD group can develop an understanding of their clients activities that previously would have been infeasible due to the workload involved in manually collecting and analyzing large quantities of data. The type of IT known as an interorganizational system (IOS) lies at the heart of the ability of IT to support the logistic integration between buyers and LD provider. The logistics integration activity typically involves the sharing of very timely and vary sensitive demand and sales data, inventory data, and shipment status data. Data sharing often involves a firm giving direct access to its computerized data bases to its supply chain partners. LD use AS/400, developed by IBM, is an information system that links the provider with more members of supply chain, such as manufactures, transportation firms, retailers, or customers. This link automates some element of the logistics workload, such as order processing, order status inquiries, inventory management, or shipment tracking. The IT utilized by LD group are the following one: Transportation management systems, Warehouse management systems, Order management & fulfilment, Warehouse planning & optimization and Web traking. Without IOS these activities are carried out by personal visits, mailing of paper documents, phone or fax. In this way, the quality of information available to decision-makers at all levels is high and centralized. Optimization of information storage and use requires that the organization and storage of data throughout the supply chain be consistent so that the data are accessible to multiple entities at different levels. Accordingly, the information structure can be star-shaped, such that all nodes are directly connected to the information medium. The implementation of information networks through IOS improves the efficiency of gathering and communicating information among the participating organizations, which creates such efficiencies as better management of inventory levels, higher levels of interorganizational communication, and lower coordination costs. A survey of purchasing and warehouse managers found that the implementation of EDI required degree a direct relationship between information availability, responsiveness to customer requests, and operating performance. Indeed, information sharing should allow firms to reduce their inventory levels across the supply chain. The partnership approach is not suitable for all interfirm relationships, some of which are best managed at arm's length. Extensive trust and commitment are needed to develop and maintain a partnerships longevity.

Case Analysis: Discussion and Implications

This study contributes to the research stream on logistics integration by specifically investigating the relationships between strategic buyer-3PL relationships, performance and satisfaction. In reality however, the literature is still very fragmented and although several studies purport to discuss supply chain issues, most of the existing research only examines one link of the chain, or more importantly only focuses on one element in the supply chain performance mix. The model, linking strategic buyer-3PL relationships, performance and satisfaction is depicted in Fig. 2.

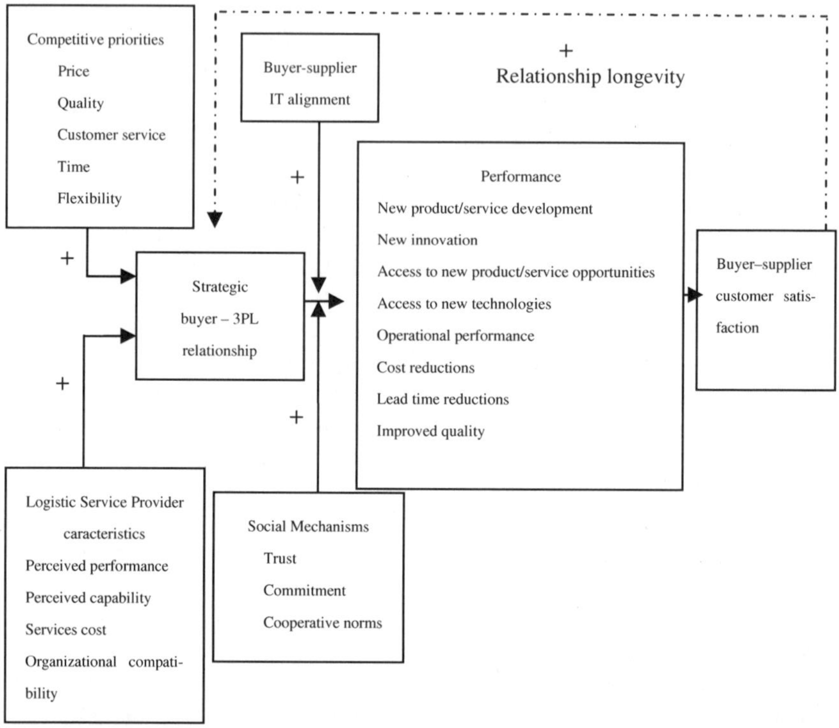

Fig. 2. Motivational process

Buyer-3PL integration is a construct defined as an effective, mutually shared process where two or more firms work together, have mutual understanding, have e common vision, share resources and achieve collective goals. But the link between strategic buyer-3PL relationship, performance and satisfaction is not directly and linear. Indeed, different are the elements who impact on each one. The results support the contention that the exchange of information through interfirm communication is an essential condition for realizing the potential benefits of collaborative relationships (performance). The embeddedness of the IOS allowed EDI to play a central role in Supply Chain coordination. The increased speed and flexibility of informationand knowledge transfer allowed for more efficient coordination for all members of the supply chain, reducing communication errors, facilitating information knowledge sharing and increase integration between the supplier and buyer firms. More specifically, by providing real-time information regarding product availability, material requirements forecast, inventory level, shipment status, production requirements, production and delivery schedules, information technology can greatly enhance the ability to further narrow delivery windows or make adjustments to the existing schedules, thereby ultimately boosting the supply chain logistics efficiency. The study suggests that external logistics integration could be one of those strategic options that lead to higher percentage of agile and on-time delivery of products and service to customers. The result also shows that the seamless integration of the logistics activities such as distribution, transportation and/or warehousing facilities between supply chain partners is crucial for responsiveness, flexibility and dependability. The results further provide empirical evidence to the value-added potential of the logistics function, suggesting that external logistics should be managed as a vital strategic activity and that its coordination can ultimately generate a sustainable win–win strategic advantage through the improvement of agility performance of both the supplier and buyer firms. But developing strong, long-term partnerships required also design managerial components and relationship activities that support the development of intangible connections (trust, commitment, cooperative norms, etc.) with partners. By doing so, the provider may also be able to achieve some of the desired outcomes from investing in a partnership. In particular, obtaining referrals, higher degrees of customer retention, and an increased perceived ability to recover from service failures are shown to be associated with stronger partnerships. In order to strengthen the partnership, the customer should perceive that the provider is focusing on the interaction between the companies and is concerned with winning and keeping the customer by maintaining links between quality, and customer service. This can be achieved by both the investment in tangible assets that are particular to the relationship and by understanding the key relationship marketing elements that have the potential to strengthen the connection between the partners. In conclusion, the application of the SCM concept leads manufacturers and retailers to outsource significant parts of their logistics, as well as to select and reduce the number of logistics providers with which to establish long-term relationships. We acknowledge some limitations of this study that might provide opportunities for future research. In this study a limitation concern the sample population. The future research aim will include a broader population. Third logistics service provider in order to expand the scope of generalizability of the results. Finally, this study focused on the buyer-supplier dyad as the unit of analysis, and assumed the supplier firm's perspective. Thus, there is a need to more fully examine the nature of the exchange relationship from the supplier's perspective so as to establish whether or not the relationship is reciprocal and mutually beneficial. Despite these limitations, this study paves the way for researchers and managers to more fully capitalize on the potential of external logistics integration in creating collaborative advantages for both buyer and supplier firms.

References

1. Andraski JC (1998) Leadership and the realization of supply chain collaboration. *J Bus Logist* 19(2):9–11
2. Stank TP, Keller SB, Daugherty PJ (2001) Supply chain collaboration and logistics service performance. *J Bus Logist* 22(2):29–47
3. Andersen MG, Katz RB (1998) Strategic sourcing. *Int J Logist Manage* 9(1):1–13

4. Mentzer JT, DeWitt W, Keebler JS, Min S, Nix NW, Smith CD (2001) Defining supply chain management. *J Bus Logist* 22(2):1–25
5. Novack RA, Langley CJ, Rinehart LM (1995) *Creating logistics value: themes for the future*. Council of Logistics Management, Oak Brook
6. McDuffie JM, West S, Welsh J, Baker B (2001) Logistics transformed: the military enters a new age. *Supply Chain Manage Rev* 5(3):92–100
7. Lee HL, Billington C (1992) Managing supply chain inventory: pitfalls and opportunities. *Sloan Manage Rev* 33(3):65–73
8. Cheng L, Grimm CM (2006) The application of empirical strategic management research to supply chain management. *J Bus Logist* 27(1):1–57
9. Maloni MJ, Carter CR (2006) Opportunities for research in third-party logistics. *Transport J* 45(2):23–38
10. Selviaridis K, Spring M (2007) Third party logistics: a literature review and research agenda. *Int J Supply Chain Manage* 18(1):125–150
11. Lai FXZ, Wang Q (2007) Taxonomy of information technology strategy and its impact on the performance of third-party logistics in China. *Int J Prod Res* 45(10):2195–2218
12. Sauvage T (2003) The relationship between technology and logistics third-party providers. *Int J Phys Distrib Logist Manage* 33(3):236–253
13. Carr AS, Pearson JN (1999) Strategically managed buyer-seller relationships and performance outcomes. *J Oper Manage* 17(5):497–519
14. Kotabe M, Martin X, Domoto H (2003) Gaining from vertical partnerships: knowledge transfer, relationship duration, and supplier performance improvement in the U.S. and Japanese automotive industries. *Strateg Manage J* 24(4):293–316
15. Prahinksi C, Benton WC (2004) Supplier evaluations: communication strategies to improve supplier performance. *J Oper Manage* 22(1):39–62
16. Sanders NR (2005) IT alignment in supply chain relationships: a study of supplier benefits. *J Supply Chain Manage* 41(2):4–13
17. Giunipero L, Handfield RB, Eltantawy R (2006) Supply management's evolution: key skill sets for the supply manager of the future. *Int J Oper Product Manage* 26(7):822–844
18. Earl MJ (1993) Experiences in strategic information systems planning: editor's comments. *MIS Q* 17(3):2–3
19. Kathuria R, Anandarajan M, Igbaria M (1999) Linking IT applications with manufacturing strategy: an intelligent decision support system approach. *Decis Sci* 30(4):959–992
20. Galliers R (1992) *Choosing information system research approaches. Information systems research: issues, methods and practical guidelines*. Blackwell, Oxford
21. Orlikowski B (1991) Studying information technology in organizations: research approaches and assumptions. *Inf Syst Res* 2(1):1–28
22. Dubois A, Gadde LE (2002) Systematic combining: an abductive approch to case research. *J Bus Res* 55:553–560
23. Yin R (1984) *Case study research: design and methods*. Sage Publishing, Beverly Hills
24. Eisenhardt KM (1989) Building theory from case study research. *Acad Manage Rev* 14(4):532–550
25. Lewis MW (1998) Iterative triangulation: a theory development process using existing case studies. *J Oper Manage* 16:455–469

Generating Knowledge by Combining Prediction Models with Information Technology

Luciano Marchi* **and Carlo Caserio**†

Abstract The process of planning is largely based on the way the Information Technology supports decision makers to formulate the future objectives from the past results, and, at the same time, managing knowledge development. In this perspective, the past business dynamics are very important in order to estimate the future ones; this way, taking some aspects arising from the variance analysis, can improve the understanding of past data and, consequently, improve the reliability of estimation. The aim of the paper is to discuss how different modelling approaches allow the process to evolve from supporting decisions to generating knowledge.

The Role of Knowledge Based Decision Support Systems Versus Knowledge Generating Decision Support Systems

The problem we are dealing with is how to integrate the process of decision making by combining, in a strategic perspective, Information Technology and Business Modelling. Some applications in the specific fields of prediction/planning and variance analysis models, give evidence that the process can evolve from supporting decisions to generating knowledge. In this perspective, information becomes knowledge when communicated and internalized into the mental patterns [1, 2].

First we will try to summarize the elements that characterize the Decision Support System (DSS), and determine their evolution versus both Knowledge Based Decision Support System (KBDSS) and Knowledge Management (KM).

In our opinion, the principal elements that have to be considered to guarantee such a decision process, are the following: (1) the large quantity of data and complexity of calculations, that characterize the problem, make it necessary to base the decision process on IT; (2) the solution of the problem, on the other hand, involves some subjective evaluations to recognize the essence of the problem or to manage

* Department of Business Administration, University of Pisa, Pisa, Italy, lmarchi@ec.unipi.it

† Department of Business Administration, University of Macerata, Macerata, Italy, c.caserio@ec.unipi.it

A. D'Atri et al. (eds.), *Management of the Interconnected World*,
DOI 10.1007/978-3-7908-2404-9_36, © Springer-Verlag Berlin Heidelberg 2010

its different solutions [3]; (3) the conceptual model, based on the relevant variables of the business, may be formalized in order to create a mathematical model of the reality; (4) the conceptual model and the mathematical model are manageable by the interactive communication between the decision maker and the computer and related software; (5) by integrating the IT in the decision making process is possible to gain knowledge (a sort of feed-back) on the relevant economic and financial variables of the business [4].

The hypothesis we formulate for this discussion is that the growing role of IT determines knowledge development only when the Technology follows, step by step, the conversion process from the conceptual model to the mathematical model. In order to describe a DSS that largely contribute to generate knowledge into the decision process we will use the term "Knowledge Generating Decision Support System" (KGDSS).

Starting from the basic assumption that "using Information Technology (computers, communication and databases) is an active part of a decision process" [5], we want to examine how to integrate IT and decision making, in order to improve the effectiveness of management and the ability of humans to deal with complex mental tasks. To do so, our aims are: (a) transforming conceptual models into mathematical models; (b) elaborating such a model with decision support interactive software and (c) managing the "knowledge feed-back".

In our opinion, the strategic role for designing and implementing the mentioned decision process is not based on the quality of the IT itself, but mainly on the way the integration between the IT and the decision maker can generate knowledge. In other words, even a simple worksheet can create a good KGDSS by enforcing the interactive elements of the decision process.

Regarding the quality of IT, the characteristics of the software instruments related to KBDSS were already well defined 20 years ago [6]. The interactive elements of the decision process that can generate knowledge are mainly related to the way the conceptual and formal models are defined and integrated with the IT, in some specific application areas.

An Application Area of Knowledge Generating Decision Support System: Prediction and Planning Models

The process of prediction and planning includes activities in which managers elaborate decisions about the future business management, taking into account the relations between the variables of information system and the past trends [7]. In order to obtain reliable predictions, in fact, past results can assume the role of starting point to carry out hypothesis with the intention to estimate the future dynamics.

This type of decisions is included into the semi-structured category of tasks [8, 3, 9]. At the same time, we can insert the type of decisions referred above into the field of strategic planning and control [10, 11]. We can distinguish three principal parts of the prediction and planning model, starting from the analysis of the past results, correlations and trends: (1) the prediction of data, (2) the simulation of the hypothesis, (3) the planning of the objectives.

The first part of a prediction and planning models is related to the predictions of the future dynamics. By combining the prediction model with the Information Technology, the past results may be projected in the future in various ways: (a) a first way (usually adopted for sales) is to replicate or elaborate the absolute or percentage trends, measured in the past periods; (b) a second way, is referring to the simple or weighted average of the past results; (c) other ways can consider other elements in the calculation, as inflation rates or cash flows. Therefore, the very important question is: how can we create participation and generate knowledge managing the prediction and planning model with the IT? The possibility to empower the process of decision making with generating knowledge is essentially related to the possibility to manage directly the conceptual model of the reality into formal terms; this can be allowed by the interactivity of the software, which allows to convert tacit into explicit knowledge and vice versa [1, 12]. This process can be empowered by on-line evidence of some control variables and coherence indicators. The principal coherence indicator can furnish the level's variation of the balance between investment flows/stocks and financing flows/stocks, for any combination of prediction formulas, generating knowledge on the best way to relate the economic and financial predictions with the past results.

The second part of the prediction and planning model is related to the formulation and verification of different hypothesis for the future, which can adapt the prediction values to different economic scenarios. These hypothesis may be able to limit the surprise, sudden shifts in preferences and goals of the strategy [13, 14]. IT can support decision makers with features such as: easy interactivity, immediate interpretation, information process acceleration, rapid learning (visualization of trends and indicators) [15]. In other words, IT can help to present the most appropriate analysis levels of the key variables and relations, assures iterative simulations, furnishes the critical evaluation of the results, and generates knowledge redefining and verifying the economic and financial elements of the prediction and planning model.

The third part of a prediction and planning model is typically related to the formulation of the objectives by integrating data together with technology and individuals in the organization. This part of the model represents the final output of a KGDSS, but may also generate further knowledge up to the process of putting in actions the decisions, motivating individual for reaching the objectives, measuring the results and analyzing the variances of them on the objectives.

An Application Area of Knowledge Generating Decision Support Systems: Variance Analysis Model

Many studies have exposed the relations between IT and management control [16–22]. Management control is conduct through both technical and social elements. In that regard some works have dedicated attention on *how* management control systems are used [23], rather than *whether* the systems are used; the results underline the benefits of interactive use of control systems [24, 25]. Some studies have underlined the need to anticipate, recognize, evaluate, resolve, control, document, and learn from past experiences in a way that supports the decision making process of all managerial levels, using the Business Information Systems (BIS) [26–31]. In our viewpoint, BIS not only allow access to knowledge but also generate it. Therefore, a classic DSS tool design is composed by a database, powerful modelling functions accessed by a management system, and an interface that enable interaction between decision maker and the computerized model [7]. Variance analysis is the final part of a prediction and planning model. It allows to obtain a *knowledge feed-back* which improves the understanding of information, generating knowledge usable to formulate reliable hypothesis on the future. Thus, the analysis of feed-back is both a management control technique and a cognitive process. The following features can improve the understanding of the past, in order to make more reliable predictions:

1. *Feed-back analysis and the concept of relevance*

It is fundamental to guarantee the selectivity and the relevance of information, [11] therefore, the actual problem is selecting the relevant information, in order to avoid overloads that may paralyze the analysis [32].

The approach that allows to detect the relevant variances is called management by exception and its objective is to identify exceptional conditions as soon as possible after they occur [33–38]. This approach involves the decision maker, who has to identify the most strategic variables and to define the levels of acceptability, and the techniques of business intelligence used like supports. The decision maker can enlarge or reduce the range to obtain different relevant values according to his informative and control needs, risk and uncertainty perception, combining statistical models with personal experiences [39, 21]. In our perspective, the analysis of relevant gaps might also favour a process of generating knowledge when the gaps are considered information that have to be integrate and well-established into the know-how of the firm [11].

2. *Feed-back analysis on product/market combinations*

In a multi-product company, variances can be broken down on the basis of product and market combinations [40–43]. The results achieved are combinable with the concept of relevance in order to improve the significance of the information obtained and to enhance its conversion in knowledge. In this case, knowledge arises from the division of synthetic variable into its "internal and external" components, concerning respectively in product and market. The detection of a synthetic relevant variance does not guarantee the relevance of the product/market variances. Even in this case, it is possible to define acceptability levels referred to dimensions of market and product.

3. *Feed-back analysis of volume, price and mix*

In a similar way, we can break down the synthetic variables into volume, price and mix, examining the causes of detected variances [44]. According to this analysis, it is possible to generate knowledge referred to the pricing, sales and mix policies, in order to define future objectives in a better way.

About the volume analysis, we can observe two perspectives: sales and production and acquire knowledge from each one. In a cognitive perspective, the feed-back analysis performed on the variances of prices, can provide information connected to bargaining power and to the efficiency of production.

Since we are analyzing a multi-product company, we also have to consider the variances of mixes, comparing the final mixes detected with the expected product combination. To do this, it is helpful to observe that a change of mix might bring about a variation of turnover due to the different "weight" of each product.

The measurement system produces information that can influence the decisional processes of the managers and it have to avoid informative distortion [44] that can influence the generating knowledge.

4. *Feed-back analysis in a temporal dimension*

After the works conducted on the effects of advanced information technologies referred to organizational design and decision making [45], some authors show that the use of information technology increases the speed and quality of problem identification and decision making [46].

The restriction of temporal dimension represents a very relevant support in the planning and control processes [47]. It is very significant to consider the frequency of observation in a combined use with relevance concept. In fact it is possible to define a continuous monitoring system that detects variances in certain time intervals. The frequency of observation and comparison assumes great importance because: (1) the more the observation is frequent, the sooner it is possible to obtain the information; (2) the sooner we acquire the information, the more we are able to anticipate the cognitive process to generate knowledge.

Even thought the feed-back analysis is an *ex-post* model, the restriction of the temporal interval improves the usefulness of the information. In fact, it enhances the possibility to align management and strategic objectives through prompt interventions [44]. The continuous analysis on brief temporal intervals allows to keep in mind the strategic intents and it prevents managers from making corrections without adequate reasoning [48] basing their decisions on the knowledge generated from the brief time analysis.

Conclusions

In this paper we have discussed about how to generate knowledge into the decision-making process integrating the use of IT instruments with the conversion of conceptual models in mathematical models for a predictive/simulative aim, and for an improving of the managing knowledge feed-back. In order to give evidence to a DSS that can generate knowledge we have used the expression "Knowledge Generating Decision Support System".

The creation of knowledge is allowed by the interaction between the decision maker and the software, which consents to manage directly the conceptual model of the reality and to convert it into formal terms. Through the use of some coherence indicators, the software gives results for any combination of prediction formulas, generating knowledge on the different modelling solutions which link the economic and financial predictions with the past values (modelling knowledge or *knowledge on the future*) (Fig. 1).

After this phase, the prediction and planning model is used to formulate and verify some different hypothesis for the future which define different economic scenarios. Integrating the data together with technology and individuals in the organization, the model can be used to define the objectives.

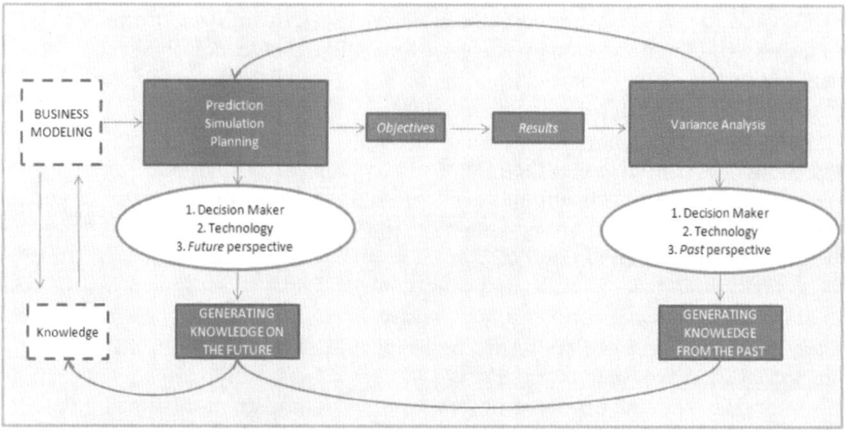

Fig. 1. A representation of *knowledge generating decision support system*

In this way, it is also possible to generate further knowledge: evaluating the results of the executed actions and analyzing the variances between the results and the objectives. Generating knowledge from the past, in this context, can depend from the pursued techniques of detection. In order to let this "feed-back knowledge" emerge it is possible to take into consideration some aspects arising from the analysis of variances, which improve the understanding of past data and, consequently, improve the reliability of estimation: the relevance concept, the analysis of internal and external dimensions (product/market), the analysis of the elementary components, the restriction of time interval.

The highest degree of "feed-back knowledge" is obtained combining: the relevance concept, the product and market analysis, the elementary component analysis and the brief-time analysis. Therefore, the knowledge acquired in this phase can be re-invested into the business modeling process, furnishing knowledge elements that the decision maker has to take into consideration when he defines model formulas and future perspective hypothesis. This potentiality becomes useful in case the decision maker iterates the business modeling process, investing the generated knowledge from the past (feed-back knowledge or *knowledge from the past*) to the generated knowledge on the future, supporting his decision-making process of the new future evaluations, even interacting with software tools. This model has been submitted to a panel of decision makers who have used it and confirmed that this model can be useful in two different ways: operating use, supporting decision for example in drawing up a business plan; "learning by modeling" use, helping to understand and to explicit the relations between the variables, and generating knowledge. These are only initial results, but the inquiry is still in progress.

References

1. Nonaka I (1991) *The knowledge-creative company*. Harv Bus Rev (November–December) 69(6):96–104
2. Quagli A (1995) *Introduzione allo studio della conoscenza in economia aziendale*. Giuffrè, Milano
3. Keen PGW, Scott Morton MS (1978) *Decision support system: an organizational perspective*. Addison-Wesley, Reading
4. Favotto F (1990) Simulazione dell'assetto economico-finanziario d'impresa mediante l'uso del calcolatore elettronico. In: Brunetti G, Coda V, Favotto F (eds) *Analisi, previsioni, simulazioni economico-finanziarie d'impresa*. Etaslibri, Milano
5. Scott Morton MS (2007) *Reflections*. DSSResources.COM
6. Favotto F (1988) Financial statement analysis and information technology: from calculation to simulation to knowledge-based support. *Economia Aziendale* 1:112–119
7. Shim JK, Siegel JG (2004) Handbook of financial analysis, forecasting and modeling. 2nd ed., CCH Incorporated, Chicago
8. Gorry GA, Scott Morton MS (1971) A framework for management information systems. *Sloan Manage Rev* 13(1):55–70
9. Ciborra C (1989) *Tecnologie di coordinamento. Informatica, telematica e istituzioni economiche*. Angeli, Milano
10. Anthony RN (1967) *Sistemi di pianificazione e controllo: schema d'analisi*. Etas Libri, Milano
11. Marchi L (2004) *I sistemi informativi aziendali*. Giuffrè, Milano
12. Nonaka I, Takeuchi K (1995) *The knowledge creating company: how Japanese companies create the dynamic of innovation*. Oxford University Press, Oxford
13. Ciborra C (1993) *Teams, markets and systems: business innovation and information technology*. Cambridge University Press, Cambridge
14. Ciborra C, Associates (2000) *From control to drift: the dynamics of corporate information infrastructures*. Oxford University Press, Oxford
15. Rossignoli C, Ferrari A (2008) Organization processes monitoring: business intelligence systems role. In: D'Atri A, De Marco M, Casalino N (eds) *Interdisciplinary aspects of information systems studies*. Physica, Heidelberg
16. Quattrone P, Hopper T (2001) What does organizational change mean? Speculations on a taken for granted category. *Manage Account Res* 12:403–435
17. Quattrone P, Hopper T (2005) A time-space odyssey: management control systems in two multinational organizations. *Account Organ Soc* 30(7–8):735–764
18. Granlund M, Malmi T (2002) Moderate impact of ERPs on management accounting: a lag or permanent outcome? *Manage Account Res* 13(3):299–321
19. Chapman CS (2005) Not because they are new: developing the contribution of enterprise resource planning systems to management control research. *Account Organ Soc* 30(7–8): 685–689
20. Dechow N, Mouritsen J (2005) Enterprise resource planning systems, management control and the quest for integration. *Account Organ Soc* 30:691–733
21. Berry AJ, Coad AF, Harris EP, Otley DT, Stringer C (2009) Emerging themes in management control: a review of recent literature. *Br Account Rev* 41:2–20
22. Chapman CS, Kihn LA (2009) Information system integration, enabling control and performance. *Account Organ Soc* 34:151–169
23. Simons R (1995) *Levers of control, how managers use innovative control systems to drive strategic renewal*. Harvard Business School Press, Boston
24. Abernethy MA, Brownell P (1999) The role of budgets in organizations facing strategic change: an exploratory study. *Account Organ Soc* 24:189–204
25. Vaivio J (2004) Mobilizing local knowledge with "proactive" non-financial measures. *Eur Account Rev* 13:39–71
26. Davenport T, Prusak L (1998) *Working knowledge: how organization manage what they know*. Harvard Business School Press, Boston

27. Negash S, Gray P (2003) Business intelligence. In: *Proceedings of the 9th American conference on information systems*, Tampa, Florida, 4–6 August 2003
28. Arain FM (2005) Strategic management of variation orders for institutional buildings: leveraging on information technology. *Proj Manage J* 36(4):66–77
29. Kemper H, Baars H (2006) Business intelligence und competitive intelligence – IT – basierte managementunterstutzung und markt-/wettbewerbsorienterte anwendungen. In: Kemper H, Heilmann H, Baars H (eds) Business and competitive intelligence. Dpunkt, Heidelberg
30. Eckerson WW (2006) *Performance dashboards.* Wiley, Hoboken
31. Clark TD, Jones MC, Armstrong CP (2007) The dynamic structure of management support system: theory development, research, focus and direction. *MIS Q* 31(3):579–615
32. Anthony RN, Hawkins D, Macrì D, Merchant K (2001) *Sistemi di controllo.* McGraw-Hill, Milano
33. Taylor FW (1911) The principles of scientific management. In: Taylor FW (ed) *Scientific management.* Harpen & Row, New York
34. Trigg DW (1964) Monitoring a forecasting system. *Oper Res Q* 15:271–274
35. Simon M (1965) *The shape of automation for men and management.* Harper and Row, New York
36. Brown RG (1959) *Statistical forecasting and prediction of discrete time series.* Prentice Hall, Englewood Cliffs
37. Bastia P (2001) *Sistemi di pianificazione e controllo.* Il Mulino, Bologna
38. Gorr WL (2009) Forecast accuracy measures for exception reporting using receiver operating characteristic curves. *Int J Forecast* 25:48–61
39. Anderson JR (2000) *Cognitive psychology and its implications.* Worth, New York
40. Ansoff HI (1968) *Corporate strategy: an analytical approach to business policy for growth and expansion*, McGraw-Hill, New York
41. Coda V (1981) Impatti ambientali e potenzialità di crescita imprenditoriali. *Sviluppo e organizzazione* (68):26–39
42. Marchi L, Paolini A, Quagli A (1995) *Strumenti di analisi gestionale – il profilo strategico.* Giappichelli, Torino
43. Quagli A (1996) Imprese, prodotti e mercati: l'analisi dei risultati economici. *Amministrazione and finanza* (22):iii–xix
44. Brusa L, Dezzani F (1983) *Budget e controllo di gestione.* Giuffrè, Milano
45. Huber G (1990) A theory of the effects of advanced information technologies on organizational design, intelligence, and decision making. *Acad Manage Rev* 15:47–71
46. Molloy S, Schwenk C (1995) Effects of information technology on strategic decision making. *J Manage Stud* 32(3):283–311
47. Marchi L, Quagli A (1997) *Il quadro di controllo delle imprese industriali.* Maggioli, Rimini
48. Lorange P (1990) *Pianificazione strategica.* McGraw-Hill, Milano

Part VI
IS Quality, Metrics and Impact

Chiara Francalanci[*] and Aurelio Ravarini[†]

This part of the book presents original research contributions on measurable impacts of information systems within organizations. While it is widely recognized that information technology impacts on organizations along multiple dimensions, the assessment of the actual costs and benefits of information systems raises a number of research questions that are still largely unanswered.

What are the real costs of key Information Systems projects? How can I assess these costs ahead of time? What are the tangible benefits delivered by Its and what evidence exists on the measurable impacts of these benefits, both at an organizational and at an industry level?

The three papers published in this part addresses these problems and try to provide insights on the methodologies and the techniques that can be applied to assess the quality of modern Information Systems.

[*] Politecnico di Milano, Milano, Italy, francala@elet.polimi.it

[†] University Carlo Cattaneo LIUC, Castellanza, Italy, aravarini@liuc.it

From IT Compliance Cost to IT Governance Benefits: An Italian Business Case

Renata P. Dameri *

Abstract IT compliance is one of the main challenges for Information Systems, not only because it is difficult to implement compliant applications, but because it requires very high investments and expenditures. Companies involved by IT compliance can pursue two different behaviours: the *Compliance view* considers IT compliance merely like a duty to accomplish with, and related cost as a necessary expenditure. The *Governance view* on the contrary considers IT compliance rules like an opportunity to improve administrative processes and information quality, and related cost like an investment able to create satisfactory returns.

In this paper, these two views are described, especially focusing on *Governance view* and benefits deriving from its implementation in companies. A business case is also examined, describing the implementation of IT compliance applying the *Governance view* in a large and global Italian group.

Compliance View and Governance View

The world in which companies are living nowadays is very complex. The context changes very fast and uncertainty is more and more increasing. It determines more pressure on business and the need of rapid decisions, based on confused data. Therefore, the importance of information and its availability is crucial.

Moreover, quality and transparency of information systems and financial reporting are necessary for companies to be appreciated on the financial markets. It needs a cultural change in IT management, that should orient its own activity towards IT governance, to better support business decisions and affordability of information and financial disclosure.

The main source of IT governance has been the introduction of laws and rules regarding the defence and protection of listed companies' shareholders, after the scandals of Enron in USA and Parmalat in Italy [1]. The first of these laws is the Sarbanes-Oxley Act (SOx) in 2002, then inspiring similar laws in Europe and Italy too; European laws are therefore called Euro SOx. In Italy, the law regarding accounting compliance is called "The Savings Law" (no 262/2005).

This law states a set of rules about the corporate governance and also some very general rules regarding IT compliance. These rules has generally been interpreted like a reduced set of the SOx rules, especially about the application of the

* Department of Business Administration, University of Genova, Genova, Italy

A. D'Atri et al. (eds.), *Management of the Interconnected World*,
DOI 10.1007/978-3-7908-2404-9_37,

COBIT Sox, that is the IT governance framework conceived to accomplish with Sarbanes-Oxley Act in USA [2].

However, COBIT SOx is a very detailed framework, requiring a difficult and heavy implementation; as it is not necessary in Italy to implement COBIT SOx to accomplish with law 262, Italian companies generally prefer to apply only their own selection of COBIT controls, as the law doesn't state how to implement IT controls, but only the results to obtain.

Anyway, the implementation of IT controls for accounting compliance is a very expensive activity, and it is therefore important to understand if and how it could become a part of the IT governance, able to create benefits for the information system and finally for the company itself [3].

For this reason, we can define two different companies behaviours:

- Compliance view;
- Governance view.

The Compliance view aims to govern IT just to comply with laws and rules about accounting and financial disclosure, data affordability and information systems security. Instead the Governance view aims to realise an IT governance framework applied to the whole information system and not only to the accounting information system, to obtain from IT compliance benefits in terms of effectiveness and affordability, beyond the mere respect of the laws [4].

The behaviours characterising these two Views could be described as follow.

Compliance view

- Focuse only on the compliance needs.
- Considers IT compliance like a business cost.
- Applies IT governance and compliance only to the accounting information system.
- Tries to avoid IT infrastructure change.

Governance view

- Considers IT compliance like an opportunity to improve information systems.
- Aims to increase the transparency, affordability, availability of financial information.
- Uses IT compliance also to improve the effectiveness of business processes.
- Tries to improve the corporate organisation.

The Benefits of IT Governance and Compliance

For listed companies, forced to implement IT compliance, it is very difficult or impossible to evaluate the return from compliance investments. However, it is at least possible to understand how to implement IT compliance, in order to obtain further benefits for the company, and not only to accomplish with compliance rules. It means, not to consider IT compliance cost merely like necessary expenditure, but like IT investments able to improve the quality of IT applications, processes and information [5].

To investigate about IT compliance returns, we use a framework designed by Gartner, showing that the IT governance and compliance implementation:

- in the first phase produces higher cost and expenses, but…
- in the second phase permits to reduce cost and risks deriving from the daily functioning of information systems [6].

In Fig. 1 we can see the three phases of IT compliance implementation and the related cost levels. At the phase 0, *Business as usual*, we have several types of cost, including the average cost of risks assumed by the company. At phase 1, that is, during the IT compliance implementation, the company has higher cost, but after the implementation (Phase 2) the company begins to realise the benefits. They derive from the reduction of the Total Cost of Ownership (TCO) along with the whole life cycle of IT, including the IT compliance expenditure but also the savings deriving from the reduction of the average risks.

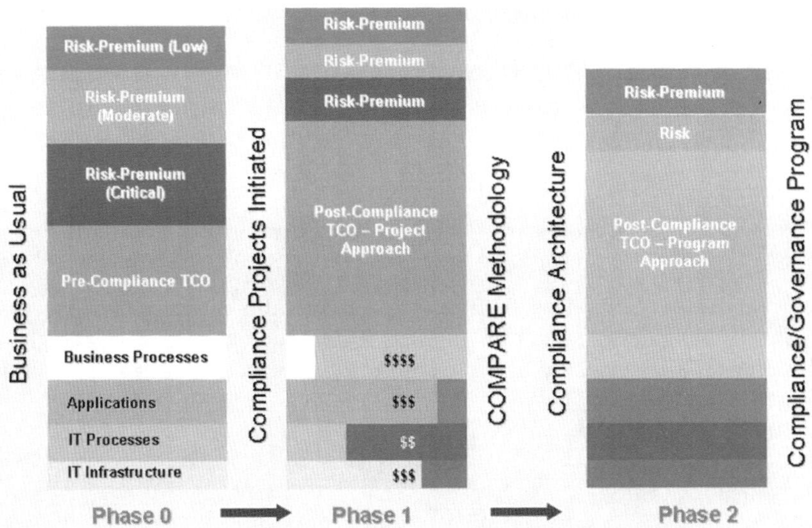

Fig. 1. Costs of IT before IT compliance implementation, during the implementation and after it

Indeed, if the risks are faced and mitigated, they produce tangible cost, otherwise they produce intangible cost. Therefore, the tangible TCO before IT compliance implementation depends on the faced risks, but the intangible cost of not faced risks is not included in this TCO. During the phase 1, the TCO increases, depending on the IT compliance implementation expenditure; however, when the system is rolled out, the company has a higher tangible TCO but a lower intangible risks cost, therefore a lower tangible + intangible TCO. This framework is difficult to evaluate with financial metrics, but it expose the benefits deriving from the reduction of risks produced by the IT compliance implemented architecture. However, there are two types of benefits deriving from IT compliance easy to measure: the access to financial markets and the insurance cost.

(1) IT compliance permits a better access to financial markets [7].
    (a) A more transparent corporate governance architecture means more trust by the investors; Moody's, S&P and Fitch have published studies regarding the evaluation of the IT compliance in companies rating;
    (b) IT compliance permits the access to the STAR segment of listed companies in Italian Stock Exchange (that is, the higher quality list of companies).
(2) It compliance grants savings in insurance costs.
    (a) Reduction of global risk premium.
    (b) Reduction of IT and IS security risks and costs related with viruses, frauds, disaster recovery, and so on.

However, these benefits are the ones a company could gain from the IT compliance view, not from the IT governance view. To implement the IT compliance requires to analyse all business processes, to individuate the potential risks and to remediate by changing the business operations and IT applications [8]. To gain more benefits from all these activities, it is necessary also:

- to reduce the complexity of information systems and the cost of their use;
- to reduce the cost of IS maintenance and evolution;
- to improve IT affordability;
- to improve the rapidity of IS changes, to better align with business.

Moreover, IT compliance is not a project, but a lifelong program, because it requires to be maintained and up to dated. To reduce the cost of IT compliance maintenance, it is necessary to apply automated IT control systems [9], focusing on three key areas (Fig. 2):

- documentation;
- monitoring;
- analysis.

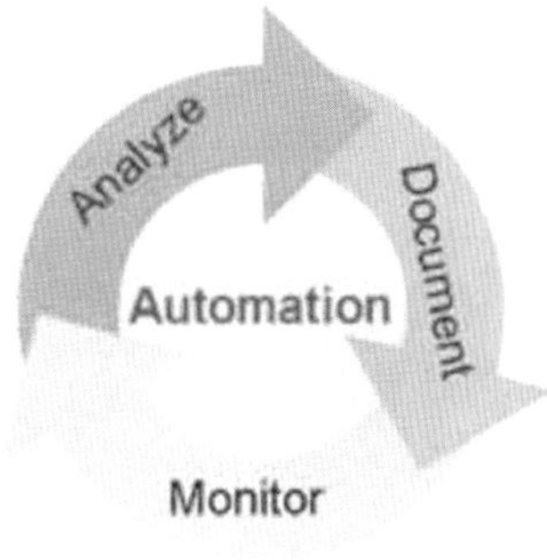

Fig. 2. IT control automation: document, monitor, analyse

IT Compliance and Governance Implementation

To guide IT compliance implementation, several standards have be designed, regarding both the accounting and the IT compliance. For the accounting and auditing area the standard is COSO II, whereas for the IT compliance the standard is COBIT. COBIT defines a set of IT controls acting on all the processes regarding information systems management. However, COBIT is too detailed for Italian companies, so that they generally choice a subset of IT controls to implement IT compliance in accomplishment with Italian law and rules [10].

Finmeccanica, a very larger and global Italian business group, has adopted the Governance view and now includes IT compliance in the larger corporate IT governance architecture. Therefore:

- IT governance in Finmeccanica is the set of processes to grant the contribution of IT to value creation, strategies realisation and business goals reaching;
- IT governance implementation in Finmeccanica applies a subset of COBIT controls and processes, linked with a subset of COSO II controls to assure the accounting compliance;
- In this way, Finmeccanica accomplish with Italian law no 262, but also support the corporate IT governance architecture and its strategic view.

In Finmeccanica, therefore, the IT governance is conceived not only like a mere duty to realise IT compliance, but like a govern activity acting between formal requirements and business goals. It implements two different but strictly linked aspects: the implementation of secure information systems processing affordable data and information, on one side; the delivering of the right information to support business decisions, on the other side (Fig. 3). For this reason, IT governance in Finmeccanica is driven both by control policies, assuring the quality of data, and by strategic needs, granting the adequateness of data. To obtain this double result, both rules application and the responsibility of managers are necessary [11].

Now, the most important step was to define how to insert IT compliance in IT governance, as to obtain an integrated way to govern IT. COBIT suggests a set of control to be applied to IT, but each company should implement them in an adequate manner, to satisfy they specific needs. Finmeccanica analysed COBIT framework and choiced 77 controls to be applied to its business units. The IT controls implementation is made defining a set of directives, drivers, rules, procedures and instructions, stated in a hierarchical structure from less to more detailed, to be applied along with the corporation.

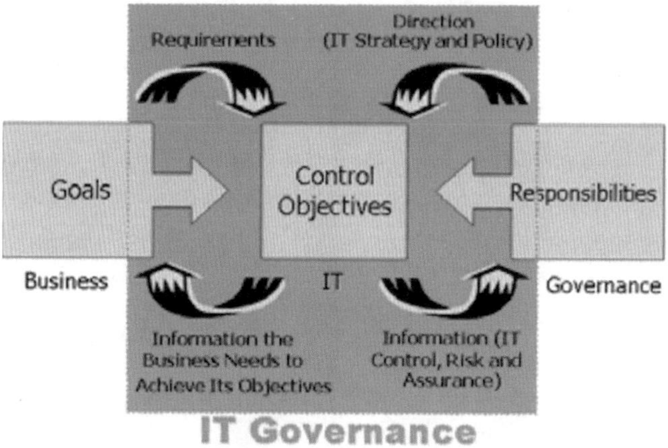

Fig. 3. IT governance drivers and processes in Finmeccanica

The implementation activities are classified also respect to the area to be applied to, that is:

- Entity Area, regarding the system general architecture;
- Application Area, focused on the development, maintenance and management of applications;
- Infrastructure Area, aimed to the management of technical IT infrastructure.

To pursue the Governance view instead of the Compliance view, Finmeccanica decides to apply all these activities not only to the accounting IT applications, as required by the law, but to ALL the IT processes and applications forming the company's information system, with the aim to obtain more benefits from IT governance. The integrated Governance view impacts on all the company's IT processes and realises a higher and more homogenous qualitative level for the information system.

To realise this Governance view, Finmecanica started from the IT strategic goals, that are not limited to IT compliance, but includes strategic benefits such as business integration and the strategic coordination of all the business units. The basis for this approach is the processes standardisation all over the group; it permits homogenous information systems and an easier control above them; it permits also the reuse of standard processes and applications and therefore savings in IT expenditure and investments, especially related to applications maintenance and up to date.

To realise a well integrated and effective information system for all the corporation, Fimneccanica implemented some IT strategic choices such as:

- formalised processes models;
- common IT skills;
- standard IT instruments;
- IT governance centralisation.

It produces also a well documented information system, therefore easier to control, at lower cost and with higher benefits in terms of business processes efficiency and effectiveness and information quality.

To obtain these results, Finmeccanica focused on responsibility like a crucial success weapon for the IT governance and compliance program. It means to strongly stress the accountability all along the organisation. In Finmeccanica, accountability has been defined as follows:

Accountability *is a concept in ethics with several meanings. It is often used synonymously with such concepts as responsibility, answerability, enforcement, blameworthiness, liability and other terms associated with the expectation of account-giving.* ***As an aspect of governance, it has been central to discussions related to problems in both the public and private (corporations) worlds.***

The IT governance and compliance framework has therefore been built enforcing both internal accountability, and external compliance. Internal accountability means the clear definition of responsibility and mansions, but also individuals' competencies and ability to be in charge for the right answers to the needs of the company IT. External compliance means transparency and affordability of financial disclosure to the company's stakeholders.

Conclusion

Instead of merely pursue the IT compliance, Finmeccanica decided to pursue an IT Governance view, that is, to apply IT controls not only to the administrative information system, but to all the information system, all over the corporation and the business units, with the aim to improve the quality of business processes, IT applications and information, and to create more benefits from IT compliance.

So, the IT compliance expenditures have been considered as investments, to implement an IT governance and compliance program, during the IS life cycle, aiming to reduce systems TCO and to permit a better and faster alignment between IT applications and business strategies.

To realize these goals, Finmeccanica applied a subset of the COBIT standards, adapting these standards to its own specific characteristics and integrating them in a comprehensive view about the objectives of the IT governance and compliance program.

To improve the benefits of its program, Finmeccanica aimed not only at the IT accomplishment with laws and rules, but at pursuing of several qualitative return such as:

- to reduce inefficiencies in IT controls, thanks to their automation and standardization all over the company;
- to reuse business processes design and IT applications;
- to better exploit IT functions, grace to their centralization;
- to improve the quality of administrative accountancy and therefore of internal and external financial reporting;
- the better define individuals' mansions and responsibility;
- to increase the involvement of top managers about IT controls decisions.

References

1. Damianides M (2005) Sarbanes-oxley and IT governance: new guidance on IT control and compliance. *Inf Syst Manage* 22(1):77–85
2. Cantino V (2007) *Corporate governance, misurazione della performance e compliance del sistema di controllo interno*. Giuffè, Milano
3. Broadbent M (2005) *Why governance matters*. CIO Insight II
4. Dameri RP, Privitera S (2009) *IT governance*. Franco Angeli, Milano
5. Dameri RP (2009) *Le determinanti dell'IT governance e la creazione di valore, impresaprogetto no 1*. www.impresaprogetto.it
6. Gartner (2006) *Understanding the cost of compliance*, July
7. Botosan C (2000) Evidence that greater disclosure lowers the cost of equity capital. *J Appl Corp Finance* 12(4)
8. Weill P, Ross M (2004) *IT governance. How top performers manage IT decision rights for superior results*. Harvard Business School Press, Boston
9. Dameri RP (2008) *Governance, risk and compliance management suite. A software selection for implementing an integrated compliance framework in listed companies*, Genova, 2nd April 2008
10. ITGI (2004) *IT control objectives for Sarbanes-Oxley*. www.itgi.org
11. Dameri RP, Garelli R (2006) IT governance in international business group. In *Proceedings of the 13th European conference on information technology evaluation*, Università di Genova, Genova, Italy, 28–29 September 2006

The Evaluation of Information Systems: Lessons Learned from Practice

Angela Perego*

Abstract IS Performance Management Systems seem to be the right solution for the CIO and IS department's problems, but they are not so widespread in companies due to the difficulties that companies have in the design and implementation process. This paper attempts to address this issue by investigating what factors affect the design and implementation of IS Performance Management Systems and how these factors influence their shape in terms of IS performance dimensions and measures. The majority of previous studies dealing with this issue sought to develop an *algorithm for selecting the appropriate dimensions and measures*. This scope implied clarity and a willingness to pursue organizational goals and that only one appropriate set of dimensions and measures exists for a company. This paper points out how it is arduous to define such an algorithm because several "soft" factors, e.g. climate and private goals, affect the final shape of IS Performance Systems.

Introduction

IS Performance Management Systems which can be defined as the set of metrics used to quantify both the efficiency and effectiveness of IS actions [1] can help IS departments to evaluate the outcomes of IS activities, practices and processes at all levels of the IS organization. They can also help IS departments to face a serious credibility problem due to lack of management practices that can provide real benefits in business operations and grant investment return. Therefore IS Performance Management Systems seem to be the right solution for the CIO and IS department's problems, but they are not so widespread in companies [2]. The lack of a robust and complete model with which to evaluate IS Business Value [3] does not seem to be a sufficient reason. We believe that the difficulty in implementing this type of systems has been determined by internal "soft" factors such as culture and power balance that affect the design and implementation process, and the shape of IS Performance Management Systems in terms of a set of dimensions and measures used to assess IS performance. Thus this paper attempts to investigate

* SDA Bocconi School of Management, Milan, Italy, angela.perego@sdabocconi.it

A. D'Atri et al. (eds.), *Management of the Interconnected World*,
DOI 10.1007/978-3-7908-2404-9_38, © Springer-Verlag Berlin Heidelberg 2010

how these factors affect the design and implementation of IS Performance Management Systems and so the shape of these systems.

Theoretical Framework and Methodology

The assessment of IS Business Value has been widely debated among both business scholars and practitioners. Academic Community has attempted to provide practitioners with several models suggesting IS Performance dimensions and measures or criteria to build an appropriate IS measure set. In particular the criteria or better still the variables that a company should take into consideration during the definition of its appropriate IS performance measure set can be summarized in the following three categories: contingency variables; IS variables and relational variables.

According to Weill and Olson [4] the contingency variables are: business strategy, organizational structure, size, environment, technology, individual and task. Several researchers introduced these types of variables in their Selection Model of IS success dimensions and measures [5–8]. The second type of variables is IS variables which refers to specific characteristics of the IS department. In their IS assessment selection model Saunders and Jones [5] included variables such as IS Executives Hierarchical Placement and the size and structure of the IS department. Other researchers suggested that other variables also referred to the IS department may impact on the relevance and usefulness of IS Performance measures: the maturity of the IS department [9], IS management expertise, IS end-user skills, IS strategic role, IS budget size, climate [4, 7, 10–15], IS operational and managerial capabilities [16–19] and the IS sourcing strategy [20, 21]. The last category of variables, i.e. relational variables, refers to the existing relationship between the IS department and User departments. Previous studies suggest considering variables like Top management support, user participation/involvement, power balance and the delegation system with regard to IS contents and managerial decisions [5, 7, 8, 22, 23].

Reviews of the literature reveal the majority of selection models aim at defining "appropriate" dimensions and measures. In particular the final goal is to develop an *algorithm for selecting the appropriate dimensions and measures* [7] in order to provide the most relevant, reliable, and representative set of IS performance dimensions and measures that refers to the specific internal and external environment of the organization considered. This scope implies clarity and a willingness to pursue organizational goals rather than private aims, and that only one appropriate set of dimensions and measures exists for a company. We do not believe this assumption to be completely true, thus this research aims at investigating how individual, unit or department interests affect the choice of the "appropriate" set. We attempt to study this phenomenon investigating the IS and Relational variables which mainly affect the climate inside the IS department and between the IS department and User Departments and the existence of organizational tension which can lead people to take the defensive rather than promote a collaborative context.

The research methodology was defined considering two aspects: (a) the nature of the variables considered in this research that requires a long period of observation in order to be investigated and (b) the companies necessity of help to face problems in order to improve the rate of successfully delivering IS Performance Management Systems.

According to previous considerations, action research methodology was chosen to undertake this research. As a matter of fact, action research methods place researchers in a helping role within the organizations that are studied [24]. This link between theory/practice and research/consulting has been considered to be essential in undertaking this research and collecting consistent and reliable data on the design and development process. Furthermore the discipline of IS seems to be a very appropriate field for the use of action research methods [25] due to the fact that IS is a highly applied field. In particular, in our research we have applied the canonical form [25].

Action Research Projects

The research consists in four action research projects which have been undertaken in the following companies[1]:

- AudioEntertainment, the Italian subsidiary of a global electronic equipment corporation.
- MedicalSound, the headquarters of a global producer of health-related products.
- HomeMarket, a no-food retailer.
- MRI, a big Italian insurance group.

We conducted the four action research projects following the interventionist approach based on a cyclical process which consists of five stages [26]: diagnosing, action planning, action taking, evaluating, and specifying learning. The approach first requires the establishment of the client-system infrastructure which is the specification and agreement that constitutes the research environment. Table 1 describes the client-system infrastructure in detail.

In all the action research cycle stages researchers collected data by document analysis, interviews and observation and sought to relate behaviour, actions, and results to variables analyzed in this research and investigate what factors affect the choice of IS performance measures, and consequently the shape of IS Performance Management System. To reduce bias in the researchers' interpretations of the interview results, each researcher individually analyzed data and coded it so as to

[1] The names of the companies are fictitious names in order to not have limitations in the use of the results coming from the analysis of the four action research projects.

retrieve information on the analyzed variables. Finally, the researchers compared their analyses and discussed about the differences so as to reach a common result.

Table 1. Client–system infrastructure of action research projects

		Audio entertainment	MedicalSound	HomeMarket	MRI
Control pattern	Control over initiation	By the researchers	By the researchers	By the researchers	By the researchers
	Authority	Client dominant	Client dominant	Client dominant	Client dominant
	Degree of formalization	Formal contract	Formal contract	Formal contract	Formal contract
	Use of research results	Free if the company name is undisclosed	Free if the company name is undisclosed	Free if the company name is undisclosed	Free if the company name is undisclosed
Project boundaries	Purpose of evaluation	IS performance data collection for Internal Audit	IS service level agreement establishment	Customer satisfaction evaluation	IS performance assessment
	Project sponsor	CIO	CIO and CEO	CEO	CIO
	Evaluation perspective	CIO and department directors	CEO, subsidiary managers and CIO	CIO and CEO	CIO and managing directors of group companies
	Domain under evaluation	Italian IS department and all Italian IS services	IS corporate department and all IS corporate services	IS department and all IS services	IS department and all IS services
	Unit/level of analysis	Organizational and individual	Organizational and individual	Organizational and individual	Organizational and individual

Discussion

In order to investigate if and how IS and Relational variables affect the shape of IS Performance Management Systems, we have analyzed the evidence from the four action research projects.

IS Variables

The first IS variable is the *hierarchical placement of the IS department.* In the four action research projects it does not seem to affect the shape of the IS measure set. On the contrary, the *role of IS* appears to be extremely relevant in the design of IS performance measures. In the MedicalSound and MRI cases, IS played a strong strategic role, and as a result IS departments were able to translate Business strategy into IS strategy and link IS activities and projects to Success Key Factors. The perception of relevance and the motivation to design specific measures connected to Business Strategy were higher than in the other cases.

The *Size* and *Structure of the IS department* directly affect measures related to the Organizational Climate, Permanent Education and skill of IS staff. As a matter of fact, in small departments, like HomeMarket's IS department, measures such as the index of turn over and absenteeism are not meaningful as they generally equal zero; measures relating to permanent education could also be less relevant because the IS budget allocated for these activities is usually low and thus the opportunity to attend training or management courses is not so frequent; finally in such a small department it is not so common to perform an analysis of IS staff skill and plan skill development courses. The Size also has an indirect influence on the shape of the IS Performance Management System for two reasons. The first reason is that it affects the Maturity level of the IS department in terms of standards and policies definition, procedures formalization, and use of management tools. The second is related to internal relational complexity that increases with the size of the IS department. As a result the size of the IS department also affects the *climate inside the IS department*. In the AudioEntertainment and HomeMarket IS departments, which are the smallest ones, the climate inside the IS department was rather good and relational problems were directly managed by the CIOs. The effect of a good climate on IS performance measures is evident: if there is a good climate IS staff will be in favour of the delivery of an internal customer survey, as in the AudioEntertainment case. In the same way, a good climate avoids the likelihood of the IS staff considering the IS evaluation project as an exam, as occurred in MedicalSound case, and the IS Performance Management System as a Control tool seeking to manipulate the design of the measures, especially referred to the efficiency of IS processes, so as to highlight only some aspects and not others, as in the MRI case.

Another IS variable which has been shown to affect the IS measure set is *IS sourcing Strategy*. Its effects are clear and evident in HomeMarket and MRI case. In the former, the outsourcing of a relevant part of the IS activities, e.g. the Help Desk and new software development, led to these activities not being considered for measurement; in the latter it determined the introduction of a specific dimension, i.e. IS sourcing efficiency, with its corresponding measures (Concentration index of IS suppliers and Percentage of contracts with the IS supplier including SLA), and again the body rental use led to add a new measure, i.e. the percentage of external FTE. In the other cases its effects do not seem so evident as the main activities were done in-house and the use of external IS professionals was not as high as in MRI, and thus no gaps are noticed in the IS measures.

The last IS variable is the *maturity of the IS department*. This variable affects the shape of IS Performance Management System in an extremely strong way because the availability of input data necessary to calculate the measures depends on it. Therefore the design of the IS performance measures is an opportunity to verify and improve the supervision and the management of IS processes. According to the analysis of the action research projects, one of the main results of the design and development of the IS Performance Management System is not only the definition of IS measures but the development of a solid system of IS governance and systems that produce input data. The four CIOs involved in the projects did not consider it to be a by-product of the project but rather one of its main outputs.

Relational Variables

The analysis of the Relational variables shows that the *climate between the IS department and user departments* has an impact on the decision to share the results of the IS evaluation with users, such as in the AudioEntertainment and HomeMarket cases. However, the MRI case shows that an apparent good climate is not enough because *power balances* are also relevant in order to decide whether or not to involve users in the project. MRI's IS department decided not to involve users because doing so would have given them useful information which could have changed the power balance. As a matter of fact, MRI's IS department was more powerful than user departments due to the lack of users' interest, which led users to not negotiate better IS service levels with IS department. Therefore IS department wanted to maintain this advantage. Whereas, in the other cases user departments were more powerful than IS department and thus IS department sought to build trustworthy relationship with users through IS performance measures. This is evident in MedicalSound where IS department would have had objective data on which to discuss with user departments and define the quality value threshold beyond which users would have been satisfied. Also HomeMarket's IS department wished to improve relationship with users through the sharing of IS performance measures.

In MedicalSound and HomeMarket the *Top Management support* was also important. On the one hand, they considered the Top Management support to be a guarantee that this project was the starting point of a change process and they were also confident that Top Management would have helped them to manage critical situations with user departments; on the other hand this factor forced them to speed up the design of the IS performance measures and extend the set of measures which would have been shared with user departments.

Finally in the AudioEntertainment case, the power of user department was stronger than in the other cases because user departments had an own IS budget which they could spend without involving Local IS department, and thus the context was rather critical. Therefore IS department decided to introduce a new dimension, i.e. IS preferred supplier. However the relationship between EMEA IS department and local IS department affected the design of IS performance measures more than the relationship between IS department and user departments. As a matter of fact, this critical relationship appeared to be the real reason of the project and thus all the measures were built in order to highlight the added value of activities performed by local IS department and consequently to show that Italian Country could not achieve the same business outcomes without a dedicated local IS organization. Furthermore, power can affect the choice of IS measures in order to maintain, as long as possible, the existing *information asymmetry* between the IS department and user departments. Therefore, IS department seeks to highlight not all possible process measures in order to have no controlled part of process which can guarantee buffer where to hide possible inefficiencies. In all the four cases, IS department behaved in this way. Finally the analysis of the four cases shows that the design of IS Performance Management System triggers the opportunity to start activities of communication and internal marketing of IS to internal customers.

To sum up, the analysis shows that "soft" factors have a significant impact on the final set of IS performance dimensions and measures. The nature of these variables makes arduous to develop an algorithm for selecting dimensions and measures. Furthermore "soft" factors can affect the relevance of IS performance measures and introduce bias in the IS performance evaluation, so companies have to try to prevent this phenomenon improving their understanding of these factors.

Limits and Further Research

The research has the limit to be conducted involving only IS staff in decision making process. We believe that the users' involvement would have changed the final IS Performance measure set because the user perspective would have been more relevant and the role of power balance would have been different. As a matter of fact, the interaction between IS department and user departments would have changed relational variables evaluation continuously. Therefore further research could involve both IS staff and users in order to investigate how the impact of variables analyzed in this research changes. Furthermore future research could enlarge the sample of companies in order to attempt to draw general conclusions and conduct cross-country studies so as to investigate the differences in corporate culture. In order to improve the understanding of IS Performance Management Systems, we also suggest that future research investigates the impacts of these systems on IS Management activities over time.

References

1. Neely A (1999) The performance measurement revolution: why now and what next? *Int J Oper Prod Manage* 19(2):205–228
2. Perego A (2006) *I.S. performance management e misure dell'IT in azienda*. In: Proceedings ItAIS, Milano
3. Gable G, Sedera D, Chan T (2008) Re-conceptualizing system success: the IS-impact measurement model. *J Assoc Inf Syst* 9(7):377–408

4. Weill P, Olson MH (1989) An assessment of the contingency theory of management information systems. *J Manage Inf Syst* 6(1):59–85
5. Saunders CS, Jones JW (1992) Measuring performance of the information systems function. *J Manage Inf Syst* 8(4):63–82
6. DeLone WH, McLean ER (1992) Information systems success: the quest for the dependent variable. *Inf Syst Res* 3(1):60–95
7. Myers BL, Kappelman LA, Prybuto VR (1997) Comprehensive model for assessing the quality and productivity of the information system function. Toward a theory for information systems assessment. In Garrity E, Sanders L (eds) *Information systems success measurement*. IDEA Group Publishing, Hershey, pp 94–121
8. Sugumaran V, Arogyaswamy B (2004) Measuring IT performance: "Contingency" variables and value modes. *J Comput Inf Syst*, Winter 44(2):79–86
9. Mahmood MA, Becker JD (1985) Effect of organizational maturity on end-users' satisfaction with information systems. *J Manage Inf Syst* 2(3):37–64
10. Davis GB, Hamann JR (1988) In-context information systems assessment: a proposal and an evaluation. In Bjorn-Anderson N, Davis GB (eds) *Information Systems Assessment: Issues and Challenges*. Elsevier Science, North-Holland, pp 283–296
11. Harris SE, Katz JL (1991) Organizational performance and information technology investment intensity in the insurance industry. *Organ Sci* 2(3):263–295
12. McKeen JD, Guimaraes T, Wetherbe JC (1994) The relationship between user participation and user satisfaction: an investigation of four contingency factors. *MIS Q* 18(4):427–451
13. Premkumar G, King WR (1994) Organizational characteristics and information systems planning: an empirical study. *Inf Syst Res* 5(2):75–109
14. Scott WR (1977) Effectiveness of organizational effectiveness studies. In Goodman PS, Pennings JM (eds) *New perspectives on organizational effectiveness*. Jossey-Bass, San Francisco, pp 63–95
15. Zmud RW (1979) Individual differences and MIS success: A review of the empirical literature. *Manage Sci* 25(10):966–979
16. Francalanci C, Galal H (1998) Information technology and worker composition: determinants of productivity in the life insurance industry. *MIS Q* 22(2):227–241
17. Tippins MJ, Sohi RS (2003) IT competency and firm performance: is organizational learning a missing link? *Strateg Manage J* 24(8):745–761
18. Banker RD, Bardhan IR, Lin S, Chang H (2006) Plant information systems, manufacturing capabilities and plant performance. *MIS Q* 30(2):315–337
19. Tanriverdi H (2006) Performance effects of information technology synergies in multibusiness firms. MIS Q 30(1):57–77
20. Bardhan IR, Whitaker J, Mithas S (2006) Information technology, production process outsourcing and manufacturing plant performance. *J Manage Inf Syst* 23(2):13–40
21. Rai A, Patnayakuni R, Seth N (2006) Firm performance impacts of digitally-enabled supply chain integration capabilities. *MIS Q* 30(2):225–246
22. Weill P (1992) The relationship between investment in information technology and firm performance: a study of the value manufacturing sector. *Inf Syst Res* 3(4):307–333
23. Perego A (2008) The role of IS performance management systems in today's enterprise. In D'Atri A (ed) *Interdisciplinary aspects of information systems studies*. Springer, New York, pp 233–240
24. Schein EH (1987) *Process consultation*, 2. Addison-Wesley, Reading
25. Baskerville R, Wood-Harper AT (1996) A critical perspective on action research as a method for information systems research. *J Inf Technol* 11:235–246
26. Susman G (1983) Action research: a sociotechnical systems perspective. In: Morgan G (ed) *Beyond method: strategies for social research*. Sage, Newbury Park, pp 95–113

Towards a Classification of Maturity Models in Information Systems

Tobias Mettler[*], Peter Rohner[†], and Robert Winter[‡]

Abstract Over the past years, a wide range of maturity models have been developed by practitioners as well as academics for the purpose of measuring and prescribing certain aspects of information systems "maturity". Since, to our knowledge, no classification system for maturity models exists to date, the rising number of maturity models implicates problems with respect to retrievability and reusability. Aiming at enhancing the time consuming and exhausting search and selection process of appropriate assessment models, a classification approach for IS maturity models is presented in this paper. Based on a broad literature review that yields 117 maturity models which are analysed in detail, the following classification characteristics are proposed: (a) a set of general model attributes that describe basic characteristics (such as the topic addressed by the model, the primary source or the targeted audience), (b) maturity model design attributes (relating to the construction and organisation of the model) and (c) maturity model use attributes (such as application method or tool support).

Introduction

Maturity models are increasingly being applied within the field of Information Systems (IS), both as informed approach for continuous improvement [1, 2] or as means of benchmarking or self-assessment [3, 4]. Since the initial finding of the concept in the 1970s [5, 6], a multiplicity of different instantiations have been developed in science and practice with the purpose of evaluating and comparing the maturity (i.e. level of sophistication, capability, availability of specific characteristics) of a particular domain or artefact. The most well known maturity model is doubtless the Capability Maturity Model (CMM) from the Carnegie Mellon Software Engineering Institute (SEI). Its introduction in the early 1990s is surely one reason for today's broad proliferation of the concept. The need for and the de-

[*] University of St. Gallen, St. Gallen, Switzerland, tobias.mettler@unisg.ch
[†] University of St. Gallen, St. Gallen, Switzerland, peter.rohner@unisg.ch
[‡] University of St. Gallen, St. Gallen, Switzerland, robert.winter@unisg.ch

A. D'Atri et al. (eds.), *Management of the Interconnected World*,
DOI 10.1007/978-3-7908-2404-9_39, © Springer-Verlag Berlin Heidelberg 2010

velopment of new maturity models will certainly not diminish in the future, given that these models help managers to balance divergent objectives with regard to obtaining and retaining competitive advantage, assembling new products and services, reducing costs and time to market, and enhancing quality. However, the rising number of maturity models implicates some problems with respect to its retrievability. As no classification for precisely allocating different kinds of maturity models exist, the search for and the selection of specific models is time consuming and exhausting. Furthermore, reusability is impaired when the maturity model is "trapped in its own circles".

In practice, first attempts to enhance retrievability and reusability have been made by simply listing maturity models on a website or wiki [7]. Although useful to get a brief overview of the existing model base, the itemisation of maturity models has been done in an unsystematic manner, for instance, leaving decision makers with the interpretation of the model's function and scope (e.g. do you know what the broccoli maturity model is good for?). To enhance the future retrievability and reusability of maturity models, detailed information about the application method, accessibility, reliability, and origin are required. In doing so, and to systematise the search and selection process, it is the aim of this paper to present a classification system for IS maturity models.

Definition of Maturity Models in IS

In general, "maturity" can be defined as "the state of being complete, perfect or ready" [8]. Maturity thus implies an evolutionary progress in the demonstration of a specific ability or in the accomplishment of a target from an initial to a desired or normally occurring end stage. The purpose of maturity models is to give guidance through this evolutionary process by incorporating formality into the improvement activities. According to [3], all maturity models share the common property of defining a number of dimensions at several stages of maturity, with a description of characteristic performance at various levels of granularity. Basic components of maturity models are [3]: (1) a number of levels (typically three to six), (2) a descriptor for each level (such as the CMM's differentiation between initial, repeatable, defined, managed, and optimising processes), (3) a generic description or summary of the characteristics of each level as a whole, (4) a number of dimensions (such as the "process areas" in CMM), (5) a number of elements or activities for each dimension, and (6) a description of each element or activity as it might be performed at each level of maturity.

Research Design

For the purpose of thoroughly exploring the field, it was recognised that multiple sources of information would need to be examined. While investigating the potential subjects of maturity models in IS was an essential goal, the published research literature presents a filtered record of activity and thinking and, given the fast-moving pace of the field and its importance beyond academia, non-research sources are likely to yield rich information about further topics and future trends. For this reason we conducted two parallel reviews, one focusing on the scientific literature and the other drawing on alternative sources available via the World Wide Web.

In view of the scientific part, the following databases were searched, using "maturity model", "capability model", and "assessment model" as search terms in titles and abstracts: ACM digital library and IEEE Xplore with the intention to cover rather technical aspects such as systems development, use and support of ISD, and technology perspectives, AISeL to locate core IS topics such as the use of information in organisations or management of IS/IT, and EBSCOhost to address predominantly commerce and business administration topics (e.g. financial and cost management, marketing, business law).

The ACM digital library yielded 186, IEEE Xplore a total of 357 results. Although relatively new, 10 maturity model papers were found in AISeL. Due to the thematic breadth of EBSCO, a total of 846 hits were listed. After subtracting inappropriate entries as well as double counts (i.e. the same article listed in several databases or the same maturity model as subject of multiple papers – for example CMMI), a total amount of 117 papers were analysed into more detail. This included the reading of each paper's abstract, introduction and conclusions section, the elicitation of the date of construction, as well as the assignment to a topic of the defined IS framework by [9].

Proposition of a Classification System

A classification system is defined as a system, which creates relations between a classification scheme and classification objects such as chemical elements, animals, plants, or as in this case maturity models [10]. A classification scheme on its part consists of a set of characteristics, which are suitable to assort these objects using a specific classification principle [10].

Whatever classification principle is used, the main problem in developing an appropriate classification lies in limiting the scope to as few descriptive characteristics as possible which should at the same time explain the diversity and be as mutually exclusive as possible. For our purpose, we used the characteristic-based approach to develop the classification scheme as we think that an unambiguous placement is not always possible.

For the classification we propose three different viewpoints: *General model attributes* (1) are used to describe the basic characteristics of a maturity model. The purpose of the selected attributes is to provide users as well as model developers a first overview of the maturity model relating to its addressed topic/domain, the targeted audience, and the primary sources, where the maturity model is described in more detail. Comparable attributes also have been applied for reference models [11]. In addition, and along with the maturity model development life cycle [12], further characteristics concerning the design and use of maturity models are provided (the list is not exclusively). For the m*aturity model design* (2) attributes pertaining to the construction and organisation of the model such as the used concept of "maturity" or the basic structure of the model are proposed. The intention here is to help potential users or model developers to better understand the concepts behind a maturity model. For the *maturity model use* (3) differentiating attributes with respect to the deployment of the model such as the application method or tool support are proposed. The identified attributes should help users in the selection of a proper model as well as show developers possibilities for improvement of their model.

Table 1 illustrates the application of the classification scheme by using the E-learning maturity model as example [13]. A detailed description of the differentiating attributes is given in the following subsections.

Table 1. Example of a classified maturity model

Dimension	Attribute	Example
General model attributes	Name	E-Learning maturity model
	Acronym	eMM
	Primary source	Marshall and Mitchell 2004
	Secondary source	http://www.utdc.vuw.ac.nz/research/emm/
	Addressed topic	Knowledge management & organisational learning
	Origin	Academic
	Audience	Management-oriented
	Year of publication	2004
	Access	Free
Maturity model design	Concept of maturity	Process-oriented
	Composition	CMM-like
	Reliability	Verified
	Mutability	Form of maturity model
Maturity model use	Method of application	Self-assessment
	Support of application	Excel workbook
	Practicality of evidence	Implicit recommendation

General Model Attributes

The identified general model attributes are used to rapidly give potential model users an overall overview of the maturity model. Basic attributes are the name and acronym (where existent) of the maturity model, the primary source and other secondary sources if available, the addressed topic categorised in terms of the IS framework, the origin of the model (academic or practice), the targeted audience of the model (management-oriented versus a technology-focused audience, or no clear distinction), the year of publication, and finally the mode of access (freely available or liable to pay a fee). Typically, these attributes are easy to define, without having a deeper knowledge about the detailed content of the model. However, this is just the reason why further attributes are needed when a sound decision in respect to the model appropriateness is to be made. Hence, we distinguish further attributes relating to the design of the model, and attributes concerning the application of the model. These additional characteristics are especially important when an enterprise already uses some maturity models and tries to synthesise an integrated model base in order to take advantage of synergy effects in respect of training, appraisals and improvement activities (e.g. only applying CMM-like maturity models).

Maturity Model Design

Maturity model design attributes are used to describe the form and organisation of a maturity model. For this purpose, we propose the attributes *concept of maturity*, *composition, reliability*, and *mutability*.

The concept of maturity is in most instances reflected on an one-dimensional manner by the constituent literature, either focusing on (1) *process maturity*, i.e. to which extent a specific process is explicitly defined, managed, measured, controlled, and effective [14], (2) *object maturity*, i.e. to which extent a particular object like a software product, a company report or similar reaches a predefined level of sophistication [15], or on (3) *people capability*, i.e. to which extent the workforce is able to enable knowledge creation and enhance proficiency [16].

The concept of maturity often motivates the composition of the model. Three basic maturity model designs can be distinguished [3]: (1) *Maturity grids* aim at illustrating a number of levels of maturity in a simple, textual manner (normally not exceeding a few pages of text), (2) *Likert-like questionnaires* are comparable with maturity grids, but the focus is more inclined on to scoring specific statements of "good practice" and not to describing the overall levels of maturity, and (3) *CMM-like models*, which are based upon a more formal architecture, specifying a number of goals and key practices to reach a predefined level of sophistication.

Although more elaborate, CMM-like models also entail a greater complexity due to a wide range of scales and subscales for the assessment of maturity.

Another important characteristic to enhance the reusability of a maturity model is its degree of reliability [17]. Conwell et al. differentiate between *verified* and *validated* maturity models. Verification is thereby the process of determining that a maturity model "represents the developer's conceptual description and specifications with sufficient accuracy" and validation is the degree to which a maturity model is "an accurate representation of the real world from the perspective of the intended uses of the model" [18]. If we examine the identified maturity models, it can be concluded that most of them cannot be categorised as validated (perhaps at most as verified). Thus, in order to enhance the reusability and reduce criticism on the poor theoretical grounding of maturity models [19], the emphasis on developing new maturity models should lay on extensively testing these models in terms of validity, reliability and generalisability [17].

The last characteristic concerning the design of the maturity model is the level of mutability. This is of particular importance – but for all that sometimes neglected – as, on the one hand, the maturity of the phenomenon is growing and therefore the model's solution stages and improvement activities have to be refaced from time to time (e.g. modify requirements for reaching a certain maturity level due to the emergence of new best practices and technologies), on the other hand, changes in the form and function are needed to ensure the standardisation and global acceptance of the model (e.g. amend the model schema from a CMM to a CMMI-compliant structure). Therefore we propose two subjects of design mutability: the *form* (e.g. the underlying meta-model or model schema, the descriptions of the maturity levels or question items), and the *functioning* (e.g. how maturity is assessed). However, not any of the suggested conditions must be used, for instance when it is unclear if changes of the design of a maturity model can be made or when design mutability simply is not part of the model.

Maturity Model Use

To describe the maturity model use, we propose the attributes *method of application, support of application*, and *practicality of evidence*. In most cases, the method how data is collected to assess the maturity of a specific domain is an important criterion for the selection of a model. Basically, three distinct approaches can be distinguished [17]. *Self-assessment* refers to a systematic and comprehensive process of gathering information about the own capabilities and level of maturity. A slight modification of the prior described application method is the *third-party assisted assessment*, where external specialists support the appraisal. Finally, by reason of the increasing complexity of organisations and technology, the appraisal is completely "outsourced" to *certified practitioners*. As most of the identified maturity model papers were concerned with the description of the design of the model (leaving the application of the model mostly unconsidered) it was impossible for us to discover a tendency which application method is commonly accepted.

As regards the support of the model application, we differentiate three stages of assistance. In the first case, the users are given *no supporting materials* at all. When reviewing the indentified papers, this is sadly to say very often the case. Especially maturity grids tend to omit how the users should collect the data and which means they should use in doing so. The more sophisticated models, also deliver a *textual description or handbook* how to configure the deployment of the model. However, the most advanced auxiliary means is the instantiation of the maturity model in form of a *software assessment tool* as it is the case in the prior presented E-Learning Maturity (cf. Table 1).

Another interesting characteristic concerning the maturity model use is the practicality of evidence (i.e. the way how suggestions for improvement are made). In this regard, we distinguish between *implicit improvement activities*, i.e. a general recommendation on the tacit assumption of the predefined goals or maturity levels, and *explicit recommendations*, for example telling exactly what to do in order to enhance a particular activity, process or skill. In the case of the reviewed maturity models, a clear tendency to implicit recommendations exists. However, this is not astonishing given that the definition of explicit improvement activities is difficult or sometimes even futile. Nevertheless, explicit recommendations are desirable when a maturity model addresses a precisely delimited problem domain and the dissimilarity of the organisational realities does not play a major role.

Conclusion

With this paper, we introduced a classification system for IS maturity models. In order to extend retrievability and reusability of these models, we proposed a set of general model attributes as well as specific attributes with regard to the design and use of maturity models. In doing so, we expect to attain the following prospective effects: (1) Maturity models will be precisely described, making them communicable, and therefore retrievable and reusable. (2) The time spent for searching problem-specific maturity models will be reduced and decisions concerning the make or buy of a model facilitated. (3) Similarities and differences between the multiple models can be identified, and therefore making similar models capable of being integrated to a common model base.

However, we are aware that the proposed characteristics are not exclusively or final. Accordingly, there are still many opportunities for future research endeavours. For instance, retrievability and reusability will be extensively enhanced when the classification is instantiated by means of a central, online accessible repository. Additional practical insights into the relevance and usefulness of the proposed classification system are required, as it is limited in that it was exclusively constructed by means of reviewing literature and web resources. The value of the proposed classification system will certainly increase, when it is integrated in a generic methodology for the development of maturity models.

References

1. Ahern DM, Clouse A, Turner R (2004) *CMMI distilled: a practical introduction to integrated process improvement.* Addison-Wesley, Boston
2. Paulk MC, Curtis B, Chrissis MB, Weber CV (1993) Capability maturity model, version 1.1, *IEEE Softw* 10(4):18–27
3. Fraser P, Moultrie J, Gregory M (2002) *IEEE international engineering management conference. The use of maturity models/grids as a tool in assessing product development capability*, Cambridge
4. Hakes C (1996) *The corporate self assessment handbook.* Chapman and Hall, London
5. Crosby PB (1979) *Quality is free: the art of making quality certain.* McGraw-Hill, New York
6. Gibson CF, Nolan RL (1974) *Managing the four stages of EDP growth.* Harv Bus Rev 52(1):76–88
7. Sheperd E (2009) http://assessmentmaturitymodel.wikispaces.com/ Other+Maturity+Models. Accessed 12 May 2009
8. Simpson JA, Weiner ES C (1989) *The Oxford English dictionary.* Oxford University Press, Oxford
9. Bacon JC, Fitzgerald B (2001) A systemic framework for the field of information systems, *Data Base Adv Inf Syst* 32(2):46–67
10. Fettke P, Loos P (2003) Classification of reference models: a methodology and its application. *Inf Syst E-Bus Manage* 1(1):35–53
11. German Research Centre for Artificial Intelligence (2006) http://rmk.iwi.uni-sb.de. Accessed 12 May 2009
12. Mettler T (2009) A design science research perspective on maturity models in information systems. Working Paper, Institute of Information Management, University of St. Gallen, St. Gallen
13. Marshall SJ, Mitchell G (2004). Applying SPICE to e-learning: an e-learning maturity model? *In Proceedings of the 6th Australasian computing education conference.* Dunedin, New Zealand
14. Chrissis MB, Konrad M, Shrum S (2003) *CMMI: Guidelines for process integration and product improvement.* Addison-Wesley, Boston
15. Gericke A, Rohner P, Winter R (2006) *Vernetzungsfähigkeit im Gesundheitswesen – Notwendigkeit, Bewertung und systematische Entwicklung als Voraussetzung zur Erhöhung der Wirtschaftlichkeit administrativer Prozesse.* HMD-Praxis der Wirtschaftsinformatik 251:20–30
16. Gillies A, Howard J (2003) Managing change in process and people: combining a maturity model with a competency-based approach. *Total Qual Manage Bus Excell* 14(7):779–787
17. De Bruin T, Freeze R, Kulkarni U, Rosemann M (2005). Understanding the main phases of developing a maturity assessment model, *In Proceedings of the 16th Australasian conference on information systems.* Sydney, Australia
18. Conwell CL, Enright R, Stutzman MA (2000) *Winter simulation conference. Capability maturity models support of modeling and simulation verification, validation, and accreditation,* San Diego
19. Biberoglu E, Haddad H (2002) A survey of industrial experiences with CMM and the teaching of CMM practices. *J Comput Sci Coll* 18(2):143–152

Part VII
Information Systems Development and Design Methodologies

Andrea Carugati[*] and Barbara Pernici[†]

This section of the book covers topics related to system development and methodologies for system design. The aim of this section is to present the most recent research in the Italian context on a topic that lies at the core and at the intersection between two areas of study of information technology: information systems and computer science. The content of this section is based on a call for contributions for the ItAIS conference (edition 2009). The conference call was aimed at presenting research in the wide area of information systems development and design methodology, with a special focus on designing information systems in complex organizations, virtual enterprises and interconnected organizations.

There is no doubt that the area of investigation of system development and design methodologies has suffered lack of attention in the last decade. Culprit of this phenomenon was the combination of high level of failures that plagued system development and the major effort from off-the-shelf and customizable software producers to provide efficient systems with comparatively lower implementation risk. After a period of focus on standardized business systems where the mantra was "buy before you make", today's organizations are beginning to rediscover the importance of proprietary business processes and strategic data treatment. This rediscovery goes beyond reaching the ideal of appropriating best practice and integrated data promised by enterprise systems. Rather the focus turns back on strategic opportunities and innovative possibilities given by well planned business systems constructed with a combination of enterprise systems and proprietary systems.

This new wave of investment in technological innovation is happening in a world where the competitive landscape has been completely turned while businesses were laying low and the developing world was beginning a wave of insourcing never experienced before. New organizational forms and increased globalization are putting emphasis on individualism, flexibility, and adaptation rather than on stability and control. Equally, system development has to produce systems that are tailored to the organization and that are more focused on being adaptive rather than easy and cheap to maintain. This situation requires a change in the mindset of practitioners and academics alike.

---

[*] Århus School of Business, Århus, Denmark, andreac@asb.dk

[†] Politecnico di Milano, Milan, Italy, barbara.pernici@polimi.it

In the search to answer to the emerging demand for tailored and flexible systems, the purpose of this section is to present to the reader the latest studies carried out in the Italian business landscape. The topic is very wide and the papers featured in this section reflect the multiplicity of aspects and complexity found in the real world.

A total of three papers are presented in this section.

The first paper is titled *Web 2.0 Applications: Model-Driven Tools and Design* (Paolone, Liguori, Cestra, and Clementini) deals with the development of web 2.0 applications. This empirical paper describes a design process to solve software standard issues when developing enterprise applications. The contribution of this paper is in extending our knowledge of ISD to the emerging socially oriented world of the contemporary internet.

The second paper, *Design of information systems integration as research intervention: a case study* (Viscusi and Batini) presents GovQual, a methodology for planning eGovernment initiatives. GovQual is based on the experience with the Tunisian Ministry of agriculture and hydraulic resources. The methodology is truly systemic including social, economical, organizational, juridical and technological issues in the identification and ranking of eGovernment projects. The emerging needs of modern society are addressed by a quality-driven strategy which includes actual and future target quality values.

The third paper, *Professional desire, competence and engagement in IS context* (Bednar and Welch) addresses the failings of technological determinism in IS. In today's multifaceted world the acceptance of pluralism and individualism is paramount and this paper presents an interesting discussion on the myth of passive "users" of technology.

In conclusion this section includes compelling works that challenge our thinking regarding taken-for-granted assumptions, models, and research practices on the process of development of new information systems. Providing a fresh viewpoint on the nature of clients and users and including organic concepts like quality and pluralism, the articles featured provide valuable inputs for system architects, developers, and users – researches and practitioners alike – of tomorrow.

Web 2.0 Applications: Model-Driven Tools and Design

Gaetanino Paolone*, Gianluca Liguori†, Gabriele Cestra‡, and Eliseo Clementini$^{\pi}$

Abstract The development of a new web technology rises a challenge to information engineering to identify instruments and suitable techniques for the production of web 2.0 software applications. For large enterprise solutions, designing human interactions is a complex process. Products of this design process are the bridge between business requirements and solution development. This paper describes a design methodological process and a framework that implements and solves some software standard issues to develop enterprise applications and it is the basis to ensure a full continuity from the business model to system software through the physical realization of the use case. We also illustrate a real process that uses the framework for the development of an enterprise application.

Introduction

This paper shows the design phase of our proposed methodological process [1, 2]. Designing solutions with a business focus links business requirements and the IT development process at enterprise level. Software engineering is a rapidly evolving field, due to continuous changes of user requirements, platforms, technologies and environments. In recent years, researchers and developers have attempted to utilize user-centered design methodologies, which proved to be very useful for designing interactive systems [3, 4]. Also today, one of the most important challenges in computer science is the definition of software production processes that permit to reuse components and services for the application on different platforms

* Department of Electrical and Information Engineering, University of L'Aquila, L'Aquila, Italy, g.paolone@postasi.it

† Department of Electrical and Information Engineering, University of L'Aquila, L'Aquila, Italy, gianluca.liguori@bluedeep.it

‡ Department of Electrical and Information Engineering, University of L'Aquila, L'Aquila, Italy, Gabriele.cestra@bluedeep.it

$^{\pi}$ Department of Electrical and Information Engineering, University of L'Aquila, L'Aquila, Italy, eliseo.clementini@alice.it

A. D'Atri et al. (eds.), *Management of the Interconnected World*,
DOI 10.1007/978-3-7908-2404-9_40, © Springer-Verlag Berlin Heidelberg 2010

[5]. Moreover the usability of user interfaces of enterprise applications is crucial for the economy of a business and its success. However, studies [3] show that the majority of user interfaces of web-based enterprise applications suffer from usability problems. Model-based user interface development typically creates a series of declarative models, such as user tasks models, dialogs and presentations [3, 4, 6]. Moreover, to improve the efficiency in software development, many approaches for automatic user interface generation were proposed to separate user interfaces from business logic. Other approaches generate user interfaces from business processes modeled by business analysts. Also, today there are some attempts to realize methods to support the development of large-scale applications [7]. Having as objective the development of interactive Web applications, we carried out the study and definition of a methodological process that implements and solves the intrinsic problems of the Web. This lead to the implementation of a software framework, called Bluedeep, and the definition of a methodology. Bluedeep provides the developer with a set of services to efficiently develop rich internet applications. Our work focuses on model-driven business transformation and, specifically, on the techniques that enable better automation from business modeling to software solution. Through several business automation engagements, we gained experience in enterprise-level solution design process and use-case driven software development [1, 2].

Our methodology can be considered as an implementation of Model Driven Architecture (MDA) [8]. It refines It adopts relevant ideas from the process framework set by Unified Process (UP) [9] and Rational Unified Process (RUP) [10] into a domain-specific, and even company-specific, method. The new aspect of our methodology is the direct transformation of use cases into code. Our goal is to improve the solution design process to meet business requirements and reduce development time. As part of the methodology, the Bluedeep framework has an important role in how we enable designers to conform and connect application design with business domain model elements and to help maintaining the design integrity through automatic generation. This paper mainly focuses on the design phase of our software development process, which is seamlessly connected with the business modeling and analysis activities already presented in past articles [1, 2], and it also describes the use of the Bluedeep framework.

Overall, we are trying to provide an agile and flexible industrial methodology capable of transforming an analysis model to design model and to code. Based on our field experience, this research has shown an effectiveness in supplying instruments and techniques that are of valuable support to a working team. We analyze the information embedded in business and analysis model and we use the inferred information in a model-driven approach to automatically generate user interfaces of a use case from a analysis model through the framework. Research on model-driven user interface design has over the years focused on modeling user interface at a higher level of abstraction, but lacked support during the iterative development process. This paper briefly presents the context of our research: we aim to the definition of a methodology to transform a business model into a web

2.0 application. Specifically, we present a feature that helps the transformation of use cases and domain objects from the analysis model to the designed user application. Further, the Bluedeep framework automatically manages the navigation between panels of the same use case. The rest of the paper is organized as follows. In the first section we define the design methodological process that completes the methodology. After we describe the framework developed to aid the implementation of the artifacts defined in the design phase. Then we illustrate a real-world industrial enterprise application created following the proposed development process and using the framework to demonstrate the applicability of our methodology and to show the results of our research. Finally, we report a short conclusion.

The Design Process

The design process is applied to every use case realization. In this context the use case realizations could be considered atomic entity that can be "processed in the design cycle" independently from the other use cases, with the only exception of included and extended use cases. In this way every use case represents a process unit. The design cycle is composed of four activities (Fig. 1).

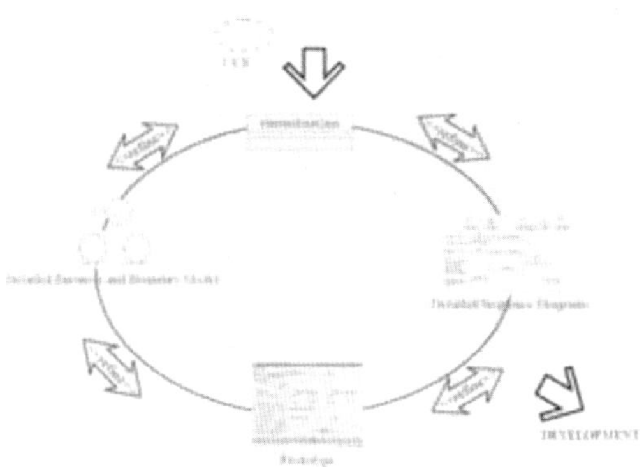

Fig. 1. The design process

Every activity is refined by the preceding and following activities. We use the word "detailed", as shown in figure, to indicate a refinement process that brings the diagrams and artifacts created before the design phase to gain an higher informative load: in this phase we introduce Business Objects attributes, the high detail degree of the class diagram imposes a transformation of analysis level patterns (such as multiple and dynamic generalization) into implementation level patterns (like Delegate, Object State…), the sequence diagrams present every single action in terms of methods and objects interactions. Once this activity cycle has ended we are ready to write the code that will implement the use case, having a description based on classes and use cases actions, a detailed diagram for every Business Object manipulated by the use case and for every Boundary or panel, an interaction or sequence diagram for every use case realization, Boundary and

Business Object. We also have a detailed and complete prototype for the use case scenarios.

The Bluedeep Framework

Our main goal in the framework development has been to create a tool capable to generate Ajax-enabled Web-based applications from analysis models [1, 2] without the need to implement in every project some commonplace facilities. Among others, the framework provides services to create a desktop-like workplace and access to heterogeneous external resources like DBMSs, Web Services or files. It also has facilities that allow use cases execution control, based on logged users privileges. The designer that uses the Bluedeep framework has at his disposal a tool that:

- allows the developer to follow an agile and flexible industrial methodology to transform an analysis model (use case and object model) to code;
- permits to develop every application element using merely Java language.

One of the featuring elements of the Bluedeep framework is its ability to automatically manage interaction between the application user and the use cases. In fact, it is able to manage navigation between scenarios, composing a use case, and between different use cases, such as included or extended ones.

Bluedeep is divided into two logical packages: Services and Elements. The package "elements" contains all elements that can be used or redefined by the developer. It aims to provide a link between the analysis model and the implementation. In order to reach this aim we need to provide the correct mapping between analysis's stereotypes and implementation. The framework provides a set of classes able to translate Use Cases into code. In the Bluedeep architecture, the use case is the fundamental element that replaces the more general controller of a classic Model View Controller architecture [11]. According to the concept of use case introduced in the analysis phase [1], the use case class is a set of scenarios and actions. For each use case, it is possible to define a set of business actions, that can be linked to the graphical components. Every sequence can be defined as a set of graphical components that refer to a single use case. The UseCaseManager provides all the services to navigate and manage the entire life cycle of use cases.

The main guideline of the framework is the following: the business model should be "pure", in the sense that it should not be contaminated by information about other layers than the "business layer". A pure model is composed of business objects without any reference to features related to the Resources layer (data sources: databases, XML files, Web Services) or to the View layer (textBox, Form, checkBox). The graphic elements offered by Bluedeep are implemented by java classes that can be extended by the developer or used as they are. Each graphic element can contain other graphic elements to produce a more complex component. The package "services" groups all the services exposed by framework (Fig. 2). Each service is designed to handle elements. All the services and their behaviour are immutable and not modifiable. The design of services adheres to the following rules:

- a service can manage (create, modify, and delete) only elements belonging to the layer of pertinence;
- a service can invoke and use another service;
- a layer's service can use, but not change, elements belonging to other layers;
- all services can be only accessed from the ServiceManager.

The service manager provides the developer with the services according to the layer that he/she is working on. Framework's guidelines define how to use services. For example business objects can be modified only from the Controller layer, particularly in the particular use case that manages the business object. The entity UseCase (that belongs to the controller layer) cannot access other layers as an entity; hence, it has to use a service to complete the required action. Let us suppose that the use case needs to manipulate a bean, called "business object". It will have to ask the ServiceManager for the ModelManager service and then call a specific function that returns the required "business object".

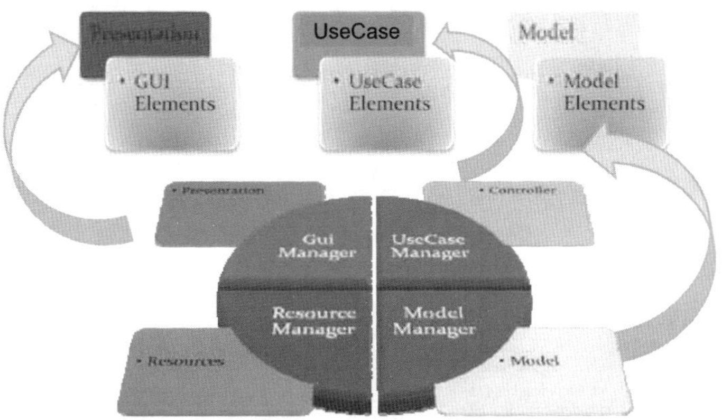

Fig. 2. The services and elements

The Service Manager represents a central access point for the other services provided by the framework. Its main task is to dispatch services upon request inside of calling Use Cases. The introduction of the Service Manager permits to control the access to the various services, forcing the developer to access those services inside the context of a use case, assuring structural robustness and avoiding access violation between different layers of the proposed architecture.

The GUI Manager exposes all rendering services, i.e., those services that generate visual elements linked to business objects. The GUI Manager can manage only graphical objects and can receive as non-editable input parameters the model elements to be rendered. The Use Case Manager is one of the most important services offered by the framework. This service handles the management of use cases in terms of opening, closing, and navigation. Specifically, it allows us to represent, during the coding phase, the inclusion and the extension of a use case. The UseCaseManager, like every other framework service, is not modifiable. Whenever the user creates a menu item and binds a use case to it, the component automatically translates that link in an action (the use case opening). If the user needs to open a use case inside another one, it is necessary to invoke the corresponding method of the Use Case Manager, which is responsible of all the tasks involving the launch of the included or extended use case. Using this approach lets the user to retain use case atomicity and cohesion. Each use case is made of scenarios. Following the framework approach, each scenario is represented by a set of panel objects. When the last panel linked to the use case has been closed, meaning that there are no more active scenarios, the use case is disposed. This process is automatically managed by the framework through the use of a specific service exposed by the UseCaseManager. The framework is capable to dispose all instances of active use cases when the application is closed or ends unexpectedly, releasing every resource associated to them. The model manager provides all services that allow the management of business elements. Supposing that the business object is stored in a database, the changes made by the designer have to be propagated to the database as well. The ResourceManager represents the link between the application and external resources; it is an interface towards databases, Web Services and any other repository.

A Real Industrial Project

In this section, we describe a system for shipment management, called Dispatch Advice Message (DAM), that we developed via the Bluedeep framework. The "layer" pattern was used, with layers presentation, use case and business object. The presentation layer is made up of the elements that allow the visualization of the necessary interfaces for the shipment management: these are implemented in java classes (panels). The use case level introduces the classes that are dedicated to the correct realization of use cases, to their navigation and interaction with domain classes. The business object includes all object classes that are dedicated to the manipulation of the necessary information for shipment management. The classes that form the DAM business object layer are: Dtd, CallUp, Purchase Order, Item, package, Shipment, Label, DAM and DAM File (Fig. 3).

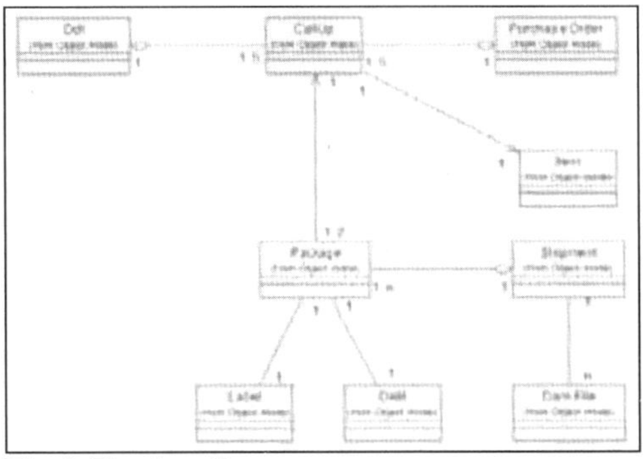

Fig. 3. The class diagram

A business use case is defined by a business analyst [2] from the viewpoint of end-users. The use case encapsulates the knowledge related to the natural work rhythms that a business user would follow when using a software application [1]. The use cases of the DAM application are: "Shipment Management", "Print Shipment", "Despatch Send", "Shipment List". For each system use case, the realization use cases are identified [1]. The application displays the interface of Fig. 4 to the user.

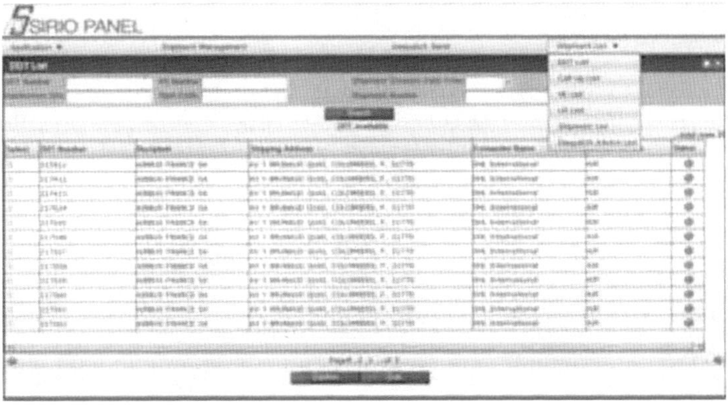

Fig. 4. The main application

To develop a software application with our methodology and framework, the developer has to implement:

- a java class for each business object [2] that implements business logic through attributes and methods; this layer is manipulated by the model manager service;
- a java class for each use case realization [1] that implements system actions for every scenario and manages the user interface navigation; the use case manager service controls these classes;

- a java class for each user interface form discovered in the analysis phase [1] and refined in the design process; they aggregate the presentation component of the framework, in a Swing-like way.

Conclusions

In this paper, we presented an approach for generating Web 2.0 applications from business and analysis models, especially regarding the design phase of the development process. The Web 2.0 applications are generated using the Bluedeep framework. In the future, we plan to extend our methodology to integrate in the design any software system based on any media. We will improve the analysis techniques by identifying additional elements to extend the framework. The current proposal of methodological process represents a further step towards defining a general methodology for the development of multimedia systems.

References

1. Paolone G, Liguori G, Clementini E (2008) Design and development of Web 2.0 applications. In D'Atri A, Saccà D (eds) *Proceedings of the 5th conference of the Italian chapter of AIS (ITAIS 2008)*, Paris, France, 13–14 December 2008, p 10
2. Paolone G, Liguori G, Clementini E (2008) A methodology for building enterprise Web 2.0 applications. In Han J, Holejsovska P (eds) *Proceedings of the 10th international conference on the modern information technology in the innovation processes of the industrial enterprises (MITIP 2008)* (pp. 228–233), Prague, Czech Republic
3. Sukaviriya N et al (2007) Model-driven approach for managing human interface design life cycle. *Lect Notes Comput Sci* 4735: 226
4. Zhao X et al (2007) A business-process-driven approach for generating e-commerce user interfaces. *Lect Notes Comput Sci* 4735:256
5. Fowler M et al (2002) *Patterns of enterprise application architecture*. Addison-Wesley, Reading
6. Pleuss A, Vitzthum A, Hussmann H (2007) Integrating heterogeneous tools into model-centric development of interactive applications. *Lect Notes Comput Sci* 4735:241
7. Leppanen K, Leppanen S, Turunen M (2007) A modelling method for rigorous and automated design of large-scale industrial systems. *Lect Notes Comput Sci* 4735:331
8. Soley R (2000) Model driven architecture. *OMG white paper* 308:308
9. Jacobson I, Booch G, Rumbaugh J (1999) *The unified software development process*. Addison-Wesley, Reading
10. Kruchten P (2000) *The rational unified process: an introduction*. Addison-Wesley Longman Publishing Co. Inc., Boston
11. Gamma E et al (1995) *Design patterns: elements of reusable object-oriented design*. Addison-Wesley, Reading

Design of Information Systems Integration as Research Intervention: A Case Study

Gianluigi Viscusi* **and Carlo Batini†**

Abstract In this paper we discuss the GovQual methodology for planning eGovernment initiatives in public administrations. In particular, the paper describes an application of the GovQual methodology for information systems integration at the Tunisian Ministry of agriculture and hydraulic resources. The key elements of the methodology are the multidisciplinary approach, which considers social, economical, organizational, juridical and technological issues in the identification and ranking of eGovernment projects, and the quality-driven strategy which considers the assessment of actual and future target quality values for services, processes, organizational systems, and technologies. GovQual aims to satisfy the requirements of the context where the methodology has been developed and tested such as e.g. the requirements of the countries involved in the methodology application during the eGovernment for Mediterranean Countries (eG4M) project and former preliminary experiences in the Italian Public Administrations.

Introduction

This paper describes a case of application of the GovQual methodology [1] for eGovernment initiatives planning. The key elements of the methodology are (i) the multidisciplinary approach, which considers social, economical, organizational, juridical and technological issues in the identification and ranking of eGovernment projects, and (ii) the quality-driven strategy which considers the assessment of actual and future target quality values for services, processes, organizational systems, and technologies. Indeed, a structured process is needed, providing a clear perspective on the different facets that eGovernment initiatives usually have

---

* Department of Informatics, Systems and Communication (DISCo), University of Milano-Bicocca, Milano, Italy, viscusi@disco.unimib.it

† Department of Informatics, Systems and Communication (DISCo), University of Milano-Bicocca, Milano, Italy, batini@disco.unimib.it

A. D'Atri et al. (eds.), *Management of the Interconnected World*,
DOI 10.1007/978-3-7908-2404-9_41, © Springer-Verlag Berlin Heidelberg 2010

to challenge, and that disciplines the complex set of decisions to be taken. The available approaches to eGovernment usually provide only a limited perspective to public managers and local authorities on the domain of intervention, either technological, or organizational, or juridical, or social [2]. Indeed, the research question of the GovQual methodology is how to develop an eGovernment initiative planning process driven by social, economic, juridical and technological issues considered in their strict relationship. Due to these issues, the GovQual systemic perspective considers both the outer context and the inner context, in order to preserve context diversity in eGovernment initiatives planning [3], where the starting points of the analysis are, among other issues (see top level of Fig. 1), the available services and the requirements expressed by constituencies, i.e. citizens and businesses.

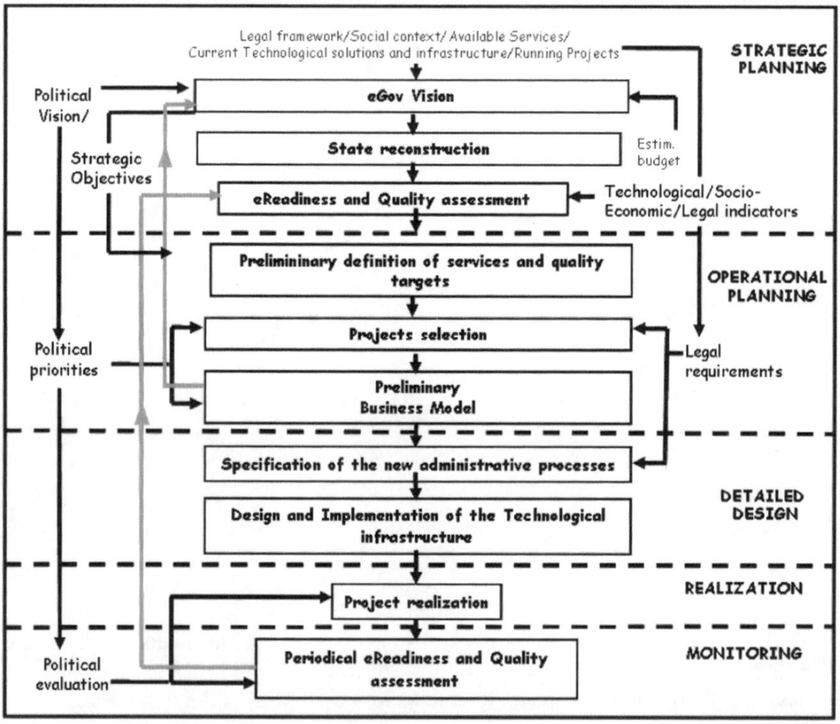

Fig. 1. The phases of the GovQual methodology

The development of the GovQual methodology follows the action research process in connection with systems design and analysis [4]. Considering the action research process, at present we have defined a methodology and we have been actively engaged in the real-world situation with diagnosis and action planning. Furthermore, according to design science requirements, on the field experiences allow the instantiation of the methodology constructs and methods [5]. In the following we describe at a glance GovQual and the interventions where methodology has been applied and developed in an evolutionary perspective.

GovQual at a Glance

The general idea of GovQual is that the planning process should be driven by social, economic, juridical and technological issues considered in their strict relationship. Figure 1 shows the high-level representation of the methodology with the inputs, outputs, and phases (for a detailed description of the phases and the steps of methodology, see [1]). The inputs are related to the scope of the project which may involve one administration, a group of administrations, a specific administrative process or service or a group of processes/services.

The GovQual methodology is composed of phases, where each phase corresponds to one or more steps, corresponding to a set of tasks. There are five main phases of the methodology: (1) *strategic planning*, (2) *operational planning*, (3) *detailed design*, (4) *realization*, (5) *monitoring*. The *strategic planning* is composed of three main steps: (1) *eGov vision definition*, (2) *state reconstruction*, (3) *e-Readiness and quality assessment* (these latter introducing the operational planning macro-phase). The *eGov vision definition* step collects the political vision underlying the eGovernment initiatives and defines their impact on the subsequent decisions. The goal of *state reconstruction* is to provide a clear understanding and knowledge of the general context in which the eGovernment intervention takes place. During this step the knowledge of the social context, laws and rules, services delivered (and administrative processes that produce them), information flows and technological infrastructures is collected and related. The outputs are a set of matrices, a simple but expressive graphical representation, showing the relationships among the types of knowledge above described. The *e-Readiness and quality assessment* step provides an evaluation of the current state of the organizations involved in the eGovernment initiatives. In particular, the phase assesses the eReadiness of the organizations by using socio-economic indicators together with metrics for the relevant quality dimensions and their interrelationships for the current legal framework, organization, services, software, hardware and network technologies and data.

The output of the strategic planning is exploited in the *operational planning* phase, contributing to the preliminary definition of the new services and related quality targets, the projects selection, and the definition of a preliminary business model. On the basis of the current eReadiness and quality levels measured above, the phase is in charge of defining realistic quality targets for the new services to be developed. Afterwards, projects are chosen and a business model is defined in order to perform a *detailed design*. In this phase, the main steps are the (i) *specification of new administrative processes*, aiming to define the automation boundary and to produce detailed specifications; the (ii) *design and implementation of the technological infrastructure* leading to the *project realization* phase where the ICT architecture is deployed. The *monitoring* phase concludes the methodological cycle, focusing on eReadiness and quality target values to control the effectiveness of the project outcome for the stakeholders (public administrations, and constituencies, e.g. citizens and businesses). It is worth noting that the methodology does not ask for an application of the complete cycle, but every phase or step can be autonomously exploited on the basis of the context requirements and needs.

The Methodology: Interventions at a Glance

A first version of the GovQual methodology was designed and applied in Italy in the 90s, resulting in one of the first national projects on cooperative architectures [6]. The application of the methodology in Italy has demonstrated several advantages. First, it enables the interplay of the ICT development plan and administrative/normative reforms, such as the simplification laws periodically enacted in Italy to reduce the amount of bureaucratic fulfillments. The application shows that normative reforms are necessary to carry out eGovernment initiatives. It offers in the short-term feasible and cost savings solutions, such as self-certification. In the long-term, it enables reforms through innovative technological solutions such as publish and subscribe layers cooperative architectures. Another positive facet of the methodology concerns the attention to social issues. The analysis of the social context (such as e.g. the one performed in 2002–2004) led to focus the attention to accessibility issues for disabled persons, resulting in the enactment of a law and several technical norms [7].

In the context of the eGovernment for Mediterranean Countries (eG4M) project, the application of GovQual focused on the Maghreb area, in particular in Tunisia and Morocco. In this context, enabling the access to government services for population is critical in particular to avoid forcing rural residents to travel to major cities for certification or other core administrative services [8]. In the cited countries, a second critical issue concerns provision of services for the urbanization phenomena, supporting citizens from rural areas to cities and suburbs of cities. Due to their complexity, these issues require planning activities, considering the social context both at the macro and micro level. This is necessary in order to promote a broad consensus among officials and citizens, and to provide a holistic perspective to senior government leadership, thus promoting their active involvement and commitment [9]. The experimentations provided further indications to improve the methodology with a right balance between the articulation of the methodology and the need for a feasible approach, by extending the phases to fully take into account juridical, organizational, and economic perspectives. In the following, we discuss the case of the methodology application to an information systems integration initiative of the Tunisian Ministry of agriculture and hydraulic resources.

Information Systems Integration at the Tunisian Ministry of Agriculture and Hydraulic Resources

The eG4M experimentations in Tunisia have been carried out from January 2008 to April 2009. Besides other central public administrations, the Ministry of agriculture and hydraulic resources (MAHR in the following) has been the focus of the application of the GovQual methodology, mainly for the strategic planning phase. MAHR is composed by a set of administrative departments. Each department has information systems integrated at vertical level, namely with decentralized agency providing data on the Tunisians regions they are in charge of administer. Considering information systems integration as characterized by three type of integration for three architectural layers, namely applications, data, and infrastructure [10], the main challenge for MAHR is the integration at horizontal level of the data bases of the central administrative departments; the goal is to have an integrated vision on the whole Ministry activity, supporting strategic and political decisions and forecasts e.g. on the productivity of the agricultural sector. Because of their role in MAHR core processes, four major administrative departments have priority in the eGovernment initiatives, namely the department of animal production, the department of the restructuring of agricultural state-owned domains, the department of veterinary services, and the department of the water resources. Several studies of feasibility and preliminary projects have been proposed in the past, but always focused only on a single department. Indeed, in this case the first goal of the GovQual methodology is to support the data bases integration for the four considered departments.

A second related goal is to provide a unified view of the interactions between each department and other public administrations, in order to evaluate the actual level of efficiency and effectiveness of current information systems for eGovernment services provision. Due to these issues, state reconstruction have been focused on the following issues:

- the conceptual schemas re-engineering of the current data bases, in order to identify the master data of the MAHR, suitable to be used for the design of the conceptual schema of the integrated information system;
- the data quality evaluation of the available data, in terms of their currency and completeness, in order to verify the correspondence with the current procedures and services provided by the public administration;
- the representation of the interactions between public administrations in terms of services and related processes, together with involved type of information and ownership of the involved data bases; the goals is to define the priority intervention areas in the integration initiative.

After a set of courses introducing the methodology and related topics, the above described three issues have been developed through participatory design workshops involving four teams composed by three civil servants (one senior manager and two middle level managers) each from the four departments. The 3 days a week workshops had a monthly frequency from January 2008 to March 2009. ICT skills and computer literacy among the participants were not homogeneous, where a major divide were mainly related to the age of the attendees, and to their functional role in the organization (some departments being represented by IT staff while others by non-IT human resources).

Table 1. Decision table for the participatory choice of suitable technologies

Condition of use (advantage)	Condition of use (inconvenience)	Department	Technology
▪HIGH AUTONOMY OF MANAGEMENT ▪HIGH ECONOMIC VALUE OF THE INTEGRATION ▪LOW RELATIVE IMPORTANCE OF THE QUERYING WITH RESPECT TO THE UPDATE	▪LOW OVERLAPPING OF THE DATA BETWEEN THE DIFFERENT DATABASES	1) The department of animal production; 2) The department of the restructuring of agricultural state-owned domains; 3) The department of veterinary services; 4) The department of water resources management	Enterprise Application Integration/Publish & Subscribe
▪LOW AUTONOMY OF MANAGEMENT ▪HIGH COST OF HETEROGENEITY ▪HIGH ECONOMIC VALUE OF THE INTEGRATION ▪HIGH COMPLEXITY OF MANAGEMENT	▪HIGH AUTONOMY OF MANAGEMENT	-	Central Database
▪LOW AUTONOMY OF MANAGEMENT	▪HIGH NUMBER OF LOCAL QUERIES	-	Distributed Database
▪HIGH AUTONOMY OF MANAGEMENT ▪LOW VOLATILITY OF SOURCES ▪HIGH IMPORTANCE FOR THE ACCESS TO HISTORICAL DATA ▪HIGH RELATIVE IMPORTANCE OF THE QUERYING WITH RESPECT TO THE UPDATE ▪HIGH ECONOMICAL VALUE OF THE INTEGRATION ▪HIGH COMPLEXITY OF THE QUERYING	▪LOW RELATIVE IMPORTANCE OF THE QUERYING WITH RESPECT TO THE UPDATE ▪HIGH VOLATILITY OF SOURCES	1) The department of animal production; 2) The department of the restructuring of agricultural state-owned domains; 3) The department of veterinary services	Datawarehouse
▪HIGH AUTONOMY OF MANAGEMENT ▪ HIGH VOLATILITY OF THE QUERYING ▪HIGH RELATIVE IMPORTANCE OF THE QUERYING WITH RESPECT TO THE UPDATE ▪HIGH COST OF HETEROGENEITY ▪HIGH ECONOMIC VALUE OF THE INTEGRATION	▪LOW RELATIVE IMPORTANCE OF THE QUERYING WITH RESPECT TO THE UPDATE ▪HIGH VOLATILITY OF SOURCES	-	Enterprise Information Integration

Workshops were dedicated mainly to a participated design [11] of the reengineered conceptual schemas for the databases of each department and of the final integrated conceptual schema; besides this activity, a check of the matrices filled by each department representing information flows has been carried out. Participatory design of the departments conceptual schemas and of the integrated conceptual schema (using the Entity-Relationship as formalism [12]), started from the current logical schemas of the department databases, previously designed by external (often private) agencies. Furthermore, participatory design activities pointed out a misalignment of the data required by the current services related to the administrative procedures, impacting on the effectiveness of the information systems on supporting decision both at political and accounting level.

It is worth mentioning the following case. Once designed a reengineered conceptual schema for a department, one of the managers attending the workshop pointed out that the schema was wrong due to the lack of a relationship between the entity *farmer* and the entity *agricultural product* (which is a strategic information in the case of MAHR). Once noticed by one of the other attendees that the produced schemas represent exactly the one produced by the external agency for the current database, all the attendees became aware of the final goal of the participatory work and of the usefulness of the methodology in providing an effective instrument to manage information and knowledge of the public administration in order to maintain the control over outsourcer and their services. In particular, the on the field test of GovQual in Tunisia, besides a conceptual schema of the integrated information system of the four departments of MAHR, provides guidelines to change the governance of the lifecycle management of the information systems, where one of the considered alternatives is to leave the deployment and maintenance activities to the market (namely, private vendors), while the public administration retains the planning, design and quality evaluation of the eGovernment projects. Besides these results, the use of the methodology, and in particular of the state reconstruction and assessment steps supports a shared definition of suitable solutions customized on the basis of the requirements defined by the departments employees and managers. Table 1 shows a decision table for the participatory choice of technologies suitable to support the exploitation of the integrated systems for service provision by the different departments.

Conclusion and Future Work

In this paper, we have described the application of the GovQual methodology at the Tunisian Ministry of agriculture and hydraulic resources. Besides the above discussed results, the analysis of the GovQual matrices pointed out the number of interactions between the departments and other public administrations, where the relevance and the volume of the information flows support the definition of priority for organization and for horizontal projects involving other ministries to be planned. Finally, at learning process level the workshops support the share of IT skills among the participants, improving knowledge and computer literacy in some attendees with no previous IT capability. In terms of *absorptive capacity*, the GovQual methodology seems to be a support for the *absorption* and *assimilation* of IT related knowledge [8]. In future work, we evaluate the results of the application of the methodology in other Tunisian public administrations and in other Mediterranean countries. In future work, we also evaluate the effective absorption of the methodology by civil servants and public managers involved in the above described experiences, through the analysis of the methodology application to other eGovernment initiatives carried out without our external support. Finally, former versions of the planning methodology were not supported by tools, and the absence of automatic documentation and design functionalities is a significant weakness of the present version of GovQual. Due to these issues we are now committed to the design and production of a tool that supports the adoption of the methodology.

Acknowledgments The work presented in this paper has been partially supported by the Italian FIRB project eG4M (RBNE0358YR).

References

1. Batini C, Viscusi G, Cherubini D (2009) GovQual: a quality driven methodology for e-government project planning. *Gov Inf Q* 26:106–117
2. Heeks R, Bailur S (2007) Analyzing e-government research: perspectives, philosophies, theories, methods, and practice. *Gov Inf Q* 24:243–265
3. Avgerou C (2002) *Information systems and global diversity*. Oxford University Press, Oxford
4. Baskerville RL, Wood-Harper AT (1996) A critical perspective on action research as a method for information systems research. *J Inf Technol* 11:235–246
5. Hevner AR, March ST, Park J, Ram S (2004) Design science in information systems research. *MIS Q* 28(1):75–105
6. Bertoletti M, Missier P, Scannapieco M, Aimetti P, Batini C (2003) The service to businesses project: improving government-to-business relationships in Italy. In Traunmüller R (ed) *Electronic government* (pp. 468–471), vol 2739. Springer, Berlin, Heidelberg
7. Italian Government (2004) Legge Stanca 9 gennaio 2004, n.4 "Disposizioni per favorire l'accesso dei soggetti disabili agli strumenti informatici". http://www.w3.org/WAI/Policy/#it. Retrieved 1 Aug 2009
8. Arfaoui J, Mahdi A (2006) *E-government making headway in the maghreb*. Magharebia Web site
9. Scholl HJ (2003) E-government: a special case of ICT-enabled business process change. In *Proceedings of the 36th annual Hawaii international conference on system sciences (HICSS'03)*, vol 5. Computer Societry Press, Island of Hawaii (Big Island)
10. Francalanci C, Morabito V (2008) IS integration and business performance: the mediation effect of organizational absorptive capacity in SMEs. *J Inf Technol* 23(4):297–312
11. Iivari J, Lyytinen K (1999) Research on information systems development in scandinavia – unity in plurality. In Currie WL, Galliers B (eds) *Rethinking management information systems an interdisciplinary perspective*. Oxford University Press, Oxford
12. Batini C, Ceri S, Navathe SB (1992) *Conceptual database design: an entity-relationship approach*. Benjamin/Cummings, Redwood

Professional Desire, Competence and Engagement in IS Context

Peter M. Bednar* **and Christine Welch†**

Abstract This paper attempts to address the failings of a predominant paradigm in IS research and practice that emphasises technological determinism. This paradigm makes use of a false belief in the power of rationality in organizational decision-making, and a mythology in which organizational actors can be viewed as passive "users" of technology. We wish to create a discussion of the nature and role of professionalism as an expression of more than technical competence. Both system analysts and organizational stakeholders (e.g. "users") are to be viewed as professionals. We discuss desire, exercise of will and their role in professional judgment in relation to transcendent values espoused within communities of practice. We go on to relate this to the environments of Information Systems research and practice. It is pointed out that many researchers, over a number of years, have dealt with these issues in relation to effective management of technological development and organizational change. The paper attempts to encourage renewed attention to interpretivist perspectives on IS development and organizational change, including recognition of the importance of contextual dependencies.

Professional Desire and Will

This paper is concerned with the nature of professional competence – how it is acquired, how it is demonstrated and how it is maintained. These issues are explored and discussed with particular reference to the field of Information Systems. We problematise a prevailing paradigm of technological determinism, involving a false belief in the power of rationality in organizational decision-making [1–12], and a mythology in which organizational actors can be viewed as receiving passive "users" of technology [13–16]. We argue that professionalism is demonstrated through a combination of factors. While these will include possession of appropriate, job-relevant skills and knowledge these are insufficient in themselves without

* School of Computing, University of Portsmouth, Portsmouth, UK, perter.bednar@ics.lu.se

† Department of Strategy and Business Systems, University of Portsmouth, Portsmouth, UK, christine.welch@port.ac.uk

A. D'Atri et al. (eds.), *Management of the Interconnected World*,
DOI 10.1007/978-3-7908-2404-9_42, © Springer-Verlag Berlin Heidelberg 2010

a desire to engage. A professional is someone who is able to reflect upon practice of certain skills in context, and to relate these reflections to a body of standards and values that transcend the immediate job role in which she finds herself at a given time. Often, this involves membership of a wider community of practice – formal or informal. For instance, an accountant may become qualified through an examination system provided by a professional association (e.g. an Institute of Chartered Accountants). Having passed the examinations, she has demonstrated technical competence but membership of the Institute (conferring the designation "Chartered Accountant") requires further evidence of probity and ability to learn through reflection, demonstrated through work experience and sponsorship by existing members. This status can be lost if the person is later found to lapse in ethical standards or conduct. If, for instance, the accountant's current employer were to ask her to "cook the books", her loyalty to her community of practice should prevail so that she would give up the job rather than her pride in her professional standards. It is clear that a number of dimensions contribute to the professional conduct of the person described above. First, acquisition of technical skills and knowledge enable her to act in her formal role, e.g. to prepare a balance sheet or appraise alternative investments. However, why would she act in a particular way? How would she improve her professional practice over time? What would govern whether she complies with any particular instruction to act in a certain way? We suggest that professional competence implies not only skill/knowledge in a particular field, but desire to apply that knowledge in accordance with certain values, and engagement with the context of application such that reflection can lead to a productive learning spiral [12–18]. It might be expected then that a professional would engage in extra role behaviour, such as suggesting innovative methods [7, 8, 19, 20]. It is through attachment to a transcendent system of values and standards that we recognise a professional at work, as opposed to a capable amateur or a charlatan. This attachment constitutes what we tend to refer to as professional pride.

These matters have long been recognised in the fields of organizational behaviour and human resource management through the phenomena of formal and informal organizations [1–3, 9–11, 21–25]. Within the formal structure, a person may have a job description expressed in terms of appropriate skills, knowledge and roles. However, the everyday experience of a professional is likely to bear only a loose resemblance to this description, as the actual role carried out is created and re-created in conjunction with colleagues and taking into account professional standards. The desire to demonstrate skills in context according to particular standards and values is demonstrated in part through the informal organization. Sometimes, when faced with a dilemma, a person will justify an action by the words "I had no choice!" e.g. this is an excuse that has sometimes been put forward by concentration camp guards who claim they took actions normally deemed unacceptable because their own families were threatened otherwise. The suggestion that there is no choice here is a fallacy [2, 3, 26]. What the person is actually saying is that, weighing up the potentially unpleasant consequences of each available choice, they took the line of least resistance. Of course, we cannot assume such choices always result from (conscious rational reflection of) resignation of responsibility, e.g. if a judge who disapproves of the death penalty nevertheless imposes it on a convicted person, he might say "I have no choice; that is the penalty laid down by law". This could be an abrogation of his responsibility as a human being to follow his conscience. On the other hand, he might be thinking that the alternative (to resign) would result in more prisoners being condemned in the future (by his replacement) in circumstances where the sentence was not mandatory. Professionalism requires that we recognise the choices we make, their relationship to a wider value system, and their impact upon the contexts of professional life.

Turning specifically to an IS context, we can observe that system failures often have their origins in ignoring emotional engagement, informal communication, personal investment by professionals in the values and standards attaching to their work. In this context, it is relevant to consider the difference between theories that are espoused, what people may believe that they do; and theories in use, what it is observed that they actually do in practice [1–3, 7–13, 19]. Williams [27] also supports this proposition with his discussion in the view of evidence gathered from approx 1,600 IT projects. An example of this arises, for instance, when actors in the field of Information Systems appear to ignore, or be confused by, the difference between applications of technology resulting from demand (pull), and applications developed because it is believed that demand will arise once they are available (push). They fail to perceive that there is a need for balance between these two forces. Related arguments are also made in discussions on socio-technical system development [12–18, 25, 28]. Technologically deterministic assumptions appear to prevail, at least in part. For example, "if we only knew what stakeholders (users) find useful and easy to use they would actually use the technological solutions we develop". This aspect is visible in, for instance, in applications of TAM (the Technology Acceptance Model) [29, 30]. This model is based on a theory of reasoned action and entails measurement of two factors – perceived use fulness of technology and perceived ease of use. TAM can be criticized because it is based upon simplifying assumptions of pure rationality. It ignores context of use and a crucial factor which is desire to engage with the technology concerned. Thus, although it is easy to imagine that someone might reject technology that she perceived to be both useless and difficult to use, TAM fails to address what is involved in determining "usefulness" for particular individuals in their contextual roles [e.g. 12–18, 31, 32]. McGrath [33] discusses emotion in the context of the much-researched failure in the London Ambulance Service Computer Aided Despatch System, from the early 1990s. In this project, the prevailing culture of public service and empathic support for patients within LAS came into direct conflict with a rational planning ethic intended to increase "efficiency". McGrath reflects that: *The case reveals that existing, even apparently latent, conflicts and emotions may surface or heighten when IS innovation is attempted. In the LASCAD case, these subjugated knowledges and emotions emerged during efforts to achieve cultural change of the LAS through the use of ICTs inscribed with government-driven efficiency logic* (p. 297). In the sections that follow, we discuss professional commitment to action as involving more than rational, role based activities but involving exercise of will to adhere to a value system. The impact of extra role behaviour [34–36] in this context will be highlighted as a key factor in achieving beneficial organizational change.

Rogers [37], in his discussion on diffusion of technology, does distinguish between different types of threshold. One type, for example, would be the difference between ignorance and knowledge of how a technology might be applied as a solution for a particular problem. This could be viewed as a key aspect of professional competence. Another threshold could be the difference between thinking about engagement and engagement itself. This is similar to the distinction between theory espoused and theory in use [19]. The difference between feeling positive about the idea of engagement and actually engaging is significant and something that for example exponents of TAM often fail to take into account [30]. The problem of engagement, and lack of reflection over this as a problem, can be viewed as a kind of self-deception. This is often promoted through use of certain language. For example, describing individuals who may engage with technology as "users" has been problematised by researchers in the IS discipline [13–18]. Failure to challenge prejudices such as this have also been recognized [19, 26, 31]. Specifically, the discourse about intention often fails to take into consideration the real investment of personal resources needed to address the required "unlearning" [13–18], and an unwitting belief in rational behaviour as if professional life could be conducted without any emotion. This is ironic, as engagement is explicitly dependent on emotional status and process. As suggested above, an important factor in professional life is a desire to espouse a transcendent system of values that we describe by the term "professional pride". However, it is possible to draw a distinction here between desire and the will to realise that desire in practice. Consider an alcoholic. He possibly has more than one "desire". On the one hand, he desires a drink. On the other, he desires to escape from the negative consequences of being addicted to alcohol. It is his will that determines which of these desires is acted upon, i.e. the will to go to the bar and satisfy one desire or the will to attend a meeting of Alcoholics Anonymous and address the other. Thus, we can see that the interaction between desire and exercise of "free will" is not to be viewed as straightforward. We can detect a process of navigation between alternative desires, assessment of risks, weighing up of consequences; or refusing to consciously weigh up consequences [2, 3, 14, 22, 23, 26]. Sometimes, a person may find himself entrapped in a double bind situation where he feels that there are no choices open to him that will meet his desires [2, 3, 14, 16, 26]. This might be due to a lack of recognition of choices that are available, or perhaps his ability to create choices is inhibited by factors he has not learned to navigate. Louis Brandeis, US Supreme Court Justice, is often quoted in relation to his dissenting judgment in Olmstead v United States 1928, which related to Government tapping of telephone wires [38]. He suggested that *The greatest dangers to liberty lurk in insidious encroachment by men of zeal, well-meaning but without understanding*.

Engagement (desire and will to act) is not sufficient in itself. Competence in judgment is also required. However, this will not necessarily lead to engagement on its own. Dogmatic, closed-minded thinking (e.g. "my country", right or wrong) leads to action without (personal awareness or recognition of) judgment. In the examples above, the impact of desire, will and their roles in creating choices for action may appear obvious. It is not always so obvious in organizational life [7, 8, 14, 16]. However, the interactions between competence, desires and exercise of will are quite similar. This is highlighted by Maister in writing about business strategy [39], who suggests: *Discussing 'strengths, weaknesses, opportunities and threats' ... is fun, but gets nowhere near the real questions. Improving the quality of the analysis is not where the problem lies. The necessary outcome of strategic planning is not analytical insight but resolve. ... Discussing goals is stimulating, inspiring, and energizing. But it feels tough, awkward, annoying, frightening, and completely unpleasant to discuss the discipline needed to reach those goals* (p. 6). In the light of these comments, it becomes easier to recognize the importance of commitment to a set of values (professional "pride") that guides our judgment and exercise of will in a work context. The next section of this paper examines the interaction between competence and exercise of judgment in context.

Engagement and Competence

Possession of relevant skills and knowledge for a work role is not sufficient to support professional practice without ability to exercise judgment in exercising those skills, related to a system of values that transcend the immediate context. This is fundamentally concerned with professional engagement. An illustration of the interplay between engagement (desire/will) and competence can be found in the field of music. Competence relates to ability to play a particular piece of music on an instrument. Engagement would relate to a wish to play in certain circumstances. The two aspects are related but possibly only loosely. For instance, people may gather around the piano in a bar for a "sing song". Someone who knows how to play the piano seats himself to pick out the tune for them. He may not be the most competent pianist in the room, but the person with the best combination of competence to play and desire to join in the fun! Sometimes, people are technically competent to play but play without feeling, e.g. a child who has been compelled to learn by his parents who duly practices the exercise set by his teacher but has no desire to express himself through music and so plays "mechanically". Competence in technique and competence in expression arise through exercise of will, motivated by different aspects of desire.

In relation to Information System, as in music, desire relates to exercise of will only as we open up space to create choices for ourselves. In a professional context, reflection is needed to negotiate such creative spaces [16–18, 39, 40]. These can become blocked through inappropriate management assumptions [40–43]. There is a need for design practice to address the whole work system and not just systems for use of particular artefacts. It is necessary to reflect upon one's professional role, on one's engagement in that role, and on engagement of the "others" in order to avoid becoming entrapped in a double bind [2, 3, 13, 14, 44]. Williams' [27] commentary on failure in IT projects is interesting here. He observes that a cognitive discourse is often used to explain behaviour which is actually only explicable through the affective domain. Williams is able to see this because he is emotionally detached himself from the situations upon which he is reflecting. However, surprisingly enough, in his conclusion he then falls into the same "modus operandi" as those he criticizes; in his recommendations Williams turns to a rational proposition for "more of the same". Engaged actors are caught in a double bind in which they cannot create those choices that would empower escape. It is possible to observe "disconnectedness", i.e. failure to reflect. Engagement within a professional context is related to the phenomenon of extra role behaviour. It is possible that roles themselves can only be sustained through exercise of extra role behaviour. We are faced with complexity of multiple, competing desires in many contexts [2, 3, 19, 45]. This is partly due to the impact of opportunity cost – any choice to expend finite resources, including time, involves choosing between priorities. Boundary setting [2, 3, 28, 42] is also involved, however. Channeled desire (i.e. exercise of will) comes about through commitment to certain values and consequences. Efforts to recognise boundaries of competence involve extra role behaviour (e.g. consider the difference between playing the piano and "playing with the piano" as a jazz musician does when he extemporises from the original melody). The potential to go beyond the basic requirements of a role in order to create new boundaries involves a higher level of reflection. See Ciborra's comment [10]:2 on the MIR space station in relation to bricolage. *A good example is the adventurous (and long) life of the Russian MIR space station Up there, revolving in space, one could find, hand in hand, advanced, robust engineering solutions, rustic deign, and widespread virtuoso tinkering ... to keep the equipment and the system going as a whole. MIR has been a staccato technology, able to defy the passing of time, the inevitable downgrading of performance, and major and minor breakdowns, providing another opportunity for all to see the approximations of science and technology in use.*

Such "extra role behavior" becomes possible only through commitment to ongoing reflection upon competence. The distinction between theories espoused and theories in use [19] is relevant here. How do we reflect upon our extra role behaviour? There is also paradox in that a professional engaged in such extra role behaviour must reflect upon "the future" whilst still involved in creating it. Such reflection involves higher orders of learning [2, 3, 16] in which the individual concerned is reflecting not only upon experience, but upon the process of reflecting on exercising judgment. This may be regarded as an exercise in practical philosophy as part of professional competence in action.

In this paper, we have looked at the nature of professional commitment and how transcendence value systems, professional "pride" and the exercise of judgment are important in creation of beneficial organizational developments. We suggest that individuals acting within their role contexts should be viewed through such a lens, rather than as receiving "users" of technology whose individuality and commitment disappear within a deterministic view of organizational life, in which rational models are privileged. Our conclusion is that it is of utmost importance that efforts made within IS must engage contextual dependencies from a critical perspective, in order to promote systems that are experienced as contextually relevant. What Klein and Meyers [46] describe as an explicit critique and improvement of social condition is necessary to develop richer meanings and understandings. Most importantly, it is necessary to entice people to speak out. In the absence of such an agenda, how are we to evaluate our efforts to support organizational change perceived to be beneficial by involved stakeholders? Only if those on whose behalf we speak are given appropriate opportunities to judge the results of their own and our activities can progress be made. A renewed emphasis on professional competence as including exercise of judgment, through engagement in extra role behaviour, is needed. The myth of the passive receiving "user" needs to be abandoned in favour of recognition of organizations as communities of professionals, all of whose perspectives are relevant to the arena of decision-making and creation of beneficial change.

References

1. Lindblom CE (1959) The science of muddling through. *Pub Admin Rev* 19(2):79–88
2. Bateson G (1972) *Steps to an ecology of mind*. University of Chicago Press, Chicago
3. Bateson G (2002) *Mind and nature: a necessary unity*, 5th edn. Hampton Press, Cresskill
4. Mintzberg H (1979) *The structuring of organizations: a synthesis of the research*. Prentice-Hall, Englewood Cliffs
5. Mumford E, Hirschheim R, Fitzgerald G, Wood-Harper T (eds) (1985) *Research methods in information systems*. North-Holland Publishers, New York
6. Nissen H-E, Klein HK, Hirschheim R (eds) (1991) *Information systems research: contemporary approaches and emergent traditions*. Elsevier Science, The Netherlands
7. Weick KE (1995) *Sensemaking in organizations*. Sage, Thousand Oaks
8. Weick KE (1998) Improvisation as a mindset for organisational analysis. *Organ Sci* 9(5):543–555
9. Ciborra C (2000) *From control to drift*. Oxford University Press, Oxford
10. Ciborra CU (2002) *The labyrinths of information*. Oxford University Press, Oxford
11. Ciborra CU (2004) Encountering information systems as a phenomenon. In Avgerou C, Ciborra CU, Land F (eds) *The social study of information and communication technology*. Oxford University Press, Oxford
12. Whitaker R (2007) Applying phenomenology and hermeneutics in IS design: a report on field experiences. In Nissen H-E, Bednar PM, Welch C (eds) *Use and design in IS: double helix relationships?* Informing Science Press, Santa Rosa
13. Nissen H-E (2002) Challenging traditions of inquiry in software practice. In Dittrich Y, Floyd C, Klischewski R (eds) *Social thinking-software practice*. MIT Press, Cambridge, pp 71–89
14. Bednar PM, Welch C (2008) Bias, misinformation and the paradox of neutrality. *Inform Sci* 11:85–106
15. Bednar PM, Welch C (2009) *Paradoxical relationships in collaboration, competition and innovation: a critical systemic perspective*. Proceedings WOA 2009, Cagliari, Italy
16. Bednar PM, Welch C (2009) Inquiry into informing systems: critical systemic thinking in practice. Chapter 14 in Gill G (ed) *Foundations of informing science*. Informing Science Press, Santa Rosa
17. Bednar PM (2000) A contextual integration of individual and organizational learning perspectives as part of is analysis. *Inform Sci* 3(3):145–156

18. Nissen H-E, Bednar P, Welch C (2007) Double helix relationships in use and design of informing systems: lessons to learn from phenomenology and hermeneutics. *Inform Sci* 10: 1–19
19. Argyris C (1990) *Overcoming organizational defenses*. Prentice Hall, Englewood Cliffs
20. Mumford MD, Scott GM, Gaddis B, Strange JM (2002) Leading creative people: orchestrating expertise and relationships. *Leadersh Q* 13:705–750
21. Etzioni A (1968) *The active society*. The Free Press, New York
22. Churchman CW (1968) *The systems approach*. Dell Publishing, New York
23. Churchman CW (1979) *The systems approach and its enemies*. Basic Books, New York
24. Lawler EJ (2001) An affect theory of social exchange. *Am J Sociol* 1007(2):321–352
25. Baskerville R, Land F (2004) Socially self-destructing systems. In Avgerou C, Ciborra C, Land F (eds) *The social study of information and communication technology*. Oxford University Press, Oxford
26. Gilovich T (1991) *How we know what isn't so*. The Free Press, New York
27. Williams P (2007) *Make sure you get a positive return*. Computer Weekly, 13 Nov 2007
28. Langefors B (1995) *Essays on infology*. Studentlitteratur, Lund
29. Davis FD, Bagozzi RP, Warshaw PR (1989) User acceptance of computer technology: a comparison of two theoretical models. *Manage Sci* 35:982–1003
30. Lee Y, Kozar KA, Larsen KRT (2003) The technology acceptance model: past, present, and future. Commun *AIS* 50(12):752–780
31. Bednar PM, Welch C (2006) *Incentive and desire: covering a missing category*. MCIS 2006. Proceedings, Università degli Studi di Trento, San Servolo, October
32. Bednar P, Welch C (2007) A double helix metaphor for use and usefulness in informing systems. *Inform Sci* 10:273–295
33. McGrath K (2006) Affection not affliction: the role of emotions in information systems and organizational change. *Inf Organ* 16:277–303
34. Organ DW (1988) *Organizational citizenship behaviour: the good soldier syndrome*. Lexington Books, Lexington
35. Nemeth CJ, Staw BM (1989) The tradeoffs of social control and innovation in groups and organizations. In Berkowitz L (ed) *Advances in experimental social psychology*, vol 22. Academic Press, New York, pp 175–210
36. Van Dyne L, LePine AJ (1998) Helping and voice extra-role behaviour: evidence of construct and predictive validity. *Acad Manage J* 41, 108–119
37. Rogers EM (2003) *Diffusion of innovations*. The Free Press, New York
38. Brandeis L (1928) Dissenting judgment of Justice Brandeis in Olmstead v United States 277US479(1928):29 May 2009 at http://caselaw.lp.findlaw.com/scripts/getcase.pl?court=US&vol=277&invol=438
39. Maister D (2008) *Strategy and the fat smoker*. Spangle Press, Boston
40. Bednar PM, Welch C (2006) Structuring uncertainty: sponsoring innovation and creativity. In: Adam F, Brezillon P, Carlsson S, Humphreys P (eds) *Creativity and innovation in decision making and decision support*, vol 2. Decision Support Press, London, pp 867–886
41. Friis S (1991) *User controlled information systems development*. Lund University Publications, Lund
42. Checkland P, Holwell S (1998) *Information, systems and information systems*. Wiley, Chichester
43. Mumford E (2003) *Redesigning human systems*. IRM Press, London
44. Bednar PM, Welch C, Depaoli P (2007) *Transformation of information systems: relevance of expectations*. MCIS 2007, Università degli Studi di Trento, Venice. October
45. Bednar PM, Welch C (2007) Loitering with intent: dealing with human-intensive systems. In: D'Atri A, DeMarco M, Casalino N (eds) (2008) *Interdisciplinary aspects of information systems studies*. Physica, Heidelberg, pp 33–41
46. Klein HK, Meyers MD (2009) *A set principles for conducting and evaluating critical field studies in information systems*. Working paper

Part VIII
Human Computer Interaction

Maria Francesca Costabile* **and Laura Tarantino†**

Human–computer interaction (HCI) is an interdisciplinary research and practice field that deals with the design, evaluation, and use of interactive technologies. The field has gained increasing attention in the last decades due to the pervasiveness of Information Technology (IT) in our lives. HCI topics, going from the traditional ones, like user-centred system design, usability engineering, accessibility, to recently emerging topics, such as improving the user experience, allowing users to customize the application they use, supporting collaboration, are very much relevant for information systems, since their users are not anymore IT experts, they are people of different skills, background and needs, who access services and information via Web.

The HCI Track at ITAIS 2009 has attracted researchers that reported on methodologies, techniques and applications about the interaction among humans, information and technology. Among the papers presented at the conference, six of them have been selected to be included in these proceedings.

A first group includes three papers focusing on the involvement of end users and/or domain experts in system design or customization. The first paper, by Daniela Fogli and Loredana Parasiliti Provenza, titled "From User Practice to ERP Customization: Reversing the Process", discusses ERP system customization, which is a critical problem due to the fact that the characteristics of the company are not properly considered. The authors present an approach to ERP customization based on user-system dialogue specification and participatory design, so that ERP users participate in creating a more appropriate customization that will provide a successful interaction experience. In the second paper, titled "A User Study on How to Render Criticality in Interfaces that Visualize Process Maps", Federico Cabitza reports on a questionnaire-based empirical user study conducted with respondents of heterogeneous expertise on the importance of representing the criticality dimension in software applications that visualize processes. The results, statistically significant, show the inadequateness of current process modelling notations and highlight the efficacy of some graphical solutions for conveying flow criticality. The third paper, by Paloma Diaz, Pablo Acuña, Ignacio Aedo and Alessio Malizia, titled "A Design Patterns Catalogue for Web-Based Emergency Management Systems", discusses the role of design pattern catalogues in the design of domain specific information systems that relies on the participation of experts with different backgrounds, like in the case of Emergency Management Systems (EMS).

* Università di Bari, Bari, Italy, costabile@di.uniba.it

† Università degli Studi dell'Aquila, L'Aquila, Italy, laura.tara@gmail.com

Multi-disciplinary process of this kind are often characterized by misunderstandings and communication problems that may be overcome by using a language understandable by a general audience with no technical knowledge. The authors introduce a catalogue of design patterns for web-based EMS, collected from a variety of sources, as a tool to communicate ideas, and deployed as a collaborative web application offering a pattern space that can be not only navigated but also enriched by the various experts in the design team based on their own experiences.

The second group of two papers concerns web application design aspects. The first paper, by Anna Lisa Guido, Luca Mainetti, Roberto Paiano and Andrea Pandurino, titled "Transforming Legacy Systems into User-Centred Web Applications", reports on authors' experience within the framework of the (MIGRation Open Source) project. MIGR.O.S. aims at outlining a re-engineering path for legacy systems, involving both technological and methodological aspects and including human interaction factors as important quality factors for the transformation of information system into a web information system. The second paper, by Rosanna Cassino and Maurizio Tucci, titiled "VALUTA: A Tool to Specify and Verify Interactive Visual Applications", presents a software tool to specify and verify the visual interface of web applications. It permits to check the interface usability at a formal level, allowing a designer to perform feedback analysis of the environment under consideration.

The last paper, by Monica Sebillo, Luca Paolino, Giuliana Vitiello, Genoveffa Tortora, Alessandro M. Martellone and David Tacconi, titled "Dynamic User Modeling for Personalized Advertisement Delivery on Mobile Devices", deals with personalized delivery of advertisements, an important issue of companies that wish to advertise their products without annoying the users while interacting with a system. This problem is even more complex when advertisements are presented on mobile devices, where the reduced screen size considerably limits users' capability to continue their tasks. The authors' proposal is based on a dynamic user modeling technique that takes into account user's interests over time.

From User Practice to ERP Customization: Reversing the Process

Daniela Fogli* **and Loredana Parasiliti Provenza**†

Abstract ERP systems are complex software packages, generally composed of a core part and a set of modules to be customized according to the company's characteristics, needs and target market. However, ERP system customization is often a critical problem because it is usually carried out by "shaping" the company and its business processes according to a predefined ERP model, rather than vice versa. As a result, company's managers and employees using an ERP system are often forced to reason about and work in some way different from what they are accustomed to. Such a situation frequently leads to ERP failures. This paper advocates the adoption of HCI methods to address these problems. Specifically, the paper presents an approach to ERP customization based on user-system dialogue specification and participatory design, in order to allow ERP users to participate in creating the interaction experience they would like to live with the system.

Introduction

Enterprise resource planning (ERP) systems are information systems designed to integrate and optimize business processes and information flows within different companies and organizations. Current research in this field has shown that interacting with ERP systems is, for most users, very difficult and frustrating. To understand these problems, several studies have been carried out investigating ERP usability issues [1] and highlighting the need of usable ERP systems [2, 3].

The approach adopted to ERP customization is, in our opinion, one of the causes of poor usability of ERP systems. The customization approach is usually "shaping" the organization and its users according to a predefined ERP model, rather than vice versa. As a result, ERP users, like company's managers and employees, are often forced to reason about and work differently from what they

*Dipartimento di Ingegneria dell'Informazione, Università di Brescia, Brescia, Italy, daniela.fogli@ing.unibs.it

†Dipartimento di Ingegneria dell'Informazione, Università di Brescia, Brescia, Italy, loredana.parasiliti@ing.unibs.it

A. D'Atri et al. (eds.), *Management of the Interconnected World*,
DOI 10.1007/978-3-7908-2404-9_43, © Springer-Verlag Berlin Heidelberg 2010

would naturally do. In many situations, users are required to perform unnecessary complex tasks and not rarely receive inadequate system support in case of errors [1]. Furthermore, it often happens that users are unaware of some useful functionality the ERP system offers, because they are not able to find it or even to recognize it among the available options [4].

These situations are documented in several work and project reports. For example, Soh et al. [4] performed a study in seven public hospitals in Singapore that adopt an ERP solution. This study allowed identifying different types of misfits – data, functional and output misfits – between what is offered by the ERP package and organizational requirements. To cope with these misfits, the authors' proposal is asking users for assimilating the package functionality in some depth. They say that users "must now consciously 'get into the ERP software' to evaluate the appropriateness of the new configured system or the alternatives adopted" [4, p. 51]. This position assumes that users should become expert also in information technologies and in the specific package characteristics, besides being expert in their own application domain. Actually, this is a usual attitude of software developers and software vendors generally, who consider users as some people to be educated. A similar recipe is suggested in [5], which presents tips "on how to prepare pare and enable your users", by considering user education as a key business process. While, in principle, we can agree on most of the tips, what we question here is the undervaluation of users' competencies, knowledge, and work practice.

In this paper, we advocate the adoption of human-computer interaction (HCI) methods that give value to users' experience, perspective and work practice. Our proposal is to reverse the usual customization philosophy by directly involving ERP users in building a model of user-ERP system dialogue according to their needs and goals. The aim is to give users a voice that allows them to communicate their perspective to developers and consultants, and to actively participate in ERP customization and, particularly, in designing user-ERP system dialogue.

In HCI, participatory design methodologies are being proposed since the eighties [6], offering methods and techniques to bring together different and controversial perspectives, with the aim of avoiding misunderstandings and communication barriers that may compromise the collaboration among the different stakeholders. Scenarios and prototypes are techniques used to concretely involve users in participatory design [7]. Scenarios represent an informal way of investigating current practice and triggering ideas for future uses of the system. Prototypes, besides permitting evaluation of hypothesis, also encourage exploration of design alternatives. Additionally, formal methods and tools, e.g. language tools [8], have been proposed over the years to describe current practice and envisaging future practice in a more rigorous way with respect to scenarios.

The present paper proposes an approach that goes in this direction: on the one hand, it promotes the use of formal and semi-formal methods for specifying the user-system dialogue according to the different stakeholders' perspectives and usual notations; and, on the other hand, it proposes a participatory design methodology properly defined on the basis of the above specification methods, which allows a true engagement of users in carrying out the ERP customization.

A Multi-Facet Approach to ERP Customization

Customizing an ERP system should take into account several perspectives, particularly that of its target users, who have their own competences, experience, work practice, and a deep knowledge of the application domain in which the system will be used. Users' knowledge complements the ignorance of ERP experts, e.g. developers or consultants, and not only vice versa, as these experts are used to think. Indeed, according to the Rittel's "symmetry of ignorance" principle [9], each stakeholder collaborating to an activity has specific knowledge and experience, but none is more important than the others. Therefore, the knowledge owned by every stakeholder involved in ERP customization must be shared and integrated with the knowledge owned by the other stakeholders, by establishing a peer-to-peer collaboration among them.

The approach we present here for customizing ERP systems aims to give value to the different stakeholders' perspectives involved in, and affected by, the customization activity, and, at the same time, to support their convergence toward a shared understanding of the interaction with the information system. In this sense, the approach is multi-facet.

At least three perspectives should be considered: (i) the users' perspective, where ERP users are employees and company managers; (ii) the perspective of software engineering (SE) experts, as software professionals like ERP developers and consultants; and, last but not least, (iii) the perspective of HCI experts, who should ensure usability requirements while playing the role of mediators between users and SE experts.

To properly express these different perspectives, there is the need to adopt three different languages suitable to the users, the HCI experts and the SE experts respectively. To this aim, our multi-facet approach to ERP customization includes a framework of languages for specifying the user-system dialogue from the different perspectives and a participatory design methodology that states how the different stakeholders should collaborate to converge toward a shared model of the user-system dialogue.

User-System Dialogue Specification

In our experiences of designing domain-specific interactive systems [10], we have observed that each stakeholder (domain expert as representative user, HCI expert and SE expert) looks at and describes the interaction experience from her/his own point of view and according to her/his goals. These observations have led us to formalize a specification framework based on three visual languages, called *visual command language* (VCL), *transformation rule language* (TRL) and *state-chart*

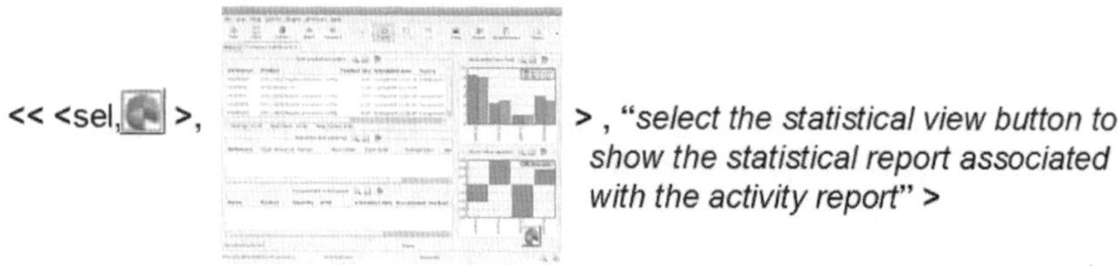

Fig. 1. A visual command specifying how to generate a statistical report

language (SCL). Domain, HCI and SE experts use these languages to specify their different perspectives on the user-system dialogue [11]. Each visual language is defined according to the notation a stakeholder usually adopts in her/his domain. Such language represents the set of (finite) rules that specify the corresponding model of the dialogue, we referred to as the conceptual model (for domain experts), the state-based model (for HCI experts) and the computational-oriented model (for SE experts). These languages can be used for a multi-facet specification of the user-system dialogue during ERP customization activities.

The first language, VCL, is a set of visual commands that express, through commands meaningful to domain experts, the strategies users typically employ to achieve their goals. Visual commands follow proper syntactic rules that are based on the rules usually adopted for system description in user manuals, from those describing simple appliances to those describing complex systems like geographic information systems [12] or CAD systems [13]. Specifically, a *visual command* is a pair <<activity, reaction>, description>, where activity denotes a user activity, namely a physical operation on a widget; reaction denotes the changes in the screen image as a consequence of the execution of the activity and the description component is a description of the pair <activity, reaction> expressed by means of natural language. Figure 1 illustrates a visual command for an open-source ERP. The command describes, from the user point of view, how to obtain the statistical report associated with the current activity report.

The second visual language, TRL, for HCI experts, is the set of transformation rules defined as the visual rewriting rules coupled with the user activities causing them [11]. Specifically, a *transformation rule* is a pair <a, r>, where r=<ant,cond,cons> is a visual rewriting rule [14], being ant the part of the current state of the system that is affected by the execution of the activity a if condition cond is satisfied, and cons the part of the subsequent state of the system resulting

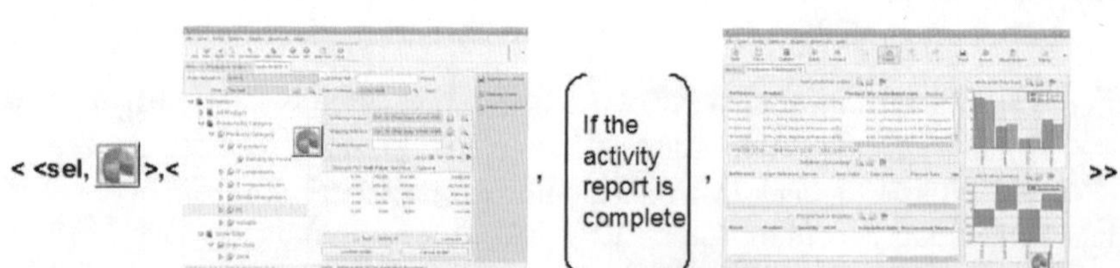

Fig. 2. The visual part of the transformation rule corresponding to the command shown in Fig. 1

from the execution of the activity a. Figure 2 shows the visual part of the transformation rule corresponding to the visual command shown in Fig. 1. It describes from an HCI expert's point of view how to generate a statistical report. With respect to the command in Fig. 1, the transformation rule makes the current state of the system explicit; it also provides HCI experts with a more formal, and machine-oriented description of user-system dialogue. Each visual representation of a system state is also described by an attributed symbol, which consists of a symbol and a tuple of attributes that uniquely describe the visual representation [14]. This is to allow HCI experts to analyze the user-system dialogue description from a usability point of view to check, for instance, the consistency of the states, or if adequate system feedbacks are provided.

The third visual language, SCL, for SE experts, is the set of state-charts [15] specifying all possible user-system dialogues. Figure 3 shows a portion of the state-chart specifying, at the highest level of abstraction, the interaction process between a user and the considered ERP system. Specifically, states 1, state 2 as well as the transition, labeled <sel, >, correspond to the example visual command and transformation rule previously described.

It is worth noticing that the above visual languages are not independent. They share the same pictorial language, as the set of visual messages the ERP system sends to its users, as well as the language of user operations, i.e. the set of names of operations users can perform on the system. They are called *animated pictorial elements* (APEs) and are the boundary objects that each stakeholder reasons about and discusses during the interaction.

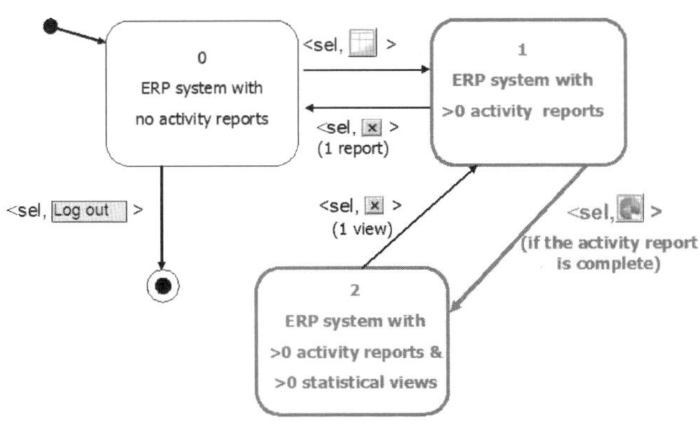

Fig. 3. A portion of the state-chart specification of the user-system dialogue

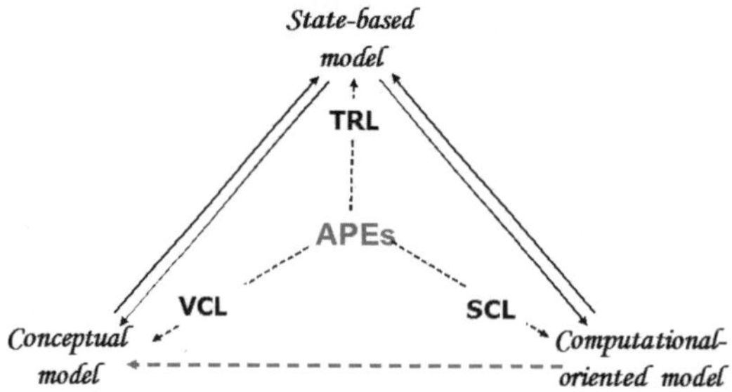

Fig. 4. An overview of the specification framework

Starting from common APEs, our framework thus encompasses a set of translation procedures that enable one model of the user-system dialogue to be mapped onto another [4]. Such procedures link the user view and jargon to the HCI and SE views and jargons (and vice versa) and bridge communication gaps that arise in the design process, thus allowing the three different stakeholder communities to discuss, modify, and evaluate the customized ERP system according to their respective cultures and languages, as it will be described in the next section. Figure 4 illustrates the specification framework for the three categories of stakeholders.

Participatory Design Methodology

Our design methodology is a procedure that establishes how the different stakeholders in the design team should work together to design the user-system dialogue by providing three different but related specifications according to the specification framework. We assume that, at the beginning, a set of functionality and APEs are available to be tailored and composed for creating such a dialogue, as it usually happens in ERP customization.

The procedure consists of the following steps:

1. Domain and HCI experts work together by discussing scenarios that describe current work practices and possible future system usages with the purpose of providing the conceptual model of the system. Specifically, they firstly choose and possibly tailor the APEs, on which the interaction process will be based, according to users' notation and system of signs. Then they collaborate each other to define the conceptual model by specifying it through the VCL, which they build progressively; in this way, while actively participating in designing user-system dialogue, domain experts also contribute to creating system documentation meaningful for users;

2. HCI experts analyze the VCL obtained in the previous step from the usability point of view; then they translate the conceptual model into a state-based model of the user-system dialogue. To this end, they use the procedure for translating the visual commands belonging to VCL into transformation rules, and thus obtain the TRL. Then, HCI experts submit this specification to SE experts;
3. SE experts analyze the state-based model provided by HCI experts and produce a computational-oriented model of the user-system dialogue being designed. They use the TRL built during the previous step to create the state-chart specifying the dialogue. During this activity, SE experts could notice problems in the state-based specification that may ask for a revision; this requires a new collaboration phase with HCI experts, and thus to go back to step 2. Whenever this revision also affects the conceptual model, HCI experts need to collaborate again with domain experts to decide the necessary modifications in the model, thus going back to step 1;
4. The state-chart specification derived from the previous steps is thus used to develop a prototype of the user-system dialogue, which is given to domain experts in order to be tested;
5. Domain experts can thus analyze the prototype physical appearance and behavior, possibly noticing interaction problems due to misunderstanding, incompleteness, lacking in consistency, etc.;
6. To solve the above problems, domain experts must ask for the collaboration of HCI experts to revise together the conceptual model and the VCL specifying it. This situation will also occur at use time whenever users, as well as their work environments, organization procedures and adopted technologies, evolve. In both cases, it is necessary to go back to step 1.

Conclusion

In this paper we have presented a multi-facet approach to customizing ERP systems, which has been derived from our past experiences in designing and developing domain-specific interactive systems. The approach supports an effective communication among different stakeholders, by permitting the expression of each stakeholder's perspective and its translation into a language comprehensible to the others, and by sustaining the iterative and participatory design of the user-system dialogue. Even though the adoption of participatory design promises to offer solutions to users' resistance to (or even rejection of) ERP introduction, it has been observed that "users tend not to fully engage until the system's impact on their working life is apparent – generally when the system 'goes live'" [16, p. 52]. For this reason, to make participation more powerful, users should be involved on topics really salient for them. This suggests considering participatory design and participatory development as two interrelated activities [17]. In our approach, the languages in the framework are formal tools that may facilitate system development, since they can be used for creating proper software environments that support system specification and prototype generation from the specification. The prototypes can then be directly tested by the users, who can thus ask immediately for system refinement. In this way, a true engagement of users in carrying out ERP customization can be obtained. In order to evaluate the effectiveness of the proposal, we plan, as a future work, to apply our approach to a real ERP context and perform usability studies with different kinds of users.

Acknowledgments The authors wish to thank Piero Mussio for his contribution to the approach presented in this paper. This work capitalizes also on the collaboration with Maria Francesca Costabile and Antonio Piccinno, who are herewith acknowledged.

References

1. Topi H, Lucas W, Babain T (2005) Identifying usability issues with an ERP implementation. In *Proceeding of the ICEIS 2005*, Miami, pp 128–133
2. Matthews D (2008) Usability as an ERP selection criteria, IFS white paper. http://www.managingautomation.com/uploadedimages/downloads/WP-Usability.pdf
3. Singh A, Wesson J (2009) Improving the usability of ERP systems through the application of adaptive user interfaces. In *Proceedings of the ICEIS 2009*, Milan, Italy, pp 208–214
4. Soh C, Kien SS, Tay-Yap J (2000) Cultural fits and misfits: is ERP a universal solution? *Commun ACM* 43(4):47–51
5. Simosko N (2008) The IT transformation process – 5 tips on how to prepare and enable your users. SAP insider, Apr–May–Jun 2008. http://www.SAPInsederonline.com
6. Schuler D, Namioka A (1993) *Participatory design – principles and practices*. Lawrence Erlbaum Associates, Hillsday
7. Bødker S, Iversen OS (2002) Staging a professional participatory design practice – moving PD beyond the initial fascination of user involvement. In *Proceedings of the NordCHI 2002*, Arhus, Denmark, pp 11–18
8. Paula MG, Silva BS, Barbosa SDJ (2005) Using an interaction model as a resource for communication in design. In *Proceedings of the ACM CHI 2005*, Portland, Oregon, USA
9. Rittel H (1984) Second-generation design methods. In: *Cross N (ed) Developments in design methodology*. Wiley, New York, pp 317–327
10. Costabile MF, Fogli D, Mussio P, Piccinno A (2007) Visual interactive systems for end-user development: a model-based design methodology. *IEEE Trans SMC* 37(6):1029–1046
11. Fogli D, Marcante A, Mussio P, Parasiliti Provenza L, Piccinno A (2007) Multi-facet design of interactive systems through visual languages. In Ferri F (ed) *Visual languages for interactive computing: definitions and formalizations*. IGI Global, Hershey, pp 174–204
12. Minami M (2000) *Using ArcMap*. Environmental Systems Research Institute, Redlands
13. Leach L (2006) *AutoCAD 2006 Instructor*. McGraw-Hill Science/Engineering/Math, New York
14. Bottoni P, Costabile MF, Mussio P (1999) Specification and dialogue control of visual interaction through visual rewriting systems. *ACM TOPLAS* 21(6):1077–1136

15. Horrocks I (1998) *Constructing the user interface with statecharts*. Addison-Wesley, Reading
16. Wagner EL, Piccoli G (2007) Moving beyond user participation to achieve successful IS design. *Commun ACM* 50(12):51–55
17. Pekkola S, Kaarilahti N, Pohjola P (2006) Towards formalised end-user participation in information systems development process: bridging the gap between participatory design and ISD methodologies. In *Proceedings of the PDC 2006*, Trento, Italy, pp 21–30

A User Study on How to Render Criticality in Interfaces that Visualize Process Maps

Federico Cabitza*

Abstract This paper addresses the main shortcoming that was reported by the users of ProDoc, an electronic document system that we developed to enable users to navigate electronic documents according to predefined process maps: how to render criticality. Criticality is a dimension that pertains to process modeling and for which a graphical way to represent it in flowcharts and process modeling notations does not exist. We report a questionnaire-based empirical user study where we sound out respondents of heterogeneous expertise and attitude on the importance of representing this dimension, as well as on the efficacy of some graphical solutions to integrate it in flowcharts representing work processes. The results we obtained are statistically significant: they show that current notations are inadequate and that a solution to convey flow criticality exists and can be used in software applications that visualize processes.

Process-Oriented Access to Organizational Documents

In organizational settings, documents and activities are deeply intertwined: usually specific records are to be completed and forms filled in in specific activities for other activities to begin. This natural entanglement suggested us to design an application that would help actors align their practices to intended reference models of action for quality and accountability's purposes by making organizational documents and work processes more integrated. To validate this idea, we developed ProDoc, a full-fledged prototype that enables users to browse, get access to and use their electronic documents in the light of work processes they have externalized in flowcharts and visual process models [1]. We firstly deployed ProDoc in a hospital setting: in that context, the documents that ProDoc displayed to users (doctors and nurses) were sections and forms from the patient record therein adopted; the processes that doctors used as maps to get access to the patient record were those clinical processes they used to refer to in routinary case management.

The main functionality of ProDoc is the following: ProDoc allows users to load only a significant subset of the whole organizational documentation according to what activity of a specific work process users have put their focus on; in

* Dipartimento di Informatica, Sistemistica e Comunicazione, Università degli Studi di Milano-Bicocca, Milano, Italy, cabitza@disco.unimib.it

A. D'Atri et al. (eds.), *Management of the Interconnected World*,
DOI 10.1007/978-3-7908-2404-9_44, © Springer-Verlag Berlin Heidelberg 2010

other words, ProDoc displays in the bottom pane of its main interface (the so called Data Panel) those forms, records and electronic documents that have been previously associated to the single activity that users select in the active process map depicted in the top pane of the interface, the so called Process Panel (see Fig. 1). In so doing, users are constantly reminded of what they are supposed to do in each activity they indicate as either "current" or just "under focus", they can glance documents regarding the activities that follow the current one, and they can glance documents pertaining to any other activity represented in the process model, if they want to use the Process Panel just for reference's sake and need to get flexible access to documents irrespectively of what activity they are currently on.

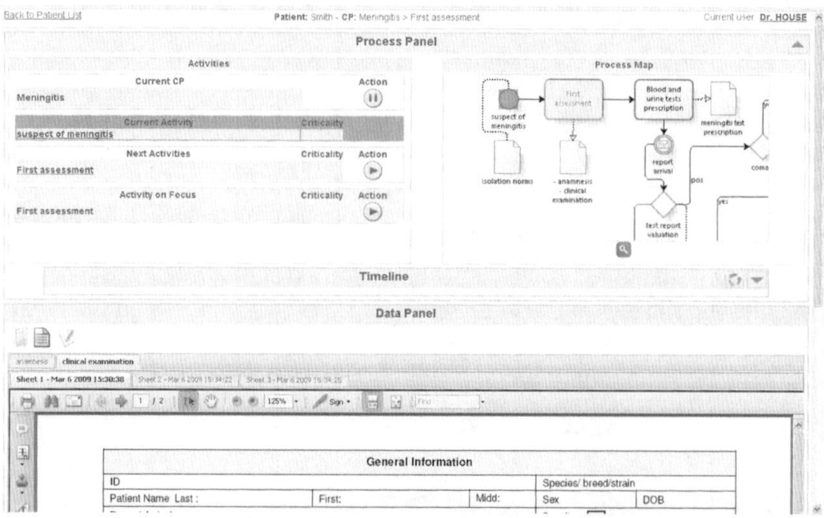

Fig. 1. The main page of ProDoc. Process panel on *top*; data panel *below*

In the ProDoc project, we considered a priority objective to have users actively involved both in building the templates for their electronic documentation (if this were still to be digitized) and, especially, in externalizing their reference process models. To this aim, we invited users build their process maps by means of a visual editor (namely the Process Modeler by BizAgi): this free editor enables users draw process models in the Business Process Modeling Notation (BPMN), associate templates' names to activities and assign a weight to both activities and flow relations. We used the latter weight to quantitatively represent what in [2] we called Activity Criticality and Flow Criticality respectively. The users involved in [2] related criticality to process activities and flows between activities for a number of reasons: e.g. they considered critical an activity that should be accomplished with as few interruptions as possible; that requires a particular ability or experience; that that can have a direct and significant impact on the patient's conditions; or that refers either to recommendations with strong evidence or to strict protocols and procedures. Flow relations were deemed critical either when the order of tasks could not be changed and tasks could not be by-passed, without compromising the process performance and its feasibility, or when actors should be particularly careful in the task handover and shift (e.g., patient transfers) to minimize timeliness and safety issues. In the next section, we will describe the Process Panel of ProDoc and introduce the main shortcoming that was reported by the users involved in the validation panel: how criticality was represented. Then, we will describe the user study we performed to achieve an apt way to represent it and discuss the main results of this study.

The Process Panel of the ProDoc System

The Process Panel allows users to have a quick glance of the process map, to assess and set the current state of the work process, and consult the process history. To this aim, the panel is divided into three sections (see Fig. 1 above). Two of these sections, the Process Map and the Activity List are fixed and discussed in what follows. The third, the Timeline, is collapsable as the whole Process Panel and is described in [1]. The Process Map is a window where a portion of the graphical BPMN-based representation of the current process is displayed after that ProDoc has imported the graphical image and computational representation (an XPDL[1] file) that users created with the Process Modeler. The process map is an active map: this means that the diagram elements depicted therein are active links that make an activity "on focus" and its associated documentation be displayed in the Data Panel. The Process Map works in combination with the Activity List on its left. This is a panel that reports textual information about (i) what the current activity in the process is and its criticality; (ii) what activity/ies follow/s the current one, and their criticality; (iii) what activity is currently on focus and whose documents are presented in the Data Panel.

We had an overall positive feedback on the usability of the Process Panel: in [2] we reported about the validation panel of key users that was selected from the staff of the hospital hosting the study. The main shortcoming reported by the panel regarded the indication of criticality. First, users said that neither Activity Criticality, nor Flow Criticality was displayed in the Process Map, although they expressed it in the Process Modeler. Flow Criticality was neither represented in the Activities Section. Second, users agreed that expressing criticality in numbers, without making explicit the scale, or even in letters, would end up by resulting pretentious: in fact, doctors usually provide activities and related recommendations with a value of strength just as a qualitative and indicative way to weight their importance and criticality in the process of care. Users emphasized the first

[1] XML Process Definition Language, standard developed by the Workflow Management Coalition (WfMC) to interchange process definitions between different management tools.

complain, suggesting that the lack of criticality indications could lead them underrate the consequences of deviating from the process model. Therefore, we recognize that criticality should be expressed, especially in the Process Map and in terms of purely indicative and graphical indications, both for activities and flow relations. Therefore, we designed the empirical user study outlined in the following section in order to understand how the dimension of criticality could be expressed in the Process Panel of ProDoc. Since the study involved general users of process representations, we believe its findings can also be applied to flowchart editors (like the Process Modeler) and in workflow software applications.

The User Study on Criticality Visualization

Method

To the author' knowledge, no process modeling notation addresses conveyance of criticality both explicitly and in a graphical way (e.g., BPMN, UML, Petri Nets, PERT diagrams) and no study has been presented on how to convey this dimension. Therefore, we first undertook an exploratory study designed in a Delphi-like manner. We conceived fourteen diagrammatic representations, seven alternative proposals for each dimension (Activity Criticality – AC, and Flow Criticality – FC). We proposed these alternatives to a panel of six experts including both academic researchers proficient in process modeling and professional practitioners from the private sector proficient in clinical process representation, software diagramming and business project management. This panel selected seven solutions, three to convey AC, and four to convey FC (see Fig. 2), on the basis of their intended simplicity, plainness and easiness of reproduction on paper by hand. Once the seven solutions had been identified, we proceeded to carry out the empirical user study. To assess the effectiveness and appropriateness of the identified solutions, we created an online self-administered questionnaire: this encompassed nine items divided in two sections, one for each dimension (four items for the AC and five for the FC dimensions, considering also "neutral solutions", i.e., solutions used as "control group" and indistinguishable from the symbols used in regular flow charting). Each item encompassed a brief question relating to a corresponding object. Objects were small sketches depicting three activity blocks – for the AC dimension – to express three different levels of activity criticality; and short four-step sequential flow diagrams – for the FC dimension – to express three different levels of flow criticality. Respondents were asked to assess the effectiveness of each object in conveying criticality information in the context of short and simple work scenarios. Each item was associated to a different dependent variable, namely the (subjectively perceived) effectiveness of the corresponding graphical solution. For the assessment of the dependent variable, we proposed an ordinal and visual six-point scale [3], with an explicit indication of the extreme anchors (from "no effective at all" "−3", to "very effective" "+3"). We adopted a scale with an even number of choices in order to reduce the risk of "diluting" the results due to the central tendency bias, which otherwise would have had a significant impact in the subsequent analysis. Yet, we did not adopt a forced choice design, since the typical middle option of "I don't know" was made available as a separate option.

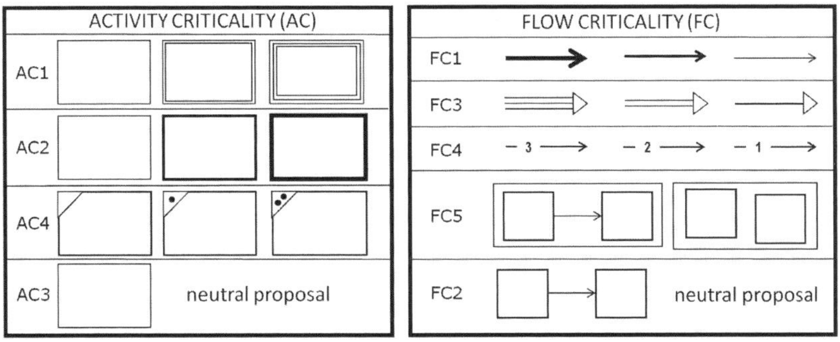

Fig. 2 The alternative graphical solutions conceived to convey criticality (AC3 and FC2 depict the regular ways to render activities and flows. The numbering of the alternatives has been assigned randomly to limit order bias.)

Our empirical user study can be divided in two parts, each associated to a different research hypothesis, $H_1(1)$ and $H_1(2)$. In the first part, the explanatory (i.e., independent) construct is the (in)adequacy of traditional flowcharts in conveying criticality-related information and therefore in providing adequate support for process description and interpretation when this kind of information must be considered. The independent and grouping variable of the second part is the (in)adequacy of the graphical solutions that we proposed as alternative to traditional flowcharts. To verify $H_1(1)$ and $H_1(2)$, we adopted the usual approach to gain (statistically) significant evidence that the corresponding null hypotheses, $H_0(1)$ and $H_0(2)$, can be rejected. Namely the null hypotheses can be expressed as follows: (i) $H_0(1)$: "Traditional flowcharts are adequate to express criticality"; (ii) $H_0(2)$: "Alternative proposals are not effective in expressing criticality". In order to reject $H_0(1)$, we proposed to the respondents "neutral proposals" in addition to the set of novel solutions that had been selected by the expert panel; the neutral solutions (see AC3 and FC2 solutions in Fig. 2) were but excerpts of regular flowcharts that have not been modified to express criticality so as to act as "control group". In so doing, we aimed to limit the risk of having results biased by acquiescence bias.

In particular, $H_0(1)$ holds if respondents consider the neutral notation effective in describing the proposed clinical vignettes. More formally, $H_0(1)$ holds if the average effectiveness evaluated for the neutral proposal is 1 or greater: accordingly, we can reject $H_0(1)$ in favor of $H_1(1)$ if the median effectiveness is lower than 1. On the other hand, $H_0(2)$ says that, among the alternative proposals we presented to respondents, there is no solution that they prefer with respect to the others in a significant way, i.e., beyond fluctuations in preference due to chance. Formally put, $H_0(2)$ holds if the real distribution of the frequencies is uniform between the solutions. Otherwise we can reject it.

The respondents of the questionnaire were contacted via mailing lists, direct emails to friends and colleagues, announcements in various classes and through a post in the blog of our lab web site. Word of mouth did the rest. The test was anonymous. To ensure that the results from our sample could hold for a general population of potential users, we have attempted to get a representative sample of people both from the general population of prospective practitioners (students in cognitive psychology, human factors, organizational psychology and computer science) and from that of professional practitioners with higher education and predisposition to conceive work in terms of processes and tasks. Professionals came both from the academic domain (they were researchers in process modeling and management, interaction design, knowledge representation and theoretical computer science); as well as from the private sector (they were practitioners involved in project management, software development and administration). The sample we got has a higher than proportional number of respondents from the university domain (either students or academics) and we are aware that such a sample may yield to technically-savvy and process-aware participation and that this could bias the study results with respect to broad generalization.

Results

When we closed the survey, we had collected 78 questionnaires, for a total of 648 ratings. Descriptive statistics of the collected data are reported in Table 1. In order to ascertain if the distribution of the collected data was normal, we applied in Minitab (v. 15.0) the Anderson-Darling test, which is more sensitive to extreme assessments than the Kolmogorov-Smirnov Test. The survey data resulted non-normal even according to the Monte Carlo significance level (as = 0.000). Therefore, since the normality assumption does not hold, we used distribution-free tests and did not consider mean values to perform comparisons and draw conclusions [4]. Our results are reported in the following: in regard to $H_0(1)$, we can reject it in favor of $H_1(1)$, i.e., traditional flowcharts cannot be considered adequate to express criticality, irrespectively of what they are used for. We applied a one-sided 1-sample sign test for median to the AC3 and FC2 variables (i.e., the neutral proposals) since this test makes no assumption about the shape of the population distribution. As a result, we are able to reject the null hypothesis $H_0(1)$ in favor of $H_1(1)$ with a highly significant confidence level (p = 0.0000, 0, 13 and 3% above, respectively). Moreover for each dimension, the neutral proposal was deemed as the worst one with respect to the alternative solutions in a significant number of cases: i.e., the solutions proposed by the expert panel are anyway better. A χ^2 test confirmed that is highly likely that the real distribution of the frequencies by which the neutral proposal was considered as the least effective one is not uniform between the alternative solutions (AC3: χ^2=114.3, degrees of freedom=3, asymptotic significance =0.000; FC2: χ^2=51.33, df=3, p=0.000). Summarizing, we can conclude that traditional flow charting is deemed inadequate to properly represent differences in criticality, especially as regards activity criticality.

Table 1 The descriptive statistics of the assessments of effectiveness

	AC1	AC2	AC3*	AC4	FC1	FC2*	FC3	FC4	FC5
N	72	70	72	72	72	72	72	72	70
Mode	2	–1	–3	–2	–2	–3	–2	–2	2
Mean	–0.2	–0.6	–2.9	–0.3	–0.5	–1.6	–0.5	–1.2	1.0
Median	–1	–1	–3	–1	–1	–2	–1	–2	1
σ	1.9	1.8	0.4	1.8	1.9	1.9	1.7	1.7	1.6

In regard to $H_0(2)$, we can reject it in favor of $H_1(2)$ for one dimension, while for the other three we did not collect statistically sound evidence. We considered for each dimension the number of times that respondents considered an alternative solution better than the others and then applied the χ^2 test to find whether the apparent differences in frequencies were real and not due to chance. The results tell us that respondents manifested a clear preference in regard to the FC dimension (FC: χ^2=47.50, df=3, p=0.000); while there is much more balance (i.e., no clear preference) in regard to activity criticality (AC: χ^2=3.75, df=2, p=0.154). By applying a residual analysis, we see that respondents tended to prefer AC1 and AC4 solutions as regards activity criticality; and FC5 for flow criticality. Summarizing, we can conclude that some graphical alternatives stand out from the others.

Discussion and Conclusions

In this paper, we reported an empirical user study on a subject that usually does no receive the attention it deserves: how to properly convey different degrees of criticality/severity in process diagrams. Adding criticality information to a process diagram means to add an explicit indication of how prescriptive, strict or approximate the modeler intended the process model for its later use by who uses the model as a reference or map for her action. In the healthcare domain where ProDoc was first deployed, conveying criticality properly can make a significant difference in either health outcomes, treatment appropriateness and result comparability [5]. Moreover, clinicians made a point that can be generalized also in other domains: the lack of criticality indication in the process maps could have a relevant impact on what could be considered a significant variation from the intended model of action, and hence on how to tune the process to make it a tool more compliant with actual work practices and standard operating procedures.

This study was aimed at reaching statistical evidence about two questions: do users consider traditional flow-charts sufficiently effective to support the description and interpretation of processes? Our study allows us to answer this question with a clear and negative answer and to generalize this finding well beyond the scope of our sample. The second question is: do the proposed notations reach the necessary compromise between graphical simplicity and effective conveyance of criticality? To this regard, we found statistical evidence that only FC5 in Fig. 2 is an effective solution. In this case, and quite surprisingly, respondents chose the concept of "activity inclusion" to properly convey flow criticality: specifically, if two activities are included in a super-activity and are related, their order is strict; if they are unrelated, they can be executed in any order; if they are related but not included within a super-activity, their execution order is not too strict or critical. On the other hand, no statistically valid conclusion can be reached on how to render criticality about single activities: to this regard, the user study suggests that preferences about this dimension are given according to just a matter of tastes. To fill this gap, we aim our future work in the domain of process diagramming and protocol visualization at finding proper and effective ways to express activity criticality. The solution will be adopted in two next projects: it will be used in the Process Panel of ProDoc, the process-oriented electronic document system we presented in [1] for a further validation in a more in-depth study with its intended users. And within the MedicinExplicit project, a research activity that follows the initiative published in [6] and that is aimed at leveraging Internet-based technologies to facilitate the externalization of medical procedural knowledge and the formulation of consensus-based guidelines in the healthcare domain.

References

1. Cabitza F et al (2009) PRODOC: an electronic patient record to foster process-oriented practices. In *Proceedings of ECSCW09*, Springer, London, UK
2. Cabitza F et al (2007) Providing awareness through situated process maps: the hospital care case. In *Proceedings of GROUP07*, ACM, New York
3. Birkett NJ (1986) Selecting the number of response categories for a likert-type scale. In *Proceedings of the American statistical association* 1987 Annual Meeting, ASA, Alexandria, VA, USA
4. Hill T, Lewicki P (2005) *Statistics: methods and applications*. StatSoft, Tulsa
5. Panella M et al (2003) Reducing clinical variations with clinical pathways. *IJQHC* 15(6):509–521
6. Randelli et al (2010) Infectious and thromboembolic complications of arthroscopic shoulder surgery. *JSES* 19(1):97–101

A Design Patterns Catalog for Web-Based Emergency Management Systems

Paloma Diaz[*], Pablo Acuña[†], Ignacio Aedo[‡], and Alessio Malizia[π]

Abstract The design of domain specific information systems, like Emergency Management Systems, has to rely on the participation of experts with different backgrounds. Such multi-disciplinary process is often characterized by misunderstandings and communication problems. In this context, design patterns might be a useful tool to communicate ideas since patterns collect solutions to recurrent problems in a domain using a language that should be understandable by a general audience with no technical knowledge. In this paper we introduce a catalog of design patterns for Web-based Emergency Management Systems (WEMS). We have used three sources to find out patterns: design principles for WEMS, existing WEMS and design patterns from related design areas including interaction, ubiquitous computing or security. Furthermore, the catalog is deployed as a collaborative web application so that designers can navigate through the patterns space but they can also make the collection grow adding their own expertise.

Introduction

Developing Web Emergency Management Systems (WEMS) is a multi-disciplinary design endeavor where knowledge on web design and its different perspectives (including information architecture, interaction design, security and personalization) is not enough. Experts on emergencies are required not only to provide knowledge on the problem but also on the suitability of the potential solutions. Emergency workers perform their activities under pressure and stress, so any tool interfering with their protocols or imposing any kind of burden will be immediately rejected. In this context, meta-design techniques [1] aimed at making of emergency workers real co-designers should be a must.

---

[*] Laboratorio DEI, Universidad Carlos III de Madrid, Madrid, Spain, pdp@inf.uc3m.es
[†] Laboratorio DEI, Universidad Carlos III de Madrid, Madrid, Spain, pacuna@inf.uc3m.es
[‡] Laboratorio DEI, Universidad Carlos III de Madrid, Madrid, Spain, aedo@ia.uc3m.es
[π] Laboratorio DEI, Universidad Carlos III de Madrid, Madrid, Spain, amalizia@inf.uc3m.es

A. D'Atri et al. (eds.), *Management of the Interconnected World*,
DOI 10.1007/978-3-7908-2404-9_45,

On the way to elaborate a conceptual framework supporting efficient and active co-design, design patterns might contribute to create some level of common understanding or common ground among inter-disciplinary participants and, in this way they can help to soften the endemic communication problems in inter-disciplinary teams that as reported in [2] have a huge impact in the final product quality. The role of design patterns to improve communication in inter-disciplinary teams has been sustained under the hypothesis that patterns document established solutions to recurrent problems using a language characterized by its cross-discipline readability [3]. In addition to improving communication among team members with differing expertise, design patterns may be of particular benefit to end-users and other nonprogrammers who wish to contribute to the development of a web system, because they may help to address the technical challenges of the web development process [4].

In this paper we introduce a design patterns catalog for WEMS that has been built by studying three basic sources: (1) well-known design principles for WEMS like [5], which are less systematic and complete than patterns but that provide useful hints to look for patterns; (2) existing WEMS that are a basic resource to identify common designs applied and how they are applied in practice; and (3) patterns applied in related design areas, including web design [6], ubiquitous computing [7, 8], security [9] and usability [10]. The catalog has been deployed as a Web-based collaborative application to support not only navigation through the collection but also edition. In this way, designers and emergency workers can make the collection grow by including their own expertise whether as new patterns or as modifications to the existing patterns. The paper is organized as follows. First we describe the mining process followed to create the patterns catalog and the catalog and groups defined, followed by an example pattern with the format defined. Then the collaborative application used for developing and navigating the patterns collection is introduced. We end with some conclusions and final works.

Pattern Mining Process

Design of WEMS involves various related areas that should be taken into account in order to provide a more or less complete solution. Domain areas like website design, usability and ubiquitous computing contribute with concepts and definitions that can be useful when developing an application. Furthermore, developers can consider design principles that provide general guidelines applicable to these types of system [5]. Consequently, for the creation of the design patterns catalog we have studied three main sources: design principles for WEMS, existing WEMS, and patterns languages and catalogs from related design areas.

WEMS development is not a brand new discipline so there is some knowledge about design practices in the form or guidelines and principles. For instance, the authors in [5] define 8 basic design principles that address important aspects of an emergency management system, based on the use of the "Emergency Management Information System and Reference Index" (EMISARI). These design principles deal with concepts like directory structures, information content and display, data source and timeline, data authority and accountability, etc. Compared to guidelines and principles, design patterns are relatively more structured and they provide much more information that can help a designer decide whether or not to apply a specific pattern. Moreover, design patterns are always grounded in a number of real examples of application and they also include information on multiple and probably competing concerns that help to understand when the pattern should be applied [11]. In these work, we have used the design principles reported in [5] as a checklist to look for common practices in existing WEMS that could suggest the existence of design patterns.

We also analyzed the following existing WEMS: SAHANA[1], SIGAME[2], ESA6[3], ReliefWeb[4], Ushahidi[5] and GDACS[6]. We studied them in order to discover useful patterns that provide a solution to common emergency problems. These systems might have different goals and deal with different phases and processes during the emergency situation but all of them are a very valuable resource to look for common designs and realize how they are applied in practice.

Moreover, we studied and analyzed a set of design patterns and catalogs from related areas in order to identify design areas that could contribute in a WEMS design. We considered the design pattern language from Van Duyne et al. [6], included in the book "The Design of Sites", that describe 107 patterns for different types of web sites, divided into site genres and inter-related according to their functionality. Additionally, we studied design patterns for ubiquitous computing in [7, 8] that include 45 general patterns providing solutions for different aspects of ubiquitous development. Furthermore, we considered design patterns language for safety-critical interactive systems [9], which based on a set of "safety-usability" principles, provides solutions for tasks regarding usability terms in a safe way for critical systems. Finally, a web usability patterns catalog [10] was also taken into account for the construction of our own catalog.

Considering all the sources, our pattern mining process consisted in observing the functionality needed in a particular emergency situation and defining which techniques might be helpful or were applied in each case. It's worth noting there that an emergency has four different phases: Preparedness, Emergency Opera-

---

[1] www.sahana.lk
[2] www.sigame.es
[3] www.esa6.es
[4] www.reliefweb.info
[5] www.ushahidi.com
[6] www.gdacs.org

tions, Rehabilitation/Recovery and Mitigation Activities [12]. Each phase faces different problems and might require different solutions. Moreover, during emergency situations people can assume roles that are classified according to event types and activities to perform [5]. For instance, "First Responders" deal personally and in the field with the situation whilst "Command Control Operators" are in a specific location or center managing information about the emergency, generally with more powerful terminals and displays. Therefore, we described the functionality required for each emergency phase related with the roles that users can assume, including situations applicable for more than one phase or role. Moreover, we observed the existing design patterns from the sources and design principles from [5] and classified them according to their applicability in each case. Consequently, we were able to group such requirements and define a set of design patterns that provide specific solutions to the problems described. Table 1 summarizes the proposed patterns for the different emergency phases and roles.

Table 1. Patterns according emergency phases and user roles

	First responders	Command control operators
Preparedness		- C.2 Emergency alerts/notifications - D.2 Web feeds indicators
Emergency operations	- A.1 Navigation for first responders - A.4 Searching and filtering information - B.1 Style sheets for multiple media types - B.2 Site accessibility - B.4 Handheld devices - C.1 Fast loading sites - C.6 Direct manipulation	- A.2 Navigation for command control operators - A.3 Map-based navigation - A.4 Searching and filtering information - B.1 style sheets for multiple media types - B.3 Printable pages - C.1 Fast loading sites - C.5 Links and action buttons
Rehabilitation/ recovery	- A.1 Navigation for first responders - C.3 Error prevention - C.4 Data authoring - C.6 Direct manipulation	- A.2 Navigation for command control operators - A.3 Map-based navigation - B.3 Printable pages - C.4 Data authoring - C.5 Links and action buttons - D.1 Collective memory/data archives
Mitigation activities		- D.1 Collective memory/data archives - A.4 Searching and filtering information

The Catalog of WEMS Design Patterns

Applying the process described above, we have built a first version of the WEMS design patterns catalog that includes 16 design patterns. In this first collection we have only included patterns for First Responders and Command-and-Control users. Our intention is to use this catalog as a seed that can be improved by real emergency workers and designers with their expertise, following the Seed-Evolution-Reseed model described in [1]. WEMS patterns are classified into 4 groups according to the main functionality they address:

A. **Situational Awareness.** This category includes those patterns that could help emergency workers to understand the situation, that is, to develop some level of situational awareness [13] that might eventually support them in making more rational decisions. With this purpose a number of patterns that support access to the information in a fast, accessible and ordered way are presented here.
B. **Accessibility for all.** Users may access the WEMS using different devices that might impose usability constraints. For example, First Responders may access the information from handheld devices so their interface has to be carefully designed considering the platform and the context conditions. Information must be correctly structured and presented in order to be accessible for every user regardless the device or browser used.
C. **Efficient Navigation.** Patterns in this category include usability techniques for an efficient access to the information and services provided in WEMS.
D. **Information access and memory.** This group is concerned with patterns dealing with fast and efficient access to data both from a current emergency event, as well as from possible related events from the past. Collective memory archives should be provided with accessible navigation [12].

Table 2 shows the patterns included in the catalog. Each design pattern has an identifier, which is made up of a letter representing its category and a sequence number within the category (thus A3 represents the third pattern in the Situational Awareness category), in the tool we use colors to distinguish between patterns groups as in [6]. Each pattern has the following sections: a context or background that describes the scope where the pattern can be applied; the definition of the problem and its relationship with the requirements described in the context; a solution including real examples and techniques to apply; and finally, related patterns from our catalog or from external sources that may contribute to the solution. Even though each pattern belongs to a unique category, there are relations among patterns from different categories whenever these patterns combined can provide a solution to a more complex problem. For instance, the pattern "D.1.Collective Memory/Data archives", which deals with the way information can be adequately stored in order to be useful in future events as a source of collective memory as suggested in [12], is related with pattern "A.4.Searching and Filtering information", which provides solutions to organize information in different ways to satisfy different visualization needs.

Table 2. Patterns catalog

Group	Design patterns
A. Situational awareness	A.1. Navigation for first responders
	A.2. Navigation for command control operators
	A.3. Map-based navigation
	A.4. Searching and filtering information
B. Accessibility for all	B.1. Style sheets for multiple media types
	B.2. Site accessibility
	B.3. Printable pages
	B.4. Handheld devices support
C. Efficient navigation	C.1. Fast loading sites
	C.2. Emergency alerts/notifications
	C.3. Error prevention
	C.4. Data authoring
	C.5. Links and actions buttons
	C.6. Direct manipulation
D. Information access and memory	D.1. Collective memory/data archives
	D.2. Web feeds indicators

Using the Catalog

An important aspect to consider when defining a design pattern catalog or language is the way users can interact with the patterns. Since our goal was to collect knowledge that might be shared by inter-disciplinary teams we decided to use a Web-based collaborative application to deploy the patterns catalog. In this way, users cannot only navigate through the patterns space to look for solutions to their requirements but they can also modify the patterns on the catalog to share their expertise with other members of the group. More specifically, we have implemented the catalog as a wiki. A wiki is a configurable Web application that allows developing and presenting a set of information, providing the users with tools to create, edit and delete content in a collaborative way. We used the MediaWiki[7] platform for including our patterns catalog because of its editing and display capabilities. First of all, MediaWiki platform allows embedding and displaying multimedia information, useful for including images in the pattern description, as shown in Fig. 1. Additionally, it is possible to specify access rights for creating and editing the information, allowing us to develop the patterns in a collaborative yet controlled way. This is a crucial issue since the wiki is expected to provide design knowledge that has to be trustable and verifiable.

[7] http://www.mediawiki.org/

Fig. 1. A design pattern in the wiki

An initial version of our catalog was presented to a group of 14 people in order to receive feedback. This group included experts in the development of WEMS, Web usability, human–computer interaction, and pattern mining and definition. The group was asked to analyze the content and structure of the patterns during 15 days and their comments were used to improve the catalog. In particular, most comments were about the categorization used to organize the patterns that according to the participants should match the expectations and needs of WEMS designers and in some cases was quite oriented towards the user interface design. Indeed, although some of the patterns names and categories were modified an expert evaluation is still required to improve their understandability by an inter-disciplinary audience. Given the number of participants we consider this experience as a first step in the development of a WEMS patterns catalog. As stated before, we want to use this catalog as a seed in the SER model [1].

Conclusions and Future Work

We have presented our design pattern catalog for WEMS aiming at providing guidelines for approaching common requirements in this type of applications. We considered design pattern catalogs and languages from related areas, a set of design principles, and observable solutions from existing applications. Additionally, we described the wiki tool used for constructing and presenting our catalog. As future work, we plan to perform a heuristic evaluation with experts from emergency management and usability in order to validate the patterns as well as the usefulness of the wiki. Our goal is to use this catalog as a seed that provides useful solutions that might have some impact in having a fluent communication among the members of inter-disciplinary WEMS development teams; a seed that can be improved by real emergency workers and designers with their expertise thanks to the use of a collaborative application like the wiki.

Acknowledgments This work is funded by grants UIA4SIGE (Ministry of Science and Innovation TSI2007-60388) and Explore (Community of Madrid and Universidad Carlos III CCG08-UC3M/TIC-4487).

References

1. Fischer G (2007) Meta-design: expanding boundaries and redistributing control in design. Baranauskas C et al (eds) INTERACT 2007, *LNCS* 4662, Part I, pp 193–206, Rio De Janeiro
2. Safoutin MJ, Thurston DJ (1993) A communications-based technique for interdisciplinary design team management. *IEEE Trans Eng Manage* 40(4):360–372
3. Borchers J (1999) *Interdisciplinary design patterns*. INTERACT'99 7th international conference on human–computer interaction. Position Paper, Workshop on Usability Pattern Language, Edinburgh
4. Rode J, Rosson MB, Perez M (2006) End user development of web applications. In Lieberman H, Paterno F, Wulf V (eds) *End-user development*. Springer, Berlin, pp 161–182
5. Turoff M, Chumer B, Van de Walle B., Yao X (2004) The design of a dynamic emergency response management information system (DERMIS). *J Inf Technol Theory Appl* January, 5(4):1–36
6. Van Duyne DK, Landay J, Hong J (2007) *The design of sites*, 2nd edn. Prentice Hall, Inc, Upper Saddle River
7. Landay J, Borriello G (2003) Design patterns for ubiquitous computing. *IEEE Comput* 36(8):93–95
8. Chung E, Hong J, Lin J, Prabaker M, Landay J, Liu A (2004) *Development and evaluation of emerging design patterns for ubiquitous computing*. Designing interactive systems (DIS2004), ACM Press, New York, pp 233–242
9. Mahemoff M, Hussey A (1999) *Patterns for designing safety-critical interactive systems*. Technical report No. 99-23, Software Verification Research Centre
10. Lyardet F, Rossi G (2001) *Web usability patterns*. European conference on pattern languages of programs (EuroPLoP 2001), Universitätsverlag Konstanz (UKV), Irsee
11. Díaz P, Aedo I, Rosson MB (2008) *Visual representation of web design patterns for end-users*. AVI 2008, Naples, Italy, pp 408–411
12. Klenk J (1997) *Emergency information management and telecommunications*. UN disaster management training programme (DMTP), DHA, Madison
13. Endsley MR (2000) Theoretical underpinnings of situation awareness: a critical review. In Endsley MR, Garland DJ (eds) *Situation awareness: analysis and measurement*. LEA, Mahwah, pp 3–32

Transforming Legacy Systems into User-Centred Web Applications

Anna L. Guido[*], **Roberto Paiano**[†], **Andrea Pandurino**[‡] **and Luca Mainetti**[π]

Abstract The web revolution makes outdated preexisting Information Systems (legacy systems). Companies need to update their Information Systems without lose neither investments on design and implementation made in the past nor the know-how acquired during years. The modern trend is to activate a reengineering process for the legacy systems. It is important that the reengineering process consider both technological aspect and definition of the Human Computer Interaction as important quality factors for the Information System transformation into a Web Information System. The process requires a methodological approach oriented to the application of a specific methodology for each reengineering phase. In this paper, we present a reengineering path that involves both technological and methodological aspects. The idea was born during the MIGR.O.S (MIGRation Open Source) project that aims to transform legacy systems into modern Web Information Systems.

Introduction

In the last 20 years, there was a wide use of ICT for the business organization, both for public and private administration. With the coming of networking and web, a lot of Information Systems went in crisis since they was unable to support the features of the new models of development needed to remain competitive on the market. Information Systems, that are often characterized by proprietary solutions developed ad-hoc, required enormous resources for their accomplishment and they continue to be an important voice of costs because of the evolutionary maintenance (normative adaptations, extension of functionalities).

The entire reengineering/migration toward more modern solution (technological, platforms, architectures and so on) is an expensive process because of their

[*] Department of Engineering Innovation, University of Salento, Lecce, Italy, annalisa.guido@unisalento.it

[†] Department of Engineering Innovation, University of Salento, Lecce, Italy, roberto.paiano@unisalento.it

[‡] Department of Engineering Innovation, University of Salento, Lecce, Italy, andrea.pandurino@unisalento.it

[π] Department of Engineering Innovation, University of Salento, Lecce, Italy, luca.mainetti@unisalento.it

A. D'Atri et al. (eds.), *Management of the Interconnected World*,
DOI 10.1007/978-3-7908-2404-9_46, © Springer-Verlag Berlin Heidelberg 2010

size, obsolescence of code, lack of documentation; therefore, rather than to carry out a substitution of such systems, the companies prefer to invest a considerable part of their annual budget to evolve them even if were conceived, planned and developed using methodologies and technological standards very far from the actual ones. The systems of which the companies are provided, named Legacy System could be described [1–3]. From the usability point of view, the Legacy System were designed and realized to be used only by the employees, and they required to be used for a suitable period of training.

The migration approaches, could be of white-box type [4] or black-box type [5]. In the white-box approach, the modules are analyzed in detail to identify functionalities, structure and relations. When there is a large gap between old and new environment, the analysis of the existing modules could carry out just to the formalization of the requirements because the automatic or semi-automatic translation of code could be impossible for the deep difference between the environments. The black-box approach avoids the understanding of the inside structure of the system that is always subdivided in functional operating units, with a well defined interface according to the Object Oriented concepts. Such approach does not allow the evolution of the single functionalities that however remain tied to the use of defined interfaces and to their execution in the original environment than cannot going off. The best migration strategy depends on the dimension, on the environment, on the code documentation of the source application. In every way, in the most reengineering projects the Human Computer Interaction aspects are not considered. The projects are focused on the code migration with the goal of execute it on a more modern environment without take in care that the application quality provided to the final users is strictly connected with the usability of the migrated application.

In this paper, we present an innovative approach (still in phase of verification) for the reverse engineering that it is inspired to the approach of white box type and it uses different methodologies and technologies to support the migration of legacy software applications to the web environment. The proposed solution starts from the essential requirement that isn't enough to transpose a code from a language to another one or to use the Web software to encapsulate the legacy user interface in order to migrate from a legacy system towards a modern web application, that, instead, it is needed to make a true re-modulation and/or re-design of the knowledge embedded in the source system. In such way the migrated application will be technically advanced (because in a more modern technological environment), but also it will be more usable and effective, because aligned to the modern standard of human computer interaction. In other words, the main effort concerns about the re-design of the use of the information from the user and the effective way to navigate among the information. For this reason, the IDM (Interactive Dialogue Model) [6] methodology will be the design methodology for the target system.

In this paper, we present a reengineering path for legacy systems. In the next section we define the main problems to face in the reengineering approach and in the section "from legacy system to user-centered web application" we discuss about a possible solution that consider the introduction of the HCI problems in the reengineering path.

The Legacy System Transformation Problem

The migration problem of the legacy Information System is very complex and the complexity increase when the target is a web based system aligned with modern design and implementation techniques.

Until now, there are incomplete solutions that solve only some Reverse Engineering problems such as the definition of not used lines of code or the existence of relationships between the modules.

It is possible to classify these approaches [7] into the three operational modality defined by OMG (Object Management Group): (i) business architecture oriented to the re-design of the business process; (ii) Application & Data Architecture related to the business architecture implementation. It requires to analyze application and to make an automatic or semi-automatic porting (using appropriate tools) towards a more modern and technological environment. (iii) Technical Architecture it does not require to modify the software but only a change to the technological environment (server and infrastructure). Leaving out the approaches that involve the Business Architecture, other approaches (industrial and academics) are of type Application & Data Architecture and are oriented to a migration process that starts from the source code analysis and allows to execute the features of the source project into a new and modern environment. These approaches deal with the technological aspects of the system. The phase of the understanding the code is useful for the decomposition where the single migration units (MU) will be used for the following phase of coding.

The single MUs will be translated (automatically or manually), and they will be used in the target environment. The output of this migration process is a version aligned to the modern technological trends of the source system, and it uses the same interaction rules of the source system. Obviously, this isn't correct because the source system doesn't consider the new needs of the web paradigm. Another problem is that the old systems use a procedural logic (based on functionalities) so they don't consider the semantic aspects that allow to link different information objects between them (this is specific of a modern web system).

The limits of the approach are clearly evident when the target Information System is web based and so the semantic relationships and an efficient HCI approach is a key aspect of the target system.

From Legacy System to User-Centered Web Application

Starting from these requirements and from the lack of a unique approach coherent with the migration of legacy application, in this paper we present an approach to the migration of the legacy application that is designed specifically to consider not only the technological point of view (as in the state of the art), but also the conceptual one: the migrated application is not a simple translation into a modern environment of legacy code, but it is the output of a specific reengineering task in which the user interaction is re-designed. In the reengineering phase, specific methodologies designed to model the human computer interaction are used.

The proposed approach is based on migration phases proposed by Wu [8]:

- system comprehension,
- decomposition,
- migration management,
- encoding of the application in the target environment.

These phases are extended with new ones in order to consider expressly the human computer interaction aspects. In detail, two main aspects are taken into account: the extraction of the knowledge from the source applications through the use of the ontology and the intensive use of formal ontology in order to have an abstract description of the applications (source and target) independent of the development aspects. The approach is based on an abstract representation of source code obtained through the use of formal ontology. This description has the important advantage to be free from the technological aspects and, thus, allows to manage in the re-engineering process not the information as its is coded in the source application (text, table, ...) but the information extracted such as bank account (in bank applications).

The introduction of the intermediate ontological level allows to rethink the data of the source application in order to consider the semantic aspect. It is clear that the phase of source on one hand aim to understand the source technological architecture and on other one aims to recover the semantic links between the information domain object (lost during the coding of legacy application). The semantic link recover is obtained using a specific domain ontology (near to the ontology of source application) able to link together the several information objects.

On this bases, considering the methodological aspects related to the definition of the human computer interaction, the approach introduces in the last step of the reengineering the use of the Interactive Dialogue Model (IDM) methodology. It's clear that IDM model is a complete design of the target application based on the source application knowledge. This design takes in care the dialogue with the final user using the application information objects and not on the coded object of the legacy application.

The IDM methodology can be represented in ontological format and, thus, it is possible to have "machine-readable" models that could be used from prototyping tools to produce the target application.

The advantage to use the ontology language is, on the one hand the knowledge hidden in the source application, and on the other the model of the target application allows to make the conceptual migration using a suitable set of rules that allow to translate the model of the source application into the IDM model of the target application.

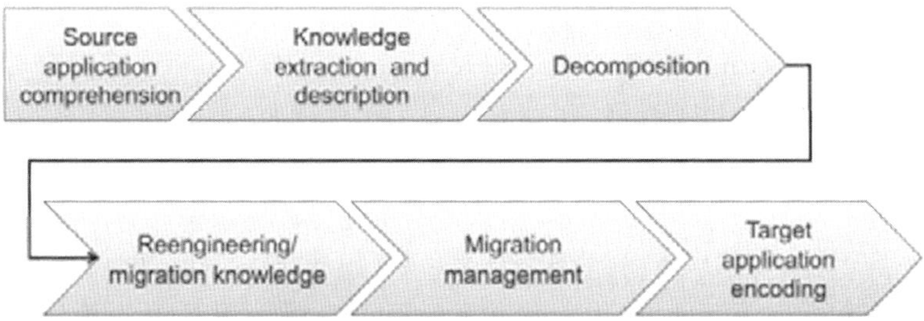

Fig. 1. Migration process of the MIGR.O.S. project

The idea here presented is the main goal of the MIGR.O.S project that aims to define a set of methodological and operative tools (framework) that can support the migration of legacy system to open source environment. The MIGR.O.S. migration process is shown in Fig. 1. In details:

- In the *comprehension* phase of the source system, the approach uses techniques and algorithms based on the solution available in the literature. In order to consider the knowledge, the preferred algorithms will be based on the domain analysis of the source application such as the variable's categorization [8] and the analysis of the variable types [9] This analysis describes not only the syntactic aspects of the source code but, if it is possible, supports the knowledge extraction phase.
- In the *knowledge extraction* and *description phases*, the application know-how will be modeled. In this phase, the specific domain ontology (near to the source application) is used to recover the semantic links between the coded information of the source application. The proposed approach, in fact, in a different way from the standard migration process in which the source code is migrated, has the aim to make the migration using the modeled knowledge that will be reengineered in user-centered point of view. The definition of semantic links improve considerably the quality of the decomposition phase; in fact, the MU are based not only on the technological aspects but also on the semantic one.
- In the *decomposition phase*, the sliding techniques widely used in the migration process will be adopted. Unlike the standard approach, this decomposition is based not only on the source code (using the modules relationships) but will

take advantage from the extracted knowledge too. The output phases are the migration units that, in the following phases, will be migrated.

- The *reengineering/migration* phase uses as input the MUs and will produce as output the MUs in the target environment. The migrated MUs will be described using the IDM methodology primitives. The IDM application model uses the semantic aspects defined in the knowledge extraction and description phases. In this step, the conceptual migration will be done and the focus is on the HCI aspects of the new Web Information Systems.
- The *migration management* phase uses the techniques defined in the standard approach because it is a classic project management.
- The *encoding phase* into the MIGR.O.S. project will be supported by a prototyping environment that uses.

The proposed solution has some innovative methodological aspects such as:

- The intensive use of the ontological language as an abstraction level to represent the source and target application and to describe the rules of migrating the legacy systems;
- The use of a domain specific ontology in order to recover the semantic links between the source information objects. The use of this ontology improves considerably the HCI aspect of the target application because the reengineering is based on the application information object and not on the coded objects of source;
- The knowledge extraction from the source application in order to describe its features and its know-how;
- The definition of a migration process that is standard, uniform and independent of the technological aspects.

Conclusions

The migration of the legacy systems through new systems more advanced from the technological point of view and more oriented to manage the human-machine interaction has been made, until today, using a code migration without to consider aspects oriented to obtain an high quality system in a special way when the target system is web-based: the HCI. In this paper we have presented a reengineering path that allows to obtain, starting from a legacy system, a modern web-based Information System where the human computer interaction is a key quality factor. To reach this goal we introduce in the reengineering path two main aspects: the introduction of formal ontology to capture the implicit knowledge of the legacy systems often complex to define and to store; the introduction in the reengineering path of a design methodology (IDM) specific for the design of the human-machine interaction.

Acknowledgments We would like to thank the Data Management SpA (the industrial partner of the project MIGR.O.S.) and Franco Di Ferrante, Angelo Rondine and Giuseppe Bava for the sharing of their experiences in the legacy system development.

References

1. Curtin DP, Foley K, Ken K, Morin C (2008) *Informatica di base*, McGraw Hill, New York
2. Batini C, Mecella M. (2001) Enabling Italian E-government through a cooperative architecture. In: Elmagarmio, W. J. Mccver Jr. (eds): special issue on digital government. *IEEE Computer,* 34(2):40–45
3. Batini C, Pernici B, Santucci G (2001) *Sistemi informativi vol. I, II, III, IV, V* Franco Angeli Editore, Milano
4. Mehta A, Heineman GT (2002) Evolving legacy system features into fine-grained components. In *Proceedings of the 24th international conference on software engineering* (pp. 417–427), 2002. ICSE 2002
5. Comella S, Wallnau K, Seacord RC, Robert J (2000) A survey of black-box modernization approaches for information systems software maintenance. In *Proceedings of the international conference on volume* (pp. 173–183)
6. Bolchini D et al (2005) IDM – a user-centred model shaping user interaction as a dialogue. In *Proceedings of the HCII 2005 international conference on human–computer interaction*, Las Vegas
7. Ulrich,W (2008) Architecturesssss-driven modernization: transforming the enterprise DRAFT V.5, (White paper) – http://www.omg.org/cgi-bin/apps/doc?admtf/07-12-01.pdf (2001). Accessed June 2008
8. Wu L, Sahraoui H, Valtchev P (2005) Coping with legacy system migration complexity. In *Proceedings of the 10th IEEE international conference on engineering of complex computer systems* (ICECCS 2005). (pp. 600–609)
9. van Deursen A, Moonen L (2000) Exploring legacy systems using types. In *Proceedings 7th working conference on reverse engineering* (pp. 32–41)

VALUTA: A Tool to Specify and Verify Interactive Visual Applications

Rosanna Cassino* **and Maurizio Tucci** †

Abstract This paper presents a system to specify and verify web applications, based on previous results on usability evaluation of interactive visual interfaces by means of checking their corresponding formal specification. In Cassino and Tucci we have described a methodology to design, specify and evaluate interactive visual interfaces, based on the SR-Action Grammars formalism, and we have presented a bottom – up approach to guide the designer to develop graphical user interface which respect any usability metrics before the software is released and tested by standard methods. TAGIVE (**T**ool for the **A**ided **G**eneration of **I**nteractive **V**isual **E**nvironments) is a visual environment for the implementation of interactive visual applications (html, xml, java applications), and for the generation of the underlying SR-Action Grammar specification. Now, we present **VALUTA** (**A**utomatic **T**ool for the **U**sability **V**erification at **A**bstraction **L**evel), a tool that supports the generation of the formal specification of existing interactive visual applications in an automatic manner, so to perform the related usability controls. Checking the usability of interactive applications at a formal level, allows a designer to perform feedback analysis of the environment under consideration.

Introduction

The evaluation of interactive visual environments is traditionally performed by means of expert-based evaluations or by testing with end users. Formal specification methods are recognized to provide a valuable aid in the design of components of a system, such as command languages and data-entry sequences. This is also true when dealing with visual interactive systems, for which user-interface architects, designers, managers, and software engineers can profitably exploit the abstraction models underlying the interactive components, to analyze the design, and to manage possible problems of the system in advance.

---

* Dipartimento di Matematica e Informatica, Università di Salerno, Salerno, Italy, rcassino@unisa.it
† Dipartimento di Matematica e Informatica, Università di Salerno Salerno, Italy, mtucci@unisa.it

A. D'Atri et al. (eds.), *Management of the Interconnected World*,
DOI 10.1007/978-3-7908-2404-9_47, © Springer-Verlag Berlin Heidelberg 2010

In the literature several formal models have been proposed in order to describe graphical applications at various abstraction levels, as well as to formally represent human computer interaction properties [1].

Grammar formalisms have been extensively used to specify visual representations adopted during software development, as well as in the construction of visual language compilers. In general, grammar formalisms for diagrammatic language specification extend traditional string grammars in that they rewrite sets or multisets of symbols rather than sequences, and specify several relationships between objects rather than the concatenation relationship only [2, 3]. An example of formal approach to the specification of diagrammatic languages is represented by graph grammar models [4–6]. A graph structure underlies traditional graphical formalisms, ranging from dataflow diagrams, to flow graphs, to Petri nets, to state charts, to class diagrams, etc. So, the use of graph grammars has often been considered a natural choice for their specification. Moreover, graph grammar principles have been widely adopted as a basis for the generation of visual environments [7–9]. Close to grammar-based approaches, are the formal specification methods based on rewriting systems [10]. An example of such approach is Chistoph's rule-based design transformation framework GREAT, which relies on a graph rewriting system and can be used to describe in a formal way static aspects of design (e.g., expressed in terms of UML class diagrams), and generate code from aspect descriptions [11].

The formalism proposed in [10] is based on the notion of dynamic visual language, defined as a weakly ordered set of visual sentences characterized by the presence of common elements. The interactive process characterizing a dynamic visual language is modelled at a low abstraction level, in terms of any image which composes a sentence. The production of visual sentences during an interaction is formalized as a rewriting process, which allow the incremental production of visual sentences respecting some specific order. However, the effective use of the proposed rewriting systems for the generation of visual interactive languages is still subject to designer's familiarity with those formalisms.

In a previous work, we have proposed the SR-Action Grammars [12] to develop formal specification of interactive visual application suitable for automatic or semi-automatic usability analysis. In this work we present an effective tool, VALUTA, that we have implemented to generate the formal specification of a visual interface and to perform several usability controls by means of the analysis of the grammar, in an automatic manner. The VALUTA tool works in a top-down approach, in the sense that takes in input web application, generates the related formal specification and performs the particular usability controls. In this perspective, we have slightly modified the proposed methodology so to allow formal specification analysis at an abstract level. In this paper we show the effectiveness of this approach by implementing the automatic verification of web applications with respect to a subset of the Nielsen heuristics: completeness, correctness, aesthetic and minimalist design, user control, consistency, metrics desirable in an interactive visual interface.

The paper is organized as follow. In section "Formal Evaluation of Usability" we present the implemented usability formal evaluation: the process of obtaining a formal specification of an interactive system by means of a SR-Action Grammar, and how the specification is used for performing usability checks of the specified environment. In section "The VALUTA Tool" we present **VALUTA** (**A**utomatic **T**ool for the **U**sability **V**erification at **A**bstraction **L**evel), the implemented tool to generate the formal specification of the visual interface to evaluate and to achieve the usability controls at a formal level. Section 4 presents some conclusions and final remarks.

Formal Evaluation of Usability

In this section, we describe an algorithmic process to perform usability controls of an existing visual application, based on the analysis of the corresponding SR-Action grammar. In particular, we concentrate on a subset of the Nielsen heuristics [13]: completeness, correctness, aesthetic and minimalist design, user control, consistency and we describe how it is possible to evaluate each property by the analysis of non terminal and terminal symbols, the set of the actions and the productions rules of the corresponding grammar.

From an evaluable point of view the *correctness* property corresponds to the frames or pages not achievable in the application; the *completeness* can be evaluated in terms of the page or scene provided in the application but never implemented; the *aesthetic and minimalist design* can be evaluated in terms of the number of scenes recalled in the application or by the complexity of the actions to perform a task, or in terms of the widgets present in each scene; the *error prevention, user control and freedom* properties correspond to the presence of an entry point scene in the application and to the number of the tasks to back return and the number of the tasks to return at the start scene; the *consistency*, defined also as *recognition rather than recall* usability property can be evaluated in terms of the check of the presence of a text linked to each icon which identifies a component and then, the check of the location of connected elements in a scenes (e.g., an icon and the related label).

Taking a visual application (in particular web interfaces) as an input, we generate the related formal specification in terms of SR-Action Grammar following an approach proposed in [12]. In particular, the derivation process consists in the generation of:

1. the set of the non terminal symbols V_N, standing for the frames of the pages of the interface (the application scenes): $V_N = \{Scene_1, \ldots, Scene_n\}$;
2. the set of the terminal symbols V_T, considering the external components callbacks from the application (.pdf, wave, movie, pictures, txt files, ecc…): $V_T = \{File_1, \ldots, File_m\}$;
3. the start symbol S (the initial scene of the interface);
4. the set of the actions related to each dynamic object in the scenes of the application: $\Delta = \Delta_1, \ldots, \Delta_q$ where $\Delta_i = \{\delta 1_{Scenej}, \ldots, \delta k_{Scenej}\}$, for i, j > 0, is the set of the actions outgoing from the non terminal symbol S_i.

At this specification level the performed controls are related to:

c1.1 the number of non terminal symbols – a large number corresponds to an excessive amount of scenes in the application that might confuse the end user. This control allows to manage *aesthetic and minimalist design problems.*

c3.1 The start symbol indicates the presence of the home page of a web application or of an entry point of the application to test – if this not exist, it is breached the usability principle of the *user control*.

c4.1 The type and the number of actions performed from any scene of the application – a large number of *single_left_click*, *single_right_click* or *double_click* may confuse the end user, violating the *aesthetic and minimalist design usability metric*.

From each non-terminal symbol, we derive the formal specification of any scene of the application [2]. For any implemented scene a production rule is generated as follows:

5. $<\mathbf{M},\mathbf{R},\alpha_{\mathbf{M}}> = <\{X^{1,b1},\ldots,X^{n,bn}\}, \{r_1(Y_1,Z_1),\ldots,r_m(Y_m,Z_m)\}, \{\alpha(X^{1,b1}),\ldots,\alpha(X^{n,bn})\}>$

Analyzing this specification it is possible to perform the usability checks described below.

c5.1 At first, if a scene is not implemented, but only named in the application (for example inside of a link) it is not possible to derive the related formal specification, then this indicates *incompleteness* problems. Otherwise:

c5.2 from the subset **M** of symbol occurrences it is possible to check the type and the number of elementary components in a scene – a large number of buttons or labels makes the application unreasonably complex. In this way it is possible to manage problems of *aesthetic and minimalist design.*

c5.3 From the set of the relational items it is possible to verify if a particular component is arranged correctly in relation to another (an image icon to the related label, for example), or if two element are overlapped so to confuse the end user. In this way it is possible to manage any *consistency* problems.

c5.4 The set of the function $\alpha(X^{j,bj})$ allow to check the type and the number of action linked to each dynamic symbol occurrence of a scene. This allows to manage non deterministic problems if two type of actions are linked to the same component.

For each dynamic element in the specified scene, the action-rule and the related r-productions are generated as follows:

$$l\!: \ \delta.Y^{0,1} \rightarrow S_i \text{ where } S_i \in V_N \cup V_T$$

Analyzing the right-hand side of the production we can perform the following usability controls:

c6.1 in the specified scene (except the initial scene) there should be at least one dynamic element $Y^{0,1}$ where S_i corresponds to the start symbol S – if not, the *user control* usability metric is violated;

c6.2 for all the specified scenes there should be at least one action rule where $S_i \in V_N$, *for each* $0 \leq i \leq N$ *– otherwise incorrectness problems are reported. This means that there is a scene in the application unreachable by any part of the interface.*

c6.3 The user control usability metric is managed by the presence of an undo function, so to allow an end user to cancel a task and to return back to the previous scene. This is verified if among the action rules there is one in which the right-hand side is equal to $\varnothing$ *or* S_{i-1}, *where* $Y^{0,1} \in S_{i-1}$.

c6.4. The type and the number of terminal symbols in the right-hand side of the r-productions allow to check the amount of times an external file is called from the application: if the same files are called many times, the performances of the interface may be affected and non-optimized problems may arise.

The VALUTA Tool

The proposed methodology is supported by the VALUTA environment (**A**utomatic **T**ool for the **U**sability **V**erification at **A**bstraction **L**evel**)**. The implemented system allows a designer to perform a set of usability checks of interactive visual interfaces in an automatic manner. Figure 1 shows the VALUTA architecture.

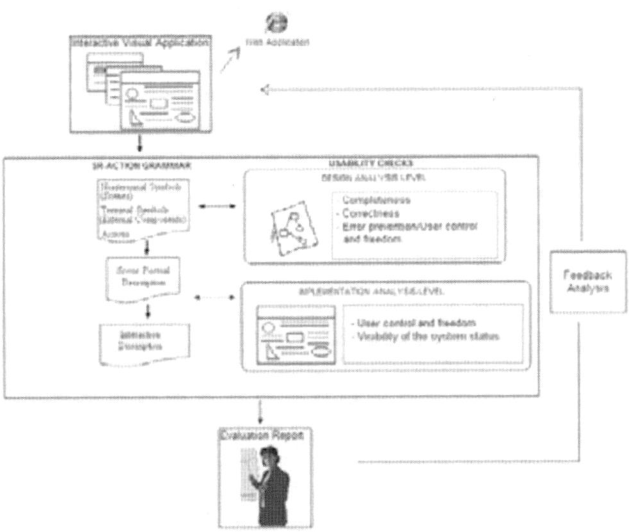

Fig. 1. The VALUTA architecture

The idea underlying VALUTA is to take in input a visual application, generate the related formal specification in terms of SR-Action Grammar and perform usability checks on the generated grammar. The current implementation of the tool is able to evaluate web applications. Then, the designer fills in the url address of the interesting site and the system generates the non terminal symbols, the terminal symbols and the set of the actions by an html parser (see Fig. 2).

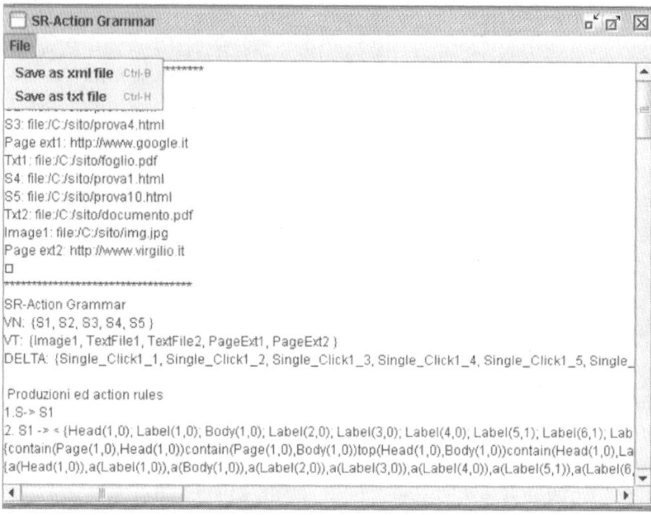

Fig. 2. The generated grammar

This phase corresponds to the design analysis level where the controls c1.1, c.3.1, c4.1 (described in the previous section) are performed. The c.1.1 and c4.1 controls are performed on the base of the parameters (the number of the pages and the actions permitted for the particular examined web application) which the designer can customize modifying the tool options. However, the system proposes any default values.

From any page the formal description of the scene and the interaction description is generated. To this level the c5.1, c5.2, c5.3, c5.4, c.6.1, c.6.2, c6.3, c6.4 (described in the previous section) are performed.

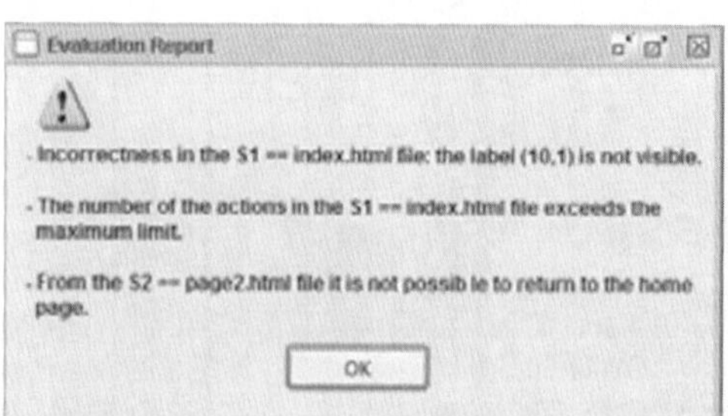

Fig. 3. The evaluation report

The result of the evaluation is a report that shows all the usability problems found (see Fig. 3). Based on the "Evaluation Report" the designer can perform feedback analysis of the application and redesign the interface consequently.

The tool works in a transparent manner to the analyzer, meaning that he/she can choose to see the generated SR-Action grammar or just the result of the usability controls. VALUTA has been tested to evaluate html applications and it is implemented in Java by the Model-View-Controller (MVC) architecture. The automatic generation of the grammar is implemented by the HTMLParser library. It has allowed to analyze the html of web pages in linear and nested manner. As a matter of fact, the parser takes in input a web page and identifies all the present links: if the target of the link is a new web page of the analyzed site, it will repeat the procedure recursively, otherwise it will examine the linked object. Then, the input of the parser is the index.html file (the home page of the web site), which corresponds to the start symbol S of the grammar. All the target elements of the link outgoing from S and corresponding to the other page of the web application, allow to define the non terminal symbols of the grammar V_N, all the target components as mailto, txt files, url of external web site, images, JavaScript, ecc…) define the terminal symbols V_T. For each non terminal symbol, the set of the actions Δ is generated inserting the number of the "single left clicks" related to the links present in the analysed web page.

Conclusions

In this paper we have described how the formal specification of an interactive visual application in terms of the SR-Action grammar can be used to perform automatic usability controls of a user interface. We have presented the VALUTA tool, that has been implemented to allows for the generation of a formal specification and to perform usability verification of an interactive application.

We have tested the system to evaluate html applications. By the implemented tool we have shown its effectiveness by verifying a subset of the Nielsen heuristics: completeness, correctness, aesthetic and minimalist design, user control, consistency in automatic manner at an high abstraction level of analysis. This implies that usability checks can be performed earlier than other canonical testing techniques. One of the major limitations of manual user testing is that the situation created for the observation can never be equivalent to an actual situation of use. Motivations, attitudes, predisposition respect to the application changes radically if the user is observed in a "test" or is under "natural" condition. Moreover, while the costs are clear from the outset, the benefits appear more nebulous and more difficult to assess, especially for an increasingly careful management to the profitability of investments in the short or very short term.

Further work will address the extension of the proposed technique to test XML, VRML, and Java applications.

References

1. Ferrucci F, Tortora G, Vitiello G (2000) Visual programming. In Marciniak JJ (ed) *Encyclopaedia of software engineering*, 2nd edn. Wiley, New York
2. Costagliola G, De Lucia A, Orefice S, Tortora G (1995) Automatic generation of visual programming environments. *IEEE Comput* 28(3):56–66
3. Della Penna G, Intrigila B, Orefice S (2001) Generating graphical applications from state-transition visual specifications. *Int J Human Comput Stud* 55:861–880
4. Bottoni P, Taentzer G, Schurr A (2000) Efficient parsing of visual languages based on critical pair analysis and contextual layered graph transformation. In *Proceedings of the 2000 IEEE International Symposium on visual languages*, pp 59–60
5. Minas M (1997) Diagram editing with hypergraph parser support. In *Proceedings of the 13th IEEE symposium on visual languages*, Capri, Italy, pp 226–233
6. Rekers J, Schürr A (1997) Defining and parsing visual languages with layered graph grammars. *J Visual Lang Comput* 8:27–55
7. Bardohl R, Minas M, Schürr A, Taentzer G (1998) Application of graph transformation to visual languages. In Rozenberg G (ed) *Handbook on graph grammars: applications*, vol 2. World Scientific, Singapore, pp 105–180
8. Ferrucci F, Tortora G, Tucci M, Vitiello G (2001) A system for rapid prototyping of visual language environments. In *Proceedings of the IEEE symposia on human-centric computing languages and environments (HCC'01)*, September 2001, pp 382–389
9. Minas M (2002) Specifying graph-like diagrams with dia gen. *Electron Notes Theor Comput Sci* 72(2):102–111
10. Bottoni P, Chang SK, Costabile MF, Levialdi S, Mussio P (2002) Modelling visual interactive systems through dynamic visual languages. *Syst Man Cybern A IEEE Trans* 32(6):654–669
11. Christoph A (2003) Design aspect and GRS-based AOD the GREAT transformation framework. *Electron Notes Theor Comput Sci* 82(5)
12. Cassino R, Tucci M (2009) Checking the consistency, completeness and usability of interactive visual applications by means of SR-action grammars. Springer book – In D'Atri A, Saccà D (eds) *Information systems: people, organizations, institutions, and technologies.* Physica-Verlag, Berlin Heidelberg
13. Nielsen J (1994b) Heuristic evaluation. In Nielsen J, Mack RL (eds) *Usability inspection methods.* Wiley, New York

Dynamic User Modeling for Personalized Advertisement Delivery on Mobile Devices

Luca Paolino*, Monica Sebillo†, Genoveffa Tortora‡, Giuliana Vitiello$^{\pi}$, Alessandro M. Martellone§, and David Tacconi#

Abstract With the advent of broadband connections, the Internet service providers have begun to charge users with fees in order to cover the higher infrastructural costs due to the management/rental of broadband networks. However, the user is often left the chance for a free Internet connection, provided that he/she accepts to be invaded by banner ads, which arbitrarily, in terms of time and position, appear on the screen. In order to make effective the latter, the Internet service providers have been studying the most appropriate advertisement (*ad*, for short) supply policy, in order to satisfy companies who wish to advertise their products without annoying the user while he/she is interacting with the service. In this paper we present an approach for the presentation of personalized *ad*s on mobile devices, which is based on a user model that takes into account user's interests over time. The approach has been adopted within the LUNA wireless network project, which is targeted at realizing a business model such that the services provided in the area of Trento, in the North of Italy, are accessible and usable by everybody, at a very low cost.

The Issue of Advertising in Ubiquitous Environments

The online advertising market has experienced a rapid growth in the last years thanks to a broader diffusion of the Internet among citizens in the areas of Americas, Europe and Asia and in general all around the world. According to [1] , the Internet usage growth from year 2000 to 2008 is around 300%, with a worldwide population penetration of 21.9%, a data that reaches 73.6% in North America and 48.6% in Europe.

In the 2007 the European online advertising market was worth €11.2 billion, with a growth rate of 40% compared to 2006 and with a gap on the US of only €3.5 billion.

---

* DMI, Università di Salerno, Salerno, Italy, lpaolino@unisa.it

† DMI, Università di Salerno, Salerno, Italy, msebillo@unisa.it

‡ DMI, Università di Salerno, Salerno, Italy, tortora@unisa.it

π DMI, Università di Salerno, Salerno, Italy, gvitiello@unisa.it

§ Futur3 srl, via A. Abondi 37, 38100, Trento, Italy, a.martellone@futur3.it

Futur3 srl, via A. Abondi 37, 38100, Trento, Italy, d.tacconi@futur3.it

A. D'Atri et al. (eds.), *Management of the Interconnected World*,
DOI 10.1007/978-3-7908-2404-9_48,

The Europe association Interactive Advertising Bureau (IAB) [2] have created a measure “Spend per user” to illustrate how much European advertisers spend for one Internet user. As illustrated in Fig. 1, the European average is at €80.6 respect to 91.9 invested by American advertiser. In Europe, the trend is highly different, namely only Norway, UK and Denmark overcome US, whereas Finland, France, Austria and Italy invested much less.

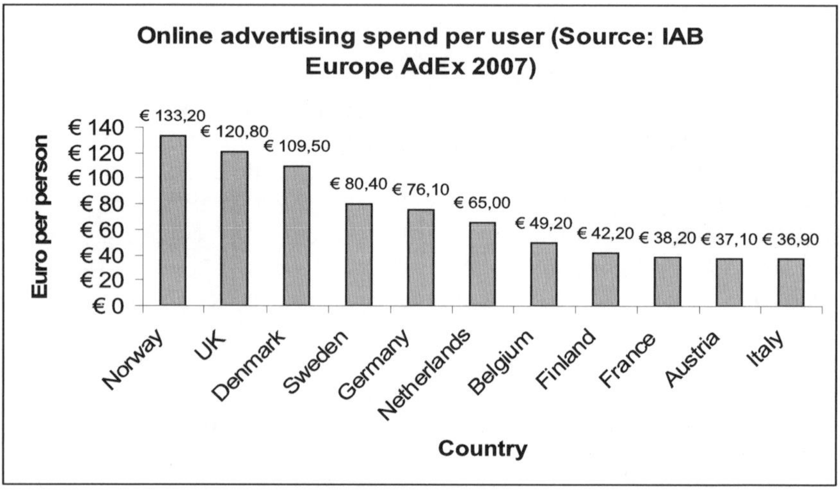

Fig. 1. Online advertising spend per user

In this context, an emerging access to the Internet by mobile devices can be observed, stimulated by a trend that creates new opportunities for brands to reach consumers in a new manner.

With respect to conventional advertising, online advertising has a promising advantage that is pushing the market to a non stop growth, namely the measurability. Whenever an *ad* is published on the web, several parameters can be measured, such as how many times a page with the *ad* has been seen, how many users have clicked on a suggested link with respect to those that have visited the page, how long a user has been watching a commercial video on the web. Obviously, there are several forms of online advertising and for each of them a proper measure exists.

Currently, online advertising formats are defined by the IAB with the goal of reducing and simplifying the amount of advertising formats [3].

Banner is the most common form of advertising on the Internet. A banner is typically a rectangular image with size ranging among the following (all dimensions are in pixels): 300×250, 250×250, 240×400, 300×100, 720×300, 468×60 (full banner), 120×240, 728×90 (leaderboard), 160×600 (wide skyscraper). The banner is usually designed to capture the viewer’s attention and leads her/him to the advertisers web page. Banners can be realized with moving images, sounds and videos or even games, known as “rich media advertisements.”

Recently, the impact and revenues of the web advertising forms on the market has been deeply investigated. A research conducted by DoubleClick [4] is based on hundreds of advertisers, thousands of campaigns and ten billion opinions about *ads*. The following metrics have been used:

- the interaction rate which is the ratio of ad interactions to the number of ad opinions;
- the average interaction time, which corresponds to the average amount of time in seconds, that a user interacts with an ad;
- the average expanding time which is the average amount of time in seconds, that an ad is viewed in an expanded state. It is proven that the rate improves when the ad is shown as a video;
- the video complete rate which is calculated by counting the number of times a video has been played to its completion.

Interactions is counted when the user performs one of the following actions:

- clicks an exit link,
- makes the ad display in Full Screen mode,
- mouse over the ad for 1 continuous second.

The Mobile Advertising World

According to [5], 60% of mobile users considers the mobile Internet access as "important" or "very important". The importance of being able to access the mobile Internet decreases with age. Younger participants (<44 years old) are more likely to consider mobile Internet access as "very important"/ "important". Participants are most likely to claim that they use the mobile Internet for functional activities (e.g. "Checking information" 45%), for communication purposes ("Sending/receiving emails", 38%) and for entertainment features ("browsing for fun/entertainment", 27%).

Following these numbers, mobile advertising is a rapidly growing sector providing brands, agencies and marketers with the opportunity to connect with consumers beyond traditional and digital media and directly on their mobile phones.

The mobile phone is an extremely personal device and this makes it a precisely targeted communication channel, improving the effectiveness of advertising campaign.

When designing a mobile advertising campaign, it is important to remember to provide a non-intrusive consumer experience and to ensure that *ads* are effectively displayed on the majority of mobile phones, without compatibility problems.
The recommended *ad* units for mobile web are defined as follows:

- Mobile Web banner ad is the default colour graphics ad type (animated banner are also available)

- Text ad is displayed instead of an image. It may be used in conjunction with a graphical banner.

The recommended aspect ratio for *ads* are 6:1 (default) and 4:1(extended) [6]. Table 1 describes sizes typically used for mobile web banner.

Table 1. Mobile web banner *ad* sizes

Total banner dimension	120	166	216	300
Max weight for basic static banners	1 kb	2 kb	3 kb	5 kb
Max weight for enhanced banners	1.5 kb	3 kb	4.6 kb	7.5 kb

A Dynamic User Model for Personalized *Ads* Delivery

The *ads* available for the publication on the mobile device through the LUNA system are chosen or discarded by associating them with a rank value which both takes into account long-term as well as short-term user interests, and periodically verifies if the dynamically updated ranks satisfy a specific *pleasure* threshold.

In this section we describe the dynamic user model adopted in LUNA *Ads* Management module, and explain how long-term and short-terms interests are computed and then combined to derive a user-oriented rank.

Long-Term User Interest Frameworks

Long-terms user interests are modeled with respect to two reference frameworks. The former is based on a classification of the domains and the latter is based on *ad* contents mapped onto user's general interests.

As for the first framework, when building a user profile, the system stores for each domain, the score the user assigns to each of its derived subcategories. For our purpose, we considered the classification of 35 product categories adopted by the *ebay©* platform. As an example, the domain *car* has the item subcategories sportive, limousine, city car, etc. When a user initially registers to the LUNA services, s/he is asked to assign a score $S_{CAT}(u)$ to each general categories *CAT*, and a score $S_{Ci}(u_j)$, to each of its subcategories.

For every domain, information concerning scores assigned by user to specific item subcategories are stored as a matrix, where rows correspond to the subcategories and columns corresponds to users (see Fig. 2).

CAT	u_1	...	u_m
C_1	val_{11}	...	val_{1m}
...	...	...	...
C_n	val_{n1}	...	val_{nm}

Fig. 2 User specified scores for CAT item subcategories

As each *ad* has a pre-assigned sub-category, selection with respect to this reference framework is immediate. Each *ad a* is assigned the score associated with the corresponding specific category in the corresponding user profile. Thus, the relevance of the *ad a* for a user profile *u*, classified as belonging to subcategory C_i, corresponds to the score assigned to C_i by the user *u*. Namely:

$$Rel_u(a) = S_{Ci}(u). \qquad (1)$$

A similarity value *sim*(*a, CAT*) is then computed between the *ad a* and the general category *CAT* to which C_i belongs, by exploiting the cosine similarity formula for the vector space model [1].

Consequently, the relevance between an *ad a* and all the general categories of a user model *u* is computed using the next formula:

$$REL_u(a) = \frac{\sum_{i=1}^{35} sim(a, CAT_i) S_{CAT}(u)}{\sum_{i=1}^{35} S_{CAT}(u)} \qquad (2)$$

The second reference framework for long-term interests further specializes user's profile It is based on a set of user-specified keywords, which are weighted on the basis of their relevance for the user. For each user, these keywords are stored as a term weight vector (k_u), as illustrated in Fig. 3.

k_u	k_1	...	k_t
U	k_{1u}		k_{tu}

Fig. 3. User specified scores for keywords

Again, the relevance between the *ad* and the keywords of a user model is given by the similarity cosine of the vector space model:

$$rel_{ku}(a) = sim\ (a, k_u). \qquad (3)$$

Thus, the long-term interest *LT*(*u,a*) of a user *u* in a given *ad a* can be computed by combining formulas (1) and (3) as follows:

$$LT(u,a) = \frac{w_1 rel_u(a) + w_2 REL_u(a) + w_3 rel_{Ku}(a)}{w_1 + w_2 + w_3},$$

where w_1, w_2, w_3 are the weights representing the importance assigned to the three relevance measures, referred to the specific category, to the general category and to user's keywords, respectively.

The value calculated on the basis of the long-term user interests is successively updated by combining it with a short-term rank which is based on the feedback the user provides during the navigation.

Short-Term User Interest Framework

Short-term interests are represented by means of feedback terms. Such terms are obtained from the user-provided feedback over the web documents s/he receives while browsing. That is to say, the user provides positive or negative feedback (*f*) over the document, and a set of representative terms is extracted from them. These information are processed and the resulting value is a term weight vector (*t*). By fixing a *p* value, representing the number of the last web documents which should be considered for the short-term value, we define:

$$r_{ad} = sim(a, t_d),$$

as the similarity degree between an advertisement *a* and the web document *d*, and:

$$r^t_{au} = \frac{\sum_{i=1}^{p} f_i r_{ad_i}}{p}$$

The r^t_a value is used to represent the current short-term interests of that user. Short-terms interests tend to correspond to temporary information needs whose interest for the user vanishes after the connection session.

Another value which has been considered crucial to determine the short-term interest of the LUNA user model is the location where the user is at the time the *ad* should be delivered. As a matter of fact, it seems reasonable that *ads* related to easily achievable places may be more interesting with respect to those far away. For this reason, we decide to involve the proximity value calculated as the inverse of the distance between the current position and the closest location where the advertised product could be purchased (see Fig. 4).

Thus, the short-term interest *ST*(*u*,*a*) of a user *u* for a given *ad a* can be computed as the sum of r^t_{au} and the corresponding proximity value *pv*(*a*,*u*).

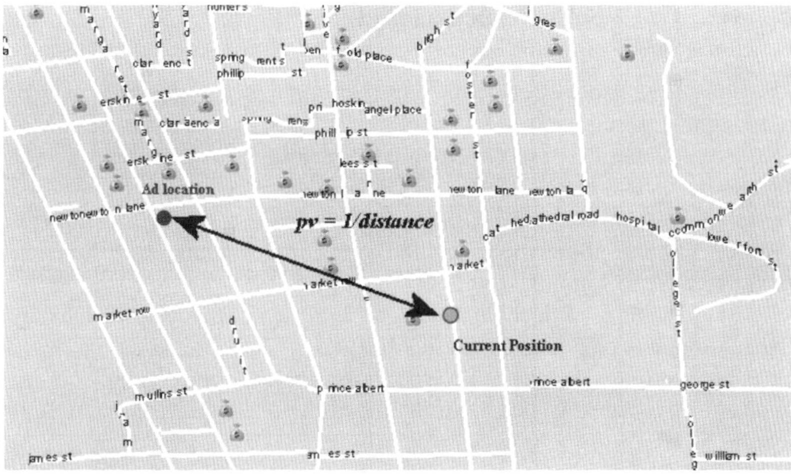

Fig. 4. User's proximity value wrt an *ad*

By combining long-term and short-term interests, the total relevance between an *ad* a and a user model u is computed by the following formula:

$$Int(u,a) = \frac{w_1 rel_u(a) + w_2 REL_u(a) + w_3 rel_{Ku}(a) + w_4 ST(u,a)}{w_1 + w_2 + w_3 + w_4},$$

where w_4 is the weight representing the importance given to the short-term interest in the given user model.

Conclusion and Future Work

In this paper we have faced the issue of establishing an adequate thread-off between the requirements elicited from advertising companies and the degree to which a user may accept to be bothered while performing some tasks. In the specific case of a wireless service network explicitly conceived to reduce access costs by means of adverts delivery, we have proposed a dynamic user modeling technique that may effectively support personalized *ad* delivery, within an ubiquitous interaction style. In the future, we plan to perform experimental studies meant to validate and properly calibrate the proposed approach. We will exploit a specific usability testing equipment that has recently enriched the HCI laboratory of the Department of Mathematics and Computer Science, where some of the authors work. The equipment includes different samples of ubiquitous devices (including an Apple i-phone), and an advanced eye tracking system, that will allow us to derive reliable data from the experiments we will perform by involving a meaningful sample of LUNA users population.

Appendix: The Vector Space Model

The Vector space model (or term vector model) is an algebraic model for representing text documents (and any objects, in general) as vectors of identifiers, such as, index terms. It is used in information filtering, information retrieval, indexing and relevancy rankings. A document is represented as a vector, where each dimension corresponds to a separate term. If a term occurs in the document, its value in the vector is non-zero. Several different ways of computing these values, also known as (term) weights, have been developed.

Relevancy rankings of documents in a keyword search can be calculated by using the assumptions of document similarities theory and comparing the deviation of angles between each document vector and the original query vector.
In practice, it is easier to calculate the cosine of the angle between the vectors instead of the angle:

$$\cos\theta = \frac{\mathbf{v_1} \cdot \mathbf{v_2}}{\|\mathbf{v_1}\| \, \|\mathbf{v_2}\|}$$

A zero cosine value means that the query and the document vector are orthogonal and do not match (i.e. the query term do not exist in the document being considered).

References

1. Internet world statistics http://www.internetworldstats.com/stats.htm
2. "Online advertising in Europe surges 40% to €11 billion in 2007", Available at http://www.iabeurope.eu/
3. IAB Ad Unit Guidelines http://www.iab.net/iab_products_and_industry_services/1421/1443/1452
4. DoubleClick, http://www.doubleclick.com/, "Creative insights on rich media", September 2008
5. Mobile Internet usage and attitudes study, dotMoby & AKQA, May 2008
6. Mobile marketing association (MMA), "Mobile advertising guidelines", October 2008

Part IX
Emerging Issues in a Globalized and Interconnected World

Cecilia Rossignoli*[*] and Daniela Baglieri[†]

Due to the rapidly increasing speed of technological changes, the world is becoming more and more globalized and interconnected. Firms can no longer rely on internal technology development. Under these circumstances, they need to widen their approach in order to exploit technological and business opportunities emerging in the globalized and interconnected world [1–3] coined the term "open innovation" to describe the manner in which large companies combine externally and internally developed technologies in a flexible way to develop new businesses.

Therefore, a systematic scanning of the available technologies and ideas inside the company as well as within the current environment, for example technology and market scouting, consultants, customers, exhibitions, universities, patent inspection etc., is becoming a strategically important activity, due to the increasing technological complexity of products and the business opportunities related to emerging technologies.

Another stream of product innovation literature emphasizes the role of lead users in developing technology [4, 5]. In this vein, we underlined a deeper understanding about the role of emerging communities of users which can be identified as lead users or as user innovators. These communities can be involved in the design process and the development of toolkits to support the design, innovation and production processes of user capabilities.

In this track, we collected papers which address the ongoing debate around the multiple interconnections between organizations and technologies which encourage innovation.

The first deals with how to manage co-opetitive actors in open innovation. This paper analyzes information platforms like e-Bay which allow actors to adopt new forms of collaborations.

The second investigates the theme of the role of ICT in clinical risk management, highlighting the critical points associated with the utilization of procedures in clinical healthcare institutions.

The third analyzes the cross-level antecedents of dynamic capabilities development. The contribution focuses on network exploitation capability.

[*] Università degli Studi di Verona, Verona, Italy, cecilia.rossignoli@univr.it

[†] Università degli Studi di Messina, Messina, Italy, dbaglieri@unime.it

The fourth explores the subject of information system and service research. The authors conduct a review of the literature in the field of Information System and service research.

References

1. Chesbrough H (2003) *Open innovation: the new imperative for creating and profiting from technology.* Harvard Business School Press, Boston
2. Chesbrough HW (2007) Why companies should have open business models. *Mit Sloan Manage Rev* 48(2):22–28
3. Chesbrough HW, Vanhaverbeke W, West J (2006) *Open innovation: researching a new paradigm.* Oxford University Press, Oxford and New York
4. Baldwin CY, Hienerth C, von Hippel E (2006) How user innovations become commercial products: a theoretical investigation and case study. *Res Policy* 35(9):1291–1313
5. von Hippel E, von Krogh G (2003) Open source software and the "private-collective" innovation model: issues for organization science. *Organ Sci* 14(2):209–223

Respecting the Deal: How to Manage Co-opetitive Actors in Open Innovation

Riccardo Bonazzi*, Lotfi Hussami†, Pius Bienz‡, and Yves Pigneur^Π

Abstract Platforms like E-bay allow product seekers and providers to meet and exchange goods. On the same way in open innovation, as defined by Chesbrough, an enterprise can collect ideas from outside the company. But on E-bay, the seeker can return the product if it does not correspond to the expectations, since E-bay is the third-party actor in charge of assuring that the agreement between seekers and providers will be respected. So who does provide the same service for what concerns open innovation, where specifications might not fully defined? In this paper we shall describe the business model of an organizational structure to support the elicitation and respect of agreements between actors, who have conflicting interests but that gain from cooperating together. The concepts of the model will be illustrated to derive a set of propositions and a simple example will illustrate one of its possible instantiations. The description of our first evaluation phase shall find place at the end.

Introduction: Problem Identification

In this paper we deal with co-opetition in open innovation. According to Brandenburger and Nalebuff [1] a **co-opetition game** can be defined by means of five components, i.e. Players, Added Values, Rules, Tactics and Scope.

On what concern the **players,** one can refer to the adaptation of Michael Porter's five forces made by Branderburger and Nalebuff [1]:30 to quote the four key roles that relate to the main actor: customers, suppliers, complementors and competitors. The authors list a set of strategies to motivate new players to enter the

* Faculty of Business and Economics, Information Systems Institute, University of Lausanne, Lausanne, Switzerland, riccardo.bonazzi@unil.ch

† Faculty of Business and Economics, Information Systems Institute, University of Lausanne, Lausanne, Switzerland, lotfi.hussami@unil.ch

‡ Faculty of Business and Economics, Information Systems Institute, University of Lausanne, Lausanne, Switzerland, pius.bienz@unil.ch

Π Faculty of Business and Economics, Information Systems Institute, University of Lausanne, Lausanne, Switzerland, yves.pigneur@unil.ch

A. D'Atri et al. (eds.), *Management of the Interconnected World*,
DOI 10.1007/978-3-7908-2404-9_49,

game, and West and Gallegher [2] refers to expectancy theory to suggest the reasons that push enterprise to contribute in open source software developments.

The assessment of the **added values** of actors raises two issues: how to calculate such value and how to increase it. In this sense Simard and West [3] name a set of metrics, while West and Gallegher [2] list three major challenges of open innovation, i.e. maximizing returns to internal innovation, incorporating external innovations and motivating spillovers.

The **rules** in this kind of game deals with the risk of not addressing properly the challenges previously mentioned. One can mention West and Gallegher [2] to underline the risk of wrong coordination between actors, which Doz and Hamel [4] address by suggesting the design of an interface between actors. We also recall the work of Simard and West [3] and their definitions of different ties (formal VS informal and deep VS wide). In particular, the deep and wide ties address the risk of exploitation of the future outcomes of the innovation.

The inventors of the term "co-opetition" list three different **tactics** to deal with information asymmetry between actors. Referring to open innovation Doz and Hamel [4] assess the shift in the kind of relationship between actors, while West and Gallagher [2] describes four business models used by software companies to capitalize their contributions to open sources programs.

On the matter of **scope**, following the indications of Vanhaverbeke [5]) open innovation can be studied at the intra-organizational and firm level, as well as at the dyad and inter-organizational level. In our work we shall consider a network of actors which deals with each other. Indeed we consider the legal boundaries as hard to be defined, since different business units in the same enterprise could be submitted to different regulations and deal with each other by means of internal service level agreements.

Referring to what has been said so far, from an agency theory point of view co-opetition is the best strategy for those game in which asymmetry of information does not allow complete trust between actors, but yet there is a partial common good that can be achieved only by cooperating.

Our contention is that **co-opetition works for projects where there is a high risk of failure**, which a single actor is not ready to stand, and there is a promise of high potential returns, high enough for the actor to be contented even if it receives only a part of it. Indeed mentioned by Wagner and Layton [6], there are two kinds of risk: the unrewarded one, which is a sort of cost to be paid in advance to enter the game, and a rewarded one, which is the promise of potential returns. We believe that co-opetition aims at sharing the unrewarded risk. This would aim to reduce what Khan and Blair [7] defines as the total cost of failure. On the other hand this form of partnership requires coordination, which the transaction cost theory links to transaction costs.

In this study we will propose a framework that supports management decisions concerning the information system – intended as the interaction between the information technology and the social setting [8] – to achieve the best **trade-off between trust and control**, in order to achieve what Cox et al. [9] refers as confidence at a minimum cost.

A large amount of literature has been previously focused on information technologies to automatically perform negotiation between enterprises; hence we will rather focus on the risk management process in the context of regulatory compliance, i.e. the definition of the objectives of the partnership, the assessment of the risks of failure and enforcement of a set of controls.

We believe that a viable tactic for an actor should be to **define rules that would shape** the game in an advantageous way, and we will follow Hegel's [10] suggestion and we will focus on ways to shape the shared platform to exchanges information between actors.

In doing so we will seek to **find an equilibrium between the different requirements of all stakeholders**, in order to achieve a solution that is **sustainable** over the time, i.e. which pushes all actors to not quit the game.

Following what has been said so far, our research question is the following:

How to support risk management in multi-actor contexts of information system regulatory compliance, such as co-opetition in open innovation, in order to achieve efficiency, consistency and sustainability?

The rest of the paper proceeds as it follows. The next section lists and motivates the requirements we set for the solution we wanted to obtain. The following section illustrates our design and describes its development process. The fourth section presents the design in action by mean of an example. Then a short section presents the evaluations of the design that we have already done and the tests that will follows. The last section ends the papers with discussions and conclusions.

The Objectives of the Solution

We shall assume that the unrewarded risk between co-opetitive actors will be shared by means of a formal agreement concerning the service that each actor shall deliver. In this sense one can identify the set of risks that occurs while signing a contract. Referring to the three categories of risk in signing a contract described by Willcocks et al. [11], we assess that a consistent number of works have been published on the first two sets of risk, namely the contextual risks and the ones related to the design of the contract.

According to what said so far our solution shall address the post-contract issues. Hence the information system to be in place shall include the required capabilities and skills to manage the relationship between co-opetitive actors; it shall include activities required to perform the required business and technical changes; it shall rely on proved standards based on best practices; it shall have a system to manage power between co-opetitive actors; and it shall support the monitoring of the supplier performance without forgetting the informal ties previously mentioned.

Referring to our research question, to obtain efficiency the solution in place should include an information system that reduces manual work and combines functionalities to allow data monitoring to assure respect of the SLA and information to support the rules management. A list of capabilities of the user of the information system should be given. To achieve consistency such rules management should be represented at a strategic level, in a standard way. On what concerns the sustainability of the solution, the information system should be able to evolve in time, while the compliance function itself should be able to adapt to environment change in a profitable way.

Design and Development

We decided to start with the most general case and to consider the compliance function as a business unit, which could be positioned within or without the reference companies, and we defined its business model accordingly, adopting the guidelines presented in Osterwalder et al. [12].

Proposition 1: the proposed model allows it to obtain a consistent solution, since it manages at the strategic level the rules to enforce.

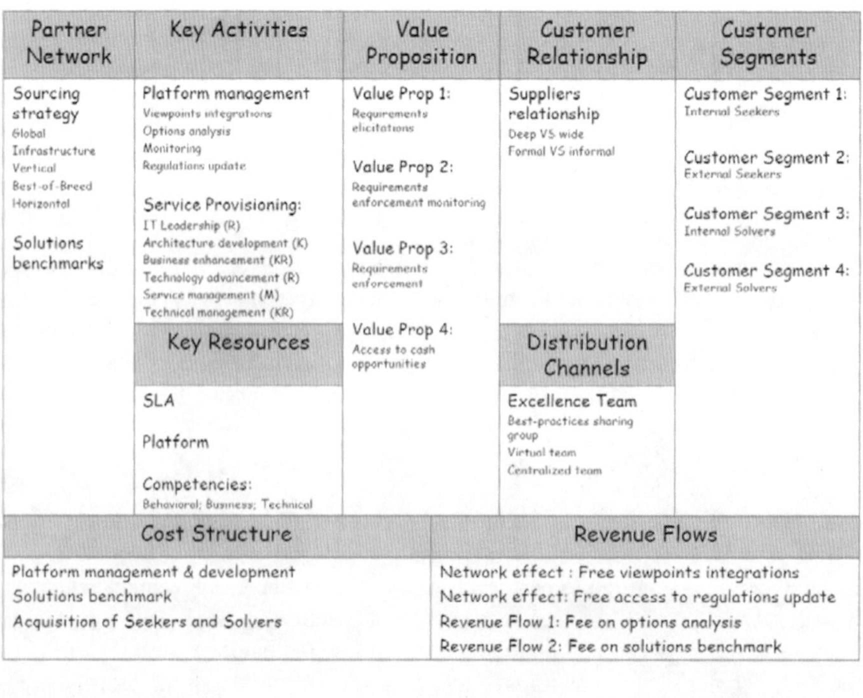

Fig. 1. Business model for the holistic compliance management function

We designed our solution as having a double-sided business model [13], i.e. basing its value proposition on the alignment of different customer segments, which gain from the network effect of converging in the same platform. In this sense we listed the four customer segments according to two dimensions: those that seek for a service against those that provide it, and those that belong to the same company as the business function against those who do not (Fig. 1).

Four value propositions have been deduced from a work on compliance presented last year at ItAIS [14]: on what concerns the solution seeker, support should be delivered regarding the requirements elicitation and the monitoring of requirements enforcement. On the other hand, the solution providers shall be supported in accessing to cash opportunity and deciding which applications use to enforce the regulatory requirements. The relationships between the seekers and providers follow the idea of ties illustrated in Simard and West [3].

Regarding the distribution channel one could see this business unit as a center of excellence, which can take the three shapes presented by Cullen [15]: a best-practices sharing group, a virtual team or a centralized service. According to the shape, the distribution channels offered by the platform will increase their complexity.

From what said so far, the revenue flows appear composed by four elements related to the four customer segments. One can assume that some component might imply a fee to be accessed, while other components might be free to access, to attract users in the platform and gain from network effects. More in general the idea of a revenue flow for the compliance process recalls the proposal of Volonino et al. [16]: if companies view the new regulation as opportunity to improve operations, they can get better returns from the longer-term strategic value of business improvement and competitive advantage.

On what concerns the key activities, beyond those related to the platform management, we took inspiration from the existing work of Cox and De Jong [17] and Joha [18] in outsourcing regarding the so-called "retained organization", i.e. the portion of the company that is kept to assure the interface with the new suppliers. According to the authors five activities should be in place:

1. The contract management: it involves a support on everything concerning the design and management of new formal agreements between the solution seeker and the providers.
2. The service management: refers to technical problems experienced by the solution seekers, which have to be solved by inter-mediator, who contacts the provider.
3. The technological advancement: this refers to the support to the projects management that the provider has in place to deliver the solution.
4. The business advancement: it deals with support on business process analysis and design, and process management.
5. Architecture development: this usually implies consulting activities regarding the development of the architecture of the solution seeker, by producing the requirements for the solution provider.

Proposition 2: the mentioned activities of the business unit allow it to reduce the post-contractual risk, since they support the required business and technical changes, and they monitor the solution provider.
Proposition 3: the use of standard approach like IPW for the activities of the business unit allows it to reduce the post-contractual risk.

The key resources include the service level agreement, the platform (for an example of its functionalities one can refer to the recent work of Bonazzi and Pigneur [19]), and the capabilities of the employees of the business unit. In this sense a large list of capabilities can be found in Cox and De Jong [17] and Joha [18], which class them in three groups: technical, business and behavioral.

Proposition 4: the mentioned capabilities of the business unit allow it to reduce the post-contractual risk, since it manages the relationship between co-opetitive actors.
Proposition 5: the proposed platform allows it to reduce the post-contractual risk, since it manages the power relationship between co-opetitive actors.
Proposition 6: the proposed platform allows it to reduce the cost, since it performs most of the tasks automatically.

The partners of the center of excellence are also its customers and the cost structure reflects that: the major costs involve the platform development and management and the acquisition of new solution seekers and providers, to gain from network effects.

Proposition 7: the proposed approach allows it to obtain a sustainable solution, since its cash flows are greater than the cost.

Instantiation of the Artifact

We applied our design to an existing case of open innovation, i.e. Innocentive (www.innocentive.com). In this case the co-opetitive actors are the problem solution seekers, who need a punctual solution, and the problem solvers, who have the required skills to deliver the solution. The solvers get profit from their knowledge, so they will try to solve the problem while explaining the solving process as less as possible, while the seekers will try to minimize their dependency from an external source.

Both actors are external to the business unit. In this sense we shall have only two customer segments, two value proposition and two revenue flows (the reader shall note the access to problems is free to gain new platform users). The distribution channel is Internet and Incentive can be defined as a centralized service offered to the users.

Regarding the key activities, one can find the platform management, while the activity 1 and 2 of our list can be deduced by the list of services offered. The key resources are the platform, the set of contracts between seekers and solvers, and the three groups of capabilities, which can be deduced by the requirements for job applicants. The cost structure is not given. Yet one can suppose that in this case, with the data available, propositions 2, 4 and 7 would find a confirmation.

A First Evaluation

In this first stage we have decided to evaluate our model by means of experts' opinion. We have already presented our design to a small panel of experts to collect their opinions concerning its efficiency, consistency and sustainability.

Starting from the feedback received a second version of the model has been developed and a survey has been prepared to let the experts rate each proposition of ours in a five-point Likert scale. The new data collection will be done on a larger scale (some 50 experts) in the following months.

Discussion and Conclusions

The presented work addressed a part of the literature regarding the link between open innovation, co-opetition and risk management, which has been only partially covered so far. By looking for a suitable solution design we crossed different domains, i.e. open innovation, outsourcing and more in general enterprise networks governance. Our goal was to start defining the IT managerial, methodological and technological capabilities and processes aiming at answering our research question. In doing so we hope to rise the interest of information system researchers in this direction of investigation, since we believe that such issues fall into the nomological net defined by Benbasat and Zmud [20].

The business model we obtain is still a work in progress, but in its final form it will aim at being a pattern for those companies, which find themselves having to address the problem of co-opetition in open innovation. Concerning the contributions of our work for practitioners one can refer to second section of the article: our solution addresses the post-contract issues and indicates the required capabilities and activities to manage the relationship between co-opetitive actors. On what concerns theoretical contributions, this paper explores the link between co-opetition as a form of sharing unrewarded risks, and compliance as a way to gain competitive advantage in a more and more regulated business environment.

In this stage of development we have decided to rely on experts' opinion to evaluate our design. Yet we consider the lack of a formal validation a limitation of the current stage of our research. In the next iteration we shall apply the model to real cases by mean of a qualitative study.

References

1. Brandenburger AM, Nalebuff BJ (1997) *Co-opetition: a revolution mindset that combines competition and cooperation: the game theory strategy that's changing the game of business*. Currency, New York
2. West J, Gallagher S (2006) Challenges of open innovation: the paradox of firm investment in open-source software. *R&D Manage* 36(3):319–331
3. Simard C, West J (2006) Knowledge networks and geographic locus of innovation. In Chesbrough HW, Vanhaverbeke W, West J (eds) *Open innovation: researching a new paradigm*. Oxford University Press, Oxford
4. Doz YL, Hamel G (1998) *Alliance advantage: the art of creating value through partnering*. Harvard Business School Press, Boston
5. Vanhaverbeke W (2006) The inter-organizational context of open innovation. In Chesbrough HW, Vanhaverbeke W, West J (eds) *Open innovation: researching a new paradigm*. Oxford University Press, Oxford
6. Wagner S, Layton M (2007) The two faces of risk. Available at http://www.deloitte.com
7. Kahn R, Blair BT (2004) *Information nation: seven keys to information management compliance*. Wiley, New York
8. Lee AS (1999) Inaugural editor's comments. *MIS Q* 23(1):v–xi.
9. Cox RA, Marriott I, Seabrook D (2003) *Trust and control: the key to optimal outsourcing relationships*. Gartner Inc., Stamford
10. Hagel J (2002) Leveraged growth: expanding sales without sacrificing profits. *Harv Bus Rev* 80(10):68–79
11. Willcocks LP, Lacity MC, Kern T (1999) Risk mitigation in IT outsourcing strategy revisited: longitudinal case research at LISA. *J Strateg Inf Syst* 8(3):285–314
12. Osterwalder A, Pigneur Y, Tucci CL (2005) Clarifying business models: origins, present, and future of the concept. *Commun Associat Inf Syst* 16(1):1–25
13. Eisenmann T, Parker G, Van Alstyne MW (2006) Strategies for two-sided markets. *Harv Bus Rev* 84(10):92–101
14. Bonazzi R, Hussami L, Pigneur Y (2008) Compliance management is becoming a major issue in IS design. In *ITAIS 2008 proceedings*. Springer, Paris
15. Cullen A (2008) *Current practices for IT centers of excellence (CoEs)*. Forrester Research Inc., Washington
16. Volonino L, Gessner GH, Kermis, GF (2004) Holistic compliance with sarbanes-oxley. *Commun Associat Inf Syst* 14(1):457–468
17. Cox R, De Jong B (2005) *The right retained team is critical for successful outsourcing*. Gartner Inc., Stamford
18. Joha A (2003) *The retained organization after IT outsourcing. The design of its organizational structure*. Faculty of Technology, Policy and Management. Delft University of Technology, Delft
19. Bonazzi R, Pigneur Y (2009) Compliance management in multi-actor contexts. In *GRCIS09 proceedings. Amsterdam*. Available at http://ceur-ws.org/Vol-459/paper7.pdf
20. Benbasat I, Zmud RW (2003) The identity crisis within the IS discipline: defining and communicating the discipline's core propertie. *MIS Q* 27(2):183–194

The Role of ICT in Clinical Risk Management: First Evidence from an Italian Experience

Gustavo Barresi * **and Carmelo Marisca** †

Abstract Clinical risk management may be considered as a set of actions with the aim of raising performance and health-care safety, through error learning. Most studies carried out and guidelines introduced give ample scope, to information and communication technology in clinical risk management. The assumption, in this case, is that human errors are an inevitable component in real life. Although this component can never be totally eliminated, the risk of error can be greatly reduced, if precise codes of behavior, shared by all health-care workers, are backed-up by suitable information and technological support. With all of the above in mind, referring to the case in hand, we will try to pinpoint critical points associated with computerization of procedures and introduction of new technological instruments to manage clinical risk in a health-care institution, and how they should be dealt with. In particular, we will try to identify the key factors in related organizational change.

ICT and Clinical Risk Management

Adverse events in Medicine have priority over many other issues in current public health-care. The problem is of interest both in clinical terms – quality of assistance, and in financial terms – higher costs associated to adverse events.

Clinical risk is defined as the possibility that a patient, due to health-care treatment, suffers involuntary injury or harm leading to an extension of the period of hospitalization, a worsening of psychophysical conditions, or death [1].

Risk management aims at reducing the probability of an error, or other events occurring, which could lead to the above-mentioned consequences. Given this, an

---

* University of Messina, DDEA, Messina, Italy, gubarresi@tin.it

† University of Messina, DDEA, Messina, Italy, cmarisca@tiscali.it

This paper is the result of a theoretical effort of both the Authors. However, Gustavo Barresi wrote the second paragraphs, while Carmelo Marisca wrote the first and the last.

A. D'Atri et al. (eds.), *Management of the Interconnected World*,
DOI 10.1007/978-3-7908-2404-9_50, © Springer-Verlag Berlin Heidelberg 2010

adverse event is defined as an unexpected event associated with treatment, which provokes unintentional and undesired harm or injury for the patient [2,3].

Problems associated to the possibility of an adverse event occurring, in the health-care field, can be tackled in two ways:

(a) First, identify the exclusively human element of the cause of the adverse event and propose better training for both health-care and non-healthcare workers, as a solution in the primary phase;
(b) Second, give more prominence to organizational and environmental conditions where the adverse events may arise. Here, the event can be traced back to an error in the system, from a combination of technological, human and relational factors. The remedy is to adopt specific behavioural models and organizational procedures [4,5].

This distinction highlights the difference between active failure and near miss event. The former is more easily identifiable and has a strict cause-effect relationship with the adverse event; for instance, it can occur due to malfunction of a machine or misuse on the part of the operator. Near miss events, instead, stem from organisational and systems failures which could lead to active failures.

Given that it is impossible to eliminate all active failures, an increase in safety levels necessarily foresees revision of potential criticalities, where active failures can be triggered.

Clinical risk management may be considered as a set of actions with the aim of raising performance and health-care procedure safety, through error learning. Correct implementation of this technique should include, at least, the following phases: (i) Identification of risk profile, specific for each Operating Unit or area of activity; (ii) Establishment of risk prevention interventions; (iii) Activation of monitoring systems for introduced measures; (iv) Introduction of additional improvement interventions for adopted measures.

Most western countries have been engaged in defining rules and regulations to tackle the above-mentioned problems. In Italy, the Ministry for Public Health has undertaken several initiatives to create a system of prevention and monitoring of high risk clinical and treatment activities. The aim is:

- To focus attention of health-care workers on potentially dangerous procedures;
- To provide health-care workers with the technical and organizational backing for risk limitation;
- To promote systems change through assumption of responsibility on the part of workers.

Five years ago, the Italian Ministry for Public Health appointed a committee with the task of producing guidelines and recommendations for health-care institutions, based on highly reliable international scientific studies. More recently, the Ministry, referring to leading articles on the topic, has drawn up a list of adverse events which, even if they only occur once, need to be identified, so as to help determine the causes and formulate possible, corrective interventions (cd. "sentinel events"; Protocollo per il Monitoraggio degli Eventi Sentinella, 2008) [6,7]. According to the aim of this paper, the most relevant adverse events are:

1. Treatment on the wrong patient;
2. Surgical procedure on the wrong part of the body (side, organ or part);
3. Wrong procedure on correct patient;
4. Instrument(s) or other material left inside the surgical site, which requires an additional operation or procedure to rectify;
5. Transfusion reaction due to AB0 incompatibility;
6. Death, coma or serious damage due to pharmacological therapy errors.

Many Italian Regions have set up diverse programmes for clinical risk management, generally aimed at training courses in health-care risk management, organizing safety procedures during treatment and activating voluntary reporting systems of adverse events [8,9]. A coordination programme for clinical risk management has been set up by the Health Commission for local Health Departments with the aim of standardizing ministerial guidelines in the various Regions, and promoting exchange of experiences between operators [10].

It is useful here to underline how most studies carried out and guidelines introduced give ample scope, in clinical risk management, to information and communication technology (Italian Ministry for Public Health [6]).

The assumption, in this case, is that human errors are an inevitable component in real life. Although this component can never be totally eliminated, the risk of error can be greatly reduced, if precise codes of behavior, shared by all health-care workers, are backed-up by suitable information and technological support.

With all of the above in mind, referring to the case in hand, we will try to pinpoint critical points associated with computerization of procedures and introduction of new technological instruments to manage clinical risk in a health-care institution, and how they should be dealt with. In particular, we will try to identify the key factors in related organizational change.

First Evidence from an Ongoing Experience

The study refers to a private hospital in the province of Messina (Sicily). The entire unit is characterized by certain conditions with are considered relevant in the study:

- Heterogeneity of conditions treated, with diverse specialties, both surgical and medical;
- Reduced size (less than 100 bed places), making the study experience more manageable;
- Advanced phase of technological innovation and process computerization.

The hospital, which was founded 50 years ago, operates as an accredited structure within the Regional Health-care Service (SSR). Heath-care specialties include: General Medicine, Cardiology, Respiratory Diseases and Medical Oncology,

General Surgery, Oncologic Surgery, Orthopaedics and Traumatology Surgery. There is also a wide range of outpatients' services backing up hospitalization activities. The structure employs 140 staff, including 36 doctors. In 2008, some 5000 people were treated (full admissions, day hospital and day surgery).

Company strategy has always been characterized by significant investment in process innovation and technological updating. The result is that, today, the hospital employs what is deemed as state-of-the-art equipment in biomedical "high technology". This includes NMR, multi-layer spiral CT, a Gamma camera for scintigraphic exams, a PET-CT and a Pacs-Ris (Picture Archiving and Communications Systems – Radiology Information Systems) for intranet management of diagnostic images.

Since 2003, in line with company strategy, the hospital had redefined its internal organization, both with a view to the then upcoming deadlines for institutional recognition (June 2007), and for obtaining ISO 9001:2000 quality certification (obtained in 2005).

With regard to computerization of procedures, the management opted to use tailor-made software, developed – contemporarily to a gradual revision of internal procedures – by a local software company with whom they work regularly. It was considered essential that computerization take place gradually, with wide participation, carried out in the following phases:

1. Medical personnel training and computerization of clinical records with revision of associated organizational procedures. After a long period of specific training for all medical personnel, computerized clinical records (subject to periodic revisions), accessible through Wireless technology directly from the patient's bed, were introduced in 2003;
2. Rationalization and integration of nursing documentation into a single document (nursing records) and revision of all associated procedures. Since 2007, a radical process of analysis and revision of nursing activities has been implemented (with a view to successive computerization), backed-up by an extensive training programme of relevant personnel;
3. Computerization of nursing records and integration into a single database, of all health-care procedures. This phase initially required a long period of software development, carried out with continual input from nursing staff.

Therefore, company management decided to let ICT play a primary role in clinical risk management.

In 2004, an internal work-group was set up to manage clinical risk, which included various professions, (health-care managers, administration managers, surgical Operating Unit chiefs, nursing coordinators, quality and safety chiefs and IT consultants). The work-group's activity (subsequently formalized in applying measures which had, in the meantime, been introduced), was characterized as follows:

1. Risk mapping and consequent revision of relevant procedures;
2. Further development of computerized procedures and adaption of same to management of identified risks;

3. Targeted training of health-care personnel according to operating procedures and newly introduced IT support (software and hardware).

Risk mapping was carried out through critical analysis of internal processes, documentation and recommendations that were progressively produced by institutional bodies (Ministry of Public Health and Local Authority Health departments), as well as international publications.

Particular attention was paid to involving all health-care personnel, who were approached in every phase and encouraged to put forward suggestions and proposals.

The above-mentioned risk mapping was accompanied by a revision of the organisation of relevant technical procedures. Keeping in mind the aforementioned list of sentinel events drawn up by the Ministry of Public Health, risks which have, to date, been dealt with directly, through the drawing up/revision of specific organizational procedures, include:

(a) Treatment of wrong patient, in the wrong part of the body or wrong treatment of correct patient;
(b) Transfusion error;
(c) Pharmacological therapy error;
(d) Instrument(s) or other material left inside the surgical site;
(e) Mix-up of test tubes and/or anatomic samples.

Process re-engineering was carried out, leaving ample space for the possible use of ICT with regard to every type of adverse event. There follows, briefly, a list of procedures in which ICT played a major role.

Patient identification error – The hospital is equipped with an Rfid (Radio frequency Identification) system – a disposable electronic bracelet with a tag transponder. This permits immediate identification of the patient during every important moment of hospitalization (administration of therapy, diagnostic tests and/or blood sampling, entry to operating area, etc). This system, which permits accessing and updating of patients' information in real time, allows unambiguous correlation between patient and relevant computer files. Operating theatres are also equipped with automatic identification devices (Rfid). Patients' records can be visualized on the monitor, and all information necessary for a correct surgical operation can be easily accessed. The use of this technology permits safer management of risks associated with patient-clinical diagnostic processes to be carried out.

Pharmacological therapy error – International guidelines recommend the use of ICT aids to avoid misinterpreting unclear instructions given by medical personnel, both regarding the drug(s) to be administered (above all regarding drugs of similar sounding names) and method of administration. The system used allows prescription of medication that is selected from a medical nomenclature, with a contemporary visualization of the therapy in the computerized nursing file. Electronic notice boards in the infirmary provide chronological instructions on therapy to be administered, with acoustic and visual alarm signals in case of omission. The operator, who reads and enters the drug bar code, confirms administration. This system, which allows traceability during each phase of therapy, highlights possible differences between the drug to be administered and the drug actually prescribed. Particular attention is also paid to the risk of prescribing/administrating drugs that the patient has declared himself to be allergic to. The system foresees the insertion of specific "warnings" which pop up every time clinical/nursing records are accessed, blocking all operations if these warnings are not read first.

Mix-up of test tubes and/or anatomic samples – The procedure is based on the association of test tubes with each patient, sticking adhesive bar-coded labels on test tubes when taking the blood sample. The bar code is then scanned, computerized clinical records are automatically updated, and test results are shown in real time.

Transfusion errors – To avoid possible errors that could arise from handling complex papers regarding transfusion procedures, all relevant information is now automatically computerized.

To date, all treatment activity, both medical and nursing, has been completely computerized. However, while computerization of all medical procedures can be considered complete, with regard to nursing procedures, the system, although fully operative, is still to be considered as experimental.

The principal ICT procedures, technologies and instruments used by the hospital in risk management are presented below (Table 1).

Table 1. Principal ICT procedures, technologies and instruments used

Errors/adverse events	Patient identification error
	Pharmacological therapy error
	Mix-up of test tubes and/or anatomic samples
	Transfusion error
Procedures involved	Therapy preparation and lot traceability
	Therapy administration
	Traceability of transfusions and hemocomponents
	Identification and traceability of samples
	Automated management of analysis laboratory in the phases: test request, identification and placing of test tubes in the machines, forwarding of work lists and results
DBMS	Oracle
	Sybase
Developer languages	Html
	Java
	PowerBuilder
	Webservice
Technology	Barcode
	Rfid
Instruments	Tablet PC
	Personal computer

	Rfid readers/players
	Barcode readers
	Barcode label printers
Communication systems	Wireless network
	Lan network

Conclusions

Keeping in mind what we have previously said, it is evident that correct clinical risk management must include continual analysis and revision of the adopted procedures. As widely observed in international literature, the use of ICT is indispensable. However, with regard to the case in hand, the experience is probably too recent to be used as empirical evidence for the current association between ICT and safety in health-care processes.

The above case, however, does allow us to give some evaluations on identifying critical points and key factors for the implementation of ICT support in health-care institutions.

It has been seen how, even in hospitals, process reengineering, relying heavily on ICT, requires deep cultural, as well as organizational, change [11]. In our case study, the company consciously adopted an incremental approach to the problem, in the medium term, first of all providing a gradual but complete revision/implementation of the relevant procedures and, only then, proceeding to computerization.

With regard to computerization, the key factors in change can be summarized as follows:

Gradual implementation – Unlike what has been seen in other areas of this sector, management thought it necessary to proceed gradually, first of all computerizing the medical area and, only then, proceeding with the nursing section. In both phases, the area of application of computerized procedures was progressively extended.

Involvement and participation – The entire computerization process was characterized by the aim of obtaining the widest participation of all relevant professions. Many meetings and briefings were held with specific groups of personnel, often on a very informal basis, to promote communication, and with the precise aim of highlighting the potential benefits of computerization and overcoming initial resistance.

Tailor-made solutions – After having carefully examined various options, management preferred to use a local software company to develop the required, new software. This enabled them to take suggestions into consideration that had been put forward, along with satisfying the need for progressive/continual revisions and broadening of the ICT procedures themselves. In this way, ICT worked for the needs of the company and not vice versa, thereby limiting the possibility of rejection of the procedures introduced.

Training – In line with what has been said above, all phases of implementation of computerized and organizational procedures went along with relevant training. After assessing company needs, management held that basic training in computer know-how was essential for many staff members who had no previous computer experience, before beginning the actual computerization procedure.

In conclusion, it is clear that ICT can be considered an extremely useful tool in clinical risk management. The use of ICT, however, must be an integrated part of a wider process of organizational change which, to be efficient, must be knowingly managed by the company. With this in mind, the willingness of management itself, right from the planning phase, to lead change is at least as important as the participation and cooperation on the part of the whole staff.

References

1. Tartaglia R, Bagnara S, Bellandi T, Albolino S (2005) *Healthcare systems ergonomics and patient safety*. Taylor and Francis, London
2. Helmereich R (2000) On error management: lessons from aviation. *Br Med J* 320:781–785
3. Reason J (2000) Human error: models and management. *Br Med J* 320:768–770
4. Brusoni M, Trinchero E (2008) Soluzioni aziendali e competenze emergenti per la ge-stione del rischio e della sicurezza. In Anessi Pessina E, Cantù E (eds) *Rapporto OASI 2008 – l'aziendalizzazione della sanità in Italia*. Egea, Milan, pp 421–440
5. Daft LR (2004) *Organizzazione aziendale*. Apogeo, Milan
6. Italian Ministry for Public Health (2007) *Raccomandazione per la prevenzione della reazione trasfusionale da incompatibilità AB0,* Italian Ministry for Public Health, Rome
7. Italian Ministry for Public Health (2008) *Protocollo per il Monitoraggio degli Eventi Sentinella,* Italian Ministry for Public Health, Rome
8. Anessi Pessina E, Cantù E (2005) *L'aziendalizzazione della sanità in Italia*. Rapporto OASI 2005. Egea, Milan
9. Brusoni M, Cosmi L, Trinchero E (2006) Prospettive regionali per la gestione del rischio clinico: una prima indagine esplorativa. In Anessi Pessina E, Cantù E (eds) *Rapporto OASI 2006 – L'aziendalizzazione della sanità in Italia*. Egea, Milan
10. Tartaglia R, Albolino S, Bellandi T (2005) Il modello toscano per la gestione del rischio clinico. *Clin Governance* 11:38–43
11. Vichi MC (2002) Aspetti informatici del monitoraggio dei percorsi. In Casati G, Vichi MC (eds) *Il percorso assistenziale del paziente in ospedale*. McGraw-Hill, Milan, pp 451–522

Information Systems and Service Research: A Co-citation Analysis

Maria Chiara Di Guardo* **and Marco Galvagno**†

Abstract In this paper, authors focus on those contributions to the IS and Service literature recognized as being the most influential, using co-citation analysis. The aim is to explore and review the research domain in order to better understand the origins, the current state of development and future trends.

Introduction

The impact of Information Technology (IT) on services and services quality has rapidly grown since firms worldwide embraced emerging technologies to restructure archaic bureaucratic procedures [1]. The increasing availability of IT has provided an opportunity for the diffusion of e-services and many private and public organizations currently employ or are planning to implement electronic service delivery through the use of modern IT. Such developments are changing the way service firms and consumers interact, and are raising a host of research and technical issues related to the delivery of services through Information Systems (IS).

Despite the importance e-services is assuming for firms and public administrations, the academic research on this issue is still in its infancy [2]. Furthermore, since the nature of e-service is likely to vary depending on the type of activity, a general agreement on its definition is missing [3].

While research depends for its lifeblood on the flow of information through the publications of people working in a specific field, knowledge can be substantially enriched by the scattered, inter-disciplinary, and sometimes contradictory contributions that have explicitly or implicitly studied related issues. In this paper, we focus on those contributions to the IS and Service literature recognized as being the most influential, and use co-citation analysis to trace the linkages among them, search for broad research fronts or subfields, and determine the relationships, if any, among the subfields. By reviewing these contributions, we propose a state of the art that might guide future research avenues in the broader field of IS and Service.

* University of Cagliari, Cagliari, Italy, diguardo@unica.it
† University of Catania, Catania, Italy, mgalvagno@unict.it

A. D'Atri et al. (eds.), *Management of the Interconnected World*,
DOI 10.1007/978-3-7908-2404-9_51,

We believe that a comprehensive understanding of the influence of IS on services is motivated by the increasing interest these issues have gained in the last years.

Our chapter is organized as follows. We present the methodology adopted for the analysis, and the selection of the most interesting contributions to the field. Than we examine the co-citation profiles by means of factor analysis, multidimensional scaling and cluster analysis. On the basis of this analysis, some critical reflections are presented.

Methodology

This work explores the structure of the Information Systems and Service research domain, to better understand its origins, current state of development, and future trends. In order to meet these goals, we based our literature review on co-citation analysis. This is a bibliometric technique used to analyze publication patterns in a field or body of literature. By using statistical techniques, co-citation analysis makes it possible to map research on a topic and to identify the dominant approaches in the field, thus shedding light on social structures and uncovering the "vast interpersonal network that screens new ideas in terms of central theme or paradigm, permitting some a wide audience and consigning many to oblivion" [4]. In co-citation analysis the data compiled are counts of the number of times two documents are jointly cited in later publications. The fact of having been cited together in the same paper establishes a quantifiable link between the earlier papers, the strength of the link depending upon the number of times that a pair of documents are cited together. The structure, and consequently the meaning, of a co-citation graph is strongly influenced by operational uncertainties associated with two fundamental assumptions. First, it is assumed that "highly" cited papers represent "important" concepts and methods in science. Second, it is assumed that "frequently" co-cited papers are related by content. A graphic representation of which published works tend to be cited together by researchers helps identify research streams and other cluster of scholarly work. Studies focusing on cited works try to establish the general structure of the discipline (what types of works are dominant), as well as the discipline's boundaries and relations to other disciplines [5]. Our analysis, following the method prescriptions [6], comprises six steps: (1) selecting the unit of analysis; (2) retrieving co-citation frequencies; (3) compiling the raw co-citation matrix; (4) converting the raw co-citation matrix into a correlation matrix; (5) multivariate analysis; and (6) interpreting the findings.

The unit of analysis can be defined in terms of articles or authors, depending on whether the analysis aims to identify the structure of specific or broad fields of inquiry [7, 8]. In particular, for the studies targeted at specific research areas (as in our case), it is preferable to analyze articles, so that the results will not be biased by the fact that the same author may have published in different fields [9]. In our case, this method makes it possible to identify the connections between the most influential contributions regarding the relationship between Information System and Service in order to systematize them in a consolidated model, thus overcoming the fragmentation and specialization of the different research streams and providing indications for future research. We based the analysis on the Social Science Citation Index (SSCI) of Thomson-ISI, with a time span from 1990 to 2009, available on the on-line database and consistent with the aim of our analysis. This database, which covers over 1,700 of the world's leading scholarly social sciences journals in more than 50 disciplines, provides access to bibliographic information, author abstracts, and cited references. The analysis was performed in May 2009, since ISI takes some months to complete the data entry at the end of each calendar year [10]. Given the aim of our analysis, we defined a criterion to search for papers. The criterion adopted crossed two subsets of key words: this ensured that the retrieved articles would refer to at least one of the key words for each subset. The first subset limited the search to the field of Information System with the words: Information System (system/systems); Information technology, IS, IT. The second subset limited the search to Service, with the words: "service" (service/services); "e-service" (e-service/e-services); "eservice" (eservice/eservices). The search was performed by selecting the papers whose title, abstract, and keywords matched our criterion. By screening the Thomson-ISI SSCI database according to the above search criteria, we obtained a set of 3,100 contributions. Among these, we selected only published articles (excluding proceedings, or working papers) in the fields of business management, finance, information systems and economics. Given our interest in defining the hard core of the discipline, we selected the most cited papers, setting the selection threshold at 50 citations, for papers between 1990 and 2005 and a threshold of 10 citations for articles published after the 2006. This resulted in a total of 34 papers, which are presented in Table 1.

Table 1. The set of articles

Goodhue & Thompson, ***MISQ***, 1995 (P1)	Boudreau, Gefen, Straub, ***MISQ***, 2001 (P18)
DeLone, WH; McLean, ER, ***JMIS***, 2003 (P2)	Chau & Hu, ***I&M***, 2002 (P19)
Bhattacherjee, ***MISQ***, 2001 (P3)	Benaroch & Kauffman, ***ISR***, 1999 (P20)
Pitt, Watson & Kavan, ***MISQ***, 1995 (P4)	Choudhury, Hartzel, Konsynski, ***MISQ***, 1998 (P21)
Lee, ***MISQ***, 1994 (P5)	Broadbent, Weill, St Clair, ***MISQ***, 1999 (P22)
Kettinger & Lee, ***DS***, 1994 (P6)	Mukhopadhyay, Rajiv, Srinivasan, ***MS***, 1997 (P23)
Lacity & Willcocks, ***MISQ***, 1998 (P7)	Kettinger, Teng & Guha, ***MISQ***, 1997 (P24)
Feeny & Willcocks, ***SLOAN MR***, 1998 (P8)	Bhattacherjee, Premkumar, ***MISQ***, 2004 (P25)
Liu & Arnett, ***I&M***, 2000 (P9)	Kettinger & Lee, ***MISQ***, 1997 (P26)

Straub, ***Isr***, 1994 (P10)	Straub & Watson, ***ISR***, 2001 (P27)
Pavlou & Gefen, ***ISR***, 2004 (P11)	Dewan & Kraemer, ***MS***, 2000 (P28)
Lacity & Hirschheim, ***SLOAN MR***, 1993 (P12)	Devaraj & Kohli, ***JMIS***, 2000 (P29)
Dewan & Min, ***MS***, 1997 (P13)	Venkatraman, Henderson, ***SLOAN MR***, 1998 (P30)
Chatterjee, Grewal, Sambamurthy, ***MISQ***, 2002 (P14)	Benaroch, Kauffman, ***MISQ***, 2000 (P31)
VanDyke, Kappelman, Prybutok, ***MISQ***, 1997 (P15)	Saarinen, ***I&M***, 1996 (P32)
Lacity, Willcocks, Feeny, ***HBR***, 1995 (P16)	Martinsons, Westwood, ***I&M***, 1997 (P33)
Chan, Huff, Barclay, Copeland, ***ISR***, 1997 (P17)	Lyytinen & Yoo, ***ISR***, 2002 (P34)

Analysis

After selecting the unit of analysis, each of the 34 papers was paired with every other paper and the co-citation frequency of each pair was computed from the total references in the Social Sciences Citation Index (SSCI) online. The result of this procedure was a 34 by 34 matrix of co-citation counts: the rows and columns represent the articles included in the set and the cells represent the number of times each pair of documents has been cited. Consequently, cells on the main diagonal report missing values [6], since they should represent the times a document has been cited together with the document itself.

In order to standardize the data and avoid possible scale effects, as well as reducing the number of zeros in the matrix, the Pearson correlation matrix was estimated [11]. Correlation coefficients represent a measure of similarity between two papers: the higher the positive correlation, the higher the perceived similarity between the two works. Following similar studies [8,12], we proceeded to apply three multivariate statistical techniques to the correlation matrix. First of all, non-metric Multidimensional Scaling (MDS) was employed, allowing us to generate a map in order to observe the relationship between the papers. Second, we applied a cluster analysis, which lets us obtain a series of groups of significant papers. Finally, a Factor Analysis was used to identify which works make up each factor and their degree of contribution or *loading* as an approximation of the relative influence that each of them has within the stream of research.

Figure 1 shows the map obtained through Multidimensional Scaling. This analysis consisted in projecting the papers on a two-dimensional map, using the data from the correlation matrix as input data. The result of this analysis was obtained using the ALSCAL routines of the SPSS statistical program. The values obtained in the statistical analyses that exhibit goodness of fit (STRESS=0.22) and the estimated variance percentage (RSQ=0.85) permits us to state that this representation is a good approximation of reality. The purpose of this representation is twofold [12].

On the one hand, MDS shows co-citation links among contributions. Points positioned at the centre of the map represent contributions linked to many different schools of thought and thus with heterogeneous citation profiles. On the other hand, MDS reduces the data space, by positioning the articles on a bidimensional space, making it easier to interpret the relative positioning of the clusters of contributions.

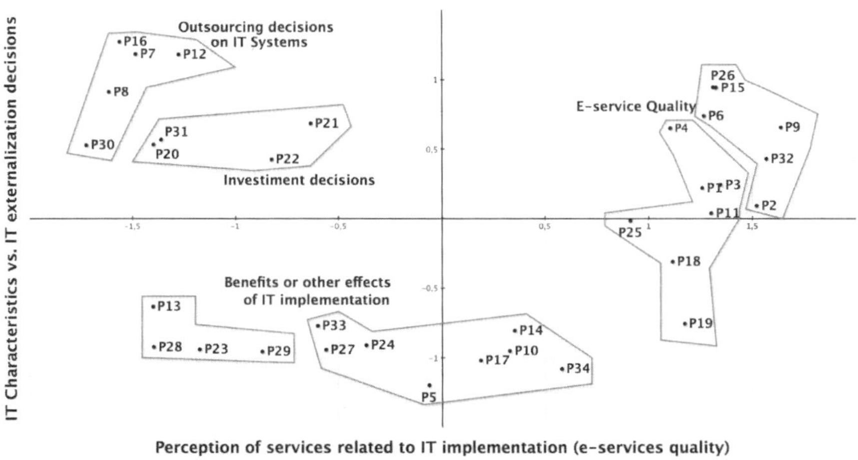

Fig. 1. Multidimensional scaling

Consequently, in order to interpret MDS maps, both the point placement of the articles and the orientation of the clusters of articles along the two axes have to be interpreted. The grouping of the authors and their labels appearing on the map were produced using the results obtained from the cluster analysis as the basis (using Ward's hierarchical method). Although the construction of the axes is arbitrary, the position of the papers on the map suggests a meaning for the axes. That is, the horizontal axis seems to refer on "perceptions of service related with IS implementations or e-services quality" that ranges, from the right to the left, from the more micro or individual level to the more macro or social level of analysis. On one hand, the papers located in the quadrants to the left of the vertical axis analyze "internal or organizational perceptions of services related with IS implementations". On the other hand, the papers located to the right of the vertical axis focus on "customer perceptions of services related with IS implementations". With respect to the vertical axis, the works located in the quadrants above the horizontal axis adopt a "IT externalization decision". While those below the horizontal axis, are mostly related with "IT systems' characteristics". The results obtained reflect the fact that the IS field applied on the study of Services is an eclectic discipline. This is generally positive, since the multidisciplinary approaches for understanding the field provide a more thorough explanation than single-track theories.

Nevertheless, it may well be turned into a weakness, as it might compromise the future development of the discipline, by producing an excessive fragmentation of the field. In this sense, the absence of papers at the centre of the map indicates a lack of research that serves as a basic reference for the entire field of study. Along with the two previous techniques, we also employed correspondence factor analysis in order to identify the papers that constitute each factor and discover the influence of each one of the papers within their respective schools, using factor's loadings analysis.

The relevance of Factor Analysis in this context is based on the notion that papers which are related to one another will, in general, be repeatedly cited together in subsequent publications, while works which are rarely or never cited together will not. If this assumption is true then Factor Analysis can use the correlation between the co-citation entries to determine which contributions are grouped together and therefore share a common element. It does so by producing a number of "factors", each of which captures a common element of the documents that are grouped together. It is also capable, by producing numerical indicators of the relevance of the factors (i.e. eigenvalues), of telling us something about the relative importance of these underlying elements.

This analysis was carried out using the Varimax rotation, following previous works [11]. The rotation of the axes in the factor analysis aims, as its ultimate goal, to obtain factors endowed with theoretical significance, as well as to achieve the simplest possible factorial structure [13]. The data to be used in this analysis were obtained from the correlation matrix [8,11]. Factor analysis allowed us to identify the factors explaining most of the variance observed (83.5%) and to identify groups of strongly correlated papers so that we could define the structure of the field of research. We have considered that a contribution should be included in a trend when its loading is equal to or greater than 0.5, and if the loading is greater than 0.7 then the paper is of great relevance within the corresponding paradigm. Table 2 lists the four factors along with the authors that had a factor loading of at least 0.5. All 34 papers, but two (P12, P21), loaded on at least one factor. Significantly, most of the contributions are loaded with a weight greater than 0.7, corroborating the relevance of these works within their respective paradigms. Likewise, it can be observed that some of the works exhibit considerable loading in more than one factor (greater than 0.5). These works are of even greater interest, as they represent bridges between paradigms and allow us to observe a broader spectrum of influences among those works that belong to the different research fronts, thus helping us to understand their evolution and the ties that have been forming between the different research trends.

By analyzing the contributions loading on each factor, we named the four factors according to the following definition: (1) IT impact in processes (e.g. procurement, invoicing, payments); (2) IT cultural effects; (3) IT impact on internal process output; (4) IT impact on service sectors or specific service areas (e.g. health care, tourism, government, banking). Factor 1 is the richest of the four extracted components in terms of number of papers.

Table 2. Rotated factor analysis – authors loadings

	Components			
	IT impact in processes	IT cultural effects	IT impact on internal process output	IT impact on service sectors or specific service areas
P32	0.968			
P9	0.968			
P6	0.939			
P1	0.923			
P3	0.921			
P26	0.911			
P4	0.909			
P15	0.907			
P2	0.859			
P11	0.830			
P18	0.742	0.504		
P25	0.732			
P30	–0.674			0.618
P16	–0.535			
P7	–0.510			
P34		0.870		
P5		0.833		
P10		0.786		
P19	0.592	0.732		
P24		0.705		
P33		0.646		
P27		0.626		
P29			0.919	
P28			0.875	
P23			0.870	
P13			0.786	
P17		0.518	0.624	
P14			0.550	
P22				0.632
P8	–0.546			0.584
P31				–0.551
P20				–0.513

Conclusion

The present findings suggest that co-citation analysis provides a potentially illuminating and valid way to represent the patterns of "invisible colleges" or "scientific communities" that characterize a field of study of IS and services research. Specifically, we have focused on the 34 more cited published papers and we have produced a two-dimensional MDS space that suggests two key underlying dimensions for the intellectual structure of the field. One dimension represents a disciplinary choice of focus that ranges from the more macro or social to the more micro or individual level of analysis. The second dimension captures the distinction between articles who lean toward externalization decision or IT characteristics approach. Cluster and Factor analysis show the existence of various "specialties" or "sub-disciplines", representing a variable field. Within this variable field, literature on seems to be polarized between individual level (customer interaction) and firm level (implementation's effects) and between a strategic management point of view and a more technical point of you (related to technological effectiveness of IS or IT systems). Concluding, our exploration of the theoretical roots of the service and IS literature reveals a heterogeneous theoretical basis for the construct and the lack of central articles (so-called seminal paper). This suggests a rich set of theories to draw upon in building a clearer, stronger, and more robust theoretical foundation for research, but it also suggests the complexity of the task. Our findings may promote a greater understanding of differences and a research agenda capable of exploiting the complementarities available from a combination of perspectives.

References

1. Moon MJ (2002) The evolution of e-government among municipalities: rhetoric or reality? *Public Adm Rev* 62(4):424–433
2. Santos J (2003) E-service quality – a model of virtual service dimensions. *Manag Serv Q* 13(3):233–247
3. Rowley J (2006) An analysis of the e-service literature: towards a research agenda. *Internet Res* 16(3):339–359
4. Crane D (1972) *Invisible colleges: diffusion of knowledge in scientific communities*. University of Chicago Press, Chicago
5. Pierce, SJ (1990) Disciplinary work and interdisciplinary areas: sociology and bibliometrics. In Borgman CL (ed) *Scholarly communication and bibliometrics*. Sage, Newbury Park, pp 84–106
6. McCain KW (1990) Mapping authors in intellectual space: a technical overview. *J Am Soc Inf Sci* 41(6):433–443
7. White HD, Griffith BC (1981) Author co-citation: a literature measure of intellectual structure. *J Am Soc Inf Sci* 32:163–171
8. Culnan MJ (1986) The intellectual development of management information systems, 1972–1982: A co-citation analysis. *Manage Sci* 32(2):156–172
9. Acedo FJ, Barroso C, Galan JL (2006) The resource-based theory: dissemination and main trends. *Strateg Manage J* 27(7):621–636
10. Podsakoff PM, MacKenzie SB, Bachrach DG, Podsakoff NP (2005). The influence of management journals in the 1980s and 1990s. *Strategic Manage J* 26(5):473–488
11. Rowlands I (1999) Patterns of author co-citation in information policy: evidence of social, collaborative and cognitive structure. *Scientometrics* 44(3):533–546
12. Brown LD, Gardner JC (1985) Using citation analysis to assess the impact of journals and articles on contemporary accounting research (CAR). *J Account Res* 23(Spring):84–109
13. Hair JF, Anderson RE, Tatham RL, Black WC (1999) *Analisis multivariante*, 5th edn. Prentice-Hall, Madrid

The Cross-Level Antecedents of Dynamic Capabilities Development: The Case of Network Exploitation Capability

Francesca Cabiddu*

Abstract This study will conceptualize antecedents of dynamic capabilities at the individual and organizational level. My focus is on network exploitation capability, defined as the ability of an organization to effectively "orchestrate" the combination of traditional and technology-enabled distribution channels for its product or service. My analysis has allowed me to reach four main results: (1) to distinguish individual antecedents from the organizational ones; (2) to list the individual and organizational antecedents in terms of sensing, seizing and reconfiguring; (3) to underscore the existing relationship between individual and organizational antecedents; to provide a small theoretical contribution to the literature concerning dynamic capabilities[1].

Introduction

The dynamic capability perspective provides an extension of the resource-based view by addressing the way in which valuable, rare, difficult to imitate and imperfectly replaceable resources can be created and how the current stock of valuable resources can be updated in changing environments [1, 2]. The central issue regarding capabilities-based work is that organizational capabilities are the fundamental units of analysis, and that the organization should be conceptualized as the repository of routines and capabilities [3]. The emphasis on collective constructs has led other authors to focus their attention on the micro-foundations of collective structures as they arise from individual action and interaction [4, 5]. Despite the

* University of Cagliari, Cagliari, Italy, fcabiddu@unica.it

[1] Financial support from the Italian Ministry of University through PRIN 2007 "The Role of Dynamic Capabilities in Fast Changing Environments: Their Upshots on Innovation Strategies and Organizational Processes" are gratefully acknowledged.

A. D'Atri et al. (eds.), *Management of the Interconnected World*,
DOI 10.1007/978-3-7908-2404-9_52, © Springer-Verlag Berlin Heidelberg 2010

importance of establishing links between individual and organizational levels, there is a considerable lack of theory development [2, 6], and corresponding empirical investigation into the interaction among the different levels of analysis and suggesting that antecedents to dynamic capabilities, can be found at the individual, firm, or network level. I address this gap by integrating the dynamic capabilities literature [7, 1] with the literature on IT capabilities [8–10], thus conceptualizing antecedents of dynamic capabilities at the individual and organizational levels. This multi-level approach enables original explanations as to how and why dynamic capabilities are born and develop. More specifically, I ask: (a) What individual characteristics influence the firm's ability: (1) to sense and shape opportunities and threats, (2) to seize opportunities, and (3) to maintain competitiveness through enhancing, combining, protecting, and, when necessary, reconfiguring the business enterprise's intangible and tangible assets? (b) How do individual-level factors (such as traits, abilities or motivation) aggregate in order to create collective capabilities?

My focus is on network exploitation capability, defined as the ability of an organization to effectively "orchestrate" the combination of traditional and technology-enabled distribution channels for its product or service. The rest of the paper is structured as follows. First, I explore the theoretical framework of my model. Secondly, I develop my model and propositions. Finally, I close with a discussion of the theoretical contributions of the paper.

Theoretical Framework

Dynamic capabilities. Dynamic capabilities [2, 11] are a learned and stable pattern of collective activity through which an organization systematically generates and modifies its operational routines in pursuit of improved efficiency [12].

Teece [7] defines dynamic capabilities as the capacity (1) to sense and shape opportunities and threats, (2) to seize opportunities and (3) to maintain competitiveness through enhancing, combining, protecting, and, when necessary, reconfiguring the business enterprise's intangible and tangible assets. The first, the ability to sense and shape opportunities and threats, refers to the process of understanding the environment and market conditions, identifying market needs, and spotting new market opportunities. The second, the capacity to seize opportunities, describes the process of creating new products, processes, or services when a new opportunity has been sensed. This capacity requires the selection or creation of a particular business model: "Once adopted it defines the way the enterprise goes to market" [7]:1327. The third "is the ability to recombine and to reconfigure assets and organizational structures as the enterprise grows, and as markets and technologies change, as they surely will. Reconfiguration is needed to maintain evolutionary fitness and, if necessary, to try and escape from unfavourable path dependencies" [7]:1335. However, the general framework advanced by Teece [7] considers dynamic capabilities as the foundation of enterprise-level competitive advantage in circumstances of rapid change, it offers a number of conceptual tools which help us to distinguish the individual antecedents of dynamic capabilities from organizational antecedents.

IT capabilities. The role of information technology (IT) in creating competitive advantage has been hotly debated over the last two decades [10, 13]. Some authors consider IT competence (or capabilities) as a critical antecedent for firm to generate more competitive actions and greater action repertoire complexity [14]. Indeed, there is a recent emphasis on facilitating dynamic capabilities by effectively using ITs [15]. In particular, dynamic capabilities have been conceptualized as knowledge-intensive processes and, also, as information-intensive routines [12]. As such, rapid, accurate, and reliable knowledge sharing can be facilitated by adequate IT support. IT can also increase the processing of information and the accessibility and availability of new knowledge [16]. In line with the literature [10], I assume IT infrastructure, IT business experience, and relationship infrastructure as organizational antecedents of dynamic capabilities. IT infrastructure is the technological backbone of the firm. A quality IT infrastructure can provide firms with the ability to share information across different functions, innovate and exploit business opportunities, as well as the flexibility to respond to changes in business strategy. The IT Infrastructure varies in reach and range [13]. As the reach and range of the IT infrastructure increase, the IT infrastructure's ability to support capability development increases as well. Sambamurthy and Zmud [17] argue that IT business experience allows a firm the ability to integrate IT strategy and business strategy, develop reliable and cost-effective systems for the business, and anticipate business needs sooner than its competitors. Some authors posit the importance of individual IT propensity as a significant antecedent to the firm's ability to rapidly develop for the long-term competitive advantage [18, 19]. Relationship infrastructure reflects the ability of the IT group to understand business needs and create a partnership with business groups to work together to meet them and exploit new business opportunities. The ability of a company to leverage IT resources critically depends on the interaction of the IT function with the business units [20]. Integrating the dynamic capabilities literature [7, 1] with the literature on IT capabilities [10]; my emphasis falls on one specific dynamic capability: the network exploitation capability.

Definition of Network Exploitation Capability

Although, a number of studies have addressed the opportunities related to channel interactions and channel synergy [21–23] the importance of how one specific organization (e.g. a Hotel) can build new dynamic capabilities by exploiting the synergies and interactions among an organization's multiple channels remain underspecified. I define Network Exploitation Capability as the dynamic capability of an organization capable to "orchestrate" the combination of traditional and technology-enabled distribution channels for its product or service. In particular, orchestration describes the ability of an organization: to integrate information throughout its traditional and electronic distribution channels, to share knowledge across channels, and to coordinate channel strategies. My conceptualization is consistent with Teece's [7] notions of dynamic capabilities. NEC is a dynamic capability because it is based on the capacity (1) to sense and shape opportunities and threats, (2) to seize opportunities and (3) to maintain competitiveness through enhancing, combining, protecting, and, when necessary, reconfiguring the business enterprise's intangible and tangible assets. The need to sense and seize opportunities, as well as reconfigure when change occurs, requires the allocation, reallocation, combination, and recombination of resources and assets. My conceptualization is also consistent with IT capabilities. In order to manage multiple distribution channels, actors must learn to manage the interactions that take place within their relationships, both internally and externally. IT capabilities form the foundation for the effective and efficient flow of information, experience, knowledge and ideas.

Theoretical Model

In this phase, I start off by considering the specific individual antecedent of sensing, and the drive to use IT's, and then move on to the individual antecedent of seizing (self-efficacy and risk propensity) and lastly I consider the individual antecedent of reconfiguring (individual learning) and point out the relationships that exist between such antecedents and the organizational ones (Fig. 1).

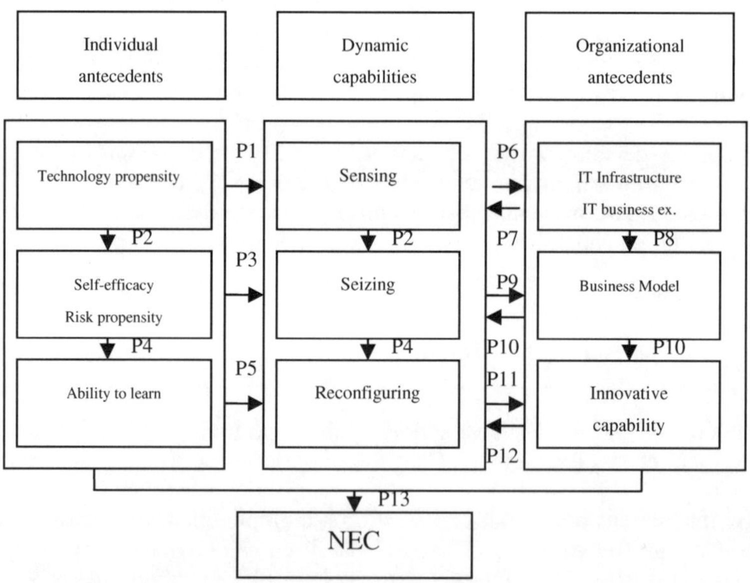

Fig. 1. Relation between individual and organizational antecedents

Individual Antecedent of NEC

Individual antecedent of sensing: Technology propensity. In an environment characterized by growing information technology the tendency to use that technology seems to be a vital requisite for the adequate spreading of information and knowledge at an organizational level. In other words, to manage information effectively, the modern firm must adopt and use information technology resources. Selecting, designing, and managing these resources is the shared responsibility of all organizational actors. Applied to NEC, the individual propensity to use IT supports the efforts of one organization to orchestrate the combination of traditional and technology-enabled distribution channels for its product or service In other words, by referring specifically to NEC, I must necessarily highlight that the propensity to use information technology becomes crucial in order to sense within the environment new opportunities related to the distribution channels: i.e. the emerging of the electronic channel. Therefore,

P1: Technology propensity will be positively related to the individual's sensing ability.

Individual antecedents of seizing: Risk propensity and self-efficacy. The sensing capacity of individuals must be interrelated to that of seizing so that the perceived individual opportunities can be transformed into real actions. In particular, there are two individual antecedents that I believe deserve being highlighted in this case, which are from my standing point, in line with the goals of this research: risk propensity and self-efficacy.

Sitkin and Pablo [24] defined risk propensity as "the tendency of a decision maker either to take or to avoid risks" (p. 12). The greater the inclination of individuals to assume risks, the greater their tendency to transform perceptions into real actions. Similarly, the less their inclination to risk , the less their willingness to undertake new initiatives, and consequently, their seizing capacity. Self-efficacy is one's perceived ability of accomplishing a task [25]. Individuals with high self-efficacy beliefs are more active, they attempt to proactively manage situations, and creatively solve problems as opposed to those with low self-efficacy beliefs who avoid difficult tasks and are passive. Accordingly, individuals tend to develop general self-efficacy expectations due to prior success and failure that they carry to new situations. From the above mentioned definition it may be stated that high levels of self-efficacy will favour the seizing ability. Therefore,

P2: Individual antecedents of sensing will be positively related to individual seizing activity

P3: Risk propensity and self-efficacy will have a positive and direct impact on seizing

P4: Individual antecedents of seizing will be positively related to individual antecedents of reconfiguring.

Individual antecedents of reconfiguring: the ability to learn. One of the foremost antecedents contemplated by literature is the individuals' ability to improve their knowledge. The role of individuals in knowledge creation is highlighted by Rothaermel, Hess [6], who argue that intellectual human capital can be conceptualized as consisting of two components: star scientists and nonstar scientists. They understand a star scientist as being someone who is both more productive in and more influential on a specific research field than the average (nonstar) scientist active in this field. Through specific reference to NEC, I would argue that in order, for organizational actors, to identify the new up-coming opportunities regarding multi-distribution channels within the market, they need to have a basic knowledge of them, to build new thinking and generate new knowledge and pursue new initiatives and solutions; they also need to identify their potential in terms of development and reconfiguration possibilities. Therefore,

P5: The *ability to learn* will have a positive and direct impact on reconfiguring.

Organizational Antecedent of NEC

Organizational antecedent of sensing: Information Technology. The propensity to use IT technologies on behalf of individuals must be sustained at an organizational level by the presence of adequate IT tools. Normally, if individuals operate within a specific organization they have a good tendency towards the use of IT's. This is normally due to the fact that the organization will certainly be well-equipped with adequate IT tools. In accordance with the literature on IT capabilities [15, 17], I assume that IT infrastructure, IT business experience and Relationship infrastructure are organizational antecedents to: Network exploitation capability. Therefore:

P6: Technology propensity will be positively related to IT;

P7: IT infrastructure, IT Business Experience and relationship infrastructure will have a positive and direct impact on sensing.

Organizational antecedent of seizing: Business model. The antecedents considered above together with IT competences will have a direct influence on the seizing capacity at an organizational level. According to Teece [7] the organizational antecedent of seizing may be summarized as the architecture of the products business models; to which the selection of enterprise boundaries and the management of complements and "platforms" are closely related. The design and performance specification of products and the business model employed, reflect management's hypothesis about what customers want and how an enterprise can best meet those needs, and get paid for doing so. In reference to NEC it appears clearly evident that the choice of Business model will be conditioned by the choice of IT's made in the sensing phase. In detail, the business model chosen will need to take into consideration the possibility of integrating information throughout their traditional and electronic distribution channels, to share knowledge across channels, and to coordinate channel strategies. Therefore,

P8: IT will be positively related to Business Model;

P9: Self efficacy and risk propensity will be positively related to Business Model;

P10: Business model will have a positive and direct impact on reconfiguring.

Organizational antecedent of reconfiguring: Innovative capability. The ability to reconfigure at an individual level is mirrored at the organizational level by the concept of *innovative capability*. Innovative capability refers to a firm's ability to develop new products and/or markets, by aligning strategic innovative orientation with innovative behaviours and processes. In other words, the more innovative firm is, the more it possesses dynamic capabilities. When referring specifically to NEC, the activation of the activity of reconfiguring at an organizational level requires new methods of coordination, of allocating resources, assigning tasks to people, and coordinating activities. Therefore,

P11: The ability to learn will be positively related to the firm's innovative capability;

P12: Innovative capability will have a positive and direct impact on reconfiguring.

P13: Individual and organizational antecedents will have a positive and direct impact on NEC.

It should be clear from the preceding discussion that the antecedents of both levels (individual, and organizational) are necessary to ensure that the NEC is successful. More subtly, the antecedents of NEC do not work in isolation, but instead interact with one another.

Conclusions and Future Research

This study has conceptualized antecedents of dynamic capabilities at the individual and organizational level. My analysis has allowed to reach four main results:

1. To distinguish individual antecedents from the organizational ones;
2. To list the individual and organizational antecedents in terms of sensing, seizing and reconfiguring;
3. To highlight the existing relationship between individual and organizational antecedents
4. To provide a small theoretical contribution to the literature regarding dynamic capabilities.

Acknowledgments I'm grateful to Gabriele Piccoli for his helpful comments on earlier drafts of this paper.

References

1. Teece DJ, Pisano G, Shuen A (1997) Dynamic capabilities and strategic management. *Strateg Manage J* 18(7):509–533
2. Eisenhardt KM, Martin JA (2000) Dynamic capabilities: what are they? *Strateg Manage J Special Issue* 21 (10–11):1105–1121
3. Nelson RR, Winter S (1982) *An evolutionary theory of economic change*. Harvard University Press, Cambridge
4. Felin T, Hesterly WS (2006) The knowledge-based view, heterogeneity, and new value creation: Philosophical considerations on the locus of knowledge. *Acad Manage Rev* 32(1): 195–218

5. Felin T, Foss NJ (2005) Strategic organization: a field in search of Microfoundations. *Strateg Organ* 3:441–455
6. Rothaermel FT, Hess AM (2007) Building dynamic capabilities: innovation driven by individual, firm, and network-level effects. *Organ Sci* 18(6):898–921
7. Teece DJ (2007) Explicating dynamic capabilities: the nature and microfoundations of (sustainable) enterprise performance. *Strateg Manage J* 28:1319–1350
8. Bharadwaj A (2000) A resource-based perspective on information technology capability and firm performance: an empirical investigation. *MIS Q* 2:169–196
9. Wade M, Hulland J (2004) The resource-based view and information system research: review, extension and suggestions for future research. *MIS Q* 28(1):107–142
10. Bhatt GD, Grover V (2005) Types of information technology capabilities and their role in competitive advantage: an empirical study. *J Manage Inf Syst* 22(2):253–277
11. Winter SG (2003) Understanding dynamic capabilities. *Strateg Manage J October Special Issue* 24:991–996
12. Zollo M, Winter SG (2002) Deliberate learning and the evolution of dynamic capabilities. *Organ Sci* 13(3):339–351
13. Piccoli G, Ives B (2005) Review: IT-dependent strategic initiatives and sustained competitive advantage: a review and synthesis of the literature. *MIS Q* 29(4):747–776
14. Sambamurthy V, Bharadwaj AS, Grover V (2003) Shaping agility through digital options: reconceptualizing the role of IT in contemporary firms. *MIS Q* 27(2):237–263
15. Pavlou PA, El Sawy O (2006) *The nature and role of dynamic capabilities: conceptualization and measurement.* Working paper, Anderson School of Management, University of California, Riverside
16. Alavi M, Leidner DE (2001) Research commentary: technology-mediated learning. A call for greater depth and breadth of research. *Inf Syst Res* 12(1):107–136
17. Sambamurthy V, Zmud RW (2000) Research commentary: the organizing logic of an enterprise's IT activities in the digital era. A prognosis of practice and a call for research. *Inf Syst Res* 11(2):105–114
18. Ross JW, Beath CM, Goodhue D (1996) Develop long-term competitiveness through IT assets. *Sloan Manage Rev* 38(1):31–45
19. Clark CE, Cavanaugh NC, Brown CV, Sambamurthy V (1997) Building change readiness capabilities in the IS organization: Insights from the Bell Atlantic experience. *MIS Q* 21(4):425–455
20. Bassellier G, Homer B, Benbasat I (2001) Information technology competence of business managers: a definition and research model. *J Manage Inf Syst* 17(4):159–182
21. Neslin SA, Grewal D, Leghorn R, Shankar V, Teerling ML, Thomas JS, Verhoef PC (2006) Opportunities and challenges in multichannel customer management. *J Serv Res* 9(2):95–112
22. Balasubramanian S, Raghunathan R, Mahajan V (2005) Consumers in a multichannel environment: product utility, process utility, and channel choice. *J Interact Mark* 19(Spring):12–30
23. Verhoef PC, Neslin SA, Vroomen B (2007) Multichannel customer management: understanding the research shopper phenomenon. Int *J Res Mark* 24(2):129–148
24. Sitkin SB, Pablo AL (1992) Reconceptualizing the determinants of risk behavior. *Acad Manage Rev* 17:9–38
25. Bandura A (1997) *Self-efficacy: the exercise of control.* WH. Freeman, New York

Part X
IS Theory and Research Methodologies

Antonio Cordella[*] and Lapo Mola[†]

Information Systems and Information and Communication Technology are becoming increasingly pervasive in human affairs, reshaping all domains of work, business and daily life.

The encounter of Information and Communication Technology and human practices is a complex phenomenon which takes place at different levels, both at the technical-instrumental, and at the cognitive-ontological level. However, our current theories and research methodologies lag behind the complexities of the interactions between Information and Communication Technology and the domains of practice.

The track devoted to this topic in the conference was intended to be an "agora" for the presentation and discussion of novel and interesting ideas on how to conceive and study Information and Communication Technology and Information Systems in the contemporary world.

Both sound theoretical contributions and empirical studies have been invited to submit to the track. Out of the papers presented for the track, only one has been chosen to appear in this book.

[*] London School of Economics, London, UK, a.cordella@lse.ac.uk

[†] Università degli Studi di Verona, Verona, Italy, lapo.mola@univr.it

Learning Computer Supported Collaborative Problem Solving: A Case Study in Postgraduate Education

Paola Adinolfi[*], **Luca Tateo**[†] **and Vittorio Scarano**[‡]

Abstract The paper presents a case study about the first introduction of the collaborative environment CoFFEE and its educational approach within the DAOSan Masters course in Leadership in Health-care Services. First, the pedagogical and technological aspects of CoFFEE-supported activities are presented. Then, the context of the DAOSan problem-solving-based approach is described. The case study of a training scenario is discussed, in order to draw a methodology fostering reflexivity, collaboration and situated learning in management training.

Collaborative Problem Solving in Higher Education

A challenge in higher education is to provide in-depth theoretical knowledge combined with the ability to apply knowledge to real contexts. Teaching should improve students' ability to make decisions and solve problems, both individually and collaboratively, to better face real world situations. Well-chosen case studies support students in acquiring such a competence at a higher level compared to learning context-independent rules [1]. This educational approach requires learner-centered training programs, such as Mintzberg's IHML, supporting students in developing "mind tools" [2], reflective and planning skills. Students must be able to apply theoretical knowledge to real-life problems and experiences in the field. This requires creating a space for collaboration and reflection, as well as continuous monitoring and evaluation of improvements. One of the training methods that fulfill these requirements is Problem-based Learning (PBL) [3]. PBL enables students to work on authentic tasks, to maintain ownership of the solution process and to experience the complexity of the environment they are preparing to work in [4]. PBL, developed since the 1970s in medical education, has been incorporated into DAOSan teaching methodology. It includes, for instance,

* Department of Business Studies and Research, University of Salerno, Salerno, Italy, padinolfi@unisa.it

† Department of Economy, Institutions and Society, University of Sassari, Sassari, Italy, ltateo@unisa.it

‡ Department of Computer Science and Applications, University of Salerno, Salerno, Italy, vitsca@dia.unisa.it

A. D'Atri et al. (eds.), *Management of the Interconnected World*,
DOI 10.1007/978-3-7908-2404-9_53,

training activities such as case-study discussions, group work, classroom exercises, role-playing and simulations, in addition to traditional lectures and seminars with experts from the health-care sector. The DAOSan educational philosophy is oriented towards achieving a context-based professional competence and a more general set of life skills through case-based learning.

The University Masters course in Leadership in Health-care Services (DAOSan) is a post-graduate degree provided by the University of Salerno and organized by the Department of Business Studies Research, in partnership with other University Departments and the Regional Health Agency for the Campania Region. The DAOSan approach is related to a more general ongoing reflection within health-care organizational studies, questioning the technocratic and bureaucratic managerial approach that dominated the last two decades of the twentieth Century [5]. This change leads to a *new health governance*, that goes beyond *managerialism* to develop a *patient-centered* approach. Following this approach, which seeks to re-establish the centrality of the individual, the objectives in higher education become more complex. The goal is no longer to simply acquire knowledge and skills. Rather, these are means for managing *change*. From this perspective, the focus is on the development of collaborative, reflective and creative skills rather than learning the ability to solve specific problems, the latter becoming a conceptual tool to experience those skills. This vision has been instantiated in a new collaborative environment, named CoFFEE.

CoFFEE Supported Collaborative Problem-Solving

It is widely accepted that computers can support collaborative problem-solving. But putting this theoretical concept into practice in a real class is not an easy task. The first requirement is to make the structure and context of the problem that students are required to solve visible. The interaction between different perspectives leads to more in-depth thinking, better information management and participation in the process of information sharing through discussion and argumentation [6]. Time management, materials, participation and group work in classroom are also affected. Collaboration requires communication between participants (students and teacher), during their attempts to solve problems, in order to reach a shared understanding about what a given question means, how to answer it, how to check the answers and how to coordinate group work. Within this general framework, CoFFEE (Cooperative Face2Face Educational Environment) was developed by the LEAD project, funded by the EU VI FP [7]. CoFFEE is an open-source suite designed to enhance multi-modal, face-to-face (F2F) and computer-supported collaborative problem-solving. It has already been used in several studies, testing a wide range of collaborative problem-solving educational activities [6].

CoFFEE comprises four main applications, which will be described briefly. The **CoFFEE Controller** is the teacher application that coordinates class activities. Each student runs a **CoFFEE Discusser** client application. The classroom activity is described in an XML *session* file, which contains a sequence of steps and a set of tools. A session can be designed using the **Lesson Planner**, a quick-and-easy design tool that offers a set of session templates, including step and tool configurations. A new session can also be created from scratch using the advanced **Session Editor**. CoFFEE provides students with several collaborative tools to support effective problem-solving in the classroom (Fig. 1). The core tools are: a threaded chat which enables participants to post, categorize and label contributions organized in threads; a graphical tool, in which posts are placed within a two-dimensional visual space of debate, using boxes, labels and connectors. CoFFEE also provides other collaborative tools, such as a co-writer, a voting tool (named positionometer), a streaming and videoconferencing tool, a shared repository, etc.

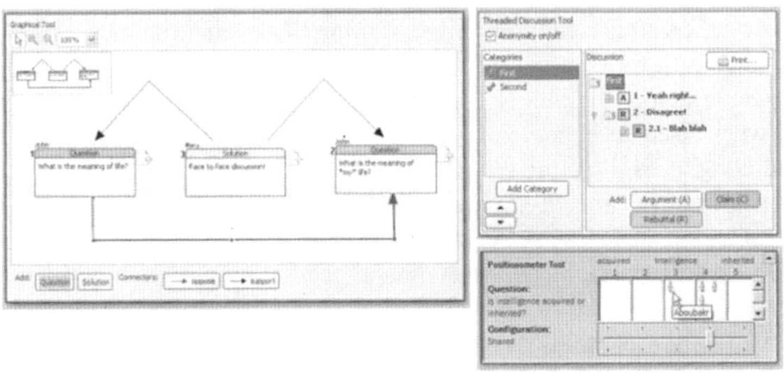

Fig. 1. The graphical tool (*left*), threaded chat (*right*) and positionometer (*bottom right*)

CoFFEE has been designed to improve the effectiveness of F2F collaborative problem-solving activities in educational contexts along four main dimensions [6]:

- *flexibility*: the software can be used for a wide range of educational activities with students of different ages and can be used with different subjects;

- *parallel interaction*: parallel discussions enhance participation and knowledge construction. Comparing F2F discussions with CoFFEE-enhanced discussions shows that the latter produce a higher number of contributions, in which students engage in a more intense exchange of opinions;

- *productivity:* productivity is enhanced by keeping a permanent trace of interactions. Everybody can take notes and everything that happens during the computer-mediated discussion is recorded, together with the digital artifacts produced. This helps students and teachers to reflect upon the knowledge they collectively generate;

- *anonymity*: the possibility of anonymity reduces students' status inequalities and shyness. Anonymity can be also very useful when discussing sensitive topics, such as those related to healthcare.

The integration of F2F and CoFFEE-supported interaction allows students to engage in a richer and more productive form of communication. The effectiveness of this approach in enhancing collaborative learning has been assessed mainly in the school context (see 6 for further readings). Less data exist with respect to higher education and professional training. The case study presented in this paper seeks to bridge this gap by exploring how CoFFEE can be used to enhance collaboration within a higher-level Masters course.

CoFFEE in the DAOSan Masters Degree

The positive role of collaborative problem-solving, with respect to students' "life skills" – reflecting, creating new knowledge, linking theory and practice – can be improved by the use of CoFFEE – enhanced collaborative problem-solving. It indeed provides more flexibility, parallel interaction, productivity and participation when used to support Master students in argumentative discussion aimed at generating ideas, arguing and reflecting upon them. We will now explore how a collaborative F2F and digital educational environment can be useful in order to enhance students' ability to reflect, participate, collaborate, debate and apply knowledge. The descriptive case-study approach will be used to outline the educational intervention and related phenomena within their real-life context [8].
The data source for the case study are:
(a) the students' evaluations of teaching and tutoring: students are required to complete evaluation forms, indicating their own satisfaction, teacher's performance and proposals for improvements;
(b) the transcripts of one collaborative problem-solving session: CoFFEE keeps a trace of the session, including the participants, group composition, all the messages and products created;
(c) researchers' field notes: field notes about classroom's atmosphere, the students' participation and teaching and tutoring styles were taken during the session and are used to provide a scaffolding for the case-study analysis.

The Context

The DAOSan Masters degree enrolls graduate students (from the fields of Healthcare, Law, Economics, Engineering, etc.), healthcare professionals (i.e. surgeons) and administrative professionals (managers and administrative staff from the healthcare field). Each class contains approximately 40 students. Lessons cover Healthcare Systems, Human Resource Management, Marketing, Communication and Quality Management, as well as Law, Computer Systems and Case Management. Students also carry out project works and stages in healthcare organizations. Students' achievements are constantly monitored. At the end of each class, students anonymously evaluate teacher's performances on a five-point scale with regard to clarity, completeness and attention to students' needs. These dimensions generally receive high scores, indicating a high level of satisfaction with the overall teaching approach. Students can also offer their own comments on the course. These comments permit an in-depth evaluation of the general teaching approach. Students' notes highlight both their commitment during debates and need to apply knowledge to real-life cases. Students also point out that, during debates, certain colleagues tend to monopolize the discussion, leaving little room for others to contribute. In order to overcome these problems, it was decided to evaluate CoFFEE with a view to improving the quality of collaborative activities in the classroom and to encourage participation.

Example of CoFFEE Sessions of Argumentative Discussion

CoFFEE-supported activities are based on a pedagogical scenario: a description of a sequence of steps and a set of "tools". The scenario we refer to for this case study was specifically designed to involve students in an argumentative discussion about the criteria to be applied in the choice of the general manager of a healthcare institution. In particular, the teacher wished to evaluate students' pre-conceptions about this topic and to foster reflection about the main dimensions involved in the choice of a manager in the healthcare sector. The outcome of the discussion was later used as a starting-point for a traditional lesson.

The activity consisted of a 50 min discussion organized in 3 phases: introduction, knowledge consolidation and restitution [6].

(1) Brainstorming: the class was asked to provide a set of criteria that could lead to the choice of a general manager, to categorize them and to argue for or against each specific criterion. Students discussed both F2F and using the *threaded chat tool*. At the end of this step students were asked to use the *positionometer tool* to vote for the most relevant criteria that should be retained during the following step. This phase had a duration of 20 min.

(2) Knowledge consolidation and organization: students, divided into 5 small groups, were asked to work collaboratively to draw up a conceptual map – using the *graphical chat tool* – of the most relevant criteria, identifying the *pros* and *cons* of each, and to connect them by arrows. Once again, this phase had a duration of 20 min.

(3) Restitution: in the final step, students were asked, anonymously, to reflect upon the discussion and to synthesize individually the "lesson learnt" using the *threaded chat*. They were also asked to evaluate the teacher's performance at the end of the lesson using the *positionometer*. The duration of this phase was 10 min.

Session Analysis

For the sake of brevity, a few excerpts of the session will be presented as examples of the processes that occurred during the exploratory study. The question of how to enhance students' ability to reflect, participate, collaborate, debate and apply knowledge by using a collaborative F2F and digital educational environment is discussed using the scenario referred to above.

The main goal was to present a collaborative problem-solving task: "*We have to choose a general manager for a healthcare institution. What are the most suitable selection criteria?*". The session involved brainstorming, the development of a conceptual map and argumentative discussion as well as classroom restitution of knowledge. The session was productive with respect to both students' parallel interaction (166 contributions posted during the 20 min brainstorming session) and outcomes (students found the relevant selection criteria by themselves: candidate's background, recruitment procedure, who should have responsibility for making the decision). In excerpt 1, an example of a discussion thread is presented.

Excerpt 1[1]*:*

```
[P] St. 1: the training background must be both management and medical because
the organizing choices concern the medical domain.
          [A] St. 2: I agree, but management has priority
          [P] St. 3: must come from the management of a large company
          [A] St. 3: I mean a private company
```

Students try to single out the most suitable background of a candidate to a healthcare management position. The first point is that all the students properly employ the contribution labels provided by the threaded chat. They build a worthwhile argumentative debate by organizing and arguing their proposals. In 4 turns they reach agreement about the need for a managerial background. This is an example of how the visual representation of the debate – using threads and labels – leads to productive and parallel interaction. The second example (Excerpt 2) is taken from another step of the session. Students were asked to reorganize and synthesize the discussion, building a conceptual map of the candidate's profile, using the graphical tool provided. The graphical representation of the debate is clear and well-organized (Fig. 2).

[1] Square brackets indicate the label that the student gave to his/her post [P]=proposal; [A]=argument.

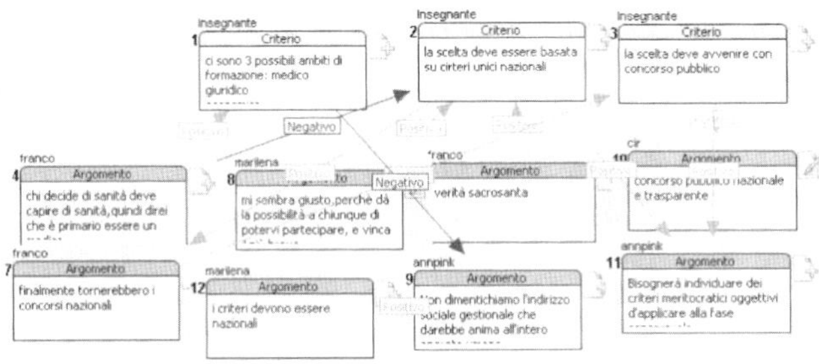

Fig. 2. Graphical representation of the argumentation

The group of students is able to organize the relationships between concepts in a short space of time, building a graph of the criteria (yellow boxes), the arguments (light blue boxes), and the pros and cons (respectively, green and red arrows).

Excerpt 2:

```
[Criterion] Tea: there are 3 possible educational backgrounds: medical,
economic, legal
[Argument] St. 1: do not forget the social aspect of management
[Argument] St. 2: finally we could have national open competitions
[Argument] St. 3: it seems right to me, because it gives the opportunity to
everybody to apply, and may the best win
[Argument] St. 4: do not forget the social aspect of management background
which will give a soul to the human conduct
```

Excerpt 2 shows how students can apply some basic principles of DAOSan philosophy – meritocracy and a human-centered approach in healthcare – during the classroom debate. They are not directly prompted by the teacher, who merely synthesizes the "educational background" issue. Nevertheless, they can link the practical issue of education with the more abstract concept of human-centered healthcare. The recording of the session was used by the teacher as a starting point for the lesson on the management of health-care and was saved on the e-learning platform of the course for use as didactic material for the prosecution of the class. Finally, anonymity was used in order to enable students to self-evaluate their activity and to evaluate the teacher. Students' comments evidence an improvement in participation and the absence of complaints about the fair distribution of speech turns. It now seems that everybody is participating and the risk that a few students monopolize the discussion is avoided.

Conclusions

It was possible to carry out a dense collaborative problem-solving activity with a large number of post-graduate students during the course of a short lesson. The result of this activity was that students were enabled to work and reflect upon a real problem of healthcare management.

Despite the exploratory nature of this case-study, it seems that the CoFFEE-enhanced approach to collaborative problem-solving can foster student reflexivity and involvement, enabling students to better understand the relationship between both theoretical and case-based knowledge acquired during the course and the real problems that they will face in healthcare organizations.

Students seemed to improve some of the "life skills" that will be part of their professional identity, such as collaboration, reflection, communication, creativity, etc. They seemed more aware of the relevant aspects of the human-centered approach in healthcare. These preliminary results require further analyzes but an initial, positive evaluation of the activity encourages the integration of the CoFFEE-enhanced problem-solving approach within the DAOSan curriculum.

References

1. Flyvbjerg B (2006) Five misunderstandings about case-study research. Qual Inq 12(2):219–245
2. Jonassen DH (1999) Computers as Mindtools for schools: engaging critical thinking. Prentice Hall, Columbus
3. Woods DR (1994) Problem-based learning: how to gain the most from PBL. Donald R. Woods, Waterdown
4. Duffy TM, Lowyck J, Jonassen D (eds) (1993) Designing environments for constructivist learning. Springer, Heidelberg
5. Glouberman S (2005) Changing conceptions of health and illness: three philosophical ideas and health. Workshop shaping the future of home care, Sutton Place (Toronto, Ontario), March 29
6. Ligorio MB, Andriessen J, Baker M, Knoller N, Tateo L (eds) (2009) Talking over the computer: pedagogical scenarios to blend computers and face to face interaction. Scriptaweb, Naples
7. De Chiara R, Di Matteo A, Manno I, Scarano V (2007) CoFFEE: cooperative face2face educational environment. In: Proceedings of the 3rd international conference in collaborative computing: networking, applications and worksharing. New York, November 2007
8. Yin RK (2003) Case study research: design and methods, 3rd edn. Sage, Thousand Oaks

Part XI
Accounting Management and Information Systems

Luciano Marchi*[*] and Renata P. Dameri[†]

Management and Accounting practices are one of the key issues for companies, to face complexity and to sustain value creation in today's business environment. However, these practices are continuously impacted by several events, such as:

- The globalization of the markets and increasing competition;
- The ongoing change of the national and international regulations;
- The recent financial crisis and unprecedented corporate scandals

All these aspects forced all the organization to rethink their Accounting and Management practices and to empower them, aiming to help organizations execute their strategies and deliver desired results to their stakeholders.

Advances in Information and Communication Technologies (ICT) are a great opportunity, to improve the ability and the role of Accounting Information Systems (AIS) for the success of the companies. Moreover, the link between ICT and AISs is a crucial driver for innovation of Accounting and Management practices.

Accounting information systems are often considered a standard instrument for accounting automation. However, they have a strong impact on business strategic activities, such as:

- operational activities and process management, because AISs are crucial drivers in business process improvement and reengineering;
- internal reporting, as AISs are the basic instrument to collect and analyse business data and support decisions along with all the organisation levels;
- external reporting, because AISs realise all the accounting activities in business and are the data repository, functional for the balance sheet and all the financial disclosure, therefore they should be efficient, effective and compliant, to assure the best quality of financial information.

Also the papers included in this track reflect the impact of AISs on business processes, such as financial disclosure, or innovative behaviours. "ICT and Procurement: The E-sourcing Systems of an Italian Bank Group" analyses the relations between Management practices and purchasing in a large financial company;

[*] Università di Pisa, Pisa, Italy

[†] Università di Genova, Genova, Italy, dameri@economia.unige.it

"IT Training: Impacts and Decision Drivers" describes the behaviour of companies in IT training; "The Impact of Law on AIS: An Analysis of IAS/IFRS Adoption in Some Italian Companies" studies the relations between the type of AIS adopted by a company and its behaviour in compliance with international accounting standards.

ICT and Procurement: The E-sourcing Systems of an Italian Bank Group

Lapo Mola[*], **Cecilia Rossignoli**[†] **and Alberto Rigodanza** [‡]

Abstract The purpose of this work is the analysis of the benefits that the enterprises may enjoy with the adoption of e-procurement solutions. In particular the analysis concerns the e-sourcing solutions implemented by an Italian bank group and the main organizational implications connected to the use of such systems within the purchasing department.

The peculiarities detected by this study through the administration of interviews to a few department managers confirmed that the e-sourcing systems adopted by the group have allowed large saving in terms of lower purchase prices and most of all in terms of rationalization of the procurement process.

Introduction

In a time of economic recession, all organizations are trying to improve their results adopting solutions that consist almost always of the centralization of purchases to create economies of scale and of the adoption of enabling systems to improve the effectiveness of commercial transactions. The objective is a total cost reduction, improving the performance of the entire value chain.

The implementation of e-procurement solutions constitutes one of the possible solutions adopted by a few enterprises to achieve valid results in a short time [1, 2]. The term e-procurement denotes the whole of technologies, procedures, operations and organizational methods that, thanks to the recent developments of the net and in particular of the electronic commerce, allow users a more effective and efficient purchase of goods and services.

E-procurement therefore is one of the many services belonging to the e-business family, and in particular to Business to Business, which includes all tools supporting e-sourcing, i.e., the search of potential suppliers on the web, as well as bidding and negotiation, e-catalog of goods and services, that is, from the process-

[*] Management Department, University of Verona, Verona, Italy, lapo.mola@univr.it

[†] Management Department, University of Verona, Verona, Italy, cecilia.rossignoli@univr.it

[‡] Management Department, University of Verona, Verona, Italy, alberto.rigodanza@gmail.com

A. D'Atri et al. (eds.), *Management of the Interconnected World*,
DOI 10.1007/978-3-7908-2404-9_54, © Springer-Verlag Berlin Heidelberg 2010

ing of a purchase request to the submission of orders to suppliers and related invoicing. Therefore, e-procurement is the macro-class (container), while e-catalog and e-sourcing are the two possible solutions to the procurement problem.

An e-procurement system, if correctly implemented, involves the entire procurement process of a company, and implies a comprehensive re-design, with clear advantages in terms of rationalization of purchasing procedures and reduction in the total cost of supplies.

E-sourcing

E-sourcing can be defined as the whole of activities that include all the phases of the value chain, from the search of potential suppliers to their qualification and negotiation and subsequent invoicing.

In the specific Italian reality, there are several e-sourcing models [3, 4], which may be classified based on the *implemented technical solution* and *used tools.* Technical solution refers to the methods by which a single organization manages the technological infrastructure for the search of suppliers with which it operates.

There are two management methods:

Internal solution. In this case, enterprises develop and manage internally the technological search platform or uses the platform of the group to which it belongs (in-sourcing).

External solution, which is divided into external solution through *Application Service Provider (ASP),* and external solution through global *outsourcer*.

External solution through ASP. The technological platform is personalized and is made available by an enterprise against the payment of a fee. The Provider manages technical and information support services as well as aggregation services of the various buyers and sellers, reporting of the various values declared during negotiation and printing of final reports. This approach is used by buyer enterprises which want to maintain a certain degree of decisional autonomy within their negotiation processes and which at the same time do not have the economic and/or technical capabilities to provide these services internally.

External solution through global outsourcer. In this case, specialized operators manage on behalf of their customer enterprises the entire e-sourcing process, that is, all the activities involving the search of new suppliers, their certification and qualification all the way to the real negotiation phase. The objective of this strategic choice is to improve the efficiency of the entire purchase process, even though, on the other hand, it reduces the decisional autonomy of the outsourcee.

The Advantages Afforded by the Use of E-sourcing Solutions

The enterprises that adopt e-sourcing solutions (and more in general e-procurement) can achieve significant advantages, such as:

- Cost reduction with respect to traditional procurement processes [5]. According to a few studies [6] the administrative costs for each issued purchase order vary from $100 to $250, while using a fully implemented effective e-procurement system the costs allegedly drop to €30, which is equal to a reduction in some cases of approx 85%. These costs include personnel, offices, telephone charges, inefficiencies in the system of orders/warehouse, non-conformity costs, supplies' management costs, authorizations on paper, faxes, phone calls, confirmations, etc.
- Reduction in the time necessary to complete the entire operation. E-procurement systems allow improvement of company performance even in terms of supply cycle time (procurement cycle completion time) and warehouse costs. According to a few studies [7] conducted on a large sample of major companies that have implemented e-procurement systems, it has emerged that the average time to complete a traditional/manual procurement cycle was 7.3 days, which dropped to approx 2 days following the implementation of the e-procurement system, while the warehouse costs dropped by 25–50%.
- Using e-procurement systems results in great price savings. Thanks to a greater efficiency in the control of purchasing activities and prices, e-procurement allows a more efficient centralization of the management and a more accurate selection of privileged/strategic suppliers and, consequently, strengthening of the contractual position towards them.
- Increased effectiveness of processes and reduction in the number of people employed in the purchasing department.
- Greater integration with the other company processes.
- Reduction in the number of key suppliers and their strategic management.
- Mitigation of the so-called "maverick effect" (out-of-control purchases), i.e., a phenomenon whereby employees tend to avoid the traditional purchasing procedure, procuring some materials personally and then filling out the related expense report.

Case Study

Methodology

The case study of this contribution regards the introduction of e-sourcing solutions in a large Italian bank group which was one of the first companies in the industry to adopt this type of systems.

In 2004 the Group was able to catch a glimpse of the potentialities offered by the Internet on the purchasing side. These opportunities were not so famous among the operators of the Italian banking industry.

Multiple investigation techniques over a long period of time have been used for the analysis. A number of interviews have been conducted several times over a 6-month period. These interviews have been addressed to main managers, buyers, partners of consulting companies and employees of the group that in several capacities were involved in the project. Furthermore, starting from archival data (specifications, standard contracts, bid logs, etc.), a few bids have been traced over. It was also possible to observe two negotiations directly *on-line* during their real performance. Finally, thanks to the analysis of a large number of company documents, it was possible to fine tune the case study.

The E-procurement Systems of a Well-Known Italian Bank Group

This bank Group wished to acquire a tool that could help it improve efficiency, also in consideration of a constant increase in the amount of work of the purchasing department, due to the expansion of the group following a number of acquisitions and mergers that have involved the entire Italian banking industry since 2004.

In particular, in the adoption of the e-sourcing solutions that will be described further on, the Group set the following main objectives:

- An efficient and integrated management of the entire procurement process of goods and services
- Reduced operating costs
- A centralized, direct and specialized management of purchase activities of goods and services for the banks of the group, which in this way are able to focus on their core activities
- Improved service level offered to the banks of the group, to suppliers and consequently the clientele.

Based on these objectives, the Group has implemented an e-sourcing system (the website) which allows support to all the procurement process phases. The system allows the following:

- Management of the roster of suppliers. The system enables the search of new suppliers thanks to the possibility to contact, with utmost ease, potential candidates sending them an "On-line Request for information". If the supplier is interested he/she may access a specific section of the portal to register, filling out a convenient form whose purpose is the registration of the most relevant information of the supplier company.
- Search and selection of suppliers fulfilling the agreed requirements. The platform uses an internal database, which is daily updated.
- Support to the preparation of a Request for Price Quote and drafting of supply specifications. Through the use of certain forms, the purchasing department communicates by email to the suppliers the technical data of the goods/services it wishes to buy.
- Analysis and alignment of offers. With this application, each individual seller is associated with a number of parameters (quality, price, general company information, delivery time, etc.), which enable and speed up the choice of the buyer.
- Automated management and control of the entire on-line negotiation
- Reverse electronic bidding. This dynamic negotiation tool allows the purchasing department to have a higher number of suppliers compete with each other than it was possible with the traditional contract awarding procedure.
- Automated transmission to all suppliers of the necessary information to actively participate in the on-line negotiation and real-time communication of main events of the negotiation.
- Assistance to suppliers during negotiation. These are numerous services supporting the activities of buyers and suppliers such as for example technical/information, organizational and procedural assistance in the management of the various negotiation phases.

The Afforded Benefits

The above described tools allow the purchasing department to enjoy several benefits, some of which in the short term, such as saving on purchase prices, and some of which are more difficult to assess in terms of money although equally relevant.

Based on the interviews administered to personnel of the purchasing department in the Summer 2006/Spring 2009 period, three main benefits have emerged:

- Reduced purchase prices (13–17% per year, on average), which may be due to multiple factors, such as:

  - The possibility to involve in the negotiation a high number of suppliers. In the initial phase of the request for a price quote, the number of involved suppliers had already gone from 4–5 to 20–25, a possibility that up to a short time ago was not convenient due to the fact that the preparation of the negotiation required a long time.
  - The specific psychological dynamics induced by the real-time on-line negotiation system [8, 9]
  - The possibility to take utmost advantage of a few contingent market situations, such as the need to dispose of excess stock or to saturate the production capacity of new competitors.
- Increased process efficiency, as a consequence of:
  - Reduced time needed to communicate and interact with suppliers during the bidding and negotiation phase. The time and cost correlated to the preparation and forwarding of documents on paper were eliminated (for example: mailing costs, fax, toner, etc.). The time for the preparation, management and closing of the bidding procedures has decreased on average by 70%, fostering a better organization of the resources dedicated to the performance of these activities. This is possible thanks to simplification of procedures, a direct consequence of the use of the portal, and to the creation of standard forms.
  - Evaluation and comparison of multiple offers and pre-qualification of suppliers through the passive scouting section (a function that must be performed by the supplier before the event).
- Greater transparency, traceability and, therefore, expenditure control. Through specific functions of the website, it is possible to:
  - View any element of the carried out negotiations, thus allowing traceability of occurred transactions and therefore efficient availability of a thorough and in-depth information base.
  - Use statistics that allow the analysis of one's own expenditure model and therefore a better support to future decisions.
  - Access, thanks to the availability of a single database, to all documents and communications with the suppliers. Retrieval of the documents relative to a bidding procedure becomes easier and more orderly. The information stored in the e-procurement platform has also allowed improvement of budgeting and control tools, making them more efficient and, in particular, adequate to the initial draft estimate of purchase costs.

The Emerging Costs

On the other hand, computer costs increase, such as the purchase of hardware, software license, consulting services, IT personnel, connections and housing/hosting. Furthermore, the costs relative to the restructuring of procurement and organizational company processes increase, as well as the costs relative to the training and assistance of both personnel and suppliers, in the innovative adjustment process.

The greatest difficulty in the implementation of an e-procurement system seems to be related to the possibility to purchase complex goods and services. In fact, the purchase of raw materials or standardized services can certainly occur on the Internet while a real revolution in the procurement on the net of non-standardized products or services appears more difficult. In this case, in fact, the purchase price does not play a primary role, but customers look for a large basket of performance and quality characteristics of the product/service.

Organizational Changes in the Purchase Department

Within the purchasing department, major organizational changes have also been observed.

In terms of human resources, it has been found that the introduction of the e-procurement system implied an effective reduction of approx 30% in the number of staff employed in the purchasing department. It should also be considered that as a consequence of the above staff reduction, the number of companies of the group have increased and consequently the amount of work of the purchasing department. To this regard, the objective of process cost reduction results in improved organization of processes and containment of personnel cost.

As regards the activities, the use of e-sourcing solutions has led to a new configuration of the procurement process, which continues to include traditional activities although with a new type of relevance. Strategic activities become important, especially scouting and negotiation activities, while the administrative phase becomes less important. Furthermore, when the e-procurement system is integrated with the management system, the whole administrative activity becomes fully automated.

Thanks to the time that becomes available when the number of transactional activities reduces, the buyer is better able to organize his/her work and tackle more strategic and less routine aspects.

Conclusions

The peculiarities detected through this work, in part emerged during the administration of qualitative *face-to-face* interviews with a few managers of the purchasing department, have confirmed that the possible price reductions through an "open" negotiation on the web seem to prefigure the achievement of a situation that is "close" to that of a perfect market. Full information availability and existence of many actors in the supply market are the two basic elements for the achievement of minimum purchase prices.

Retrievability of information on the web and its easy transfer and diffusion through the systems being studied allow achievement of relevant reductions in time and cost of the procurement process. Furthermore, the simplification of administrative activities connected to the purchase process becomes particularly relevant since these can be fully automated when the e-procurement system is integrated with the management system of the company.

References

1. Rappaport A (1998) *Creating shareholder value*. The Free Press, New York
2. Emiliani M (2001) A mathematical logic approach to the shareholder vs. stakeholder debate, *Manage Decis* 39(8):618–622
3. Politecnico di Milano (2003) *Dai marketplace ai servizi di sourcing, procurement e supply chain collaboration*. Report dell'Osservatorio B2B, Milano
4. Politecnico di Milano (2004) *Il B2B in Italia: Finalmente Parlano i Dati*. Report dell'Osservatorio B2B, Milano
5. Lim BL, Wen J (2002) The impact of next generation XML. *Inf Manage Comput Secur* 10(1):33–40
6. Doyon T et al (2001) *E-procurement: perspective, preparation and selection*. Strategy/Tactics/Trends & Direction, May 7. Gartner Group, Lowell
7. Bartolini A (2006) *The 2006 E-procurement benchmark Report: E-Procurement 2.0*, Aderdeen Group
8. Emiliani ML, Stec DJ (2002) Realizing savings from online reverse auctions. *Supply Chain Manage Int J* 7(1):12–23
9. Marbert V, Skeels J (2002) Internet reverse auctions: valuable tools in experienced hands. *Bus Horiz* 45(4):70–76

IT Training: Impacts and Decision Drivers

Paola Bielli*[*] and Pier Franco Camussone[†]

Abstract Training is one of the key activities for Information and Communication Technologies (ICT) adoption processes in organizations. Literature emphasizes the importance of training to assimilate new technologies and to take the highest benefits from them. But we do not know enough about decisions drivers for launching ICT training programs, both to support the ICT introduction and later to reinforce the use of installed ICT. Besides, literature and business practice seem to ignore what happens when the pure training activity is over. E.g., what is the return for the company of the training effort? Based on this assumption, SDA Bocconi and AICA[1] launched a multiyear research program in order to understand the impact of ICT training on organizational performance and to investigated ICT training propensity among CIOs and HR managers.

Introduction

Information Systems (IS) literature often identifies the lack of training as one of the reasons for ICT are not really adopted and assimilated in organizations [1]. Despite this awareness, research projects and papers on ICT training are not numerous. In particular, the authors did not find much evidence on studies aimed at measuring the impacts of ICT training on organizations and industries. This is the reason why SDA Bocconi and AICA launched a multiyear research program in order to understand the impact of ICT training on organizational performance and to investigated ICT training propensity among CIOs and HR managers.

The key point is: the insufficient ICT training has a direct impact on the performance of an organization, an industry sector and a country as a whole? In the previous years the research project investigates the effects of ICT training in several industry sectors (like manufacturing, banking and health). In the 2008 the research project took in consideration the Public Administration (PA) and the results are presented in this paper.

The research is based on the theoretical frameworks developed in the previous research years and validated in terms of consistency with the scope of this year

---

[*] Università L. Bocconi, Milan, Italy, paola.bielli@unibocconi.it

[†] Università di Trento, Trento, Italy

[1] SDA Bocconi is the Business School of Bocconi University (Milan), while AICA (Associazione Italiana per l'informatica e il Calcolo Automatico) is the most important association of ICT professionals in Italy.

A. D'Atri et al. (eds.), *Management of the Interconnected World*,
DOI 10.1007/978-3-7908-2404-9_55, © Springer-Verlag Berlin Heidelberg 2010

project, the Italian public administration. The main research questions addressed by the study were:

- What are the impacts of ICT training at the individual and organizational level? What is the cost of insufficient training?
- What are the decision drivers for ICT training in organizations?

The paper introduces the research areas aimed respectively (a) at measuring the impact of ICT training and (b) at identifying the determinants of P.A. managers'[2] decision to adopt ICT training. In terms of methodology, in the first research area, we applied a quantitative approach, collecting data among public servants about their training experience and the perceived results. For the second area (decision drivers), through a survey the research team collected judgments and personal evaluations in a sample of public decision makers.

The paper first presents the two research areas, with their background literature, methodology and main findings, and then ends with some lessons learned on the whole research program.

Training and Productivity in Italian Public Administrations

White and blue collars in the digital society need a relatively high computer literacy and they use at any level the most common software applications, such as Internet browser, e-mail, word processing, spreadsheet, etc. ICT knowledge increases not only process speed, but also the quality of the outcome, which is more complete and richer [2, 3].

Besides, the link between growth and training has been analyzed from different perspectives, e.g., macroeconomic [4–6] and micro economic [7]. It is generally agreed that the economic growth of an industry, or of a country, is positively influenced by the effective and efficient use of ICT.

The rapid evolution of ICT implies frequent update of ICT competencies and ICT training should not stop at the end of the schooling system, to enable to worker to adapt to changes over time [8]. Surveys [9] demonstrated that increased productivity originates from the way people use ICT, to simplify their job and to get more time for higher value activities.

Previous studies in Italy [10–12] calculated a significant cost for the country as a whole and for specific industries, deriving from the low ICT literacy of the workforce.

In Italy central P.A.[3] accounts for 550,000 computer users[4]. Data collected in this study show that 51% of the sample employees spend more than 60% of their

[2] We found that ICT training decisions are taken either by CIOs (Chief Information Officers) or, less often, by HRM (Human Resource Managers). Therefore, in the rest of the paper we refer to CIOs to generically mention the decision makers.

[3] The Italy central PA is represented by National Government and his institutions like Social security, Civil protection, Economic & Statistical Agency, and so on.

[4] Source CNIPA (Department of the Central Government responsible for the coordination of the ICT Public investment of Italian National Administration).

working time on a computer; for an additional 14% of the sample computer time is more than 80% of the daily routine[5].

The relevance of these data for the present study is high: a low computer readiness of the employees can easily jeopardize the productivity of the administration.

The respondents were asked to estimate the average time they wasted weekly because of technical problems. The majority of the respondents declares they waste less than 60 min (with 11% of the respondents estimating more than 240 min). On average we calculated 69 min of unproductive time per week. Malfunctioning causes resulted to be technical (HW crashes or SW problems), insufficient user's knowledge, time wasted in supporting other ICT users. This survey calculated that technical problems represent 65% of unproductive time, while user illiteracy 35% (Fig. 1).

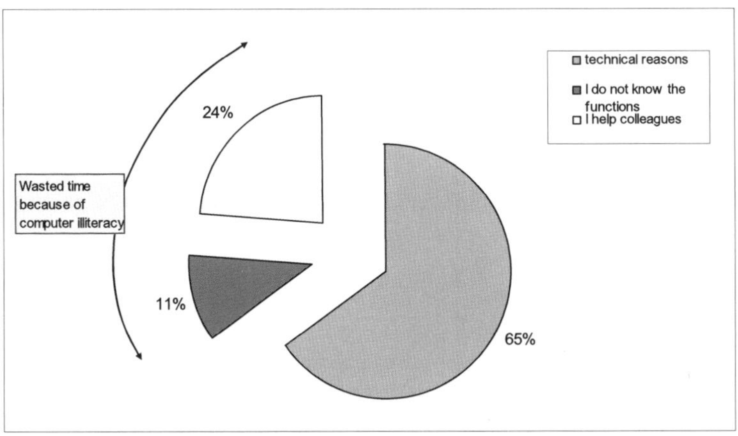

Fig. 1. Sources of unproductive time

Both factors are necessary to estimate in monetary terms the value of wasted time (around 1 h and 10 min a week per employee, which corresponds to 3.2% of the weekly working time). This value is 1.439€ a year per person and close to €280 million extending the mean value to the whole Public Administration in Italy (Table 1).

The previous paragraphs suggest that one possible way to increase efficiency in Italian P.A. is through a better use of ICT. In fact, this is coherent with one of the hypotheses of the whole research program, which states the following:

> *ICT training can increase the level of ICT knowledge and therefore, it contributes to reduce the cost of ICT ignorance in P.A. and can improve*

[5] The survey involved three ministries in Rome and other public employees who filled in an on line form. Altogether the usable questionnaires were 780.

individuals' productivity (reducing time needed to complete activities), and therefore the efficiency of the whole public sector.

Table 1. Total cost of unproductive work in central Public Administration in Italy

ICT users	Annual cost of unproductive computer work per person (€)	Total cost of unproductive computer work in central P.A. (€)	working time wasted for ICT illiteracy (€)	Annual cost of ICT illiteracy per person (€)	Total cost of ICT illiteracy in central P.A. (€)
550,000	1,439	791,239,931	35%	504	276,933,976

Previous researches had proved that a cause-effect relationship between ICT training and users' productivity does exist, and that improved ICT knowledge reduces illiteracy dependent wasted time [10]. Therefore, also in the case of Italian P.A. the researchers aimed at measuring ICT training impacts and they organized training sessions about ECDL[6] (European Computer Driving License) for about 200 P.A. employees. Before the training course the average ICT knowledge in the sample was already relatively high, reaching 50–60% of the maximum value for the different modules, scoring on average 53 points over 100. At the end of the course this average score reached 82 points, with an increase of more than 29 points over 100.

The last step links training impacts and productivity. As revealed in other researches [10] trained personnel can better accomplish activities which brought troubles before the course; needs lesser time to complete a task, wastes less time to solve problems deriving from limited ICT knowledge. Aware that just some of the benefits are measurable in monetary terms, the research team followed the approach developed in other similar works [9]. In this sample, time needed to complete the ECDL tests after the training course reduced (Fig. 2).

Generalizing these results to the whole central P.A., the increased profitability per employee might produce an annual benefit of 755 million of euro at the country level (Table 2). Tangible training benefits refer not only to increased productivity, but also to reduction of wasted time as seen before. The loss deriving from ICT ignorance amounted to €504 a year per employee (Table 1) and based on it can be estimated the total value if all P.A. employees would reach higher ICT literacy.

[6] ECDL is the standard assessment of the skill's level of PC usage ability according to EU Commission (http://www.ecdl.org).

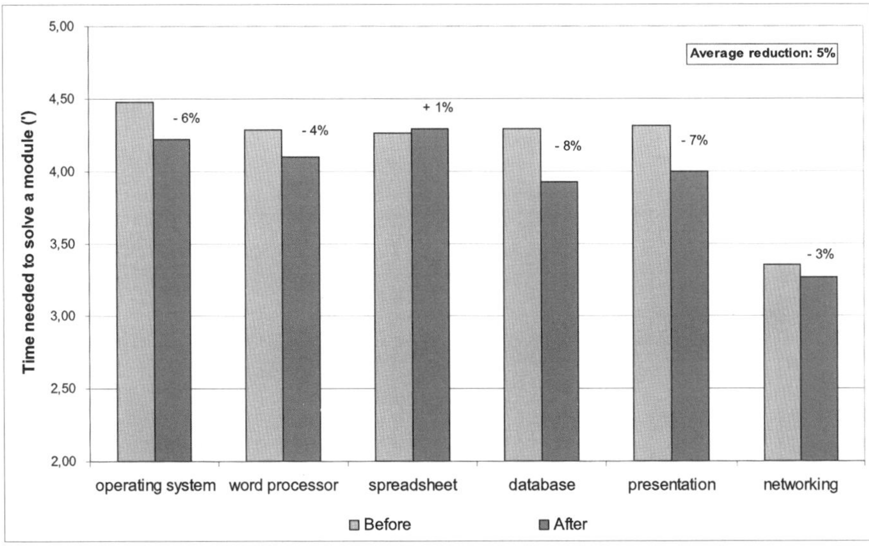

Fig. 2. Time needed to complete the exam before and after the training course

Table 2. Estimating ICT training impact on central P.A. productivity

Working hours on PC (% of total working hours)	5% increased productivity (hours)	Increase in the yearly working days	Daily cost per employee (€)	Monetary value of the increased productivity per employee (€)	Total increase in productivity (€)
22 (61%)	1,10	5,9	232	1,374	755,462,125

Basic assumptions are 550,000 users, with a working week of 36 h and an average annual cost of €45,035.

Using the results of the ECDL tests – where the participants improved by 29% the level of their knowledge – the research team came to an annual saving of €146 per person thanks to higher literacy, based on the assumption that the cost of ignorance would be reduced in the same proportion of the increment of knowledge. Table 3 sums up the total impact both at the employee and country level: evidently the benefit from increased productivity is almost 10 times bigger than time savings.

In synthesis, this research area clearly suggests that ICT training can have a financial return: the initial expenditures (some 100€ per person) to launch an ECDL course are compensated by cost savings and productivity gains for more than 1,500€ a year. If we assume that the benefits of training last more than 1 year, the financial impact is impressive.

Table 3. Annual value of the return on ICT training for the Italian central P.A.

P.A. ICT users	Increased productivity per employee (€)	Cost of ICT illiteracy avoidable with training per employee (€)	Annual return of ICT training per employee (€)	Annual return of ICT training for the central P.A. (€)
550,000	1,374	146	1,520	835,850,125

ICT Training Propensity

The first part of the research suggests that CIOs and HR managers should invest in ICT training to boost productivity, but often this does not happen. In the present session we discuss a model to analyze the determinants of ICT training propensity in Central PA in Italy. The ICT training propensity is examined in terms of intention to future use training services by a decision maker. Therefore, literature on customer loyalty [13] is useful in framing the issue and it enables to: (1) measure an index of the tendency for customer loyalty relative to each type of organizations operating in the same sector, but with different institutional and organizational structures; (2) construct and measure a valid, reliable system of indices of CIOs' beliefs on different aspects associated with determinants of ICT training in organizations. Previous studies [14] underlined the presence of a sort of concurrence between economic rationality and non-economic rationality in training decision. Based on this, the distinction or co-presence between technical environment and institutional environment [15–17] as settings conditioning managerial practices, their dissemination and adoption was introduced.

In synthesis, the main research propositions are: (1) the propensity toward ICT training is influenced by technical pressure (i.e. from the technical environment) and institutional pressure (i.e. from the institutional environment) in a *concurrent* manner; (2) this concurrence and/or competition is influenced by the presence/absence of practices and tools for measuring outcomes of ICT training; (3) the presence of measuring tools also conditions perceptions about past outcomes of ICT training.

For what the methodology is concerned, a model was developed including seven categories of variables: (1) technical variables, (2) institutional variables, (3) variables linked to the decision making process which lead to the implementation of ICT training initiatives, (4) variables linked to the process of measuring ICT training, (5) variables linked to past results, (6) organization variables, (7) technological variables. A *questionnaire* used both for direct or phone interviews was developed translating the above variables into *items* and into questions.

A total of 58 questionnaires were collected by phone and direct interviews with CIOs and HR managers from public administrations in Italy and processed with PLS techniques. On a 0–100 scale, the propensity toward ICT training is 47, lower than the figures calculated for the healthcare (51) and banking (58) industries in Italy.

The structural equation model obtained shows solid prediction power, since the variance (R^2) explained by the endogenous variable (ICT training propensity) is higher than 0.5. This would suggest that the latent variables hypothesized as antecedents influence propensity to a very substantial degree. The significance level of the *impacts* is 90%.

The applied model: (1) has taken into account and measured a spectrum of CIO beliefs and evaluations (as latent indices/variables) which explains most of the variance in their propensity to invest in ICT training, (2) it is useful to provide an accurate estimation of which CIOs' evaluations most strongly condition the propensity to invest in ICT training, and which have little or no effect on this intention. The matrix in Fig. 3 shows how latent variables are mapped on the axis of evaluations (vertical axis) and on the axis of impacts (horizontal axis). On the two axis, from high to low, the discriminant values are respectively 55 and 0.5.

Briefly, observing the four areas resulting in the matrix, we can divide the variables in some classes. In the first area (I) we find those variables which get high agreement by the sample, but which do not significantly impact ICT Training propensity. We might call them "myths", where managers do agree (by common sense or rationality) that they are important, but they have not the strength to eventually activate the training decision. We find here the importance of training to have effective ICT users or the impact of training of the administration's image. For this group of variables suggestions refer to creating the awareness about the real results they can achieve. In fact, the decision makers already believe in their importance; if they have data or facts showing the positive influence of ICT Training on performance and other variables, they would easily increase their propensity to invest in training.

In the second area (II) we have the factors eventually driving the ICT propensity, the real "training levers". This group has both a high level of agreement and high impact on propensity. Therefore, we might consider them as decision enablers and specifically, we list here the assimilation of technologies both already in place and new technologies (training supports ICT assimilation), externally driven changes require training and user driven decision processes imply higher training. As the Fig. 3 shows the higher impact derives from the need to increase the assimilation of present technologies and to face external changes, while users' preparation and new ICT are relatively lower.

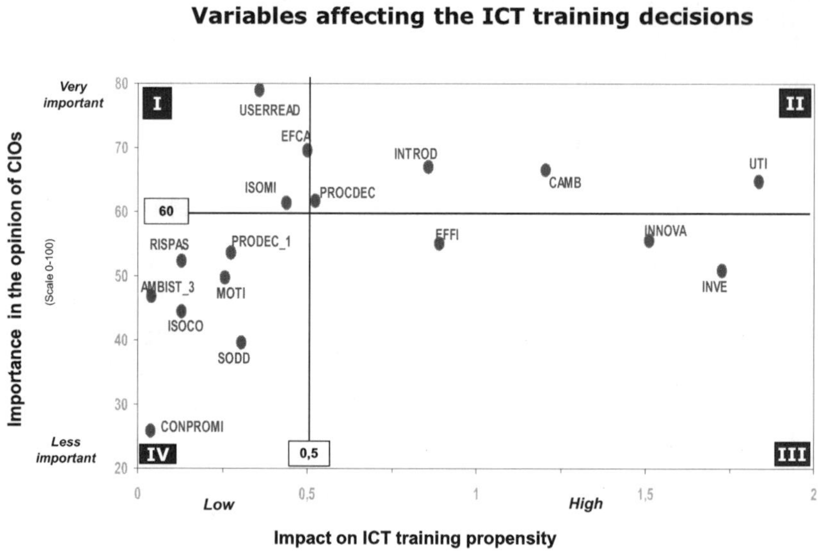

Fig. 3. The evaluation/impacts matrix

The third area (III) hosts those variables with a high impact, but low agreement (in other words they are not able to trigger the decision to launch a training program). We include three variables in this group: the level of IT investments, IT portfolio innovativeness in that administration and the efficiency gain through better users (the latter two variables at the border line with area 2). At one side, these results are a consequence of a certain reduction of public investments occurred in Italy in the recent years; at the other side it underlines again a lack of awareness about the real impact of training on organizations. We call this area "opportunities" to suggest that a growing effort in communication and measurement might help in moving these variables in area II.

Finally, the last area (IV) includes the variables whose impact and agreement are both low. Some variables (e.g. users' motivation and satisfaction) are perceived as potentially important, but they are too weak to activate a decision. Using a label, we might call this group "patter" as all its members are perceived as moderately important, but do not help in practice.

Conclusions

The research shows the relevance that ICT training play and might play for P.A. Despite that the survey shows that (1) the propensity toward IT training in the Italian P.A. was low; (2) the rationality of investment choices in this area was only one of the numerous factors that prompted training; (3) decision making processes regarding investments in ICT training did not appear to be hindered by any explicit and recognizable obstacles, such as limits in available resources, or organizational and cultural barriers. Instead, such decisions seemed to be influenced by a non-economic rationality, whereby training was implemented "because everyone knows it's good for you," and in any case "you know it could be useful." This situation seems to support the hypothesis that the development of more sophisticated measurement systems would allow organizations to activate a decision making process in a context characterized by a higher degree of economic and/or technical rationality.

A series of *limitations* are inherent to this study. Undoubtedly the first is linked to the number of respondents, which did not allow researchers to fully exploit the potential of *cluster analysis*. The second involves the data collection tool of choice, the questionnaire. In fact, answers given to each *item* (manifest variables) regarding latent institution-based variables might have been underestimated, given the need to express an opinion on external conditioning/influence. The third limitation may relate to the heterogenic nature of the variables being measured.

In terms of *directions for future research*, the study highlights the complexity of decision making processes leading to the adoption of managerial practices. Prior research conducted in the context of the health sector has underscored the "crisis" of economic rationality, and brought to light a sort of *competitive coexistence* between the institutional environment and the technical environment. The present study suggests that the concept of rationality can be broken down further, moving beyond the dichotomy of institutional environment vs. technical environment and economic rationality vs. non-economic rationality. The importance of variables, relating to user-readiness, corporate innovation, and technological change, suggest there is room for developing a rationality which is more aptly technological, midway between "real" knowledge and "superstitious" knowledge of training in information technology.

References

1. Camussone PF, Occhini G (2003) *Il costo dell'ignoranza nella società dell'informazione*. ETAS, Milano
2. Borgonovi E, Camussone PF, Occhini G (2004) *Il costo dell'ignoranza nella sanità*. ETAS, Milano
3. Brynjolfsson E, Hitt LM (2003) *Computing productivity: firm-level evidence*. MIT Sloan working paper, June
4. Scott WR, Meyer JW (1994) The rise of training programs in firms and agencies: an institutional perspective. In: Scott WR, Meyer JW (eds) *Institutional environments and organizations: structural complexity and individualism*. Sage, Thousand Oaks, London
5. Becagli R, Pagliari A (2004) La formazione informatica nella aziende della Sanità in Italia: un'indagine empirica. In Borgonovi E, Camussone PF, Occhini G (eds) *L'ignoranza informatica: il costo nella Sanità*. McGraw-Hill, Milano

6. Johnson MD, Anderson EW, Fornell C (1995) Rational and adaptive performance expectations in a customer satisfaction framework. Journal of Consumer Research 21:695-707
7. Danziger JN, Jenning JA, Park SC (1999) *ICT training, center for research on ICT and organizations*. University of California, Irvine
8. Dedrick J, Gurbaxani V, Kraemer K (2003) Information technology and economic performance: a critical review of the empirical evidence. *ACM Comput Surv* 35(1):1–28
9. Jorgenson D, Ho M, Stiroh K (2003) *Lessons from the U.S. growth resurgence; presented at the first international conference on the economic and social implications of information technology*. Department of Commerce, Washington, January 27–28
10. Stiroh KJ (2002) *Reassessing the impact of IT in the production function: a meta-analysis*. Federal Reserve Bank of New York, November
11. Hitt L, Brynjolfsson E (1996) Productivity, profit and consumer welfare: three different measures of information technology value. *MIS Q* 20(2):121–142
12. McKinsey Global Institute (2001) *US productivity growth – 1995–2000*. Washington, October
13. Camussone PF, Occhini G, Santececca D (2006) *Competenze digitali e produttività nel settore bancario*. McGraw-Hill, Milano
14. Fichman RG, Kremerer CF (1999) The illusory of diffusion of innovation: an examination of assimilation gaps. *Inf Syst Res* 10:255–275
15. Danziger JN, Wang YC (2000) *Enhancing end users' ICT skills in the new economy*. Center for research on ICT and Organizations, Irvine University, Irvine
16. DiMaggio PJ, Powell WW (1991) The iron cage revisited: institutional isomorphism and collective rationality in organization fields. In: DiMaggio PJ, Powell W (eds) *The new institutionalism in organizational analysis*. The University of Chicago Press, Chicago
17. Scott WR (1991) Unpacking institutional arguments. In: DiMaggio PJ, Powell W (eds) *The new institutionalism in organizational analysis*. The University of Chicago Press, Chicago

The Impact of Law on Accounting Information System: An Analysis of IAS/IFRS Adoption in Italian Companies

Katia Corsi* **and Daniela Mancini†**

Abstract Recently, several laws (38/2005, 231/2001, 262/2005) have been revising the corporate internal control legislation system in Italy, consequently requiring the accounting information system (AIS) to adapt[1]. Accounting systems and financial reporting must comply with new law requirements which generate a "corporate impact". The object of this paper is to examine this corporate impact. Analyzing four Italian listed companies, authors investigate the effects of the adoption of the International Accounting Standard-International Financial Reporting Standard (IAS/IFRS) on the information process, tools, accounting and procedures. The analysis shows that firms use different approaches to implement law requirements; authors develop a model to identify their determinants.

Introduction and Literature Review

AIS change can be interpreted according to two main theoretical approaches, which are both adopted in this paper. The first is described by the known and wide literature of the contingency theory [1–6], that, initially, considers the effectiveness of organization structure from a rational evaluation of the enterprise's environment, the strategy and the technology. In the subsequent developments many contributions relate the information system changes to external environment characteristics and to resulting strategic choices [7–11]. The second theoretical approach to the AIS change is the institutional isomorphism, that considers change as an adaptation, more or less obligatory (coercive, mimetic, normative) to external practices and procedures [12, 13].

---

* University of Sassari, Economy, Business and Regulations Department, Sassari, Italy, kcorsi@uniss.it

† Parthenope University of Naples, Business Studies Department, Naples, Italy, mancini@uniparthenope.it

[1] This research is carried out from both authors, however the first, the second and the fourth paragraph can be attributed to Katia Corsi, the third and the fifth paragraph to Daniela Mancini.

A. D'Atri et al. (eds.), *Management of the Interconnected World*,
DOI 10.1007/978-3-7908-2404-9_56,

Recently, several Italian laws restructured the corporate financial communication to markets: Law 231/2001 provides the specific model of internal control; Law 262/2005, similar to the US-Sarbanes Oxley Act, emphasizes the role of accounting control system, and Law 38/2005 imposes the adoption of the IAS/IFRS on the operating and consolidated balance sheets of Italian listed companies. All these legislator interventions have generated different impacts on the internal control system and its components, including the AIS [14–16].

The main object of this work is to verify the possible patterns of behavior in the Italian companies, in response to laws that have impact on information systems, and secondly to identify possible determinants of these patterns. This analysis, in particular, takes into account rules (IAS/IFRS) introduced in Italy by Law 38/2005, because they act more directly on the balance sheet and on the AIS, with consequent impacts on the data processing, on the accounting procedures, on the skills and on technical tools [17–19]. Authors assign to this legislative act a coercive nature, complying with institutional isomorphism framework, but the underlying process is wide and complex: it is interesting to examine the presence of a rational evaluation in the management process and the determinants which guide the changes of AIS, complying with contingency theory.

Method of Analysis

Authors conducted an empirical investigation on four case studies of large listed companies, in different sectors, among the industrial companies listed on Italian Stock Exchange. The case studies were selected on the base of the greater willingness to take part in this research. Table 1 highlights some financial and non financial information about the companies. For each company authors conducted one long semi-structured interview with those responsible for the IAS/IFRS project. All the interviewees were chief of accounting office and/or chief of internal auditing department. The interviews took place in December 2006, the first year of the adoption of IAS/IFRS in Italy.

In this work, authors followed a qualitative research method, consistent with traditional literature on case studies [20, 21], that allowed the authors to examine deeply the context in which the phenomenon was manifested [22].

Table 1. Main features of examined companies (2006)

	Organization 1	Organization 2	Organization 3	Organization 4
Sector	Gambling activities	Chimical-pesticides	Industrial machinery for woodworking	Industrial motors and pumps
Listing year	2004	2003	2001	1996
Number of employees	201	826	1,956	1,617

Sales (€/000)	619,078	156,102	396,733	364,876
Subsidiaries' number	15	13	25	26
Foreign markets	No	Yes	Yes	Yes

Discussion Results

The case studies confirmed the widespread impact of the IAS/IFRS on AIS, in particular, on every phase of the information and accounting process (Table 2):

- collecting data phase: data are taken, not only from corporate transactions, but also from management accounting (MIS) and general economic system;
- elaboration of data phase: this is getting more complex with the introduction of the risk component into the evaluation process and with a more detailed principle of recognition of some balance sheet's items;
- value representation phase: IAS/IFRS generate additional information supply, a different process to draw the consolidated balance sheet and an improvement financial reporting from a quality and quantity point of view.

Table 2. Summary research results about IAS-IFRS impact on AIS

	Organization 1	Organization 2	Organization 3	Organization 4
AIS/MIS integration	No	No	No	Yes
tools	Sap, easy report, easy finance, Ms-Excel	ERP formula, Business object, Ms-Excel	ERP formula, Ms-Excel	Enterprise, hyperion
Accounting changes	Chart of accounts	Chart of accounts Accounting procedures Knowledge in accounting area	Chart of accounts Elaboration processes of non-accounting data	Chart of accounts Consolidation manual Corporate accounting standard

Adoption of IAS/IFRS requires significant changes in AIS and involves a high exploitation of time, human resources and skills. Therefore, their implementation, like other coercive changes related to the Legislator acts that impact on AIS, is a costly project. Companies may consider this investment in term of cost/risk/opportunity for the redesign of administrative procedures and for the management of accounting information. The results of the case studies analysis are synthesized in the following statements of the examined companies and summarized in Table 3.

Organization 1: "We observe the law but we do not share it"

"Twice the work but zero clarity in return. The balance sheet became matter for specialists: in the past the figures were more raw but now they are much more sophisticated. One thing is to read four pages and two tables, another thing is to read 250 pages of notes".

The company grasps the elements of simplification without too much enthusiasm and without the top management commitment because it doesn't believe in the new IAS culture and is anchored to the previous tradition. The change of AIS is made carefully, but it is often determined by the audit firm and its positive judgement on balance sheet. Stress is put on the formal enforcement of the law.

Organization 2: "We must limit the damage"
"The IAS/IFRS adoption was seen as a nuisance. Rather than taking a pro-active approach it was preferred a defensive one, to avoid excessive changes and complexity. Costs and benefits analysis did not lead to consider the project as an investment but as a threat".

The company tries to make the AIS as compliant as possible to IAS/IFRS, limiting the changes required and minimizing costs and administrative complications. The IAS/IFRS project is seen as an administrative problem, without any particular involvement of other functions. People involved look again at the auditing firm and its know-how with suspicion. Stress is put on the costs generated to comply with the regulation in force.

Organization 3: "We must keep business under control"
"Our approach to the IAS/IFRS transition was to limit the damage because of: - at the beginning we had a very vague idea of the project and of the gap; - we are a company which needs to continue to work. We tried not to upset things too much for everyone else, otherwise we will not be able to read the business".

The company limits the damage of IAS/IFRS adoption not because it is necessary to keep the same information (as in the past) in order to guarantee continuity of external communication, but rather to preserve the understanding of the internal results and controlling over business and information.

Organization 4: "We want to seize the opportunities"
"We lived the IAS/IFRS project well. It was an opportunity to look around the companies of the group, to study again the group accounting principles, the opportunity to join together the group. It was a way to grow up together and to confront each other"

The company considers the IAS/IFRS implementation as an opportunity to audit at corporate level the balance sheet accounting communication from three points of view: accounts, informational and organizational. The IAS/IFRS experience is pervasive under a strong commitment of top management and the relationship between this company and the consultant/audit firms is managed as a partnership. Stress is primarily put on the benefits arising from being compliant in the best way, not only outside but also inwards.

Table 3. Summary research results about IAS/IFRS project

	Organization 1	Organization 2	Organization 3	Organization 4
Top management role	Involvement with skepticism	Strong disinterest	Informed	Active partecipation
Project leader	A function	Single office	A function	Inter functional
Subjects involved	Administrative responsible, balance sheet and consolidated responsible, Controller, KPMG	Balance sheet and consolidated responsible, IA, IR, E&Y	CFO, Administrative responsible, IA, Controller, IR, SIA, Deloitte	CFO, Administrative responsible, IA, Controller, IR, SIA, KPMG
Audit company role	Conditioner	Training	Support/advice	Support/advice

Patterns of Behavior for IAS/IFRS Project

Case studies analysis, outlined in the section before, shows that companies adopt different approaches and different behavior to implement law requirements. As illustrated in Table 4, according to interviews' results, we identify three behavioral approaches, which can be represented along a continuum. In the transition from first to third approach we can highlight the following aspects [23–26]:

- the focus of the management of AIS changes moves from efficiency (saving costs) to effectiveness (gathering all the opportunities);
- the focus of the integration of AIS and MIS moves from the use of both office automation tools and accounting information software, to the implementation of an integrated information system that automatically generate financial reports;
- the growing of horizontal integration of the organization involves the administrative level of all the company functions (finance, management control, human resources, etc.), to retrieve data and to gain skills necessary for financial report assessment;
- the growing of vertical integration of the organization: a greater discretion and a higher level of risk on the evaluation process leads to an involvement of the functional middle management in accounting information process;

- the growing of the integration of internal and external information: the increase of data sources coming from the management accounts generates an integration between financial and accounting management, in this way the financial information for the market is no longer a constraint but it is similar to the internal reports.

Table 4. The behavioural approaches to IAS/IFRS adoption

Approaches	Attitude towards the IAS/IFRS	Areas involved	Focus
Accounting approach (Organization 1 and 2)	Passive: the companies adapt themselves to IAS	Accounting	The balance sheet procedures
Administrative/ managerial approach (Organization 3)	Active/defensive: the companies adopt the IAS	Administrative area/accounting process	The administrative and managerial procedures
Strategic approach (Organization 4)	Active/proactive: the companies exploit the IAS	Most of the business functions at different organizational levels	The risk management in the accounting evaluation process

Determinants of Law Adoption Approach on AIS

The study presented in this work shows that firm behaviours caused by coercive changes on AIS are different and characterized by an increasing pervasiveness and effectiveness. Therefore it is useful for legislators and companies to understand the determinants of effectiveness of these changes.

The first hypothesis concerns how IAS project is conducted, in terms of time spent, phases developed, methodology and people involved. Interviews show that there are no relevant differences between the companies among these aspects. The second hypothesis is to consider the elements of difference between case studies examined in IAS project conduction. Authors isolated the following aspects: (a) top management commitment; (b) project team composition; (c) corporate international profile; (d) information asymmetry between the competitors; (e) length of quotation.

The first significant element is the degree of involvement of the top management in such project. In cases of greater involvement, the project is managed with a wide and prospective vision, aiming at an in depth review of the balance sheet information process. The results are the improving of financial communication, the involvement of a number of business functions in the balance sheet process and the review of "the ways to do" the administrative process.

The second aspect is connected to the previous. When the project team composition involves different skills, not only the administrative ones, the project is managed with an integrated and rational vision of information process.

The third factor is the number of subsidiaries outside Italy (the international profile of the groups). In this context the administrative culture is used to draft the consolidated balance sheet according to different rules and legislation. Therefore the international groups have an open and flexible approach to the IAS adoption problem, while national groups are tied to the past and "old" standards.

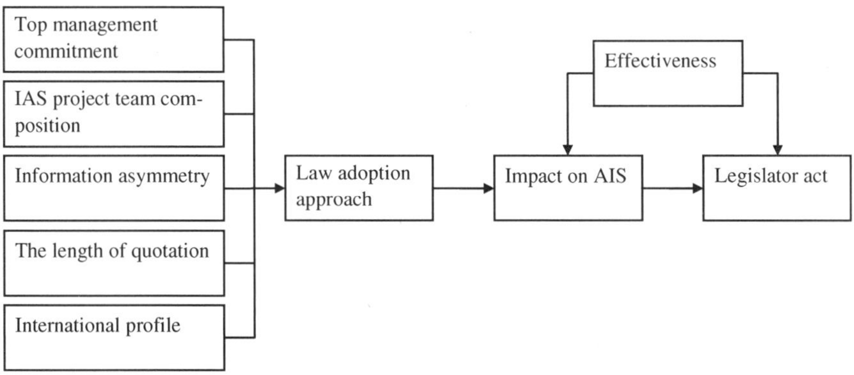

Fig. 1. The determinants of law adoption approach

A high specific weight is assigned to the information asymmetry between listed and not listed companies in the same sector. In some cases, companies prefer a soft implementation of IAS/IFRS in order to prevent the diffusion of sensitive information that could somehow benefit directly not listed competitors which are not required to provide such information (Fig. 1).

Finally a significant differentiation point is the length of time quotation, in fact the "best practice" company is also the most time listed on the Stock Exchange.

Conclusions and Further Research

Based upon data from case studies operating in Italy, this study revealed the different ways to manage the IAS/IFRS implementation. The impacts on the AIS have different importance and the difference is due to some factors, such as commitment of top management, composition of the IAS project team, international profile of the group, the information asymmetry between the competitors and the length of time quotation.

The results of this work can have useful implication for the legislator and the companies. The legislator learns that it isn't sufficient a law to induce an effective behavioral change, but he must act on the determinants factors. The companies, knowing the determinants factors, have a tool to implement effectively the changes required by the legislator.

In the future researches, we will extend the same analysis to other Italian regulatory requirements which affect more or less directly on AIS, such as L.262/2005.

References

1. Burns T, Stalker GM (1962) *The management of innovation*. Tavinstock, London
2. Chandler AD (1962) *Strategy and structure – chapters in the history of American industrial enterprise*. MIT Press, Cambridge
3. Lawrence P, Lorsh J (1967) *Organization and environment*. Irwin, Homewood
4. Thompson JD (1967) *Organizations in action*. McGraw-Hill, New York
5. Woodward J (1965) *Industrial organization: theory and practice*. Oxford University Press, London
6. Perrow C (1967) A framework for the comparative analysis of organizations. *Am Sociol Rev* 32(2):194–208
7. Abernethy MA, Guthrie CH (1994) An empirical assessment of the "fit" between strategy and management information system design. *Account Finance* 34(2):49–66
8. Gordon L, Miller D (1976) A contingency framework for the design of accounting information systems. *Account Organ Soc* 1(1):59–69
9. Chenhall RH, Morris D (1986) The impact of structure, environment, and interdependence on the perceived usefulness of management accounting systems. *Account Rev* 61(1):16–35
10. Waterhouse J, Tiessen P (1978) A contingency framework for management accounting system research. *Account Organ Soc* 3(1):65–76
11. Thomas AP (1991) Towards a contingency theory of corporate financial reporting systems. *Account Audit Account J* 4(4):40–57
12. Di Maggio PJ, Powell WW (1983) The iron cage revisited: institutional isomorphism and collective rationality in organizational fields. *Am Sociol Rev* 48(2):147–160
13. Corsi K (2008) *Il sistema di controllo amministrativo-contabile. Prospettive e dinamiche evolutive alla luce degli IAS/IFRS*. Giuffrè, Milano
14. Coopers & Lybrand (1997) *Il sistema di controllo interno. Progetto di Corporate Governance per l'Italia*. Il Sole 24. Ore, Milano
15. D'Onza G (2008) *Il sistema di controllo interno nella prospettiva del risk management*. Giuffré, Milano
16. Mancini D (2005) *Le condizioni di efficacia del sistema di controllo aziendale. Qualità e sicurezza nel governo delle aziende*. Giappichelli, Torino
17. Andrei P (2006) *L'adozione degli IAS/IFRS in Italia: impatti contabili e gestionali*. Giappichelli, Torino
18. Cantino V, De Valle A (2005) *Impatto degli IAS/IFRS sui processi gestionali*. Ipsoa, Milano
19. Marchi L, Paolini A, Castellano N (2008) *Principi contabili internazionali e sistemi di controllo interno*. FrancoAngeli, Milano
20. Eisenhardt KM (1989) Building theories from case study research. *Acad Manage Rev* 14(4):532–550
21. Yin R (1994) *Case study research. Design and methods*. Sage, London
22. Franceschi Ferraris R (1998) *Problemi attuali dell'economia aziendale*. Giuffré, Milano
23. Merlyn V, Parkinson J (1994) *Development effectiveness strategies for IS organizational transition*. Wiley, New York

24. Cantoni F, Mangia G (2005) *Lo sviluppo dei Sistemi informative nelle organizzazioni.* FrancoAngeli, Milano
25. Ravagnani R (2000) *Information technology e gestione del cambiamento organizzativo.* Egea, Milano
26. Marchi L (1993) *I sistemi informativi aziendali.* Giuffré, Milano

Part XII
Innovation Transfer of IT Research Projects

Domenico Saccà[*] and Michele Missikoff[†]

Nowadays, the current global economic crisis calls for a profound reogranisation in all productive sectors. To face this crisis, ICT firms must introduce more innovations within their technologies, products and business processes. Therefore, the cooperation with public and private partners for the development of research activities or system integration, for the implementation of their innovation capabilities and technology knowledge transfer, become a key factor.

In ICT fields, a great opportunity is given by co-operative projects focused on research and development technologies and innovation transfer, provided that technology-based innovation processes be adapted to deep changes in organizational contexts.

On the other hand, conventional models, methods and tools used to support technology transfer and diffusion of IT domain are becoming obsolete. Advanced ICT tools offer a set of new possibilities to facilitate the use of open cooperative and decentralized models where different entities asynchronously cooperate by adapting transfer/diffusion processes and roles to specific cases, situations, countries and cultures.

In this context, the track this part refers to, focused on the new open cooperative technology transfer and diffusion models needed to handle ICT based innovation, and addresses new theories and tools, and best practices in cooperative and network-based ICT transfer and diffusion. Relevant topics discussed in the track were:

- Cooperative IT transfer and innovation theory and practice;
- Public–private partnerships for ICT transfer and diffusion;
- Public procurement of IT services and other demand-side policies as catalysts or open innovation;
- Open innovation models for networked organizations;
- Technological and scientific districts;
- IT tools to support cooperative technology transfer and diffusion in the context of Web 2.0 and future 3.0;

[*] Università della Calabria, Rende, CS, Italy, sacca@unical.it

[†] CNR, Roma, Italy, missikoff@iasi.cnr.it

- Case studies and best practices for specific technologies, geographical contexts, or organizations related to ICT or ICT-supported fields;
- Best practices and experiences of innovations transfer of ICT research projects

Among all papers presented for this track at the conference, only five have been selected to appear in this book.

Transferring FAME, a Methodology for Assessing Open Source Solutions, from University to SMEs

Filippo E. Pani[*], Daniele Sanna[†], Michele Marchesi[‡] and Giulio Concas[॥]

Abstract We present FAME (Filter, Analyze, Measure and Evaluate), a simplified approach for Open Source software assessment. This approach has been derived by more heavyweight, proven approaches developed in a University research environment, to match the needs of small organizations. The proposed approach has been developed by CC-ICT-SUD, a consortium for the delivery of technology transfer services, and for transferring advanced methodologies for software evaluation and assessment from academic to industrial contexts, in particular for Small and Medium Enterprises (SME). The FAME methodology is briefly described, and a case study involving the choice of a document management system for a SME is presented, showing how the approach can be used.

Introduction

Nowadays, information systems are crucial to organizations, because they influence practically all their businesses processes. Therefore, the optimal choice of their architecture and of their software components is of paramount importance. A wrong choice can lead to dire consequences, such as inefficiencies, information loss, higher maintenance and redesign costs, stop of operational activities, and so on. In recent years, free/open source software (F/OSS) emerged as a viable solution for software applications [1, 2]. The increasing interest in F/OSS is patent in many

---

[*] Electronic and Electric Engineering Department, University of Cagliari, Cagliari, Italy, filippo.pani@diee.unica.it

[†] FlossLab Srl, Cagliari, Italy, daniele.sanna@flosslab.it

[‡] Electronic and Electric Engineering Department, University of Cagliari, Cagliari, Italy, michele@diee.unica.it

[॥] Electronic and Electric Engineering Department, University of Cagliari, Cagliari, Italy, concas@diee.unica.it

A. D'Atri et al. (eds.), *Management of the Interconnected World*,
DOI 10.1007/978-3-7908-2404-9_57, © Springer-Verlag Berlin Heidelberg 2010

different contexts – communities of individual users, private firms focusing their attention on this kind of approach, and public institutions. The reasons of the success of F/OSS software include:

1. Cost: F/OSS is usually available at no cost for public download.

2. Quality: F/OSS source code is available to all. This transparent approach enables to produce high-quality products, achieved through an elaborate peer-review process performed by a large community of users, who act as co-developers to identify and correct software defects and add features [3–6].

The European Commission is currently funding several research projects related to open source and quality, namely, QUALOSS [7] FLOSSMetrics [8], SQO-OSS [9] and QUALIPSO [10]. However, it is very difficult to decide which F/OSS application to adopt inside an organization, because the number of open source projects is strongly increasing. Some products have their own web site as the main distribution mechanism for the software. However, the huge part of F/OSS products are available through portals, which act as repositories of projects. On SourceForge alone, one the most important repositories, more than one hundred thousand projects are hosted. So the myriad of F/OSS products makes actual adoption a real challenge, and it is necessary to have methods to assess and compare these software products [4, 5, 11–13]. In the last years, many F/OSS evaluation methodologies have been proposed to address this issue. All these methodologies have effectiveness as their main goal, and this goal led to a hardly sustainable increase of their complexity, from both the perspective of their costs and needed competences. All evaluation frameworks reported in the literature were devised using an analytic research approach, trying to analyze very many factors [11–13]. For this reason, such frameworks are often not easily applicable to real environments, especially in the case of small organizations.

This paper presents a new F/OSS maturity and reliability evaluation methodology, called FAME for "Filter, Analyze, Measure and Evaluate". FAME is aimed to reduce the evaluation complexity, and thus to be easily usable also by SMEs and small public bodies. FAME was born from the experience of CC-ICT-SUD, a consortium for the delivery of technology transfer services aimed to improve demand and offering in ICT technologies, and to offer technology advanced solutions in ICT field. This consortium chose to support SMEs in selecting F/OSS applications, using a simple, structured and scientifically tested approach. The FAME approach is derived from previous studies performed at the University of Cagliari, partner of CC-ICT-SUD, characterized by a rigorous, but heavyweight approach to F/OSS selection [14, 15, 11]. CC-ICT-SUD worked to devise a simpler approach, more suited to be applied by small organizations. The goals of FAME methodology are to aid the choice of high-quality F/OSS products, with high probability to be sustainable in the long term, and to be as simple and *user friendly* as possible. The evaluation is not only about technical features of the product and quality of its development community, but it also takes into account a cost-benefit analysis specific of the involved organization. The paper is organized as follows: in the next sections we first describe some of the main F/OSS evaluation methodologies; then we describe the origin, motivation and main features of FAME; eventually, we describe its application in a case study and provide some conclusive remarks.

Software Assessment Methodologies

Many studies [3, 4] investigated whether the maturity of the processes employed by distributed, volunteer projects is linked to their success. The results of these studies clearly showed that the maturity of open source processes are correlated to the success of a project. This study identified the importance of the use of version control tools, effective communication through the deployment of mailing lists, and found several effective strategies related to testing. In spite of the widespread use of open source products in academic and industrial environments, only recently first attempts have been made to evaluate open source products. Some significant contributions are mentioned in this section. All these methodologies have common criteria; they also present various phases and are based on scores. The main elements of F/OSS evaluation methodologies are:

Assessment Model: there are several levels of details or assessment granularity; Some predefined criteria are usually provided; the methodology permits the use of domain specific criteria, based on technical information or features.

Scoring Model: each criterion/aspect of the evaluated product is evaluated through a score, according to a given scale; the assessment can be performed and refined using several steps, each improving the detail level; it is possible to apply weighting on the assessed criteria, as part of the methodology scoring model

Evaluation Elements: The common Evaluation element of these methodologies are: Software Quality, Support, Documentation, Training, Product integration, Professional Services, Seniority, Functionality, Adoption, Popularity. Some of them use a comparison process defined by the methodology. Some among the main F/OSS evaluation methodologies are the following.

Business Readiness Rating

Business Readiness Rating (BRR) is being proposed as a new standard model for rating open source software. It is intended to enable the entire community (enterprise adopters and developers) to rate software in an open and standardized way [16].

The Open Source Maturity Model

The Open Source Maturity Model (OSMM) is designed to help organizations to successfully adopt and implement open source software. It consists in a three-phase process for selecting, assessing and implementing F/OSS products [17].

Open Source Maturity Model by Capgemini

In order to be able to determine if an open source product is suitable for an organization, Capgemini developed its Open Source Maturity Model (OSMM) [18]. The OSMM describes how a F/OSS product should be assessed to ensure that the product meets the IT challenges companies face today. The OSMM accomplishes this by linking an extensive product analysis with a thorough review of the company and its IT issues. Capgemini's knowledge and experience serves as the glue that links these two parts together to product a clear, independent and reliable overview of the use of an Open Source product within a specific company.

QSOS

In order to have a method of qualification and selection of open software, Atos Origin built an original methodology to evaluate F/OSS software called QSOS [19]. The general process of QSOS is made up of several interdependent steps.

EFFLOSS

This approach is intended to help IT organization assess which open source software would be most suitable for their needs [15]. The main limit of the frameworks described above is that they are based on qualitative metrics. The key idea of EFFLOSS is to systematically use quantitative metrics that can be automated, taking advantage of the information that can be found in the Web. In order to allow an easy usage of EFFLOSS, the assessment process is divided in three steps, which are performed sequentially: step 1 determines the features that characterize an open source product [20]; step 2 identifies the success metrics; step 3 assigns a score for each metric.

FAME: Filter, Analyze, Measure and Evaluate Approach

FAME methodology originates from two methodologies developed at University of Cagliari to evaluate the maturity of F/OSS projects. The first of these is NVAF (Needs, Values, Assessment Framework) [14], intended to support the choice of software applications. NVAF is mainly addressed to public administrations and has a neutral approach to assure impartiality in the adoption of IT solutions based on proprietary software or F/OSS. The framework accounts also for the social impact of the choice. The second methodology is EFFLOSS mentioned above, aimed also to use quantitative metrics gathered on the Internet about the projects to evaluate. Both NVAF and EFFLOSS, however, are quite heavyweight approaches, suitable for large organizations or research studies, but difficult to adopt by SMEs. For this reason, in the context of the activities of CC-ICT-SUD, a consortium aimed to improve demand and offering in ICT technologies, we decided to devise a new methodology to support SMEs in selecting F/OSS applications, using a simple, structured and scientifically tested approach, building on the previous experience of Cagliari University. The main idea behind FAME is that the users should evaluate which solution amongst those available is more suitable to their needs by comparing technical and economical factors, and also taking into account the total cost of individual solutions and cash outflows. It is necessary to consider the investment in its totality and not in separate parts that are independent of one another. This principle is strictly related to a set of conditions to account for, its constraints, disadvantages and benefits. First, the goals of the project need to be defined, and the planning approach has to follow a strategic investment choice. In particular, we also consider all the positive effects registered in the area where the investment takes place. The required activities to obtain these results are:

- identify and evaluate the main constraints and risks;
- identify and evaluate the needs of the involved organization;
- identify and prioritize the key objectives;
- provide a priority framework.

The stakeholders with strategical information are considered as users of the framework. They are in charge to make changes and to approve the choices of a specific project. The methodology is structured according to four distinct phases:

- ***Filtering***, aimed to reduce up-front the number of candidate solutions, thus simplifying the whole process; it includes the creation of an "identity card" for each candidate project, holding all the data that can be gathered on it, mainly through the Web.
- ***Analysis***, to elicit the needs of the organization, and consequently the element important for the evaluation and their relative relevance. To this purpose, we use the GQM (Goal-Question-Metrics) approach, derived from software engineering studies [21].
- ***Measurement***, to define the quantities to measure, and to perform such measurements, building on the previous analysis phase.
- ***Evaluation***, includes the normalization of the measurements using a Cost-Benefit Analysis approach, and performs the relative comparison, up to the final result.

Validation of FAME Methodology

To validate FAME we used as test case a real need of a SME, which decided to enter the Document Management System (DMS) market with a F/OSS approach. To this purpose, they had to choose the open source DMS best suited to their needs. The skills of the firm were mainly in Java. In the followings, we will briefly describe how the four phases of FAME were applied to this specific case.

Filter Phase

In this phase, key prerequisites of the programs to choose are selected, with the goal to reduce the number of potential candidates for the next phase. These prerequisites can be linked to strategic issues, such as quality and sustainability of the project, and to technical issues, such as the target operating system, programming language, and so on. In our case, we set a filter to restrict the DMS projects to those written in Java and PHP, because of their portability. Another filter was set to consider only highly popular – and hence highly downloaded and with a high activity index – projects. Since Java is the language used by the SME, we set a preference towards Java by lowering the latter filter requirements in the case of Java projects with respect to PHP ones. We searched SourceForge and Ohloh F/OSS repositories, and came out with a list of five projects, namely Alfresco, Contineo, e-prot, KnowledgeTree and Nuxeo. Among these, only KnowledgeTree is a PHP project, all others being Java ones. We also allowed for two more projects: Adam, an Italian DMS promoted by Italian Center for Open Source in Public Administrations (CNIPA), and Hummingbird, a proprietary project evaluated for comparison purposes. The last part of this phase was to create an "identity card" for all pre-selected projects, gathering the most relevant information about them, as found in the Internet.

Analyze Phase

This phase was the most critical and effort-prone. It consisted in eliciting the key *needs* of the SME, as regards the DMS to choose. Following FAME guidelines, we performed an analysis of technical-functional and economic requirements, and associated to them suitable metrics – a need corresponds to one or more metrics. A typical metric scale for the need relevance is:

1: not relevant
2: not much relevant
3: fairly relevant
4: relevant
5: very relevant

We set high priority to the programming language, security (using popular protocols, including LDAP), quality of documentation, and community "strength".

Measurement Phase

The various identified metrics were evalued using different units, depending on their specificity. Some of them were simply Boolean (yes or no, corresponding to 1 and 0 respectively), denoting the presence or absence of a specific feature. Some had a score between 1 and 5, while others had a three-valued score (0, 1, 2). For the sake of simplicity, the relative weights were chosen identical to the relevance factor for the relative need, that is between 1 and 5. The metrics were then applied on the relevant features of the pre-selected projects, using data found in their "identity card", SourceForge and projects' Web sites and source code repositories, yielding a set of scores for each candidate product.

Evaluate Phase

In this phase, we normalized the measured values in such a way to become consistent with each other, and to reflect comparable values in economic terms. We then weighted them according to the relevance of the respective needs, obtaining the total scores for each area (technical and economic). The final result was obtained by summing up the partial scores. The DMS with the highest score was Alfresco, in both the technical and economic areas, and it was therefore the chosen project.

Conclusions

In this paper we presented a FAME, a simplified methodology for F/OSS project assessment, and its applications to a specific case study. FAME is derived from quite heavyweight methodologies, but was simplified in order make simpler its use. FAME is a new-generation evaluation methodology, able to be tuned to specific needs and without fixed and pre-defined score systems. Its main original characteristics are: a filtering phase to pre-select project candidates, easing the whole evaluation process; an analysis of the needs of the organization performed using a GQM approach and in practice able to configure the evaluation process according to the actual organization's needs, both technical and economic; a phase that explicitly considers various viable metrics, including possible quantitative measurements of software repositories and Web hits related to the projects; a final evaluation phase that blends together different metrics, making them comparable and consistent, and performs the final evaluation. Presently, we are working on the application of the methodology to other case studies, in the context of CC-ICT-SUD technology transfer consortium, also in order to get feedback for improving FAME itself. We are also considering the automation of the evaluation process of some the identified metrics, taking advantage of the information that can be found in the Web.

Acknowledgments CC-ICT-SUD funded this technology transfer experience.

References

1. Feller J, Fitzgerald B, Hissam S, Lakhani K (2005) Perspectives on free and open source software. The MIT Press, Cambridge
2. FLOSS (2003) Free/Libre and open source software: survey and study: final report. Available at: http://FLOSS.infonomics.nl
3. Senyard A, Michlmayr M (2004) How to have a successful free software project. In: APSEC, IEEE Computer Society, Los Alamitos, pp 84–91
4. Michlmayr M (2005) Software process maturity and the success of free software projects. In: Zielinski K, Szmuc T (eds) Software engineering: evolution and emerging technologies. IOS Press, Amsterdam, pp. 3–14
5. Crowston K, Annabi H, Howison J (2003) Defining open source soft ware project success. In: ICIS, Association for Information Systems, Atlanta, pp 327–340

6. Crowston K, Annabi H, Howison J, Masango C (2004) Towards a portfolio of floss project success measures. Open Source Workshop of the International Conference on Software Engineering
7. QUALOSS (2008) http://www.qualoss.org
8. FLOSSMetrics (2008) http://flossmetrics.org
9. SQO-OSS (2008) http://www.sqo-oss.eu
10. QUALIPSO (2008) http://www.qualipso.org
11. Cau A, Concas G, Marchesi M (2006) Extending OpenBRR with automated metrics to measure object oriented open source project success. The workshop on evaluation frameworks for OSS, collocated in the second international conference on OSS2006
12. Ciolkowski M, Soto M (2008) Towards a comprehensive approach for assessing open source projects. In: Dumke RR et al (eds) Proceedings of the international conferences on software process and product measurement. Munich, Germany, November 18–19. Lecture notes in computer science, vol 5338. Springer, Heidelberg, pp 316–330
13. Deprez, JC, Alexandre S (2008) Comparing assessment methodologies for free/open source software: OpenBRR and QSOS. Lecture notes in computer science, Springer, New York
14. Mannaro, K Concas G, Marchesi M (2006) NVAF: un Framework per una valutazione di tipo comparativo delle soluzioni software nelle Pubbliche Amministrazioni. Esperta 2006, Como, Italy
15. Cau A (2007) EFFLOSS: an evaluation framework for Free/Libre Open Source. PhD Thesis
16. Business Readiness Rating (2005) A proposed open standard to facilitate assessment and adoption of open source software. http://www.openbrr.org
17. Golden B (2004) Succeeding with open source. Addison-Wesley Information Technology Series, Addison-Wesley Professional, Boston
18. Open Source Maturity Model (2000) Published on: http://www.seriouslyopen.org
19. QSOS (2006) Method for Qualification and Selection of Open Source software (QSOS) version 1.6 Atos Origin, April 2006. http://qsos.org
20. Jones C (2000) Software assessments, benchmarks, and best practices. Addison-Wesley, Boston
21. Basili V (1995) Applying the Goal/question/metric Paradigm in the Experience Factory. Software quality assurance and measurement: a worldwide perspective, Chapter 2. International Thomson Computer Press, London, pp 21–44

Innovative Strategies to Knowledge Transfer in a Context of Open Innovation

Angela Sansonetti * **and Alessandro D'Atri** †

Abstract In a conventional way, we refer to "open source" as the set of tools achieved without licensing, and available to every user in open environments oriented toward democratization of innovation. In another meaning, it is possible to assume open sources as the set of material and immaterial resources shared in open environments to produce innovation. Thus, the open innovation phenomenon is multifaceted and may be used to explain various issues related to the sharing of knowledge, know-how and competencies in a lot of contexts. In this new framework, this paper explores the open innovation paradigm as an innovative and pervasive method to transfer knowledge from research organizations to industrial world. Among the different ways to transfer innovative knowledge, this paper focuses on spin-off phenomenon, as one of the most effective and suitable approach to transfer innovation from research organizations to industrial world and to capitalize on tangible and intangible outcomes. The main attention concerns inter–intra organizational issues of IT spin-offs created within European cooperative research projects.

Introduction

In the last years, an important change in innovation processes is occurring due to the increase of collaborative research and sharing of knowledge and intellectual property among different organizations, that they traditionally produced and coordinated research and innovation processes sole and without ecosystem exchange [1].

---

* LUISS Guido Carli University, Rome, Italy, asansonetti@luiss.it
† LUISS Guido Carli University, Rome, Italy, datri@luiss.it

A. D'Atri et al. (eds.), *Management of the Interconnected World*,
DOI 10.1007/978-3-7908-2404-9_58,

The growth of an "user-centered" approach induces to an important change of innovation processes from "the traditional manufacturer-centric model, in which products and services are developed by manufacturers in a closed way, with the manufacturers using patents, copyrights, and other protections to prevent imitators from free riding on their innovation investments" [2] to an open innovation approach characterized by the sharing of knowledge among communities operating in distinct organizations.

In this new framework characterized by the sharing of knowledge and intellectual know-how to produce new knowledge in a not always codified way, the interaction between public research organization and industry has significantly increased through collaborative research, structured partnerships and other forms of cooperation [3]. In such context embodied by a sort of open innovation, knowledge acquires a strategic value in the processes to create, development and exchange innovation. Knowledge transfer and the linked economic and inter-organizations implications, become key factors for the development and the diffusion of such innovations and the exploration of new field of science. The adoption of this open innovation paradigm allows to "outstrip the knowledge endowment of an individual contributor" and to build consensus "around issues such as technology standards that have permitted whole business ecosystems to flourish" [4]. Furthermore, this new approach allows to design new solutions aimed at managing research results and capitalizing on tangible and intangible resources developed into. According to the European Commission, "knowledge transfer involves the processes for capturing, collecting and sharing explicit and tacit knowledge, including skills and competence" [1], and it includes commercial and non-commercial activities such as research collaborations, consultancy, licensing, IP management and spin-off creation. Therefore, in this new framework of "open innovation", European universities and other public research organizations play a key role in "fostering technology transfer and encouraging innovation for growth" [1]. In order to remain attractive, to open up new businesses and international cooperation, to leverage new funds and to support technology transfer, Universities and other research organizations are developing a complementary system of new activities to attract researchers and industrial partners [5]. Among the different ways to transfer knowledge from research organizations to industries, this paper focuses on spin-offs phenomenon as one of the most effective and innovative strategies to capitalize on long-period outcomes and to transform basic research into successful innovations [6–9]. Specially, the focus will be on the analysis of inter-intra organizational issues and the linked relationships between spin-off companies and parent organizations.

Background

Innovation is the application of knowledge to produce new knowledge [10, 11]. Therefore, a better use of existing knowledge and more effective acquisition and assimilation of new knowledge becomes the business imperative [12]. The development and valorization of human intellect and skills, "more than managing and deploying physical and capital assets", will be the dominant matter of innovative and successful companies [10]. In an increasingly internationalized and globalized turbo-economy, innovation become the heart of productivity [13] and technological changes, interactive learning, knowledge development and knowledge integration, key factors of innovation for growth [1, 14, 15]. The analysis of knowledge-intensive economic systems evidences the tendency of knowledge companies to focus on few tangible assets and several intangible ones with a high number of well qualified and talented professionals that use their own competencies and creativity, to convert information to knowledge [10, 15, 16]. In such contexts, the research on technologies, productions and other supply-side domains can provide new knowledge elements that foster product and process innovation by increasing variation in the problem-solving repertoire and raising chances of finding valuable new combinations [17–19]. However, the sole knowledge or information availability doesn't totally explain the innovation; it is "the ability to creatively use knowledge that is the key to promoting innovation and creating competitive advantage" [20]. Information efficiencies facilitate innovation by improving the initial base of knowledge and creates a "larger and richer pool of codified knowledge for any given employee to draw from, reducing the cost of information search" [21]. On the other hand, Prahalad and Hamel [22] suggest that it is not the absolute level of knowledge a firm possesses which leads to competitive advantage, but the velocity with which it is circulated in the firm. Knowledge optimization depends by human resources and by the way in which individuals and groups interact. Thus, the information synergies possible through IT will only be realized when the firm is able to move further and actually utilize knowledge in its optimal location within the organization. This implies that organizations must move beyond knowledge circulation as described by Prahalad and Hamel [22] and actually reallocate knowledge resources to the place where they can add the highest value to the organization as the need arises [21]. According to Dewett and Jones [21], project based work provides a vivid example of this process. As a project progresses, the needs for someone team members waxes and wanes. In an effort to optimize the overall value added of each employee and, in turn, optimizing knowledge use and the potential for "information synergies", the resources will be allocated in relationship to the really expertise required.

European Policies to Support Knowledge Transfer

In the European context, the main problem is "the transformation of results into new products more than the scientific production" [23]. According to the European Commission, an important problem is "how to make better use of publicly funded R&D" considering that compared to North America, "the average universities in Europe, generates far fewer inventions and patents" [1]. Research cooperation and knowledge transfer between research organizations and industry represent one of the weak points of the European research and innovation system [1], and transnational knowledge transfer remains an important goal of European Programmes. The development of a well-defined and organized knowledge transfer system in Europe is hindered by a range of different issues related to the management of knowledge and intellectual property by European universities and other research organizations: a fragmented market for knowledge and technology, legal barriers and cultural differences between the scientific and the industrial community represent an obstacle to the knowledge and innovation harmonization. In order to reduce this gap and to increase knowledge transfer, several European countries have developed numerous initiatives – such as new laws, IPR regimes, guidelines, Technologies Transfer Offices, Industrial Liaison Office and Business Angels – to promote collaboration between research organizations and businesses within the framework of the Lisbon strategy. However, "these initiatives are often designed with a national perspective, and fail to address the transnational dimension of knowledge transfer" [1]. Encouraging innovation and transnational knowledge transfer is a top priority for EU policies, which have always been at the heart of the UE Research & Technological Development Framework Programme (FP). To achieve this goal, the European Commission promotes a transnational cooperation among different public and private partners for the development of collaborative research projects. In this respect, the best performance, in terms of research organizations and industry cooperation, has been achieved by the IT sector: more than 90% of projects involved a collaboration between public and private spheres. Thus, more technologies that are ready for the commercial use are being developed in this sector. On the other hand, to facilitate transnational clustering activities and knowledge sharing between research organizations and companies (in particular SMEs), the Competitiveness and Innovation Programme (CIP) provides a suite of complementary activities for R&D projects and supports all forms of innovation, public–private partnerships and measures to improve access to finance. The current framework is vastly changing. In many countries, research institutions have created reward systems whereby the inventor receives a share of any profits generated when licensing or spinning off inventions [1].

Furthermore, the development of various transnational networks for knowledge transfer and the sharing of knowledge and results has allowed an increase in the number and the types of innovations used. When analyzing the results obtained by ProTon Europe, one of the largest European Technology Transfer network, a significant increase of innovation activities and results can be detected in the last 5 years. The increase is significant in comparison to the US framework; data are provided in the following Table 1. The total number of spin-off companies created with the support of European KTOs in 2006 was 473, with an increase of +338% if compared with 2004, specifically in the field of spin-offs. This result is particularly significant in comparison with the total number of 553 spin-offs generated from US KTOs in 2006 [24]. These results, and the related economic implications, are very important for the development of an integrated system of knowledge transfer.

Table 1. A comparison about innovation transfer between UE and US in KTO

Overall figures	ProTon Europe			AUTM U.S.
	FY 2004	FY 2005	FY 2006	FY2006
Total number of invention disclosures	2,373	4,475	5,261	18.874
Average number of invention disclosures for TTO	31.6	15.3	18.3	99.9
Total number of priority patent applications	943	2,162	2,496	15.908
Average number of priority patent application for TTO	12.7	6.4	8.7	84.2
Total number of patent granted	123	176	687	3,255
Average number of patent granted for TTO	2.1	1.3	2.5	17.2
Total number of licenses executed	423	295	3,174	4,963
Average number of licenses executed for TTO	6.3	2.4	11.2	26.3
Total number of spin-off created	108	435	473	553
Average number of spin-off created for TTO	1.7	1.4	1.6	2.9

Source: Proton Europe Survey (FY 2006); AUTM Licensing Activity Survey (FY 2006).

The Spin-off Strategy for Knowledge Transfer in the European Open Innovation framework

In a context of open innovation – such as the European framework linked to cooperative research projects – "by collaborating, young firms are able to combine distinct pieces of knowledge by tapping into the resource base of their partners" [25]. In order to achieve this target and grow, young firms need to establish learning relationships with external sources of knowledge [26, 27]. According to learning theories, "knowledge held in common" is important for an absorptive capacity of the firm, and therefore, for an effective learning and new knowledge generation from external sources [25, 28]. This sort of open knowledge improves the ability of the firm to evaluate effectively the value of external knowledge, to discard irrelevant knowledge, and to concentrate its learning efforts on valuable knowledge sources [14]. In short, considered that "firms learn most efficiently close to their existing knowledge domains" and "local optimization contributes to a higher operational efficiency" [29], it's possible to conclude that the intensification in knowledge overlap with the parent company "should increase the productive capacity of the spin-off firm and the related potential for growth" [25]. From a holistic perspective, the spin-off becomes a new "space" to share knowledge, cultures and competencies among different categories of partners. In this context, the common use of knowledge and results provides an added value.

In the European framework, many research activities are developed within multi-annual Framework Programmes (FPs) that are planned, organized and co-financed by the European Commission. The European research projects provide an integrated partnership between public and private organizations that cooperate for the development and the implementation of research activities aimed at achieving pre-competitive research outcomes. Inside the framework of well-defined consortium agreements, FPs provide different rules to manage the projects and to use the results. The lack of industrial partners interested to exploit the research outcomes, related to inadequate funding and the complex administrative procedures of public research organizations, reduce the chances of a long-term exploitation of research results. On the other hand, in the specific field of IT, research results usually concern prototypes, demonstrators or other kinds of products and/or services "ready for use" and ready to be commercialize. Therefore, the definition of innovative approaches to implement the industrial exploitation and to commercialize IT outcomes, is determinant.

An Innovative Configuration of Research Spin-offs in Open Innovation

Under the specific context of the collaborative research projects developed within European research FPs, a new spin-off framework may be defined. In this contest, the spin-off may be considered a new company created by parents organization in order to exploit knowledge and innovative contents and outcomes obtained by cooperative research projects. The following Fig.1 describes a possible configuration of the research spin-offs in a context of open innovation, characterized by an open cooperation among different players [6]. Within this framework, the "parent organization" is the Consortium of partners of research projects – companies, universities, research centers and other institutions; the "spin-off entrepreneurs" are the employees – manager, researchers, consultants – and other project team involved in the project. This new configuration evidences the impact of an open innovation approach related to the exploitation of research outcomes within European project: the different competencies and know-how, developed during the project life, may be exploit in the new spin-off company. In this way, researchers, scholars and research organization on one hand, and managers and companies on the other, can capitalize the set of knowledge and experience developed and implemented within the project in a new "open space", characterized by the continuous sharing of knowledge and expertise among different individuals and it able to guarantee the long period industrial exploitation and the dissemination of the research results.

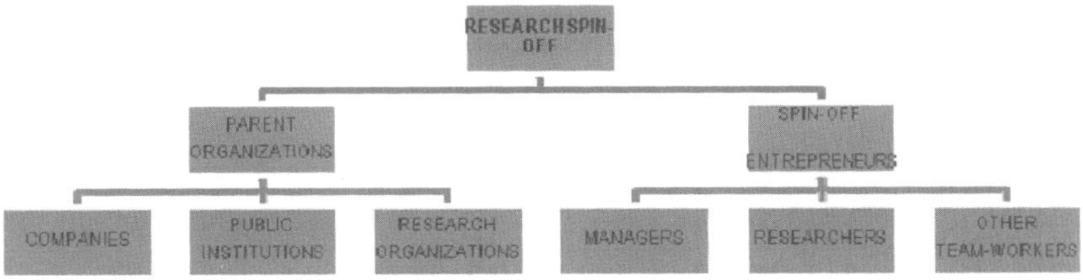

Fig. 1. Research Spin-off configuration

Conclusion

In the current context characterized by a sort of "open innovation", universities and research institutions play a strategic role in knowledge transfer and innovation results [1, 5]. The adoption of the "open innovation" paradigm allows to design new solutions aimed at managing research project results and capitalizing on tangible and intangible know-how. Into the European Framework the main problem is the transformation of results into new products, thus innovation and transnational knowledge transfer is a top priority for EU policies. To achieve this goal, the European Commission promotes multi-annual FPs for the development of collaborative research projects and the transnational cooperation between public and private organizations. In this framework of open innovation – such as the European framework related to cooperative research projects – characterized by open cooperation among different players, the spin-off strategy may represent an effective solution to exploit research outcomes. Hence, in the specific field of IT, research results usually concern prototypes, demonstrators or other kinds of products and/or services "ready for use" and ready to be commercialize. Therefore, the definition of innovative approaches to implement the industrial exploitation and to commercialize IT outcomes, is crucial. Under the specific context of the high-technology collaborative research projects developed within European research FPs, is possible to hypothesize a new spin-off framework related to the research spin-off.

References

1. European Commission (2007) *Improving knowledge transfer between research institutions and industry across Europe: embracing open innovation*. COM(2007) 182 final
2. Von Hippel E (2005) *Democratizing innovation: the evolving phenomenon of user innovation*. MIT Press, Cambridge
3. Sansonetti A, D'Atri A (2009) IT spin-offs into the European research framework: an innovative configuration. *In Proceedings of the Americas conference on information systems 2009*, San Francisco

4. Chesbrough HW, Appleyard M (2007) Open innovation and strategy. *Calif Manage Rev* 50:1
5. European Commission (2006) *Putting knowledge into practice: a broad-based innovation strategy for the EU.* COM(2006) 502
6. Dodgson M (1993) *Technological collaboration in industry.* Routledge, London
7. Siegel DS, Waldman D, Link A (2003) Assessing the impact of organizational practices on the relative productivity of university technology transfer offices: An exploratory study. *Res Policy* 32:27–48
8. Degroof J, Roberts EB (2004) Overcoming weak entrepreneurial infrastructures for academic spinoff ventures. *J Technol Transfer* 29(3–4):327–354
9. O'Shea RP, Allen TJ, O'Gorman C, Roche F (2007) Delineating the anatomy of an entrepreneurial University: the MIT experience. *R&D Manage* 37(1):1–16
10. Jonnansen JA, Olsen B, Olaisen J (1999) Aspects of innovation theory based on knowledge-management. *Int J Inf Manage* 19:121–139
11. Drucker PF (1993) *Post-capitalist society.* Butterworth Heineman, New York
12. Thurow LC (1996) *The future of capitalism.* Nicolas Brealey Publishing, London
13. Freeman C (1995) The national system of innovation in historical perspective. *Cambridge J Econ* 19:5–24
14. Grant R (1996) Toward a knowledge-based theory of the firm. *Strateg Manage J Winter special issue* 17:109–122
15. Sveiby KE (1997) *The new organizational wealth: managing and measuring knowledge-based assets.* Berrett-Koehler. San Francisco
16. Archibugi D, Michie J (1995) Technology and innovation: An introduction. *Cambridge J Econ* 19:1–4
17. Ahuja G, Lampert CM (2001) Entrepreneurship in the large corporation: a longitudinal study of how established firms create breakthrough inventions. *Strateg Manage J* 22:521–543
18. Fleming L, Sorenson O (2001) Technology as a complex adaptive system: evidence from patent data. *Res Policy* 30:1019–1039
19. Sidhu S, Commandeur HR, Volberda HW (2007) The multifaceted nature of exploration and exploitation. *Organ Sci* 18(1):20–38
20. Leavy B (1998) The concept of learning in the strategy field, review and outlook. *Manage Learn* 29(4):447–466
21. Dewett T, Jones GR (2001) The role of information technology in the organization: A review, model and assessment. *Manage* 27:313–346
22. Prahalad CK, Hamel C (1990) The core competence of the corporation. *Harv Bus Rev* 3:79–91
23. Chiesa V, Piccaluga A (2000) Exploitation and diffusion of public research: the case of academic spinoff companies in Italy. *R&D Manage* 30(4):329–340
24. Proton Europe (2006) *ProTon Europe. Fourth Annual Survey Report,* Brussels
25. Sapienza HJ, Parhankanga A, Erkko A (2004) Knowledge relatedness and post-spin-off growth. *J Bus Venturing* 19:809–829
26. Liebeskind J (1996) Knowledge, strategy, and the theory of the firm. *Strateg Manage J Winter issue* 17:93–107
27. Zahra S, George G (2002) Absorptive capacity: a review, reconceptualization, and extension. *Acad Manage Rev* 27(2):185–200
28. Cohen M, Levinthal D (1990) Absorptive capacity: a perspective on learning and innovation. *Adm Sci Q* 35(1):128–152
29. Levinthal DA (1997) Adaptation on rugged landscapes. *Manage Sci* 43(7):934–940

An Approach to Digital Business Ecosystems based on Process Models

Nicola Boffoli[*,†,‡,Π,§], Marta Cimitile[†,‡,Π,§], Fabrizio M. Maggi[‡] and Giuseppe Visaggio[Π,§]

Abstract The Digital Business Ecosystem (DBE) is an organizational approach which allows competitive enterprises to cooperate with each other. It is necessary to put aside the operating realizations to formalize this new approach in order to build up a theory to base the empirical experimentation. This work is a contribution to the formalization with the goal of understanding how competitive enterprises with heterogeneous organizations and belonging to different areas, can coexist in a same DBE. The formalization proposed has a logical reading based on processes models. Thanks to the use of the process models it is possible to organize some tools which allow to quickly build platforms for DBE management and governance and to make this flexible to comply with the different operating modes foreseen by the management of the enterprises which are part of the DBE.

Introduction

A Digital Business Ecosystem (DBE) is a network of organizations, also in competition with each other, which will come together in structures organized as biological ecosystems [1–3]. Many authors have discussed about the advantages deriving from the DBE model [1–6]. In a DBE, organizations offer or require from the community excellence capabilities and capacities. The excellence is increased through the exchanges among the organizations that provide and require innovations formalized as knowledge into applications, competences, practices, and tools. The DBE diffusion encourages to study the DBE formalization model in the way to manage the cooperation among organizations automatically with the adoption of ICT technologies.

This work introduces a formalization of the DBE in the way to facilitate its governance using a process based software. The proposed approach is based on the idea that a DBE can be represented as a network of organizations offering their capabilities as digital species that must be integrated according to specific requirements expressed by a process model. It implies the formalization of the digital species, of the organisms containing them and of the related DBE. All these

* Department of Informatics, University of Bari, Bari, Italy, boffoli@di.uniba.it
† Department of Informatics, University of Bari, Bari, Italy, cimitile@di.uniba.it
‡ Department of Informatics, University of Bari, Bari, Italy, maggi@di.uniba.it
Π Department of Informatics, University of Bari, Bari, Italy, visaggio@di.uniba.it
§ SER&Practices spinoff of University of Bari, Bari, Italy

A. D'Atri et al. (eds.), *Management of the Interconnected World*,
DOI 10.1007/978-3-7908-2404-9_59,

elements must be coordinated to systematically accomplish one or more business goals. The coordination of the available resources is expressed through the choreography of one or more processes. The use of the process models as coordination mechanism allows to integrate the proposed approach with other works of the same authors [7, 8] about the Business Process Lines (BPL). In this paper we also present an applicative example of the approach. The remainder of this paper is structured as follows: the following section recalls the conceptual model of DBE clarifying the necessary definitions; successively the corresponding logical model is presented. Such model is based on the formalization of the DBE and allows to define a DBE reusing primitive components appropriately composed. Finally conclusions and final remarks showing prospective works complete the paper.

Conceptual Model

The following paragraphs define all the concepts used and the formalism which it is possible to produce with them.

Capabilities

The *capability* (Cb) is the property to supply an action, a service, a product, etc. A person, a software component, a knowledge package can be carriers of one or more capabilities. For example if we consider the auction selling activity, the auctioneer has the capability to execute an auction. He is able to negotiate with one or more customers and select the best bid.

Digital Species

Any capabilities carrier can be generalized with the concept of *Digital Specie*(DS). Formally, a DS is defined in the following way: $DS=CY(Cb_1,Cb_2,.., Cb_n)$ (1)
Where: CY is a choreography concerning the capabilities Cb_i required for the systematic accomplishment of the DS goal, Cbi is the generic *capability of CY.*

A digital species can be *primitive* or *composed.* It is *primitive* if it can not be further divided to preserve its capabilities. It is *composed* (DSc) if it can be divided in more DS (primitive or/and composed). Often, in a primitive digital species DS, the function CY is implicit. It means that the relation among all the associated Cb_i is tacit. Instead, in a DSc the function CY is usually, explicit.

Generalizing, we can have: $DSc=CY(DS_1, DS_2,.., DS_n)$ (2)

According to (1): $DS_i=CY_i(Cb_{i1}, Cb_{i2},..Cb_{in})$ (3)

So we have: $DSc=CY(CY_1((Cb_{11}, Cb_{12},..Cb_{1n}), CY_2(Cb_{21}, Cb_{22},..Cb_{2n}),.., CY_n(Cb_{n1},..Cb_{nn}))$ (4)

In the way, to explain the digital species formalizations, we can consider as example the digital species involved in the realization of an "auction selling" goal. The auction selling requires the adoption of the following DS:

$DS_{\text{Auction service}} = CY_{\text{Auction service}} (DS_{\text{Auctioneer}}, DS_{\text{Auction software service}})$

Where $DS_{\text{Auctioneer}}$ and DS_{Auction} software service according to (3) can be represented in the following way:

$DS_{\text{Auctioneer}}=CY_{\text{Auctioneer}}$(Execute Auction, Select best bid);

$DS_{\text{Auction software service}} =CY_{\text{Auction software service}}$ (Register Auction Results, Synthesize and visualize results);

According to (4) we can have the following $DS_{\text{Auction service}}$ formalization:

$DS_{\text{Auction service}} =CY_{\text{Auction service}}(CY_{\text{Auctioneer}}$(Execute Auction, Select best bid), $CY_{\text{Auction software service}}$ (Register Auction Results, Synthesize and visualize results));

$DS_{\text{Auction service}}$ is an example of composed DS. It is composed by two digital species and its choreography. $CY_{\text{Auction service}}$ relates to all these resources in a process.

$DS_{\text{Auctioneer}}$ is a primitive DS, in fact it cannot be divided. Moreover, $CY_{\text{Auctioneer}}$ is tacit. In fact it is hard to formalize the auctioneer behavior. $DS_{\text{Auctioneer}}$ is composed by two capabilities:the capability to Execute Auction consisting of the sequence of activities that the auctioneer perform during the negotiation with its customers, the capability to Select the Best Bid consisting of the capability to select the best customer during the auction execution

$DS_{\text{Auction software service}}$ is a primitive DS composed by other two capabilities: the capability to Register the Auction result in an electronic format and the capability to Synthesize the Results and Visualize them in the most significant way.

$CY_{\text{Auction software service}}$ can be explicated and this explication corresponds to the Auction software service workflow.For clearness, according to the previous formalization, a primitive DS cannot be changed each time it is implied in a DBE, it must be used as it is. Instead, a composed DS can vary, according to its use, although same primitive DS components to other contests are used.

Organism, Organization and Capacities

Organism (Org) is an entity containing one or more digital species managed to achieve business goals of the organization where the organism itself is active.

An *Organization* could contain one or more organisms. For example: according to the selling auction example we could have a Software Organization S (Fig. 1) that includes three different organisms: *ERP System Management* that is the set of digital species for the ERP specialization, installation and administration, *Marketing Software Development* that is composed by the set of digital species to marketing software design, testing, analysis, programming and for marketing services. Finally there is a digital species of *Selling* that is primitive and includes the sellers. Within each organization there are DS constituted by men, software components, tools and whatever can be useful to realize goals assigned to it. Such digital species are managed in compliance with modes defined by the organization. The organizations, in turn, are managed and coordinated by the organization management to ensure that the whole goals achieved by the organizations, properly arranged, realize business goals of the whole organization. To be more precise, the

Org in the example produces two owners' tools: marketing software and ERP application. Besides, in the same organization we have a system made by a single digital species, *Selling*. In this last Org the management is not specified because the $CY_{selling.}$ is implicit anyway. Alike organism and organization are defined, they can be also defined in terms of digital species. In fact the organism is a composite digital species where CY integration of each DS belonging to the organism is defined and realized in the organism management. The organization is in turn a DS where the management integrates the CY of any organism belonging to the organization.

The definition of organism and organization allows to feature all DS contained in them with another size which is capacity. In fact, each organism has a capacity associated to each DS. The capacity measures the production quantity each DS in the organism can dispose for each capability.

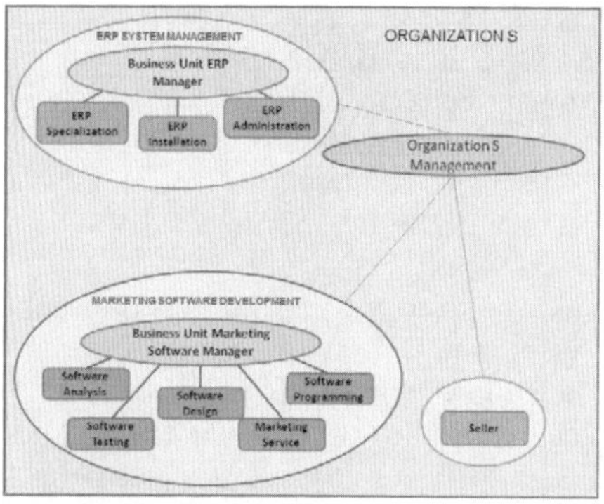

Fig. 1. Example of organization and digital species

The *capacity* associated to a generic capability Cb_j in DS_t is Cc_{tj}. It can be represented in the following way: Cc= (q, u) (5)

Where u represents the measure unity of the capacity (for example human hours) and q is the number of u for $Cc_{t.}$. For example: $DS_{Auctioneer}$ the following capacity: $Cc_{Auctioneer}$=(4, Hours/day).

To be more precise, two organisms belonging to the same organization could have digital species in common. In such case the capacity for this species can be associated to each organism, or to the whole organization. It means that two DS in the same organism have different capacities and then the organism has capacities which correspond to the sum of the two DS.

There are capacities which can be linked only to the organization. They express themselves in the same way but they are not able to be separated per organism. Such capacity is the *financial* one. An organization has a financial capacity which characterizes it but this cannot be split between the organisms included in the same organization.

Given the formalization of capacity, an organism may not be able to provide the necessary capacity for one o more capabilities, although it has a part available. In this case, the DBE must include two or more organisms with the same capabilities for reaching the total capability. Each makes part of the capacity available so that the sum equals to the one requested by the DBE. The organisms involved will belong to different organizations which may be in competition. Although they are in competition, they must collaborate in the DBE to provide the requested capacity.

Digital Business Ecosystem

The organizations which offer some or all their own organisms for the cooperation with other organizations constitute an ecosystem. Whenever the ecosystem aims to realize a business goal, it constitutes a digital business ecosystem. A DBE must compose the available digital species in choreography CY that integrates the choreography of all the DS of the DBE realizing the DBE goal. It is formalized as:

$DBE=CY[DS_1, DS_2,...DS_n]$ (6)

Where: $\exists$ $(DS_i, DS_i) \in DBE$ with $DS_i \neq DS_i$ and $DS_i \in Org_A$ and $DS_i \in Org_B$ and $Org_A \neq Org_B$, Org_A and Org_B are two different organisms; they could belong also different organizations.

According to this definition, DBE is in general a network of organizations that can offer the organisms necessary with their corresponding capacity. When an organism is within a DBE, it is managed by the DBE through the CY of the same DBE and loses its dependency from the management of the organism it derives from. This makes each DBE able to exploit capabilities and capacities of the organisms even being independent of them. We can consider the example proposed in Fig. 2. It shows two different DBE related to each other. DBE 1 is a Fish Seller DBE. It is composed by four digital species: *Fish Auctioneer, Fish Seller, Auctioneer Software Service and Marketing Service*. Each digital species can be offered by a different Organism. For example according to Fig. 1, Marketing Service is offered by Marketing Software Development Organism. The DBE 2 is a food market DBE. It is a network composed by the four DS: *Auctioneer Software Service, Marketing Service, Food Auctioneer and Food Seller*. The two sellers exchange their experiences and their best practices about food seller market. The two DBE are connected in the following way: Software Service and Marketing are in both the DBE.

Logical Model

The DBE conceptual model allows to define all the actors and entities involved in a DBE considering their rules, their relations and their characteristics. Starting from the conceptual model in this session we propose a logical model for the DBE governance. More precisely, a DBE can be considered as a set of digital species that provide the capabilities needed to satisfy a specific customer business needs which are the aim of the DBE. The choreography CY according to the DS and DBE definitions (1), (3) and (6) can be expressed through a Process Model. Indeed a process model is able to formalize the relation that manages the collaboration between the entities involved, and that can be processed by a computer and therefore digitalized. Considering the example proposed in the Digital Species session, we can represent CY as shown in the fig. 3 (the input and output are represented in blue, the activities are in grey).

As observed in fig. 3 the capabilities sequence is obtained towards the definition of the process input and output. The input and output represent some results and some starting point for a DS or capabilities execution.

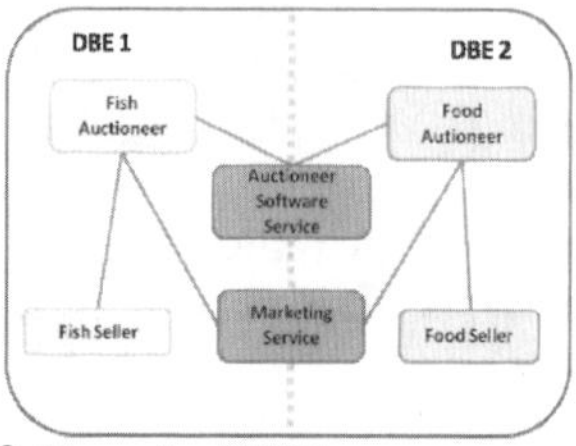

Fig. 2. Example of DBE

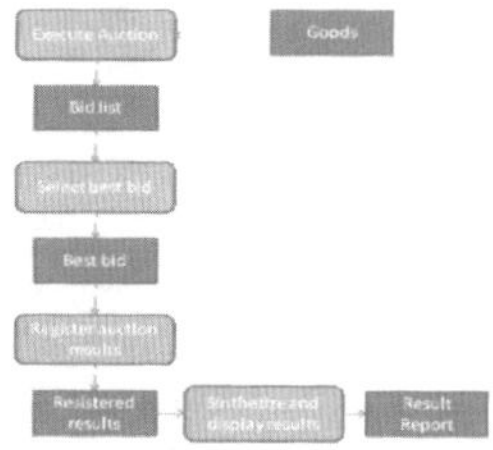

Fig. 3. CY process

BPL and Digital Species

The previous paragraph points out that with the proposed formalization in this work, the DBE can be formalized through a process model. As so, the variability needed for the composed DS to adapt the DBE to different operational contexts can be expressed through a Business Process Line (BPL) [7–9]. A BPL is a set of similar business processes (*assets*) sharing a common part (*commonality*) and characterized by a variant part (*variability*) depending on the specific context where the process will be applied. Each process of a BPL can be applied in a specific context and it is modeled composing activities, inputs and outputs needed in that specific context. So a BPL facilitates the process flexibility management and consequently it allows to integrate the primitive digital species in different ways for different applicative contexts.

More precisely, the commonality is a set of invariant assets and the variability is a set of variant assets. When a business process is defined, the associated commonality is defined and consequently the assets that realize the commonality are selected. Successively when the business context is selected, the corresponding variability and the associated assets are fixed. Commonality and variability are then integrated in order to obtain a process variant to be applied in the fixed context. The BPL is selected based on the process that has to be modeled. For example: instead of many "Sell" processes for each satisfying user contexts we will use a "Sell BPL"; the invariant assets of "Sell BPL" will be "Obtain Order", "Deliver product" and "Receive Payment"; each one of these process assets is composed by the basic assets, inputs and outputs needed for its own purpose within the "Sell" process; variant assets are added to these ones depending on the context to sell via electronic store, by adding the asset "Organize the web site to interact with customers". Obviously, variant and invariant assets are integrated to obtain a specific process of the context considered. Starting from this formalization, the authors are experimenting a technology to manage this model. The technology is the *decision table* supporting the assets selection when a context profile is specified [10, 11].

Application of the DBE and BPL Based Model

The proposed approach was adopted in a research project. The project consists of building various DBE which involve food, agricultural and software companies. The companies all aim at carrying out a *supply-chain* of various products each having as a competitive factor the verifiable *traceability* from production to distribution. The DBEs to compose are various because each type of food product requires different variants. The challenge of the research project consists of identifying the minimum number of DS needed to compose all targets DBE, in order to have a unique platform to manage all the DBE, independently of their variants. According to the DBE modeling, the DBE is organized towards the DS offered by all the organizations involved. In particular each organization built its digital species basing on their excellence capabilities. DBE administrators drive the DBE organizations in the digital species building. They ensure that the DS are realized according to the formalization model described in the previous session. In order to extract a list of business processes, their activities and their corresponding digital species the MIT library was considered [12], The MIT library has been represented through decision tables.

Conclusions

The formalization of the DBE elements, pointed out in this work, promotes the research of DS primitives which can be combined to build a composed DSs. The combination of DSs is expressed through a choreography that can be composed itself by simpler choreographies. This model allows to use the same DS in various ways, according to the characteristics of the user context.

Implementing a DBE with a process, this can be transformed into a workflow which arranges capabilities. Therefore the model suggested allows to efficiently handle the cooperation among the organizations. When a composite digital species is included in a DBE which requires a specific behaviour, the model proposed suggests to specialize the process which implements the CY through the use of decision tables. In this way a set of primitive digital species remains unchanged while their arrangement is modified; as a consequence the behaviour of the composed digital species is changed but the goals it can reach are the same and are guaranteed by the primitive digital species. In other words, a set of DS primitives can, appropriately orchestrate and combine, constitute a set of DBE with various aims. The DBE, as it has been defined, leads the organizations belonging to the ecosystem, to specialize and be excellent on few capabilities. The excellent capabilities to make up a DBE are selected in the ecosystem, then organizations which compete in the same business areas will cooperate to complete their own excellences with the other ones.

As future works, we will conduct empirical investigations to generalize the results, to improve the model proposed and to confirm it empirically. Actually, we are applying the proposed approach in the real DBE. We are interested to share our research experience with other researchers.

Acknowledgments This research has been funded within the project "Distributed Production Innovative System" grant PS_092 Apulia Region

References

1. Peltoniemi M, Vuori E (2004) *Business ecosystem as the new approach to complex adaptive business environments*. Frontiers of e-business research, Tampere, Finland
2. Nachira F, Nicolai A, Dini P, Le Louran M, Rivera Leon L (2007) *Digital business ecosystems*, European commission digital business ecosystems, luxembourg: office for official publications of the European communities. ISBN 92-79-01817-5
3. Nachira F (2002) Towards a network of digital business ecosystems fostering the local development. http://www.digital-ecosystems.org. Retrieved on 16 Aug 2007
4. Chang V, Uden L (2008) Governance for E-learning ecosystem. *In Proceedings of the 2nd IEEE international conference on digital ecosystems and technologies (IEEE DEST 2008)*, Phitsanulok, Thailand
5. Wang J, De Wilde P (2008) A model for digital business ecosystems and topological analisys. In *IEEE international conference on services computing*, Honolulu, Hawaii
6. Doukidis GI, Mylonopoulos N, Pouloudi N (2003) *Social and economic transformation in the digital era*. Idea Group Int ISBN: 1591402670, 2003
7. Boffoli N, Cimitile M, Maggi FM (2009) Business process lines: an approach to a flexible, process modelling. In *Proceeding of the 4th conference on software and data technologies (ICSOFT)*, Sofia, Bulgaria
8. Boffoli N, Cimitile M, Maggi FM, Visaggio G (2009) Managing SOA system variation through business process lines and process oriented development. Workshop on service-oriented architectures and software product lines (SOAPL 2009). In *Proceedings of the 13th international software product line conference (SPLC)*, San Francisco, California
9. Clements P, Northrop L (2001) *Software product lines: practices and patterns*. SEI Series in Software Engineering, Addison-Wesley, Boston
10. Yao Q, Chen Z, Wang H (2006) Improving flexibility and reusage of business process management: the role of cased-based reasoning technique. In *Proceedings of the IEEE international conference on e-business engineering (ICEBE'06)*. IEEE Computer Society, Shanghai, China
11. Yang Z, Yang N, Zhang Y (2005) The application of reusable pattern-based business modeling in equipment management. ACM international conference proceeding series vol 113 archive. In *Proceedings of the 7th international conference on electronic commerce table of contents*, München, Germany
12. Malone TW, Crowston K, Herman GA (2003) *Organizing business knowledge*. The MIT process handbook. MIT Press, Cambridge

Intelligent Agents in a Logistics Domain: The PROMIS Project

Maurizio Colica[*], **Marco A. Mastratisi**[†], **Fabio Palopoli**[‡], **and Sergio Greco**[Π]

Abstract Logistics companies have faced in recent years the challenges imposed by globalization. The thinning of the margins and the enormous costs have forced companies to review and modify their product offerings and services and their business processes. One of the most feasible and reasonable way for improving port competitiveness of logistics companies is to make better use of available resources through the adoption of information technology.

This paper presents the results of some research activities of a research project called PROMIS (*logistic PROcess Management and Intelligence*). The PROMIS research project has been started by the R&D.LOG (*Research and Development Logistics*) Consortium, that operates in the area of Gioia Tauro terminal container, and that is characterized by public–private partnerships for ICT transfer and diffusion. In particular, the paper proposes an agent-based model of the entities involved in berthing, shipping, yard planning and straddle carriers routing processes and describes its implementation as a multi-agent system using constraint programming (OPL) to find re-planning problem solutions.

Intelligent Agents in Logistics Domains

One of the goals of logistics systems is the optimization of resources usage during transport of materials and goods. This goal is limited by various constraints, such as the time window within which the asset is delivered, or a particular sequence of deliveries to be respected, etc. Furthermore, often it is also necessary to make decisions, in absence of a complete knowledge, so that scheduling and routing activities satisfy time constraints.

These issues are suitable to be dealt with the use of agent technologies and multi agent systems. To justify this claim, some characteristics of the logistics do-

[*] Exeura s.r.l., via P. Alvares Cabrai, contrada Lecco, 87036 Rende, CS, Italy, maurizio.colica@exeura.com

[†] Exeura s.r.l., via P. Alvares Cabrai, contrada Lecco, 87036 Rende, CS, Italy, marco.mastratisi@exeura.com

[‡] Exeura s.r.l., via P. Alvares Cabrai, contrada Lecco, 87036 Rende, CS, Italy, fabio.palopoli@exeura.com

[Π] Dipartimento di Elettronica, Informatica e Sistemistica (DEIS), Università della Calabria, via P. Bucci, cubo 41/C, 87036 Arcavacata di Rende, CS, Italy, greco@deis.unical.it

A. D'Atri et al. (eds.), *Management of the Interconnected World*,
DOI 10.1007/978-3-7908-2404-9_60,

mains will be highlighted below and, subsequently, some properties of multi-agent systems will be presented. Shortly, a logistics domain is typically characterized by being:

- *Decentralized.* The involved organizations are geographically distributed, and they need to cooperate to achieve their goals. Thus, each organization uses its logistics processes (services) and the decentralization of a logistics domain is not exclusively caused by geographic distribution, but also because the involved organizations are characterized by a high degree of autonomy.
- *Dynamic.* The goals, the capabilities of organizations (the type and the availability of the services they provide) and the knowledge and information available change often.
- *Open.* Participants could frequently enter and leave the logistics domain.

Logistics systems are modular, and they could be viewed as the composition of separate entities, such as production instrument, machineries, operators, etc. Moreover, it is necessary to coordinate the activities executed by participants and the allocation of resources which are, usually, limited.

Agent technologies seem to be particularly suitable to be effectively used in domains with these characteristics [1, 2]. Indeed, multi agent systems are typically characterized by ensuring support for parallelism, and they are robust and scalable. These systems also show great utility in contexts where it is desirable to have technologies that make efficient and effective exchange of information between heterogeneous software systems [3]. These characteristics are of fundamental importance in the contexts in which there are distributed data, distributed control and distributed skills. The agent technology seems particularly suitable to handle distributed data and to enable parallel processing of large amounts of data more quickly than a centralized approach. Furthermore, the use of agents makes it generally easier to devise algorithms for rapid processing (with sub-optimal solutions).

In conclusion, multi agent systems seem particularly suitable in logistics applications. They also seem to find natural application in contexts where the use of a centralized approach is not effective. Obviously, the agent technology presents similar advantages in the terminal container domain, which is a kind of logistics domain.

One of the most useful applications of agent technology in a terminal container could be the planning and re-planning tasks [4]. A plan is a sequence of actions to be performed in order to achieve one or more goals, whereas the planning is the process of creating plans [5]. Generally, the plan's goal is reachable under the following conditions: (i) the plan is correct; (ii) the environment in which the plan is executed is static and deterministic; (iii) it is not executed any other action not included in the plan during its execution. Unfortunately, in real contexts the environments in which the plans are executed are not static and, often, we must consider it as non-deterministic environments. Furthermore, during the plan execution, unexpected events could happen. So, there is no guarantee that the plan execution causes the goal achievement [6]. On the other hand, when unexpected events occur such that it is impossible to continue the execution of the current plan, it is necessary to generate a rapid re-planning. The use of multi-agent systems, due to their above discussed features, seems to be one of the best approaches to provide quickly a good solution to planning and re-planning problems in dynamic environments.

The PROMIS Research Project

Ports are very important nodes in the trades of goods from thousands of years, and recently, due to the advent of a globalized economy, they are acquiring a crucial role in commercial activities and their traffic is rapidly increasing. Nowadays transport of goods by sea is based on standard *containers* exchanged using a global network of *terminal containers*. In such rapidly expanding field it is of vital importance to increase productivity, achieving a more rapid exchange of goods through a faster turn around of vessels and containers [7]. These needs inevitably stimulate the design of new technical solutions for managing the container. On the other hand one of the most feasible and reasonable way for improving port competitiveness is to make better use of available resources through the adoption of information technology [8].

From this business scenario comes the PROMIS research project, realized by R&D.LOG Consortium, that operates in the area of Gioia Tauro terminal container. The overall goal of the PROMIS research project is the definition of an innovative *TOS* (*Terminal Operating System*) and its implementation as a research prototype.

The research project is structured into nine work packages (WPs):

- WP1: Scenario analysis and definition of the characteristics of the system;
- WP2: Optimization models for integrated management of the quay operations and the yard operations;
- WP3: Optimization models for tactical/strategic and technological innovation of container terminals management;
- WP4: Event Simulation and Scenario Analysis;
- WP5: Methodologies and computer based techniques for supporting logistics processes;
- WP6: Methodologies and computer based techniques for supporting decisional processes;
- WP7: Technologies and wireless devices for data transmission and for system interfacing;
- WP8: Innovative software architectures and integration of software demonstrators;
- WP9: Models and algorithms for supporting operational decisions for the handling of containers.

In this paper we present some of the research and pre-competitive development activities of WP5, and, in particular, we show an agent based model of the portual entities involved in planning and re-planning processes (more specifically, in berthing, shipping, yard planning and routing processes) and the use of constraint programming in joint with agent technologies.

An Agent Based Model

Below we present the modelled agents [9], which play a role in the processes of *berthing* (which defines an allocation of the ships at the quay), *yard planning* (which defines where the containers have to be temporarily stored within the yard), *shipping* (which defines a sequence of load/unload of the containers) and *routing* (which assigns the jobs to the straddle carriers). Every re-planning process (about which we give some outline in the description of the agent based model) are based on the auction paradigm. An auction takes place between an agent known as the auctioneer and a collection of agents known as the bidders. The goal of the auction is for the auctioneer to allocate the good to one of the bidders. The auctioneer desires to maximize the price at which the good is allocated, while bidders desire to minimize price. The auctioneer will attempt to achieve his desire through the design of an appropriate auction mechanism, while bidders attempt to achieve their desires by using a strategy that will conform to the rules of encounter, but that will also deliver an optimal result [10]. In the modelled context, we design mechanisms to assign a cost to every task (appropriately decomposed in sub-task). In the following part of this section, for each type of agent, we propose a description, in which we specify their behaviour in the berthing, yard planning, shipping and routing processes and their interactions with other agents and with the environment in which they are placed.

Ship Agent

Every ship that is involved in the activities of the container terminal is modelled by a ship agent. The system generates a new ship agent when a ship begins interacting with any entity belonging to the domain of the container terminal. Next we describe the behaviour and the iterations that characterize a generic ship agent, for each process in which it is involved:

- *Berthing*. In this process, each *ship agent* can interact with the *quay agents* (which will be presented later) and other ship agents. In particular, these agents will be involved in re-planning processes caused by the occurrence of unexpected events. In this context, an example of unexpected event could be the delay of a ship that is already allocated in a certain location. In this case, the quay agent that represents the quay, receives communication about the delay by the ship agent. As a consequence of the delay, the quay agent generates a new allocation plan of the ships.

- *Yard Planning*. In this process, the role of the ship agent is to provide information about the container cargo to the other agents that are involved in the process, responding to appropriate requests. They interact with the yard agent, which have to reallocate the containers in the yard when unexpected events occur.
- *Shipping*. In this process, the ship agent interacts with crane agents, that model the crane involved in unloading and loading of containers.

Crane Agent

Each crane that is used to load and unload goods from a ship is modelled by a crane agent. In particular, when the shipping algorithms assign a crane to a vessel, the system automatically generates a crane agent. A new agent will replace the previous one when the associated crane is allocated to a new ship. During its lifetime, a crane agent interacts with other crane agents, with ship agents, the yard agent and routing agents. Crane agents are involved in shipping, yard planning and routing processes and are organized in pools (i.e. the set of cranes is partitioned into pools of cranes). Now, we describe in more detail the interaction of crane agents with other agents, and we define their behaviour for each process analyzed:

- *Shipping*. Immediately after that the cranes have been assigned to a certain location of the bay, the system generates a crane agent for each crane. If an unexpected event occurs (for example, if a delay in the activities of loading or unloading of containers occurs) it is often necessary to generate a new plan. The crane agent, in this case, interacts with other crane agents and, in particular, with “adjacent” ones, in order to appropriately reassign the tasks. In addition, the crane agents, in this process, interact with ship agents.
- *Yard Planning*. In this process, if an unexpected event happens and a crane agent percepts its occurrence, it sends a description of this event to the yard agent with whom it interacts.
- *Routing*. Crane agents provide to the routing agent (which is the only agent that does not model any entity and that is responsible for assigning the containers that have to be moved to the straddle carrier agents) a sequence of sets of variables that identify the containers.

Yard Agent

A yard is typically divided into smaller rectangular areas, into which containers are temporarily stored. The system generates an agent that manages that areas. During its lifetime, a yard agent interacts with ship agents, crane agents and routing agents. Next, we describe the behaviour of the yard agent in the processes under consideration:

- *Yard Planning*. Unlike other agents, the yard agent is generated at the start of the system and remains active for the whole session. Even in the context of yard planning unexpected events may occur. For example, a location could be unexpectedly busy. In this case (and in other cases in which unexpected events happen), the yard agent generates a reconfiguration of the allocation of the containers in the yard, and communicates it to other agents involved in this process. Moreover, the yard agent interacts with crane agents and ship agents, receiving from them the appropriate communications about the occurrence of unexpected events.
- *Routing*. In the context of the process of routing, the yard agent interacts with the routing agents. In particular, the yard agent communicates to the routing agents the locations of the yard in which the straddle carriers have to move the containers, whereas the routing agents send to the yard agent the information about the straddle carriers which are in charge to transport the containers.

Routing Agent

The Routing Agent manages the routing of the straddle carriers. In particular, a routing agent, during its life cycle, interacts with crane agents, straddle carrier agents and yard agent. The only process in which the routing agents are involved is the routing process:

- *Routing*. A routing agent, in the context of this process, interacts with a pool of crane agents. In addition, it interacts with straddle carrier agents (those assigned to the cranes of the current pool) and with the yard agent. The routing agent receives the information regarding the jobs to be allocated from the crane agent and the yard agent, and on the basis of these data, it interacts with the straddle carrier agents, assigning each one a list of jobs to be performed.

Straddle Carrier Agent

The system generates a straddle carrier agent for each active straddle carrier. The straddle carrier agents are active only in the routing process. They interact with other straddle carrier agents and with a routing agent. In particular, they are involved in the routing process as follows:

- *Routing*. The straddle carrier agents interact with a routing agent which assigns to them the jobs to be executed (during the allocation of job sequences to the straddle carriers). These agents are also involved in the re-planning processes, which are necessary if the occurrence of unexpected events do not allow to continue to successfully execute the current plans. For example, an unexpected event could be a failure in a straddle carrier, which could become unable to execute the jobs assigned. In this case, the straddle carrier agents interact each-others to produce a reallocation of the jobs.

Quay Agent

The quay agent, during its life cycle, interacts with ship agents. The quay agent is active only in the context of the berthing process (for more detail, see the ship agent description).

Implementation Notes

The agent based model described in the previous section is currently under implementation using the framework *Repast Symphony*. Repast is a widely used free and open-source agent-based modelling and simulation toolkit based on Java technologies that provides features for model development and an execution environment. The Repast runtime is designed to include advanced features for agent storage, display, and behavioural activation, as well as innovative facilities for data analysis and presentation [11].

Starting from other research results of PROMIS project we are using the OPL language, based on the Constraint Programming paradigm, for the rapid prototyping of agents components which are in charge of planning activities. Constraint Programming [12] represents a powerful technology for expressing and reasoning about planning problems and allows to express complex constraints (e.g. constraints on resources, time constraints and space constraints, constraints on sequences) using simple and intuitive syntaxes, such as they can be used effectively in various forms of reasoning [13].

Conclusions ad Future Works

In recent years, transport of goods by sea is quickly increasing. This growth has led to severe congestion of sea ports, reducing productivity and increasing costs, making them less competitive. A possible solution for this congestion is represented by the introduction of ICT technologies in order to make better use of available resources.

The agent technologies, in particular, seem to be suitable to address some typical issues of the container terminal application domain. An agent, indeed, is a software based computer system that enjoys the properties of: (i) autonomy, (ii) social-ability, (iii) reactivity and (iv) pro-activeness [14]. Due to these characteristics, agent technologies seem to be particularly useful in container terminal domains, which are typically modular, decentralized and complex. In this paper we have proposed a possible agent-based model of the port entities involved in berthing, shipping, yard planning and routing operational processes. A first prototype of the system implementing a very restricted subset of agent functionalities has been implemented. The next step is the implementation of additional features.

References

1. Moore LM, Reyns RB, Kumara SRT, Hummel JR (1997) Distributed intelligent agents for logistics (DIAL) In *Proceedings of the IEEE international conference* on Systems, Man, And Cybernetics, Orlando, Florida, USA, October 12–15, 1997
2. Yuan Y, Liang TP, Zhang JJ (2001) *Using agent technology to support supply chain management: potentials and challenges.* Michael G. DeGroote School of Business, Working Paper No. 453, Hamilton, ON, Canada, October 2001
3. Santos E, Zhang F, Luh PB (2003) Intra-organizational logistics management through multi-agent systems. *Electron Com Res* 3(3/4):337–364
4. De Weerdt M (2002) Combining planning and coordination to improve efficiency in transport. In *Proceedings of the 7th congress on transport, infrastructure and logistics* (TRAIL-02), Delft, The Netherlands, November 2002
5. La Valle M (2006) *Planning algorithms.* Cambridge University Press, Cambridge
6. Guestrin CE (2003) *Planning under uncertainty in complex structured environments.* Doctoral dissertation, Department of Computer Science, Stanford University, Stanford
7. Strandenes S, Marlow PB (2000) Port pricing and competitiveness in short sea shipping. *Int J Trans Econ* 27:315–334
8. Cullinane K (2002) The productivity and efficiency of ports and terminals: methods and applications. In Grammenos CTh (ed) *The handbook of maritime economics and business.* LLP, London
9. Mastratisi MA, Palopoli F, Colica M (2008) *Documento di descrizione di un ambiente multi-agente per la gestione di attività di CT.* Rapporto Tecnico 26. R&D.Log
10. Wooldridge M (2002) *An Introduction to multiagent systems.* Wiley, Chichester
11. North MJ, Howe TR, Collier NT, Vos JR (2005) Repast simphony runtime system. In *Proceedings of the agent 2005 conference on generative social processes, models, and mechanisms*, ANL/DIS-06-1, Chicago, IL, USA, October 2005
12. Kumar V (1992) Algorithms for constraint satisfaction problems: a survey. *AI Magazine* 13(1):32–44
13. Van Hentenryck P (1989) *Constraint satisfaction in logic programming.* MIT Press, Cambridge
14. Jennings N, Wooldridge M (1995) *Agent theories, architectures, and languages: a survey.* Intelligent agents: ECAI-94 workshop on agent theories, architectures, and languages. Springer, Berlin

Towards Management Guidelines for Collaborative Research Projects on Information Systems – Learning from Project Management Contingency Theory

Jan vom Brocke* **and Sonia Lippe†**

Abstract Large scale publicly funded research projects involving both academia and industry have gained tremendous importance in information systems research. However, little knowledge is available on how to suitably manage these projects. Project management contingency frameworks can help to characterize the specific type of a project and offer guidelines for its management. In this paper we apply these frameworks to collaborative research projects. As a result we present a first set of management guidelines derived from each framework and highlight further directions of research towards a comprehensive management approach for collaborative research projects.

Introduction

Today a major challenge in project management is the adaptation of conventional practices to the needs of a specific project type. Despite the growing understanding that project success largely depends on the suitability of the management method [1–3], most projects are still managed via a uniform approach. It is seen a necessary step for each project to conduct an upfront analysis of its type in order to provide a basis for the adoption of managerial attitudes and styles [4]. The evolving field of project management contingency theory has developed various classification frameworks in order to categorise existing project types. While no commonly accepted framework exists to be solely used and each framework addresses a certain perspective, collectively they offer a formal framework to categorise and describe projects. Even more, it is expected that the categorisation into a

* University of Liechtenstein, Vaduz, University of Liechtenstein, Vaduz, Fürstentum Liechtenstein, jan.vom.brocke@hochschule.li

† Sap Inc (Switzerland), St. Gallen, Switzerland, sonia.lippe@sap.com

A. D'Atri et al. (eds.), *Management of the Interconnected World*,
DOI 10.1007/978-3-7908-2404-9_61,

certain framework gives first insights into an appropriate project management approach.

In this paper, we focus on public funded, collaborative research projects in the information systems discipline. Encouraged through expanding funding opportunities, e.g. from the European Union, public funded research projects take up an increasing role in the portfolio of public and private organisations, especially in the area of IT[1]. Despite the growing economic importance, little knowledge has yet been gained on the management of these projects. Project management is a challenging and often neglected task since specific project management practices and tools that take into account the distinct nature of this project type are largely missing. Drawing from both literature and practical experience we first give a more detailed characterisation of collaborative research projects in information systems. We then introduce selected contingency frameworks that seem to be most promising to further analyse these projects. Against this background, we arrive at drawing first specific guidelines for the management of collaborative research projects, which we then discuss regarding their applicability and practical relevance. We conclude highlighting further directions for research.

Collaborative Research Projects

Design science research has proven successful in information systems in order to align both business needs and research objectives. The essential element of the approach is to pick relevant problems from business, design rigorous solutions in academia and then bring them back to practice in order to evaluate the result [5]. In collaborative research projects, this work is executed jointly in a consortium of independent project partners from industry and academia. This kind of projects shows certain features which differentiate them from other project types. The most prominent are listed in the Table 1.

Table 1. Characteristics if collaborative research projects

Nature of research work	
Novelty of results [6]	• High degree of creativity, uncertainty and risk • Balance of creative environment and need for project planning and controlling
Systematic investigation [7]	• Research method ill-defined and subject to change [8] • Milestones and timelines less rigid • An essential part of each research activity to demonstrate the utility, quality, and efficacy of a research result and to test various alternatives before finding an answer
(Economic) Impact	• Results often only understood within research community

[1] For example, the currently running EU 7th Framework Programme has a budget 53.2 billion euros of which 9.1 billion euros are solely reserved for research in the area of IT.

	• Difficult to judge project success and to pre-determine the net present value of project results [9]
Project set up	
Extended project boundaries	• Cross- organisational, multi-national consortium • Inter-disciplinary research topics
Heterogeneous partner set up	• Mix of industry, academia, end users, SMEs, etc. • Unexpressed agendas of project partners
Public funding	• Additional constraint through public funding and high bureaucracy through funding body
Governance structure	• No direct authority of consortium lead: High importance of trust and socio-emotional relationships • "Shared" management of all partners • Weak team structure: organisational influence on each project team member is much higher than the identification with the project [10]
Nature of research personnel	
Culture of researchers	• Self managing nature of researchers and need for self directed responsibilities [10] • Orientation towards professional or even academic recognition rather than project work [11, 12] • High individual spirit and thus low team orientation [12]
Skill dependency	• Researchers are usually highly skilled experts in a certain field and this offer a project resource that is hard to replace. The loss of a researcher in a project can therefore lead to a shift in project scope if no equal skill set can be found.
Divided project management team	• Knowledge asymmetry between the project manager and the individual researcher [10]

In the next section we will use the above characteristics to classify research projects by drawing from contingency classification frameworks discussed in literature.

Application of Classification and Contingency Frameworks

Project management contingency theory has developed various frameworks in order to categorize project types. An overview of existing frameworks is given in Crawford, Hobbs and Turner [1] and Sauser, Reilly and Shenhar [13] and thus will not be repeated in this paper. To derive management guidelines for collaborative research project we have chosen a subset of existing frameworks based on two criteria. First they consider research projects independent of development projects and second they do not only offer a classification scheme but conclude with suggestions on the management style for each project type. The actual assessment of each framework is performed in a two step approach. First, the framework is applied to collaborative research projects in order to determine the respective project category. Second, the management guidelines given for this specific category are outlined and evaluated.

Turner and Cochrane

The starting point of Turner and Cochrane's [8] framework is their criticism on the assumption that the project results and steps towards them are well defined at the project start [8]. Although this might be the case for construction or engineering projects, a lot of other project types exist for which either goals or working methods are ill-defined. Based on this observation they identify four different types of projects:

- Type 1: Both goals and methods are well defined. Examples are engineering projects.
- Type 2: Goals are defined, however not the method of achieving them. Examples are product development projects.
- Type 3: Methods are defined, however not the goals. Examples are software development projects where often the goals in terms of the user requirements will only be determined during the project.
- Type 4: Neither method nor goals are defined. Research projects are commonly positioned in this category, whereas this follows a simplification, as also research projects to not entirely lack goals and methods but they are comparably less precisely described.

Start-up and implementation techniques for each project type are discussed and management guidance is given. The start up-process for type-4 projects is based on creativity and inspiration and should involve a first negotiation of methods and goals. They further elaborate that "the process is inevitably iterative, cycling between goals and methods and between purpose and objective, as the level of definition improves" [8]. Along the innovation process, type-4 projects would thus typically become type-3 projects as research outcomes such as concepts, architectures and designs are evaluated in prototypes and customer pilots. Type-3 projects can be initiated through informed negotiation during which the purpose and the objectives are defined among all stakeholders. The outcome can then be implemented as type-1 projects. Techniques for the execution phase are hindered by the fact that neither the work breakdown structure nor the product breakdown structure can be determined. Milestone planning based on activities or deliverables is challenging and should therefore only be done for decision points where goals are refined and go/no-go decisions are taken. Thus their main suggestion is to gradually define methods and goals and thus turn projects into more manageable types for which basic techniques, such as work breakdown and product breakdown structure can be applied. On a high level this approach sounds applicable and will allow for application of common project management methods to ill-defined projects. However, also the initial and more creative phases require dedicated management techniques which fail to be described in this framework.

Shenhar and Dvir

Shenhar and Dvir [14] developed a multidimensional framework that classifies projects based on novelty, technology, complexity and pace [14]. The dotted lines show our classification of collaborative research projects. Collaborative research activities, especially under public funding conditions, usually have a time horizon of 3–5 years and research projects are not immediately critical to the organisational success. Thus they can be classified as regular in terms of the pace. Technology-wise research projects would be classified as super high-tech or high-tech as mostly new technologies are used or applied. The classification of collaborative research projects into this framework in terms of novelty and complexity largely depends on the project objectives in terms of concrete technical results (Fig. 1).

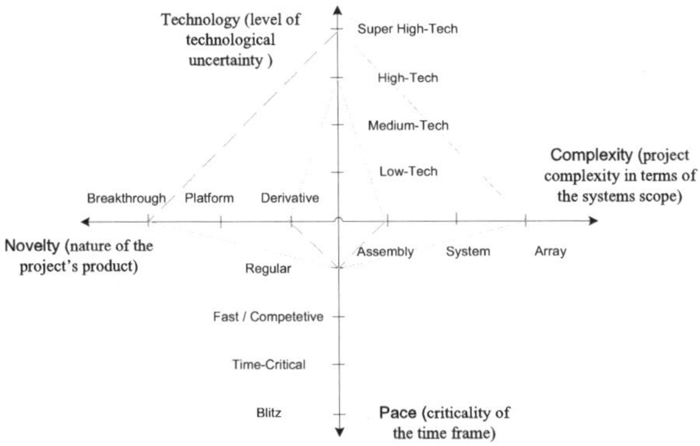

Fig. 1. Our classification of collaborative research projects into the NTCP framework of Shenhar and Dvir [14]

For each dimension of the framework dedicated management guidelines depending on the project classification are given:

- Pace: More formal project management practices, strict deadlines, and continuous decision making are required for fast or critical projects. For projects with a regular pace Shenhar & Dvir suggest more informal project management practices such as management by exception [3].
- Technology: "A higher technology level requires increased design and development activities, more design cycles, later design freeze, and better interaction among team members. A high technology level also requires that team members have higher technical skills and that you hold frequent technical reviews in addition to the usual managerial reviews." [14].
- Novelty: A high degree of novelty means basically nonexistent market data. Thus with increasing novelty fast prototyping is necessary to include customer feedback early on. Requirements are frozen at a much later stage in the project life cycle which increases the level of uncertainty and risk.
- Complexity: The greater the complexity of a project, the more complex the organization will be and the more formal management is required. Planning for assembly projects can be done using simple tools or even manually while array projects require advanced computerised tools and a central master plan. Analogous is the application of controlling and reporting and documentation practices.

Concerning the management guidelines, this framework is seen as the most advanced of those evaluated within this paper. Although no direct reference to existing project management methods is made, the suggestions allow for an assessment and application of commonly used standards, such as PMI and PRINCE 2 [15, 16].

Crawford and Pollak

Crawford and Pollak [17] develop a seven-dimensional framework for project classification based on the assumption that hard and soft issues in projects require different, although not mutually exclusive project management approaches. Each of the dimensions follows a 0 to 100 scale where 0 represents ultimately hard and 100 ultimately soft projects. Collaborative research projects clearly tend towards the soft dimension of this framework. Figure 2 depicts the framework along with our classification of collaborative research projects.

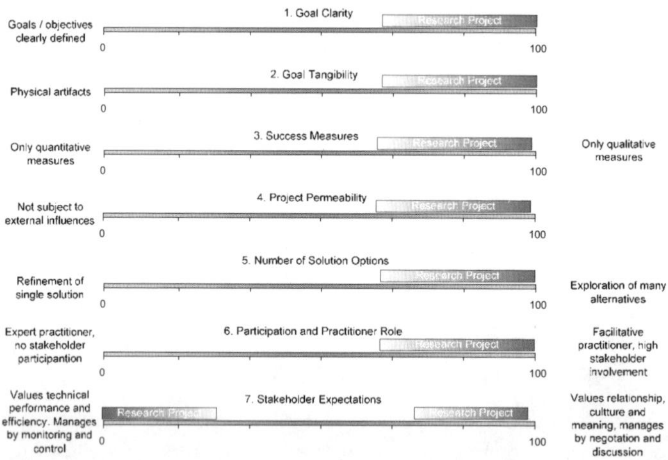

Fig. 2. Soft and hard dimensions framework of Crawford and Pollak [17]

Although the broad objectives are agreed upon, research projects are characterized through the definition of a research question rather than a concrete outcome, usually explore various possible solutions and will rather produce concepts than physical artifacts. However, as already discussed for the framework of Tuner and Cochrane, goals and objectives become more defined and less exploratory as the project moves along the innovation process. To deal with goal ambiguity and the high number of possible solutions Crawford and Pollak suggest to focus on "learning, exploration and problem definition" through negotiation, debating and accommodation. To measure project success research projects would use qualitative goals rather than quantitative. Project permeability refers to "the degree to which a project goals, processes and outcomes are affected by influences outside project control" [17]. Especially collaborative research projects are characterized through a large and influential group of external stakeholders and are thus highly subjected to external influences. In addition, management strategies should allow deliverables to be tailored to the local environment and newly emerging knowledge. In terms of the practitioner role, project teams are equipped with experts in the relevant fields. For the stakeholder expectations, research projects cannot be clearly classified and tend towards the hard as well as the soft side of the framework. This can be explained with the large heterogeneity of stakeholders in public funded collaborative projects. The focus of the given guidelines is clearly on the soft side of the framework and this on techniques such as negotiation and discussion of common goals that the use of formal management methods.

Conclusion

Project management is a challenging and often neglected task in collaborative research projects. As a step towards a tailored management approach we set out analysing existing contingency frameworks with respect to contribution to the management of this specific type of project. Based on two criteria, namely (1) the differentiation of research and development projects and (2) existing recommendation of management guidelines, four frameworks have been chosen to be evaluated in this paper. For each framework the classification of collaborative research projects has been discussed and the related management guidelines have been extracted. Our research has shown that there are certain guidelines that can well be derived from contingency theory helping to better manage collaborative research projects in information systems (Table 2).

Table 2. Management guidelines from selected frameworks

Authors	Suggestions on management style for research projects
Turner and Cochrane [8]	• Project initiation is driven by creative negotiation and strategy definition. • Milestone planning for decision points where goals are refined and go/no-go decision are taken. • Gradually define methods and goals and thus turn type-4 projects into more manageable types.
Shenhar and Dvir [14]	• Use of informal project management practices such as management by exception. • Allow for more design cycles and later design and requirement freezes. • Hold frequent technical reviews in addition to the usual managerial reviews. • Foster frequent communication through multiple communication channels.
Crawford and Pollak [17]	• Focus on learning, exploration and problem definition • Use of qualitative instead of quantitative success measures

However, our study has also revealed that these recommendations are in general on a very high level. In particular they miss the link to the concrete implementation and application of project management techniques and thus lack practical applicability. A logical next step is the evaluation of existing project management practices and their adaptation or extension to the project types and given recommendations.

References

1. Crawford L, Hobbs B, Turner JR (2006) Aligning capability with strategy: categorizing pro jects to do the right projects and to do them right. *Project Manage J* 27(2):38–50
2. Dvir D, Shenhar A, Alkaher S (2003) From a single discipline product to a multidisciplinary system: adapting the right style to the right project. *Syst Eng* 6(3):123–134
3. Shenhar AJ, Dvir D (2004) How projects differ and what to do about it. In: Morris PWG, Pinto JK (eds) *The Wiley guide to project, program and portfolio management*. Wiley, Hoboken, pp 1265–1286
4. Shenhar AJ (2001) Contingent management in temporary, dynamic organizations: the comparative analysis of projects. *J High Technol Manage Res* 12:239–271
5. vom Brocke J, Buddendick C (2006) *Reusable conceptual models. Requirements based on the design science research paradigm*. Paper presented at the 1st international conference on design science research in information systems and technology (DESRIST 06), Claremont, CA
6. Frank U (2006) *Towards a pluralistic conception of research methods in information systems*. ICB research report, vol 7, Duisburg-Essen
7. Creswell JW (2009) *Research design: qualitative, quantitative and mixed methods approaches*, 3rd edn. Sage, Thousand Oaks
8. Turner JR, Cochrane JR (1993) Goals-and-methods matrix: coping with projects with ill defined goals and /or methods of achieving them. *Int J Project Manage* 11(2):93–102
9. Keegan A, Turner JR (2002) The management of innovation in project based firms. *Long Range Plann* 35:367–388
10. Erno-Kjolhede E (2000) Project management theory and the management of research pro jects. In: *MPP working paper* (ed) vol 3. Copenhagen Business School, Copenhagen
11. Clarke TE (2002) Unique features of an R&D work environment and research scientists and engineers. *Knowl Technol Policy* 15(3):58–69
12. Brown CJ (1993) Can research be project managed? *S Afr J Bus Manage* 30(3):72–77
13. Sauser BJ, Reilly RR, Shenhar AJ (2009) Why projects fail? How contingency theory can provide new insights – a comparative analysis of NASA`s Mars Climate Orbiter loss. *Int J Project Manage* 27(7): 665–679
14. Shenhar AJ, Dvir D (2007) *Reinventing project management: the diamond approach to successful growth and innovation*. Haward Business, Boston
15. Office of Government Commerce (2005) *Managing successful projects with PRINCE2, 4th edn*. The Stationery Office, Londons
16. Project Management Institute (2004) *A guide to the project management body of knowledge* (PMBOK Guide). Project Management Institute, Newton Square
17. Crawford L, Pollak J (2004) Hard and soft projects: a framework for analysis. *Int J Project Manage* 22:645–653

Printed by Printforce, the Netherlands